OLIVER CROMWELL.

your most humble servant

Oliver Cromwell

OLIVER CROMWELL:

The Man and His Mission.

BY

J. ALLANSON PICTON.

WITH STEEL PORTRAIT.

CASSELL, PETTER, GALPIN & CO.:
LONDON, PARIS & NEW YORK.

1882.

𝔗𝔬

SIR JAMES ALLANSON PICTON, J.P., F.S.A.,

WHO, LIKE THE SUBJECT OF THIS MEMOIR,

HAS EVER REGARDED "PUBLIC SERVICES" AS THE END

"FOR WHICH A MAN IS BORN,"

AND ALSO, LIKE HIM, HAS RECOGNISED

IN DEVOTION TO HUMANITY THE PRACTICAL WORSHIP OF GOD,

THIS BOOK

IS, WITH MUCH GRATITUDE AND AFFECTION,

𝔇𝔢𝔡𝔦𝔠𝔞𝔱𝔢𝔡

BY HIS SON.

PREFACE.

THE great work of Thomas Carlyle has not entirely excluded the need of humbler efforts to tell the story of Cromwell's life. There is a large and increasing class of readers who by first reading a more commonplace narrative would be better prepared to appreciate not only the " Letters and Speeches," but also the series of dramatic pictures that illustrate them.

Besides, the place of Cromwell in English history is too great, and has too many aspects, to be exhaustively treated even by a master, especially if the master have favourite doctrines of his own to set off by the light of a great example. In such a case humbler students may do service by showing that other points of view are possible.

The subject of the book has a special interest for these times, because on many issues of contemporary politics—always excepting ecclesiastical questions—it seems as though the age were strongly inclined to the opinions of Cromwell's soldiers. I have not hesitated to point out where modern Liberalism departs, whether for better or for worse, from Cromwellian ideas. On the whole, we have much even yet to learn from the unconventional vitality of conviction characteristic of those days.

The present work makes no pretension to original research,

and is indebted to the late Mr. Bruce, to Mr. S. R. Gardiner, to Mr. Sanford, and in one point also to the late Mr. John Forster, for facts not known when Carlyle wrote. Of course Carlyle's work (third edition) has been the chief mine of facts and references; but it will be seen that I have made my own use of his authorities.

I have not felt able to make use of the " Squire Papers." They certainly appear congruous with their alleged origin; but if genuine, they add nothing to previous knowledge beyond trivial details, and their story is so extraordinary that I cannot pretend to be a judge of it.

In a work of this kind multitudinous references would be inconvenient; but, as far as practicable, all needful indications of the authorities relied upon have been given.

J. ALLANSON PICTON.

Nov. 1st, 1882.

⁎ For the sake of some readers, of a class specially desired, it may be as well to explain that where a date is given with alternative figures—*e.g.*, 1643–4—the last figure is according to the modern style, reckoning January 1st as New Year's Day; the previous figure is according to the old style, reckoning March 25th as New Year's Day. Where one figure only is given—*e.g.*, 1643—it is according to the modern style.

CONTENTS.

OLIVER CROMWELL.

CHAPTER I.

ANCESTRY AND HISTORIC HERITAGE.

The history of England during the seventeenth century was like a long stormy day relieved by one brief interval of splendour at noon. During that interval, it is true, there was thunder in the air; but, at any rate, the clouds were rolled back, the sun of prosperity shone, and the commercial progress, as well as the military and naval power of this country moved the envy and admiration of the world. Undoubtedly many causes united to make the alliance of the British Commonwealth so eagerly sought by the chief nations of Europe during the sixth decade of the century; but the most conspicuous among those causes was the concentration of all powers of government in the hands of one extraordinary man.

An incident of March 4th, 1654, illustrates both the singular form and the proud position of the English Government of that day. A stately procession of carriages, outriders, and attendants entered the court of Whitehall Palace to present the desires of the United Netherlands for the completion of a treaty of peace. Confident in the supposed weakness of a rebellious and distracted nation, the Dutch had charged their most renowned admirals to seize the opportunity for shaking off British claims to rule the narrow seas; and now, after two years of desultory war, they were so beaten and humbled that they had much ado to escape a federal incorporation with the English Commonwealth, and short of that were prepared to concede almost any terms imposed. These ambassadors descended from their coaches, and being ushered into the banqueting-room, approached with repeated and pro-found obeisances a raised daïs at the end of the chamber. On this daïs, with great officials and military officers disposed on

B

either side about the steps, stood the chief magistrate of the Commonwealth. He was a man just passing middle life, of a stature rather above than below the average, while indomitable vigour was evident in his furrowed and weather-beaten face. Velvet attire could not disguise the uncourtliness of his figure, but the bearing of a soldier gave dignity to his roughness. His light-brown hair, touched with grey, fell around his capacious head in flowing locks, symbolic of his independence of precisian rules. Beneath his broad forehead and heavy eyebrows, divided by deep lines, his eyes were luminous with keen vitality, and suggestive of a sincere, eager, passionate soul. His large nose, and rough red complexion allowed him no claim to beauty; but his strong jaw, and lithe, capacious mouth showed that the secret of his rule over men was strength rather than grace.

As the ambassadors drew near, he uncovered and gravely bowed. They presented credentials addressed to his Highness Oliver, Lord Protector of the Commonwealth of England, Scotland, and Ireland. At the conclusion of the presentation, forty attendant gentlemen desired the distinction of kissing the hand of his Highness. But this royal ceremony was politely declined, and he bowed to each instead. After their retirement the foreign party had much to say and write about the unparalleled career of this strange potentate, who from being a small grazier in the Fens, had risen to be the sovereign ruler of three kingdoms, and to sway the balance of power in Europe. They were not alone in soliciting his favour. Sweden was showering honours on his special ambassador. Denmark followed suit with Holland. France and Spain were bidding against each other. Portugal surrendered a brother of its envoy to the stern justice of the Protector, and on the very day of his execution signed a treaty of amity advantageous to the Commonwealth.

Nor was the Protector's fame abroad obtained by the sacrifice of his power at home. No monarch who ever reigned over England—not even Henry VIII. or Elizabeth—ruled so directly by decrees of an imperial will as did this man. By a stroke of his pen he repealed ancient statutes and made new laws. He called up an army, reformed a Church, remodelled Chancery, regulated roads, emancipated debtors, created schools, enriched universities, stimulated commerce, restrained bigotry, and inspired zeal, all by his mere word. Nor was it only a fragment of a distracted realm that obeyed him. In the remotest corners of Scotland and Ireland his word was law. Yet, absolute as he was, the very men who had shed their blood to abolish a weak tyranny were content to accept his strong sovereignty as the embodiment of ordered freedom, or, at least, as the nearest approach to it possible for the time. It is the purpose of the following pages to show by what concurrence of personal character with contemporary conditions and precedent causes the reign of this uncrowned king became not only possible but inevitable.

The point up to which Oliver Cromwell's ancestry is ascertainable coincides very conveniently with the date from which events began to make clearly inevitable an ultimate struggle for life between Parliament and Crown. Inevitable,—but not perhaps to contemporary observers, unless gifted with superhuman foresight. For when Henry VIII. in 1531, in addition to his new-fangled despotism, forced on an unwilling clergy the acknowledgment of his spiritual supremacy, it might have seemed that the prospects of English liberty were blighted for ever. Fortunately, however, for after times, King Henry found in Parliament a convenient make-weight against the clergy; and the subserviency of the House of Commons in this reign concealed the growth of an influence afterwards fatal to the royal prerogative.

The chief instrument of the King in moulding Parliament to his purposes was Thomas Cromwell, the son of a Putney blacksmith. By a singular union of strong will with instinctive understanding of the times, he became for ten years the supreme administrator of the realm. He made a fatal mistake at last in attempting to use the king's passions, as he had used popular feeling, for the promotion of his policy. But he kept his power long enough to leave his influence indelibly stamped on English history; and amongst its results we may reckon one which perhaps he did not foresee—a more conscious appreciation of the House of Commons as the meeting-place of popular impulse and royal will. His adventurous and brilliant career, together with its tragic close, was the theme of wondering comment amongst his contemporaries and immediate successors. And there is some reason for thinking that the curious confusions of popular tradition have transferred to a greater Cromwell some of the

B 2

gossiping stories formerly told about this Thomas Cromwell, Earl of Essex. At the beginning of the seventeenth century a play appears to have been frequently acted of which Thomas Cromwell's adventures formed the subject. And in the ambitious soliloquies attributed to the blacksmith's son, impatient of the noise and fumes of his father's forge, we have possibly one origin of stories told about the soaring ambition of Oliver's youthful thoughts.*

The noblest trait in the character of the Earl of Essex was the bravery with which he stood by his fallen master, Wolsey. Such a man deserved to have faithful followers of his own; and indeed he seems to have had the gift of securing them.

So at least we should judge from such records as we have of the only one amongst his followers with whom we need to concern ourselves. This was a certain Richard Williams, a Welshman, who was introduced to his service through some family connection. Richard was born in Glamorganshire, the son of Morgan ap-William, who showed his leaning to English fashions by exchanging his Welsh patronymic for the permanent surname of Williams. And so the son, instead of being Richard ap-Morgan, became Richard Williams. This man was the great-grandfather of Oliver Cromwell. What was the precise relationship of Richard Williams to Thomas, Earl of Essex, and how it was that he assumed the name of Cromwell, are disputed questions. The connection was apparently not by blood but by marriage.† As to the assumption by the latter of the name of

---

* "The Life and Death of Thomas, Lord Cromwell," was published in 1613, under the initials W. S., as though the unknown author had desired to insinuate a distinguished origin for a very mediocre production. The following lines form part of a soliloquy of young Thomas fretted by the obtrusive clang of his father's forge :—

"Why should my birth keep down my mounting spirit ?
Are not all creatures subject unto time,—
To time, who doth abuse the cheated world,
And fills it full of hodge-podge bastardy ?
There's legions now of beggars on the earth,
That their original did spring from kings ; (*sic*)
And many monarchs now, whose fathers were
The riff-raff of their age ; for time and fortune
Wears out a noble train to beggary ;
And from the dunghill minions do advance
To state and mark in this admiring world.
           *   *   *
Then Cromwell, cheer thee up, and tell thy soul
That thou may'st live to flourish and control."

† Bishop Goodman, in offering to Oliver the dedication of a book on " The Two Great Mysteries of the Christian Religion," published in 1653, referred in complimentary terms to Thomas, Earl of Essex, as " your lordship's great uncle;"

Cromwell, that need not occasion much difficulty. Richard scarcely possessed a surname in the English sense. His father's change of the patronymic ap-William into Williams was of course quite recent, and could not create the fixity or the associations of an established family name. When, therefore, his services and his personal qualities raised him to the intimate favour of the great man, it was not unnatural that the Earl should grant, and very natural indeed that Richard should eagerly accept, a permission to take his name. Lady Essex must have been very unlike most other wives if she did not try to induce her powerful husband to treat her needy kinsmen as his own. He continued, however, to sign himself in formal documents as " Cromwell, alias Williams," and this custom was maintained by his descendants even down to the earlier days of his great-grandson.

This Richard Cromwell, as we may now call him, showed himself trustworthy and energetic in carrying out his master's orders. He was employed in the suppression of the monasteries in 1536. In the same year Lincolnshire rose in riotous opposition to the religious innovations of the time; and he was very active in restoring order. One of the only two letters of his which survive seems to belong to this year, and suggests a restless energy, a vigour and a swiftness in action, curiously prophetic of his great descendant's character. In 1537 his services were very handsomely rewarded by the manor of Hinchinbrook, near Huntingdon, formerly the possession of a convent. He must have been a man of considerable bodily strength as well as mental activity, for in a tournament at Westminster, on May-day, 1546, he greatly distinguished himself, and attracted the attention of the King.

Sir Richard Cromwell was succeeded by his son, Henry, who enjoyed for half a century the fruits of the father's keenness and energy. Sir Henry—for he, too, was made a knight—seems to have been specially fitted to appreciate the pleasant places in which the lines of his inheritance had fallen. For he took more

whereupon Oliver observed, according to Fuller, " My family has no relation to his." Carlyle assumes that Fuller was misled by an impatient remark of Oliver's to the effect that his flatterer had misstated the relationship. " You are quite wrong as to all that; good morning." This is not satisfactory. It is not likely that Oliver would have cavilled as to the precise number of removes of the uncleship. But if there was no consanguinity, we can quite understand the repudiation of it. And in this sense we may fairly take the words, " My family has no relation to his."

pleasure in building and planting than in reforms of public
abuses; and a local reputation for munificence entirely satisfied
his desires for fame.   He rebuilt the mansion at Hinchinbrook,
turning the old convent buildings into kitchens and offices.
He was returned to Parliament as knight of the shire for his
own county in 1563; and in the following year he had the
burdensome honour of entertaining Queen Elizabeth in one of
her progresses.   But to a man whose lavishness earned him the
name of the "Golden Knight" such an opportunity for expenditure was welcome rather than otherwise.   And even royalty
was gratified, while courtiers were amazed, at the magnificence
of the entertainment.   In addition to Hinchinbrook he had
a residence at Ramsey, which he preferred in the summer time;
and there, when the bright days of May or June brought him
back, he would signalise his arrival by scattering small coin,
to be scrambled for by the villagers as he rode towards the
great house.

He was twice married; and the death of his second wife, in
1592, was the occasion of proceedings for witchcraft, which form
a significant indication of the condition of public opinion on the
very threshold of the great Puritan revolution.   Some peculiarities of the poor lady's illness aroused suspicion of evil spells
at work.   The doctors and attendants could not understand the
symptoms, which were not in accordance with the legitimate
course of disease, and therefore must needs be put down to
preternatural influence.   Suspicion fell on one John Samwell,
with his wife, and his daughter Alice.   They were all three
lodged in gaol, and the mother, broken down by misery, confessed impossible guilt.   According to the law, the property of
the condemned wretches was forfeited to the lord of the manor;
and Sir Henry founded with it a lectureship in the parish church
for the delivery of an annual sermon against witchcraft.   The
vigorous survival of so cruel a superstition, at a time when
the opposing forces of political light and darkness were being
silently marshalled for a deadly struggle, should be a warning
against a thoughtless use of nineteenth century standards in
judging the people of those days.

Similarly the anti-papal passion, which had grown up in
England since Sir Henry Cromwell's father had turned the nuns
out of Hinchinbrook, is not to be hastily confounded with the

theological sectarianism of modern times. The art of controversial wrangling had not then been popularised. But the people at large were deeply moved by aspirations, the ultimate scope of which they could not themselves understand. All that is now called Liberalism in politics and opinion, the tendency to new ideals, impatience with old abuses, hopefulness concerning the future, and enterprise both in thought and action, was symbolised by abjuration of the Pope and all his works. On the other hand, an adherent of the Papacy was in the general view necessarily a " malignant," an opponent of spiritual independence for the nation, and of political freedom for the people. The triumphant security of progress in our day favours a calmer judgment. And the wider knowledge of human nature, given by the accumulation of recorded experience, teaches us not only that men's motives are often very much better than their acts, but also that in the settlement of complicated questions it is better to leave full liberty even for stupidity and malignancy to exert whatever moral or immoral force they have.

These differences between our own century and the sixteenth should be borne in mind as we try to conceive the murmurs of conflict and change and growth that broke in now and then upon the drowsy silence of Huntingdon during the long and peaceful incumbency of Sir Henry Cromwell. He was hardly more than a boy when Edward VI., a sickly, amiable child, succeeded to the throne; and only ten years had then elapsed since Lincolnshire and Yorkshire had risen in defence of the old religion. The seed sown by Wycliffe and the Lollards in the fourteenth and fifteenth centuries had never been wholly extirpated. But the new convictions had scarcely as yet dominated the current of opinion; and when, on the accession of Edward VI., political power fell into the hands of statesmen with strong Protestant leanings, the changes, too rapidly effected, in national forms of religion awakened a reaction that had much to do with the popular decision in favour of Queen Mary.

A popular landowner did not perhaps require the genius for accommodation to circumstances ascribed to the Vicar of Bray, in order to survive unscathed the revolutions of the time. But it may fairly be assumed that the golden knight of Hinchinbrook was troubled by no such wistfulness of conscience as sometimes overwhelmed his grandson with self-condemnation and despair.

The news at times retailed by servants from the talk of the town, and the London letters they occasionally brought for their lord must have caused some anxious hours in the grand new rooms, with the Williams-Cromwell blazonry in their windows. News of Parliamentary subserviency in the repeal of all the religious legislation of the previous reigns, and in the authoritative restoration of the Mass, was accompanied by rumours affecting perhaps far more painfully the comfortable possession of convent lands. The Queen, it was whispered, was obstinately bent upon making the spoilers of the Church disgorge their gains; and whoever might be spared, it was unlikely that any leniency would be shown to the son of an adventurer, whose whole wealth had been earned by zealous complicity with the destroyer of Mary's Church, the enemy of Mary's mother, the guilty counsellor of Catherine's divorce. Most welcome, then, were the tidings dropped by pack-horse drivers, and confirmed by letters from the capital, that the Parliament, which kneeled before the Pope's legate, remained firm on the question of Church lands, and refused to surrender an acre.

But the tales of terror brought to Hinchinbrook after the Statute of Heresy was re-enacted, when funeral pyres were re-lit round living men, because they would not deny their faith, helped there, as elsewhere, to quicken a counter-reaction, which brought Britain out of the fire of persecution the most stubbornly Protestant country in the world.

In Huntingdon, and at Hinchinbrook, and elsewhere, the death of the bitter and gloomy Mary lifted a weight from the spirits of men. And though the state of the country was depressed, the character of Elizabeth inspired the national courage. Reviving confidence was justified by that great Queen's practical appreciation of the tone and temper of her times, and by her perception that the glory of supreme power is most fully realised by the prince, whose stately assumption of autocracy disguises obedience to national impulse. She loved despotic airs, as when she haughtily reminded the "proud prelate" of Ely of his abject dependence upon her. Nevertheless, no sovereign who ever lived was less willing than Elizabeth to sacrifice for the querulous strife of personal self-assertion the vast joy of embodying in herself the loyal might of a nation. If the Stuarts had understood as well as she the true delight of sovereign power, Oliver Cromwell might have died a tithe-farmer at Ely. Still, it was during the reign of Elizabeth that the issues of the coming struggle were rapidly matured. For the House of Commons began somewhat to presume upon the assured position acquired through the readiness of Henry VIII. to make a convenient tool of it.

Sir Henry Cromwell, already returned as knight of his shire to the second Parliament of Elizabeth, was soon to have proof that there were in the conditions of the time some elements of discord which even the great and popular Queen might have some difficulty in controlling. The language of the House of Commons, whenever the Sovereign was concerned, was obsequious, fulsome, even slavish. Still, they now and then assumed a position which courtiers denounced and the Queen rebuked with masculine vigour of language. So long as Elizabeth did not marry, the papistic Queen of Scots was heir presumptive to the crown of England; and should she succeed, in her train would come all the abominations of superstition, now dreaded with the horror inspired by the late reign. Under such circumstances, the fear of royal displeasure at their meddling with matters too high for them was overcome by the sharper terror of her childless decease. But her imperious rebuke overwhelmed them with a sense of their presumption.

Still, a spirit was now abroad which, after every dissolution and fresh election, always had its irrepressible representatives in the House. In 1575 the Queen sent a peremptory message, not for the first time, that Parliament should not meddle with religion, unless the clergy moved first. Whereupon Mr. Peter Wentworth, of Tregony in Cornwall, delivered an outspoken speech, worthy of note for several reasons, but here in particular for its indication of the growing sense of Parliamentary responsibility for the welfare of the State.

"There is nothing," he said, "so necessary for the preservation of the Prince and the State as free speech; and without this it is a scorn and mockery to call this a Parliament House; for in truth it is none but a very school of flattery and dissimulation, and so a fit place to serve the devil and his angels in, and not to glorify God or benefit the Commonwealth. . . . The King ought not to be under man but under God, and under the law, because the law maketh him a king. Let the King therefore attribute to the law what the law attributeth to him, that is, dominion and power; for he is not a king in whom will, and not law, doth rule.

. . . . I have heard of old Parliament men that the banishment of the Pope and Popery, and the restoring of true religion had their beginning in this House, not from the bishops. And I have heard that few laws for religion had their foundation from them. And I do surely think— before God I speak it—that the bishops were the cause of that doleful message."

The maxim that the king can do no wrong was not understood in those days of personal rule ; and Mr. Peter Wentworth presumed to say that "there was none without fault, no, not even their noble Queen."

In such an age these surely were brave words, of which the inspiration needs to be pondered, if we would understand the upheaval they presaged. The House that listened in dumb amazement might censure the speech, and order the speaker into custody; but probably there was not a man amongst them who did not feel that here were truths which sounded startling only because expediency, and pretence, and cowardice made falsehood more familiar.

While the political forces of a yet unforeseen struggle were thus being prepared, the household at Hinchinbrook was occupied by the cares and joys of a growing family. Sir Henry Cromwell was very young when he succeeded to the property, and some years elapsed before he had children about him. His eldest son was Oliver, who was knighted by Queen Elizabeth before the death of his father, and who survived far enough into the next century to mark with horror the sinister fame of his great namesake and nephew. He seems to have grown up in simple loyalty to Church and Queen, and never to have been affected by the religious or political speculations of his time. The expensive tastes of his father were so faithfully imitated by him that soon after succeeding to the estate he was compelled to sell Hinchinbrook, and to content himself with the house at Ramsey. The second son was Robert, who died comparatively young, leaving the one son with whom this book is concerned. What traits of Robert's character have been preserved will be considered in the next chapter. They are such as to suggest probable differences of promise, even in boyish days, between him and his lavish, lordly brother. There were still other three sons, and three daughters, only one of whom needs to be mentioned.

Elizabeth, the second daughter, born in 1574, was married to Mr. William Hampden, of Great Hampden in Buckinghamshire. She was left early a widow with two infant sons, John and Richard. She survived for sixty-seven years in her widowhood. She saw her nephew and her sons play such a part in the world's history as is given to few. She mourned her eldest son slain in battle, but leaving an undying name. Her nephew she saw, with such wonder as we can easily conceive, rise to more than kingly power, fill the world with his fame, and rule the country by a dying whisper, potent even after he was dead. Then her second son left her utterly alone; and still she lived on for fifteen years more, to ponder the memory of such a family history as the world had never seen before, and never will see again. Napoleons of various degrees of genius are common enough. But Cromwells and Hampdens are scarce indeed.

With such a father as the " Golden Knight," and in such a residence as the renovated Hinchinbrook, the childhood of that generation of the family was no doubt a very happy one. The popularity of their father, as well as his position, would secure them many friends anxious to add to the pleasures of frequent holidays. Among those friends we must reckon the Stewards of Ely, an undubitable branch, as genealogists hold, of the Scotch royal family of Stuart. Prince James of Scotland, held prisoner by Henry IV. of England, was accompanied in his involuntary sojourn by a kinsman, Walter Stewart, or Steward, who found the southern land agree with him, and did not return home. Robert Steward, his descendant, was Prior of Ely in the reign of Henry VIII., and proving complaisant, became Dean of the reformed Cathedral Church. He left, among other relatives enriched by his politic conduct, a nephew, William, who had the farming of the tithes at Ely. Between the Cromwell and the Steward families there had been occasional intercourse ever since Richard Williams had expressed doubts, happily unjustified, of the readiness of the Prior of Ely to fall in with the views of the Earl of Essex. And at any rate it is permitted to us to think, without any improbability, that amongst the girl playmates of the Cromwell children little Elizabeth Steward was sometimes found, the future mother of Oliver Cromwell.

It would be of great interest to us to know how far the Cromwell children of that generation and their friends were subject in any direct and special manner to the influence of that earnest religious spirit, commonly termed Puritanic, which, at this period, was rapidly acquiring predominant influence. But having no sufficient information on that point, we must content ourselves with the indirect evidence afforded by the after lives of some of them, and with an estimate of the spiritual tendencies with which the very air around them was alive. That the household at Hinchinbrook was ever much affected by Puritan feeling or opinion seems very unlikely from all that we know of Sir Henry or his son Sir Oliver. But the reputation of the Protector's father, Robert Cromwell, though not suggestive of fiery zeal, certainly implies a quiet earnestness of character, and a serious feeling of responsibility in life, which were rarely found in those days except under the inspiration of Puritanism. Mrs. Hampden, the Protector's aunt, if she was not Puritanically inclined before her marriage, must soon have acquired the views of that school. For not only had she sole charge of the education of her sons, but she seems to have followed with her approval and sympathy the whole career of them and their cousin. Puritanism was in the air; and the rising generation of Cromwells and Stewards were affected by it just in proportion to their individual susceptibilities. It remains, therefore, to estimate the nature of this great influence, as prominent, and perhaps chief, among the gifts conferred upon the subject of the following biography by the conditions of his birth.

Puritanism was not so much a set of theological opinions as a spiritual temper and a moral tone. This is, indeed, suggested by the name. The earnestness and reality of the doctrinal opinions of Puritans are not for a moment to be ignored. But everything substantial in these opinions was held equally by their opponents; and somehow their descendants, though very zealous for the theology of the "Puritan Fathers," do not exactly exhibit the same results in corporate character. The Puritans were distinguished from other contemporaries and other generations holding the same opinions by a spiritual temper and moral tone on which it is more profitable to concentrate attention.

Wycliffe and his followers did much to awaken the conscience of England. They tore away the dusty veil of once translucent form, then thick with accretions of superstition, and brought men face to face once more with the eternal facts of the divine life. Direct responsibility to God, undisguised by ministrations of the Church, was one of the chief lessons they taught. And with this went, as it always does, the sense of an immediate divine inspiration, helping the soul in its struggles against sin. Through all the persecutions of the Lollards, the distractions of the wars of York and Lancaster, and the exhaustion, both bodily and spiritual, that followed them, the living seed sown by Wycliffe was preserved. And when Henry VIII. for his own purposes threw off the priestly yoke of Rome, the hopes and aspirations quickened here and there amongst such receptive elements of the population went far beyond his intentions. The cruelties of the Marian persecution roused an heroic temper in the inquirers after truth, who were more and more discontented with the compromises of Elizabeth's reign. Thus it came to pass that in the later years of this queen there were throughout the land groups of devout men and women, who, though rarely organised as "separatists," formed centres of spiritual fervour, requiring only a stir in the heavy air of choking worldliness above them to burst into a general flame of reforming zeal.

The deepest distinguishing characteristic of these people was an overmastering sense of the nearness of the soul to God whether as Judge or Saviour. This gave them a horror of sin; this made the question, What must I do to be saved? the directing aim and pervading thought of their lives. But to conclude that they must, therefore, have been always pre-occupied with a self-centred anxiety for the deliverance of their own souls from hell, would be to adopt in its worst form that confusion between theological opinion and spiritual temper against which we have protested. Logically, or illogically, they thought more about salvation from the power of sin, and present triumph in the grace of God, than about ultimate safety from the condemnation of the wicked. They held, indeed, to the doctrines of "divine sovereignty," "election," "effectual calling," and whatever else goes therewith. But, as the letters of Cromwell sufficiently show, with the best of them such opinions, far from inducing spiritual pride, were valued because they gave extreme expression to the utter unworthiness, helplessness, and absolute dependence realised in their inmost souls.* As the living organism selects unconsciously from the surrounding medium the elements that feed its growth, so these people, who had a spiritual life transcending all creeds, took in, without knowing how or why, the inspiring truths disguised in their creeds; while the falsehood or injustice discerned therein by a later generation left them comparatively unharmed. And so doctrines, which some in these days rightly or wrongly interpret as necessarily suggestive of capricious tyranny in heaven and abject cowardly slavery on earth, were in these men associated with an unconquerable faith in the supremacy of an eternal Father, and with a quenchless longing to be pure and useful members of His family below.

The words of Jesus to his first followers, "Ye know not what manner of spirit ye are of;" have a very wide application to all apostles of reformed methods, whether in politics or religion. Such people feel strongly the reasonableness and justice of some particular aspects of a newly apprehended principle. But rarely, indeed, do they realise its full scope. And when they take to writing theoretic discourses about it, they are almost sure to exaggerate the importance of temporary and accidental questions. So the Puritans, whose deepest inspiration was a sense of immediate personal responsibility to God, were naturally, in their controversies, concerned most with accidental questions of prelacy, and vestments, and the cross in baptism. In politics the issues they raised were more substantial, involving the right of the commonalty to a voice in deciding their own spiritual destinies, and in the establishment of laws under which godly conduct would be secure. But even in such matters, not their theories, but rather their spirit, was of chief importance in their influence on the coming age. Cartwright's learned arguments have now fallen utterly dead; but the spirit evinced by Peter Wentworth in Elizabeth's Parliaments is now the very soul of British liberty.

We have already quoted from this man's speeches in illustration of the the growing boldness of the Commons. But he also

---

* "By Christianity," says Mrs. Hutchinson, "I intend that universal habit of grace which is wrought in a soul by the regenerating Spirit of God, whereby the whole creature is resigned up into the Divine will and love, and all its actions designed to the obedience and glory of its Maker." This is Puritanism at its best; but then it is also Anglicanism at its best, and Romanism at its best likewise.

shows us at what an expense of inward conflict, and by what supreme efforts of heroism, the first leaders of this new spirit took up their position. When committed to custody and examined by a committee of the House, mainly for the assertion that even the Queen's Majesty was not without fault, he exposed the struggles of his soul in language that puts to shame the cheap heroics and gainful platitudes of much modern Liberalism. In its very inconsistencies, now repudiating and now pathetically acknowledging the terror of his position, it has the moving power of living truth.

"Why do your honours ask," he pleads, "how I dare tell a truth to give the Queen warning to avoid her danger? I do answer you thus; I do thank the Lord my God that I never found fear in myself to give the Queen's Majesty warning to avoid her danger. Be you all afraid thereof who will; for I praise God I am not, and I hope never to live to see the day. And yet I will assure your honours that, twenty times and more, when I walked in my grounds revolving this speech to prepare against this day, my own fearful conceit did say unto me, that this speech would carry me to the place whither I shall now go, and fear would have moved me to put it out. Then I weighed whether in good conscience and the duty of a faithful subject I might keep myself out of prison, and not warn my prince from walking in a dangerous course. My conscience said unto me that I could not be a faithful subject if I did more respect to avoid my own danger than my prince's danger. Here withal I was made bold, and went forward as your honours heard. Yet, when I uttered those words in the House, 'that there was none without fault, no, not our noble queen,' I paused, and beheld all your countenances, and saw plainly that those words did amaze you all. Then I was afraid with you for company, and fear bade me put out those words that followed; for your countenances did assure me that not one of you would stay me of my journey; yet the consideration of a good conscience, and of a faithful subject, did make me bold to utter it in such sort as your honours heard. With this heart and mind I spake it, and I praise God for it; and if it were to do again, I would with the same mind speak it again." *

Brave soul! These were not the days of luxurious clock-tower seclusion, with deputations of admiring friends, and walks on the terrace, and only the danger of insomniency from Big Ben booming overhead. "The place whither he should now go," was of more evil repute than that, and the possibility of exit save by the ministry of the hangman very dubious. But the divine spirit of truth had got possession of him; and speak

* Given in Cobbett's "Parliamentary History."

he must, be the issues what they might. The tones of such a
mood must have had an eloquence no art can give, and the
silent stare of amazement, bristling into horror, was not the
frigidity of indifference, but the momentary paralysis of consciences appalled by the greatness of manifest duty.

When such voices were uplifted for the freedom necessarily
involved in the sense of direct responsibility to God, the hearing
ear might recognise the clear signal of coming battle.

" I was, amongst others in the last Parliament," said Wentworth, " sent
to the Archbishop of Canterbury for the articles of religion that then
passed this House. He asked us why we did put out of the book the
articles for the homilies, consecrating of bishops, and suchlike ? Surely,
sir, said I, because we were so occupied in other matters that we had no
time to examine them how they agreed with the word of God. What!
said he, surely you mistook the matter; you will refer yourselves wholly
to us therein ? No; by the faith I bear to God, said I, we will pass
nothing before we understand what it is ; for that were but to make you
Popes. Make you Popes who list, said I, for we will make you none."

Such words as these, such conduct as this, give a far deeper
insight into the real meaning of Puritanism than volumes of
controversy about Prelacy, Presbyterianism and Independency.
And this spiritual temper, this moral tone, more human and
more abiding than any accidental vestment of theological
doctrine, was perhaps the noblest gift in all the historic heritage
that devolved on Oliver Cromwell.

CHAPTER II.

CHILDHOOD AND YOUTH.

ABOUT 1590 Robert Cromwell, the second son of the Golden Knight of Hinchinbrook, began to think of marriage and a settlement in life. Elizabeth Steward, mentioned in the previous chapter, had married William Lynne, styled Esquire, which in those days meant something, of Bassingbourne in Cambridgeshire. Of this union one child was born. But the joy of her young married life was suddenly blighted. Within a few weeks she lost both husband and child. Distance of time and oblivion of all but the bare fact have reduced that sorrow to a matter of formal record now. But she was not a woman over whom grief so terrible could pass without leaving solemn influences behind.

By this young widow the heart of Robert Cromwell was won. Where the wooing began, or how it grew, no record lives to show. But her portrait, though it represents her in mature years, makes her earlier attractions conceivable enough. Sweetness, that comes not of fawning weakness, but of loving strength ; calmness, not of indifference, but of resignation to eternal powers; force of character, most unobtrusive, but clearly there when wanted; and withal a touch of wistfulness, as though the mystery of things answered not fully to the desires of the heart,—such are some of the characteristics of that silent face. In the regularity of its oval outline and smoothly chiselled features it presents a singular contrast to the burly roughness of Oliver's countenance. On the other hand, the eyes of the mother are not nearly so fine and open as those of the son. The exquisite neatness of the " cardinal," and lace kerchief lying close to the shapely throat, suggest that the slovenliness attributed to Oliver did not come from the female side of the house. It is difficult to point to any feature in common, unless it be the fair hair that both exhibit. Still there is a certain likeness in character, making allowance for difference of sex. The firmness of the womanly face is bold vigour in the man's. The pure simplicity of the mother's expression becomes down-

C

right daring in the son's. But beyond the simplicity of the one and the boldness of the other, there is in both a hinted depth of mystic pondering, fathomless not only to others but to themselves.

Robert Cromwell seems to have been a quiet serviceable man, content to do his duty in his own neighbourhood, and distracted by no ambitions. His fame in the Huntingdon region was that of a good man, contented with his lot in life, diligent in such business as fell to him, upright in all his dealings, a useful citizen and a kind neighbour.

The lordly life at Hinchinbrook was not destined to last many more years. But the generous old knight was able to make a very fair, and even liberal provision for his second son. Away from the paternal manor, across the flat fields through which the Hinchin reaches the Ouse, there stood a substantial stone* house at the entrance to Huntingdon town. This house was either bought or rented for the young couple; for it does not appear to have belonged to the estate. And in addition to the house and court-yard attached, they were endowed with possessions in Huntingdon, formerly belonging to a monastery of Augustine Friars. These, together with the tithes of Great Hartford, brought in an income of about £300 a year—in those days a very handsome provision for the younger son of a country gentleman.

To this house Robert Cromwell brought his wife, Elizabeth, in 1591.† We may imagine the kindly old Sir Henry, looking in upon them with his blessing, and visits of brothers and sisters from across the fields. But the life that was so vivid and happy to them, with its daily interests and its little excitements, its presents from the paternal mansion, its news from Ely, its town gossip and its political rumours, has for us dried up into a few crabbed entries in dusty registers.

Their first child was born in September, 1592, and baptised by the name of Joan on the 24th of that month.‡ She died in childhood. The second, also a girl, Elizabeth, was born almost

---

* The house now occupying the site is of brick, but Noble says that Robert Cromwell's house " was certainly built of stone."

† No register has been found; but the date is tolerably well fixed by the death of Mr. Lynne, in 1589, and the birth of Robert Cromwell's first child, in 1592.

‡ Carlyle, from Noble.

within a year of the first. Then, no doubt to the great joy of his parents, came a boy, who was called after the grandfather, being baptised on August 31st, 1595, by the name of Henry. Again, within eighteen months, a third girl, Catherine, was born at the beginning of 1597.

But though his household was thus rapidly increasing, family affairs had not wholly engrossed the attention of Robert Cromwell during these years. Owing partly to his father's position, but partly also we may imagine to the esteem in which he was himself held by his fellow-townsmen, he was returned in 1593 to Queen Elizabeth's seventh Parliament as one of the representatives of Huntingdon. There is no record of any part taken by him in the proceedings.

And so when, on April 25th, 1599, a second boy was born, his welcome, though doubtless cordial, was not such as is given to the first born, nor to any recognised heir of promise. His elder brother having been named after the grandfather, the new arrival was naturally called Oliver, after the uncle and future head of the family. He was christened four days afterwards in All Saints' Church, and the register, in its pedantic Latin, may be read to this day : " Oliver, son of Robert Cromwell, gentleman, and of Elizabeth, his wife, born on the twenty-fifth day of April, and baptised on the twenty-ninth of the same month."

Above the entry in the register some later incumbent, zealous for Church and King, has written the words, " *England's plague for five years.*" But some one else, probably a more liberal successor, has run a pen through this unauthorised addition. So has posterity wrangled over the name and fame of Oliver; but little did the friends and relatives assembled for the christening think of the possibility of that, as they watched their parson enter the new Church member in his book.

Of anything that happened to the boy we know very little for seventeen years, except only what we can infer with reasonable probability from the annals of the neighbourhood and the customs of the time. Still the local and the national records enable us to conceive, with a probability almost approaching to certainty, the surrounding influences and the course of development by which the man was prepared for the work allotted him in the world.

c 2

While Oliver was learning to walk and talk,* perhaps even advancing as far as his A, B, C, Queen Elizabeth was passing away, and with her the institution of Tudor royalty. In January 1602–3, the "Golden Knight" died, and his son Oliver reigned in his stead. The chief distinction of little Oliver now was that he was name-sake to the master of Hinchinbrook.

On March 25th—New Year's Day according to the old style —the bells in Huntingdon that rang the new year in were hardly silent when the street was startled by the flying hoofs of more than one headlong horseman racing for the north, to announce to the Scotch King the old Queen's death and his own accession. Few but children and drunkards would get much sleep in the town that night. Any fool could understand that the change of dynasty was portentous; but what it portended, not the wisest could foresee. The Puritans had their hopes of a king trained by Presbyterians. "As the twig is bent," they thought, "so the tree's inclined." There was no Darwin to teach them that pressure, applied at a certain point to the germinating plant, determines its growth *towards* the side of pressure instead of *away* from it.

But, whatever may have been the case with Oliver's parents, the uncle at Hinchinbrook thought more of the revival of the royal honours of his house than of any sectarian issues. An early post down the north road bore the humble and loyal offer of his mansion for the new Sovereign's lodging on his way southward. He had almost a prescriptive right to receive majesty on its travels; and preparations on the most sumptuous scale commenced before the gracious acceptance could arrive. On Wednesday, April 27th, the British Soloman reached Hinchinbrook; and all Huntingdon crowded the approaches to gaze with awe upon the new monarch. In the pedantic eloquence of the King himself we may read what delight it was to him to find himself at every point of his journey gazed upon as one of the wonders of the world; and that Huntingdon did not come short in enthusiasm we may well believe. Amongst the gazers was no doubt the little Oliver, who, as the nephew and namesake of his

---

* The story of his being carried off by an ape to the roof of Hinchinbrook rests on no authority. Apes of the size supposed were no commoner in a domesticated state then than now. In all probability the story is based on popular myths of Oliver's dealings with the devil.

Majesty's host, would be a privileged spectator. Thus, his first ideas of royalty would be a confused vision of a tottering, stuttering, staring man, grandly dressed, with the gallant uncle, the child's ideal of greatness, bowing low before him, a crowd of gentlemen talking gibberish,* and in the background a raving, shouting mob, thronging around flowing beer-barrels, or rolling in the gutter. The King was pleased, and more than pleased with his entertainment. He staid two nights before he resumed his journey. And amongst the subjects of mutual congratulation which little Oliver heard talked of by his elders after the pageant had rolled away, was this, that uncle Oliver was henceforth to be Sir Oliver, as his grandfather had been Sir Henry; and that uncle Thomas Steward was now Sir Thomas.

Sir Oliver seems to have gone up to London for the coronation ceremony, which took place July 25th. At any rate about that time he received the Order of the Bath, an honour, doubtless, much talked of in the family circle.

When Parliament met, he was one of the knights chosen for the county, and Henry Cromwell, Robert's younger brother, of Upwood, near Ramsey, was elected for the town, events which would cause much family activity, and must surely have awakened in young Oliver's mind some wonder as to the nature of the big talking-house up in London where his uncles were going to sit.

The issue of the Hampton Court Conference considerably lessened the suspense with which the opening of the new King's first Parliament would otherwise have been awaited. For the Puritans now knew what they had to expect. Still they had some hope from the great assembly to whose respectful urgency even the imperious Elizabeth had yielded. But the effusive speech of the royal pedant at the opening of Parliament, justified the worst forebodings. It showed that the nation had crowned a hypocrite, who would be a despot, if only duplicity could smooth the way for cowardice. The grandiose condescension with which he affected to treat the consultation of Parliament as a flattering compliment from an all-sufficient giant to impotent pigmies, suggested that there would be other questions besides that of religion to be fought over presently. But the tenderness shown to Romish reaction, and the intolerance exhibited towards pro-

---

* The Scotch dialect was not easy for English people to follow then.

gressive Protestantism, must have smitten many a Puritan soul with the sickness of despair.

What effect such language from the throne would have on a people, to the majority of whom the Papacy was the abomination of desolation, is easily conceivable. But this was not the only point of dissidence between the King and his new subjects. He assumed a right to decide on disputed elections, and this, if conceded, would have reduced the Commons to nominees of the Crown. He presumed on an interference with free speech in Parliament, such as had been barely tolerated from Queen Elizabeth, and was insufferable from this stranger. He seemed to consider it an impertinence for the people's representatives to deal with anything but supply, and showed a strong disposition, by his proclamations and his "impositions," to take both legislation and taxation entirely into his own hands. Indeed, it was evident from the very beginning of his reign that the accession of the Stuart dynasty had set up, between the Crown and Parliament, a conflict which, if not arranged by some satisfactory compromise, must end in the destruction of one or the other.

It is of the utmost importance to any conception of the probable development of Oliver Cromwell, to remember that he grew up in a society interested and agitated, throughout the whole period of his youth and early manhood, by this long-continued strain of the relations between King and people. The traditions of the family were strongly Protestant; and we may well believe that occasional letters of mild dissatisfaction from the county and borough members suggested, in little Oliver's home, many grave forebodings of coming evil, such as make a far more serious impression than is often supposed on the minds of children. And such impressions may well have grown to a panic terror when the Gunpowder Plot of 1605 horrified the whole land with the limitless possibilities of spiritual wickedness.

But in the meantime it is said that Oliver renewed his experience of royalty in the persons of the King's children, who, some time in 1604 are believed to have lodged at Hinchinbrook on their way south. It is credible, indeed highly probable; for the mansion was conveniently situated for the purpose, and, to a host who had so nobly entertained himself, the King would not grudge the expensive honour of entertaining his children. That Oliver, who was very nearly of the same age with Prince Charles, would be sent for on such an occasion, is also likely. But when tradition adds that the two infants quarrelled over their toys, and that the sturdy Oliver drew blood from the royal nose of the more delicate Charles, it is far more likely that we have here mythopœic fancy at work, than that children so young, and in such circumstances, should have been left without judicious attendance.

If Oliver as a child was rough and violent, it was not for want of sisters. There were three of them, as we have seen, when he was born. Then came three more sisters in succession, Margaret, afterwards Mrs. Walton, whose son was killed at Marston Moor ; Anna, afterwards Mrs. Sewster; and Jane, afterwards Mrs. Desbrow, whose husband was well-known in the civil wars. The ninth child of this numerous family was a boy named after his father, Robert, but dying within three months. Then, finally, came another girl, the seventh, whose name, Robina, gives a pathetic hint of the grief felt for Robert, and of the fond wish of the father to perpetuate his name. No other boy was likely to come to this house; so this last baby girl must take a feminine variation on her father's name. So far as her worldly lot was concerned this Robina was more fortunate than any of her sisters. She became the wife of the Rev. Dr. French, and on his death married Bishop Wilkins. Her only child, a daughter by her former marriage, became the wife of Archbishop Tillotson.

The demands of so large a family must surely have sometimes strained the moderate resources of the father. Perhaps this may have had something to do with Robert Cromwell's disinclination to service in Parliament. And, certainly, it would be a strong reason for adding to his income by all legitimate methods. With this purpose, it is said, that he carried on a brewing business, an assertion which has caused far more controversy than such a matter is worth. The real fact seems to be this. Mrs. Cromwell, like most good housewives of the time, was in the habit of brewing for the consumption of her own family. The water of the Hinchin, flowing through the court-yard of her house, was very suitable to the purpose, as, indeed, had probably been known to the Hinchinbrook Cromwells for three generations. The combination of good water, skill and care, resulted in such brewing that Mrs. Cromwell's ale became famous among the neighbours, and people having less convenience in their own homes would take it as a favour to be allowed to buy from her. Thus, a quiet little business grew up, which proved of great advantage when the father was taken away. Amidst all the falsehoods of the Restoration biographies we find them generally disposed to recognise the quiet virtues of Oliver's parents. And in the absence of any other known resources, beyond some £300 a year from land and houses, it seems probable enough, as asserted by one of them,* that the brewing business enabled Mrs. Cromwell to "give each of her daughters a fortune sufficient to marry them to persons of genteel families."

Oliver's elder brother, Henry, died in boyhood, thus leaving him the one boy among seven surviving sisters. Such a position does not seem very likely to have produced ungovernable roughness and rudeness. It would be more likely to make of him what is vulgarly called a "milksop." Still, the tremendous energy he exhibited as a man must have shown premonitory symptoms in the boy, and he may have been troublesome enough. All we can say is, that the stories of his orchard robbing and street fighting rest on no tangible evidence; and are precisely the sort of fiction likely to be bred of local gossip, instructed by after events. On the other hand, there were elements of tenderness and affection in Oliver's mature character, which we may well trace in part, at least, to the predominance of female influence over his earliest life.

The Huntingdon Grammar School was at that time presided over by Dr. Beard, a clergyman of moderately Puritanic leanings, or, as we should say, of Low Church views. He wrote books which attracted some attention in their time. When Oliver, as a new boy, was brought to school by his father, it would have been difficult for the reverend doctor to conceive that, in two hundred years, the only possible interest attaching to his books would arise from the indirect light they might cast on the sort of influence he exerted over this fair-haired, bright-eyed, sturdy-limbed boy. The fate of England stood meekly by his knee, looking from father to master and back, not without anxiety. But the doctor—small blame to him—could see nothing more than an ill-instructed pupil, at whose imperfect grounding in the rudiments he probably "pished" and "pshawed," as schoolmasters generally do.

* Quoted by Noble; apparently Heath.

Restoration biographies say that the boy had fits of application alternating with fits of idleness. This may have been so. But as in mature life his attainments were quite up to the average of his time, and his interest in learning and literature considerable, we may be sure that he made reasonable progress at school. For he went from school direct to the University, where he stayed only about fourteen months, and he never had any other opportunity for study.

Among the stories most persistently told of Oliver's boyhood, are those of his alleged presages of future greatness. The Rev. Mark Noble, after dismissing other idle tales, says :—

"It is more certain that Oliver averred that he saw a gigantic figure which came and opened the curtains of his bed, and told him that he should be the greatest person in the kingdom, but did not mention the word king. And though he was told of the folly, as well as the wickedness of such an assertion, he persisted in it; for which he was flogged by Dr. Beard at the particular desire of his father. Notwithstanding which, he would sometimes repeat it to his uncle Steward, who told him it was traitorous to relate it."

This story shows such barbarous ideas of education, both on the part of Robert Cromwell and of Dr. Beard, that we may be permitted to hope it is more than doubtful. The variety of forms assumed by the tradition betrays the absence of any clear and definite source. When a man's career excites so much wonder as Cromwell's did, gossips have an inveterate tendency to find omens and presages in the most ordinary experiences of his youth. And it would be strange if an only son, the father's hope, idolised by a mother and seven sisters, had never said anything which betrayed ambitious whims and fancies.

It is also said that at one of their festivals the pupils of the Huntingdon Grammar School acted a fantastic allegorical comedy called *Lingua*, in which the characters represented the tongue and the five senses. The part of Tactus (or Touch) was, it is alleged, assigned to Oliver at his very earnest desire, and the reason suggested for that desire is the attractiveness of a scene in which Tactus, entering, stumbles over a crown and sceptre, then puts the crown on his head and declaims some lines, declaring its appropriateness to his worth. Obviously there is nothing very improbable in this. Any schoolboy would like a part made conspicuous by a crown and sceptre. And if there is anything in such a story illustrative of Oliver's character, it is surely the force of will by which he succeeded in getting his own way.*

But, indeed, doubt is thrown upon the whole story of the performance by the circumstance that the comedy, first printed in 1607, was said, by way of recommendation, to have been first acted at Trinity College, Cambridge,† and afterwards at the Free Grammar School in Huntingdon. Before 1607 it is of course impossible that Oliver can have taken such a part.

The manner of the boy's life during these years can only be guessed from surrounding circumstances. School and its studies occupied a great part of his time. His parents were certainly diligent attendants at church, and he with them. Holidays would often be spent with his cousins at Hinchinbrook. In 1611 his sister, Joan, would appear to have been married to Mr. William Baker, of whom we know nothing more. But the marriage would, no doubt, be a time of rejoicing for Oliver amongst the rest. Each year he would be able to understand more of the uneasiness pervading the country because of the King's leaning to Romish traditions, and his arbitrary treatment of the House of Commons. In 1612 came the news of the death of Prince Henry. Charles now became Prince of Wales, and both boys and men who had seen him on his passage through Huntingdon would be set speculating as to what sort of a king he would make. Next, all the country heard with joy of the marriage of James's daughter Elizabeth to the Elector Palatine; for now, surely, her father would feel himself committed to the Protestant interest. Then Huntingdon received a new archdeacon, but probably saw little of him, and did not like what it heard of him; for this was Dr. Laud, already marked and prominent amongst the Romanisers of the Church.

Two days before his seventeenth birthday, that is, on April 23rd, 1616, Oliver was admitted a fellow-commoner in Sidney Sussex College, Cambridge. The reasons for the selection of this College are probably given correctly by Mr. Sanford :—

---

* The readiness of prejudice to convert commonplace facts into portents is shown by Mr. Symonds' memorandum in the Harleian collection (991, p. 22). Assigning the occurrence to Cambridge, he seems to treat the assumption of the crown, and the question, " if it did not become him," as an extempore addition to the performance, suggested by the youth's morbid longing for his own coronation.

† Noble says this is stated in the first edition of the play. Neither in that nor in any other edition in the British Museum can I find any such statement.

" Sidney Sussex College counted among its benefactors the landed family of Montagu in Huntingdonshire, and members of several branches of that family entered as students. The families of Montagu and Cromwell must have had frequent intercourse, being the two leading county proprietors, and nothing was more natural than that young Oliver should join the College with which they were connected."*

Mr. Sanford adds that Cromwell's future commander, Edward Montagu, then Viscount Mandeville, entered the same College in January 1618. The tutor to whose oversight Oliver was committed, was Mr. Richard Howlet, who was known to, and favoured by, the Montagu family. The master of the College was Dr. Samuel Warde, who was so far of Puritan tendencies that years afterwards he attracted the disapproval of Laud, though the good man also fell into trouble with the Parliament, near the end of his life, for helping the King to a hundred pounds out of the College funds. He had the reputation of being a strict disciplinarian, and the College under his rule was distinguished above others by the correctness of its manners.

We may believe that the fame of the College in the latter respect very much strengthened in Mr. Robert Cromwell's mind the arguments possibly drawn from the favour of the Montagues. Under such supervision he might leave his son for the first time alone among strangers, with comparatively little anxiety.†

The Restoration biographies naturally pursue the youth to Cambridge with relentless zeal. He is said never to have attained a degree, because he had not the " worth and merit" for it.‡ He is described as " throwing himself into a dissolute and disorderly course," as becoming " famous for football, cricket, cudgelling, and wrestling," and as acquiring " the name of royster."§ We

---

* " Studies on the Great Rebellion," p. 202.
† The entry in the College books is as follows :—

" A Festo Annunciationis, 1616. Oliverius Cromwell, Huntingdoniensis admissus ad commeatum Sociorum Aprilis vicesimo tertio ; Tutore Magistro Ricardo Howlet." (Given by Carlyle). That is—" From the Feast of the Annunciation, 1616. Oliver Cromwell of Huntingdon, admitted a fellow commoner, April 23rd ; Tutor Master Richard Howlet." Between this and the next entry (Carlyle) a note is interpolated, which may be Englished thus :—" This was that archhypocrite, that most abandoned murderer, who having, by shameful slaughter, put out of the way the most pious king, Charles the First, grasped the very throne, and for the space of nearly five years, under the title of Protector, harassed three kingdoms with inflexible tyranny."

‡ Heath.   § Sir William Dugdale.

are told that he " never reached any good knowledge in the Latin tongue ; "* " made no proficiency in any kind of learning." Against these vague assertions we have to set, first, the fact that he left the University for family reasons before he could have been examined for a degree, which is a very sufficient cause for his not obtaining one.   Next, we have the testimony of foreign ambassadors in his later years that he was able to understand spoken Latin, and to reply in the same tongue.   Again, it may well be believed that under Dr. Warde's rule, as described above, such a " roystering " student would speedily have been dismissed.   On the whole, the account adopted with approval by Noble from Harris's " Life of Cromwell," is probably a fair statement of the truth : " It is far from being improbable that he was fonder of active amusements than of learning ; but it is certain that instead of totally neglecting his studies, his tutor, by discovering the bent of his disposition, had address sufficient to persuade him to become a proficient in the Latin language."

Early in the next year (1617) King James visited Hinchin-brook again on his way towards Scotland, to force bishops on a Church described by himself as " the sincerest kirk in the world."   He was accompanied by his new favourite, George Villiers, whom cunning courtiers had thrown in his way to draw off the royal affections from the justly detested Somerset. On this occasion, also, Huntingdon saw once more its arch-deacon, who was in the royal retinue.   But rumours of the law's shameful subserviency to royal caprice in dealing with the villainies of the late favourite and his wicked wife pre-ceded the King everywhere on his progress, and cooled the ardour of loyalty even more than James's arbitrary rule in matters of religion and taxation.

The reception of majesty by the knight of Hinchinbrook must have been much less splendid than on the previous occa-sion.   For the extravagance of the father having been too well imitated by the son, the retention of the great house threatened to become an impossibility.†

* Heath.

† During the revels occasioned by this visit, Heath relates that the young Oliver displayed the vulgarity of his manners in so offensive a form that his uncle ordered him to be ducked in a horse-pond. By other unfriendly biographers this is said to have taken place during a Christmas festival. Apparently none

Robert Cromwell was already under the shadow of approaching death. If, as is by no means unlikely, his son did come over from the neighbouring University to be present at the King's reception, the decaying health of the father must have cast a gloom over the occasion, so far as Oliver and his mother and sisters were concerned. The purpose of the royal visit to Scotland would certainly be the subject of talk in the town. And as the King and his train swept northwards, the dying man may well have had his forebodings about a possible religious conflict in the near future, when his family might sorely miss a father's care. At the beginning of June he felt that his end was near. On the sixth of that month there came by appointment to his house his brother Richard, his nephew, John Cromwell, son of Sir Oliver, his old friend Dr. Beard, and one Paul Kent, unknown to us. The schoolmaster found his former pupil in great trouble; his father very ill; mother, we will suppose, unable to come down to them; all conversation sad and whispered. Then comes the lawyer, grave, but curt and prompt. Would they step into Mr. Cromwell's room, as they are desired to be witnesses to his will? So they tread softly, and with constrained face and voice greet their dying friend, whom yet they hope to see well again, if it be God's will. And they watch the thin hand trace for the last time the earthly name. In robust letters they append their own signatures, and take their farewells. As they part in the street, or pace in groups to Huntingdon, they have their reminiscences of the dying to tell, and their regrets for children left fatherless—specially, perhaps, for that big-boned, large-headed boy, who looks as if he might need a strong curb. On the 24th of the same month Oliver's father was laid in his grave at All Saints.*

The chill of bereavement, like frost on the verge of harvest, often suddenly ripens an undeveloped faculty in the young. Boys in their teens too often rely upon the control and care of a father, instead of exerting their own powers of self-guidance. At the

of them had any evidence other than country-side gossip. That the lad was fond of practical jokes is probable enough, for he showed such a propensity even in mature age. And some excesses of boisterous mirth might be remembered and exaggerated to his discredit. But that a youth with his training and associations should ever have given way to mere indecent buffoonery, is so unlikely that we should require clear evidence before believing it; and such evidence has never been even alleged.

* Provisions of the will and names of witnesses from Noble, p. 84.

same time they sometimes chafe against his authority, and assert their manhood by self-willed caprice, with an inward, though unconscious assurance, that the very authority they dispute will keep them from going far wrong. But when they are bereaved of their natural guardian, they awake to the necessity of guarding themselves. Their incipient manhood has no need to assert itself by mere petulance. The demands upon it have suddenly become serious. And thus it often happens that wayward boys, for whom friends have prophesied destruction on the death of their father, have been changed by such a loss into wary and determined men. This is the case, of course, only where there is a latent power and worth responsive to the obvious demands of changed circumstance.

Oliver was just eighteen; an age at which he might be boy or man according to circumstances. It strikes us that he changed all at once from one to the other. This is probably the significance of his quitting Cambridge, which he did at this time.* The reason for this step is not at first sight obvious. The income of the family was not in the slightest degree affected by the father's death; while, on the other hand, their expenses would necessarily be diminished. If, then, it had been possible to maintain Oliver at the University before, it was not more difficult, perhaps, indeed, easier, to do so now.

The strong probability is that he left the University, not by his mother's wish, but by his own determination. He had no ambition to be a scholar, and he was the only man left to take care of his mother and sisters. He had no thought of other destiny than the management of the little property and such municipal activities as had been his father's. He might be a Parliament man, of course, as so many of his relatives had been. But the preparation for such a position was not to be found in Cambridge; it must be got by experience of town and county affairs. We may picture him, then, in his home, trying to step into his father's shoes, and finding them at first too large. Even his widowed mother would relent into a wan smile now and then as she noted the mingling of boyish vanity with manly intent. The sisters found the new domestic sovereign

---

* As Carlyle says, it is a matter of " inference." Oliver may possibly have gone back for a term or so, but not for longer.

perhaps at times insufferable, but they could well protect themselves, and, besides, was he not "our Oliver"?

By the will signed shortly before his death, Robert Cromwell left to his wife, in addition to her jointure, two-thirds of his property for the term of twenty-one years, for the purpose of bringing up the daughters and establishing them in life. There was a sum of £600 owing to him by his brother-in-law, Richard Whalley, which money was to go to the daughters. The remainder of the property, and ultimately the whole of it, excepting of course his mother's jointure and the above amount of £600, went to his only son.* The arrangement seems a singular one. The sudden change in his wife's circumstances, after a term of twenty-one years, appears arbitrary. But the marriage of all the daughters, and the happy relationship which, to the very end of Mrs. Robert Cromwell's long life, subsisted between her and her son, prevented any practical inconvenience. In the course of this same year, 1617, a most eventful one for the family history, her father, William Steward, died at Ely, leaving his son, Sir Thomas, to succeed, both to his office of farmer of tithes, and also to his property.

The will of Robert Cromwell was proved in London on the 21st of August. Oliver may have gone up with the executors and seen the great city for the first time. Either then, or shortly afterwards, it was decided that he should, for the present, remain there. The object apparently was that he might study law; at least Noble found a very general tradition to that effect, and goes so far as to say that he was entered at Lincoln's Inn. But his name has not been found either in that or any other Inn, and Carlyle is probably right in the supposition that he was admitted to the chambers of some lawyer, with a view to his gaining such knowledge as a country gentleman might need. We may surmise that there was also another purpose in his mother's mind, and that was to provide some temporary occupation for a lad who was disinclined to the University, who thought himself too old to be at school, and was yet too young to manage affairs at home.

During the two years that Oliver was in London no Parliament sat. The last, after a single session of only two months, had been dissolved in 1614 because of its impracticable deter-

* Noble.

mination to have grievances redressed before supply was granted.
Some members had timidly suggested that it would be well to
oblige the King, "lest he should lay a heavy hand upon them."
For, said they, what was now threatened was "a dissolution, not
of this, but of all Parliaments." These gloomy prophets might
have found much to justify their predictions at the time when
Oliver Cromwell came to town. The King had already begun
his pet project of a Spanish marriage for Prince Charles, which
he knew to be an insult to the nation's faith, an abomination
and a terror to all the best elements of the population. He was
laying on imposts—impositions, as they were called—by no other
authority than his own arbitrary will. He was extorting money
by an odious enforcement of nearly obsolete feudal rights ; and,
being still embarrassed by debt, he had swallowed the gilded
bait of Raleigh's proposed voyage in search of treasure ; but, at
the same time, true to his Spanish infatuation, he had given a
warning to the Most Catholic King which ensured the failure
that the veteran navigator expiated by his death.

The city of London, in which the Puritan party was strong,
was seething with discontent at a system of government not less
inimical to Protestantism than vexatious to trade and commerce.
And Oliver Cromwell's nearest associates in London would
certainly appear to have been found in city circles. Sir James
Bourchier was one of the merchant princes of that time. He
had a town house on Tower Hill, and also an estate near Felsted
in Essex. There was a connection between the Hampdens and
Bourchiers, and it is not assuming too much to suppose that the
former introduced their young kinsman to the prosperous city
knight. In the family of Sir James Bourchier, Oliver found a
stronger attraction than even that of pleasant friendship. There
was a daughter, Elizabeth, who won his heart, and whom he resolved to make his wife. But the love of youths and maidens
does not shine so conspicuously in history as it does in romances,
and of this wooing there lives no record except the prosaic and
almost dumb entry in the registers of St. Giles's, Cripplegate,
under the date of August 22nd, 1620—"Oliver Cromwell to
Elizabeth Bourchier." This is meagre enough ; but, nevertheless,
it has an eloquence of its own sufficient to dispel the slanders
with which the resurrection men of the Restoration strove to
add falsifications of the Protector's character to the indignities

wrought on his corpse. We are asked to believe that in London he gave free rein to the vicious inclinations which had caused his banishment from home. Without even the pretence of any shadow of evidence, except an unauthenticated story of his having restored, in after life, some money won in gaming, it is insinuated that he spent his days in sloth and his nights in debauchery.

On the other hand, let these facts be weighed. He was little over eighteen when he came to London, and hardly four months more than twenty-one when he took his wife home to his mother in Huntingdon. It would seem also very probable that Noble is right in asserting that he returned to his native town some time before his marriage. Now boys of eighteen are often wayward, foolish, and unsteady; but rarely, indeed, especially when brought up as Oliver had been, do they rush headlong into the vices of men. Unless in exceptional natures, there is always some touch of shyness, some relic of the child, some tender fastidiousness to be overcome, before the young soul can lie down and wallow in the mire of vice. If, coming from a home where he was idolised by a mother and seven sisters, Oliver was without any vestige of such delicacy of feeling, then he must have been a young brute who could by no possibility have developed into the historic character we know, and the writer of the letters we possess. Nothing we know of his mother justifies us in thinking she would have been so wanting in motherly instincts as to send a lad like that to certain perdition in the dissolute capital of King James the First. We are bound to believe that she had confidence in his power to withstand temptation, and her reasons for such confidence must have been found in his previous conduct. Even if we assume, then, what is no doubt very reasonable, the possibility of his yielding to evil, we must allow a few months to elapse before he reaches the depth imagined by "Carrion" Heath. But at the other end of his short career in town we find him married to the daughter of a city magnate. Such a marriage, at the age of twenty-one, surely implies a previous engagement of some duration; for otherwise the father of the girl would have been very exceptional if he had not insisted on the delay of a year or so, that such very young people might be quite sure they knew their own minds. Indeed, as already said, the connection between the Hampdens and Bourchiers makes it pretty certain that

D

young Cromwell was made known to the latter on his first
coming up to town.* If all these considerations are duly
weighed, it will be seen that the dissolute courses attributed to
him are extremely improbable, and as they rest on no evidence
but malignant rumour we may confidently acquit him.

Expressions of his religious experience have been thought, by
some who do not understand such things, to point to his remembrance of wild days in youth; but these it is better to leave to a
later stage. That the young man should have taken his wife to
his mother's home, where several of his sisters still remained unmarried, and that this arrangement should have continued for
eleven years while children were rapidly filling the house once
more with shouts and laughter not unmixed with wailings, is
surely suggestive of strong family union and sincere mutual
affection. The home-coming, the mother's welcome to the new
daughter, the eagerness of the girls to show their new sister
everything in the neighbourhood, and especially their uncle Sir
Oliver's mansion and grounds; the pride of the young husband
in the impression made by his wife on all the home circle,—all
these have been, and we may picture them to ourselves; but
that age had other things to think of, and forgot them.

* It is even possible that Oliver was received into the Bourchier family during
his residence in London. The remarkable honour in which he was held at
Felsted, even before his public fame—as will be afterwards shown—seems to
imply something more than occasional visits after his marriage.

CHAPTER III.

EARLY MANHOOD.

FOR eight years after his marriage Oliver lived quietly at home, occupied, so far as we know, only with the management of the family property, and perhaps seconding his prudent mother's efforts to increase the profits of the brewery. What dowry Elizabeth Bourchier brought with her, if any, is not recorded. But before leaving London her husband had covenanted to secure to her, as her jointure, certain portions of his estate, consisting of the parsonage-house, glebe, and tithes of Hartford. When it is remembered that by his father's will the mother was to possess two-thirds of the property for twenty-one years, we cannot suppose that there was much left at the personal disposal of the young husband. But mother, son, wife, and sisters were apparently on such terms that it was easy to have all things in common.

It is usual, but without any adequate ground, to refer Oliver's " conversion " to the time immediately following his marriage. His early traducers, who, on the subject of his vices are inconsistent with themselves and with each other, do, indeed, speak of a change that came over him in his early manhood. But they assign no definite limits of time; and some of them, entirely overlooking the date of his marriage, describe him as behaving with more recklessness than ever after his despairing mother had recalled him from London with the vain idea that she might control him better at home.* On the other hand, the only trustworthy records of Oliver's real spiritual history are to be found in his letters and speeches. Now the first letter extant, written six years after his marriage, affords no indication at all of religious enthusiasm, though the occasion was certainly one appropriate enough for its expression ; and the later letters and speeches, in which the language of spiritual experience abounds, suggest no sharp and sudden crisis of decisive change, such as could be referred to a definite moment, or even to a particular

* Heath. *Flagellum.*

D 2

year of his life. That he did pass through terrors of conviction, and sloughs of doubt, and storms of conflict, is certain enough. But the medical testimony, reasonably interpreted as referable to such mental troubles, would seem to belong to the period of Oliver's first Parliamentary experience.

At twenty-one years of age it is very improbable that he was the victim of morbid melancholy, especially as he had just secured the wife of his choice. Bad as the times were in which he lived, life could hardly have seemed to him stale or unprofitable just then; and at his age so much vital force is still expended in growth, if not in actual stature, at least in general development both mental and physical, that the misery of self-consuming energy could hardly yet be realised. On the whole, we think of Oliver Cromwell at this time as a stalwart lad, in whom unmistakeable signs of breeding and culti-vation appeared through the homely guise of a Huntingdon burgess. His capacious head and fine eyes might well arrest attention, and suggest the question, Whom have we here? But his features were indicative more of undeveloped power than of easy grace. His manner, we conjecture, was at this early age shy and retiring rather than obtrusive. But changeful flashes of anger and of fun showed an eager life behind this reticent exterior. Opposition would engender a gloom suggestive of sleeping thunder; and if persisted in unreasonably, would provoke a passionate will. Otherwise the instructions of good Dr. Beard, and domestic pre-cept and example, aided by the growing inspiration of the times, had given the young man devout thoughts, and prompted in him a desire to serve God rather than the devil, if only the way could be shown him.

The facility and apparent suddenness with which his military capacity asserted itself in middle life would suggest that drilling and practice in the use of arms must have been among the exercises of his youth. And sufficient opportunity for this would be afforded by the military system of the times. Every county had its " trained bands," officered by the local magnates and gentry according to their degree.

Before the end of his twenty-third year his first son was born, and was baptised at St. John's on October 13th, 1621, by the name of Robert, after the grandfather. A second son, Oliver, was born at the beginning of 1623. And the father must have been indebted to these infants for a deeper sense of his responsibility in the world. For children have a mission to their parents long before the latter can give any instruction to *them.* The sense of having a young soul to defend and guide aright through the world is often the final touch of education which constrains the man to put away childish things; and we need not doubt that Oliver, the youthful father, began to have more anxious thoughts than ever about the world into which he had brought his children.

It was not a promising state of things. The saying of Solomon about "an old and foolish king who will no more be admonished," must have had a special significance for the people of England in those days. Constrained by the failure of all arbitrary impositions to furnish him with sufficient means, James, after five years' interval, called a Parliament in 1621. The Commons protested against monopolies and consequent unnatural prices; against the despotic imposition of duties without their consent, a clear infraction of time-honoured charters; against favour to the Papists, which, it was declared by one member, had brought things to such a pass that "it would grow soon to an equal balance, which were the greater number, Papists or Protestants." Above all, the House protested, in tones now rising to manly indignation and now passing into as manly a pathos, against the cowardly neglect of Protestant interests on the continent, and the unnatural abandonment of a daughter of England. " It hath been the honour of England," exclaimed Sir Robert Phelips, " not to bear an ill *word;* and shall we now take such a *blow* as that which hath been given to the King of Bohemia, and our King's children, who, we may say, are relieved by the alms of others ? "

But King James preferred the way of match-making, and was very angry that petty knights and low-born burgesses, whose proper office was to fill his coffers, should presume to meddle with matters beyond their understanding. " The far distance of our person," he wrote from Newmarket, " hath emboldened some fiery and popular spirits in our House of Commons to debate and argue publicly* on matters far beyond their reach or capacity." What follows may help us to understand the courage required to be a " popular " man in those days. Much complaint

---

* This is, of course, an exaggeration. The debates were supposed to be secret; and it was an offence against the House to reveal them.

had been made of the imprisonment of Sir Edward Sandys after the previous Parliament, and the royal rebuke might well have shaken the resolution of men who, the moment after dissolution, would be helplessly at the King's mercy. " We think ourself very free," wrote this sceptred pedagogue, as though he were toying with a birch in the sight of naughty boys, rather than wielding the sword of State among men of the breed of Eliot, Pym, and Hampden, " we think ourself very free and able to punish any man's misdemeanours in Parliament, as well during their sitting as after ; which we mean not to spare hereafter, upon any occasion of any man's insolent behaviour there, that shall be ministered unto us. And if they have already touched any of these points, which we have forbidden, in any petition of theirs, to be sent unto us, it is our pleasure you shall tell them, that except they reform it before it comes to our hands, we will not deign the hearing or answering of it."

The stand taken by the Commons in face of this letter of the King was an ominous sign of the inspiration now beginning to stir the better part of the nation to an heroic temper. The insulting missive met with no hot rejoinder ; it aroused no hysteric eloquence about the rights of man. There was a solemn pause, as if for a full realisation of the danger to be met, until the suppressed emotion of the House found short but dignified expression in the words of Sir Dudley Digges, who moved " That they should now rise, but not as in discontent, but rather to resort to their prayers, and then to consider of this great business."

" Now," said Sir Robert Phelips, " is the time to justify the affection of the people to the king, and to defend the privileges of this House which our ancestors have delivered us. . . . But since we have broken our privileges in yielding our obedience . . . I know not what hath caused this soul-killing letter from the king ; soul-killing, I mean, in respect of the earnest desire of our souls in that petition."

But the deep pathos of the strait in which these men now found themselves between loyalty to the sovereign and faithfulness to the people, received most touching expression from Sir George Moore, the member for Surrey.

" We now stand," he said, " between the indignation of our king and the privileges of our House, which are the spirit of the blood of the liberties of the common weal. Whereas the king is misinformed that we have meddled with things above our reach and capacity; we have not done otherwise than the Samaritan woman, who out of her faith did but touch the hem of Christ's garment; for which Christ did not blame her, but said that her faith had saved her. And I hope when the king shall be rightly informed, he will, seeing our humility, love, and care for his honour, encourage us to proceed."

But it was impossible to "rightly inform" a man who was wholly wrong-headed. And the apologetic petition on which the House agreed was met with another scolding message because it referred to freedom of speech in Parliament as "an ancient and undoubted right." Thereupon arose fresh debate, and an attempt of the King to explain his position. "The plain truth is," he wrote, "that we cannot with patience endure our subjects to use such antimonarchical words to us concerning their liberties, except they had subjoined that they were granted unto them by the grace and favour of our predecessors." But, "as for his intention," he added that he had neither purpose nor desire to infringe on their privileges. He was, or seemed to be, quite incapable of understanding that in some cases title may be of more importance than actual possession. On the other hand, the Commons felt that to allow the treatment of their liberties as a matter of royal grace would be political suicide for themselves, and a paralysis of the constitution at a vital crisis of its growth.

They therefore went into committee of the whole House "to consider of privileges." And notwithstanding assurances "full of oil," as Sir Thomas Crewe said, concerning the gracious intentions of their Sovereign, they held an unusually late sitting* for the purpose of drawing up and entering on their journals a solemn protestation of their constitutional rights. In this protest they asserted, as the "ancient and undoubted birthright and inheritance of the subjects of England, full freedom for parliamentary discussion, in any order commending itself to their own discretion, of all arduous and urgent affairs concerning the king, state, and defence of the realm, and of the Church of England, and the making and maintenance of laws, and redress of mischiefs and grievances." The immediate result of this proceeding was that the King demanded the journals of the House, as a schoolmaster might order up a peccant exercise book, and in the presence of his council, with his own hand plucked out the

* Dec. 18, 1621.

protest, and cast it contemptuously aside. The Parliament was instantly dissolved, and Coke, Phelips, Selden, Pym, and others were committed to prison to receive the penalties they had deliberately faced.

Such were the immediate issues of this conflict between the Crown and the Commons. But there were others that were of slower growth. What was the effect when snatches of heroic speech, such as we have heard, were repeated in homes like that at Huntingdon? This is what we must needs picture to ourselves if we would understand the influences that played on the soul of the young Oliver Cromwell. Great as is our loss in the oblivion that has swallowed up almost every record of his early growth, we need not increase that loss by ignoring what is absolutely certain—the traditional interest of his family in public affairs, and the eagerness with which the Spanish match and the opposition of Parliament were then discussed throughout the land. Our judgment on the extent to which personal ambition ruled the life of this man, will necessarily depend in part on the notion we may have of the effect of such events as we have glanced at on his young heart and mind.

But in 1623 the Puritan party, or perhaps we should rather say the nation generally, was suddenly relieved from the dread of Spain and the Inquisition by the return of Prince Charles and the Duke of Buckingham from their romantic expedition, and their determination to break with Spain. For the moment, joy at the conversion of the Court to a deadly hostility against Spain superseded all other considerations; and when James's last Parliament met in February 1624, the whole nation was too eager for action to scrutinise the transparent falsehood of the King's account of the futile negotiations with Rome and Lisbon. Sir Oliver of Hinchinbrook attended this Parliament as knight of his shire, and his nephew would hear from him personally how Prince Charles had kindled the enthusiasm of both Houses in a conference of Lords and Commons on the critical state of relations with Spain. "If in this ye shall fail me," said the Prince, "ye shall not only dishonour me, but bring dishonour upon yourselves. But if ye go on with courage, and show alacrity and readiness in this business, you shall so oblige me unto you now that I will never forget it here-after; and when time doth serve, ye shall find your love and your labour well bestowed." The loyal Sir Oliver, in relating this to his home circle, would be quite of a temper to echo the words of Viscount Mandeville, the future Parliamentary General :—"This conclusion did so take us that we all prayed to God to bless him, as we had just cause to honour him."

But though the King, in his alarm and necessity, showed no disposition now to regard foreign affairs as entirely "beyond the reach and capacity" of his Commons, yet things did not go smoothly. The substitution of a French papistical princess for a Spanish one cast a damp on Puritan rejoicing. An important, and perhaps unprecedented, condition was attached by the Commons to the vote of a subsidy. They required that it should be "paid into the hands, and expended by the direction, of such commissioners as shall hereafter be agreed on in this present session of Parliament." It was a futile arrangement, for the commissioners were obliged to honour all drafts of the Crown; but it showed the temper rising in the House, and the impeachment of the Lord Treasurer was a similar indication.

Meanwhile Oliver's domestic cares and joys went on accumulating as such things do. Through successive marriages of his sisters and the birth of two boys in succession, the feminine character of the household seemed likely to be exchanged for an opposite extreme. But in August 1624 the first daughter, Bridget, was born, and was welcomed with the joy due to the assurance she brought that the monopoly of girls in a former generation was not to be balanced by a monopoly of boys in this. If the proud father, as he took her in his arms, could have read her destinies and their connection with his own, would his joy have been equally pure? That he would not have blenched nor shrunk from his grand doom we may be sure. But of how many innocent delights in home life should we be robbed by that knowledge of the future which men have often foolishly craved!

In the end of March 1625, before this baby girl was a year old, the news flew throughout the land that James was dead and that Charles was King. The new monarch's first Parliament met in June, and Sir Oliver of Hinchinbrook was sent once more, and for the last time, as member for his county.*

---

* By a clerical error he is described as Oliver Cromwell, Esq , in Willis's list of this Parliament ; and this has occasioned the mistaken assertion that his nephew entered the House at that time.

The plague was rife in London and Westminster. In that year it carried off more than thirty-five thousand people. The passing bell was tolling every minute during the early sittings of Parliament, and this in the mood of the times must have added a peculiar solemnity to their deliberations. In July, doubtless to the great relief of the families of members, the Houses adjourned from so dangerous a neighbourhood, and held their remaining sittings at Oxford. But, short as the session was, it proved ominous of discord for the new reign. In finance, in religion, and in foreign politics alike, it was sadly clear that the King was of one mind and the nation of another. In former reigns the duties called "tunnage and poundage" had been granted to the Sovereign for his life-time. But the Commons now ventured to establish a new precedent by giving them only for one year. This course has been sometimes blamed as showing an ungenerous distrust of the young King. But it would have been a very cheap generosity to gratify a private sentiment at the expense of a public trust. And the young King had been so active as Prince of Wales that the Commons may be credited with a reasonably accurate knowledge of the man with whom they had to do.* The gift under such conditions was spurned, indeed was rejected by the Lords, and so began the fatal issue as to the right of taxation.

The King's marriage, and the concessions made to the ecclesiastical train of Queen Henrietta Maria, increased the watchful jealousy of the Puritans against all encroachments of Popery. On the other hand, the known inclinations of the Court encouraged many clerics to sail very close to the popular wind. Prominent among these was the Reverend Dr. Montagu, with his two books "A New Gag for an Old Goose" and "Appello Cæsarem." The "old goose" was a Romish controversialist, and the "gag" was a professed apology for Protestants. But unfortunately this defence of Protestantism consisted mainly in

---

* In November 1621 Charles wrote to Buckingham, " Steenie, the Lower House has this day been a little unruly; but I hope it will turn to the best, for before they rose they began to be ashamed of it. Yet I could wish that the king would send down a commission here that (if need were) such seditious fellows might be made an example to others by Monday next, and till then I would let them alone. It will be seen whether they mean to do good or to persist in their follies; so that the king needs to be patient but a little while. I have spoken with so many of the council as the king trusts most, and they are all of his mind, only the sending of authority to set seditious fellows fast is of my adding." Quoted by Sanford (Studies, &c.) from Halliwell, vol. ii., p. 157.

explaining it away. Montagu's second book was an appeal to the King against the accusations brought upon the author by the former treatise; and it repeated the offence of minimising to the utmost the differences between the Anglican and Roman Churches. If we think of the effect of "Tract XC." in our own times, we may form some conception of the storm thus produced in an age when theological beliefs were far more intense, and when confidence in the power of law to suppress error was far stronger than it is now. The Commons would have summoned Montagu to their bar and committed him to prison. To this course they were strongly urged by Sir Thomas Wentworth; but even more explosive questions arose, and Montagu was for a time forgotten.

With the money granted to James on breaking off the Spanish match, an army of 12,000 men had been raised, but dwindled away and perished without striking a blow against any one except the unfortunate British subjects on whom they had been billeted, and the towns that lay in their line of march to the sea. The disorders caused were the source of bitter complaints, and the Commons, with an eye to Buckingham's evil counsels, insisted on getting some account of the expenditure of the subsidies granted.

Meantime seven or eight ships, supposed to be equipped against Spain, were sent over to Dieppe; and on their arrival the commander, John Pennington, was informed, with a due display of authoritative documents, that he was to put himself and his vessels under the orders of the French king for the reduction of the Protestant rebels of La Rochelle. The order was so astounding, so contrary to all public professions of the Government, and to all English feeling, that the blunt seaman could make nothing of it, and point blank refused to carry it out. Twice the secretary of the French ambassador in England came on board Pennington's ship to denounce him as a rebel against his King. But on the second visit, when he added threats to reproaches, the crews and the soldiers on board took matters into their own hands, and decided the question by hoisting anchor and making sail for England. They declared " they would rather be hanged at home than surrender the ship, or be slaves to the French, and fight against their own religion." *

* Rushworth, Part I., vol. i., p. 175.

King Charles, however, sent Pennington peremptory orders
to transfer the ships, and, accordingly, he returned to Dieppe;
but he had to fire at some of his consorts in order to bring them
back, as they were making off, and all the men on board, except
one gunner, deserted.   Pennington himself then returned to
England, and made his way to Oxford, where the Parliament was
assembled, but he was, in some way or other, suppressed and
kept in concealment till the dissolution. This story told in all
the country towns considerably helped the process of popular
education which ended in the election and arming of the Long
Parliament.

The Parliament was dissolved in August, 1625, without any
redress of grievances, and, the year's grant of tunnage and
poundage having been rejected, without any legal provision for
adequately meeting the expenses of government. An attempt was
made to meet the difficulty by forcing a loan from all men of
substance, in proportion to the estimate formed of their means
by Lords-Lieutenant and other local officials. Recusants were
to be punished by impressment, or even by imprisonment.

The expedient did not answer, and in less than twelve months
from the dissolution of his first Parliament, Charles felt that he
had no option but to summon a second. Thus, at the very time
when the Crown and Court began to conceive the design of dispensing with Parliaments altogether, events brought about, for
the present, a more frequent recurrence of elections than usual,
and so familiarised the constituencies with the exercise of the
franchise, that when the royal conspiracy against the Constitution
was begun in earnest, the people felt the deprivation of their
powers much more than they would otherwise have done.   Huntingdon sent Arthur Mainwaring and John Goldsborough, whose
politics we may perhaps suspect to have been more courtly than
Oliver liked. The Lord-keeper (Sir Thomas Coventry) exerted a
servile eloquence to overwhelm the Commons with a sense of
the honour done them in being brought within the effulgence
of the throne. If they "considered aright, and would think
of that incomparable distance between the supreme height and
majesty of a mighty monarch and the submissive awe and
lowliness of loyal subjects," they would receive "exceeding
comfort and contentment" to know that they were brought
into such high company.

But the temper of the Commons was now too high to be soothed by grandiloquent servility. More peremptorily than ever precedence was claimed for the redress of grievances. And Sir John Eliot took the lead in attacking the unconstitutional influence of the Duke of Buckingham, as the head and fountain of all other grievances. There is a loftiness and lustre in the character of Eliot unparalled even in the heroic annals of his time. Perhaps because he did not live till political perplexities bewildered all directness of aim, perhaps because no turbid element of mysticism clouded his chivalrous devotion, perhaps because, though great, he had not the vastness and variety of powers by which simplicity is endangered,—he certainly commands an unreserved and unqualified admiration such as is never likely to be conceded to Oliver Cromwell. The two characters seem contrasted, like those of Jonathan and David in the portraiture of the Old Testament, the one all fervour and light, the other having the gloom and power of thunder, as well as the swiftness and vividness of lightning. The inspiring effect of Eliot's pure courage and of his cruel fate upon the generation for whose liberties he died, can hardly be overestimated; and already during this Parliament of 1626 the echoes of his impeachment of Buckingham reached all corners of the land.

Residing near to Cambridge, and connected with the University and town by ties of association and friendship, Oliver, no doubt, shared fully in the feelings of helpless indignation revealed by letters of the period at the obstinate enforcement of Buckingham's election as Chancellor. All such influences helped to ripen Oliver's political convictions; but there is no evidence that up to this time he entered fully into the religious enthusiasm by which such convictions were generally sustained. His earliest extant letter is dated October 14th, 1626, and the occasion for writing it might naturally have suggested the expression of religious feeling. The absence of anything of the kind is, therefore, the more noteworthy. Oliver's fourth child, Richard, destined to become his feeble and incompetent successor in the Protectoral office, was born about this time; and, in accordance with the usual custom, an early day was fixed for the baptism. One of the godfathers selected was Mr. Henry Downhall,* fellow

* The account of Mr. Downhall is taken from Appendix I. to Carlyle's Letters and Speeches of Cromwell. 3rd edition.

of St. John's College, Cambridge. He was afterwards vicar of
St. Ives, where Oliver attended his ministry, and was by no
means satisfied with it. He had been elected to his fellowship in
1614, and must have been already in holy orders when he was
invited to become godfather to Richard Cromwell. He came of a
good family in Northamptonshire, and was probably known to the
Cromwells before Oliver's residence at Sidney Sussex. During
that residence the acquaintance ripened into friendship which had
continued ever since. But it is, to say the least, very improbable that this man had any strong sympathy with Puritanism.
Not only was Oliver, when a parishioner of St. Ives, unsatisfied
by his preaching; but in 1642 Downhall was ejected as a
" malignant," and continued to the end of a very long life, a
devoted son of the Anglican Church as restored under Charles II.
He was Archdeacon of Huntingdon when he died in 1669. Now
if at this time Oliver had been as fervent in spirit as he certainly was within a few years afterwards, it is difficult, indeed
impossible, to think that he would have selected such a man as
godfather of his child.

But the notion that Cromwell's religious character was at this
time fully formed becomes still more unlikely when we turn to
the letter of invitation itself. In later years he could hardly
write or speak on the most secular subjects without betraying the
religious feeling that permeated all his thoughts. But now, when
his child is to be declared " a child of God and inheritor of the
kingdom of heaven," nothing occurs to him but the ordinary
civilities of a ceremonious invitation.

" *To my approved good friend, Mr. Henry Downhall, at his chambers
in St. John's College, Cambridge, these :*

" *Huntingdon, 14th October, 1626.*

" LOVING SIR,—Make me so much your servant by being godfather unto
my child. I would myself have come over to have made a formal invitation; but my occasions would not permit me: and therefore hold me in
that excused. The day of your trouble is Thursday next. Let me entreat
your company on Wednesday.

" By this time it appears I am more apt to encroach upon you for new
favours than to show my thankfulness for the love I have already found.
But I know your patience and your goodness cannot be exhausted by

" Your friend and servant,

" OLIVER CROMWELL." *

* Carlyle's Letters and Speeches of Cromwell, Appendix I., vol. iv., p. 406.
(The references are always to the 3rd edition.)

The style of this brief note is quite in accord with the writer's own account of himself, that he was " by birth a gentleman." It suggests also a sensitiveness to the claims of friendship and the courtesies of life such as we should scarcely expect from the rude "royster" of restoration myths. But it is impossible to believe that the man who on such an occasion could write to a valued friend without one word of gratitude for divine favours, or any reference to his growing responsibilities in life, could have been already so full of religious fervour as his later letters show that he became. He had his perplexities and anxieties about his personal salvation. But no complete surrender to God's will, no influx of "marvellous light" had yet made the language of Puritan experience natural to him. He could not make the professions he heard around him. They rather repelled him, and induced in him an attitude of recalcitrance, which in St. Paul's case is described as "kicking against the pricks."

This view of his state of mind at that time is not based only on the preceding letter. Writing from Ely to his cousin, Mrs. St. John, in 1638, he says: "You know what my manner of life hath been. Oh, I lived in and loved darkness, and hated light; I was a chief, the chief of sinners. This is true; I hated godliness, yet God had mercy on me." These words have been taken as an acknowledgment of vicious conduct. But such an interpretation shows a misapprehension of the language of religious experience. He does not say that he loved iniquity or impurity, but that he "loved darkness." In other words, the glory of an ideal life in entire surrender to God's will, redeemed from the bondage of corruption into the glorious liberty of God's children, was glimmering upon him. But clouds generated by humours of self-will gathered to shut it out, and for the present he liked the listless gloom better than the stimulating and tantalising brightness. It is probable that this mood of indecision was maintained for some years after the time of which we are speaking. Indeed the letter to Mrs. St. John would seem to imply that his complete emancipation was even then, in 1638, only a recent experience.

In 1627 the head of the Cromwell family, the Knight of Hinchinbrook, was so far involved in debt that he was compelled to sell the estate, and retire to his other residence at Ramsey

Mere, where he survived in obscurity for thirty years longer. The estate was purchased by Sir Sidney Montague, brother to the Earl of Manchester and uncle to the Viscount Mandeville, Oliver's future colleague. Such a change must have made a difference in the social position of the younger branch in Huntingdon town. They no longer lived on the outskirts of an uncle's estate in the reflected lustre of ancestral wealth. And though it will soon be clear that Oliver needed no patronage— even if he had been likely to get it—to give him factitious importance, yet, in the local squabbles that followed, he probably felt some of the disadvantages of belonging to a decayed and impoverished house.

Two incidents of local or family interest which it is impossible to date accurately, may be most conveniently mentioned here, as at any rate they cannot have happened much later. Oliver's schoolmaster, Dr. Thomas Beard, still continued to hold his post at the hospital of St. John's, and " painfully preached the word of God in the town of Huntingdon on the Sabbath-day duly, to the great comfort of the inhabitants of the said town." * That is, the doctor held one of the lectureships by which the religious reformers of the time tried to supplement the neglect or incompetency of the parochial clergy. But it does not appear that there was much, if any salary, attached to it. For, in recognition of his services, the bailiffs and burgesses made an agreement, dated March 23rd, 1625, with the doctor, granting the power of appointing as his successor in the hospital some learned preacher, who might continue the lectures. This provision was made with a view to the appointment of Henry Cooke, " a faithful and learned preacher, and minister of God's word, whom both the said Thomas Beard and all, or the most part of, the inhabitants of the said town do very much like and approve of." But, between the date of the agreement and the year 1630, some effort, the source of which may be easily guessed, was made to suppress the lectureship. Later on, in 1633, Laud, then raised to the episcopate, succeeded in putting it down, and there is no want of charity in attributing the previous attempt to him. For, as Archdeacon of Huntingdon, he must have been offended by the establishment of so Puritanic an institution. But the local oppo-

* Indenture between the corporation and Dr. Beard, given by Mr. Sanford in "Studies and Illustrations of the Great Rebellion," p. 240.

sition to his interference proved for a time too strong even for his imperious will. And in dedicating to the corporation of Huntingdon his book on " The Theatre of God's Judgments," Dr. Beard says his chief motive is " to show his thankfulness to all that stood faithfully for him in the late business of the lecture, notwithstanding the opposition of some malignant spirits." * Amongst those who " stood faithfully for him," we may probably reckon Oliver Cromwell. For he was keenly alive to any case of injustice that occurred in his neighbourhood, and had a remarkable power of carrying his point when he took a case in hand. It is, perhaps, more than a coincidence† that no sooner had Oliver left Huntingdon than the lectureship was suppressed.

The other incident is an alleged attempt of Oliver to get into his own hands the management of the property of his maternal uncle, Sir Thomas Steward. Sir William Dugdale states that having fallen into pecuniary difficulties by extravagance, Oliver applied to this uncle for help, and on failing to obtain it petitioned the King to have Sir Thomas declared mentally incompetent, and the management of the property committed to the petitioner. That some application was made for a judgment as to Sir Thomas Steward's competence, and that Oliver was concerned in it, is to a certain extent confirmed from another source. For Hackett, in his life of Archbishop Williams, says that in 1645, the archbishop reminded King Charles of the occurrence, in order to warn him of Cromwell's character. But, on the other hand, it is not true that Oliver ever was in pecuniary difficulties. It is also highly improbable, if such a petition was made, that Oliver alone was concerned in it, as there is a Humphrey Steward mentioned in Sir Thomas's will, who would have had a prior right. Considering the well-established character of Oliver's mother and his relations to her, it is most unlikely either that she would approve any insidious attempts on her brother's property, or that her son would take any steps in such a matter without her consent. And, finally, Sir Thomas must surely have known what took place; and he can hardly have thought himself wronged; for in his will, made towards the end of 1635, he left the principal part of his

---

* This expression, of course, would refer to Laud's local tools. The body to which this dedication was addressed was the new corporation created by a charter, to which reference will be made in the next chapter.

† This remark is made by Mr. Sanford, loc. cit.

E

property to the very nephew who is said to have treated him so disrespectfully. If we suppose Sir Thomas to have fallen into a lingering illness affecting his nerves and brain, his relatives may very well have thought some legal decision, as to the management of his property, to be required. And if the medical evidence failed to establish a sufficient reason for the application, their conduct would, of course, be open to criticism and misinterpretation, however good their intentions were.

At the beginning of 1627–8 Oliver's fifth child, Henry, the future Lieutenant of Ireland, was born. But, notwithstanding the responsibilities implied in the obvious prospect of a large family to provide for, the father was so far from feeling the pressure of poverty, that when soon afterwards another Parliament was called, he felt no difficulty in consenting to become a candidate for the representation of his native town.

CHAPTER IV.

ENTRANCE ON PUBLIC LIFE.

NOTWITHSTANDING the fallen fortunes of the Hinchinbrook family, it is probable that Oliver owed his election for Huntingdon partly to the local influence of his name. But it is tolerably certain that this would not have sufficed had he not already given proof of opposition to the courtly leanings of his uncle. The Puritan party in the town had one good candidate in the person of James Montague, a younger son of the Earl of Manchester, and nephew to the purchaser of Hinchinbrook. It was an excellent stroke of policy to join with him the nephew of the late lord of the manor. The combination was successful, and Oliver, at the age of twenty-nine years, entered on a responsibility sufficiently serious to rouse into at least incipient activity his hitherto slumbering powers.

The vacillation of Charles—now listening to his wife, and now to his favourite Buckingham—had plunged him into disastrous hostilities with France, and had, at the same time, excited the indignant distrust of the rebellious French Protestants who were his natural allies. To Buckingham's vanity and incompetence thousands of soldiers had been sacrificed before Rochelle, while the grief of the nation and its wounded pride were aggravated by the domestic miseries and constitutional wrongs incidental to the raising of the defeated and wasted forces. Regiments of gaol-birds, drunkards, and idle vagabonds, gathered by violence, had harried the country, on their march to the outports, with robberies and outrages that maddened the people more than a hostile invasion. Not only inn-keepers, but all kinds of peaceable citizens were liable to have billeted upon them ruffians who consumed their goods, insulted their wives, and frightened their children. To supply the reckless waste occasioned by folly, duties were imposed on trade and commerce by arbitrary decrees of the King in council; and not only did such exactions provoke anger by their illegality, but the imperious need for money led

E 2

to irregular extortions, rendering all business calculations uncertain.

In September of this year, 1628, Richard Chambers, merchant and hero, keen in pursuit of profit, but refusing all terms with oppression, flung in the teeth of the council at Hampton Court the reproach that "there was no part of the world where merchants were so screwed and wrung as in England, and that in Turkey they had more encouragement." Thrown into prison for his audacity, and ordered, as a condition of his release, to sign a humble acknowledgment and apology in a prescribed form set before him, he wrote at the foot that he "did utterly abhor and detest the same, and never till death would he own any part thereof." Then, after appending his signature, he went on writing words of Scripture on the lower margin of the paper :—*"Woe to them that call evil good and good evil, that put darkness for light, and light for darkness ;" "which justify the wicked for a reward, and take away the righteousness of the righteous from him." "If thou seest the oppression of the poor, and violent perversion of judgment and justice in a province, marvel not at the matter, for he that is higher than the highest regardeth, and there be higher than they."* The sturdy valour of this man, and the high source of his inspiration, may help us to understand hereafter Cromwell's insistance on enlisting only the "godly" amongst his troops.

But Charles was dazed by flattering notions of his " divine right." He had no more doubt about his claim to the absolute obedience of his subjects than about that of a father to be obeyed by a young child. The one claim seemed to him as much a part of the law of nature as the other, and, as is always the case, there were not wanting prophets to allege a supernatural sanction for injustice. Dr. Sibthorp, preaching the Assize sermon at Northampton in February 1627, openly maintained that there were absolutely no limits whatever to the right of the king to submission. " If," he said, putting the extremest case—"if princes command anything which subjects may not perform because it is against the laws of God, or Nature, or impossible, yet such subjects are bound to undergo the punishment, without either resistance, or railing, or reviling, and so to yield a passive obedience where they cannot yield an active one." He added that he knew no other case in which a subject could excuse himself in the sight of God by offering passive for active obedience. Dr. Manwaring, preaching at Court, had delighted the royal ears by arguing that "the king is not bound to observe the laws of the realm concerning the subject's rights and liberties," and that his mere demand for loans or taxes "doth oblige the subject's conscience, upon pain of eternal damnation." *

Of course such doctrines would not have been preached if they had not already been practised by the King and his Council. In addition to the illegal exaction of duties unauthorised by Parliament, large bribes were taken from Roman Catholic recusants for an unconstitutional suspension of the laws against them. The sum of £100,000 was demanded from the city of London, and it was also compelled to furnish twenty ships completely equipped. Proportionate burdens were laid upon other ports; and in answer to the plea that "the case was without precedent," the Council deigned only to reply that "the precedents of former times were obedience, not direction; and precedents were not wanting for the punishment of those that disobey his majesty's commands." "Benevolences" and forced loans were levied, and to facilitate these the Lords Lieutenants of counties were ordered to return the names of all men able to contribute, together with a report as to their property. A private memorandum of Dr. Abbot, then Archbishop of Canterbury, shows the feeling excited even amongst the mildest and most moderate men by such despotic innovations.

"At the opening of the commission for the loan," he says, "I was sent for from Croydon. It seemed to me a strange thing; but I was told then that howsoever it showed, the king would have it so; there was no speaking against it. . . . But when I saw the instructions, the refusers should be sent away for soldiers to the King of Denmark, I began to remember Urias that was sent to the forefront of the battle, and, to speak truth, I durst not be tender in it. And when afterwards I saw that men were to be put to their oath [as to the persons] with whom they had conference, and whether any did dissuade them—and yet further beheld that divers were to be imprisoned—I thought this was a somewhat new world."†

In the autumn of 1627 there were at least seventy-six men of high character and position subjected to various degrees of restraint, varying from confinement in their country houses to close imprisonment, because they refused the loan. These are all

* Rushworth, vol. i., p. 423.   † Rushworth, vol. i., p. 455.

whose names we possess, but there were probably many more; and how many humbler persons were sent for soldiers "to the King of Denmark" and elsewhere, there is no record to show. In October of that year Sir John Heveningham, Sir Edward Hampden, and other prisoners in the Fleet obtained their writ of habeas corpus, the return to which was that they were detained by "special order of our lord the King." The argument of their counsel was that this return was insufficient; what was required was a specification of the crime of which they were accused, of the law that they had broken. Magna Charta declared that "no free man shall be arrested or imprisoned unless pursuant to the law of the land." Where was the law which justified incarceration "by special order of our lord the King?" The very object of Magna Charta, of all its renewals, and of the writ of habeas corpus, was precisely to make imprisonment by mere command impossible. That such arguments were unanswerable, Sir Nicholas Hyde and his brother judges of the King's Bench must have felt. The strain on their conscience and self-respect is betrayed by the unworthy quibble that "there is not one word in the writ to demand the cause why the prisoners were taken, but only why they are detained." But, as if to prove for all time to come that the traditions of the Bench are as futile a guarantee against servility as are the doctrines of the Church, and that no earthly institutions can protect men except on condition that they help themselves, these judges decided that the "special order of our lord the King" was a sufficient return to the writ, and thus at one stroke of judge-made law converted all the noblest statutes of English history into waste rags.

Such was the condition of the country when Oliver Cromwell went home from the hustings to his house by the brookside, the elected member for Huntingdon. That he expected to play any great part in setting things right, we have no reason to suppose; but, being what he was, he could not help looking forward with eager anticipation, and with valiant resolve, to the constitutional struggle in which he was summoned to take sides.

The very fact that a Parliament was called proved that the revolutionary schemes of the Court were brought to a dead lock for want of money. And the conscious weakness of the Council was further shown by anxious efforts to make the Duke of Buckingham appear as the adviser of an appeal to Parliament, and by hasty orders for the release of prisoners illegally detained. Needless to say that wherever these prisoners offered themselves they were the most popular candidates. Sir John Eliot left the Gatehouse prison to be returned for Cornwall, and John Hampden, released from his enforced retirement, was elected for Andover. Pym was member for Tavistock, Denzil Hollis for Dorchester, Sir Harbottle Grimstone for Essex. Somerset elected Sir Robert Phelips, boiling with indignation at the unrighteous judgment in the King's Bench. Wiltshire sent Sir Francis Seymour to protest against the King's divine right to do wrong; and Downton in that county returned Benjamin Rudyard, who sturdily backed up the knight of the shire.

We may reasonably suppose that on the morning when Parliament was opened, Cromwell would seek the company of his cousin Hampden, who was already familiar with the procedure and rules of the House. Passing through the crowds in Palace Yard, not without the proud sense of privilege so natural to a Parliament man, the new member would meet here and there, in the entrance and the lobby, men whom he already knew, and to others would be presented by his cousin as a new champion of popular rights from Huntingdon. His family name and connections were familiar to all old Parliament men, and references, half jocular, half earnest, to the " hammer of the monks," would arise naturally enough, now that the further progress of the Reformation was threatened, not only with resistance, but reaction. Passing through the door of the chamber, all unconscious of the tremendous struggle with himself and with the world which this threshold was to witness, the new member took a seat most probably on the right of the chair, a little below the table,* and looking about him with natural curiosity, awaited the ceremonies of the day.

The buzz of conversation ceased suddenly. The Usher of the Black Rod was at the bar summoning the faithful Commons to the presence of Majesty. The stalwart young burgess from Huntingdon was well able to hold his own in the rout that stormed into the " Painted Chamber," and Cromwell, for the first time, saw enthroned as King of England the Prince whom he remembered as a visitor at Hinchinbrook. The face, handsome but

* This was his place in the Long Parliament, and men are curiously influenced by habit in such things.

weak; haughty, but not imposing; pleasing to the eye, but repellent of confidence; showed already, in nervous traces of anxiety and worry, the wear and tear of habitual discord with circumstance.   The tone of the royal speech that followed, and which, at that time, reflected of course not the advice of ministers, but the personal feelings of the monarch, was in marked contrast with the expectations formed of a prince " brought up in Parliaments." Cromwell could remember the loyal admiration with which his uncle Oliver had reported the diligent attendance of the Prince of Wales in the House of Lords, and the enthusiasm of both Houses in their response to Charles's declaration that support against Spain "would bind him to them for ever."   But the prince, transformed into a king, now spoke of Parliament as only one amongst other means for supplying him with money, and plainly intimated that its continuance or otherwise must depend upon obedient and speedy attention to this humble duty.   The assembly of the people's representatives was admitted to be " the ancient, speediest, and best way in this time of common danger," to furnish the King with supplies.   But Charles was careful not to acknowledge it as the *only* way.   On the contrary, he distinctly hinted that if they did not give him what he wanted, his prerogative would enable him to take it.   " Wherefore if you—which God forbid—should not do your duty in contributing what the State at this time needs, I must, in discharge of my conscience, use those other means which God hath put into my hands to save that which the follies of particular men may otherwise hazard to lose."   Here it seems to have occurred to the anxious speaker that to open Parliament with threats was scarcely a propitious beginning of business.   By way of soothing the susceptibilities of his hearers, he therefore added a singularly haughty apology : " Take not this as a threatening; for I scorn to threaten any but my equals; but an admonition from him that both out of nature and duty hath most care of your preservations and prosperities."

Did men like Eliot, Pym, and Hampden smile as they listened to this over-acted dignity of querulous self-assertion? Not at all.   It would be a total misapprehension of the position to suppose that they knew their strength or the King's weakness. Eliot might, indeed, ominously declare that " there were none who went about to break Parliaments, but in the end Parliaments had broken *them.*" But he was thinking, probably, of courtiers, not of the King. The vague notion of a divine right, and a sacred inviolable dignity inherent in a crowned head, had spread far beyond courtiers and priests, and had taken its place among the most firmly rooted superstitions of the race. If these men should have to fight the King, whether in a Parliamentary way or on the open field, they felt that they would have almost every recognised social force against them. Habit, tradition, education, the pulpit, interest, servility, horror of rebellion, legal organisation, courtly possession of the means to terrorise—all were against them ; and, on the other hand, they had nothing to look to but public spirit and conscientious conviction. Merchants and capitalists, indeed, very naturally disliked illegal taxation, and were ready enough to protest against it. But then, beyond a certain point, persistence in refusal might mean stark ruin ; and we may excuse the patriots of the time if they doubted how many of their countrymen were prepared to run such a risk for political principle.

Dismissed from the presence, the Commons chose as their speaker Sir John Finch—not a bad man for the office in calmer times, but, as it turned out, singularly unfitted to represent the Commons in any conflict with the Crown. His anti-Puritanic bias was curiously shown by his reference to the bishops in the course of his address to the King :—" On your right hand are the reverend, religious, and learned prelates, the lights of the Church, fit to be set in golden candlesticks, and not made contemptible by parity and poverty." The idea of apostolic souls being "made contemptible by parity and poverty" probably sounded almost like a satire in the ears of godly members fresh from their morning portion of the Scriptures. But Speaker Finch knew his King, and, perhaps it may be added, his bishops too.

The custom of Parliament at that time was to divide the House into a certain number of grand committees, charged with the consideration of chief public interests, and with the preparation of proposals thereon, to be submitted to the whole House. The precedent has been recommended, on high authority, for modern imitation. At any rate it had the effect of bringing the representative system to bear on the details of public interests more directly than is at all possible on the chaotic plan substituted for it. The members concerned for the purity of religion, or the redress of grievances, or the reform of finance, would have no difficulty in getting themselves appointed on the grand committee dealing with their special subject. In general the inclination of members would have to be accepted as a probable indication of their fitness for this or that committee. But, of course, where there was any pre-eminent capacity for dealing with a particular class of subjects, the desire of the House would be sure to find expression. No such reason, however, could well exist in the case of Oliver Cromwell as yet, and, therefore, we may presume it was by his own wish he was named a member of the Grand Committee on the state of religion.

But during the first session of this Parliament the reports of the committee on grievances had precedence. This was, of course, inevitable. For the House was urged to give a speedy supply, and if that were done without any redress first obtained, the Commons knew well enough that prorogation or dissolution would follow before any remedies could be even discussed. Besides, if taxation by prerogative was legal, the Parliamentary grant of subsidies was a needless form. " For," said Sir Francis Seymour, " how can we think of giving subsidies till we know whether we have anything to give or no? For if his Majesty be per-suaded by any to take from his subjects what he will, and where it pleaseth him, I would gladly know what we have to give?" Sir Robert Phelips, with pathetic humour, likened their brief opportunity for speaking their minds, under Parliamentary pri-vilege, to the one day of freedom conceded on an annual holiday to Roman slaves. The hours would soon be over, and they must return to their chains. He urged his colleagues, therefore, to let the truth appear while it was possible. Referring to the dis-graceful reversal by the King's Bench of all guarantees for per-sonal liberty, he broke into a cry of despair. Grievances through billeting and royal robbery were nothing to this supreme treason against English rights :—

" I can live, although another without title be put to live with me. I can live, although I pay excises and impositions far more than I do. But to have my liberty, which is the soul of my life, taken from me by power, and so to be pent up in a gaol without remedy by law, and to be adjudged to perish in gaol,—O improvident ancestors! O unwise forefathers! to be so curious in providing for the quiet possession of our lands, and liberties of

Parliament, and to neglect our persons and bodies, and let them die in prison, *durante bene placito*, remediless! If this be law, why do we talk of our liberties? Why do we trouble ourselves with the dispute of law, franchises, propriety, and goods? It is the sum of all miseries." *

But the impassioned speaker was animated by no malign purpose of revolution. Let these intolerable innovations be repudiated, and he would give " such a supply as prince never received. And with our money," he loyally added, " we shall give him our hearts, and give him a new people raised from the dead."

It is, of course, not with a view of attempting any complete history of the period that such anecdotes of the first Parliament attended by Oliver Cromwell are introduced here. Our purpose is simply to illustrate the influences under which was matured his idea of the national crisis, and of the duty of a Christian citizen therein. Strong, pure emotion, like that of Sir Robert Phelips, is infectious, and Cromwell was peculiarly susceptible to enthusiasm. While, therefore, we need not follow in detail the stormy course of this session, which provoked the King to his fatal attempt to govern without any recourse to Parliament at all, we must endeavour to picture to ourselves the effect produced on a daring, but susceptible temperament, unconscious yet of the meaning of the inward tumult of vast energies, awakened by the stir and conflict and terror around.

The new member watched the daily growth of the Petition of Right until it embodied a re-affirmation of Magna Charta and all analogous statutes. And he learned from royal letters and messages on the subject how incomprehensible it was to Charles that any reasonable man could possibly mean to debar the monarch from committing his subjects to prison whenever he judged it necessary to do so. The King thought there must surely be some misunderstanding, and that the force of State considerations must have escaped plain men unversed in such matters. Had he not given his royal word that no one should be deprived of liberty unless the King was convinced such a step was necessary? What more could possibly be wanted? He wrote on May 20th :

" We find it still insisted on that in no case whatsoever, should it never so nearly concern matters of State or Government, have we or our Privy Council power to commit any man without the cause showed; whereas it often happens, that, should the cause be shown, the service itself would

* Cobbett's Parliamentary History.

thereby be destroyed and defeated. And the cause alleged must be such as may be determined by our judges of our courts at Westminster in a legal and ordinary way of justice, whereas the causes may be such as these judges have not capacity of judicature nor rules of law to direct and guide their judgment in cases of that transcendent nature."

In other words, if a man committed murder, or robbery, or arson, his arrest, trial, and judgment would be conducted in a scrupulously constitutional manner. But if he declined to " lend " money to the King, and there was no law to compel him, it would be monstrous in " a case of that transcendent nature " to confine the monarch to " an ordinary and legal way of justice." Such experiences must have gone far to prepare the patriotic party, and Cromwell amongst them, for the conviction that there was no hope of ever reconciling the King's notions of constitutional government with those of the Parliament; and that the only alternatives before the country were either submission to arbitrary rule, or insistance, even at the cost of civil war, on material guarantees for the ancient charters of England.

This sad foresight of a terrible, and perhaps sanguinary issue inevitably drawing nigh helps us to understand the extraordinary scene of June 5th in this year (1628), when the House of Commons, perhaps for the only time in its history of six hundred years, sat weeping in silence. The Petition of Right had been passed and presented to the King by both Houses, after a futile attempt of the Lords to insert a clause saving the King's " sovereign power," a vague phrase which would have surrendered every point at issue. The answer of Charles had not been unfavourable, but it was not given in legal form, and this informality was held to be significant. The King might have been insidiously advised that the Petition would thus be prevented from having the power of a statute. Accordingly there was a strong disposition to renew the impeachment of the Duke of Buckingham, which had been averted by the dissolution of the last Parliament. The Commons already felt that the only effectual method of avoiding conflicts with the Crown was to hold the advisers of the monarch responsible for good government, and so to make any ministry impossible except such as had the confidence of the nation's representatives. Thus their one hope of saving at once the dignity of the throne and the liberty of the subject lay in the condemnation of the Duke of Buckingham.

But on June 5th the Speaker brought an imperious message from the King cautioning the House against any "scandal" about the State government, and warning them, not for the first time, that he would not tolerate any aspersion upon his ministers. Thereupon Sir John Eliot, untamed by past experience of royal power, and undaunted by the cruel fate he clearly foresaw, rose to lead the discussion of the House on the message they had heard. But as soon as his purpose was apparent the Speaker stopped him, pleading the command of the King that no such debate should be allowed. Sir John Eliot sat down amid a deadly stillness. Like a crew in the Arctic seas, struck by the cruel chill and gleam of ice ahead in their only avenue of escape, the House was for the moment unnerved and unmanned. Utterly baffled in a constitutional course, and overwhelmed with the vague horror of any other alternative, they felt helpless as children, and gave way to tears of despair.

Sir Dudley Digges essayed to break the silence. "Must we not proceed?" he asked. But probably at a gesture from the Speaker, who was himself overcome, he refrained. "Let us sit in silence," he said; "we are miserable, we know not what to do!" Thereupon a sad stillness continued for some moments. It was not their own fate of which they were thinking. Sentence of death against themselves would have been met in a different mood. But it was the terrible alternative —slavery, or civil war, which oppressed them with the weight of their responsibility. Such emotion, however, could not long continue speechless. "We *must* now speak," exclaimed Sir Nathaniel Rich, "or for ever hold our peace. For us to be silent when the King and kingdom are in this calamity, is not fit." But what to say?—who could think of and dare to speak the right thing?

What followed is well told in a letter of a member then present, Mr. Thomas Alured :—

"Then Sir Robert Phelips spake, and mingled his words with weeping. Mr. Prynne did the like; and Sir Edward Coke, overcome with passion, seeing the desolation likely to ensue, was forced to sit down, when he began to speak, through abundance of tears. Yea, the Speaker in his speech could not refrain from weeping and shedding of tears, besides a great many more whose great griefs made them dumb and silent. But others bore up in that storm and encouraged the rest."

Cromwell, though we have reason to believe that already he was recognised for a valiant and trustworthy man, was hardly yet of consideration enough to take much part in "encouraging the rest." More important for the present was the influence on himself. That he began to have already a shrewd suspicion as to whither all this was tending, we may very well believe. And if we should hereafter think the language of his enthusiasm somewhat high pitched, let us remember the kindling influence of scenes like these upon a nature half soldier, half prophet. The end of this incident was that the House went into committee, and the Speaker obtained leave to wait upon the King. All other members were ordered to remain, on pain of committal to the Tower. Sir Edward Coke now found freedom of utterance, and maintained that the reason for their present difficulty was a want of sincerity in dealing with the King. For his part, if he should never lift up his voice in that House again, he would at any rate now speak his mind, and so, with all solemnity, he named the Duke of Buckingham as the root of all mischief. Selden followed with the suggestion of a remonstrance against the influence of the Duke. And when the Speaker returned, late in the evening, with the King's command that they should adjourn till next morning, their minds were made up, and, as it was then eleven o'clock—at that time thought to be a most unnatural hour for deliberation—they made no difficulty about complying.

But the next day showed that even Charles had been startled by the effect of his message. The Speaker was now empowered to assure the House that their Sovereign had no wish to interfere with their freedom of speech, but had only intended to deprecate useless scandals about the past. The Commons were very grateful for the concession. But, on the same day, fresh anxieties were aroused by the examination of one Burlemack, a merchant, who had been summoned to explain the part he had taken, as agent for the King, in raising forces abroad. He said that he had been employed to buy a thousand horses in Holland, and that riders had been secured, but that the orders had since been countermanded. If the purpose of this force was foreign war, why should not the King rely on English arms? Since when had Englishmen required aliens to fight their battles? The incident looked suspicious, and suggested an intention to silence all remonstrance by the terror of foreign mercenaries.

Partly, perhaps, to allay this suspicion, and partly in the hope of diverting attention from the favourite, the King, on June 7th, gave to the Petition of Right the formal assent, which converted it into a law of the land. But, as in the case of every concession this unfortunate monarch ever made, the effect was instantly marred by a fresh discovery of his levity in the treatment of all constitutional order. For it was ascertained that a Commission for the collection of excise duties was dated after the summons of the Parliament, which he professed to regard as at least the "ancient, speediest, and best way" of obtaining a supply. The House now insisted on completing its remonstrance against the influence of Buckingham; and added another against the persistent collection of duties without their consent. But Parliament was suddenly prorogued on June 20th, and did not meet again till March in the following year.

When Oliver reached his home once more, not only his wife and mother, but his fellow townsmen, were eager to hear his experiences in his new position. Honourable members did not at that time summon their constituents to receive an account of their doings in the House; but talks in the market-place, the inn parlour, or friendly gatherings at the houses of acquaintances, would serve the purpose sufficiently well. To the good Dr. Beard it was a satisfaction that his former pupil had been on the Grand Committee of Religion. And though secular grievances had obtained necessary precedence during the session, it was a comfort to the Puritan lecturer to know that Dr. Manwaring and Dr. Montagu had not escaped censure for their servile abuse of the pulpit. When news came, as it soon did, that these very men had been singled out by the Court for preferment,—Montagu being made Bishop of Rochester, and Manwaring obtaining an additional living,—we gather, from what afterwards occurred, that Oliver had to listen to more than one private homily from his old schoolmaster on the inroads of Popery and the perilous nature of the times. More formidable still was the translation of Laud to the see of London. Things looked black, indeed, when a man bent on suppressing means of grace, such as the lectureship at Huntingdon, was on the high road to become Primate of all England.

But scandals of Church preferment, after all, troubled comparatively few. A rumour of more startling import reached Huntingdon in the latter days of August. The Duke of Buckingham was dead, stabbed by the knife of an obscure assassin. We know with what mysterious speed reports of this kind fly, trackless in their career, from mouth to mouth. And we can imagine the agitation, the doubts, the eager questionings excited in Huntingdon as throughout England; and when the rumour was verified, men did not say "it was *too* true." There can be no sadder illustration of the deep disgust and weary despair pervading the population at that time, than the fact that Englishmen could not, and did not even try to repress their satisfaction at a murder. The wild cry of the woman in the admiring crowd through which the assassin Felton was dragged, " God bless thee, little David," interpreted only the feeling of the whole country that a divine deliverance had been wrought. The feeling was insane; for wrong can never be right; and events soon furnished a practical comment on the words that " the wrath of man worketh not the righteousness of God." But if the feeling was insane, it was the fault of rulers who seemed bent on driving a whole nation mad.

The death of Buckingham did not change the King's policy. It rather tinged his obstinacy with the bitterness of revenge. A mere minion of the dead favourite's was made Lord Treasurer, as though to taunt the nation with its impotence. The month of October, to which Parliament had been prorogued, brought no summons for the despatch of business ; and Cromwell, whose private affairs could hardly give him sufficient occupation, had ample time to brood over the destinies of the nation and the condition of his own soul. From the testimony of Dr. Sincott, a physician who attended him, and whose words Sir Philip Warwick reports in his memoirs of the time, we know that Oliver about this time fell into a condition of morbid melancholy, and was specially troubled about the town-cross. Perhaps it distressed him as a relic of Romanism.* The events of his first Parliamentary session must have made a profound impression upon him, and we can well conceive that the strong religious convictions actuating his noblest colleagues would stimulate his own desire for sure grounds of faith and

* Mr. Sanford, p. 226, adduces also an entry in the journal of Sir Theodore Mayerne, a celebrated physician of the time, which shows that Sir Theodore was consulted on September 15th, 1628, by a "Monsr. Cromwell, *valde melancholicus.*" This was very probably Oliver. Parliament was not sitting then, but Cromwell, of course, might be in London on other business, or specially for medical advice.

hope. Of the intellectual uncertainties that trouble the present age there is in his spiritual history no symptom. The revelation in the Bible was for him always supremely sure, with a certainty sometimes appalling, sometimes blissful, according to his feeling of his own personal relation to it.

When Parliament met in January 1628-9 the business of religion came to the front, and Cromwell was one of a committee named to examine and report on the pardons granted for ecclesiastical offences since the prorogation. John Hampden had addressed the House on the subject, and was succeeded by his cousin. The appearance of the member who now, presumably for the first time, caught the Speaker's eye, was not at first sight prepossessing. His ill-fitting, country-made coat, and the coarse, not over clean, linen collar that fell over it, were suggestive of rustic manners. The red face, large nose, and powerful jaw, might show a strong man, but were not attractive. The light-brown flowing hair, parted upon an ample forehead, and covering a massive head, stamped the man as no precisian or narrow bigot. But the eyes showed a keen light and a directness of purpose that arrested attention. And the voice, though "sharp and untuneable," had a ring of earnestness about it that compelled the House to hear. Only the most meagre sketch of what he said is left us. A member had charged Neile, Bishop of Winchester, with advising the pardon of obnoxious Romanisers. Oliver then remembered an incident told him by Dr. Beard, and now very much to the point. Dr. Alablaster had many years ago been appointed to preach certain customary sermons from an open-air pulpit in Spital Square. To Dr. Beard had then been assigned the humble duty of recapitulating those discourses in a final sermon. Here the recorded outline of Cromwell's speech takes up the story :

"Mr. Cromwell saith that Dr. Beard told him that one Dr. Alablaster did at the Spital preach in a sermon tenets of Popery, and Beard being to repeat the same, the now Bishop of Winton, then Bishop of Lincoln, did send for Dr. Beard, and charge him, as his diocesan, not to preach any doctrine contrary to that which Alablaster had delivered. And when Dr. Beard did, by the advice of Bishop Felton, preach against Dr. Alablaster's sermon and person, Dr. Neile, now Bishop of Winton, did reprehend him, the said Beard, for it." *

* Given by Mr. Gardiner in "The Personal Government of Charles I.," vol. i. p. 76, from notes taken by Mr. Nicholas, a member at the time. The

F

A motion was immediately carried to send for Dr. Beard and hear his testimony from his own lips. But before the Doctor could appear Parliament was dissolved. It did not last many days after this debate. The ostentatious persistence of the Government in maintaining the ecclesiastical and financial abuses denounced by the Commons raised the temper of the House afresh to a dangerous height. Eliot called upon his colleagues to testify, by a solemn vow of allegiance to the Gospel, their purpose to maintain it, not only with words, but with actions. "There is a custom," he said, "in the Eastern churches, of standing at the repetition of the Creed, to testify their purpose to maintain it, not only with their bodies upright, but with their swords drawn. Give me leave to call that custom very commendable." Was not Cromwell responsive to such an appeal? May we not conceive his thoughts? "Oratory is not much in my line; but if it comes to drawn swords—well, we shall see!"

The House more firmly than ever declined to make any grants of taxes until the illegal levy of customs was disowned and withdrawn. They summoned to the bar the agents for the collection of these dues, but these men declined to give any account of their actions, and pleaded the King's command. On March 2nd the House proceeded to draw up a protest; but the Speaker declined to put it, and announced the King's orders that they should adjourn. On this occasion there were no tears save those shed by Speaker Finch in his distracted desire to serve two masters. Anger, indignation, and scorn, stormed upon him from all parts of the House. "Mr. Speaker," cried Selden, "if you will not put the question which we command you, we must sit still, and so we shall never be able to do anything. We sit here by command from the King, under the Great Seal; and as for you, you are, by his Majesty, sitting in his royal chair before both Houses, appointed our Speaker; and do you now refuse to be our Speaker?"

The miserable man essayed to leave the House, but Denzil Holles thrust him back into his chair and—strange sound for so Puritanic an assembly to hear—swore, "by God's wounds, he should sit there till it pleased the House to rise." News came

speech as given in Cobbett's "Parliamentary History," and adopted by Carlyle, contains additions from "another speech, by another speaker, on a different occasion." (Gardiner, *l.c.*)

that the Usher of the Black Rod was at hand with a summons to them to hear their sentence of dissolution. Instantly the door was locked, and the key given in charge to a trustworthy member. Presently a knock was heard, but no one answered. It was repeated, but no one had ears except for words that proved to be Eliot's dying breath. The King ordered that a file of soldiers should break open the door. And so, amid the cries and entreaties of the Speaker held down in his chair by force; amid the battery at the door, and the tramp of approaching soldiers, Eliot's final protest against tyrannic rule was adopted, and then the nation's last hope of peace was dissolved with the Parliament. Henceforward, whatever delusive delay might occur, the appeal to force was inevitable—nay, it had already begun. The obstinacy of the King had constrained the House into a revolutionary procedure, and the lesson was not lost upon the member for Huntingdon.

CHAPTER V.

OLIVER AS A LOCAL PATRIOT.

FOR eleven years following the spring of 1629 no Parliament was called in England. A royal proclamation declared that the King "would account it presumption in any to prescribe any time to him" for another election. And the more vigorously to assert his supremacy over the Great Council of the realm, in case it might suit his convenience to appeal to it once more, Charles ordered the arrest and close imprisonment of Sir John Eliot and other prominent Parliamentary leaders. Those who were not conspicuous enough for such notice were fain to continue in their safe obscurity, to watch events, and to bide their time.

Cromwell could now perhaps scarcely be considered obscure, and we shall find that the Court had an eye to his position and influence. But the traditions of his family probably suggested a hope that, like some other patriots, he might be gained over; and for some time he was left unmolested. In his private circumstances he was fairly prosperous, having recently received a welcome addition to his property. His uncle Richard, after whom his third son had been named, died at Ramsey in October of the preceding year, and left to Oliver some nineteen acres of land in the neighbourhood of Huntingdon. This bequest, together with that of his mother's brother, Sir Thomas Steward, received a few years later, would seem to indicate that, notwithstanding his political leanings, Oliver found favour with his elder relatives, and was certainly not regarded by them with the dislike and anxiety pictured by writers of the restoration period. A small addition to his means was all the more pleasant as his family appeared likely to be a large one. Towards the end of June, after the dissolution, his sixth child and second daughter was born, and received the name of Elizabeth after his aunt, Mrs. Hampden. This was the girl who became Mrs. Claypole, and was always to her father the special treasure of his household. The fact that she remained for nearly seven years the "baby" of the family, may well have helped to secure for her a very warm place in her father's heart.

Local politics as well as family interests helped to distract Oliver's attention from gloomy thoughts about his own soul, and morbid "fancies about the town-cross." The power of the reforming party in the town, as proved by the election of Montague and Cromwell, seems to have suggested to local reactionaries the desire to remodel the corporation in a sense adverse to popular power. At that time the town affairs were managed by two bailiffs and a common council of twenty-four members, all annually elected by the burgesses.* But the feelings of the more courtly inhabitants were revolted by the vulgar excitement and heat of the annual contests over this business. The reactionary party in the town had interest enough at Court to obtain a new charter, which wrought an entire revolution in the local government. This new charter, dated July 15th, 1630, after reciting the causes for change, the necessity for preventing "popular tumult" and for restoring "certainty and constant order" to the public business of the borough, ordained that the town council should henceforth consist of twelve aldermen elected for life, a recorder, and also a mayor elected annually by the aldermen out of their own number.

One of the leaders, if not the chief, of the reactionary party was Mr. Robert Barnard, whose destiny it was to suffer a little from imprudent contention with a man too strong for him, and to obtain his reward after the restoration in the shape of the recordership of his borough. Meantime the charter was a great victory for him. The document named certain justices of the peace for the borough, and one of these was Robert Barnard himself. Singularly enough, however, Oliver Cromwell and Thomas Beard were also named for the same honour. It may be, as Carlyle suggests, that these nominations were not new; but it is more probable that they were so. Once a justice, always a justice, unless a man's name be struck off the commission; and if any of these three had been appointed before, there was no need to name them again for the purpose of " confirming and continu-

---

* Mr. John Bruce, who so ably edited the Calendar of State Papers belonging to this time, was the first to set in its true light this local revolution, and to discover the record of Cromwell's summons before the Council. (See his letter in the *Athenæum* for October 13th, 1855; also his preface to the Calendar of State Papers (Domestic) for 1630.

ing " them. Perhaps the nomination of two popular men along
with Robert Barnard was expected to make the charter more
acceptable, and to soothe local irritation at the changes introduced. It may be also that Cromwell was recognised as a man
worth gaining ; and the effect of a trivial honour, to which the
position of his family fairly entitled him, might naturally be
tried first. But if any such ideas were entertained, they proved
wholly delusive. Popular irritation was very far from being
soothed. On the contrary, it broke out with such violence as to
occasion an appeal to the authority of the Privy Council.

Oliver took a prominent part in resisting and resenting this
reactionary change. The feeble compliment to himself did not
disguise from him the deliberate mischief designed. That he
had a keen sense of the importance of local organisation we know
from his earliest activity in the war. And he would have been
blind indeed had he not perceived how fatal to the liberties of the
country such despotic suppression of municipal institutions might
become. With him in this local agitation was associated Mr.
William Kilborne, who had taken a warm interest in his election
to Parliament, and had signed the certificate of his return. The
details of the disturbance have not come down to us. But the
language of Oliver and his friend caused vexation and anguish of
soul to the aldermen, and in particular to Mr. Lionel Walden,
their newly-elected mayor. These gentlemen sent up a complaint
on the subject to the Privy Council, a course which admits of
more than one interpretation. It is impossible to suppose that if
local feeling had been with them they would ever have dreamed
of defending themselves in this manner. But where men are
unpopular, and conscious that their opponents have a good case,
they are naturally very sensitive as to the language in which they
are attacked. However, the Council thought fit to interfere, and
a summons was sent down addressed to " Oliver Cromwell, Esq.,"
and " William Kilborne, gentleman," postmaster of Huntingdon,
requiring them to appear at Whitehall on November 26th. The
appearance of the official messenger with the summons would
excite no little sensation in the town, and no little fear in Oliver's
household. So long as the special order of the King continued
to be held a sufficient return to a writ of *Habeas Corpus*, a man
once committed to prison was almost as much beyond the help of
his friends as though he were dead. It would be in very painful

uncertainty about any speedy reunion that Oliver's wife and mother saw him mount and ride off once more towards London, no longer as a member of Parliament, but as a prisoner going to a sort of trial.

The accused men attended on the appointed day, and were ordered " to remain in the custody of the messenger," with whom they had apparently travelled up to town. But an early time, December 1st, was fixed for hearing the case. On that day there were present the Lord Treasurer Weston, the Lord Keeper, Sir Thomas Coventry, Lord Falkland, the Earl of Manchester, Lord Privy Seal, and Dr. Laud, Bishop of London, besides several others. To Henry, Earl of Manchester, the father of his colleague in the representation of Huntingdon, Oliver might reasonably look for favourable consideration. From Laud he could expect nothing but bitter enmity. The general feeling of the Council, of course, leaned to the side of the mayor and aldermen.

When the name of "Oliver Cromwell" was called, not a member of the Council, except perhaps the Earl of Manchester and Bishop Laud, would regard with any interest the homely rustic figure that stepped forward to the foot of the table. But the brief record of the proceedings has expressions implying that before the day was over their lordships had reason to think that the worthy mayor and aldermen had caught a Tartar. " Both sides having had this day a long hearing," so runs the minute, " there appeared much contrariety and difference in the allegations on each side."* This dry record of an evidently stubborn contest shows that Mr. Lionel Walden and Mr. Robert Barnard did not find their appeal to the Council quite such plain sailing as they had anticipated. In fact, the wind was taken out of their sails in an unexpected manner by Mr. Oliver Cromwell, whose mode of putting the case made an off-hand decision against him impossible. Accordingly "their lordships thought fit and ordered that the examination of the whole business should be referred to the Lord Privy Seal."

It is noteworthy that the question referred to the Earl of Manchester included not only the "satisfaction fit to be given to the said mayor and Mr. Barnard for the disgraceful and unseemly speeches used unto them," but also some dispute not specified "touching the charter of the said town."

* Given by Mr. Bruce.

From this we gather that while Oliver was not able to deny the use of strong language, he justified it and carried the war into his opponents' camp, charging them with unfairness and injustice, perhaps with falsehood, in support of the new charter. Against Kilborne, and against " Brooks, his man," a farther complaint was made of "much oppression to the country, and many great abuses to particular persons." This complaint also was referred to the Earl of Manchester, who seems to have been selected for this duty because of his family connection with Huntingdon county.

The selection was a fortunate one for Cromwell. The Earl made his report within a week, on December 6th, and fully justified " Mr. Barnard's carriage of the business in advising and obtaining the charter." Oliver seems to have felt that he had expressed himself too violently. For Lord Manchester reported that "for the words spoken of Mr. Mayor and Mr. Barnard by Mr. Cromwell, as they were ill, so they are acknowledged to be spoken in heat and passion, and desired to be forgotten ; and he found Mr. Cromwell very willing to hold a friendship with Mr. Barnard, who, with a good will, remitting the unkind passages past, entertained the same." * The wording of the report as regards Cromwell is peculiar, and seems to indicate a desire to settle the matter without requiring more than a polite apology. The probability is that the mayor and aldermen pocketed their injured feelings in consideration of being left in undisputed possession of their charter. We, before whom the events of that time pass like dissolving views, see already the Huntingdon burgess exalted and transformed to play a very different part within the chamber he now leaves in hardly secured safety. But who among their lordships would not have smiled at the prophecy that this plain countryman would become the arbiter of their fate ? " A sturdy fellow that ! " they say one to another, and so the matter ends, as they suppose.

But although in escaping from such a tribunal without a fine and with safety for his person Cromwell had come off better than his accusers expected, and so had won a sort of victory, Huntingdon was no longer a place for him to live in. The party of reaction kept the spoils; and social influence would be increasingly against him. The death of Dr. Beard, in January 1631, deprived him of

* Calendar of State Papers, Domestic Series, 1630.

a venerable ally, and, no doubt, helped to make his position more uncomfortable. And in these circumstances his morbid melancholy preyed on his spirits, and some change became absolutely necessary. Perhaps, also, the growth of his family made it desirable for him to seek a separate establishment, and leave his father's house to his mother and the two or three sisters who, probably, still remained unmarried.* Five miles down the river Ouse, at St. Ives, there was a grazing farm obtainable, that appeared suited for his purpose. And so, with the concurrence of his mother, his wife, and his uncle Sir Oliver, the Huntingdon property bequeathed by his father was sold for £1,800. The paternal home was still occupied by his mother; and the property received by the will of the recently deceased uncle Richard was not included in the sale.

The town of St. Ives had then, as now, a cattle market, and the business done was probably more considerable, at least in proportion to the cattle trade of the country generally, than it is at present. It consisted of one street—Carlyle thinks, of only one side of a street—ranging from north-west to south-east along the sluggish Ouse, the timber-framed houses tottering on boggy foundations, and bowing towards the river. At the upper end was the church, close by the Ouse, and at the other the street opened out on the flat fen lands of the Slepe Hall estate. " Cromwell's Barn " is still pointed out, but with what probability of genuineness we cannot say. Slepe Hall House is said to have been his residence here. But judges, better than we can pretend to be, declare that it dates from a more recent time, and occupies the site of the manor-house, which would not, probably, be let to a grazier. An industrious inquirer† who laboured upon this subject a hundred years ago, laments that even in his time very little trustworthy information on such points could be obtained. But the rows of pollard willows probably then, as now, divided the fields; the slow river still creeps by with unctuous flood; and the wide flats over which the evening shadows lengthen away to infinity, have a pensive melancholy, soothing to a mind worried with over occupation; but, surely, dangerous to a soul inwardly consumed by the ferment of unused energies.

* The Rev. Mark Noble thinks Elizabeth, the eldest surviving sister, remained unmarried to her death in 1672. Robina, the youngest, was still only about eighteen years old.
† The Rev. Mark Noble.

The lands appear to have been rented by Cromwell, not purchased ; and the money received from the sale of his property
would amply suffice to stock the farm. Here he spent five
years of his life, from the end of his thirty-second to the
close of his thirty - seventh year. It is probable that on
the removal of the family to St. Ives the eldest boy, Robert,
now ten years old, was sent to Felsted school in Essex. The
relations between Oliver and Dr. Beard would suggest a natural
desire that the Doctor should educate the sons of his former
pupil. But we know that Robert did attend Felsted school, and
it is most natural to suppose that he was sent there after the
death of the old master and the change of abode. A remarkable
testimony under the hand of the rector of Felsted * shows that
the boy gave signs of considerable promise, and was specially
distinguished for his piety. At Felsted his maternal grandfather
resided ; and not far off were the Mashams, distant connections
of the Cromwells. The father and mother, therefore, knew that
their boy would be well cared for, and they had no foresight of
the early fate that awaited him. The reports received of his
growth in favour with God and man, must often have been a
happy alleviation of the gloom oppressing the mind of his
father.

A fifth son, and seventh child, was born at the beginning of
1632, but lived only to be baptised by the name of James. It
is the mother who feels a loss like this. But Oliver was a tender
husband, and his wife's sorrow was his. Such domestic troubles,
together with the insolent and apparently resistless triumph of
the royal and ecclesiastical conspiracy against the liberties and
the religion of Englishmen, deepened the morbid melancholy of
his soul, and prompted agonising desires to lay hold of the eternal
life that ranges above earthly shadows, and subsists for ever in
the light of God.† Of this period in Oliver's life it is related
that his business was ruined by the time spent in fanatical
preachings and prayers with his servants. There is no shadow
of confirmation for the statement as to his business. But his

* See p. 84.
† "The Lord accept me in his Son, and give me to walk in the light—and
give us to walk in the light, as He is in the light ! He it is that enlighteneth
our blackness—our darkness. I dare not say He hideth His face from me. He
giveth me to see light in His light. One beam in a dark place hath exceeding
much refreshment in it. Blessed be His name for shining on so dark a heart as
mine."—*O. C. to Mrs. St. John, October* 1638.

later letters and his practice both make it easy to believe that his family prayers and private devotions were frequent and prolonged. His objection to the Laudian reaction against the Reformation did not prevent his diligent attendance at the parish church, where, if we may credit local tradition, he was frequently seen with "a piece of red flannel round his neck," suggestive of throat disease, probably brought on by the dampness of the district. The rector was the boy Richard's godfather, the Rev. Henry Downhall. But he and Oliver were taking different paths in their spiritual pilgrimage; and the latter found little help for his soul in the church services.

Under these circumstances Oliver prized highly a "lectureship" maintained in the county by the voluntary association previously mentioned. At this time the lecturer was Dr. Wells, of whom, in his second extant letter, Cromwell speaks in very strong terms of commendation as "a man of goodness and industry, and ability to good every way, not short of any I know in England. I am persuaded," he adds, "that sithence his coming the Lord hath by him wrought much good among us." Personal gratitude seems to speak in these words. The devout soldiers who at this time were passing through experiences like those of their future leader, were largely indebted to similar lectureships. England's resurrection after the political death of these years was an instructive illustration of the truth, that the revival of nations always implies precedent efforts at some form of popular instruction or inspiration.

Laud and his coadjutors knew this as well as the Puritans, and therefore they laboured to suppress these lectureships. They had succeeded already in Huntingdon, where Dr. Beard's successor was soon removed after Cromwell had left the town. And any organisation for such purposes was made so difficult, and even dangerous, that the funds fell off. The salary of good Dr. Wells was in arrear, and he found himself in a precarious position. We fancy the difficulty was the subject of conversation at Slepe Farm, perhaps over supper after an evening lecture at St. Ives, and the preacher's host, being a man with many London acquaintances, bethought him that some of them might help the poor country people in this pinch. Accordingly, "Mr. Storie, at the sign of the Dog, in the Royal Exchange," received a letter from Oliver, strongly urging him to use his influence amongst the subscribers to the fund. In this letter the Puritanic sympathies of London—" a city so renowned for the clear shining light of the Gospel "—are mentioned with satisfaction. And, on the other hand, the suppression of these lectureships " with too much haste and violence, by the enemies of God's truth," is seen to be the cause of a grave indignation, which grows ominous.

This letter, compared with the note to Mr. Downhall eleven years previously, shows a considerable change in the religious feelings of the writer. It can hardly be contended that the occasion, or the character of the correspondent accounts for the difference. Surely the baptism of his own child was at least as suggestive of devout expressions as a begging letter asking a grant of money. And a clergyman about to act as godfather was at least as proper a recipient of spiritual confidences as " Mr. Storie at the sign of the Dog." " The souls of God's children will bless you," he says to Mr. Storie, " and so shall I." Did he not then count himself amongst God's children ? " I dare not say He hideth His face from me," runs his confession to Mrs. St. John, " I live, you know where—in Meshec, which, they say, signifies prolonging; in Kedar, which signifies blackness—yet the Lord forsaketh me not." His was a troubled, stormy sky, in which deep gloom was occasionally broken by flashes of brilliant light. But he did not lose hope or faith. It was of himself he doubted, not of God. " Judgment and justice," were for him always " the habitation of God's throne." He was never touched by the heart-sickening scepticism which doubts whether the universe might not have been better made. The ultimate reality of things was essentially good, and only human folly and sin were bad. To get through the illusions of sense and passion to the eternal reality of truth and goodness—this was the struggle of his spiritual life. Of course he did not express himself in such words. His highest purposes inevitably took Calvinistic forms of expression. But this is most noteworthy, that it is not fear of hell that actuates him, not the safety of his own person, whether material or immaterial; but the desire to be right, to do right, to have a consciousness of right. This for him was light and peace.

Yet though about his sincerity there can be no doubt, he had not a simple nature. Whether the cause lay in his education, or in irremediable personal defect, certain it is that his vast energies and the perspectives of his brooding thought were never so entirely subordinated to one clear purpose as to be clarified into transparency. In this respect he was very far from the type of apostle or martyr. At each successive demand for exertion he was indeed equal to the occasion. Every faculty of his mind, every emotion of his heart, nay, every fibre of his body flashed into that white heat of energy which united watchfulness, swiftness, power, in one supreme function of his complex greatness. But when the occasion had passed by, he never had any far-reaching policy, except to be ready for the next call upon him. Thus, until action became necessary he seemed undecided, and his apparent indecision showed itself in cumbrous, awkward forms of speech. But he was really more decided than he himself knew. In a nature like his a great deal goes on beneath the surface of consciousness, and determines the future without the man himself being aware of it. This, perhaps, is only a roundabout way of saying that he was pre-eminently not a theorist but a man of action. But the reason why he was no theorist was that there was more unity in his impulses than in his thoughts. The demand for action concentrated all his powers on one point; but the demand for reflection never did. Hence he was very bad at explaining why he took this or that line of policy, even when he had the most confident assurance that he was right. And for much the same reason there was a great want of simplicity in his religious experience. The simplicity consisting in lack of variety he could not have, because his great brain was too busy for that. The simplicity consisting in unified variety he could not get, because no unifying idea commanding enough for the complexity of his thoughts ever possessed him.

Meantime the news he received year by year from his correspondents was sufficiently distracting. Wentworth's summons to the royal Council and then his elevation to the presidency of the north can scarcely have surprised Cromwell, for the self-seeking motives determining the new favourite's policy had been sufficiently evident even under the disguise of patriotism. His rapid elevation in the peerage, and his appointment in 1633 to be Lord-Lieutenant of Ireland showed his supremacy at Court, and the swift development of his daring plans. In

England Laud soon took his place as the first minister of the Crown, but the two men worked cordially together, and their letters remain an unanswerable proof of their deep treason against the constitution of their country.

Under their united influence all means of obsolete or illegal extortion were strained to the uttermost in the hope of making the King independent of Parliament. Loans were persistently enforced. Offenders out of whom money could be squeezed were not allowed to be judged according to the ordinary course of justice, but were brought before the Star Chamber, which claimed an unlimited power of fining. Monopolies, distinctly condemned, with Charles's own sanction, by the Petition of Right, were multiplied more than ever, with the usual consequences of dearness and adulteration. Tunnage and poundage were of course collected as before; and even subsidies, the grant of which had never been completed, were levied under the pretext that Parliament had intended to give them. In addition to such devices ship-money was invented by Attorney-General Noy, and Charles stretched the obsolete custom beyond even Noy's argument by levying on the whole country a form of contribution which the precedents cited only justified in sea-board districts. John Hampden's resolve, in 1634, to try the question in his own person, by flatly refusing to pay, no doubt had the sympathy of his cousin at St. Ives, but one fancies also that it would deepen the gloomy fits of the latter by the contrast it suggested with his own uselessness.*

At the beginning of 1636, soon after the letter to Mr. Storie was written, a considerable change took place in Cromwell's circumstances. His maternal uncle, Sir Thomas Steward, died towards the end of January, and his will, dated in that month, made Oliver his heir. The office of tithe-farmer at Ely being hereditary or devisable, Cromwell succeeded to it, and this necessitated his removal to Ely. His business was to collect the tithes of certain parishes, and to pay the stipulated rent to the Dean and Chapter, retaining the surplus for his own profit. The lease for the parishes of Trinity and St. Mary was running out when he succeeded, but he obtained, in October, a renewal for twenty-one years. In addition to his profits from tithe-farming,

---

* Cromwell may also have refused to pay. But the policy of the Government was to take one test case and keep all others out of the courts.

he also held various parcels of property under his uncle's will, sufficient to give him a substantial and even considerable position in the neighbourhood.

The change from St. Ives to Ely brought with it a considerable increase of occupation for Oliver, and this must have been very welcome. At Ely he exchanged the society of graziers, "whose talk is of bullocks," for that of the clergy and gentry of a cathedral town. Amongst both the latter classes there were to be found men who sympathised both with his political and religious aspirations. And even to those who differed most strongly from his Puritanism it would be an absurd anachronism to attribute the prejudice which made him an anathema to succeeding generations. On the contrary, he seems to have been freely admitted to the place his uncle Steward had occupied in society and local activities. He was at once elected one of the feofees of an important local charity,* three of his colleagues being cathedral dignitaries, who held their places *ex officio*. And, inasmuch as all vacancies were filled up by co-optation, it is certain that Oliver cannot have been in ill odour at this time even with the clergy. The accounts of the charity for that period have many leaves missing, probably because of the frequent occurrence of Oliver's name. But enough has come down to us to show that he was something more than a perfunctory feoffee. In particular, a note has been preserved, wherein he desires that a dole of forty shillings may be paid at once to a sick man, Benson, who seems to have had a good deal in that way ; and the writer adds that if the amount be disallowed "at the time of account," he will "pay it out of his own purse."†

But the most exciting topic of local politics at that time was the drainage of the fens. The swampy lands around the Isle of Ely had long been subject to a Commission of Sewers charged with the promotion of drainage.‡ On this Commission Oliver's father and uncle had served, and had supported projects for the reclamation of deluged fens. In the beginning of Charles's reign Cornelius Vermuyden, a Dutchman, drained large tracts on the Lincolnshire side of the Wash, and obtained from the King

---

* Now "Parson's Charity," then called the "Ely Feoffees' Fund." (Sanford, p. 247.)

† Carlyle, Appendix No. 2.

‡ The particulars which follow are mainly from Sir William Dugdale's "History of Embankment and Draining," 1662, p. 379 *et seq.*

a concession for similar works in the neighbourhood of Ely. The contractor was to keep for himself 95,000 acres of recovered land. But the country people objected to Vermuyden as a foreigner, and petitioned Francis, Earl of Bedford, owner of some 20,000 acres about Thorney and Whittlesea, to take the matter out of the Dutchman's hands. This was in 1630, when Cromwell was still at Huntingdon. The Commissioners, with the King's consent, agreed to the substitution of the earl as chief contractor, and articles were drawn up in that year, but it was not until 1634 that the earl and his associates were incorporated by charter. ⊦

The scheme was not matured without opposition. Besides fishers, fowlers, and others who feared a limitation of their hunting grounds, there were farmers with rights of common, and therefore jealous of enclosures ; and there were ratepayers fearful of any public works because of the risk of increased rates. In the public records of 1632* it appears that " Mr. Cromwell of Ely " had offered the inhabitants of the district to undertake the legal defence of their rights for a voluntary rate of fourpence per head of cattle. Oliver was then residing at St. Ives. But there is no other " Mr. Cromwell of Ely " known to collectors of Cromwell traditions. And it is conceivable that if Oliver made Ely the centre of his agitation, and was often a visitor at his uncle Steward's for that purpose, he might be reported to the Council as " Mr. Cromwell of Ely." †

In 1637 the whole area now known as the " Bedford Level " was adjudged by the Commissioners to have been well and sufficiently drained ; and the earl, with his fellow adventurers, claimed and received the lands apportioned to them. According to the articles of association the adventurers were to keep 95,000 acres. The whole of this was to be held liable for the completion of the work, but after completion duly declared, only 40,000 acres were to be liable in perpetuity for maintenance. The King was to receive 12,000 acres out of the Company's estate, and this royalty was to be carved out of Whittlesea manor and the marshes adjoining. The Company had expended £100,000 ; and 83,000

---

* Calendar of State Papers, Domestic Series.
† It should be remarked that the entry is referred to the year 1632 by inference only. But on such a point it is hardly probable that an error of four years can have arisen. And unless the entry could be referred to 1636 the difficulty still remains.

acres of recovered land, nearly half to be held liable for expenses of maintenance, could not be considered an exorbitant reward.

But in April, 1638, the Commissioners pronounced the works defective. The extensive overflows during the winter appeared to justify this judgment. On the other hand, the works had been authoritatively declared complete, and according to the charter no more than 40,000 acres were liable for maintenance. But the Commissioners irritated the public by levying enormous rates, varying from 6s. to 30s. an acre. And then, like a "deus ex machina," the King interposed, declaring he would undertake the work at his own charge. In compensation, however, his Majesty awarded to himself 152,000 acres of the recovered lands, while he allowed 40,000 as a *solatium* to the adventurers.

This proposal was, of course, resisted by the Earl of Bedford, and he had the country people with him. Whether they opposed the royal design in the interest of the earl or on grounds of their own is not quite clear. But there was ample reason why a Parliament man like Oliver Cromwell should resist the King. According to Sir William Dugdale, Charles estimated the value of the whole area in question, 400,000 acres, at £600,000 annual value. If that was at all accurate, then the King, who would of course take his 152,000 acres from the best parts, would thus add £228,000 a year to his revenue independent of Parliament. This consideration alone was enough to make the resistance of the Earl of Bedford popular.

The storm arose and reached its climax between April and July, 1638. On the 18th of the latter month the Commissioners, at a meeting held in Huntingdon, not without strong opposition, declared the King himself the sole undertaker. But within three days they were compelled to acknowledge that several complaints urged by opponents of the scheme had been made good ; and the Scotch troubles having already begun, the design was checkmated. The counsel for the Earl of Bedford were Mr. Holbourne and Mr. St. John, the latter of whom had married Cromwell's cousin. But unless Sir Philip Warwick and all collectors of country side traditions are in error, it was Oliver Cromwell who not only instructed and directed the counsel, but backed them up in interviews with the Commissioners by urging his view of the question

G

with resistless plainness and force.* It was his energy " as a head
of this faction," says Sir Philip Warwick, "which made his
activity so well known unto his friend and kinsman, Mr. Hampden, that he in this (Long) Parliament gave a character of Cromwell of being an active person, and one that would sit well at a
mark." He must have been mistaken in supposing that Hampden
was much enlightened by this incident as to the power of his
brooding cousin. But the words, "one that would sit well at a
mark," are graphic enough. His success on this occasion gave
him the popular title of " Lord of the Fens,"† a title which proved
very significant in after years. When he became lord, not only
of the Fens, but of all Great Britain and Ireland, the son and
successor of this Earl of Bedford completed the work now
arrested, and expressed his acknowledgments to Cromwell for
the encouragement and assistance he had received.

Meantime the family circle at Ely still continued to increase.
The household darling, Elizabeth, was nearly seven years old
when a rival, Mary, appeared, in February 1636. The new baby
was taken over to Huntingdon to be baptised, no doubt at the
desire of her grandmother. But when the last child, Frances,
was born, in December 1638, the baptism took place at Ely.
Probably Oliver's mother had already removed to her son's house,
the house where she herself had been born ; and she remained
with him to the end of her long life.

It was shortly before the birth of this last child that the letter
to Mrs. Oliver St. John was written which throws so much light
upon Cromwell's religious history. The comparative ease of his
position at Ely, and the opportunities given for a public employment of his formerly self-consuming energies had moderated his
gloom, and brought him the satisfaction of exertion in the strength
of the Lord. How deeply his forced inactivity had weighed upon
him is suggested in the words which lament " how unprofitable he
is, and the mean improvement of his talent." The last word is, of
course, simply an allusion to the parable in the Gospels, and does

* It has been suggested by Mr. Sanford that Cromwell's success on this occasion was owing to his diversion of the popular feeling on which the King had
relied. The Fen people are supposed to have been discontented with the restric-
tions imposed on them by Bedford's works, and hence to have been disposed to
side with the King, till Cromwell showed them that they would be just as badly
off, or even worse, under the new scheme.

† This, at least, is the general tradition, and it is more probable than any other
explanation.

not indicate any overweening consciousness of power. Indeed it looks rather in an opposite direction ; for he seems to class himself with the servant who had only one talent entrusted to him, and who thereupon buried it in the earth. But that he longed to be doing is shown by the words, " my soul is with the congregation of the firstborn; my body rests in hope ; and if here I may honour my God either by doing or by suffering, I shall be most glad."

The words suggest a labouring heart and a perplexed mind in a period of rest and light, desiring in vain to prolong the moments of joy. This precariousness of peace was of course partly a matter of temperament ; but, as his career develops itself, we shall see that another cause for his perplexity and lack of simplicity was an incongruity most real, though never recognised by himself, between the forms and the substance of his faith, perhaps also between his faith itself and the circumstances of his life. What was " the good work" for the perfection of which he prayed ? It would be doing him an injustice to regard it as anything less than the moulding of his character into conformity with the divine will. But the forms of his religion led him to regard it rather as perfect assurance of heaven's favour towards him—in his case an unattainable desire. Who were " the congregation of the firstborn ? " In his inmost heart he identified them with those who sought and struggled for rational liberty in England, nobility of national life, public purity, and orderly progress. But the forms of his faith required him to think only of those who had passed or were passing through his own Puritanic experiences. What was the " cause of God ? " It was to him the cause of humanity. But the forms of his belief led him to identify the interests of humanity with the triumph of a theological party, whose influence might be good or bad independently altogether of its dogmas. Besides, though his practical energies were pre-eminently fitted for war, his convictions, his sentiments, and sympathies would, in many respects, have harmonised far better with the peaceful life of an apostle. Thus the times into which he was born made it absolutely impossible that such a man as he was should ever have the charm of simplicity, or the repose of cloudless peace.

The letter to Mrs. St. John derives its most touching interest from the reference it makes to his eldest son Robert at Felsted

School. That lady was then staying at the house of Sir William Masham, not far from Felsted. Oliver sends a grateful message to Sir William's family. " I am much bound to them," he says, " for their love. I bless the Lord for them ; and that my son by their procurement is so well. Let him have your prayers, your counsel." Alas, the object of this fatherly solicitude was soon to escape beyond the need of any earthly counsel or prayer. Sad news came to Ely about the boy, nearly a man now, who had been then " so well."

The register at Felsted Church shows that he was buried there on May 31st, 1639.* He was then eighteen years old, and had continued longer at school than was usual in those times. Probably Oliver did not like the influences in the ascendant at Cambridge; and he evidently attached special value to the society of Felsted and the neighbourhood. But what makes the incident particularly noteworthy is the exceptional character of the entry made in the register by Mr. Wharton, the rector of that day. " Robert Cromwell, son of that honourable man, Oliver Cromwell, Esq., and of Elizabeth his wife, was buried on the 31st day of May. And Robert was a remarkably pious youth, fearing God above many." It was not the habit of this rector, nor of his predecessors or successors, thus to enlarge the dull records of death. No other instance has been found in the volume. There must have been therefore something to make an unusual impression upon the good man's heart, when he entered the memorial of his sad duty on that day. The overwhelming grief of the parents probably touched him, even accustomed as he was to scenes of human sorrow.

And it was, indeed, a terrible blow. The lad was their first-born. He was at an age towards which parental affection unites all the tenderness of protecting strength with the glad pride inspired by manly promise. And in this case that promise would seem to have been unusually rich and bright. At the church door Oliver had heard the words—" We brought nothing into this world, and it is certain we can carry nothing out. The Lord gave, the Lord hath taken away ; blessed be the name of the Lord." With weary longing for comfort, which neither friend nor wife could give, he turned to his Bible and read—" I

* The discovery of this entry is due to Mr. John Forster, who announced it in an *Edinburgh Review* article published in January 1856.

have learned in whatsoever state I am, therewith to be content. I know both how to be abased, and I know how to abound. Everywhere and in all things I am instructed both to be full and to be hungry, both to abound and to suffer need." But did Paul know the hunger of such a bereaved love as this? such a need as this dread void in the house? Could it be endured in calm? The reader went on and found a sudden inspiration in the words—"*I can do all things through Christ which strengtheneth me.*" The agony and relief of that moment survived all the struggle and storm of Cromwell's after-life. In the last grief he experienced before he entered into rest he went back for consolation to the memory of this time.

Slowly, no doubt, after much prayer and conflict, amidst the heartfelt sympathy of friends, hope and peace came back to the sorrowing parents. And now their huge grief has shrunk into a brief, dusty entry, scrutinised by dry eyes for the interesting hint it gives on the estimation in which poor Robert's father even then was held. *Vir honorandus*—"that honourable man;" an entirely unparalleled description in the burial register, cannot be regarded as merely conventional courtesy. The title " miles" or " esquire " added is quite enough for that. We may fairly conclude that the impression made by Oliver in his visits to Otes and Felsted, together with the reputation he had gained in Parliament and in his own county, justified the sympathetic clergyman in paying a tribute to the father, while he recorded the blighted promise of the son.

The reputation thus early recognised by the rector of Felsted assured to Cromwell some part, more or less important, in the struggle, now no longer to be delayed, between Crown and Commonwealth. The apparent success of Strafford in establishing a firm despotism in Ireland, and in getting all the resources of that country under his control, gave delusive hopes of a basis of operations for the conquest of England and Scotland. Laud would fain have emulated his success, but his difficulties were greater. The Church was increasingly Romanised ; communion with foreign Protestants forbidden ; and Puritan ministers punished for recusancy. In 1637 Prynne, a man of cantankerous temper, whom only cruelty could have made a hero, was placed on the pillory a second time, to have the remaining stumps of his ears sawn off ; and this time he was accompanied by Dr. John Bastwick, a physician, and the Rev. Henry Burton, a clergyman, who were condemned to similar torture and mutilation. But opinion in England was by no means so unanimous on ecclesiastical questions as it was in Scotland, and it was Laud's imprudence in meddling with the northern kingdom which brought matters to a head.

Eliot lay buried in the Tower, killed by confinement, because too proud to make a sufficiently abject appeal for mercy. And when his family petitioned for his body Charles wrote—" Let Sir John Eliot be buried within that parish where he died." In the case of ship-money, after a long struggle in 1637, the judges consummated the mischief of their subserviency by condemning Hampden to pay. In 1638 the Scots rejected Laud's innovations so decisively that it was clear nothing but actual force would avail. And in the days when young Robert Cromwell lay dying, a royal army, raised and supported by illegal taxation, reached Berwick. But, unfortunately for Charles and Laud, the Scots were equally quick in raising an army too formidable to be lightly attacked. Under a hollow pretence of pacification actual hostilities were prevented. But things could not remain as they were. The effort had exhausted the trickling intermittent stream of illegal revenues, which no violence could enlarge, and in these desperate circumstances Charles and his advisers were forced to try the old-fashioned method of Parliament once more.

CHAPTER VI.

IN THE LONG PARLIAMENT.

As soon as it was known that a Parliament was to be summoned once more, the question arose where Oliver was to find a seat. He had quite sufficient reputation now to mark him as a man who could not be spared; and we do not suppose that he needed any persuasion on the subject. But where was he to offer himself? Huntingdon was out of the question. The Barnard influence was still supreme there, though probably modified to some slight extent by that of the neighbouring Montagues. In Cambridge, however, Cromwell was well known, and his recent activity in the Fen question is quite sufficient to account for his election there. His colleague was Mr. Thomas Meautys, who had already served the town in Parliament without distinction, but who was afterwards dropped, probably because he did not answer sufficiently to the popular impulse. At Huntingdon Oliver's successful rival, Robert Barnard, was chosen, together with William Montague of the new family at Hinchinbrook.

The "Short Parliament" as it is called, met April 13th, and was dissolved May 5th, 1640. If anything but sheer desperation prompted Charles to summon this assembly, it must surely have been the hope that after proof of his firm resolve to uphold his own view of the royal prerogative, the people's representatives would submit themselves to the inevitable. Indeed this is apparent in the words of the Lord Keeper Finch, Speaker of the last House of Commons, "His Majesty did not expect advice from them," said this convert to courtly interests, "much less that they should interpose in any affair of mediation; which would not be grateful to him; but that they would, as soon as might be, give his Majesty a supply."

Eleven years of tyranny, however, had not broken the spirit of Englishmen. The new House of Commons imperturbably insisted on giving precedence to the question of grievances, and it was presently clear that no apprehension of any conse-

quences, be they what they might, would turn these men from
their purpose. As soon as Charles saw this he dissolved Parliament once more.

But the unsettled state of affairs in Scotland, and the warlike
counsels of Strafford compelled fresh efforts to raise money.
Once more the vacillating monarch tried the extra-parliamentary
expedients belonging, as he believed, to his prerogative. A "benevolence" was headed by the Earl of Strafford with £20,000; an
enormous sum when the relative value of money is considered. A
forced loan was pushed again, but, as before, with little result
other than friction, and smoke, and sputtering of fire. A commission of array was issued for the gathering of a new army;
and it is easy to conceive the temper in which men, who more
than half sympathised with the Scots, left their farms and shops
for a war in which the destruction of their opponents would entail
on themselves a continuance of arbitrary government. The English troops were half mutinous from their first assembly, and
melted away on the line of march. The Scots, on the other hand,
did not wait to be invaded, but promptly took the offensive; and
by the end of August they held the whole of Northumberland
and Durham.

In distracted helplessness, the weak will that claimed a divine
supremacy now sought to shift its burden to others, and demanded
the advice of a council of Peers at York. The King's anxiety
was apparent in the earnestness with which he deprecated the idea
that he wanted to substitute this council for Parliament. But
at least they might advise him what to do about those unmanageable Scots, and perhaps help him to get money. They consented
to engage the Scots in negotiation, but urged a speedy recourse
to Parliament; and on the King's concession of this point the
city of London at once gathered a loan of £200,000.

The writs summoning the most fateful Parliament of English
history were then issued, fixing November for the meeting. John
Pym knew that the crisis was now come, and he rode from town
to town, impressing upon local leaders the importance of returning
the right men. If he visited Cambridge, there is no doubt that
his influence would be favourable to Oliver Cromwell. But the
election appears to have been closely contested. Oliver's colleague
in the representation of Cambridge was no longer Meautys, but
John Lowry, a member of the town council.

When Parliament met, the bearing and conversation of the members, as they eagerly gossiped together in Westminster Hall or the lobby of the Commons, betrayed a confidence that the scale was turned in their favour, and that the King's government was now in their power if only they could agree to be bold and firm in seizing their advantage. The Court party also showed depression and a sense of impotence. There was no state pageant at the opening of the session. At the last moment the king found that Sir Thomas Gardiner, recorder of London, whom he had designed for the Speaker's chair, would fail to secure election, and William Lenthall was hastily substituted. Charles came quietly in his barge from Whitehall, and the speeches made on the occasion show a desire to cut short ceremonial because of an oppressive sense of the serious business in hand.

A biography of Cromwell does not involve any detailed history of the Long Parliament. For though he was certainly a diligent and active member, his services during the first two years are veiled from us in the obscurity of committees whose records are either totally lost or only preserved in dry reports and in fragmentary reminiscences. It was on his motion that a bill for annual Parliaments was read a second time on December 30th.* But his chief activity for a while was in the Grand Committee of Religion, which met on Mondays, and whose efforts to reform the Church and evangelise the nation were congenial to the longing of his own soul. It has been computed that he worked on eighteen committees, in all, during the first nine months of the Parliament.† Of all that he said and did, however, very little survives. It will be best therefore at once to mention two or three brief but vivid glimpses that we get of him during that time, and then rapidly to note the steps by which the now inevitable appeal to arms was brought on.

During the very first days of the session, the crimes of the Council, and the Star Chamber, and the Court of High Commission rose in judgment against the King's government as sins are pictured crowding from a forgotten past to overwhelm the sinner at the supreme assize. Victims with cropped ears and lacerated backs, and blasted health, and ruined fortune, appeared by petition before the House. And happy were they who could get a zealous member to make their cause his own. Prisoners debarred

*_ Gardiner, from D'Ewes's Diary. † Sanford, p. 306.

from their right of *Habeas Corpus* and denied any access to the outer world could not help themselves; but mourning wives, or sorrowing children, or faithful servants petitioned for them, and so secured the vigorous interference of Parliament. Amongst these prisoners was John Prynne. He was now confined in the island of Jersey, beyond the reach, as it was hoped, of justice or pity. On November 9th, six days after the opening of Parliament, two petitions, amongst others, were presented praying for a consideration of his sentence; one from his servant, John Brown, and the other from John Lilburne, who had been associated with him and shared his views and his sufferings. This Lilburne had been a " libeller " on his own account, and had received two hundred lashes at a cart's tail from West-minster to the Fleet Prison. His petition is mentioned by Sir Symonds D'Ewes, a note-taking member; and he states it was presented by " Mr. Cromwell." It was on this occasion also that Cromwell first attracted the notice of Sir Philip Warwick, a royalist, who, after the restoration, published his " Memoirs of the Reign of King Charles I." It will be seen that Sir Philip says the person whose cause Oliver advocated was " a servant of Mr. Prynne's," a description apparently more applicable to the John Brown mentioned above than to Lilburne. Possibly indeed both petitions were presented by the member for Cam-bridge, and Sir Philip, to whom the matter appeared very trifling, may have mixed them up. But what is chiefly to be noted is the worldly-minded knight's astonishment at the passion to which Cromwell was moved by the wrongs of an obscure and vulgar person.

"The first time I ever took notice of him was in the beginning of the Parliament held in November 1640, when I vainly thought myself a courtly young gentleman; for we courtiers valued ourselves much upon our good clothes. I came into the House one morning, well clad, and perceived a gentleman speaking, whom I knew not, very ordinarily apparelled; for it was a plain cloth suit, which seemed to have been made by an ill country tailor; his linen was plain, and not very clean, and I remember a speck or two of blood upon his little band,* which was not much larger than his collar; his hat was without a hat-band; his

* The "band" was the shirt collar turned down over the collar of the coat, as Eton boys wear it now. Courtly gentlemen loved to show a broad expanse of shining linen. The specks of blood were, no doubt, as Carlyle suggests, due to bad razors—and, we may add, carelessness.

stature was of a good size ; his sword stuck close to his side; his countenance swollen and reddish ; his voice sharp and untuneable, and his
eloquence full of fervour—for the subject would not bear much of reason,
it being in behalf of a servant of Mr. Prynne's, who had dispersed libels
against the Queen for her dancing and such like innocent and courtly
sports; and *he aggravated the imprisonment of this man by the council-
table unto that height, that one would have believed the very government itself had been in great danger by it.* I sincerely profess it lessened much
my reverence unto that great council, for he was very much hearkened unto."

The "sharp, untuneable voice" had evidently the searching
power belonging only to earnest conviction, and, in the words
we have italicised, there is clearly described an absorbing
possession by the subject in hand. Only a sophisticated
courtier, trained to reverse the proportionate importance of
character and dress, could wonder that a man carried beyond
himself by another's wrongs should be "very much hearkened
unto." Cromwell never was an orator ; but his unusual force
of feeling and will found a way of making itself recognised in
his words as well as in action. The union of all his faculties
under the spell of strong emotion commanded attention when
he spoke, just as it compelled success when he had work to
achieve.

Lord Digby, on descending the stairs from the lobby of
the House in company with John Hampden, saw Cromwell
below them, and asked for information about the rough,
unconventional speaker whose impassioned sympathy for Lilburne had so arrested attention. "Pray, Mr. Hampden," he
said, "who is the sloven who spoke to-day? for I see he is
on our side by his speaking so warmly." "That 'sloven'
you see before you," replied Hampden, "hath no ornament
in his speech. But if we should ever come to a breach with
the King—which, God forbid!—that 'sloven,' I tell you, will
be the greatest man in England."

In the debate on Episcopacy in February, 1641, Sir John
Strangways argued that parity in the Church would involve
parity in the Commonwealth. Cromwell appears to have been
very much irritated by this argument. As we shall see, nothing
could be farther from his ideas than the notion of a "parity"
in the Commonwealth. But his religious feelings were outraged
by the pomp and wealth of bishops, and it made him angry to

be told that this abuse could not be rectified without a revolution in the State. He answered so warmly that some
members cried, "To the bar! to the bar!" But, on the
interposition of Pym and Holles, he was allowed to proceed;
and he declared "he was more convinced touching the irregu-
larity of the bishops than ever before, because, like the Roman
hierarchy, they would not endure to have their condition come
to a trial.*

Another illustration of Oliver's temperament is given in
Clarendon's Life. This time the matter of dispute is the
Fens again, a subject which, we may be sure, Oliver understood much better than Mr. Hyde. The Queen had certain
manors near St. Ives, on the marshland called the Soke of
Somersham.† On these lands, previously subject to rights
of common, an enclosure of considerable extent had been
made with scant regard to the claims of surrounding tenants.
Experience in our own day makes us familiar with the injustice
suffered by the public through encroachments of this kind.
There may be much grumbling, but the wrong is done, and
the memory of it dies away. In this instance, however, the
injured tenants found an advocate in Oliver Cromwell. The land
had been granted to a dependent of the Queen, and from him had
been bought by the Earl of Manchester, Lord Privy Seal. To
oppose this nobleman could not have been a welcome task to
Oliver, for not only had there been some friendly association of
the Montagues and Cromwells in the past, but if Oliver himself
should ever need the aid of aristocratic influence, there was
no one in great place so likely to be available as the earl.
Besides, Lord Mandeville, the earl's son and heir, afterwards
Cromwell's companion in arms, already favoured the Parliamentary party, and in his case public policy as well as some
degree of private friendship must have suggested reasons for
avoiding a collision, if possible.

In February 1641 a bill for confirming certain grants made
by the King to his royal consort was referred by the Commons
to a committee, of which Cromwell was a member.‡ About the
same time a petition was presented from the inhabitants of

* Gardiner, "Fall of the Monarchy of Charles I.," vol. ii., p. 82.
† The identification of the land concerned is Carlyle's.
‡ For information on this subject we are indebted to the research of Mr.
Sanford. "Studies," &c., p. 367, *seqq.*

Somersham complaining of the enclosure; and, as this concerned the Queen's manors, it was referred to the same committee. Meanwhile, the House of Lords made an order to settle the possession in the interest of the Earl of Manchester and others. The result was a riot, in which the obnoxious fences were broken down. Then, towards the end of May, a petition was presented by Mr. Denzil Holles to the Commons on behalf of Lord Mandeville and Sir Thomas Hatton, praying that possession might continue, as ordered by the Lords, until the Lower House had considered the case, and that the rioters might be compelled to wait peaceably for their decision. Among others who spoke on this question was Cromwell. The summary of what he said, as given by Sir Symonds D'Ewes, is as much characterised by moderation as by decision.

" He showed that this much concerned the privilege of this House, and of all the commons of England; for after the petition by the inhabitants of the said towns preferred here, and (after) that it was in hearing before a committee of this House, the Lords made an order in the House of Peers to settle the possession, which made the people to commit this outrage, which he did not approve, nor attempt to justify; and that, since, they had made an order to settle the possession again by the sheriff and by force of arms with the trained bands."

The subject seems then to have dropped. But immediately afterwards Cromwell learned that the Earl of Manchester had sent out sixty writs " against the poor inhabitants in Huntingdonshire, for pulling down some inclosures." Many of these obscure people were, no doubt, personally known to the late farmer of St. Ives; and he interfered at once by moving, on June 9th, " that the committee for the Queen's jointure might be renewed," and that " the petition of the poor inhabitants might be considered by it." This was agreed to, and both parties were represented before the committee. On a particular day the petitioners were present in some numbers, together with their witnesses, and were advised, directed, and supported by Cromwell. Lord Mandeville was present in person, " sitting covered "—such was the deference shown to a peer—" by the direction of the committee." Mr. Edward Hyde was voted into the chair, and in his reminiscences he describes the difficulty he found in keeping Mr. Cromwell in order. How far he can be relied on for precise accuracy may be judged by his remark that Oliver " had never before been heard to speak in the House of Commons," an absurd misstatement, as his colleagues Sir Philip Warwick and Sir Symonds D'Ewes could have abundantly proved to him. But now that Oliver did speak, Mr. Hyde did not like his manners at all.

" Cromwell . . . ordered the witnesses and petitioners in the method of proceeding, and seconded and enlarged upon what they said with great passion; and the witnesses and persons concerned, who were a very rude kind of people, interrupted the counsel and witnesses on the other side with great clamour when they said anything that did not please them, so that Mr. Hyde, whose office it was to oblige men of all sorts to keep order, was compelled to use some sharp reproofs, and some threats, to reduce them to such a temper that the business might be quietly heard. Cromwell, in great fury, reproached the chairman for being partial"—an insinuation very incredible to Mr. Hyde, of course—" and (alleged) that he discountenanced the witnesses by threatening them. The other (Mr. Hyde) appealed to the committee, which justified him, and declared that he behaved himself as he ought to do, which more inflamed Mr. Cromwell, who was already too much angry. When, upon any mention of matter-of-fact, or of the proceeding before and at the enclosure, the Lord Mandeville desired to be heard, and with great modesty related what had been done, or explained what had been said, Mr. Cromwell did answer and reply upon him with so much indecency and rudeness, and in language so contrary and offensive, that every man would have thought that, as their natures and their manners were as opposite as it is possible, so their interest could never have been the same. In the end, his whole carriage was so tempestuous, and his behaviour so insolent, that the chairman found himself obliged to reprehend him, and to tell him that if he proceeded in the same manner he (the chairman) would presently adjourn the committee, and the next morning complain to the House of him, which he never forgave, and took all occasions afterwards to pursue him with the utmost malice and revenge."

Evidently Mr. Hyde thought that nothing but malice could account for a low opinion of a man with his eminent perfections. But his words throw a light, such as he little intended, both on his own character and on that of the object of his hatred. As we think of it, the picture of that afternoon comes out clearly. Hyde in his chair at the table head, the committee-men round the board, Lord Mandeville seated with his hat on near the foot of the table, the other petitioners and their witnesses standing uncovered in a throng near the door, Cromwell at times coming out to consult with them in hurried whispers, then in his " sharp, untuneable voice," questioning them aloud, cross-questioning their opponents, disputing points of order with his colleagues, and even with the chair. It is easy to gather how favourably disposed was Mr. Hyde towards the mild-mannered nobleman, how curt and peremptory he was with the " rude kind of people " who made such a contemptible business a matter of life and death. It is very conceivable also to us that Mr. Cromwell, who always bore the possibilities of storm and whirlwind within him, began to feel inwardly disturbed as he marked the difference of treatment accorded to the opposite parties. This very probably suggested a redress of the balance by special sharpness and incisiveness in his own dealing with Lord Mandeville. As the controversy grew more involved, we can very well believe Mr. Hyde that Oliver's " whole carriage " grew " tempestuous." In fact, some faint foretaste was given, could any one have understood it, of the whirlwind in which the House itself was one day to disappear.

One or two other incidents mentioned, either in the journals of the House, or in the diary of Sir Symonds D'Ewes, are suggestive of the same keen sympathy on the part of Oliver with wrongs suffered by the weak at the hands of the strong. One feels that at this period of his life, whatever might be the case afterwards —a question we may leave for the present—his heart must have responded warmly to the words of the prophet : " To turn aside the right of a man before the face of the most High; to subvert a man in his cause the Lord approveth not." Two brothers, Sir James and Sir Henry Thynne, the former a member of the House, were at loggerheads about the property left by their deceased father. The elder appears to have used his privilege as a member to obtain an unfair advantage over the younger ; at least such was the opinion of Cromwell ; and, having this conviction, he allowed no fear about meddling in a matter of no personal concern to him to interfere with his action. On June 1st, 1641, he moved that Sir James Thynne be required by the House " to show cause concerning his brother." The motion was carried. But afterwards Sir James, with the support of Hyde and Falkland, got the affair referred to a committee. What was the issue we do not know, but the incident indicates a proper jealousy on the part of Cromwell of any unjust use of a member's privilege.

The impression made upon us by the occasional light thrown

upon his comparatively obscure activity as a working member is, that he took his duties as they came, struck for right when he could, and had neither policy, nor scheme, nor ambition, apart from the restitution and security of constitutional rights, which Charles's mistaken notions of kingly prerogative had overthrown. But as to the precise securities to be insisted upon, that was a question he was for the most part content, during this period, to leave to others. There was probably far more frankness than guile in his reply to Sir Philip Warwick toward the close of this year (1641), when asked what he and his party would have. " I can tell you," said Oliver, " what I would *not* have, but I cannot tell what I *would*."

At this time Cromwell's mind was exercised on the question of uniformity in religion; for the treaty with the Scots had to be settled, and one of the articles proposed the establishment of a more complete ecclesiastical agreement between the two countries. The extent to which Oliver's attention was attracted by this subject is shown by a short note he sent off to his "loving friend Mr. Willingham, at his house in Swithin's Lane," * requesting a copy of "the reasons of the Scots for enforcing their desire of uniformity in Religion." As Oliver takes care to explain that the document he wants is "the same which he had before" of Mr. Willingham, it appears that this was not the first time he had turned his thoughts to the subject, and that he found himself rather perplexed by it. If he had but known it, this was a difficulty fated to haunt and distract him all his days. For himself, he afterwards came very near the modern method of dealing with it, but then he was practically alone.

Just now, however, he was more concerned with pulling down than with building up; and he joined with Vane and Haselrig in promoting the "Root and Branch Bill," as it was called, the object of which was the entire abolition of episcopacy.

The wariness and foresight of Oliver were shown, in accordance with the intolerant temper of the times, by a proposal he made on May 3rd, 1641, that "some course might be taken to turn the Papists out of Dublin." This is a proposal which naturally and rightly revolts our feelings. But mutual tolerance between Papists and Protestants in Ireland was then simply out of the question. The motion was not carried. The

* Letter III. in Carlyle.

feeling of the House probably was that it might precipitate the danger it was designed to avert. But the year had not passed over before a conspiracy was discovered in Dublin, that went far to justify at least the apprehensions and the foresight of Cromwell.

Meantime, the friction between the King and Parliament was slowly smouldering into open war. There was already a remarkable difference between this Parliament and any former one in the mutual bearing of the Commons and the Crown. There was no such hesitation about the impeachment of Strafford as there had been about the mere naming of Buckingham. The Commons were implacably resolved on his death; the Lords, after a little hesitation, endorsed this resolve; and the wrath of the country paralysed the King's feeble efforts to save him. It is impossible, indeed, to suppress a feeling of painful pity for the miserable monarch forced to sacrifice to a just popular instinct the dangerous counsellor whom he had praised and pampered. But our sense of the conduct that a higher sense of honour would have dictated to the King need not lessen our appreciation of the constitutional foresight which led the Parliament to insist, at all hazards, on the death of such an adviser. When the axe fell it destroyed irresponsible government; and the cruel rapture with which the people shouted in the streets, " His head is off ! his head is off !" was inspired by no ignoble delight in blood, but by the conviction that an irreversible victory had been won for constitutional rule.

From the very moment of Strafford's arrest Charles's power of resistance seemed to have been paralysed. He consented to the abolition of the courts of star chamber and high commission. He surrendered the arbitrary powers of his Privy Council, and of the Council of the North. He agreed to make the judges' commissions tenable " during good behaviour," instead of " during pleasure." Within fifteen months of the meeting of Parliament he passed twenty-four Acts to condemn and prevent the repetition of the despotic practices of the previous eleven years. Most significant of all, on the same day when he signed Strafford's death warrant, he assented, perhaps in the very faintness of agony, to a Bill putting it out of his power to dissolve Parliament without its own consent. The reason urged was that the measure was necessary to give confidence to capitalists, who

H

otherwise would not lend money. As to Church affairs, Charles had warned the Commons that he was ready to agree to reformation but not to alteration. Unfortunately it was alteration they wanted. And in February 1641 they took a bold step to prevent any farther Popish reaction, by impeaching Archbishop Laud of high treason and shutting him up in the Tower.

Was it then only in the insolence of triumph that the two Houses prepared to meet the King on his return from Scotland with a Remonstrance recalling every evil wrought under his rule? The truth is the Parliamentary leaders had good reason to fear that without some material guarantee, such as power over the militia, they would lose everything they had gained, whenever fortune or intrigue might put the King at the head of an army. And not even Parliamentary power over the militia would prevent this unless the King would consent to govern only through men possessing the confidence of Parliament. To obtain such guarantees was the main object of the " Grand Remonstrance."*

After a brief recess, from September 9th to October 20th, the completion of this document was hastened by the terrible news, reaching Westminster on November 1st, of the rebellion in Ireland. How far the horrors of massacre were exaggerated we do not here pause to inquire. It is sufficient to note that popular feeling did not wait for inquiry, and that the position of the Commons was strengthened both by the public wrath against Papists, and also by a general suspicion of collusion on the part of the Court. The Commons declared themselves in danger. The City Council sent the train bands to guard them. And amid the excitement thus aroused Pym pushed on the Remonstrance.

On November 22nd, a final decision was urged; but Lord Falkland supported an adjournment which was carried. Cromwell afterwards asked him why he had interposed; and Falkland replied that the issue would raise a long debate. "A very sorry one," said Oliver, impatient to have the question decided. Next

---

* This famous document consisted of 206 numbered paragraphs recounting all the disorders, discontents, and miseries of the time. Perhaps the hand of the "Lord of the Fens" may be traced in section 32, which runs:—"Large quantities of common and several grounds hath been taken away from the subject by colour of the statute of improvement, and by abuse of the commission of sewers, without their consent, and against it." At all events, the passage helps to elucidate the action of Cromwell concerning the Bedford Level. The reference of "their consent" is obscure; but it probably means the consent of the subject.

day the discussion was angry and prolonged beyond all precedent. At one period the tumult was such that swords were drawn, and bloodshed was threatened. At length, after midnight, the Remonstrance was finally adopted by a majority of eleven. As the members passed out, Cromwell told Falkland he would take his word another time as to the prospects of debate; and he added that had the Remonstrance not been carried, he would have sold all his possessions and left the country for the new world. Doubt has been thrown upon this declaration. But in fact this division on the Remonstrance decided whether constitutional government in England was now to be placed on a firm basis or not. And whether the words are authentic or not, at least they express the greatness of the crisis.

Charles, returning from his northern kingdom, reached London on November 25th by way of Kingsland and Moorfields. He was welcomed by the City with an enthusiasm which might have suggested to him a generous reciprocation of the loyalty of his subjects. Had he then taken the opportunity of graciously conceding guarantees for constitutional government, the Remonstrance would never have been presented, and, for a time at least, he might have been the most popular monarch that had ever reigned. Instead of that, on the very next day he expressed anger and astonishment at the presence of the Parliamentary guards in Westminster, and peremptorily ordered their dismissal. The Houses demurred with equal decision. On the 27th the King consented that the train-bands might continue their service for a time, provided it was not for long. On December 1st the Remonstrance was presented to the King at Hampton Court, and, while promising an answer, he received it, as might be expected, with expressions of anger and impatience.

Meantime the agitation against the political power of bishops, and indeed against the episcopal form of Church government, grew to a dangerous height. The bishops were insulted in coming to the House of Lords. Ten of their number declined to run the risk of attendance any longer, and drew up a protest declaring all action of the Peers void during their enforced absence. On this the Commons accused these ten bishops of high treason, and the Lords committed them to the Tower. The King, alarmed by the disorder around him, strengthened his personal

H 2

guard at Whitehall; and collisions with adherents of the Parliament became dangerously frequent.   The request of the
Commons for a guard was still denied, and on January 3rd,
1641–2 Charles answered their petition in words which, taken in
connection with the events of the following day, sound unpleasantly like mocking irony.   He assured them that they might
rely on his word for their safety; " and," he added, " if this
general assurance shall not suffice to remove your apprehensions,
we will command such a guard to wait upon you as we will be
responsible for to Him who hath encharged us with the protection
and safety of our subjects.",

On the same day he sent a sergeant-at-arms to demand the
surrender of Lord Kimbolton (Viscount Mandeville) by the
Lords, and of Pym, Hampden, Holles, and Strode, by the
Commons, to answer a charge of high treason.   This being
evaded, he did indeed command " a guard to wait upon " the
House of Commons; for next morning he headed his own
attendants, supported by a number of courtiers, in an attempt
to arrest the obnoxious members in their places in Parliament.
We need not enlarge upon the fatal folly of this hitherto unprecedented invasion of Parliament.   Oliver himself a few years
afterwards did something not wholly dissimilar, only he did it
much more effectually; and we may have to consider not only
the similarity, but the difference between the two cases.   On
this occasion he sat in his place, unconscious of his destiny.
He shared the excitement caused by rumours of the King's
approach; he joined in the peremptory order to the endangered
members to withdraw; he heard the tramp of the guards in the
lobby; he stood in silence with the rest, while the pale King,
with vain assumption of imperious majesty, dispossessed the
Speaker of his chair, and then, already conscious of mistake, had
to retreat, defeated and baffled.

After this the outbreak of hostilities was only delayed by the
unpreparedness of both sides, and by the unwillingness of either
to be chargeable with being the first to begin.   The enthusiasm
of the City defeated another infatuated attempt to arrest the five
members; and then Charles quitted Whitehall on January 10th,
1642, never to return thither again until the final scene of his
life's tragedy.   After his departure the Parliament came back in
a sort of triumph to Westminster, guarded on the river by the

watermen, and watched on land by the City train-bands. In all the weary correspondence that followed the substantial questions at issue remained the same—whether the King would govern solely through advisers approved by Parliament, and whether, as a guarantee of this, he would put fortresses, magazines, and military command into the hands of men approved by the two Houses. Our judgment of the whole following conflict must depend on our opinion of the reasonableness or otherwise of these requirements.

Already, in the middle of 1641, Sir Arthur Haselrig had brought in a Bill " to settle the militia in persons nominated by the House." It was then read a first time, but further procedure was postponed. On November 4th of that year Cromwell carried a vote, ordering that the Earl of Essex, who commanded the trained bands south of the Trent, should continue to do so until Parliament should give further orders. This was a clear assumption of power to neutralise the royal prerogative. In the posture of affairs at the beginning of 1642 the House began to act for itself. Sir John Hotham had been despatched to the north to have an eye to Parliamentary interests there; and a large magazine of military stores at Hull was the object of his special watchfulness. Parliament wanted these stores brought up to London; but, of course, the King had refused consent. Two days after the departure from Whitehall, Sir John Hotham's son, also a member of the House, was called upon to go down to Hull, and convey to his father the orders of Parliament that he should assume the governorship of the town, and hold it " for King and Parliament." From the gallery the young man exclaimed, " Mr. Speaker, fall back, fall edge, I will go down and perform your commands," and immediately left the House on his fateful errand.

Meanwhile the question of the militia continued unsettled, and on March 2nd the King peremptorily refused to concede the demand for a limited time—" not even for an hour ! " The House then resolved that " His Majesty's subjects be put in a posture of defence." On March 19th Charles reached York, and began to gather adherents around him there. On April 23rd he appeared in person before Hull. Hotham was in sore perplexity, but, resolving to stand by his orders from Parliament, raised the drawbridge, and informed the King that he could only obey such commands as were conveyed through Parliament. Charles then proclaimed him a traitor, and called upon the loyal inhabitants of the country to aid their Sovereign in capturing the town.

The House of Commons now passed a resolution that " the King, seduced by wicked counsels, intends to make war against Parliament; " and they did not hesitate to take measures of defence. In doing so they did not for a moment admit that they were raising a rebellion. They maintained that according to the constitution, royal authority did not and could not mean the personal caprice or will of the individual man, Charles Stuart. It meant his power to give orders for the carrying out of law. " And the levying of war against his laws and authority, though not against his person, is levying war against the King; but the levying of force against his personal commands, though accompanied with his presence, and not against his laws and authority, but in the maintenance thereof, is no levying of war against the King, but for him." * To some historians this distinction has appeared to be a mere superfluity of hypocrisy. Yet the distinction was a most real one, without which, indeed, constitutional monarchy would be impossible. In this sturdy defence of the Crown against the King they made such provision for the protection of Hull that Charles was baffled in his attempts to seize it. Afterwards he was repelled from Coventry, which closed its gates against him ; and so, retreating to Nottingham, he set up his standard there on August 22nd, 1642.

During these eventful months Cromwell, like all other members of the Long Parliament, had to decide whether he would still follow the resolute policy of Pym, or whether, like Falkland and others, he should be satisfied with the King's verbal concessions, and oppose any further demands. His family traditions and associations would have favoured a policy of compromise, but his religious convictions determined his political conduct. He held that the work of God in redemption was to form out of fallen mankind " a people for himself, zealous of good works." He held that England had been so singularly favoured as a special field of this work that the godly in this country might class themselves with the chosen people of old. For the further progress of God's work in England two conditions were, in his view, essential : first, the purification of the Church from

* Declaration of the Parliament, May 26, 1642.

relics of Romish superstition, so far, at least, that they should not be binding on any Englishman's acceptance; and next, the establishment of such constitutional government as should ensure public justice, protect the rights of all, and encourage the development of private virtue. He did not believe that either of these conditions was secured by any promises of the King, or by any arrangement short of the plan insisted on by Parliament, that is, government by responsible advisers acceptable to the people's representatives, and a material guarantee for the continuance of the system by the King's surrender of personal control over the militia. Hence his adherence to the most resolute band of Pym's supporters was the direct issue of his religious faith. That such was the true genesis of his political impulses—for political philosophy he had none—will, perhaps, be more apparent as we proceed.

Consistently with such practical religious and political aims, Cromwell's Parliamentary services continued to be of a strictly practical nature. We have seen how in the beginning of 1641 he moved for precautions in Dublin which would have prevented much alarm afterwards. At the beginning of 1642, ten days after the King's attempt to arrest the five members, Oliver moved for and obtained a committee to consider of means to put the kingdom in a posture of defence. In the next month (February 7th) he offered £300 towards the reduction of the Irish rebellion, an offer he afterwards raised to £500.

On June 1st he manifested his watchfulness over the Irish difficulty by representing strongly the case of Colonel Steward * and 3,500 Scots, who had maintained themselves against the Ulster rebels without assistance or supply of any kind, but were then reduced to great straits. On the same day he moved that two ships might be sent to the mouth of the Tyne to prevent the landing of arms or forces from abroad, a motion which shows that he already had foresight of the strategic conditions under which the war would be opened. On the 5th of the same month he offered to give or obtain £500 for the defence of Parliament, from which we gather that where his heart was engaged he was not sparing of his money. In July the Parliament resolved somewhat tardily to raise an army of which the Earl of Essex was to be general. Thereupon Cromwell moved that

* Probably of his mother's family.

the townsmen of Cambridge might be allowed to raise two companies of volunteers, and to appoint captains over them. But he had himself already taken time by the forelock, and, without waiting for orders, had sent down to his constituents arms to the worth of £100, which the House now resolved to repay him. On the 21st of July he was yet at Westminster; for, still interested in the affairs of Ireland, he was ordered, with Mr. Strode, to prepare a letter for the Lords Justices there, requiring them to send a thousand men for the defence of Duncannon Fort. But about that time it became clear to him that he could be of more service if actually on the spot in his own district. He therefore went down to Cambridge, and though his voice was still at intervals heard in the House, always with growing potency till at last it drowned every other, yet his place of work for the next ten years was not the council-chamber but the battle-field.

CHAPTER VII.

THE EASTERN COUNTIES ASSOCIATION.

When a great emergency arises, involving a whole community in danger, the natural course is for every man to fall into his own place, and throw his whole soul into doing his duty there. As time goes on, and events supply a test of differences in power, it will soon become apparent whether his previous fortune has set him too low or too high. This, we have said, is the natural course; for the divine order makes the strength of every organic whole dependent on the healthy vigour and due co-ordination of many parts. But self-consciousness, ambition, and fussiness tempt various members of the community in such a case to another and an unnatural course. The men who come under these influences ask themselves, not where they can do the most work, but where they can attract the most attention. They hesitate about falling back into their obvious posts, lest they should miss the chance of something higher. Their sense of self and self-interest is much keener than their loyalty to the body corporate of which they are organic parts. And therefore instead of doing with instinctive devotion to the general good what first comes to hand, they scheme and intrigue to secure for themselves the largest possible share of power and honour. Woe to the commonwealth which in any time of sudden and unusual peril counts a large proportion of such men among its members!

In the uprising of the English Commons against the arrogant unreason of the royal prerogative, very few such men took any part. Self-seekers usually thought there was more to be gained in the royal camp; and thither, therefore, they betook themselves, with the result that Charles's counsels were weakened by division, and his son was afterwards puzzled how to meet the demands of his expectant mercenaries. Much has been said and sung about the romantic sentiment of the Cavaliers; but it was no match for the ecstatic—or, if you will, the fanatic—fervour of the Roundheads. The one poured itself forth in toasts and drinking-songs, the other in prayer and prophesying. The one produced a great deal of dashing valour; but no romantic sentiment for any human person ever did or could create an army like Cromwell's Ironsides. They are unmatched in history; for the sanguinary Hebrew warfare, which they idealised as their model, had no such grand political purpose. And they must remain unrivalled for ever now; for the time has gone by when war could be carried on as an act of worship.

When war became inevitable, Oliver Cromwell, in common with many other members of Parliament, took the natural course of going down amongst his own constituents to prepare them for the coming struggle. If he was from the first bent on making his own fortune out of the troubles of his country, the mode of action he selected was, according to any forecast then possible, the least adapted to serve his purpose. It would be absurd to suppose that he was aware of his latent military genius. At forty-three years of age none but incurable visionaries would stake anything on the chance of suddenly developing unsuspected powers. And Cromwell's religious enthusiasm was singularly allied with a keen eye for practicability in all human affairs. None of the myths about his early wildness have ever attributed to him the love of soldiering commonly shown by headstrong youths. He had gone through the train-band exercises like others ; but there is no shadow of a hint that they ever roused in him the instinct of his destiny. It may be doubted whether he had ever up to this time seen a review of a thousand men. And when his cousin Hampden prophesied his greatness in case of a breach with the King, the prediction could only have been based on the signs he had given of consuming fervour, prodigious energy, and indomitable will. On the other hand, in Parliament he was a fast rising man. His "sharp, untuneable voice" always commanded a hearing, and generally secured votes. On every committee that required resolute purpose, insight into practical details, and business-like dispatch, he was increasingly in request. So that if his chief anxiety had been to push himself, his obvious course would have been to remain at Westminster, and court "King Pym," whose successor, indeed, he might easily have become.

But that was not the light in which Oliver looked at the

crisis of 1642. Unless the Parliament were speedily armed it would assuredly be overwhelmed by the military forces that would naturally gravitate round the King. And in the existing temper of the country every corps raised for the popular cause would have a moral effect equal to ten times its physical strength. His personal influence as the " Lord of the Fens " made him the best recruiting agent the Parliament could possibly have in and about Cambridge. And we may well believe that his unconscious genius taught him the strategic importance of a compact military organisation thrust like a " quadrilateral " between York and London. Besides, he could not endure that a piece of work, which he saw through from beginning to end, should be fumbled over by half-hearted and muddle-headed agents. Clearly, his place was in Cambridge, and to Cambridge accordingly he went.

His first business was to get together the men and horses for whom arms had, in part at least, been provided. A troop of horse generally numbered sixty. The townsmen of Cambridge had been authorised to raise " two companies of volunteers, and to appoint captains over them." The words may be taken as applicable either to horse or foot. What the second company was we cannot say, but certainly one of them was a troop of horse, of which, as a matter of course, the energetic member for Cambridge was elected captain. It is reasonable to suppose that in this very first effort at enlisting men he adopted, as far as possible, the principle on which he afterwards insisted so strongly, the requirement of character and intelligent conviction as a condition of engagement. But circumstances would hardly permit him to carry it out punctiliously now. So soon as the beginning of September he received orders to hold himself in readiness to join the Earl of Essex, the Commander-in-Chief of the Parliamentary forces. With the prospect of a speedy call to action he could not take undrilled men ; nor could he suddenly secure yeomen and farmers, who required time to arrange their affairs. But that he did his best is certain, for within a year of his first experiment in recruiting, his men had a character of their own, which was recognised by the news-sheets of the time. And now, having got his troop, he was only one of a mob of 210 Parliamentary captains, all of whom would come in for hard knocks, and most of them for little more. Hampden, on the other hand, was one of twenty-seven colonels. On the whole, we get the

impression that, in the outset of the struggle, Oliver contentedly
took a position lower than might have been fairly claimed by one
of his family connections and antecedent services.

But his very first piece of work was promising. Cambridge
Castle contained a small magazine of powder and arms, and the
plate of the University was no inconsiderable treasure. Such
were the sources to which the Court looked for the supply of the
King's army; and if all over the country these could be closed
against them, the conflict would in all probability be a short
one; at least such was the idea of Parliament men. The University was, as a rule, royalist in its leanings, though not so
passionately so as Oxford. Already suggestions had been made
as to the service which the plate might render to the King.
Some had gone to him, and the rest was likely to follow. Here
was a case requiring quick decision and a courageous acceptance
of responsibility. Legally, Captain Cromwell had no more right
to seize Cambridge Castle, and lay an embargo on the University
plate, than he had to break into his neighbour's house and pocket
his silver spoons. Nevertheless, he quietly took possession of
the castle before its garrison could be strengthened, and prohibited
the removal of plate from any of the colleges. When it is considered that peace still nominally existed, and that the Parliament was naturally anxious to avoid the odium of being the first
to break it, the seizure of the castle by a mere captain of a
troop will appear almost audacious. But it was characteristic
in its prudence as well as in its boldness. In this, as in more
famous transgressions of legal form, he felt the solid ground of
justice and expediency very firm beneath him before he stepped
across the line. On this occasion he needed a Parliamentary
indemnity, which was instantly granted.

The personal influence of such a captain of course extended
far beyond his own troop. It dominated the whole district, and
directed all its incipient military arrangements. The communications incessantly going on between the King at York and
officials or magnates of doubtful leanings in the south had become dangerous to the Parliamentary cause, and needed to be
closely watched. None knew better than a native of Huntingdon its importance as a station on the northern route. Cromwell
therefore had guards placed around the town, with orders to
examine all travellers, and allow no suspicious persons to pass.

About that time Chief Justice Bramston, who was in ill odour with the Parliament on account of his decision in favour of ship-money, and who yet feared to cast in his lot with the King, received a summons to leave his retirement in Essex and appear at York. His services were apparently required for the trial and condemnation of rebels who might fall into the royal power. Not liking the work, he sent his two sons to excuse him to the King on account of his age—little over sixty—and the difficulty of travelling. On their return with the King's refusal to accept these excuses, they were stopped near Huntingdon by some musketeers, who started out of the standing corn. They were told they must go before Mr. Cromwell to give an account of themselves. When informed that Mr. Cromwell was four miles away, they expostulated, as they were in great haste, and finally were allowed to pass on payment of one shilling,—a plain proof that whatever might be the case with the new captain's own troop, the Parliamentary army was not wholly beyond the influence of bribery. Notwithstanding the royal command, the incident deterred the Chief Justice from attempting the journey.

A pamphlet dated September 14th, 1642, and giving a list of the Parliamentary forces, shows that the organisation of the army under Essex must have been roughly completed during August. There were twenty regiments of foot, each reckoned at 1,200, but probably considerably under-manned. One of these regiments was commanded by Lord Kimbolton (Viscount Mandeville) soon to succeed his father as Earl of Manchester. Other colonels of note were John Hampden, Denzil Holles, Strode, and Stapylton. There were seventy-five troops of horse, besides dragoons. Amongst the captains we may mention, besides Oliver, his brother-in-law Valentine Walton, his future son-in-law Henry Ireton, Sir Arthur Haselrig, and Sir William Waller. Two cornets also interest us for the grief their early deaths occasioned. One was Cromwell's own son Oliver, the eldest now since Robert's death. He served under Lord St. John. The other was Valentine Walton, cornet in his father's troop.

In the beginning of September, as we have seen, the army being scattered principally in the eastern and home counties, Cromwell, with others, was directed to muster his men, and be prepared to follow the Earl of Essex. Where and when Cromwell

actually joined the main army we do not know,* but we shall
hear of him presently in the first pitched battle of the war. The
King, disappointed by the lack of enthusiasm for his cause in
Nottingham and the neighbourhood, retreated by Derby to
Shrewsbury. He took this course because the reports from the
west were more favourable to him, and he had good hopes of
Welsh loyalty. The desertion of the Parliamentary cause by
Colonel Goring at Portsmouth, after indignant protestations of
his faithfulness, had raised the spirits of the Royalists, only to be
damped again by the shifty colonel's speedy surrender to a besieging force. On the other hand, the peremptory refusal of the
two Houses to treat with the King except on condition of his
first withdrawing his proclamations against them, recalling his
commissions of array, and surrendering all evil counsellors for
judgment, certainly excited a reaction of feeling amongst
waverers, and helped to swell the Royalist army. But the
struggle had gone too far now for compromise. There could be
no sound and permanent peace till one side had been hopelessly
beaten.

On September 10th, 1642, the Earl of Essex left London to
take the field, and moved westwards after the King. Ten days
afterwards Charles entered Shrewsbury. Prince Rupert, who
had recently joined his royal uncle as general of cavalry, signalised
his fiery valour by defeating and scattering a detachment of
Essex's army near Worcester, but he made no attempt to keep
possession of the city, which was occupied by Essex. The royal
forces having grown considerably, the King was emboldened to
strike towards London. Essex, on learning his movement, quietly
followed again, showing no haste, nor indeed any clear purpose
except to prevent Charles from overwhelming his Parliament.
How imperfect were the means of information in those times is
sufficiently suggested by the fact that on Saturday, October 22nd,
the royal army had reached the neighbourhood of Banbury, and
the Parliamentarians Keynton, within six or seven miles, without
either being aware of the immediate proximity of the other.
Between Banbury and Keynton, separating Oxfordshire from

* Denzil Holles, in his " Memoirs," sneeringly intimates that he did not join
at all, could not find his way to Keynton field, though the artillery was loud
enough to have directed him. The clearest contemporary testimony, however,
shows that this was a *willing*—not perhaps a *wilful*—misapprehension on the
part of Holles, who was never near enough to the main battle to know.

Warwickshire, are the heights of Edgehill. The town of Banbury was held for the Parliament, and Charles had summoned it to surrender. But hearing on the Sunday morning (October 23rd) that the Earl of Essex lay about Keynton, he ordered the heights of Edgehill to be immediately secured. So unconscious were the Parliamentarians of his design, that those who lay nearest to Keynton were assembling for the church service there, when outlying troops nearer to Edgehill saw the royal forces appearing over the top.

Essex speedily drew out his army in battle array. He pushed forward about a mile and a half towards Edgehill. He stationed his foot in the centre, directly in front of Keynton, and the bulk of his horse on the left, under Sir James Ramsay, a Scotchman, with whom was Sir Faithful Fortescue. On the right were placed some musketeers conveniently sheltered by hedgerows, and a little in advance the remainder of his horse. In this right wing was Oliver Cromwell with his troop. They formed part of a regiment of which the Lord General himself was colonel, and which during the engagement was commanded by Sir Philip Stapylton. Along with this regiment was that of Sir William Balfour, in which Nathaniel Fiennes was captain of a troop. To this Nathaniel Fiennes we owe the clearest contemporary account of the battle, and it is important to note that he was in the same part of the field with Cromwell.*

The Royalists made no haste to descend the hill. They would naturally have preferred to be attacked there; but the Earl of Essex did not oblige them. When, however, they did come down, there was a moment at which, in the opinion of military critics they offered a fine opportunity to their opponents. "Their cannon and ammunition, with the rear of their foot," says Nathaniel Fiennes, "were somewhat long ere they came down, and if we had charged them (we being in battalia before them) before their cannon and all their foot were come down, we had had a great advantage over them." Captain Cromwell probably made the same observation; and years afterwards, at Dunbar, he snatched such an opportunity with a rapidity of which Essex was incapable. When the royal army finally got down to the lower ground, towards three o'clock in the afternoon, the dispo-

---

* *E.g.*, he was much more likely to be correctly informed as to Oliver's doings than Denzil Holles, who was in the extreme rear of the centre towards Keynton.

sition of their force was very similar to that of their adversaries, only reversed. Their foot was principally in the centre, the bulk of their horse under the fiery Rupert was on the right wing opposed to Sir James Ramsay, and a few troops of horse and dragoons were on the left, together with the King's red-coats, a regiment of foot-guards.

It was the Royalist army that moved to the attack, the Parliamentarians standing on the defence; and as the former advanced along their whole line, the Parliamentary left and left centre gave way, shrank together, got into confusion, and fled pell-mell towards Keynton, carrying the reserves and Denzil Holles with them in the rush. The disaster was heightened by Sir *Faithful* Fortescue and his troop, who turned round upon their own comrades, and charged with Prince Rupert, not, however, without suffering the penalties of double-dealing in shots from both sides. The result of these Royalist successes was that the battle swayed towards their left, and towards the right of Essex's army, where the musketeers kept post behind their hedges, and where the regiments of Sir Philip Stapylton and Sir William Balfour, including the troops of Captains Cromwell and Fiennes, were in the van. The rout swept by the left of these forces, and they were powerless to stay it, for they had enough to do to maintain their own ground. The swaying of the whole Royalist attack towards the Parliamentary right would expose them to the weight of the King's centre as well as the onset of his left wing. So far as we know, it was the first time that Captain Cromwell had been under fire. Such an experience after forty years of age is very different from that of a raw youth. "The bubble reputation" is not then so attractive a lure towards the cannon's mouth as at twenty; and if firmness is not given by nervous constitution or intensity of moral purpose, neither emulation nor discipline is likely to produce it. In Cromwell's case there was surely an equal absence both of fear and ostentation. He was there amid the smoke and thunder in discharge of a duty he dared not desert, and he had probably no thought but to carry it through as best he might. Words he had written four years previously were brought to the test of action now. "My soul is with the congregation of the first-born, my body rests in hope; and if here I may honour my God, either by doing or suffering, I shall be most glad." It is surely

a significant circumstance that on this day the only part of
Essex's army which never yielded for a moment was the wing in
which Captain Cromwell was stationed with his troop. Against
this right wing the Royalist horse and dragoons dashed in vain.
On the contrary, it charged and broke the King's red-coats, capturing the royal standard, and kept the ground firmly amidst
all the defeat and confusion on the left.

Meanwhile the rout had been stayed at Keynton, where the
victorious Royalists stopped for plunder. Denzil Holles and others
then managed to rally their fugitives, and brought them back to the
support of the right wing. Hampden and Colonel Grantham,
who had been left behind by the main army, brought their
regiments on to Keynton by a forced march, and opened so hot
a fire that Prince Rupert retreated to the main battle. Here,
however, his somewhat disordered troops were successfully
charged by Sir Philip Stapylton, while Cromwell's troop,
amongst others, helped to re-form the Parliamentary left.
Darkness now came down, welcome to both sides alike, for
neither was in a position to make a fresh effort for complete
victory. Each claimed the advantage in what was substantially
a drawn battle.

Hampden's opinion of his cousin as a man who "could sit
well at a mark" began from this day to be shared by many outside the Fen country; for the newswriters extensively copied the
account of the battle given by Nathaniel Fiennes, and that
account makes generous mention of certain officers who distinguished themselves.

"These persons undernamed were all of the right wing of our army,
and never stirred from their troops; but they and their troops fought
bravely till the last minute of the fight:—Of the Lord General's regiment
the Lord General himself, Sir Philip Stapylton, Captain Draper, Sergeant-
Major Gunter, Lord Brook, Captain Sheffield, Captain Temple, and Captain
Cromwell."

The King was sufficiently free from fear of molestation to
summon Banbury; and the opinion entertained by the garrison
as to the results of the battle is shown by their surrender on
condition of freedom to depart without their arms. The Earl of
Essex, on the other hand, after remaining on the field till it was
clear no fresh attack was intended, retired to Warwick, where he
took up his quarters. Fugitives from the first onset of Prince

I

Rupert spread disastrous tidings everywhere, and the Lord General's report was barely in time to prevent a dangerous panic. The Parliament, however, maintained an unbending front. The fortification of London was hurried on, and Windsor was secured for the popular cause by Colonel Ven.

In the Parliamentary army, as it lay on the field through Sunday night and Monday, carefully provisioned by the forethought of Lord Essex and the favour of the country-side, many were the discussions amongst the officers about the position and prospects. Captain Cromwell had his own views, and he imparted them after his manner to Colonel Hampden.* We may well conjecture that he had in mind the resistless onset of Rupert's horse, and the nerveless shrinking up of the Parliamentary left and centre. "Your troops," said he, "are most of them old, decayed serving-men, and tapsters, and such kind of fellows; and their troops are gentlemen's sons, younger sons, and persons of quality. Do you think that the spirits of such base and mean fellows will ever be able to encounter gentlemen that have honour and courage and resolution in them? You must get men of a spirit that is likely to go as far as gentlemen will go, or else you will be beaten still."

Such sentiments in the mouth of Oliver Cromwell may seem incongruous to those who suppose him to have been a republican theorist. But this notion of him is very far indeed from the truth. For equal consideration to all fair human claims, entirely irrespective of rank or condition, he did indeed contend with all the vehemence of his eager nature. But, with his clear eye for patent facts, he did not and could not ignore the practical influence of birth, breeding, and social habit on the English population as he knew it. There was one power, and one alone, could raise the uncouth peasant to a level with chivalrous gentlemen on the field of battle—one inspiration only that could vie with the fiery impulse of honour. That power and inspiration were to be found in religious conviction—the sense of a call from the very Spirit of God to battle against the evil in the world.

To the objection that such religious inspiration might be felt

---

* Speech XI. in Carlyle. The reasons for assigning the conversation to this date are that it took place on Oliver's "first going out," &c.; that it was occasioned by some striking instance of the untrustworthiness of the Parliamentary recruits; and that no other time so natural can be suggested up to the date of Hampden's death.

equally by the other side, Oliver would have allowed no force. In his view, falsehood, superstition, and injustice could furnish no divine flame, only the simulation of it, which would pale before the sacred fire, as earthly flames are said to do before the rays of the sun. In our day even those who sympathise most strongly with Cromwell's faith have learned that equally pure devotion may be prompted by opposite forms of opinion. But to this extent, at least, he was substantially right, that the chances for freedom of conscience, equal justice, and spiritual religion lay rather with the success of the Parliament than with that of the King; and the nature of the inspiration on either side was likely to correspond with the actual facts. In the interests of humanity Cromwell had a better cause than his adversaries, and as the redemption of mankind from their low estate was in his view the present work of the divine creative energy, he was wise in urging that the Parliament should "raise such men as had the fear of God before them, and made some conscience of what they did."

His cousin Hampden was favourably impressed with the idea; but as he looked at the blood-stained field, and mangled corpses, and coarse, repulsive scenes around him, he thought the notion impracticable. Coarse work wanted coarse men. Officers, indeed, must be men of principle; but as to the rank-and-file, how could prayer-leaders and preachers put up with the rough-and-tumble life of the camp? But Oliver knew of humble men about St. Ives, and Huntingdon, and Ely, in whose hearts there burned the same zeal that had driven him out to the war. He had "taken sweet counsel" with them in passing to or from the Sabbath services; he had joined with them in prayer; he had seen the deep glow of a sacred passion in their faces as they talked of the abuses of the Church and the need of a godly reformation. In his own troop he had some such men already, and their behaviour in the battle prompted him to try if he could not enlist others like them. It was obviously the best service he could render to the cause; and the approach of winter, with the suspension of all but insignificant operations on both sides, gave him a good opportunity.

After the battle of Edgehill the royal army moved on Oxford, and thence towards London. A fight at Brentford, rashly brought on by Prince Rupert, gave them a severe check; and if

Hampden's advice had been followed, a flank attack, cutting off their retreat to Oxford, might, perhaps, have ended the war. As this course was not taken, the King in the course of November reached his faithful university town once more in safety. The rest of the operations of the winter were a series of small local struggles which have no direct bearing on our special subject.

Immediately on Oliver's return to his own county he must have set about, or rather perhaps resumed, a work of local organisation that proved to be the salvation of the Parliament. This was the union of Cambridge county with four others— Norfolk, Suffolk, Essex, and Hertfordshire—in an association for mutual aid and co-operation in the interest of the Commonwealth. To these, under the name of the Eastern Counties Association, Huntingdon and, ultimately, Lincolnshire were afterwards added. There were several other associations of the kind; but this alone came to be of any practical importance. On the day before the battle of Edgehill (October 22nd), the House of Commons had passed a resolution approving the formation of such unions, and their committees were appointed, or at least confirmed, by Parliamentary authority. The work of these committees was to raise contributions in money, arms, and horses, to enlist men, and to nominate officers. Subject, of course, to higher military authorities, they could also direct the movements and location of troops raised and maintained in the district. If a Royalist attack from without or rising from within were apprehended at any particular place, the Parliamentarians there would communicate with the committee, and obtain the aid of such available force as happened to be within reach. If the designs of any local magnate of doubtful leanings were suspected, information would be given to the committee, who would thereupon communicate with the Parliamentary leaders, or, in case of emergency, act on their own responsibility.

Of course Captain Cromwell was from the first a member of the Eastern Counties' Committee. And if we say that he speedily became, in a manner, the committee itself, this is not because the other members were nonentities or needless, for without them he would have been as powerless as the brain when the leading nerves are severed. But he prompted their zeal, suggested their services, quickened their operations, and all results that they produced in the form of contributions, organisation, or information, passed through his mind, and were directed to the best issues. He was also a member of the committee for Huntingdonshire, and this fact, perhaps suggested, and certainly facilitated, its early union with the other counties around.

The establishment of the association must have helped Oliver in his effort to increase his own troop into a regiment, and, on on the other hand, his success consolidated the union. "The Perfect Diurnal," a sort of newspaper of the time, gives him the title of Colonel on March 2nd, 1642–3. From this we may gather that his commission followed on the raising of his regiment, which would thus have been completed during the last months of the previous year. He was not only particular as to the personal character of the men he accepted, but it is clear that he aimed at getting men of some little position, with a stake in the country, and therefore having material interests as well as spiritual convictions to fight for. Richard Baxter says that his troops were largely composed of "freeholders or freeholders' sons." This may seem almost incredible to a generation which, in rural districts, knows of scarcely any freeholders except large landowners. But in that day the race of yeomen cultivating their own fields was still numerous, and they constituted perhaps the most valuable and trustworthy class of the whole Commonwealth. Amongst these men the "Lord of the Fens" had great personal influence, and his success must have somewhat astonished his sceptical cousin Hampden; for he got together what Baxter calls "a double regiment of fourteen full troops. Taking the full troop at sixty, this means 840 men. They formed the first members of that famous body of "Ironsides" who decided the course of the English revolution. The name, was, of course, not given them until later, and seems first to have been a popular nickname for Oliver himself, from whom it was extended by association to his soldiers.

Cavalry had in the period of the Civil War a much greater proportionate importance in pitched battles than now. Artillery was singularly ineffective, considering the noise it made and the powder it burnt. The rude muskets had a very short, uncertain range. And the issue of a fight was often decided by actual cutting and slashing, and banging, and pommeling. In such a hurly-burly of hand-to-hand conflict, heavy cavalry had a great advantage, and Cromwell always preferred it to any other sort of force. Each man carried a pair of pistols, cumbrous and clumsy, but effective enough at close quarters when they did not happen to miss fire. Otherwise they had to trust to their heavy swords, of which either the point or edge might be used. "Dragooners," whom Cromwell also favoured for special services, were distinguished from cavalry, and were properly a sort of mounted infantry carrying muskets. They were dismounted for battle, and were, in fact, simply foot-soldiers with the means of rapid movement always at hand.

In drilling and training his regiment, Cromwell attached quite as much importance to moral discipline as to exactness of order, or skill in handling weapons. He was firmly determined that none of the irregularities or vices, vulgarly regarded as inevitable in a soldier's life, should sully the righteous purpose for which he and his comrades had taken arms. And not only contemporary admirers, but his most virulent slanderers have said enough to show that the moral tone of his men made them a sort of portent, in which some might see a miracle of grace, and others a masterpiece of hypocrisy, but which was in either case astounding.

While diligently engaged in raising and training his regiment, Oliver kept a watchful eye upon all influences tending to mar the unanimity of the Eastern Counties. For instance, his former rival in Huntingdon, Mr. Robert Barnard, who had obtained his arrest and appearance before the Privy Council some twelve years before, was now attempting to play a double game. Barnard had been appointed a member of the Association Committee for Huntingdon, and he must therefore have professed devotion to the Parliament. But his bearing and his actions were suspicious; and in such a time, when not merely a few human lives, but the life or death of a nation was at issue, it was impossible to stand upon ceremony. Treachery, or even doubtful allegiance, in a young county association, could not be endured, at least by Oliver. As well might one expect an anxious farmer to tolerate an experiment with Colorado beetles in a corner of his newly-planted potato ground. Accordingly about the 20th of January 1642–3 Captain Cromwell* sent his lieutenant and

---

* Letter IV. in Carlyle. The words "my Lieutenant," "soldiers of my troop," seem to imply that he was still captain. The regiment was practically raised, but he had not apparently received his commission as colonel.

some soldiers to search Mr. Robert Barnard's house. That gentleman, who seems to have been absent at the time, felt considerable indignation on learning what this troublesome tithe-farmer had been about, and appears to have written the latter an angry letter on the subject. The reply of Oliver was cool but determined. He fully accepted the responsibility, and did not deny that Mr. Barnard's reason for indignation was plausible, but insisted that his own duty had been plain, and should be discharged again if there were occasion.

"Mr. Barnard,—It's most true my Lieutenant with some other soldiers of my troop were at your house. I dealt freely to inquire after you. The reason was I had heard you reported active against the proceedings of Parliament, and for those that disturb the peace of this country * and the kingdom, with those of this country who have had meetings not a few, to intents and purposes, too, too full of suspect.

"It's true, sir, I know you have been wary in your carriages ; be not too confident thereof. Subtlety may deceive you; integrity never will. With my heart I shall desire that your judgment may alter, and your practice. I come only to hinder men from increasing the rent †—from doing hurt, but not to hurt any man; nor shall I you; I hope you will give me no cause. If you do, I must be pardoned what my relation to the public calls for.

"If your good parts be disposed that way, know me for your servant,

"Oliver Cromwell.

"Be assured fair words from me shall neither deceive you of your houses, nor of your liberty."

But Mr. Barnard was not by this letter at all convinced of the futility of "subtlety." Being ordered by the Association Committee to pay a contribution, apparently by way of fine for his double dealing, he went up to London and obtained a letter in his favour from the Earl of Manchester, which he sent to Cromwell, together with one from himself, demanding, apparently, to know whether he was to be deprived of unrestrained movement about his business in the county. But Oliver was not easily to be overawed by great names. In his reply he wrote—

"17 *April*, 1643.

" Sir,—I have received two letters—one from my Lord of Manchester, the other from yourself—much to the same effect. I hope, therefore, one answer will serve them both. Which is in short this : that we know you

* Understand county, or neighbourhood.
† Of course not rent in the landlord and tenant sense, but schism, discord.

are disaffected to the Parliament. And truly, if the Lords or any friends
may take you off from a reasonable contribution, for my part I should be
glad to be commanded to any other employment. Sir, you may, if you
will, come freely into the country about your occasions. For my part I
have protected you in your absence, and shall do so to you.

"This is all, but that I am ready to serve you, and rest your loving
friend,

"OLIVER CROMWELL." *

The letters are worth noting, because they are exceedingly
characteristic. A keen eye for the immediate practical issue,
and an intolerance of any formalities that would obscure it—an
anxiety to subordinate all personal considerations to public duty,
and a haunting suspicion that he had not altogether succeeded—
an absolute certainty that the cause he served was that of
righteousness, and that men's moral worth was to be measured
by their bearing towards it—all these are suggested by the two
letters, and they were prominent in the man.

The first actual service rendered by Colonel Cromwell's newly-
raised regiment was the prevention of a threatened Royalist raid
on Cambridge. In February, 1643, Prince Rupert was reported
to be plundering and ravaging Hampshire and Wiltshire. Lord
Capel, who served under him, was detached towards Cambridge,
where he was to rob the county and capture the town. This
Lord Capel, like many others in the Royalist army, had formerly
protested against the King's misgovernment. But he had become
frightened when he saw how his protests must be backed up if
they were to be of any avail; and he was now seeking to build
again the tyranny he had helped to overthrow. This threatened
attack was just the sort of danger against which the Association
was designed to guard; and we may easily imagine the energy
with which the chief member of the committee set himself to
prove the value of the institution he had laboured to establish.
Lord Gray of Wark had been named by Parliament commander
of the forces of the Association. But he might have been a
leader without an army had it not been for Colonel Cromwell,
who wrote and rode and wrought till he had got some 12,000
men concentrated near Cambridge; and the voice of rumour,
swelled by enthusiasm or fear, increased them to double the
number. Under the circumstances Lord Capel thought it dis-

* Carlyle : Letter VIII.

creet to turn aside; whereupon a great part of the 12,000 dispersed to their homes, undertaking to join again at any time on three days' notice.

But the alarm gave a good opportunity to raise money for the fortification of Cambridge. And so Oliver and his fellow-committee-men drew up a short appeal to the population, asking "a freewill offering of a liberal contribution . . . . for the better enabling of them to attain their desired end, viz., the preservation of their county." The amount asked was £2,000, which now seems a ridiculously small sum for the fortification of a considerable town. Even that amount, however, was not very easy to raise. Nevertheless, the work was done, and Cambridge was never lost to the Parliament even for a day. At the beginning of March the House of Commons in recognition of Oliver's services sent him down four cannon; and at that time the garrison of the town was reported in the newspapers to be 800 horse and foot, all raised in the associated counties. Cambridge, thus firmly held, proved to be an important base of operations for securing the rest of the eastern district. The security of that district, and the accumulation of military power there brought about the conquest of Lincolnshire for the Parliament. The conquest of Lincolnshire made possible the victory on Marston Moor, and Marston Moor was the turning point of the war.

At the beginning of March, 1643, some movements in Norfolk and Suffolk attracted the notice and excited the suspicion of the committee at Cambridge. Certain county gentlemen had a design to detach those counties from the Association and unite them in the Royalist interest. The decision was instant that Colonel Cromwell should march in that direction and stamp out any sparks of over-enthusiastic loyalty which might threaten a conflagration. He was in Norwich on Monday, March 13th, having probably passed the Sunday there. On Monday morning companies of soldiers were sent out to visit the suspected gentry, and returned at night with several important captives and arms that had been prepared for a rising. The same night news from Yarmouth informed Cromwell that Sir John Wentworth and a Captain Allen, from Lowestoft, had been endeavouring to change a suspicious quantity of dollars there. The obvious suggestion was that they were receiving supplies from abroad in the interest of the King; and the local authorities arrested them. But information from Lowestoft itself was more disquieting. Captain Allen might have many associates there; nay, the town was receiving a number of strangers, and, still more ominous, was fortifying itself. This afforded weighty matter for Colonel Cromwell to ponder that evening at Norwich. But he did not ponder long. " Shut the gates," he said, " and let no one in or out this night." He intended going to Lowestoft, and he preferred to carry his own message. He had five troops of his own in the town, and these, with two other troops of another regiment, and eighty Norwich volunteers, were ordered to be up betimes. Between five and six in the morning they started, and by some quick rider the colonel sent on a message to the Yarmouth volunteers to meet him with whatever ordnance they had.

When the little force reached Lowestoft they found the town barricaded; and having no fortified gate at the approach by which the enemy came, the townsmen had drawn a chain across the street, and behind it had stationed three cannon. Having halted, Cromwell summoned the town, and in the parley that followed the terms he imposed were the surrender of the town itself, all strangers within it and all armed men to be prisoners. In return, he offered favourable consideration; but if the terms were refused he would promise no favour at all. The Lowestoft authorities agreed to surrender strangers, but declined the two other points. No sooner was their answer given than some Norwich dragoons crept under the chain, avoiding the big guns, and threatened the cannoneers with cocked pistols. Thereupon the cannoneers ran away, and the dragoons turned the cannon against the town. The chain was then broken, and Cromwell entered without receiving a shot. The prisoners had no more than a local importance; but in this business of founding and securing the Eastern Counties Association local importance was everything. And, indeed, the blow was so decisive that no serious attempt was again made to destroy the union.*

---

* Vicars is worth quoting here. "About the 16th of this March came certain intelligence by letters out of Suffolk that that brave and most successful valiant commander, Col. Cromwell, with about 1,000 horse, having secret notice of a great combination held among the malignants of a brave sea town called Lastolf (*sic*) in this county .... came upon them at unawares, and suddenly set upon them and carried the town. . . . . Had this business

No sooner had Cromwell returned to Norwich with his prisoners than there was a pressing demand for his presence at Lynn, to secure the town against a municipal faction there.* The news of his success at Lowestoft made his work easier here, for not even threats or cocked pistols are mentioned. When Lynn was settled, the indefatigable colonel was wanted at once at his head-quarters in Cambridge. Prince Rupert was active in Buckinghamshire, and a raid towards the Eastern Counties was feared. The "Camdeners" also, named from their leader, Viscount Camden, had possessed themselves of Stamford, and were reported on the way to Cambridge.† "It's happy to resist such beginnings betimes," wrote Oliver to Sir John Burgoyne in Bedfordshire, asking for help. The promptitude of his arrangements appears to have once more averted the danger.

been delayed but one day longer, it would have cost a great deal of hot blood ere the town could possibly have been taken. For there were listed to have met together (as afterwards appeared, which was an admirable providence of the Lord thus to prevent it) as many more knights and gentlemen. But this cockatrice's egg was thus happily broken. . . . . This, therefore, may justly be accounted one of the best pieces of service that hath been done this long time to the kingdom, the whole county being thereby set to right."—" God in the Mount," Pt. ii. p. 265. Amongst the prisoners was Mr. Thos. Knyvett of Ashwellthorpe, on whose generosity Cromwell afterwards showed a singular reliance (see chap. xiii.).

* Cromwelliana.

† Letter VI. in Carlyle; written, perhaps, from Cambridge rather than Huntingdon.

CHAPTER VIII.

THE EASTERN COUNTIES ASSOCIATION (*continued*).

Thus, by the end of March, 1643, the Eastern Counties Association had become thoroughly consolidated, and its working had been facilitated by practice. But the work had not been an easy one, and its continuance was even then threatened by want of money. When we consider the interruptions of trade, the countless individual losses, and the disorganisation both of imperial and local revenue incidental to the war, we may form some idea of the persistence and determination needed to get money for such an association. Force, even if otherwise justifiable, would have alienated the people whom Cromwell desired to weld into one. And therefore, with the exception of windfalls in the shape of compositions from " malignants," he was generally obliged to rely on the voluntary principle. At this very time, when the Association was prospering beyond hope, and likely to be summoned to a supreme effort for the reinforcement of the Lord General in dealing a decisive blow, the people of Colchester sent their contingent without a penny of pay; and in urging the mayor of that town to make good the deficiency, Colonel Cromwell uses the argument, very astonishing to us after the event, that " one month's pay may prove all their trouble." In fact, a movement on Oxford was to end the business. But the movement was not made, and the power of the Eastern Counties had to be exerted in a different direction.

In order to understand this, it is necessary to glance at the general course of the war on the eastern side of the kingdom. When the King left York for Nottingham, he left Sir Thomas Glemham behind him, with a commission to command such forces as remained or might be raised in the county. There was, however, a general anxiety to avoid, if possible, the sufferings of war, and an attempt was made by some leaders on either side to agree to an arrangement which would keep the county neutral. This, of course, was condemned by Parliament; and Lord Fairfax levied forces to secure the district. The result was that the Parliamentarians stole a march on the Royalists, and seemed likely to command the north. But the Earl of Newcastle, holding the only port at the disposal of the King, and which, it will be remembered, Cromwell had wished to secure in the middle of the previous year, made in December a skilful march to York, connecting Newcastle and the latter town by a chain of strong communications, and thus entirely suppressed the Parliamentary interest in the north of the country. In the month of February he protected the landing of Queen Henrietta Maria in Bridlington, and the material supplies she brought were, to a certain extent, increased in value by the chivalrous devotion her presence excited. Thus reinforced, he pushed his conquests southwards, and secured the whole of the county, finally shutting up Lord Fairfax and his son, Sir Thomas, in Hull. Not content with these successes, the earl strengthened Newark, seized on Grantham, and, throwing a flying column into Lincolnshire, he practically cleared that county also of Parliamentary forces. Thus, by the time that Colonel Cromwell had completed and proved by actual trial his Eastern Counties Association, the Earl of Newcastle had won for the King the whole of north-eastern England, from the Tweed to the Wash.

But if Hampden's advice had been taken, these successes would have gone for little. He wanted the Earl of Essex to strike directly at Oxford in the early spring. Instead of this, however, the earl turned aside to besiege Reading, and notwithstanding an attempt made by the King to relieve it, that town was surrendered to the Parliament before the end of April. In this siege the earl had the assistance of 7,000 horse and foot under Lord Grey, the military chief of the Eastern Association. But Cromwell's presence seems to have been more needed nearer home.

The power of the Parliament having been firmly established in the six counties, the triumphs of Lord Newcastle in Lincolnshire were regarded by the committee with discontent and indignation. They were not satisfied with their own security; their devotion was aggressive. And once again in Oliver's experience it was seen how the fulfilment of the nearest and most obvious duty naturally suggests others when that is accomplished. Lord Willoughby of Parham had been named Parliamentary commander of the county. But though no suspicion could be thrown upon his faithfulness, his energy and ability were not satisfactory to Cromwell. On April 18th the "Perfect Diurnal" announced to the Londoners that Colonel Cromwell had marched with 5,000 or 6,000 men into Lincolnshire to aid the Earl of Lincoln and Lord Willoughby. But the news was a little premature, for there were yet some points in the Eastern Counties that needed attention, in order that the base for operations further north might be perfectly safe.

Huntingdonshire was even yet troubled with malignancy,* and needed visitation; in fact could only be cured by incorporation with the rest of the Eastern Counties. Mr. Robert Barnard had to be rebuked in a second letter already mentioned, and it seems most likely that at this time the well-known scene took place between the Royalist Sir Oliver and his "rebel" nephew. There were arms said to be stored at Ramsey Mere. The house was a focus of disaffection to the Parliament, and the evil must be stopped. The account was first given by Sir Philip Warwick from the lips of the venerable Sir Oliver himself, and is very suggestive of the nephew's anxiety to reconcile as far as possible public duty with private feeling. The nephew, now a middle-aged man, much weather-beaten, and scarred with fiery anxieties, stood uncovered before his father's white-haired brother, and masked his imperious business with gentle courtesy. But the arms must be had, and a reasonable contribution in plate or money too. For surely it would be a scandal if an accident of family connection should rob the cause of the people.

And money, as always, was very much wanted; so much so, that some pressure must be put upon the colleges at Cambridge to lend a portion of their treasure to the Commonwealth. It is profitless to discuss such proceedings with minute casuistry. The letter of the law had been inevitably rent and defaced by war. But the broad principle remained that the public good may require the use of private property. The only question was, which authority represented the public good, and that, unfortunately, had to be decided by force. So both Parliament and King took what they could get. Accordingly, as the old newspapers have it, "Lord Grey of Wark and Master

* "Cromwelliana," under date April 20, 1643.

Cromwell did deal very earnestly with the Heads of colleges to lend £6,000." But the Heads of colleges declined, even after they had been kept in custody all night. Master Cromwell was reported to have said, but on somewhat doubtful authority, it must be admitted,* that "he could have been contented with £1,000 or less for the present turn; not that so little money would have done them good, but that the people might have thought that one of the two Universities had been on their side." Many other leaders of revolt against injustice have had a similar desire, and equally in vain. But as Oliver could not get £1,000 with good-will, he insisted on having considerably more without it. Lynn also required a passing attention. Malignancy was showing itself there once more, and a small vessel of suspicious appearance came in there from Dunkirk. Colonel Cromwell, who in these months really seems ubiquitous, happily seized the vessel,† and converted its cargo of arms and war material to better uses than had been presumably intended. And now for Lincolnshire !

Such forces as could be collected were on their way, when Colonel Cromwell heard of strange deeds at Croyland, held by a garrison of Royalists. These men, in whom an unpleasantly grim humour must have been largely developed, had, in one of their sallies, captured the Rev. Mr. Ram, a godly minister, and Mr. John Harrington, " a religious gent.," as Vicars has it, also Mr. Horne and Mr. Shuter, all of Spalding, a few miles away across the fen. The Spalding people valiantly resolved to rescue their friends; but after they had been firing for some time at the Croyland defences, they found, to their horror, that they had been taking careful aim at the Rev. Mr. Ram, the religious Mr. Harrington, and the other captives, who had been set up and bound fast on the walls. Happily the aim had not been good. But wherever they shifted their attack, thither the Rev. Mr. Ram and the religious Mr. Harrington, with their friends, were instantly carried. And so irksome was the position in which they were bound that poor Mr. Ram desired to be shot dead rather than endure it longer. But after futile efforts on the part of the Spaldingers and their allies, "valiant and active Colonel

* " Mercurius Aulicus," April 22. The same paper imputes incredible atrocities to Oliver in his visitation of Huntingdonshire.
† " Cromwelliana," Perf. Diurn., April 28.

Cromwell" came to their assistance, and took Croyland, delivering their friends unharmed.

During this advance into Lincolnshire Cromwell occupied
Peterborough, and much outcry was occasioned by his treatment
of the cathedral. Certainly whatever doubtful ornaments had
escaped the fierce order of January, 1641, "for defacing, de-
molishing, and quite taking away all images," and such like
"monuments and reliques of idolatry," would receive no mercy
from Cromwell's regiment. But the cathedral as it stands at
this day is a witness that their destructive violence did not go
beyond the terms of a Parliamentary order issued eighteen months
before the war. And if the troopers' horses were stabled in the
venerable nave, as perhaps they were, we must needs make
allowance for two features of that time—first, the general indifference to sacred associations of the kind; and, next, the
passionate dread and hatred entertained by the best spirits of the
day towards the hierarchy, and creed, and symbols of Romanism.
The nave of St. Paul's was a familiar lounge and place of
gossip, where all the scandal of the day was exchanged. And
Oliver's troopers were, perhaps, of opinion that dumb horses were
less out of place in a church than slander and backbiting. On
the other hand, if we could only realise the wild ecstasy of joy
with which the destruction of Cheapside cross, "that most
abhominable idol of Rome," * had just been greeted in London,
we should feel that, however irrational and offensive hostility to
works of art may rightly be thought now, the prejudice of these
Puritan soldiers was no vulgar vandalism, but a conscientious
intolerance of the Pope and all his properties.

Newark-on-Trent was at this time, and continued to be, a
most aggravating thorn in the side of the Parliamentarians of
Lincolnshire. It had been made by Lord Newcastle a sort of
firm island amidst the midland chaos, across which the Royalists
of the north could communicate with the King. The Queen,
after visiting York, passed through Newark to join her
husband once more near Edgehill. If any headway were made
by the Lincoln County Association, a sally from Newark was
almost sure to disturb, or even destroy, their work. Newark was
in fact just then as intolerable to a Lincoln Parliamentarian as
Carthage to the Roman Cato. The one service required of enter-

* Vicars.

prising officers was the capture of Newark. This, however, even Oliver Cromwell could not accomplish. But he did the next best thing—or, perhaps, the next better thing—by emancipating Lincolnshire under the guns of the Newark garrison.

At the end of April, 1643, the position was this : the county committee sat in Lincoln, not without fears for their own security. Stamford seems to have been held by the Parliament, threatened, however, by a strong Royalist post at Burleigh House. Grantham was for the Parliament ; so was Gainsborough. But, generally, the Newarkers could ride as they pleased through the county, while the Parliamentary forces had to be very wary in their movements. Even in the towns they held there was little heartiness for their cause amongst the inhabitants.

Cromwell was trying to arrange a junction with Lord Grey, who was to come from Lincoln to Stamford ; and at the same time Sir John Gell, commander in Derbyshire, was to bring reinforcements by way of Nottingham. But the combination failed more than once. Lord Grey was afraid of exposing the town of Leicester to capture ; and Cromwell was very angry that his commander had so little discernment of the comparative importance of two incompatible objects. "Believe it, it were better, in my poor opinion, Leicester were not, than that there should not be found an immediate taking of the field by our forces to accomplish the common ends." * Yes ; for though Leicester was a county town, it was not the key, as Newark was, to a prosperous Royalist combination. And if only Lincolnshire could be well joined with the Eastern Counties, there was a prospect of a union with the Fairfaxes—possibly even with Scottish brethren—and, perhaps, a notion of something like Marston Moor, with the capture of York in the distance.

Stamford failing, Grantham seems to have been fixed upon instead, for a meeting with Lord Willoughby and the younger Hotham, now, alas, of uncertain faith. Both of them, however, failed, and Cromwell with about twelve troops, "some so poor and broken," he says, "that you shall hardly see worse," was exposed to a furious dash of the Newarkers. On the 13th of May they came out with one or two and twenty troops of horse. On this occasion Cromwell must have been badly served in regard to information, for it was evening when two outlying

* Letter IX. in Carlyle.

J

troops were surprised and routed out of their quarters.* But
the alarm having reached him he speedily drew out his men, and
met the enemy within two miles of the town. For half an hour
the two little armies faced each other, firing at a distance too
great for much execution, till Cromwell induced his party to
charge. "They came on at a pretty round trot," the enemy
standing firm. There was a momentary tussle, and then the
Newarkers broke and fled, pursued with fatal effect by the
Grantham troops for several miles. Forty-five prisoners were
taken, and a number of colours. The victory was not a great
one; but its moral effect was considerable. The name of "that
eminent soldier, Colonel Cromwell," began to be familiar to
readers of news-letters, and the remarkable discipline of his
troops to be talked of. Both officers and men of the Eastern
Counties were increasingly anxious to serve with a commander
who seemed to have the knack of victory. Immediately after
this skirmish he received some accession of force; but the combinations he desired for the reduction of Newark could not be
effected.

Increase of numbers however brought greater demand for
money; and money—at least outside of London—was very hard
to get. In a letter,† written May 28th, to the mayor and corporation of Colchester, urging additional supplies Oliver made
pathetic complaints of neglect. "Forget not money!" he writes;
"I press not hard; though I do so need that I assure you the
foot and dragoons are ready to mutiny. Lay not too much on
the back of a poor gentleman who desires without much noise
to lay down his life, and bleed the last drop, to serve the cause
and you. I ask not money for myself; if that were my end and
hope, viz., the pay of my place, I would not open my mouth at
this time. I desire to deny myself; but others will not be
satisfied." The "others" seem to have been only the foot and
dragoons, not the cavalry, of whom he had twenty-four troops
with him. These latter were principally recruited by himself,
and shared largely in his own devotion.

The reason why he was specially anxious to have both more
men and more money just now was that affairs in Yorkshire
seemed to have reached a crisis. Lord Fairfax had defeated a

* "Special Passages," May 9-16, in "Cromwelliana."
† Letter XI. in Carlyle.

part of Lord Newcastle's army at Wakefield; but Cromwell, while magnifying this "great mercy," was well aware that failure would have reduced Lord Fairfax from difficulty to despair. He foresaw that the force and generalship at the command of this lord would not suffice to keep back the energetic Newcastle. "We assure you," he says to the Mayor of Colchester, "should the force we have miscarry, expect nothing but a speedy march of the enemy up unto you." Lord Fairfax and his son were clearly destined to be shut up in Hull, and then there would be nothing between the Earl of Newcastle and London but the Eastern Counties Association. Colonel Cromwell therefore had very sufficient reason for urgency in asking "for more strength to be speedily sent for this great service."

For some weeks after this Oliver was compelled to be comparatively quiescent. Sir John Gell from Derbyshire, and Lord Grey from Leicester appear to have met him too late for the object he had in view, and their authority of course superseded his. Together they moved on Nottingham, still with an eye to Newark, but also to the movements of the Queen, who succeeded in rejoining the King. Captain Hotham, he who had made such valiant promise of serving the Parliament, "fall back, fall edge," was found to be in correspondence with her Majesty, and betrayed symptoms of a sort of mutinous lunacy. He had to be imprisoned for safety in Nottingham. Here Cromwell remained after Sir John Gell and Lord Grey had departed to Derby and Leicester respectively. But on June 30th his fears about the course of affairs in Yorkshire were realised. The Fairfaxes, father and son, disastrously beaten at Atherton Moor, were driven to seek shelter in Hull, and the father was appointed governor there in place of the elder Hotham, who, like the younger had proved faithless.

In fact it was under a persistent drizzle of discouraging news that Colonel Cromwell some time in the earlier part of July moved once more towards the south of Lincolnshire, where he was close to the head-quarters of his Association. His "noble friend" and cousin, Hampden, had fallen in an obscure skirmish, striving vainly to retrieve disadvantages incurred by the Lord General's slack and heartless strategy. And from the south and west, as well as from the north, came intelligence of military failures. The weaker spirits in Parliament showed an abject

J 2

desire to renew futile negotiations with the King ; and amidst
his weary and disheartening labours, Cromwell must have often
feared that a sudden vote might surrender everything.   But in
the spirit of St. Paul's words, " this one thing I do," he stuck to
the Eastern Counties Association and its work.

At this time Stamford town had fallen into the possession of
the Royalists.   Its position at the meeting-point of three counties—Lincoln, Rutland, and Northampton—was important ; and
the first piece of work Cromwell did on returning from Nottingham was to retake it.   As the papers of the time only mention
the fact of its re-capture by the " victorious and courageous
Colonel Cromwell," without giving any details, it was probably
surrendered without much resistance.   But the town was threatened by the two strong houses in the neighbourhood, Worthrop
and Burleigh, which afforded a refuge for guerilla bands of the
enemy.   On the other hand Lord Willoughby, who had retaken
Gainsborough, was hard pressed there by a besieging force, and
must be speedily relieved.   Of the two this was, perhaps, the
more important place, because when in the hands of the enemy
it helped to maintain their communications between Yorkshire
and Oxford.   But the presence of a thousand Cavaliers roving
and ravaging about Stamford made Cromwell try whether
swiftness and energy could not secure both positions.   He
speedily found the Cavaliers, attacked them, and chased them
into Burleigh House, which they reached on Monday evening
July 24th (1643).

Two colonels with foot and ordnance having opportunely
arrived in Stamford, Cromwell invested Burleigh House during
the small hours of Tuesday morning.   The residence, built in
Elizabeth's time, was not constructed to stand a siege, but was
still strong enough to resist such riotous attacks as might be
anticipated in times without a standing army or sufficient police.
It was " surrounded with a strong stone wall " thick enough to
receive little impression from the cannon then brought to bear
on it.   It was in the first dawn of the summer morning, about
three o'clock, that Oliver opened fire.   He did not summon the
place first.*   He was in a hurry, and probably thought the garrison would be more likely to yield if first roused out of sleep by
the roar and crash of his artillery.

* Vicars : his account is from contemporary journals.

But after he had played on the place for two or three hours, making no impression except on fragile mouldings and hastily-constructed barricades, he sounded a parley and offered terms. The holders should have permission to depart in safety, leaving their weapons behind them ; but if they refused these conditions now the commanding colonel could make no other offer, nor promise quarter. The answer was scornful and resolute. The garrison " utterly refused the notion." They did not want quarter ; would neither take nor give it. Then, storming parties to the shattered gates, scaling ladders to enclosure walls, and projecting offices, and accessible windows! And so the fight rages for hours again with hotter passion ; horsemen sallying, climbers falling, barricades cracking, cannon roaring, the ungodly cursing, the godly shouting a Hebrew watchword, and the defenders jeering from the walls and roof. In a land that had been so long at peace one fancies the horror of such a scene would be heightened by strange incongruities ; trellised walks hiding grim musketeers ; bright banks of flowers sheltering gashed and dying men ; luxurious walks furrowed with cannon wheels ; and here or there a child's ball, or hoop, or kite, dropped on the day before, when the first fugitives announced the dreaded Roundheads. An alarm of rescue was raised during the day. A military force was hurrying up from the direction of Newark, and some scouts of the besiegers had already been killed. Instantly three or four troops of horse galloped off, and found only four hundred poor clubmen coming to do their best for the great house, but scattering like frightened sheep before the rush of the Cromwellian cavalry.

The hopes of the besieged were at an end. They found they had to do with a man who did not undertake things without seeing his way pretty well through. So, piercing through the confused uproar, a trumpet was heard from within sounding a parley. There was some surprise among the besiegers that the commanding colonel should give any heed to it after his stern alternative and the haughty rejoinder of the besieged. But he made his intentions indubitable by commanding a cessation on pain of death to any one who disobeyed. The defenders then being promised their lives surrendered the house and yielded themselves prisoners. The arms, ammunition, and all armed men having been secured, the house, in accordance with the barbarous rules

of war, was handed over to pillage; and without other interval
than a brief night's rest Cromwell started northward.

Then was seen the advantage in such warfare of well-fur-
nished and highly-disciplined cavalry. On the Wednesday he
reached Grantham, a march of more than twenty miles. Here he
was joined by 300 horse and dragoons from Nottingham. On
the next day he had arranged to meet at North Scarle a detachment from Lincoln. North Scarle is twenty miles from Grantham as the crow flies, and the march must necessarily have been
more. Here he rested only a few hours on the Thursday evening,
and at two o'clock on the Friday morning, July 28th, hurried his
whole force off towards Gainsborough. This was a distance of
twelve miles,* so that by the time he encountered the enemy,
about four o'clock on Friday morning, he had marched nearly
fifty-five miles in less than forty-eight hours, including two
nights, and had effected two junctions by the way.

Though all this energy and hot haste shows how critical
Cromwell felt the occasion to be, his letter written after the
engagement proves that his information was defective, and that
he did not know how near Lord Newcastle was with the
main body of his army. About a mile and a half from
Gainsborough the relieving force met 100 horse of the
enemy. These they drove in, climbed a hill in the face of
the foe, and found at the top of it a great body of horse with
a reserve regiment, also of horse, behind it. The fight was
hand to hand, with swords and pistols, both lines for a while
well preserved even in the tug of war. But as when a sandy
embankment yields even a little all is lost, so on a slight
shrinking of the Royalist line, the relieving force rushed in like
a flood, and their opponents were scattered in flight past either
wing of the reserve regiment behind. The complete self-
command maintained by Cromwell in moments of supremest
excitement kept him from the error repeatedly committed by the
headlong Rupert. He was not going to have that reserve regiment on his rear; so Major Whalley impetuously pursuing the
chase was recalled, and three troops, including Cromwell's own,
were re-formed for a fresh attack. There were also four troops
from Lincoln on his left. General Cavendish, an enthusiastic

* Oliver, in his Letter (XII. in Carlyle), makes it only ten miles, but the real
distance is considerably more.

and chivalrous young Royalist of twenty-three, was in charge of the reserve regiment of the enemy, and he charged the "Lincolners" with fatal effect. Quick as lightning, Cromwell wheeled round his three troops and fell on the rear of Cavendish, "which," says Oliver, "did so astonish him, that he did give over the chase, and would fain have delivered himself from me." Alas, poor Cavendish! His fate was on him. He was driven headlong down into a quagmire below the hill, and there slain by a sword-thrust from the hand of Oliver's lieutenant. His death was the occasion of much poetic passion, but it does not seem to have been other than the inevitable fortune of war.

The powder and provision carried along on that hasty march having been deposited with the garrison, an alarm was brought in from another side of the town. With untiring vigour Colonel Cromwell was again to the fore beating back the enemy with his own horse and 400 of Lord Willoughby's foot. But in his pursuit of some retreating cavalry he gained a hill from which he saw an unexpected sight that sent him quickly cantering into the town. Ranging along the hollow in formidable perspective were one, two, three regiments of foot, and a great body of horse. By signs unmistakeable he recognised Newcastle's own regiment. It was Newcastle's army! After a hasty consultation Cromwell went out to call in the foot. He found them already engaged, and they were only brought off with disorder. His trusty cavalry, tired as they were, faced the enemy's fresh troops, and relieving each other by turns so protected the retreat that not a man was lost.

This is the first occasion on which we have, in a complete form, Oliver's own account of a considerable achievement by his troops; and the letter giving it is eminently characteristic. There is no mistaking his consciousness that he has done something remarkable; but there is also manifested a desire to repress anything like vainglory; and it is still more clear that what was uppermost in his mind in writing to the committee of his Association was the practical use to be made of his partial success. "The honour of this retreat is due to God, as also all the rest. Major Whalley did in this carry himself with all gallantry becoming a gentleman and a Christian. Thus you have this true relation as short as I could. What you are to do upon it is next to be considered. The Lord direct you what to do."* It is noteworthy that he makes no reference whatever to the extraordinary exertion it must have cost him to reach Gainsborough with supplies within three days of the capture of Burleigh House. He will not waste time or ink on that. " What to do upon it is next to be considered." This letter was written from Huntingdon on the third day after the fight, and at a distance of eighty miles from Gainsborough, so that his return march was much quicker than his advance.

His business at Huntingdon was to raise more men and more money. It is not to be supposed that he had brought his regiment there. They were more probably sent into the neighbourhood of Boston,† which he regarded as a good rendezvous for the work in Lincolnshire, and where he was himself soon afterwards heard of. He had no home in Huntingdon now, for his mother had removed to Ely. But the place was nearer the scene of operations than Cambridge. Mr. Robert Barnard had been suppressed, and his own influence was again paramount. He dared not go up to London, but he found means to move the House of Commons in his interest. An order was passed to raise a large additional force of foot and dragoons in the Eastern Counties, each man to have a month's pay in his pocket. The sum of £3,000 was voted to Colonel Cromwell for that service, but apparently Colonel Cromwell was expected to collect the money himself.

Meanwhile, the military affairs of the Parliament seemed falling from bad to worse. On the 26th of July, 1643, while the captors of Burleigh House were on the way to Grantham, Bristol had been surrendered by Nathaniel Fiennes to Prince Rupert. If Gloucester, too, should fall, all England and Wales would be the King's, except London and the Eastern Counties. On the top of such dismal tidings came news of the surrender of Gainsborough, and then a letter from Lord Willoughby announcing that, as most of his men had run away, he had given up Lincoln also, and was now (August 5th) in Boston. He added that he rather expected the enemy would not be long out of Norfolk and Suffolk. But zeal and faith like Cromwell's are often roused to fresh energy by discouragements that damp and chill the hopes of weaker men. He sent on Lord Willoughby's letter to the

---

* Letter XII. in Carlyle.
† "If you send, let your men come to Boston." Letter XI.

committee at Cambridge, enclosed in a few words of passionate
exhortation.*

"It's no longer disputing, but out instantly all you can ! Raise all
your bands; send them to Huntingdon; get up what volunteers you can ;
hasten your horses.   Send these letters to Norfolk, Suffolk, and Essex
without delay. I beseech you spare not, but be expeditious and industrious.
Almost all our foot have quitted Stamford; there is nothing to interrupt
an enemy but our horse, that is considerable.   You must act lively !   Do
it without distraction.   Neglect no means !"

That the committee did their best we know, for by the end
of August the collectors of news in London announce that " the
associated counties have already completed an army of about
8,000 horse and foot ; and, so soon as their harvest is once over
(which for the present much retardeth their proceedings) the
Earl of Manchester will have a very brave and considerable army
as any in the kingdom, to be a terror to the northern Popish
army if they advance southward." Think of these 8,000 cutting
their corn, and expecting in a few days to have another sort of
mowing to do.   What a universal attitude of trowel in one
hand, sword in the other, does it suggest !

But while the committee were doing their part, their leader
was doing his.   He was by no means satisfied with Lord Willoughby of Parham ; but for the present his lordship could not
be got rid of.   If, however, the Earl of Manchester were substituted for Lord Grey of Wark in the supreme command of the
Eastern Counties, Lord Willoughby, though Lincoln was outside
the Association, would have to give way to a general of such
rank and position.   And Cromwell's hand may be traced in the
arrangement by which the Commons' House, on the same day
that they ordered the new army to be raised, also resolved to move
the Earl of Essex to give this commission to Lord Manchester.

But the Earl of Manchester was not yet on the spot, and
toward the latter part of August Cromwell joined his men in the
Boston country, to order and drill the new recruits as they came
in.   Why did not the Earl of Newcastle send promptly an overwhelming force to break the weapon that was being forged to
smite him?   He did not do so, because he was bent on getting
into Hull.   The capture of Hull would not only be of great

* Letter XIV.

strategic value, but it would gratify and soothe the King more than any of the victories just now brightening his hopes.

Meantime Oliver, in addition to drilling, had the still more depressing business of begging. The £3,000 could not be got in. Half mutinous soldiers, not his own but outsiders, clamouring for pay had been considered before his grim and silent "Ironsides." At his wit's end he wrote to Oliver St. John, from whose official influence he might hope something :—

"I have a lovely company. You would respect them did you know them. No 'Anabaptists!' They are sober Christians; they expect to be used as men. . . . I desire not to seek myself. I have little money of my own to help my soldiers. My estate is little. I tell you the business of Ireland and England hath had of me, in money, between eleven and twelve hundred pounds. Therefore, my private purse can do little to help the public. You have had my money. I hope in God I desire to venture my skin. So do mine. Lay weight upon their patience; but break it not. Think of that which may be a real help. I believe £5,000 is due."

In a postscript he adds, "Weak counsels and weak actings undo all!" Oh, Lord Willoughby of Parham!

In these days Essex was marching slowly but effectually to the relief of Gloucester, and on September 5th the siege was raised. He pointedly declined to take Cromwell with him; but there does not seem to have been any other reason for this than the obvious fact that this colonel was very much wanted in Lincolnshire. The safety of Gloucester greatly relieved Parliamentary anxieties; but it did not slacken the eager efforts made to secure the assistance of the Scots. On this subject, and the conditions imposed by the kirk leaders, something must be said in another place. Here it is only necessary to note that the House of Commons and the Westminster Assembly agreed to take the Covenant, and Cromwell appears to have signed it at Westminster.* He had, no doubt, other business there. He was bringing many things to bear on the one point—the emancipation of Lincolnshire. This done, the "Northern Popish Army" might have to relinquish Hull and much else.

One arrangement made, we fancy, by Colonel Cromwell when up in London concerned Sir Thomas Fairfax. With

---

* Carlyle points out that Cromwell could hardly have signed in Westminster on September 25th if he was in Hull on the 26th. But Rushworth was perhaps as likely to be wrong about the latter date as about the former.

20,000 men under Lord Newcastle closely pressing Hull, the horse troops of Sir Thomas could do nothing but consume food and provender, which was inconvenient. Fortunately communication was open by water, and Lord Fairfax received a suggestion for putting his son's force to a practical use.* Soon after the Covenant signing Cromwell was down at Boston again, and led his own regiment by cautiously-selected roads towards Saltfleet, a fishing village facing the North Sea, beyond the Humber estuary. On the 27th of September the besiegers of Hull saw with rage a little flotilla carried swiftly beyond the range of their guns, and bearing to an unknown destination Sir Thomas Fairfax and all his cavalry. They were disembarked at Saltfleet, and either there or at Louth, ten miles inland, a junction was effected with Colonel Cromwell. The news of this movement considerably fluttered the troops of Royalists scattered through Lincolnshire. And both their excitement and their confidence were increased by the detachment from the besieging army of a large force, comprising both horse and foot, under General Henderson. The Earl of Newcastle had evidently gathered that some serious mischief was brewing. Cromwell and Fairfax managed their retreat to Boston without risking an engagement. The former thought he saw his way now to an important conflict, and it was necessary that the Earl of Manchester should be fully informed as to the position of affairs.

The new commander was then at Lynn, which had relapsed into "malignancy," and had to be delivered by force of arms. Nominally Cromwell was only one of four colonels under him. But practically Oliver's knowledge of the country, his clear apprehension of the work to be done, his influence with the Association, and not least his tremendous energy, made him the real director of the campaign. In fact he had so ordered matters that when the earl came on the field there was only one course open, which was to meet and fight the enemy before the latter could reach Boston. The internal security of the Eastern Counties was now such that when at the beginning of October Lord Manchester advanced from Lynn towards Boston, he left the town guarded by only one troop of horse and six companies of

* Rushworth (Part III. Vol. ii. p. 280) states that Cromwell himself with Lord Willoughby, visited Hu'l to make the arrangement. If so it is another illustration of his quickness in action.

foot, under Colonel Walton Cromwell's brother-in-law. The whole force at his disposal was reckoned at 14,000, nearly all being now in or around Boston, the horse somewhat scattered, and the foot about the town.

To understand what followed, it is necessary to keep the county map in view. Nearly due north from Boston, at a distance of about fifteen miles, lies the town of Horncastle, at the foot of the Wolds. Nine miles east-south-east from Horncastle is Spilsby, and about half-way between them is the hamlet of Winceby.* Thus the three places lie in the base of an acute angled triangle, of which the apex is at Boston. Within the triangle, three miles west-south-west of Spilsby, is Bolingbroke village, on a hill, then boasting a castle capable of defence, and held by a Royalist garrison. The enemy were reported to be converging in the direction of Horncastle, drawing force from Lincoln and Newark, and gathering in their outlying detachments. Lord Manchester had his eye on Bolingbroke Hill, and when he drew a part of his infantry out of Boston he sent ten companies to that place under Major Knight, with orders to take the castle. Another body was stationed three miles southward, at Stickford, under Colonel Russell; and a few companies of Manchester's own regiment were two miles still further south, at Stickney.† Thus what infantry he had was scattered in weak groups over a long distance—its right occupied with a hostile garrison and its left stretched out towards Boston, about which the General would seem to have been nervous. The horse soldiers were scattered over a wide district, including Spilsby, Horncastle, and even Thimbleby, still nearer to Lincoln.

On Tuesday, October 10th, Lord Manchester met Cromwell and Lord Willoughby by appointment, within a mile of Bolingbroke. The castle had not yielded. The garrison flouted the summons of Major Knight with the reply that "his bugbear words would not take castles." Partly perhaps for this reason, the earl decided that Horncastle should be the place of rendezvous, and that they would await the enemy there. After this

* By Carlyle Winceby is placed *west* of Horncastle, which quite confuses the account of the fight.
† The narrative of Vicars, on which I draw, is trustworthy as to main facts, but it does not account for half of Manchester's foot. The probability is the earl was anxious to keep a "firm grip" of Boston, and left a large force there.

decision, the three commanders rode on towards Horncastle to look up Sir Thomas Fairfax. They met him half-way. But hardly had they greeted him when a loud alarm arose behind him. They galloped back with him towards Horncastle, the crack of musketry and shouts of men increasing as they neared the town. The enemy were upon them unexpectedly,* and were received so stoutly that after a brief skirmish they retired; but the outlying troops about Thimbleby barely escaped capture. The earl now changed the place of rendezvous to Bolingbroke Hill, and Horncastle was abandoned to the Royalists.

All that night the scattered troops of horse were being gathered in towards Bolingbroke. Even Cromwell doubted whether both men and horses would not be too wearied for a fight. Strenuous exertion for a definite object might be cheerfully endured; but confused and worrying movements without a visible issue wear out both nerve and muscle far more. Besides, nothing like a complete concentration had been effected. The whole stress of the attack must be borne by the extreme right of the Parliamentary line, where the horse were huddled together, with scarcely a full regiment of foot to co-operate. The numbers engaged were about equal on either side, neither army bringing its whole force into action. The Royalists brought into the field ninety-five colours of horse and dragoons, which ought to have represented 6,000 men.† The Parliament army had not much more than half so many colours, but their troops were better filled up. Perhaps there were between 4,000 and 5,000 on each side.

Cromwell and his men had the van, with a "forlorn hope" of five troops in advance, and Sir Thomas Fairfax in support. About noon they pushed from the direction of Spilsby and Bolingbroke towards Horncastle. Soon the advancing lines of the enemy were seen, and about Winceby the dragoons on either side dismounted and closed up. After they had fired Cromwell sprang forward with his cavalry. But when he was within half-pistol shot of the foe the enemy's dragoons fired again. His horse fell dead beneath him, and partially rolled upon him. As he dragged him-

---

* There had been an earlier alarm, but it was believed delusive.
† *I.e.*, taking the horse at sixty to a troop, and dragoons at one hundred, besides officers.

self loose and rose to his feet, a troop of the enemy's cavalry
was upon him, and he was knocked down again by its leader.
Rising once more, shaken and dizzy, but not stunned, he received
a sorry nag from a soldier at hand, and mounting joined again
in the fight. The weight of the charge made by his men
scattered the hostile dragoons, drove in the enemy's first line
upon its supports, threw these into confusion, and produced a
general rout. The chase passed through Horncastle and beyond
it, the panic of the enemy spreading far and wide through their
whole army. One road there, called Slash * Lane, is said to
take its name from the execution done as pursued and pursuers
rushed along it on that day. Wounded and falling horsemen
were drowned in ditches; heedless fugitives were overwhelmed
in quagmires. Out of ninety-five colours thirty-five were captured. At least 1,000 Royalists were killed, 1,000 more surrendered as prisoners, 2,000 horses were obtained, and 1,500 arms
of various kinds. The result seems altogether disproportionate
to the brief struggle of half-an-hour by Winceby hamlet. But
the completeness of the disaster to the Royalists was such that
Sir William Widdington, of the defeated army, writing to Lord
Newcastle, apprehended that the siege of Hull would have to be
raised, and Yorkshire would be in danger. " Their horse," he
said, speaking of the victors, " are very good, and extraordinarily
armed. They are at present at liberty to dispose of their forces
whatever way they please, either to Hull or Derby."

But even while Colonel Widdington was writing his discon-
solate letter, Lord Newcastle had already determined to abandon
Hull. Early intelligence of the disaster at Horncastle perhaps
hastened his resolve. But that resolve was suggested by a
vigorous and victorious sally of Lord Fairfax, which showed the
siege to be hopeless; for the defenders, being supplied and reinforced by water, might renew such sallies at their leisure.
Accordingly on October 12th, the day after Winceby fight,
Lord Newcastle drew off his army. The Eastern Counties'
Association after long and laborious self-discipline and preparation had delivered Lincolnshire at one blow. And this change in
the position of affairs in the east, together with the relief of
Gloucester in the west, led to a new phase of the war.

* One cannot help suspecting that it is really " Slush Lane."

CHAPTER IX.

THE Solemn League and Covenant, inaugurated at St. Margaret's Church, Westminster, on September 25th, 1643, had a very important influence, not only on the course of the war, but on later events. It turned out ultimately to be the greatest mistake ever made by the leaders of the Long Parliament; and Cromwell particularly was embarrassed by its results. Why then did he sign it? The obvious answer is that with his usual attention to one main issue he wanted to bring the war to an end, and for the accomplishment of this he thought an alliance with the Scots to afford the speediest and surest means. But the only condition on which this alliance could be secured was the adoption of the Covenant. And accordingly Cromwell signed it, though with him probably it went against the grain.

The Scots had watched with mingled feelings the outbreak and progress of the war in England. They congratulated themselves on the security of their own kirk, while the godly in the south had to fight for Reformation. But sometimes the painful question would obtrude itself, what would become of their kirk if King Charles should get the upper hand? They knew their "native-born prince" far too well to trust him; and though they might have confidence that they would always be able to fight their own battles, it was time their Reformation should be so secured that there would be no more battles to fight. In their view the most effectual way of accomplishing this would be to extend their own ecclesiastical polity to England. And Presbyterianism was so widely favoured by English Puritans that the attempt seemed not only practicable but easy.

But it should be remembered that the document agreed upon was not the original Scotch League and Covenant. It committed no one to any detailed creed, or to any particular theory of Church government. It was certainly regarded by the Scots as promising all they wanted. Still, by whatever influences the language was moulded, it did not literally bind England to accept the Scotch model of the kirk and its activities.

Yet, when all is said, it must be admitted that the form of the agreement greatly narrowed the scope desired by the Independents for a free development of the revolution according to any fresh light they might receive, and any circumstances that might arise. It not only conferred on the presbytery an indisputable title to succeed to the spiritual throne of prelacy, but it engaged all the signatories " to preserve and defend the king's person and authority," an undertaking which, at least in reference to Charles I., had already become impossible. Far better would it have been for the English Parliament to have persisted in fighting its own battle alone than to accept aid on such terms. This fatal document was the fruitful cause of dissensions, recriminations, and plausible charges of faithlessness against the Independent army. And amongst the causes which overthrew the Commonwealth, postponing for generations the full fruition of Cromwell's victories, no insignificant place must be assigned to this Solemn League and Covenant.

If Cromwell had added to his earnest sincerity that last perfection of a great character, simplicity, he would have dared all consequences, both to himself and to the cause, rather than sign. "Subtlety might deceive him; integrity never would." But he was not simple. His great soul was a chaos of seething thoughts, impulses, and half-formed ideals, with some one immediate issue always emerging into glaring light and concentrating all his giant powers on itself. In September, 1643, "weak counsels and weak actings" were still threatening ruin. The Parliament was strong nowhere except in London and the Eastern Counties. The country was bleeding to death. Victory must be had. And the Scots could bring into the field 20,000 trained and resolute men. The document left much to after discussion and interpretation, and meantime the two kingdoms would be united against the curse of Popery and despotism.

In the interval between Winceby fight and the battle of Marston Moor, though there are traces of Cromwell's incessant activity, it is often difficult to arrange in an intelligible sequence his transient appearances here and there. We catch sight of him, not only in his proper domain of the Eastern Counties' Association, but about Bedford and Leicester and Oxford, at Westminster, and as far west as Gloucester, in hurried march, with hasty blow or with urgent word, doing all that in him lies for the triumph of the Parliament. The few incidents in any degree illustrative of his character and the growth of his influence may be rapidly indicated.

Soon after the rout of the Royalists in Winceby fight, Lincoln and Gainsborough in succession surrendered to the Earl of Manchester; and for a while nearly the whole county was at the disposal of the Parliament. But the contest was not wholly abandoned there for some time longer; and both Lincoln and Gainsborough changed hands more than once before the great concentration of contending armies at York. On a report that certain Cavaliers of Bedfordshire were intending a raid into the Associated Counties, the Earl of Manchester sent Cromwell with his horse soldiers towards Huntingdon. But the Lord-General, being at St. Albans, countermanded him, promising at the same time that the cherished district should come to no harm. Accordingly Cromwell returned into Lincolnshire to Sleaford, a place of some strategic importance, which the Cavaliers showed a disposition to seize and fortify. In the middle of November Lord Willoughby of Parham distinguished himself by taking Bolingbroke Castle, where a little Royalist garrison had stood out stoutly notwithstanding the rout at Winceby. But, as we shall presently see, this small achievement did not by any means justify in Oliver's judgment his lordship's retention of the post of Serjeant-Major-General in Lincolnshire. The inclination of victory in the east was perhaps more distinctly indicated in December by the return of Sir Thomas Fairfax with twelve troops of horse into Yorkshire, where his father had already turned the scale on the Earl of Newcastle.

Since the relief of Gloucester at the beginning of September nothing of critical importance had happened on the wider field of the war. With his usual policy of avoiding too decisive an issue, Lord Essex fell back from Gloucester towards London, and at Newbury fought a battle fatal to poor Lord Falkland, but in its issue as indeterminate as even the most irresolute waverers could have desired. Two political arrangements made during this year, 1643, had more influence on the course of events than all the battles of the campaign. One was the engagement of the Scotch alliance at the expense of the international

K

Covenant, to which we have already referred. The other was the cessation of hostilities against the rebels in Ireland. This truce was arranged with the sanction and by the authority of the King, in order that he might bring over the Protestant forces there, and probably Papists as well, to quell his more formidable rebels in England. It is difficult amid the balanced opinions of later days to realise the sacred rage excited in Great Britain, even amongst moderate Royalists, by that blind stroke of policy. If we can imagine a truce arranged in 1857 with Nana Sahib and the Cawnpore murderers, in order to recall troops for the suppression of a reform movement at home, we may also form some conception of the passion that possessed all Puritan souls at the intelligence of that " cessation." Indeed not a few devoted supporters of the crown either left the country or went over to the Parliament when they found that the incredible report was true. Nor did the King obtain any adequate compensation in military strength; for nearly the whole of the reinforcements landed from Ireland were scattered or slaughtered by Sir Thomas Fairfax at Nantwich, or by Sir William Waller in the south.

Two appointments conferred about this period on Oliver indicate the steady advance of his public influence. The " Plantations," as the American colonies were called, had not altogether escaped Royalist designs, and the colonists petitioned Parliament to protect them from interference. Accordingly, an Ordinance was passed in November 1643, designating certain commissioners, amongst whom were Pym, the younger Vane, Haselrig, the Earl of Manchester, and Cromwell, who were to appoint governors, and exercise a general superintendence over plantations and islands. The other appointment was to the governorship of the Isle of Ely, which was given him at the midsummer previous. As to the colonies, his work cannot have been much more than nominal. But the other post was more onerous. One of his duties was to see that the Acts and Ordinances of Parliament on the reform of public worship were carried into effect. His conduct in the discharge of such duties has brought upon him charges of inconsistency, irreverence, and even brutality. His manners were certainly adapted to the occasion, which scarcely permitted the roundabout procedure of hollow compliment. But at least he showed a desire to do his work without giving unnecessary pain. It was only when the alternative was suggested of leaving the work undone that the strong hand was openly displayed. And it should be remembered that, though he went as far as any one of his time in supporting freedom of private opinion and action, he never doubted for a moment the necessity of a state provision for religious worship; and this to his plain mind involved the duty of the state clergy to obey the voice of national authority. The zeal with which he asserted that authority is repellent to our feelings now. Many old customs, ceremonies, and super-stitions have for us the interest of faded leaves, glowing with colours they never showed in the season of their vigour. But if we would not be unjust, we must enter into the feelings of a generation to whom these things were a thick and deadly shade interposed between their longing eyes and the pure light of spiritual truth.

This at least was the feeling of the new Governor of Ely; and when month after month passed by without a satisfactory reformation of the Cathedral service there, he felt that he must interfere. Regiments of soldiers valiant for the truth were constantly passing and repassing, and consisted of men ac-customed to make short work of any remnants of idolatry that came in their way. It is probable, also, that Oliver had received from higher quarters a hint that he should take more active measures. The Reverend Mr. Hitch was responsible for the services at the time, and to him, in January, 1643-4, Cromwell addressed a brief note, saying that, for the prevention of possible tumult, the choir service, "so unedifying and offensive," must be discontinued. The Governor expressed a desire also for more frequent sermons and expositions, pending further ar-rangements. But the choir service went on as before. Mr. Hitch apparently did not know his Governor. So one day while he was solemnly intoning the prayers, the tramp of soldiers was heard in the nave, and presently the Governor with his guard appeared, attended of course by the sort of idlers who always scent the probability of an exciting scandal. Oliver kept his hat on, much to the indignation of all well-mannered people. In a voice that must have been in startling discord with the conventional tones it interrupted, he said, so as to be heard by all, "I am a man under authority, and I am

K 2

commanded to dismiss this assembly." He then retired "towards the communion table," which apparently had stood
in the body of the church. But Mr. Hitch would not take
the hint; and after the interruption he went on as before.
Whereupon Cromwell came back, and, according to the story
current amongst the clergy afterwards, peremptorily required
the reverend gentleman to "leave off his fooling, and come
down." It need scarcely be said that Mr. Hitch obeyed. It
was not a polite proceeding on the part of the Governor of Ely;
but it must be admitted that it was characteristic.

Soon after this scene, Oliver was in his place in Parliament
once more. Many people were discontented with the slow progress of the war, and Cromwell began to feel that, unless great
changes were made in the direction and discipline of the army,
"weak counsels and weak actings" would bring the cause to
ruin. Sir Symonds D'Ewes, on returning into the House after
some hours' absence on the morning of January 22nd, 1644,
found his friends in a considerable flutter of excitement. The
member for Cambridge had been expressing himself about the
state of things in Lincolnshire with a plainness of speech to
which even the Long Parliament was not always accustomed
when titled supporters of the popular cause were concerned. He
"stood up, and desired that the Lord Willoughby of Parham,
who had commanded in Lincolnshire as Serjeant-Major-General
of the forces there, might be ordered to stay away, and to go no
more thither; and that the Earl of Manchester might be made
Sergeant-Major-General of that county, as well as of the other
associated counties."*

Such a blunt proposal required plain reasons to support it,
and they were given. He stated "that the Lord Willoughby
quitted Gainsborough when he (the speaker) was not far off with
forces to relieve him; that he quitted the city of Lincoln, and
left powder, match, and arms there, and seven great pieces
mounted, with all the carriages, which the enemy made use of
against the Parliament's forces; that he had very loose and pro-
fane commanders under him." One of these commanders Cromwell charged with the odious offence of abusing his military
power to lay a shameful tax on the women of the district.
Thereupon ensued a "scene," such as we are too often deluded

---

* Harl. MSS., No. 165, f. 280*b*.

into regarding as peculiar to our own times. A lord rarely wants friends on such occasions; and Sir Christopher Wray, boiling with indignation, declared he had scarcely been able to keep his seat—" he had much ado to have patience to hear this out to the end." It was intolerable that a nobleman who had so well deserved of the House should be spoken of in this way. And so the wrangle went on for an hour or two. But in the end, the weight of Cromwell's reasons prevailed. Sir Christopher Wray declared that his friend was sick of Lincolnshire, and was already " resolved to go thither no more," and so a resolution was passed desiring the Lord-General to grant the suggested commission to the Earl of Manchester.

Lincolnshire was now added to the Associated Eastern Counties, and the founder of the union was raised to the rank of Lieutenant-General. The title was more in accord with his real influence; but zealous Presbyterians began to mutter that, if the truth were known, he was really the chief commander of the eastern army, and that under his patronage Independency and other obnoxious heresies had become ominously prevalent among the soldiers there. One of Cromwell's letters * throws a good deal of light on the causes of this uneasiness. There was a certain Major-General Laurence Crawford, a Scotchman, of considerable experience in foreign wars, who had joined Manchester's army with an expectation, both on the part of himself and of admiring Presbyterian friends, that he would not only give the earl some useful strategic hints, but would also guard the orthodoxy of his army from further corruption. He seems at once to have obtained a strong hold on his commander's confidence, and the " Lord of the Fens " had, perhaps, somewhat lost the decisive influence justified by his local knowledge and authority.

In February of this year (1643–4) Cromwell was employed in a cross-country expedition for the conveyance of ammunition to Gloucester. In addition to the accomplishment of this work, he succeeded in capturing various strong places, in alarming Oxford, and taking the town of Banbury, though the Royalists kept possession of the castle. Major-General Crawford was amongst the officers on this service, and under him a Lieutenant-Colonel Packer. When Cromwell returned to

* No. XX. in Carlyle.

Cambridge at the beginning of March, these men were left in Buckinghamshire, and for some cause Crawford placed his subordinate under arrest, and sent him for judgment to the Earl of Essex, who was then busy in reforming Cambridge University. Packer laid his case before the Lieutenant-General, and the latter was convinced that the real cause of offence was the man's religious opinions. He was said to be an Anabaptist, though Packer himself does not seem to have admitted this. At any rate he was loose in his notions and indiscreet in his enthusiasm. On this ground, and as the Earl of Essex was closely occupied, Cromwell sent Packer back to Crawford with a letter; and this letter is of great significance for an understanding of the writer's character. After explaining that the General had not time to hear the case at present, and that under the circumstances it seemed the best course for Packer to return to his post, the letter proceeds :—

"Surely you are not well-advised thus to turn off one so faithful to the cause, and so able to serve you as this man is. Give me leave to tell you I cannot be of your judgment—if a man notorious for wickedness, for oaths, for drinking,* hath as great a share in your affection as one who fears an oath, who fears to sin †—that this doth commend your election of men to serve as fit instruments in this work."

"'Aye, but the man is an Anabaptist!' Are you sure of that? Admit he be; shall that render him incapable to serve the public? 'He is indiscreet.' It may be so in some things. We have all human infirmities. I tell you if you had none but such indiscreet men about you, and would be pleased to use them kindly, you would find as good a fence to you as any you have yet chosen.

"Sir, the State in choosing men to serve it takes no notice of their opinions. If they be willing to serve it faithfully, that satisfies. . . . Take heed of being too sharp, or too easily sharpened by others, against those to whom you can object little but that they square not with you in every opinion concerning matters of religion."

It is obvious that in these last words the writer stated not the actual practice of the State, but rather the opinion of himself and his friends the Independents as to what was the proper thing for the State to do. Whether, when he came to greater power, he was consistent in carrying out this opinion, and, if not, what were the hindrances that prevented his being so, are questions belonging to the policy of his latter days. But for an under-

---

* These words apparently point to some individual.
† Supply here "I cannot think."

standing of the critical stage that we are now approaching in Cromwell's career, it is more important to note the evidence afforded of his determination to judge of men only by one test, and that was the degree of their faithfulness to "the cause." What that cause was we have already seen.*

The issues of the war now slowly converged towards York. The death of John Pym, which occurred in December 1643, did not apparently make so much difference to the progress of affairs as might have been expected from the greatness of the man. The forces he had evoked were developing a more complicated struggle than he had anticipated. But for the present his policy of a Scotch alliance held good. When military operations were actively resumed in the spring of 1644, there were five sectional armies in the field, without counting minor detachments that kept every part of the country in a fever of sporadic conflict. Essex and Waller had each about 10,000 men operating in the Midlands and the South, but never earnestly combining for a decisive attack on Oxford. The Scots had crossed the Tweed on solid ice in January, and were slowly feeling their way southward. Lord Fairfax had mastered all South Yorkshire, and was pushing towards York, where in May he and the Scottish army united to form the siege. The Earl of Manchester had still much to do to complete the subjection of Lincolnshire, and often found his progress hindered by forays from Newark, a town that held out with singular tenacity to the very last. Nevertheless his progress was northwards, and all eyes began to be turned towards York.

In March Sir John Meldrum besieged Newark in a mistaken and headstrong fashion. Prince Rupert, who in these months seems ubiquitous, dashed in upon him in an unexpected direction, and compelled the surrender of his whole force, who were disarmed, and dismissed in a demoralised condition to seek refuge in Lincoln and Gainsborough. The surrender of these towns naturally followed, and loud were the wailings in London. This misfortune " was ascribed by some to my Lord Willoughby, of treachery, for his envy to Manchester and desire to see his forces there broken; by others to the malcontentment of the Independent soldiers, who did mutiny; by others to the slackness of Colonel Cromwell, the great Independent, to send to Meldrum

* Chap. VI.

timeous relief." * But when it is remembered that the "great Independent" had barely completed his work in Buckinghamshire, we can quite understand how gossipping critics came to the conclusion that "when all is well considered, and Sir John Meldrum's own letters looked upon, it seems his own improvidence alone has procured that mischief."

The mischief, however, was fully repaired. The Earl of Manchester, having finished his commission in Cambridge University, got his army into the field again, and made for Lincoln. Attempts were apprehended from the Royalists upon Sleaford; but Cromwell, with 2,000 horse, speedily dissipated all fear on that account. With the same force he kept a look-out for Colonel Goring, while the Earl of Manchester advanced by Grantham to Lincoln, and retook the town at the beginning of May. Mainly by Cromwell's activity, the Lincolnshire side of the Trent was pretty well cleared of Royalists, and the Eastern Counties' army was able, in the early summer, to advance across the Humber, in order to join with Lord Fairfax and the Scots under the Earl of Leven against York.

At the end of May Essex and Waller had seemed nearer than ever before to an effective combination against Oxford; but the King, at the beginning of June, slipped between their armies and went into Derbyshire, whence he wrote an urgent letter to Prince Rupert to relieve York at all risks. When it was found that the King had gone, Essex left to his colleague the unwelcome duty of following him, while the Lord-General himself turned towards the west, and, as it ultimately proved, towards defeat and surrender. Waller, believing that Charles intended to join his nephew, moved on Shrewsbury to keep them separate. But the King, having no such intention, marched in security back to Oxford. Prince Rupert then, having received such urgent orders, was speedily on the march, and on July 1st the commanders of the united armies about York received information that he was near Knaresborough† with 20,000 men. The forces concentrated by Fairfax, Leven, and Manchester for the capture of the city did not number more than 23,000. The generals

---

* "Baillie's Letters," April 2nd, 1644. He still calls Cromwell a "colonel," but a newspaper in February announced that he had received the higher commission, and, at any rate, he exercised the powers of a Lieutenant-General.

† It seems to have been in some skirmish at Knaresborough about this time that Cromwell's son Oliver lost his life; but the matter is obscure.

therefore broke up the leaguer, and marched out in the direction of Knaresborough to intercept the Prince.

All who have ascended the central tower of York Minster are well aware that the country to the west of the city is a wide, flat plain, through which flows the river Ouse, bending to the southward after passing through York. The little river Nidd, curving round from Knaresborough, flows northward into the Ouse, about eight miles from the city. This portion of the plain is thus enclosed on three sides by water, and the quadrilateral is nearly completed by the river Wharfe to the southward. The besiegers had constructed a bridge across the Ouse on the west side of York ; but between this and Boroughbridge, sixteen miles up the river, there was no other passage. On crossing the Moor in the direction of Knaresborough, the vanguard of the Parliamentary army was confronted by detachments of Royalist horse sent out by Prince Rupert to confirm the expectation of a battle. But this was only a feint ; for meanwhile, under cover of these skirmishing troops, Prince Rupert marched northwards to Boroughbridge, and transferred his whole force to the other side of the river.

Having thus outwitted the Parliamentary generals he marched at his ease to the forest of Galtre, within five miles of York. The Earl of Manchester, to do him justice, had not been without a suspicion of this manœuvre, and had established a bridge of boats at Poppleton, half-way between York and the confluence of the Nidd. This bridge, however, being imperfectly guarded, was attacked in force by Prince Rupert, and triumphantly captured. The Parliamentary generals then, of necessity, changed their plan. They determined to continue their march to the southward, with a view of intercepting supplies and reinforcements for the Royalist army, and also of establishing communication with the reinforcements they themselves expected from the west.

On the night of Monday, July 1st (1644), they took up their quarters in the village of Long Marston, in that of Tockwith, and in other hamlets of the neighbourhood. Long Marston, so called from the length of its straggling street, is situated just where the flat land of the moor rises into a swelling ridge towards the south. Along the base of this ridge runs a lane, then probably a moorland path to Tockwith. The distance between the two villages is a mile and a half. On the morning of July 2nd the army broke up from its quarters in these villages, and marched towards Cawood, below the confluence of the Wharfe and Ouse, a large force of cavalry under Cromwell and Fairfax remaining behind to secure the rear.

The van had already marched about five miles, when the rear-guard on the swelling ground above Long Marston perceived that the Royalists were in full pursuit from the direction of York and Poppleton. Orders were then immediately given to recall the army, and to form line of battle in the neighbourhood of Marston. The rising ground was advantageous for the purpose, but the direction of the retreat, and the lines on which the Royalists advanced caused some difficulty in the extension of the Parliamentary front. As fast as the troops returned they took up ground to the left from Marston village, and by two o'clock in the day they were extended as far as Tockwith, while the enemy confronted them on the moor immediately below. They were fairly equal in numbers, each army being a little over 20,000. The weather was showery, the air thunderous, with changes of bright sunshine and deep gloom.

The disposition of the Parliamentary force was such that the centre consisted mainly of the Scotch force, under the Earl of Leven; the right wing was formed by Lord Fairfax's force, and the left by the Earl of Manchester's army. Still, there was some intermixture of troops. Thus, a brigade of Manchester's foot supported the main battle sustained by the Scotch infantry, and a detachment of Scottish foot were placed in reserve behind Lord Fairfax's foot regiments on the left of the right wing. Three regiments of Scotch horse, under General David Leslie, supported the left wing; and Scotch Dragoons, stationed amongst some trees on the extreme left, guarded that portion of the position. The three Commanders-in-Chief took up their place in the rear of the main battle. The left wing was under the immediate command of Cromwell, the centre under that of the Scotch General Bailie, and the right wing under Sir Thomas Fairfax.

The centre of the Royalist army was under General King, created Lord Eythyn; the right wing, mainly of horse, was under Prince Rupert; and the left wing, also mainly horse, was under General Goring. The Marquis of Newcastle accompanied Prince Rupert to the field, after having vainly counselled a prudent delay, and resigned to him both command and responsibility. Parallel with the path between Marston and Tockwith, a ditch, with a straggling hedge alongside of it, divided the moorland from the cultivated fields. To pass this ditch first would be a disadvantage to either side; and this slight obstacle seems to have kept the armies quiescent for several hours. A desultory cannonade was commenced about two o'clock, but it died away about five; and most began to think that the prospects of a battle were over for the day.

Meantime, a prisoner released by Prince Rupert returned to his comrades on the left wing, and was brought to the Lieutenant-General. The man related how eagerly the prince had asked whether Cromwell was in this wing, and whether they would fight, because, if they would, they should " have their bellyful." "And, please God, so shall he!" rejoined Cromwell. About seven in the evening Cromwell noticed a battery being placed on the moor for the purpose of galling his position. It was apparently a shot from this hostile battery that took off the leg of Cromwell's nephew, young Valentine Walton. The youth died in the course of the evening, but lived long enough to see victory assured. Meantime, as soon as Cromwell had noted the movement, he ordered two guns forward. The execution of this order drew the fire of musketeers stationed in the ditch, and on the extreme right of the Royalist army. A shot grazed Cromwell's neck; but, beyond drawing a little blood, did no further damage. This caused some alarm to his men; but he called out, cheerily, " A miss is as good as a mile," and turned his face to the foe.* The moment was come. The musketeers must be silenced; and this skirmish brought on the battle by the light of the setting sun. It was Cromwell's horsemen who first charged, and the eastern counties foot kept pace with them as well as they could on their right. The opposing skirmishers were swept back, the ditch was cleared, and horse and foot found themselves engaged

---

* It is just possible—nothing more—that some little delay, occasioned by this wound, may have given rise to the extraordinary story of Denzil Holles, that Cromwell played the coward at Marston Moor, and declined to charge. It need scarcely be added that the story is refuted by every eye-witness whose account has come down to us.

hand to hand on the moor with Prince Rupert's Life Guards and his regiment of infantry.* Scoutmaster Watson, in his account of the battle, recalls with enthusiasm the sight presented on the hillside as the movement spread from left to right:

"The signal being given, we marched on to the charge, in which you might have seen the bravest sight in the whole world; such disciplined armies marching to a charge came down the hill in the bravest order and in the greatest resolution that ever was seen: I mean the left wing of our horse, led on by Lieutenant-General Cromwell, which was to charge their right wing, led by Rupert, in which were all their gallant men, they being resolved that if they could scatter Cromwell, all was their own. All the Earl of Manchester's foot, being three brigades, began the charge with their bodies against the Marquis of Newcastle's foot and Prince Rupert's bravest foot. In a moment we were past the ditch upon the Moor, on equal ground with the enemy, our men going on a running march. Our front divisions of horse charged their front. Lieutenant-General Cromwell's division of three hundred horse, in which himself was in person, charged the first division of Rupert's own regiment, in which himself was in person; the rest [charged] other divisions, but with such admirable valour as it was to the astonishment of all the old soldiers of the army. Lieutenant-General Cromwell's own division had a handful of it; for they were charged by Rupert's bravest men both in front and flanks. They stood at the sword point a pretty while hacking one another. But at last it pleased God he brake through them, and scattered them before him like dust. At the same instant the rest of our horse of that wing had wholly broken all Rupert's horse on the right wing, and was in the chase of them beyond their left wing. Our foot of the right hand,† being only the Earl of Manchester's foot, went on by our side, dispersing the enemy's foot almost as fast as they charged them, still going on by our side, cutting them down, that we carried the whole field before us."

On the right rear of the Royalist position lay Wilstrop Wood, of which part remains to this day. This turned the chase towards York, and across the rear of the battle. The observer who stands now on Marston fields, and looks across the lowly flat towards Wilstrop Wood, can easily understand how, in the headlong gallop of pursuers and pursued, amidst the rattle and the roar of fire-arms, and the flight of stragglers, and the "hurly-burly" of struggling hosts scattered everywhere along the plain, this victorious left wing could form no notion of what was going on along the front, and imagined the case of all their

---

* This infantry was on the right of the Royalist main battle.
† *I.e.*, on the right of the Parliamentary left wing.
‡ This extract is copied from Harleian MSS., "D'Ewes' Journal.'

fellow-soldiers to be like their own. But their discipline was such that they were never out of hand, and having followed the chase to within two miles of York, Cromwell brought them back through the summer twilight in good order towards the battle-field.

He had not returned far when he was met by signs of disaster. It was ominous that no Royalists were flying from the centre, or from the Marston side. But what was worse, there were stragglers from the Parliamentary army declaring that, after fighting through the enemies' ranks, they found themselves alone, and they feared things had gone badly with their comrades. Presently Sir Thomas Fairfax was met, with blood streaming from a wound in his face, and riding a wounded horse. He had led a successful charge down a lane leading from Marston fields to the moor ; but owing to the narrowness of the passage his men had been divided, and part of them were involved in the general rout which was the fortune of the Parliamentary right. On returning from the charge, Sir Thomas had found himself in the midst of the enemy, but passed for one of their own officers, and so had managed to join Cromwell. Lambert, who had been on the extreme right, also appeared to tell the same story of defeat. And indeed the state of the hill-side made the case clear. The disordered crowds surging upwards and the tumult amongst the baggage-waggons showed too plainly that the centre and right of the Parliamentary army had fled, leaving both guns and baggage to the foe.

What followed is surely one of the most extraordinary incidents in the history of warfare. The eastern counties horse and foot, with their Scotch allies under Leslie, having beaten Rupert and returned from the chase, now undertook to fight the victorious Royalist centre and left, and to turn the disaster of their friends into a second triumph for themselves. Fragments of the beaten army rallied to them, and they then formed a fresh line of battle, occupying the very ground formerly taken up by the Royalist left, while the enemy faced them on Marston Fields, where the Parliamentary right had been. The Royalist commanders, King and Goring, recalled their men as well as they could from plunder and pursuit, and they charged down the hill. Thus, whatever advantages or disadvantages had previously belonged to each army were now reversed. But the result was the same. The Royalists dashed in vain against the rigid lines of the Ironsides. The guns were regained; the baggage was rescued. Troop after troop was charged and dispersed by Cromwell and Leslie. But Newcastle's foot battalion of " white-coats," who in the beginning of the battle had been on the left centre, stood together to the last, and fell dead in rank and file. The rout of the Royalists was now complete. Escaping as they could round the flanks of their pursuers, they fled towards York, followed by their victors to within a mile of the walls, and leaving a train of dead bodies three miles in length behind them.

The final ruin and slaughter went on by the light of the moon, and the dark shadows of Wilstrop Wood afforded a refuge to many fugitives. But everywhere in the open they were slain without mercy, in spite of the generous order of Sir Thomas Fairfax to spare the common soldiers. Out of their whole force of more than 20,000, it was reckoned that the Royalists would not be able to rally more than 3,000 horse and foot.

The fate of the Parliamentary Commanders-in-Chief on this day was peculiar. The Earl of Leven, after a vain effort to rally his Scotch infantry, had left the field under the persuasion that all was lost, and did not pause in his flight till he reached Leeds. Lords Manchester and Fairfax had also been carried away by the stream of fugitives, but they returned in time to see victory restored by the eastern counties army.

Amongst the Royalists slain was a Captain Charles Towneley, a Lancashire Papist. His widow was at Knaresborough, and came over on the morning after the fatal day to look for his body. She met on the field a Parliamentary officer, who inquired with sympathy the cause of her sorrow, and urged her to retire from so frightful a scene. She consented at last, and a trooper was called, who took her up behind him on his horse, and carried her to Knaresborough. On the way, she asked the name of the officer whose sympathy had touched her, and she was told it was Lieutenant-General Cromwell.

But Oliver had another and a nearer sorrow to assuage. Colonel Walton had to be informed of the loss of his eldest boy. The letter by which this sad duty was discharged is singularly touching, both in its endeavour to subordinate private grief to public blessings, in the kind suddenness of its announcement,

and in its allusion to his own experience.   It may well conclude
the story of Marston Moor :—

"DEAR SIR—It's our duty to sympathise in all mercies ; that we
praise the Lord together in chastisements or trials, that so we may sorrow
together.   Truly, England and the Church of God hath had a great favour
from the Lord in this great victory given unto us, such as the like never
was since the war began.   It had all the evidences of an absolute victory
obtained by the Lord's blessing upon the godly party principally.   We
never charged but we routed the enemy.   The left wing, which I com.
manded, being our own horse, saving a few Scots in our rear, beat all the
Prince's horse.   God made them as stubble to our swords.   We charged
their regiments of foot with our horse, and routed all we charged.   The
particulars I cannot relate now, but I believe of twenty thousand the
Prince hath not four thousand left.   Give glory, all the glory, to God.

" Sir, God hath taken away your eldest son by a cannon shot.   It broke
his leg.   We were necessitated to have it cut off, whereof he died.   Sir,
you know my trials this way.*   But the Lord supported me with this, that
the Lord took him unto the happiness we all pant and live for.   There is
your precious child full of glory, not to know sin nor sorrow any more.   He
was a gallant young man, exceeding gracious.   God give you His comfort.
Before his death he was so full of comfort, that to Frank Russell and
myself he could not express it—it was so great, above his pain.   This he
said to us.   Indeed it was admirable.   A little after, he said one thing lay
upon his spirit.   I asked him what that was.   He told me that it was that
God had not suffered him to be any more the executioner of His enemies.
At his fall, his horse being killed with the bullet, and, as I am informed,
three horses more, I am told he bid them open to the right and left, that he
might see the rogues run.   Truly, he was exceedingly beloved in the army
of all that knew him.   But few knew him ; for he was a precious young
man, fit for God.   You have cause to bless the Lord.   He is a glorious
saint in Heaven, wherein you ought exceedingly to rejoice.   Let this
drink up your sorrow ; seeing these are not feigned words to comfort you ;
but the thing is so real and undoubted a truth.   You may do all things by
the strength of Christ.   Seek that, and you shall easily bear your trial.
Let this public mercy to the Church of God make you forget your private
sorrow.   The Lord be your strength ; so prays your truly faithful and
loving brother,   OLIVER CROMWELL."

* This, no doubt, refers to the death of young Oliver.

CHAPTER X.

THE Battle of Marston Moor was an event no less important to the
personal career of Oliver Cromwell than to the course of the civil
war. It brought a complete triumph within the reach of Parliament; but it may fairly be doubted whether the prize would
ever have been boldly grasped had not the issue of that terrible
day conferred on the restorer of victory a preponderant influence,
and an inward consciousness of power to sway the destinies of
his country. The very splendour of the achievement daunted
the lordly generals of the Parliament; for they began to doubt
whither the wave of triumph on which they rode would carry
them. Hence they slackened in their zeal, delaying and tem-
porising, in the hope that some accommodation might be made
before the golden ball of kingly authority was shattered beyond
repair.

The result was that within a few months the scale of fortune
seemed to incline once more to the Royalist camp, and the year
closed with no more hope of an end to the nation's troubles than
had been felt after Edgehill. The best soldiers, those whose
hearts were in the cause, grew discontented, and a general feeling
of weariness and dissatisfaction crept over the whole Parliamentary party. Oliver shared the discontent; but he differed
from all the grumblers around him in this respect—that he had
the power to change the whole course of events, and to secure
the issue for which others only sighed and prayed. In estimating
his conduct during the year after Marston Moor, it is necessary
to remember this.

After the surrender of York, the commanders of the three
conjoined armies held a consultation, and agreed that they should
now separate their forces once more. The Scots undertook the
reduction of Newcastle; Lord Fairfax accepted the charge of
York, together with the duty of keeping an eye on the movements of Prince Rupert; and the Earl of Manchester fell back

on Lincolnshire and his associated counties, for which at this time he began to show an affection that hampered the movements of his victorious army. Amongst other reasons for returning towards Lincoln, he gave out that he intended to attempt the indomitable garrison of Newark; but the attempt was never made. While he was moving slowly southward, the Derby House Committee * wrote to him several times to urge the danger of allowing Prince Rupert to recruit himself unmolested in Lancashire. Essex and Waller, it was hoped, would be too strong for the King in the south-west. But if Rupert, reinforced by Irish troops and fresh levies, should go to the help of his royal uncle, the result would be doubtful. Again and again therefore the Committee advised, and indeed ordered, that the three generals in the north should unitedly provide against this danger, or that Lord Manchester should go himself, or that at least he should send a detachment to co-operate with forces to be collected from Nottingham and Derby. But the Earl was obstinate, and the reasons he gave for refusal were sometimes so irrelevant † that his more energetic officers became convinced he had other than strategic reasons for declining the service. In particular, his General of Horse believed that, with the strength they possessed, Newark might at least have been blockaded, and Rupert pursued at the same time. And, as Oliver afterwards stated in the House, he began to think there was "some reason to conceive that this backwardness was not from dulness or indisposedness, ‡ but from some principle of unwillingness in his lordship to have this war prosecuted unto a full victory, and a design, or desire, to have it ended by accommodation." For such a purpose, of course, "it might be disadvantageous to bring the King too low."

The Earl and his army reached Lincoln on August 4th (1644); and though the Committee were almost peremptory that he should now hasten into the west, he stayed there for a full month, doing little or nothing. From one of Cromwell's letters § we gather that during this time he had to magnify his office as Governor of

---

* A Select Committee of both Houses charged with the prosecution of the war.

† *E.g.*—On one occasion he replied that the Derby House Committee were quite mistaken about Rupert's being in Lancashire; they might make themselves easy on that score, for the Prince was gone into Cheshire; as though it were the county of Lancashire that was the special object of anxiety.

‡ That is, not from cowardice. § Letter XXII. in Carlyle.

L

the Isle of Ely, and his manner of doing it was characteristic.
The committee for the Isle, consisting of members of Parliament,
had taken it upon them, without reference to the Governor, to
release some prisoners committed by his subordinates. The tone
of his letter on the subject was ominous of the writer's conduct
in case more weighty responsibilities might seem to require
larger discretionary powers.

"I have given order to Captain Husband to see them re-committed to
the hands of my marshal, Richard White. And I must desire you for the
future not to entrench upon me so much as to release them, or any committed in the like case by myself or my deputy and commanders in the
garrison, until myself or some superior authority be satisfied in the cause,
and do give order in allowance of their enlargement. For I profess I will
be no governor, nor engage any other under me, to undertake such a charge
upon such weak terms."

During this month the affairs of the Parliament in the west
were going from bad to worse. The Earl of Essex had marched
towards Cornwall to attack Prince Maurice. The King had
watched him away, and then, just before the battle of Marston
Moor, had defeated Waller at Cropredy Bridge, and driven him
back towards London. Charles then followed in the steps of
Essex, and, in conjunction with his nephew, had pinned the Parliamentary general fast between Lostwithiel and the sea. The
Earl had never desired to humiliate the King; but the shameful
issue to which, by his indecisive tactics he had reduced himself
must surely have been a bitterness worse than death. He had to
choose between three cruel alternatives—death in a hopeless fight,
which must have involved thousands in his own fate, or a surrender with the probability of a traitor's fate, or a miserable
desertion of his own army in a flight by sea. He chose the last
as the least intolerable, getting away to Plymouth, and thence
to London, where the Parliament received him with a generosity
nobly significant of their faith and courage. His horse, under
Sir John Balfour, desperately cut their way through and escaped.
His foot, under Major-General Skippon, had nothing for it but
to lay down their arms.

It was on September 1st that this disastrous surrender was
made; and the Earl of Manchester, who by that date might
have been on the back of the King, was still fooling away his
time at Lincoln. Human life has, perhaps, few bitterer trials

than the misery felt by conscious capacity and courage when held down in a subordinate post, and forced to watch a good cause ruined by feebleness, futility, or short-sighted prudence in higher place.   And assuredly that misery was Cromwell's at this time. Witness his letter to Colonel Walton,* whose gallant son must now have seemed to have been sacrificed in vain. In heat of spirit and indignant impatience, we imagine, the bereaved father had written to Oliver, either on the first receipt of these dismal tidings, or while they were manifestly impending. Could nothing be done ?   Would the army of Lord Manchester look on in shameful idleness while the ungodly triumphed ? But the fault was not with Cromwell.

" We do with grief of heart," so he wrote, " resent the sad condition of our army in the west, and of affairs there.   That business has our hearts with it ; and truly, had we wings, we would fly thither.   So soon as my Lord and the foot set me loose, there shall be in me no want to hasten what I can in that service." . . . . " We have some amongst us much slow in action.   If we could all intend our own ends less, and our ease too, our business in this army would go on wheels for expedition."

There are other complaints in this letter, showing that the issue between Presbyterian uniformity and Independent unity in variety was rending the army with evil tempers. But Oliver, as usual, was willing to subordinate all secondary aims to the main issue.   " I hope the kingdom shall see that in the midst of our necessities we shall serve them without disputes."

It was no time to indulge in differences.   The King, having destroyed two armies of the Parliament, was now turning his face towards London ; and it was absolutely essential that the Earl of Manchester should throw himself in his way.   Still the Earl's movements were slow, and as his march brought him within easy reach of Westminster, he and Major-General Crawford came up to town in the middle of September.   Cromwell also naturally came up to watch their proceedings.   The Reverend Robert Baillie, Scottish Commissioner to the Assembly of Divines, believed that the " great Independent" made an attempt to get Crawford removed.   It would have been a happy thing for the harmony of military counsels if he had succeeded. We may doubt the information of Mr. Baillie ; for Oliver was not in the habit of attempting things impracticable.   But as he

* XXIII. in Carlyle.

did succeed in getting the Commons to pass an order for an accommodation between Presbyterians and Independents, the zealous Scottish preacher was ready to believe anything of him.

Slowly and listlessly the army crept on by Watford, by Maidenhead—waiting three days there for the repair of a bridge —till Reading was reached at the end of September. Cromwell did not cross the river, but was sent on into Oxfordshire, with his own regiment of horse and a few dragoons and foot-soldiers, to watch the Royalist head-quarters, and, if possible, capture Banbury. Up to the middle of October, the Derby House Committee kept urging on Lord Manchester a further march westward with all his force, while he, on the other hand, alleged many reasons why he should not remove further from his associated counties. Indeed, he seemed to hold himself at their service rather than the Parliament's, and, according to credible testimony, declared that, should they summon him, he would go back to them, "though he should be hanged for it." Suddenly, and apparently quite contrary to his commander's expectation, Cromwell appeared at Reading, not, perhaps, without some hint from London; and then the army moved on Basingstoke, near to which Basing House held out stoutly for the King.

Charles, meanwhile, was advancing by Weymouth, Dorchester, and Blandford, avoiding Salisbury, and driving Waller before him towards Andover. Cromwell afterwards maintained that the King might have been met west of Salisbury by the united armies, and that, if this had been done, Dennington Castle, near Newbury, with Basing House and Banbury, must have yielded, while the King would have been left without a single garrison east of Salisbury, except in Oxford, Winchester, and Wallingford.

As it was, Waller was driven to Basingstoke, sending on before him a "hot alarm" that the King was at Andover. The next move of Charles was to Newbury, where he drew up his forces in a strong position between the town and Castle Dennington; and here, at length, the Earl of Manchester was doomed to attack Majesty in person. But it was with no goodwill that he did it; and his strategy was apparently designed to prevent too decisive an engagement. The town of Newbury is situated in the fork between the river Kennet, which runs on past Reading, and the Lambourne stream that joins the Kennet from the north-west, a little eastward of the town. Castle Dennington stood on the left bank of the Lambourne; and, further down this stream, on the right or southern bank, was a house, known as Dolman's House, occupied by the King's army. Now, Cromwell afterwards maintained that the quickest and most feasible mode of attack on the King's position would have been to move from Basingstoke direct on Newbury, and either force the town from the south or cross the Kennet higher up, and come upon the royal army where it was comparatively unprotected. Instead of this, the Earl of Manchester went from Basingstoke round by Reading, consuming four days instead of one, and then approached the King's lines through lanes obstructed by breastworks, only to find a stream guarded by a castle and a fortified house between himself and the enemy. In fact, when they had fought their way so far, it was seen that the plan must be altered; and on Saturday, October 26th, the greater part of the united armies, under Waller and Cromwell, was sent to make a long detour to the north of Dennington Castle, and round by Boxford, on the north-west of Newbury, to attack from Speen, which lay on that side. This march lost another day, or rather the greater part of two days. Meanwhile the Earl was to occupy the village of Shaw on the east, and to make his attack as soon as he heard the cannon fire on the other side of the town.

The Speen party got into position and began their attack by two o'clock on Sunday. But though their shots were clearly heard, there was no co-operative movement on the other side. Cromwell declared that from the Earl's position at Shaw the enemy might have been seen "retreating from hedge to hedge in disorder;" but it was not until after sunset of that October day that the Earl fell on, and then in the dark his men fired upon each other. The attack from Speen was so far successful that the King was glad to retreat in the night; and then his forces were allowed to get away across the Lambourne, in the face of the Earl's detachment on the opposite bank. Nevertheless, two commissioners from the Parliament, who were present, reported to the House a satisfactory victory, and with characteristic piety concluded: "We desire to give God the glory, it being His work, and *upon His day.*"

On the next day, Monday, Cromwell and his horse soldiers pursued the enemy, but did not overtake them. Late at night he reached Blewberry, only to find that the King and all his forces had got clean over the Thames at Wallingford much earlier in the evening. There was no passage for the pursuers nearer than Abingdon; and both men and animals were tired out with continuous work for eight or nine days without proper refreshment or rest. On consultation, therefore, the commanders returned, and met on the way a message from the Earl recalling them. It seems pretty clear that Oliver was in no very good temper at this time. A few days afterwards, on the Earl's ordering the cavalry to a rendezvous, Cromwell asked his lordship " whether it was his intention to *flay the horses?* " And when the Earl looked astonished, he added that, through overwork, it would be only their skins that would be of any value. On another occasion, when the Earl appealed to his officers whether he had not always taken the advice of a council of war, Oliver, approaching as near an asseveration as was becoming in an Ironside, declared that the " man was a liar and a villain who would affirm the contrary." " Too much counsel, and too much sloth in action! " we can imagine him adding beneath his breath.

It was necessary to mention in some detail the symptoms of a disposition on the Earl's part to prevent too decisive an issue with the King; for this will put in its true light the action soon afterwards taken by Cromwell in the House of Commons. But having said so much, we need only add that his lordship positively declined the sensible suggestion of his subordinate to pass over the Thames and find winter quarters in Witney, Burford, and Woodstock, around Oxford; that by his dilatory and ill-conceived strategy, he allowed the King to come back to his former position for the relief of Dennington Castle, and to get away again unscathed; and that he continued to refuse every opportunity of effectively damaging the royal army. Cromwell and others argued that the success of Charles in relieving Dennington would be magnified into a great exploit, and obtain him support from abroad; whereas, if they could destroy his army now it would be his ruin. But this was just what Manchester did not want; and being at last badgered into plain speaking, he exclaimed: " If we should beat the King ninety-nine times he would still be King, and his posterity after him, and we should be subjects still; but if he should beat us only once we should be hanged, and our posterity undone!"

When language of this sort was used by military chiefs in the service of Parliament, it is not surprising if some men of uncompromising devotion to the rights of the Commonwealth began to think this sacredness of kingship might require some stern qualification. But for the present the King was suffered to get clear away, and marched to Marlborough, always on the look-out for an opportunity to relieve Basing House. The Earl of Manchester, on the other hand, notwithstanding many pretexts of an intention to defeat such a design, finally abandoned Newbury, and ignoring the danger at Basing drew all his army into winter quarters in and around Reading. The Earl of Essex perhaps had something to do with this. He took no active part in this Newbury campaign, being depressed bodily and mentally. But on November 10th Major-General Skippon wrote him an urgent letter on the miserable condition of his Excellency's own troops, entreating him to "use the best means he might think most meet that they might have a good winter quarter at Reading." *

The military commanders who were also Members of Parliament now betook themselves to Westminster, and then were begun the debates and cabals which ended in the "Self-denying Ordinance" and the "New Model Army." The part taken by Cromwell in these proceedings has been very variously judged. The upshot was that he shook off all opponents of his military policy; and though only second in command became the real director of the war. And as this success, combined with the entire break-up of the old constitution of the country, led on inevitably to his supreme elevation, those who see in his acceptance of power only the indulgence of a selfish ambition naturally look upon his conduct during the winter of 1644–5 as the beginning of his guilty intrigues to usurp the sovereignty of his country. But however plausible such a view may appear as we look back at the end of more than two centuries on events " foreshortened in the track of time," we have only to realise the actual position of affairs as they presented themselves to contemporaries in order to feel that this theory is in some respects incongruous with the facts of the case.

* Letter given by Rushworth.

The question between King and Parliament had now taken a form very different from the issue raised in 1640–1. At the beginning of the contest it was a difficulty between two equally essential elements in the constitution; and, however opinion might incline to the one or the other, the nation was unanimously loyal to both. A tolerable accommodation could then have been easily secured by the King's frank surrender of all novel pretensions to despotic power, and by his honest adherence to ancient charters. But the bitterness of the war had changed all that. There was now a desperate struggle between Crown and Commonwealth, from which it had become impossible that either could emerge unaltered. If Charles had succeeded, he would have taken good care to make himself and his posterity independent of Parliaments. And to the most far-seeing advocates of the Commonwealth, on the other hand, it was becoming plain that no peace could safely be made with the King, except on terms that had never been imposed on the Crown before. To such men as these it was intolerable that so much blood should have been shed, and so much misery endured, only to end in a weak compromise for the sake of a hollow reconciliation. This was not with them a mere matter of temper or self-will. To consent to such a course would have been in their view a crime against their country—nay, a treason against the cause of God.

Perhaps indeed the religious issues raised had changed their character more rapidly than those of secular policy. Episcopacy was now wholly gone; and the Presbyterian system elaborated by the Westminster Assembly was almost ready for authoritative establishment. But that new establishment threatened to be quite as intolerant, and far more inquisitorial than the old episcopal church. At the same time the half-dozen " dissenting brethren," who in the Assembly had vainly pleaded for a very modest and limited toleration, turned out to be the representatives of a formidable body of opinion out-of-doors. Unfortunately the rapid spread of such opinions was very little better represented in Parliament than it was in the Assembly of Divines.

But with the Army the case was different. The most permanent elements in the force were of course the regiments raised and maintained by the Eastern Counties' Association, under the diligent superintendence of Cromwell himself. While armies under Essex and Waller were alternately gathered and scattered, this eastern army retained its identity, matured its organization, and developed a powerful *esprit de corps.* Here Independency, in the sense of a refusal to be enslaved by a presbytery any more than by an episcopate, was unmistakably predominant; and to this body, by the selective operation of spiritual affinities, all men of open minds and strongly individual character were inevitably attracted. It was not merely the martial vigour of his future father-in-law that drew Ireton from Colonel Hutchinson to Oliver Cromwell. He, as well as Desborough, Harrison, Joyce, Peters, and many others, preferred service in this eastern army, because there, to an extent unknown elsewhere in the whole world at that time, fervour of spirit was found not inconsistent with diversity of operations.

But up to the autumn of 1644 the formal control of the army had been in the hands of men to whom a compromise was coming to be considered the only mode of deliverance from an intolerable position. And amongst the results of their distraction were intrigues in counsel and weakness of action, such as neutralized every Parliamentary victory, and threatened to keep open the wounds of the Commonwealth till it bled to death. Under these circumstances Cromwell felt very strongly that he must face one of two conclusions—either that he had been wrong ever to take up such a quarrel, and had spilt much blood unjustly, or else that he was bound to exert all the powers God had given him to have it prosecuted in a much more decisive manner. Of course the suggestion of the former alternative only served to clinch his adoption of the latter, and in this spirit he appeared once more in the House.

The failure of Lord Manchester to prevent the relief of Dennington Castle had given deep dissatisfaction in Parliament, even to the party most anxious for an accommodation with the King. They feared that Charles would now be less disposed to a compromise. All therefore agreed in demanding some explanation of miscarriages at Newbury. The members who belonged to the Derby House Committee were first questioned. And on November 23rd a resolution was carried requesting that Committee to prevent the advance of the King; "and likewise, upon the consideration of the present state and condition of the armies, as now disposed and commanded, to consider of a *frame or model* of the whole militia." This was the first suggestion of a complete reorganisation of the Parliamentary forces. But the time was not yet quite ripe. Through all the discussions of this and other motions the House felt that they were yet groping in the dark, and weakly avoiding the real issue. So far as we know, Cromwell was silent till nearly the end of November; but then he was ordered to give the House his account of the Newbury campaign.

Cromwell's statement,* made on November 25th, was in effect an indictment of the Earl of Manchester. He did not impute to him any insincerity or indolence, much less any want of courage, but he plainly charged him with an inclination to a weak compromise with the King, and with a disinclination to any such decisive successes in the field as would imperil this compromise. In accordance with this Cromwell alleged that ever since Marston Moor the Earl had been loth to follow up that success; that he had declined to carry out the instructions of the Derby House Committee; that he had kept his army needlessly long about Lincoln; and that, by his dilatory tactics, he had brought the King's victorious army much further east than it should have been allowed to come. As to the indecisive results at Newbury, Oliver's statement was simply a narrative of events as we have given them—a narrative in which he was afterwards confirmed by the testimony of Waller and others.† The speech made a deep impression on the House, and a select committee was appointed, with Mr. Zouch Tate, as chairman, to take evidence on the subject.

Of course the Earl of Manchester did not remain silent. On November 28th he gave in the House of Lords his own version of events since Marston Moor, and especially of the operations at Newbury. He insisted that he had never been wanting in devotion to the Parliamentary interest, and that all his strategy had received the full approval of his council of war. This assertion would on the face of it include his Lieutenant-General, who would have a prominent place in the council. On the other hand Cromwell had distinctly declared that the strategy of his commander was not only contrary to the opinion of the officers, but sometimes persisted in against their urgent entreaty. We are not, however, driven to fix upon either of them the odious

---

* See the "Quarrel of Manchester and Cromwell," &c.
† See "Notes of Evidence" taken by Tate's committee.

charge of untruth. It should be remembered that Cromwell's own branch of the army, the horse, was often detached on distant expeditions, and he would frequently be unavoidably absent from the council. On the other hand, a sullen acquiescence of the officers, under pressure of the General's authority, might be accepted by the latter as an approval, while they themselves were fretting against his decision. That any harmony of counsel in this army must have been very superficial indeed is sufficiently shown by the exhortations of the Derby House Committee against dissensions, and indeed by Lord Manchester's own complaints of the insubordination of his chief officer. Nor can we resist the impression that Oliver's despair of any effective use of his men under such direction had manifested itself in some slackness of military obedience. Submission to authority bent on ruinous compromise in a solemn issue between the life and death of a nation was a counsel of perfection to which, in truth, he never aspired.

A committee of Peers was now appointed to investigate the Earl's statement; and on December 2nd a conference was ordered between representatives of the two Houses. At this conference the Earl of Manchester's speech was supplemented by additional charges against Cromwell of sundry wild and revolutionary utterances. He was said to have expressed disaffection toward the Upper House and the whole order of nobility, and to have informed the Earl of Manchester that it would never be well in England till that nobleman was " plain Mr. Montague." Nay, he had been known to declare that in this contest he would not hold sacred the person of the King himself, but if he met his Majesty in battle would fire his pistol at the King as at another. Perhaps, in the eyes of the reverend brethren assembled in the Jerusalem Chamber, he had been guilty of even worse treason, in " speaking contumeliously of the Scots' intention in coming to England to establish their church government," to prevent which " he would draw his sword against them; also " (horribile dictu) "against the Assembly of Divines ! " And, to cap all, he had " threatened to make a party of sectaries to extort by force, both from King and Parliament, what conditions they thought meet."

There is an interesting air both of verisimilitude and exaggeration about this gossip. There can be no doubt that Cromwell had given occasion for it; and it is well to bear this in mind when we hear of the artful dissimulation with which he is said to have concealed his designs until they were ripe for accomplishment ; for, if these stories are only half true, he proclaimed openly his ultimate policy from the very beginning of his public influence.   As to his supposed design of enforcing his own religious opinions by the sword, he himself refers to the charge in a letter previously quoted.   " Because some of us are enemies to rapine and other wickednesses, we are said to be ' factious,' to ' seek to maintain our opinions in religion by force '—which we detest and abhor."*   The truth is, his opponents could not distinguish between such a design and the determination to resist by all possible means the substitution of a Board of Presbyterian Inquisitors for the Court of High Commission.

But the cabal against the irrepressible Independent was not confined to the Parliament House.   One evening in December Bulstrode Whitelocke and Serjeant Maynard received a pressing invitation to a late and very private meeting at Essex House, in the Strand.   Here they found in conclave the Scotch chancellor Loudoun with the Scots' Commissioners, also Denzil Holles, Sir Philip Stapylton, and Sir John Meyrick, all full of some urgent but mysterious business.

Lord Essex was too great a man for such an intrigue ; but the shelter of his house is significant of his favour.   When the company are assembled, Chancellor Loudoun addresses them in his high-pitched Scotch, and with words often difficult to southern ears.   But the main purport of his remarks is clear enough.   This Independent General of Horse, whose name has been so prominent since Marston Moor, is growing to be a danger to the comfortable settlement of Church and State.   His enmity to the Scots and their kirk is notorious : witness his violence towards the godly Crawford, and his patronage of the Anabaptist Packer.   Then his insubordination to my Lord Manchester—that " sweet, meek man," and his disaffection toward the Lord-General would suggest a fear that he holds all earthly authority in contempt.   But the solemn covenant, which this firebrand himself has taken, enforces the duty of putting down all incendiaries, and since this man Cromwell clearly is such it is their duty to put him down; at any rate, he would not be tolerated in Scotland.

* To Col. Walton, Letter XXIII. in Carlyle.

Then Bulstrode Whitelocke, seeing he is expected to give his opinion, does so with the caution that makes his fortune. No doubt the Chancellor was right in his views as to the deadly sin of incendiarism; and they in that room might all be convinced that Cromwell was so far guilty that he ought to be suppressed. But then, in England it was customary to require proof of such accusations. Definite words and actions justifying the epithet "incendiary" must be attested by credible witnesses. The Lieutenant-General was not without warm friends and admirers in Parliament as well as in the army; and it would be very unadvisable for the Lord-General to appear in this matter unless his proofs were very good. It is curious to note, after the gossiping stories related in the House of Peers and at the conference, that no proof seems to have been forthcoming; and after a little more head-shaking and sighs over the growth of license and insubordination, the little assembly separated in the dark night, and went home by boat, or along the muddy Strand, with a feeling of helplessness under some coming fate.

On December 4th Mr. Holles reported to the House of Commons the result of the conference held with the Lords to consider the Earl of Manchester's statement. Thereupon the Commons showed a disposition to resent the charges made against a member of their House, and a second committee, with Mr. John Lisle as chairman, was appointed to consider whether a question of privilege had not arisen. On the 9th the House itself went into committee to consider the sad condition of the kingdom by the continuance of the war; and an unwonted interval of silence, that no one cared to break, showed the depression, bordering on despair, to which all were reduced.

And now Cromwell felt the resistless impulse which always came upon him when a practical issue was clearly presented to his mind, on the decision of which depended the cause of God and the nation. He saw, as plainly as he saw the chairman in his chair, that the whole and sole cause of recent misfortunes was the predominant influence of Essex, Manchester, and the Scots. So long as this prevailed, the everlasting see-saw of victory and defeat would always go on; and there was a growing danger that the nation, in disgust and weariness, would throw the Parliament over, and let the King have his way. The one and only condition of success was the transference of power from the devotees of a futile compromise to the more resolute party, in whose eyes both King and Presbytery were as nothing compared with a free England. True, he was himself now the most formidable representative of that party, and in seeking to bring it to the front he was open to the charge of selfishly pursuing his own interest. But this circumstance could not obscure the fact that his policy was the sound and true one. Even if he could have foreseen, which is more than doubtful, how events would from this time lay him open to the charge of unpatriotic ambition, he was placed in this dilemma, that either he must submit to that, or stand self-convicted of unpatriotic cowardice. And so, with that piercing and searching earnestness which made itself felt in every vibration of his "sharp, untuneable voice," he sprang to his feet, delaring that "it was now a time to speak, or for ever hold the tongue."

The business now, he declared, was "to save a nation out of a bleeding, nay, a dying condition." If there was any more spinning out of the war, the kingdom would hate the name of a Parliament. In fact there were murmurs on all sides that members in great place found it suit their purpose to prolong the war. This might not be true; but the very fact of its being said might endanger the whole issue of the conflict. Then, with that quick perception of the line of least resistance, which may be called tact or cunning according to our leanings, he deprecated raising any personal questions.

"For as I must acknowledge myself guilty of oversights, so I know they can rarely be avoided in military affairs. Therefore, waving a strict enquiry into the causes of these things, let us apply ourselves to the remedy, which is most necessary. And I hope we have such true English hearts, and zealous affections towards the general weal of our mother country, as no members of either House will scruple to deny themselves, and their own private interests, for the public good; nor account it to be a dishonour done to them, whatever the Parliament shall resolve upon in this weighty matter."

On this hint, Mr. Zouch Tate spoke, and proposed that during the time of the war no member of either House should hold "any office or command, military or civil," granted by Parliamentary authority, and "that an Ordinance might be brought in accordingly." The resolution was opposed by

Bulstrode Whitelocke and others, who pointed out that the army would thus be deprived, by a stroke of the pen, of nearly all the commanders in whom the soldiers had any confidence; and some members went so far as to express a fear that the army would not submit to such an Ordinance. This brought out Cromwell again, who, speaking now to the resolution, professed that he had no apprehension about the army. "I can speak for my own soldiers," he said, "that they look not upon me, but upon you; and for you they will fight, and live and die in your cause; and if others be of that mind that they are of, you need not fear them. They do not idolize me, but look upon the cause they fight for. You may lay upon them what commands you please; they will obey your commands *in that cause they fight for.*"*

His arguments prevailed. The Self-denying Ordinance, as it was called, was brought in, carried, and sent up to the Lords. Here it naturally met with a cold welcome, because it excluded the whole peerage from military command. The Lords insisted on their ancient right to be leaders in war; and after a futile conference with the Lower House, rejected the Ordinance on January 15th, 1644-5.

Meanwhile the Commons were already taking up the matter by a new handle. They discussed the necessity for re-casting the whole army; and on January 28th resolved that all the Parliamentary forces should be re-organised into one body of 22,000 men, consisting of 14,400 foot, 6,600 horse, and 1,000 dragoons. Sir Thomas Fairfax was to be Commander-in-Chief, and his Major-General was to be Sir Philip Skippon; but the second place, that of Lieutenant-General, was significantly left vacant. The Lords did not resist the passage of this new model; but they strongly insisted that all officers should sign the Covenant as a condition of their engagement. To this however there was a growing objection in the Commons; and a compromise was effected by which a time of grace was allowed to those who had not already signed.

After this there seemed little to be gained by resisting the Self-denying Ordinance. Lords Essex, Denbigh, and Manchester resigned their commissions on April 2nd, and on the following

---

* Observe, *not against* that cause : the Parliament had better not try that; is not supposed at present to dream of trying it.

day the Ordinance passed the Upper House. It had, however, been somewhat modified from its original form. It was now made to apply only to members holding commands at that date, and did not exclude either Lords or Commons from future appointments. Meantime, before the Ordinance became law, hostilities had been resumed; and officers in the field were necessarily exempted from its operation until a convenient moment for superseding them. But it was ultimately enforced in every case except that of Lieutenant-General Cromwell. And why was he excepted? The answer is simply that to have enforced it against him would have been to sacrifice military success to a mere punctilio of consistency.

Surely every one who voted in the Lower House for the Self-denying Ordinance and the New Model knew very well that the real object was to get rid of Essex, Manchester, Denbigh, and Waller, with all their habits of vacillation and inefficiency. Of course it would have been a more straightforward thing to have called upon them to resign. But the other was the easier thing, and where bodies like Parliament are concerned, managers of new proposals may fairly be excused for following the line of least resistance, unless indeed that should involve some dereliction of principle. But there was nothing wrong in ruling that all members alike must give up their commands; and this mode of procedure gained the desired end better than any other could have done. Witness the Rev. Robert Baillie, who on the 26th December wrote :—

"The House of Commons in one hour has ended all the quarrels which was betwixt Manchester and Cromwell, all the obloquies against the General, the grumblings against the proceedings of many members of their House. They have taken all office from all the members of both Houses. This done on a sudden, in one session, with great unanimity, is still more and more admired by some as a most wise, necessary, and heroic action; by others as the most rash, hazardous, and unjust action as ever Parliament did."

It need scarcely be said that those only were of the latter opinion who thought the King and Presbytery of more importance than justice and freedom.

But what was Cromwell's part in it? Was he playing a cunning game for his own personal advancement, or was he honestly trying to do his duty as a Christian patriot from moment to moment, when he could not see half a dozen steps before him? The truth is, the gamester's cunning imputed to him was too deep and subtle and far-reaching for credibility. For the interest of the cause he had at heart, the course was plain. It would have been difficult to find worse commanders than Essex and Manchester. Fairfax, at any rate, was devoted, heart and soul, to the cause. But so far as Cromwell's own prospects of advancement were concerned, the decision was by no means so easy. No doubt there was talk of making him an exception, and he could not but be aware of it. But in a House where Presbyterianism was strongly predominant it was certain that nothing but overwhelming necessity would produce a majority in favour of excepting from the Ordinance so prominent an Independent; and in fact no such exception was actually made. What happened was, that the dire need of the army, and Cromwell's acknowledged ability to meet it, brought about a grudging leave of absence from the House—a leave extended from time to time, until, in the rush of events to their sanguinary end, the formality became too absurd for repetition.

CHAPTER XI.

NASEBY.*

AT the opening of the campaign of 1645 the victory of Marston Moor had been apparently neutralised, and the hopes of the Royalists had been greatly revived. Westward of a line drawn from Weymouth to Basing House and thence to Oxford the King's authority was supreme over the whole south, with the exception of a very few garrisons, notably Plymouth, Taunton, and Abingdon, which held out for the Parliament. In this district Charles had at least 14,000 men under Lords Goring and Hopton, Sir Richard Greenville, and Sir John Digby. The Parliament had no hold on Wales. The Midlands were at the King's command, with the exception of the larger towns, such as Leicester, Nottingham, Stafford, and Shrewsbury. In Scotland Montrose had gained successes which, according to his own report, would enable him soon to bring important reinforcements to the King. Even Kent and Sussex were fermenting with discontent. Indeed, the only part of the kingdom where the Parliamentary interest was both supreme and impregnable was the eastern district extending from the Thames to the Humber; the district dominated by the Association founded, organised, and inspired by Oliver Cromwell.

The royal hopes were still further encouraged by the open issue now raised between the more timid and the more resolute of the Parliamentary party. It is therefore not surprising that Charles broke off with indifference the lingering negotiations at Uxbridge, or that worldly-wise moderates, like the Rev. Robert Baillie, looked forward with dismay to the future. But Parliamentary difficulties, instead of having the effect anticipated by Charles, had driven irresolute and fearful members to surrender the guidance of affairs to men who knew their own minds. And when the Royal Commissioners stiffly declined concessions on the

* In this and succeeding chapters, to the end of the first civil war, Joshua Sprigge's "Anglia Rediviva" is generally followed.

Church question, considerable progress had already been made with the New Model Army.

The scheme for this new army was completed in February, but it could not become an accomplished fact until the old commanders had laid down their commissions. Meantime, the state of things in the west of England demanded immediate attention. Lord Goring, with his head-quarters at Bruton, in Somersetshire, was busy recruiting and organising his forces, menacing such garrisons as remained to the Parliament, and threatening a general advance eastwards. Sir William Waller and Cromwell, in accordance with a resolution of the House of Commons, were sent down to oppose him. At the beginning of April they reached Bruton. Lord Goring retreated on Wells and Glastonbury, and in the prospect of his being reinforced by Sir Richard Grenville, and joined by Prince Rupert, they did not think it prudent to follow him. They therefore retired to Salisbury. Sir Thomas Fairfax had then assumed the chief command, having his head-quarters at Windsor. To him Cromwell wrote, reporting the expected concentration of the enemy, and pressing for reinforcements to prevent " the shame and hazard of a further retreat." It does not appear what measures the new General-in-Chief took in consequence of this letter. But before the end of the month Cromwell was in some way released from this service in the west, and on the 22nd of April arrived at Windsor, to take leave of Sir Thomas Fairfax, and surrender his commission in accordance with the Self-denying Ordinance.

Whether he really expected that his resignation would be accepted is an unprofitable, and perhaps an unanswerable, question. He may very well have thought it unlikely, or, at any rate, that events would speedily compel a recourse to his services. But the only question interesting to us is that of his good faith; and opinions on this point will necessarily vary according to our estimate of the man's character, and also of the obviously imperative need for his services at the time.

Be that as it may, on the morning of the 23rd of April, before Oliver had risen from his bed, a dispatch came from the Committee of both kingdoms ordering him instantly to take the field once more. The occasion was the detachment of 2,000 men by Prince Rupert from Worcester to Oxford to convoy the King to the former town. For an attack on this convoy the

M 2

Committee naturally thought that no one was so well fitted as
the now famous General of Horse.   So far as energy and swiftness could go, the Committee had no reason for disappointment.
The order was received early on Wednesday.   Oliver instantly
fixed the rendezvous for his troops at Watlington, twenty miles
away, in Oxfordshire.   All being arrived there, he sent on
Major-General Browne to obtain information about the starting
of the convoy, and himself, with the main force, followed more
slowly to Wheatley Bridge, a distance of sixteen miles.   Some
" Oxford scholars," probably taking their " constitutional,"
were disagreeably surprised at falling in with a troop of grave,
stern soldiers, who in a tone that forbade all trifling demanded
information about the intended convoy.   From what they said
Cromwell gathered that the departure was imminent.   From
other sources he learned also that the Earl of Northampton's
regiment was at Islip Bridge, a few miles to the north of
Oxford.   The day was already declining when he hurried off a
forlorn hope to surprise this regiment.   But when the main body
came up, after a march in all of more than twenty-five miles in
that day, it was found that through some mistake the Royalists
had received warning, and were gone, no doubt to effect a concentration with others.

   That night Cromwell and his troops remained at Islip,
and the next morning, Thursday, April 24th, the Royalists,
now increased to three regiments, suddenly fell upon him.
But the discipline of his men was superior to any surprise.
Sir Thomas Fairfax's regiment, formerly Cromwell's own,
was instantly in fighting order, and the rest drew out
steadily.   A single troop charged and broke a whole squadron of
the enemy.   The whole Royalist force was soon in full flight,
vigorously pursued by Cromwell's men.   Then the enemy separated, some flying to Oxford, others to Woodstock, and a considerable part to Bletchington, to the north of Islip.   These
last found refuge in a fortified house belonging to Sir Thomas
Cogan, and kept by a garrison of two hundred men under
Colonel Windebank, son of the unfortunate secretary.   The
son, destined to a worse fate than his father, was summoned
by Cromwell to surrender, bargained and haggled till midnight, and then accepted permission to depart, leaving his arms,
ammunition, and horses.   Better for him if he had fought to the

death; for in a few days he was condemned as a coward, and shot dead as a warning to others.

On the 25th of April, Cromwell sent a dispatch to the Derby House Committee, reporting how, in obedience to their command, he had in three days marched some fifty miles, fought a battle, scattered the enemy, captured a strong-hold, and taken two hundred prisoners, besides nearly five hundred horses, arms, and ammunition. "This was the mercy of God," he wrote. And surely it is not a real insight into human nature which finds hypocrisy in his words. They are the words of a man astonished and grateful, but of one who never dreamed of boasting of his own energy and swiftness. "His mercy appears in this also," he adds, "that I did much doubt the storming of the house, it being strong and well manned, and I having few dragoons, and this being not my business—and yet we got it." On the day this dispatch was written, the spoils of victory were sent off to Aylesbury,* and Cromwell hastened off towards Radcott Bridge. At Bampton, near Witney, on the 26th, he fell in with Sir William Vaughan, commanding 350 men, every one of whom he captured or killed.

The unexpected success at Bletchington encouraged an attempt to frighten the Governor of Faringdon into surrender. But this Governor, Roger Burgess by name, was made of sterner stuff than poor Windebank, and Oliver was provoked to attempt a storm. He was, however, no better provided with the means for such an attack than he had been at Bletchington, and he had to give it up—one of the very few instances in which Cromwell attempted any military operation that he could not accomplish.

The New Model Army under Sir Thomas Fairfax was now ready to march; but almost to the last moment its Parliamentary masters had not made up their minds what to do with it. Should it march into the west, or should it besiege Oxford? After a debate the former course was adopted. The idea, no doubt, was that the Scottish army of 21,000 in the north was in a position to prevent the King's junction with Montrose, or to threaten his rear, and co-operate with the forces of the Eastern Association, if he should be bold enough to make a dash on London. In the west, on the other hand, the relief of Taunton, hard pressed by

* Sprigge. Carlyle says Abingdon.

the Royalists, seemed absolutely essential, unless the whole of that region was to be abandoned. Second thoughts suggested that the shortest way to victory was to strike at the King himself; and more by good luck than good management they ultimately accomplished both aims.

Having received his orders, the new General-in-Chief marched from Windsor through Reading, and reached Newbury on May 2nd. To this place Cromwell came over from Faringdon to meet him. That night some of Oliver's men, being out towards Marlborough, obtained information of Colonel Goring's intention to fall upon them within a few hours. Instantly they sent word to their commander, and he was back at his post as speedily as a horse could carry him. But before he could dispose his men, Colonel Goring had secured Radcott Bridge. Cromwell, however, succeeded in getting a party of horse over the river, under the command of Major Bethel; but this officer, venturing too far, was cut off, and taken prisoner. In the course of the day Cromwell passed the river by another bridge,* and Goring, either through discretion or necessity, retired.

Fairfax vigorously continued his march towards the west. But when he had reached Blandford, in Dorset, on May 7th, his advance was peremptorily stopped. He was ordered to content himself with sending a detachment for the relief of Taunton, while he himself was to rejoin Cromwell before Oxford. The reason for this change of counsel was that Prince Rupert was marching to effect a junction with the King, and the Parliament found that, after all, they had better rely for protection on their own army.

Fairfax instantly obeyed; but fortunately the news of his having done so did not reach Taunton; and the detachment he sent on was supposed by the besiegers to be the vanguard of his whole army. They accordingly raised the siege, and the town was saved. Meanwhile Fairfax retraced his steps towards Oxford, and received, almost daily, from the Committee of both kingdoms letters of command and direction, which left him little discretion. These letters showed, at any rate, the Parliament's supreme confidence in its power to control the demon of militarism which it had evoked. The Committee, according to their wisdom, detached forces hither and thither as seemed good to them, and, in par-

* "Newbridge," Sprigge.

ticular, dictated the operations of Lieutenant-General Cromwell
with the most perfect assurance that he was only a tool in their
hands. When Charles left Oxford, they ordered Cromwell to
attend him. They then directed that 2,500 of Cromwell's men
should go north, under command of Colonel Vermuyden, to
strengthen the Scots.* They recalled Oliver from attending
upon Charles, told him to put a garrison into Bletchington, and to
prevent supplies being carried into Oxford. They ordered Fairfax
to hurry forward what horse he could spare for the same purpose,
and himself to sit down before Oxford as soon as possible.

What Fairfax thought of the military genius of his masters
is perhaps suggested by the fact that, though he sat down before
Oxford, as ordered, he refrained from summoning the town,
apparently, as was thought at the time, that he " might draw off
with the less dishonour." And he had good reason for his
doubts. The King had gone north to save Chester besieged by
Sir William Brereton, and to strengthen his communications
towards Scotland. Sir William Brereton, finding himself unsup-
ported, raised the siege, and the King then turned eastward,
through the Midlands, as if making for the invincible " Association." The Parliament, knowing how much they owed to that
organization, were alarmed at this movement, and immediately
bethought themselves of the man who had not only founded the
union, but remained still its life and soul. They wrote to Cromwell, ordering him to Ely at once, and merely informed his Commander-in-Chief that they had done so. The instruction they
gave, that Oliver should only take four troops of horse with him,
shows how entirely they relied upon his personal influence and
power of inspiring others.

Nor were they disappointed. Always going straight to the
main issue, Oliver busied himself for five or six days " to secure
that part of the Isle of Ely where he conceived most danger to
be." On June 4th he was in his native town. Here we find
him writing to Sir Thomas Fairfax :—" I most humbly beseech
you to pardon my long silence. I am conscious of the fault, considering the great obligations lying upon me." Then he briefly
recounts the arrangements he has made, and concludes with a
" humble suit," that the bearer of the letter, " a most honest

---

* " Lieutenant-General Cromwell being, for I know not what reason, not so
acceptable to their army," says Joshua Sprigge.—" Anglia Rediviva," p. 20.

man," "nominated to the Model," may be reappointed captain of horse. Two days afterwards he signs—ninth among the Cambridge Committee—an urgent appeal to the Deputy-Lieutenants of Suffolk to raise horse and foot sufficient to meet the emergency.

But now the Parliament, through the Derby House Committee, had sent fresh orders to Fairfax, not without startling necessity. On May 29th the King reached Leicester from Ashby. Next morning he battered his way through the Newark* wall and at several other points, and gave up the town to pillage on his entrance. So serious a loss increased almost to a panic the alarm of Parliament for the eastern counties. Fairfax must rise instantly, and follow the royal army. This was the most welcome service which his masters had yet required from him ; and the movements culminating in Naseby Field were the most glorious passage in his life.

After refreshing his soldiers for a day or two with the plunder of Leicester, the King marched due south to Daventry, as though intending the relief of Oxford. But on June 4th Fairfax had broken up from this town, and by the 7th was at Sherringham near Newport Pagnel, his first object being to throw himself between Charles and the eastern counties. On that day he communicated with his comrade, Cromwell, that the latter might know whither to send in case of need. On the next day scouts discovered that his Majesty was hunting about Daventry. And now—a great battle being apparently imminent—an uncontrollable desire arose both among officers and men to have with them the cavalry chief, whose onset had already begun to be regarded, both among friends and foes, as resistless. A letter was despatched to Westminster, begging that Cromwell might be sent to them, and the request was instantly granted.

On the 13th, at Gilsborough, while a council of war in the early morning was earnestly debating the impending struggle, a rumour ran through the camp that Oliver was at hand, and loud and heartfelt were the cries of welcome with which he was hailed as he rode in with 600 troopers. In Fairfax's letter to Cromwell, written two days previously, he says :—

"You will find, by the inclosed vote of the House of Commons, a liberty given me to appoint you Lieutenant-General of the horse of this army

* A large outwork of Leicester Castle.

during such time as that House shall be pleased to dispense with your attendance. You cannot expect but that I make use of so good an advantage, as I apprehend this to be, to the public good."

He adds, significantly, that the enemy "are, as we hear, more horse than foot, and make their horse their confidence." This rumour had, no doubt, quickened the desire of the new army to have with them the man who had quenched the fiery Rupert as a torrent might extinguish a squib.[*]

The King had now become alarmed. For some days he had been aware that Fairfax was in his neighbourhood; but was very imperfectly informed both as to the strength and the design of the Parliamentary general. Indeed down to Friday, June 12th, the nearness of his adversaries does not seem to have entered at all into the calculations of Charles. In this security he was very rudely disturbed on the Friday by an incursion of a party of Fairfax's horse, who took prisoners and raised a momentary panic, of which however they were not strong enough to avail themselves further. That night the King fired his camp and retired on Market Harborough, apparently under the impression that he would not be followed, and that it was not worth his while to force a battle. The dilatory tactics of his former opponents, Essex and Manchester, had in a sense demoralized him.

But on that Friday he was to experience for the first time how stern and swift and resolute was the temper of the New Model Army. Major Harrison was despatched towards Daventry to make sure of the enemy's movements. Colonel Ireton was instructed to march northwards as close to their flank as he could, and, if he saw any good chance, to fall on. The whole army then broke up from Gilsborough and marched flank to flank with the King towards the north. In the evening the main body reached Gilling, in the northern border of Northamptonshire; and here Fairfax learned how Ireton had found the rear of the enemy in Naseby village, had routed them out of their

* In a letter from a Northampton gentleman (King's Pamphlets, No. 212), the writer says that, on the Thursday evening (11th), the King's army were much impressed by the news "that *Ironsides was coming* to join with the Parliament's army." This, he adds, was told to Sir Thomas Fairfax by a countryman next day. The passage is interesting, as showing that the term "Ironsides" was originally a personal *soubriquet* of Cromwell, and that by this time it was current in the Parliamentary army. It is from this letter also we learn that when "Ironsides" actually arrived the cavalry "gave a great shout for joy of his coming to them."

quarters just as they were making themselves comfortable for the
night, had forced them a mile or two further on their journey,
and had captured many prisoners. This news reaching the King
in the brief summer night somewhat alarmed him for his own
safety. He pushed on to Harborough, and, rousing Prince
Rupert from sleep, held a hasty council of war. The majority
are said to have been in favour of continued retreat. But the
King, with greater spirit, would not hear of it, and insisted on
an instant concentration towards the rear with a view to give
battle.

Almost simultaneously with this royal resolve, which must
have been announced in the small hours of Saturday morning
(June 14, 1645) Sir Thomas Fairfax with his main body advanced from Gilsborough to Naseby, and soon fixed upon the
battle-field. He was prompted in his choice by the sight of the
advanced guard of the Royalists, who appeared in successive
ranks over the top of a hill toward Harborough, and who were
evidently feeling their way toward their right. The object of
this was to secure the advantage of the wind, which was blowing
from the west. A little to the north-west of Naseby village was
a fallow field, lying along a broad ledge in the slope that falls
away to the north. Fairfax saw that he could here conceal
his line of battle from the approaching enemy by keeping his
men back from the edge of the slope.* In fact King Charles
was informed that the rebels were in full flight to Northampton.
The Royalists imagined themselves to be pursuing a demoralized
enemy, and when they found their mistake the discovery had to
some extent the shock of a surprise.

The battle was arranged mainly according to a plan of
Major-General Skippon. But such conflicts in those times
admitted of little originality, and both as regards the order of
battle and the events of the day, there was a striking analogy
to the fight on Marston Moor. The numbers engaged on
each side were a little smaller, both being, as nearly as can
be ascertained, under 20,000. The arrangement of forces was
very similar. Each army ranged its cavalry on the wings
and its foot in the centre; but on this occasion pieces of
ordnance were introduced between the different sections of the
main lines. This time Ireton had the left wing, with five

* Sprigge, p. 34.

regiments of horse, and a small division of 200 from the eastern counties. As at Marston Moor, the extreme left was protected by trees or a hedgerow, along which a party of dragoons were disposed. To Ireton's right rear was Naseby village, and between him and the village was the army train, guarded by musketeers. The centre was under Skippon, with whom was Sir Thomas Fairfax himself. Cromwell, with six regiments of horse, held the right of the position. There were also reserves in the rear, commanded by Rainsborough, Hammond, and Pride. In the Royalist army the Princes Rupert and Maurice had the right wing. The King himself, supported by Lord Barnard, commanded the centre, and Sir Marmaduke Langdale led the cavalry on the left.

In addition to his special charge of the right wing, Cromwell had the general ordering of the cavalry; and Skippon's arrangements were so incomplete when the enemy were close at hand, that it needed all Oliver's energy to get the troops into position. The historian of the New Model says, " The enemy came on amain in passing good order, while our army was yet in disorder, or the order of it but an embryo."* It was in allusion to this that Cromwell said afterwards :—

"I can say this of Naseby, that when I saw the army draw up and march in gallant order towards us, and we a company of poor ignorant men, to seek how to order our battle, the General having commanded me to order all the horse, I could not—riding alone about my business—but smile out to God in praises, in assurance of victory, because God would by things that are not bring to nought things that are; of which I had great assurance. And God did it."†

The issue of the battle justified Cromwell's faith; but it at the same time illustrated his fortunate habit of heightening enthusiasm by discipline. It was not improbably a desire to gain time which suggested to Fairfax the idea of sending forward a "forlorn hope" of 500 men, who first undeceived the Royalists as to his flight. The five hundred, when they were hard pressed, retreated, and the fight soon became general. When the Royalist right wing, under Rupert and

* Sprigge, p. 43.
† K.P., No. 217, § 18, from "The copy of Lieut.-General Cromwell his Letter to a worthy Member of the House of Commons," July, 1645; not given by Carlyle.

Maurice, came in sight of Ireton's men as the latter advanced towards the slope, the Royalists made a sudden halt, as though surprised at the attitude and order of their opponents. Ireton's men, being thrown out of line by the roughness of the ground, paused also until all had formed up. Then the Royalists advanced again; Ireton's trumpeters sounded a charge, and both sides fell on. Rupert, on the extreme flank, with his usual impetuosity broke through the regiments of Colonel Butler and Colonel Vermuyden, and, carrying all before him, pursued the chase past the army train towards Naseby. Prince Maurice found greater difficulty. Ireton's own regiment sustained the shock, and afterwards charged the Royalist centre. Then Ireton himself received two pike wounds, and was for awhile made prisoner. Thus the Parliamentary left wing was shattered and broken.

In the centre, under Fairfax, the issue was more doubtful. All except his own regiment gave way. Many of them fled behind the reserves, and were only rallied with great difficulty. But the one steadfast regiment kept the disorder from turning to a rout. Major-General Skippon was wounded in the side, but doggedly declared he would not stir so long as a man would stand.

Just as at Marston Moor, it was the wing led by Cromwell that decided the day. Dashing against Langdale's troops, the Ironsides fired their pistols at close quarters, and fought furiously at the sword's point, until they broke the ranks of their opponents, and drove them in disorder behind the main body of the Royalist foot. The strength of that foot was Lord Barnard's division, which resisted every attack, and formed a rallying point for the broken troops. Cromwell now ordered a part of his force to keep back Langdale's defeated regiments, while with the rest he attacked Lord Barnard's foot in the rear. But even thus no impression was made. Cromwell then took the liberty of hastening up the Lord-General's own regiment of foot to attack the sturdy foe in front. Fairfax's men fell upon them with the butt-ends of their muskets, while Cromwell's horse hacked at them and plunged through them from the rear. And thus these men fell in the place where they stood, not less honoured in such a defeat than in victory. The only forces King Charles now had on the field in anything like order were portions of his cavalry. Prince Rupert, unwarned by experience, had pursued too far. In returning he made an attempt on the train. But the guard offered a stiff resistance, and he could see enough of the battle-field to be sure that he was needed elsewhere. He moved off, therefore, towards his royal uncle, followed by the rallying cavalry of the troops he had previously chased.

The King now formed another line, consisting wholly of horse; and Fairfax judged it prudent to reorganize his own line as well. He formed it entirely anew, with foot in the centre and cavalry on the wings, as before. The effect showed the prudence of risking a little delay; for the Royalists, seeing they were to be charged afresh by a complete army of horse, foot, and artillery, would not abide this new adventure, but turned and galloped for life toward Leicester town, sixteen miles away. The pursuit was disastrous for them, for they were closely followed and slaughtered to within two miles of their city of refuge. The whole train of artillery was captured, also about five thousand prisoners, including many officers of rank. The number killed could not be ascertained. But in a political point of view the most important prize of the battle was the King's cabinet containing the secret correspondence, which proved his readiness to employ papists, foreigners, or any power on earth that would place an unmanageable people at his feet.

CHAPTER XII.

THE TRIUMPH OF THE NEW MODEL.

THE material results and the moral effect of the victory at Naseby were alike enormous. How completely the royal army was scattered is shown by the fact that while the King, followed only by a feeble guard, escaped into Wales and took refuge in Ragland Castle, the commander of his left wing, Sir Marmaduke Langdale, made for Newark, with the idea of joining Montrose in Scotland. The Royalists had no longer any field force worthy of consideration in all the Midlands or the north of England. At the same time the revelations of the King's cabinet, with its proofs of his intrigues for foreign assistance, and of his promise to suspend the penal laws against Catholics in return for help from Ireland, produced a moral effect that seemed to increase rather than diminish with lapse of time.

On the third day after the battle Leicester was re-captured in a miserable condition through the plunder it had suffered. After the re-establishment of order and security here, it became a question for anxious consideration what the next aim of the victorious army should be. And it will be well to give in outline the military operations designed and accomplished during the months of July, August, and September, before describing the special services in which Cromwell was specially prominent.

The idea was entertained of sending a party of horse in pursuit of the King,* and it is difficult for us to conceive why this was not done. But in those days the king's name was literally a tower of strength. The horror excited by Cromwell's blunt declaration of his readiness to fire his pistol in battle against the King as against any other foe, showed clearly that the Parliamentary party still clung to the sacredness of majesty as rather a point of religion than a political doctrine. Generally speaking, the expectation of the Parliamentary party was that, when all

* Sprigge, p. 52: "The thoughts of the west occasioned the deferring of the debate thereof for the present."

evil counsellors had been beaten away from the royal presence, the King, in sheer helplessness, would follow the advice of his Parliament. So long as such a hope could be cherished, the capture of the King could not by any means be regarded as an unmixed benefit. On the other hand, the west of England, held for his father by the Prince of Wales, and defended by Goring, Hopton, and Greenville, had resources and population enough at least to prolong the war, and perhaps even to turn the tide of success again.

But Fairfax, as faithful in his obedience as George Washington in an after age, would not take upon himself to decide the use to be made of his army, and referred the question to the Parliament. Yet, to save time, he left Leicester on Midsummer Day, and shaped his course so that on receiving directions from London, he could turn towards either Hereford or Taunton. The Committee of both kingdoms decided for a campaign in the west, and thither accordingly Fairfax hastened his march. By Salisbury, Blandford, and Dorchester he held his way, till in Beaminster, on July 5th, he heard that the siege of Taunton had been already raised. Goring's movements left it uncertain whether his intention was to retreat or to fight. But Fairfax came up with him at Langport, and after a confused and obstinate contest, compelled him to fly to Barnstaple, while the Prince of Wales, who had been in the latter town, removed for greater safety to Launceston.

On July 23rd Bridgewater was stormed, after long and earnest exhortations by Hugh Peters, who was said to be as valiant in deed as in word. Soon afterwards (July 29th, 1645), Bath surrendered to Colonel Rich, commanding only a detachment of horse and dragoons; and the circumstances of that surrender showed the demoralisation that was eating the heart out of all Royalist forces. The whole of Somerset was now regained for the Parliament, with the one conspicuous exception of Bristol; and the siege of such a place required elaborate preparations, both material and moral.

A fast was kept throughout the army on Friday, August 29th, "to seek God for a blessing on the designs against Bristol." Mr. Del and Mr. Peters prayed and preached at headquarters, the General and Lieutenant-General devoutly attending. Nor were preachers or hearers distracted from their devotions by

the noise of a sally, in the course of which Prince Rupert captured a few prisoners.   Sermons ended, a solemn council of war
was called, the purport of which seems to have been quite as
much to assault the devil and his angels as to capture Bristol;
for the first subject of consideration was the vices of the army.
It had vices, then, this army of saints!   Alas, the flesh is weak,
and soldiering is a life of temptation.   But the council severely
determined that, cost what it might, these vices should be
punished; and then with satisfied consciences proceeded to discuss the possibility of storming the town.

   While they were in debate news came that Montrose
had beaten their Scottish brethren, and was marching on
Edinburgh; also that the King instead of going north
as was expected, had made his way unmolested to Bedford,
and was turning westward again, presumably to gather force
for the relief of Bristol.   The movements of the Prince of
Wales and also of Goring showed a design of attacking the
besiegers, and Greenville was to bring up forces from the
recesses of Cornwall for the purpose.   If half of these designs
should succeed, the position of the army would be very precarious; for it was barely strong enough for the siege, and
must be consumed if placed between two fires.   But none
of these things moved either commanders or men.   The one
thing they had to do was to take Bristol.   In fact there was
no safety for them now in any other course.   If once they
turned away, Rupert, Goring, and Greenville, perhaps reinforced by all the rabble of the country, would be upon their
backs.   Therefore they resolved to storm the place.   But before
doing so, Fairfax, in a very manly letter, summoned Prince
Rupert to surrender.   There are some passages in that letter
which deserve to be repeated as often as these events are called
to mind, and the more so by us now, as it is tolerably certain
the letter would be the joint work of the General and Lieutenant-
General.   Having flatly called on the Prince to yield, Fairfax
says the consideration of Rupert's royal birth and personal virtues prompt the writer to add something more :—

   "Sir, the crown of England is, and will be, where it ought to be;
we fight to maintain it there.   But the King, misled by evil counsellors,
or through a seduced heart, hath left his Parliament—under God the best
assurance of his crown and family. . . . The King, in supreme acts, is

not to be advised by men of whom the law takes no notice, but by his Parliament, the Great Council of his kingdom, in whom, as much as man is
capable of, he hears all his people, as it were, at once advising him. . .
Sir, if God makes this clear to you as He hath to us, I doubt not but He
will give you a heart to deliver this place. . . . But if this be hid from
your eyes, and through your wilfulness this so great, so famous and ancient
city, and so full of people, be, by your putting us to force the same,
exposed to ruin and the extremities of war—which we shall yet in that
case, as much as possible, endeavour to prevent—then I appeal to the
righteous God to be judge between you and us, and to requite the wrong.
And let all England judge whether the burning of its towns, ruining its
cities, and destroying its people, be a good requital from a person of your
family, which hath had the prayers, tears, purses, and blood of its Parliament and people; and—if you look on either as now divided—hath ever had
that same party, both in Parliaments and amongst the people, most zealous
for their assistance and restitution, which you now oppose and seek to
destroy, and whose constant grief hath been that their desires to serve your
family have ever been hindered or made fruitless by that same party about
his Majesty, whose counsel you act, and whose interest you pursue in this
unnatural war."

Rupert consented to treat for a surrender on conditions, but
refused the terms offered. On the night of September 10th the
lines round the city were vigorously stormed in several places;
and part of the works having been gained, a trumpet was
sounded for a parley. Fairfax wisely conceded generous conditions, and on the next day Rupert marched out, attended for
two miles by his victorious opponent, and made his way to
Oxford.

During the time of these operations Cromwell was in almost
constant attendance on Sir Thomas Fairfax, and had little independent command. But on two or three occasions collateral
operations were of sufficient importance to justify a temporary
severance of the Lieutenant-General from his chief. Most noteworthy was the new danger that threatened the Parliamentary
cause in the rise of the " Clubmen," whose cry was, in effect,
" a plague on both your houses." They seem to have been
exceptionally strong in the track of Goring's army; and Cromwell's method of dealing with them is illustrative both of his
quickness of insight into the signs of the times, and also of his
tact and firmness.

When the army passed by Salisbury, at the beginning of
July, those who went through the town found the inhabitants
very confidently declaring themselves neutral in the conflict.

N

The reason of their boldness was their reliance on the power of a new association, founded in Wilts and Dorset, with the object of resisting the exactions either of King or Parliament, and of enabling these counties to stand aloof until the issue was decided. Once started, the idea was received with enthusiasm. Farmers with their sons, and ploughmen, and herdsmen, readily obeyed the summons to a rendezvous. Such fowling-pieces and rusty swords as they possessed were brought with them. But most of them were obliged to be satisfied with even ruder weapons ; and hence the name "Clubmen," by which they were generally known.

There can be no doubt that the Royalists amongst the gentry saw in this association an opportunity of hampering and annoying the Parliamentary army in its advance; but there is no reason for imputing any such purpose to the mob whom these gentry tried to direct. On the contrary, when Prince Rupert evacuated Bristol, he solicited and was allowed the loan of a thousand arms, on the express ground that his unarmed followers would not be able to defend themselves against the Clubmen. Besides, Lord Clarendon, with inherent probability—a support often to be required before his testimony can be taken—attributes the origin and progress of the new organisation to Lord Goring's cruel exactions. He also states in confirmation of this, that a body of five or six thousand Clubmen assembled in arms presented a petition at the beginning of June to the Prince of Wales, then at Wells in Somerset, begging that they might be relieved from the intolerable mischiefs they endured through ill-discipline amongst the royal troops. The Prince, with the good humour natural to him, had assured them of his sympathy, but had warned them against maintaining their organization, lest evil-minded men should make use of them to the King's injury.

But the rapid development of this organization was a far more formidable symptom than the young Prince of Wales was likely to understand. It was a sign of approaching social disintegration ; the beginning of the end, the sloping border of chaos. Since the Wars of the Roses, England had become much more highly organized, and a continuance of civil broils was proportionately more disastrous. An early peace was beginning to be essential to national life ; and even the most determined champions on either side were asking with deep anxiety what would become of the land if the conflict was allowed to go on. The Clubmen supplied an answer. The counties, or associations of counties, would set up for themselves. The writs, whether of King or Parliament, would alike cease to run, except where enforced by soldiery. In a word, the kingdom of England would be dissolved into a number of unfederated communities, and the days of the "Heptarchy" would return.

When the army was pressing Sherborne Castle, in the first days of August, information reached the Generals that the leaders of the Clubmen were making use of a letter from the King to raise the country people.* A large gathering was held at Shaftesbury on Saturday, August 2nd, and Colonel Fleetwood was sent to disperse it. He brought back with him as prisoners a number of local gentlemen. But the mob, though scattered for the moment, speedily rallied again, and took up a strong position near Shaftesbury, on the summit of Hambleton Hill, where there existed the relics of ancient fortifications, said to be Roman. The difficulty was now felt to deserve the special attention of the Lieutenant-General, who marched out with a thousand horse to seek the rioters. On the road to Shaftesbury he noticed some military colours glancing amongst the foliage at the top of a high, wooded hill, very difficult of access. This was not Hambleton Hill; and a lieutenant with a company of soldiers was sent to reconnoitre, and make enquiries. They found the hill occupied by another party of Clubmen, who seemed not unwilling to parley; and one of the leaders, Mr. Newman, a gentleman of the neighbourhood, voluntarily accompanied the soldiers on their return. He told Cromwell that the people were discontented because their leaders had been arrested on Saturday, and were determined to know the reason why. Cromwell replied that he did not feel bound to give Mr. Newman or his associates any account of that, as it had been done by competent authority; but being willing to satisfy them as far as possible, he might tell them that the prisoners were accused of gathering tumultuous, unlawful meetings; for this they would be duly tried by law, and such trial ought not to be questioned or interrupted by riotous assemblies. Mr. Newman then said he would carry

* See a letter in King's Pamphlets, No. 220.

N 2

this answer to his friends; and Cromwell very wisely determined to bear him company.

The Lieutenant-General evidently had a shrewd suspicion as
to the real nature of the connection between the Clubmen and the
Royalists; and had good hopes of the effect of a frank explanation
from himself. He went therefore attended by only a small
party, and held a conference with the people. What they said
to him is not detailed, but was, in all probability, a repetition
of explanations that had already been sent to Sir Thomas
Fairfax.* They were associated together to petition the King
and Parliament; and meanwhile they bound themselves "to
provide arms, to set watches, to be quiet with them that were
so, to lay hold on disorderly soldiers and bring them to the
next garrisons; not to refuse quarter and contribution till
their petitions were delivered; not to favour either party;
not to protect any not associated." As to their petitions, they
desired a "cessation of arms; possession of all garrisons in Wilts
and Dorset until King and Parliament could come to an agreement; freedom from all exactions, except for the maintenance
of those garrisons; the execution of all laws by ordinary officers;
liberty to all their countrymen to leave the armies, and to
return home." To such proposals for secession from the
Commonwealth it was impossible to give any answer other
than the written reply of Sir Thomas Fairfax—that they were
inadmissible.

But Cromwell in this interview addressed himself rather to
the feeling which he saw clearly to be the real inspiration of the
gathering—the revolt of desperation from incessant exactions that
made industry hopeless. He told them that if they desired to
save their goods they were taking very ill-devised means for the
purpose; for to leave their houses unguarded was the very
way to lose their goods. Further, he assured them that in
the army of the Parliament irregular exactions were sternly
punished, and guaranteed that if any soldiers offered them
violence they should receive speedy justice. As to the gentlemen taken at Shaftesbury, they must needs answer some accusations against them of things done contrary to law and the peace
of the kingdom.† Cromwell was not disappointed by the effect
of his reasoning, for the mob dispersed and went quietly home.

* "Anglia Rediviva," p. 58.   † "Anglia Rediviva," pp. 78–9.

But he had worse success when he came to the main body at Hambleton Hill. Here 4,000 men were gathered, and showed great confidence in the strength of their position. It was difficult for horse to reach them, and the mounds of the old fort gave them good shelter. A lieutenant, sent to enquire the cause of their meeting, could get no answer other than a volley of shot. Nor would they listen to a message sent back by an emissary of their own. Cromwell was exceedingly loath to use force; but after the failure of a third message, giving them notice that the next word would be an assault, he was obliged to fall on. For a moment his men were repulsed with some loss, but being taken in the rear by Major Desborough the poor people quickly dispersed, after the capture of 400, of whom half were wounded. On one of the colours taken was the significant motto, confirming the view we have taken of the purpose of the combination :—

> " *If you offer to plunder, or take our cattel,*
> *Be assured we will bid you battel.*"

On the next day the prisoners were assembled, and after further investigation of their objects Oliver addressed them. He told them that they were quite at liberty to defend themselves against plundering; but such dangerous assemblies as these could not be allowed. To this they heartily assented, and then being set free they departed, swearing that if they were caught in arms again against the Parliament they would deserve to be hanged.

This affair of the Clubmen has seemed to deserve careful attention, not only because it indicates the danger already existing of the disintegration of the State through the exhaustion of war, but also because the incident must have made a deep impression on Cromwell. From this time, if not before, he must have begun to feel that the victory of the Royalists and the disguised priest-craft of Presbyterianism were not the only dangers to be feared; but that all parties alike were wrestling on the brink of an abyss, in which all the accumulated results of English civilisation might be swallowed up.

It is observable that from this time forth Cromwell seems to have taken every opportunity of emphatically warning his countrymen against the perils of factious self-will, and of needless dissensions upon matters of form. About six weeks after the events just now described several congregations in London

found an unusual interest in their Sunday services, through an
order of Parliament that the Lieutenant-General's letter concerning the capture of Bristol should be read to them. The conclusion of that letter* evidently caused what modern newspapers
would call a " sensation."

"Our desires are that God may be glorified by the same spirit of faith
by which we ask all our sufficiency, and have received it. It is meet that
He have all the praise. Presbyterians, Independents, all have here the
same spirit of faith and prayer; the same presence and answer; they agree
here, have no names of difference; pity it is it should be otherwise anywhere. All that believe have the real unity, which is most glorious because
inward and spiritual—in the body and to the Head. For being united in
forms, commonly called uniformity, every Christian will, for peace' sake,
study and do as far as conscience will permit. And for brethren in
things of the mind we look for no compulsion but that of light
and reason. In other things, God hath put the sword in the Parliament's
hands for the terror of evil doers, and the praise of them that do well. If
any plead exemption from that, he knows not the Gospel. If any would
wring that out of your hands, or steal it from you under what pretence
soever, I hope they shall do it without effect."

"*Wring that out of your hands?*" "*Steal it from you under
what pretence soever?*" Alas, alas! who is thinking of it?
Who threatens it? "Is thy servant a dog that he should do
this thing?"

It would profit us little, with a view to our main purpose, to
follow in detail the events which now rapidly hastened the
military ruin of the King. They throw little fresh light on
Oliver's mind and aims, while the illustrations they afford of his
military genius, to be made effective, would need more space than
we can give. But a brief outline may conclude the present
chapter.

The grief and anger of poor King Charles on the surrender of
Bristol were not disproportionate to the severity of the blow.
After a vain effort to relieve Chester, he could henceforth do
little more than watch from Oxford the resistless triumph of his
rebels, and finally, in despair of foreign or Irish help, endeavour
to insert himself as a wedge at the splitting point between Scotch
and English, or between Presbyterians and Independents, or
between Parliament and army. But the swift, unremitting vigour
with which the operations of the army were now conducted, and

* Letter XXXI. in Carlyle.

the unwavering resolution of the Independent party neutralised all his devices.

On September 13th, the second day after the surrender of Bristol, a council of war determined that the next thing to be done was to reduce the scattered garrisons still holding out between the rear of the army and London. Of these the Lieutenant-General was charged with the capture of Devizes, Winchester, and Basing House. Devizes, held by Sir Charles Lloyd, was very strong, both through advantages of situation and the addition of works considered in those days a model of engineering skill. Having got his siege-train thither, Cromwell made all his dispositions for bombardment before he summoned the governor, on Sunday, September 21st. Sir Charles Lloyd, knowing well enough that in the then condition of the King's affairs the capture was only a matter of time, asked a delay of ten days to communicate with his master. Cromwell in reply advised him not to let slip the opportunity now offered of obtaining good terms, and suggested that if he were otherwise resolved he should at once send to a safer place his lady and any other gentlewomen who might be with her. As to the King's rights, he begged to inform Sir Charles that none were more fitting than the Parliament to keep strongholds, forts, and castles for his Majesty's use. The brief rejoinder of the governor was, " Win it, and wear it." Whereupon the cannon opened their mouths and the mortars belched forth grenades, and in an hour or two, notwithstanding the boasted skill shown in the fortifications, the powder magazine was found to be in danger. This demoralised the garrison, and next day the place was surrendered on conditions favourable to all except deserters from the Parliament, but effectually preventing any further aid to the King from the surrendering force.

The reduction of Winchester town and castle was equally speedy. On Sunday, September 28th, the besieging force reached the walls. The town was indefensible, and possession was yielded at once. The castle was summoned, and refused. The defective condition of Cromwell's poor battery of six guns, caused a delay until the following Saturday; but then, a breach having been effected, Lord Ogle the governor requested and obtained terms of surrender. One or two incidents of this siege deserve mention. Lady Ogle, who in accordance with Cromwell's suggestion had left the town and been safely conducted to a distance of four

miles, died while the battery was proceeding, a calamity which
the pious Hugh Peters interpreted as a Divine summons to the
garrison. The bishop, Dr. Curle, was in the town, and Cromwell offered him protection, guaranteeing his security. From
lack of faith however the prelate chose to go into the castle,
and after the surrender sought refuge with Mr. Hugh Peters,
with whom he "spent an hour or two"—certainly not a very happy
time for Dr. Curle. But perhaps few of the men of that period
have suffered more than the fighting preacher from the reaction
that followed the Restoration. It may be that he felt a righteous
complacency in the "tears, and importunity" with which the
haughty prelate now "desired the Lieutenant-General's favour
to excuse his not accepting the offer made unto him" on the
occupation of the town. But if there was a touch of carnal
vanity, there was also surely something of charity in the satisfaction of Mr. Peters at being able to convey the bishop safe
home under the escort of a guard, "lest the soldiers should use
violence to him and his chaplain who were in their long gowns
and cassocks." The Ironsides had, it would seem, an aversion to
the clerical garb.

But the discipline under which these triumphant soldiers were
kept was severely signalised after this capture of Winchester.
One of the conditions granted was, that all the garrison or
townspeople desiring it should remain where they were, "free
from all violence and injury of the Parliament's forces." Some of
Cromwell's own men were accused of plundering contrary to this
article. He had them tried by court-martial, and six of them
being convicted, they were made to draw lots—an ordeal frightful
to conceive—and the one on whom the lot fell was hanged. The
other five were marched off to Oxford, to be delivered over to the
mercy of the governor, Sir Thomas Glemham. Naturally, the
latter sent them back again, "with an acknowledgment of the
Lieutenant-General's nobleness in being so tender in breach of
Articles."

It was on the 6th of October that Cromwell announced to
Sir Thomas Fairfax his success at Winchester. Within eight
days he was able to add to this the capture of Basing House, an
achievement of such importance that he related it in a personal
despatch to the Speaker of the House of Commons :—"Sir, I
thank God I can give you a good account of Basing." The words

sound like the escape of a sigh of relief. And indeed from his own point of view—"*it is not of him that willeth, nor of him that runneth, but of God that showeth mercy*"—he had very special occasion for gratitude. Basing House was at once a palace and castle. The lines of fortification were a mile in circuit, and within were two separate mansions. The older was a castle in the style of the fourteenth century. The new house was built in the reign of Henry VIII. by Sir William Paulet, created Marquis of Winchester, who was thirty years Lord-Treasurer, entertained Queen Elizabeth and attendant ambassadors with lavish hospitality, and died at the ripe age of ninety-seven. The stronghold was now held by John, the fifth Marquis, with diminished wealth indeed, but still with an assumption of old baronial airs. Kept always amply stocked with provisions and strongly garrisoned, the place had defiantly held out through all the varying fortunes of the war, had humiliated several Parliamentary commanders, and still continued to harass trade and communications between London and the west. The Lieutenant-General of the Parliamentary army felt that the time was come when it must fall. But it was an enterprise demanding one of two things: either a great deal of time or a great deal of faith. The former could not be spared; but Oliver's faith was exhaustless, and therefore he faced Basing House firmly persuaded that the Lord would deliver it into his hand.

Impatient of slow operations he determined on an early storm. It is probable that many of the most famous strongholds of that time owed more to the moral effect produced by their formidable appearance than to any actual impossibility of storming. And Cromwell had the gift of imparting to his men something of his own temper—at once fiery and resolute; a temper not at all susceptible to moral impression by apparent impossibilities. Cromwell's personal preparation for the dreadful work was characteristic. He "spent much time with God in prayer before the storm." And in reading the hundred and thirty-fifth Psalm, with many fierce thoughts of the idol-furniture stored in that reputed stronghold of papistry, he felt the keen joy of contempt for an adversary's gods as he paused at the words, "*They that make them are like unto them; so is every one that trusteth in them.*"

After due battery, during which under cover of darkness

the storming parties took their places, there fell a silence in the early morning. Then, at the quick succession of four cannon-shots, the storming parties rushed on, planted their ladders, and dashed aloft like the first crest of a resistless tide. By windows, by doors, by gaps in the shattered walls, they pressed in, bewildering the defenders by their ubiquitous fury. One party, under Colonel Pickering, thus passed right through the new house, driving all before them, and reached the gate of the older castellated building. And now a parley was called by the besieged. But the tide of battle could not then be stayed. Another party, under Montague and Hardress Waller, were then fighting through the "court of guard," the very citadel of the fortification. These beat the defenders from their ramparts, drew their ladders after them, to plant them afresh against another line of works, and finally reached the house, where they met their victorious comrades.

Thus fell Basing House, "the twentieth garrison," says Mr. Peters, "that hath been taken in this summer by this army." And the seventy-four corpses that lay about the rooms and grounds betokened a fiercer assault and resistance than had been witnessed yet in this war. One of them was a woman; "only one," says Mr. Peters. "One too many!" echo succeeding times; and, indeed, the military preacher seems to have felt this a little sadly himself. "She was the daughter of Dr. Griffith," he says, "who by her railing provoked our soldiers (then in heat) into a further passion." Silver, and gold, and jewels, stores of food, with wagon loads of furniture, became the plunder of the soldiers. The very bars were wrenched from the windows, the lead stript from the roof; wantonness or carelessness added the ravage of fire, and in a few days nothing was left but a ghastly skeleton. Terrible is the pathos, whether intended or not, of the contrast between the beginning and the end of Hugh Peters' narrative. "The old house," he says, "had stood for two hundred or three hundred years, the new house surpassing that in beauty and stateliness, and either of them fit to make an emperor's court." But the hot breath of war passes, and now— "Whereas the House had ordered that the country people should carry away those buildings, God Almighty had decreed touching that beforehand—nothing remained but a blast of wind to blow down the tottering walls and chimneys." We may imagine the weary, smoke-begrimed victors looking on and inwardly revolving with cruel devoutness the divine word that had inspired their leader : *" They that make them are like unto them; so is every one that trusteth in them !"*

The remainder of the war against the King may be dismissed in a few words. The failure of Charles to relieve Chester was followed by the utter destruction of the Scottish force under Montrose, with whom the King had expected in some way to effect a junction. When Basing House fell, the Royalists had no longer in the field any force worth fighting except the army in the west; and Cromwell, with his usual grasp of the main issue, deprecated the expenditure of any more time in reducing isolated garrisons, thinking it far more important that he should rejoin Fairfax, and drive Goring and Hopton into the narrow end of Cornwall. Therefore, notwithstanding the desire of the Parliament that he should take Dennington Castle, he hastened again into Devonshire, receiving on the way the surrender of Langford House near Salisbury ; and at Crediton, on October 24th, he once more met his commander.

The army soon after went into winter quarters at St. Mary Ottery. While here, Sir Thomas Fairfax received an invitation from Lord Goring to consult on terms of peace. Goring's idea seems to have been that possibly both armies might have been united to enforce terms on King and Parliament alike. But he was mistaken in the men with whom he had to do. The New Model Army wanted peace indeed, but only on condition of the complete triumph of civil and religious liberty. Down to that time this was identified with the supremacy of the Parliament, to which Lord Goring was referred. From St. Mary Ottery the army was removed to Tiverton, because of prevalent sickness ; and Crediton also was occupied the better to straiten Exeter. Early in January Cromwell, by a sudden movement, surprised a party of the enemy at Bovey Tracy, and made many captives. The continuous successes of the Parliamentary generals hastened the demoralisation of the Royalist army. On January 12th, 1646, the siege of Plymouth was raised in a panic. On the 19th Dartmouth was stormed. At the beginning of February Exeter was left blockaded, in order that the enemy might be pushed westwards. Goring abandoned his command in despair to fly into France ; and with noble courage Lord

Hopton took over his deserted trust. The only anxiety of the victors now was so to extend their line from sea to sea that the retreating Royalists should neither escape nor break through. But the task was rendered comparatively easy by the utter decay of martial spirit among the Cavalier army. Near Bodmin four of Cromwell's troopers chased and captured forty-two musketeers; and on another occasion six troopers took four wagonloads of ammunition from the convoy guarding them. At the beginning of March Prince Charles took ship and escaped to Scilly; and by the 10th of that month Lord Hopton saw that the only course open to him was to surrender. His forces were disbanded and dispersed by treaty. Exeter was soon afterwards taken; and in the middle of April Fairfax turned his face once more towards Oxford.

The time was now come when the Lieutenant-General might be more needed in Parliament than with the army; and when Fairfax set out for Oxford, he dismissed his colleague to render to the House of Commons an account of the campaign. Thus on April 23rd, 1646, the Member for Cambridge appeared once more in his place in the House. Four days afterwards, King Charles, helpless and wearied, followed only by a single attendant, rode out of Oxford, and after a week of aimless, heartsick wandering sought refuge in General David Lesley's quarters near Newark.

CHAPTER XIII.

PRIEST, PRESBYTER, AND KING.

On the 22nd of April Lieutenant-General Cromwell arrived once more in London. The New Model Army had amply fulfilled his expectations; and in proportion as its organisation was traceable to his personal influence his reputation and political authority had been very largely increased during the campaign. We may be very sure therefore that, as he made his way to the House on the morning after his arrival, he felt very agreeably the inward glow of comfort which, at least for a brief interval after achievement, is experienced by successful men. He was received with enthusiasm; "and as a testimony of their true respect of his extraordinary service for the kingdom, it was ordered that Mr. Speaker should, in the name of the whole House, give him hearty thanks for his great services for the Parliament and the whole kingdom; which Master Speaker did accordingly." *

His reputation was indeed at this time greater than his acknowledged influence. It was impossible to ignore the obvious fact that the New Model was simply an enlargement of the Eastern Counties' Army, the special creation of Cromwell. The adoption of his methods in enlistment, drill, and discipline, had changed disaster into triumph, and in a few months had finished a war which had threatened to drag on until the nation should be exhausted. But, however admirable as a weapon of war, the New Model without Cromwell would have been like the bow of Ulysses without its master. Such at any rate was the opinion of the soldiers themselves. They had distinctly indicated that opinion before Naseby; and not only this decisive battle, but also every following achievement of the campaign had confirmed and increased their fond confidence in the leadership of Oliver. Whether he was himself aware of it yet or not, events had already decided that he

* Newspaper extract in "Cromwelliana."

should be tried by the strongest temptation a patriot can know —the passionate devotion of a resistless army.* How he bore himself under that temptation we must gather as we go along.

But, except as a victorious commander and the writer of hortatory letters increasing in frequency and earnestness on the subject of religious toleration, Cromwell was not conspicuous in the counsels of his country. Devout Presbyterians were already scandalised at the weight of his influence with the populace. But it was Cromwell as the idol of the army and the sects whom they feared; not Cromwell the Member for Cambridge.

The honours and gifts hitherto bestowed by the House upon the successful general had neither been so great as to suggest subserviency, nor so small as to indicate jealous fear. The vote of thanks accorded to him on his return from the west was not the first he had received. But except his official pay, and the repayment of sums advanced by him, we do not hear of any substantial rewards proposed for him until this winter of 1645–6. In December the Commons had agreed that in the event of peace with the King his Majesty should be requested to bestow a number of titles, and amongst those to be elevated to the lowest grade of the peerage were Fairfax and Cromwell. To support the dignity Fairfax was to receive lands to the value of £5,000 a year, and Cromwell to the value of £2,500. The estates were to be bestowed out of the forfeited possessions of Royalists ; and difficulties were raised with regard to the special victims to be sacrificed. In the end Cromwell was more fortunate than Fairfax, and received a substantial endowment. But for the present an income of £500 a year was all that could be arranged.

On the morning of May 6th authentic news came that the King had ridden into the Scottish army, and had entrusted to his northern subjects the guardianship of his royal person. Thereupon the English Parliament at once asserted their right to dispose of their King so long as he was on English soil ; and for the present ordered that he be sent to Warwick Castle, an order, however, which had no effect. Newark, impregnable even to Ironsides, was surrendered at last by royal order ; and the Scots

* See Sprigge, p. 139.

retreated northwards to Newcastle, carrying their sovereign with them.

Perhaps Oliver's inaction in public affairs about this time may be in part explained by some interesting private business affecting his children. His two eldest daughters had been asked in marriage—one of them at least by a man after his own heart ; and the suitors were not disposed to wait until times of peace. The elder of the two girls had won the heart of Henry Ireton. The masculine affection cherished by this man for the father might well predispose both sides to a closer bond. Ireton belonged to a Nottinghamshire family, and after graduating at Oxford, as a gentleman commoner of Trinity College, he devoted himself for some years to the study of law. On the outbreak of the war he took up with ardour the cause of the Parliament. After serving for a time with his own county association, he was attracted by the marvellous energy and inspiriting achievements of Cromwell in the eastern counties, and he permanently attached himself to the " Lord of the Fens." Cromwell saw his worth, and took every opportunity of urging his promotion. So long as the Ironsides were engaged in their native district, Ireton would have many opportunities of visiting the tithe-farmer's house at Ely, which was still Oliver's home. He was fourteen years older than Bridget Cromwell. But this was probably no disadvantage in his eyes ; and as by all accounts she was deeply imbued with her father's opinions, she would be easily inclined to a warrior whose heroism in the good cause would often be the subject of conversation in her home. The campaign in the west must have caused a long separation of the lovers; and the mode and circumstances of their marriage indicate some impatience. The union took place at Horton, in the neighbourhood of the leaguer before Oxford, on the 5th of June, 1646. Ireton seems to have been what his father-in-law certainly was not—a Republican by conviction. But the difference between the two men in volume and power of character was so great, that the possible influence of the weaker over the stronger has not the importance sometimes attached to it. We may well believe that the marriage of Henry Ireton to Bridget Cromwell was brought about almost as much by the mighty attraction exercised over the bridegroom by the father-in-law as by the charms of the lady herself.

About the same time Oliver's second daughter, Elizabeth, was married to John Claypole of Narborough in Northamptonshire. The girl was yet very young, being in fact under seventeen years of age. Her husband also was very young, scarcely more than twenty. So far as we are aware, he had nothing either in character or circumstance to give him any exceptional claims to consideration. At the same time, he was a kindly, amiable man; and it is to his credit that, though he lost his wife early, he afforded a home to her mother in her desolate widowhood. The union was probably one of pure, unworldly affection between two child-like lovers.

The military wedding being over, the father soon went back to London. He probably remained in the camp till the surrender of Oxford, which took place on June 24th, under conditions far too favourable, said some irate patriots. Along with Ireton, Fleetwood, and Lambert, he was deputed by Fairfax to draw up a plan for disposing of part of the army to unsettled districts. But the sittings of this select council seem to have been in London, and Whitelocke acted as their secretary. For the present there was no more fighting to be done by the great General of Horse, and he stayed for the most part quietly in London, doing nothing that we know of, except keeping an eye on the course of events, and writing a few letters, which reveal something of the inner man. He had a lodging in Drury Lane, then unapprehensive of its present squalor. His wife cannot have been much with him. There were two little girls at home, Mary and Francis, aged respectively ten and eight, who needed a mother's care; and Oliver's mother, who lived with them, was verging into extreme old age. Of this period there remains a touching letter. It is addressed to the elder of Oliver's married daughters, and it shows how his affection followed them in their new career. The old fashion, so tenderly preserved by the Germans, so unfeelingly abandoned by ourselves, of keeping "thou, thine, and thee," for the dear ones of life's inner circle, adds much to the pathos of this still living utterance of an honest, human love, touched by mystical emotions :—

"FOR MY BELOVED DAUGHTER, BRIDGET IRETON.
"DEAR DAUGHTER,   "LONDON, 25th October, 1646.
"I write not to thy husband, partly to avoid trouble, for one line of mine begets many of his, which I doubt makes him sit up too late, partly

because I am myself indisposed at this time; having some other considerations. Your friends at Ely are well: your sister Claypole is (I trust in mercy) exercised with some perplexed thoughts. She sees her own vanity and carnal mind. Bewailing it, she seeks after (as I hope also) that which will satisfy. And thus to be a seeker, is to be of the best sect next a finder, and such an one shall every faithful humble seeker be at the end. Happy seeker, happy finder! Who ever tasted that the Lord is gracious, without some sense of self, vanity, and badness? Who ever tasted that graciousness of His, and could go less in desire, and less than pressing after full enjoyments. Dear heart, press on; let not husband, let not any thing cool thy affections after Christ. I hope he will be an occasion to inflame them. That which is best worthy of love in thy husband, is that of the image of Christ he bears. Look on that, and love it best, and all the rest for that. I pray for thee and him; do so for me. My service and dear affections to the General and Generaless. I hear she is very kind to thee; it adds to other obligations. My love to all. I am thy dear father,   "O. CROMWELL." *

The first words of this letter are very significant of Ireton's devotion to Cromwell. Few fathers have to complain that " one line" from them " begets many" from a daughter's husband. But it is the " sister Claypole" that is at present most on his heart. Though married, she was yet but a child; and it seems hard that she should have to " bewail her own vanity and carnal mind." But the mental trouble was a very real one to her, and therefore to her father. Yet he can take comfort from the memory of his own gloomy days at swampy St. Ives, by the sluggish Ouse. " Whoever tasted that the Lord is gracious without some sense of self, vanity, and badness?" How strange is this eternal controversy between the atom and the Infinite, between base self and supreme Goodness! The shibboleths of that struggle change, but the issue is ever the same—" that God may be all in all."

During the interval between Bridget's marriage and the writing of the above letter, the question of the re-settlement of the two kingdoms was tending towards new and unanticipated issues. It is not our business to follow the national history of the time except so far as the development of Oliver Cromwell's character and aims is distinctly associated therewith. Now for nearly a year at this period there is little open manifestation of his individual action upon public affairs. It will be sufficient therefore to indicate the chief problems coming into view, and

* Letter XLI., in Carlyle.

O

the light in which they must needs have presented themselves to a man such as we have seen Cromwell to be. In brief, those problems concerned the Church and the crown. The army and its rights became indeed the more obvious subject of conflict between rival parties. But this was only because of the different attitudes assumed by Parliament and army respectively towards Church and crown. If then we can get a clear view of the true issues in the re-settlement of these two, we ought to be the better able to understand the conduct of Oliver in following years.

A pregnant hint of the issues to which the Church question was drifting is given by a letter written in the interest of religious freedom from Drury Lane in July of this year. About this time Cromwell heard of some petty persecution waged by one Robert Browne, a tenant-farmer, of Hapton, in Norfolk, against some poor village sectaries, whose conventicles and prayer-meetings were not apparently authorised either by priest or presbyter. Mr. Thomas Knyvett, the landlord of this Browne, had been formerly Cromwell's captive; and it will be conceded that Oliver shows a high opinion of his former prisoner's generosity in appealing to him on the subject. The letter itself is a very noble one, and must here be given entire, not only for the light it sheds on the approaching ecclesiastical crisis, but for the insight it ought to give into the writer's character :—

"SIR,—I cannot pretend any interest in you for anything I have done, nor ask any favour for any service I may do you. But because I am conscious to myself of a readiness to serve any gentleman in all possible civilities, I am bold to be beforehand with you to ask your favour on behalf of your honest, poor neighbours of Hapton, who, as I am informed, are in some trouble, and are likely to be put to more, by one Robert Browne, your tenant, who, not well pleased with the ways of these men, seeks their disquiet all he may.

"Truly, nothing moves me to desire this more than the pity I bear them in respect of their honesties, and the trouble I hear they are likely to suffer for their consciences and humour—as the world interprets it. I am not ashamed to solicit for such as are anywhere under pressure of this kind; doing even as I would be done by. Sir, this is a quarrelsome age; and the anger seems to me to be the worse where the ground is difference of opinion; which to cure, to hurt men in their houses, persons, or estates, will not be found an apt remedy. Sir, it will not repent you to protect these poor men of Hapton from injury and oppression, which that you would (do) is the effect of this letter. Sir, you will not want the grateful acknowledgment, nor utmost endeavours of requital from your most humble servant,

"OLIVER CROMWELL."*

It is almost certain that in writing these words, Oliver had in his mind the formidable claims at that time urged by the Assembly of Divines on behalf of the new ecclesiastical discipline. Within six years the Presbyterian form of belief and Church order had apparently won over the whole kingdom of England. But the victory was more apparent than real. It was not due so much to intelligent conviction, as to a passionate revolt against everything that savoured of the old tyranny. The adoption of Presbyterian forms was by no means the natural issue of an English revival of religion. However, the chances of war had thrown power into the hands of Presbyterian leaders in Parliament, and they were determined to use it. The Assembly of Divines, with the assistance of a few Scottish brethren sent for their better instruction, had elaborated a formidable creed and a still more formidable system of Church government, while ritual, so essential to any permanently popular religion, had been reduced to a minimum. The devoutness and the learning of those excellent men are indisputable. But they laboured under the common delusion that what was good for themselves must needs be good for every one else; and in this conviction they were benevolently resolved that no misguided sinner should have any choice as to the means to be used for his soul's health. The few Independents who pleaded in the Assembly for some relief to erratic consciences were regarded as sentimental enthusiasts without clearly-grounded convictions. How far the Independents were actuated by the fact that they were in an insignificant minority may fairly be questioned. But the time they wasted in discussing whether the three thousand converted at Pentecost could or could not have worshipped habitually under one roof, may well be pardoned to them in consideration of the sound doctrine they laid down, in a very limited and imperfect form, that the Government has nothing to do with a man's theological belief or disbelief.

The Presbyterians had no other difficulty than the pro-

* Letter XXXVI., in Carlyle.

o 2

lixity of debate in carrying their whole scheme through the Assembly. But the House of Commons had never dreamed of regarding the divines in any other light than as advisers; and the ideas of the latter upon spiritual censures appeared objectionable, and even dangerous. It was no light matter in those times to be excluded from the communion of the Lord's Supper. Religious feeling on the subject was inflamed by morbid associations of superstition; and part of the ecclesiastical discipline was the exclusion of such an outcast from social sympathy. Now the Assembly of Divines held and insisted that the infliction of such a sentence rested by divine right with the Church, and they would not hear of any interference on the part of the secular power. Not only so, but they were not disposed even to define the faults for which the ban was to be inflicted. It was not to be expected that the House of Commons would suffer this. They amended the suggestions of the Assembly by appending a definition of offences for which excommunication should be legal, and also by retaining an ultimate appeal to Parliament.

Meantime the City Presbyterians were petitioning the House to quicken the establishment of the godly and thorough reformation so long promised; and they were supported by letters from the Scottish Parliament, which, in the month of February, 1646, almost peremptorily required that the Solemn League and Covenant should be carried out in the Scottish sense of it. "It is expected," wrote Lord Crawford and Lindsay, the Scotch President of Parliament, "that the Honourable Houses will now, after so mature deliberation, add their authority and civil sanction, without further delay, to what the pious and learned Assembly of Divines, upon mature and accurate debates, have advised to be most agreeable to the Word of God."* Such appeals were answered by the passage, on March 14, of an Ordinance concerning suspension from the sacrament; but this Ordinance embodied all the objectionable rules in limitation of the spiritual power of the Elders. Thereupon, the Assembly petitioned in high language sounding rather like commands than prayers, and asserted once more the divine right of the Church to set aside all earthly rule in anything it chose to regard as its own province. No Pope nor Œcumenical Council ever

* Rushworth, Part vi., Vol. I., p. 234.

claimed larger powers over the individual Christian—at least in this world—than did these Presbyterian preachers. Happily they had to do with men of simpler purpose and less wily suppleness than Macchiavellian princes. The Commons were angry. They referred the petition to a committee, who came to the conclusion that it amounted to a breach of privilege, and, in fact, went far to deserve the penalties of Præmunire. In this temper it was that Oliver found the House when he resumed his place in it on the 23rd of April.

But though the Parliament were unwilling to consign Englishmen to the tender mercies of priestcraft under a new name, they were by no means prepared to surrender their own empire over human souls. They would not surrender the right of considering appeals on spiritual cases; yet they showed no mind to encourage the undisciplined aspirations of Independents. Down to the middle of 1646 there was no reason to doubt that, whatever differences might exist as to the relations of the Church and the secular power, the Assembly might safely count on the willingness of Parliament to use its whole resources for the substantial embodiment of the ideal establishment conceived by the Presbyterian ministers. Such an establishment would have contrasted with prelacy, as Rehoboam's threatened scourge of scorpions with the milder instruments of discipline ascribed to his father. If prelacy was tyrannical, it contented itself, for the most part, with tyrannising over outward acts and uttered words. Presbyterianism, with amazing unconsciousness of presumption, would have pierced to the dividing asunder of soul and spirit, and to the discernment of the innermost thoughts and intents of the heart. Prelacy, never very metaphysically inclined, left about its creeds a lazy vagueness, which good nature on the inquisitor's bench might interpret with safe laxity. Presbyterianism, on the other hand, elaborated its beliefs about the Infinite with a loving nicety, under an evidently sincere conviction that a syllable more or less might make all the difference between salvation and perdition. Under the abolished prelates it undoubtedly went hard with a small minority of conscientious people. But under the new priesthood it was likely to go hard with the vast majority, to whom conscience is for the most part a latent faculty. In the old days, if a man were only worldly and jovial enough—a condition not difficult of fulfilment—he could get off with a minimum of church-going, and without many impertinent questions as to the state of his soul. But if presbyteries and synods—congregational, classical, provincial, and national—were to spread their ingeniously woven meshes over the land, not a peccadillo would escape rebuke, not an amiable weakness would be shielded from exposure. Temper, bearing, appetite, the very fashion and quality of clothes —all would be subjects of censorious gossip in the presbytery, and of judgment from the presiding Elders. In truth the world has never seen a more admirably contrived instrument of spiritual tyranny than that which the reverend assembly at Westminster had elaborated by the spring of 1646. Only in some States of America was the experiment of such discipline ever tried, even on the smallest scale*; and, however good some of the results might be in that nursery of nations, the attempt to wrap a full-grown Commonwealth in such swaddling-clothes must always and everywhere be absurd and impossible.

What, then, was the feeling of the English people generally towards this preposterous design, in the age with which we are dealing? The true answer probably is, that the English people generally knew little, and cared less, about the matter. Their grievance against the King and his advisers, Laud and Strafford, had been mainly that of illegal impositions, and only secondarily that of religious persecution. With the leaders of the insurrection, of course, the case was different. With most of them religion was their inspiration, and if they cared for political liberty it was because they believed it to be a healthier atmosphere for religion. But it would be a mistake to attribute this heroic attitude of mind to the general public. They, for the most part, did not understand what the Assembly of Divines were about, and they were not likely to do so until the new ecclesiastical harness began to gall them.

Besides, a considerable number of the religious enthusiasts amongst the obscure multitude had never been converted to Presbyterianism at all. They thought the simplicity of the Gospel to be less disguised under Presbyterian than under Anglican forms. But in reality they cared for no forms of

---

* In Scotland the Presbytery has never had the full power of the State at its back as was then threatened in England, and realised in the American colonies.

any kind. What they valued in the religious excitement of the age was the inward stir, the stimulating emotions, the moral renewal it brought with it; and their experience was, that such gifts of the Spirit were not confined to any forms whatever. Such men generally were the Independents and "sectaries" of various kinds. The Independents indeed for the most part believed that a system of Church government had been authoritatively laid down in the New Testament, and therefore they were under strong temptation to contend for it with carnal weapons—a temptation to which they succumbed in the only States where they ever constituted a majority of the population. But in the minds of the greatest Independents, such as Cromwell and Milton, theological precisianism on the subject of Church polity does not appear to have been strongly developed.

Now Independents and sectaries, though represented only by a small minority in Parliament, had an overwhelming majority in the victorious New Model Army. This was certainly due to Cromwell's method of recruiting, and his insistance on preferring men of marked character and strong individual convictions. These men fought for freedom from spiritual tyranny as much as for the supremacy of Parliament. They had never asked themselves which of these two objects they placed first. They had never suspected the possibility of their clashing. But if those ends should turn out to be incompatible, there ought never to have been a doubt on the minds of disinterested observers as to which these soldiers would prefer. Reasonable liberty of conscience they believed to be worth fighting for. By the essential necessity of free religion to the higher life of a nation they justified the bloodshed they bewailed. But to find that they had risked blood-guiltiness before the bar of the Most High, only to fasten on the country a system of spiritual slavery more searching, engrossing, and remorseless than even that of Rome, was an irony of fate in which they could hardly be expected to acquiesce. That consistency required submission to the Parliamentary majority might be true enough, but in such extremes of torture to talk of consistency is useless. What the Presbyterians demanded from the New Model Army was not to be expected from flesh and blood.

The question as to the disposal of the King's person became accidentally involved in the issues between Presbyterianism and the sects. For if the King had been a man to be trusted, and if he had frankly accepted the army programme of free religion, a free Parliament, and responsible advisers, there is little doubt that he might have kept his crown and his Anglican ritual—at least for his own worship—and might yet have concluded his reign prosperously as the first constitutional King of England. Instead of this, he angered the army by making their most sacred purposes mere cards in a game, to be played or held as he thought most to his own advantage in dealing with the Presbyterian Parliament.

On July 11th, 1646, Commissioners from both Houses were appointed to lay certain propositions for peace before the King at Newcastle. These of course involved everything for which the Parliament had contended, and in a form developed and exaggerated by the altered position of affairs. All armed forces were to be absolutely under the control of Parliament for a period of twenty years. Speaking generally, all public acts done by the Parliament, or by its authority, were to be confirmed; and all public acts done by the King or his Oxford anti-Parliament, without due authorisation from Westminster, were to be void. As to the first condition, it is substantially what is now accepted as a matter of course by every British sovereign, not for a limited period, but as the regular course of things. The forms may run differently, but every one knows that the armed forces of the realm are entirely at the disposal of Parliament, and not at the disposal of the monarch's personal will. This was all that Charles's Parliament required. As to the latter conditions, they were hard and humiliating; but it is difficult to see how else the matter could have been adjusted. Both sets of public acts could not stand; and to suppose that those of the victorious Parliament should have given way is absurd. The religious conditions of peace were, however, put in the forefront of the proposals, and these more than anything else show how the ground of both sides had been changed in the course of conflict. At the beginning of the war, Parliament would have been satisfied with the abolition of the Courts of Star Chamber and High Commission, together with the reduction of the bishops to superintending elders, and the protestantising of the liturgy. Now, nothing would satisfy them but a ruthless eradication of the whole Anglican system. Moreover, the King must take the

Covenant; the religion of Englishmen must conform to that of Scotchmen; and provision must be made for a diligent persecution of papists, not without an eye to " innovations " from a very different quarter.

On August 10th the Commissioners who had been sent to the King returned to Westminster. It was late in the day when they arrived, but Cromwell, eager to learn how their mission had sped, had an interview with two of their number.* He could, however, only obtain very general information. The King had given no distinct answer. It was a suspicious circumstance that the Duke of Hamilton had gone into Scotland; especially as Cromwell learned that, in spite of an ostensible order from the King, Montrose's force had not been disbanded. The labyrinthine web of royal intrigue in Ireland was beginning to be discovered. Altogether, Cromwell was very uneasy, and wrote a brief letter full of trouble to Sir Thomas Fairfax, who was reposing at Bath. It is said that Oliver himself had taken part in a scheme to secure the King's rejection of the Parliamentary proposals. The story is that, together with other leading Independents, he had contrived the escape of Dr. Hudson, the attendant of Charles in his flight from Oxford, and had sent this clergyman to Newcastle to represent that much better terms might be obtained from the army. The evidence on which this rests, however, is of a very suspicious character, being that of Colonel Bamfield, a renegade of doubtful reputation. When the Commissioners offered their report to the House, it was not allowed to be read, because it did not comply with the instruction that they were to bring only a categorical answer—yes or no.

The death of the Earl of Essex on September 14th increased the growing danger of a fatal schism in the victorious party. The Presbyterians had hoped to restore him to the head of the army, and so sheathe or blunt the terrible weapon they had forged and could not wield. They were now left without a man to rival in military authority the commanders whose exploits overwhelmed their employers with a too complete success.

Not only were the political and religious opinions of the soldiers a cause of anxiety, but the burden of their sustenance and pay was pressing heavily on the country. A deputation from Staffordshire came up to Cromwell, pressing him, " with

* Letter XXXVIII., Carlyle.

more than ordinary importunity," to help them in getting pay for the forces in the county, and in obtaining their despatch to Ireland. Fairfax's army complained of arrears, and money was difficult to obtain. In York there was an open mutiny.

No wonder that the City of London, always sensitive as to public security, began to urge upon the Parliament the necessity for diminishing or disbanding the army in England. But a petition presented with that purport on December 19th irritated the soldiery in their best susceptibilities. For it was burdened with groans and lamentations over prevalent heresies, over the unblushing effrontery of " separate congregations," and over the danger of allowing officers to retain their commissions without signing the Covenant. " We have had a very long petition from the City," wrote Cromwell to Fairfax two days afterwards ; " how it strikes at the army, and what other aims it has, you will see by the contents of it ; as also what is the prevailing temper at this present, and what is to be expected from men. But this is our comfort, God is in Heaven, and He doeth whatsoever pleases Him. His, and only His counsel shall stand, whatsoever the designs of men and the fury of the people be." Now if Oliver believed that the counsels of the Eternal were concerned chiefly with his own personal interest and advancement, those latter words are blasphemy. But if he was thinking of a reasonable religious freedom, the want of which had so cruelly harassed the best elements in the nation, the ring of strong conviction and burning passion here tells of a true soul animated by supreme loyalty.

The Parliament, however, could not deal with the army, for two reasons : First, the negotiations with the Scotch lingered ; and next, they could not pay the men. The first difficulty was overcome, at least for the time, by the middle of January, 1647, when a train of wagons carried £200,000 to Newcastle in discharge of the English debt to the Scottish army. But the successful accomplishment of this only increased the remaining difficulty of the Parliament—that of paying their own soldiers. We need not notice the charge made against the Scotch of selling their King further than to say, that it is unfairly based upon only one subordinate feature of a very complicated negotiation. If the King would have taken the Covenant, and guaranteed to them their precious Presbyterian system, his Scottish subjects would have fought for him almost to the last man. The firmness of Charles in declining the Covenant for himself is, no doubt, the most creditable point in his resistance. But his obstinacy in disputing the right of two nations, in their political establishment of religion, to override his convictions by their own, illustrates his entire incapacity to comprehend the new light dawning on the relations of sovereign and people. The Scots did their best for him. They petitioned him, they knelt to him, they preached to him. Poor Alexander Henderson, it is said, died of chagrin that he could not convince Charles, and thus ensure his sovereign's salvation in body and soul. Even baffled as they were by the King's imperturbable confidence, they warned the English Parliament boldly of the danger that must arise from any forgetfulness of the interest which the northern kingdom, equally with the southern, had in the Lord's anointed. But to have carried with them an intractable man to form a wedge of division amongst themselves, at the same time that he brought against them the whole power of England, would have been sheer insanity. Accordingly, they made the best bargain they could both for him and themselves ; and, taking their wages, they left him with his English subjects, who conducted him to Holdenby House, in Northamptonshire, on the 6th of February, 1647.

CHAPTER XIV.

THE REVOLT OF THE ARMY.

In the autumn of 1646, Lieutenant-General Edmund Ludlow met Oliver Cromwell at Sir Robert Cotton's house, where they adjourned to the garden, and paced to and fro in familiar but not cheerful converse. Ludlow was an idealist and a sincere republican. His companion was neither. Hence they did not understand each other very well. What vexed the soul of Cromwell was the unworthy use the Presbyterian leaders were preparing to make of their victory. He inveighed against them with extraordinary strength of language, much to the wonder, apparently, of his milder and more philosophic friend. "If thy father were alive," said Oliver, "he would let some of them hear what they deserve." What was the precise significance of this allusion to Ludlow's father it is hard to say, unless it was intended to excite the son by his supposed example. But Cromwell went on fretting and fuming, as impatient men will do, against the conditions under which he served his country. "It is a miserable thing," he said, "to serve a Parliament! Let a man be never so faithful, yet if one pragmatical fellow rise up and asperse him, he shall never wipe it off. Whereas when one serves under a general, he may do as much service, and yet be free from envy." Following events brought back this conversation very vividly to the placid, self-contained thoughts of Ludlow; and he came to suspect that the tamer of Parliaments had been sounding him to ascertain how far he might be a suitable tool. Yet who that has served under a committee, board, Parliament, or any other many-headed master, has not had similar fits of impatience? If every time we long for a healthy despotism we must needs be suspected of treason it would go hard with us all.

But Cromwell had good reason to think well of service under a general, for he and Fairfax were literally like hand and glove, he being the hand and his nominal superior the glove. And the time was now coming when both would have to decide whether they would go with the Parliament or with the army in the clear divergence of purpose that arose. But that time had not quite come even in the beginning of 1647. There was general uneasiness at the monopoly of physical force now possessed by the victorious New Model, and also at the prevalence of perverse heresy in the ranks. But there was not yet any expectation of an open rupture either on one side or the other. On February 9th the question how to dispose of the army was raised in the Commons. All members hoped and believed that there would be no further need for an army in England. The subject was debated at great length on the 17th and 18th, and it was finally resolved that only certain garrisons should be maintained; that a force of 5,000 horse and 1,000 dragoons should be kept up; that volunteering for Ireland should be encouraged; and that £200,000 should be borrowed to pay the soldiers an instalment of their arrears. During this debate some doubt appears to have been expressed that the army might not be altogether amenable to orders. Against this insinuation Cromwell protested with great warmth. He solemnly declared that such fears were groundless, and that the army would disband and lay down their arms whenever the Parliament should give the order.[*] The sincerity of this declaration has been questioned. But few, if any, have ever doubted the honesty of Fairfax; and in a paper addressed to the Parliament many months afterwards, with his sanction and under his authority, the writers point their criticism on the treatment the soldiers had received by the reproach that it had roused a rebellious spirit in "this army, which until the middle of March last was ready to disband."[†] Indeed, in a despatch to the House of Commons, dated April 1st, Fairfax expressed himself as still confident of the men's obedience.

Why the month of March was mentioned as a crisis in the temper of the army will be presently apparent. The head-quarters were now at Saffron Walden, in the extreme north of Essex, and within the limits of the Eastern Counties Association. On March 6th, the Lords, alarmed by their own instincts and urged by the uneasiness of Presbyterian London, ordered

[*] Walker's "Independency," p. 33. The time of this declaration is very distinctly assigned by Walker, yet it is constantly asserted to have been made at a later time when Cromwell must have known the contrary.

[†] Rushworth, part iv., Vol. I, p. 570.

that Fairfax should keep his soldiers outside what may be called the "quadrilateral" of Independency. On the 11th a petition was presented to the Commons from the county of Essex, complaining, not without reason, of having an army quartered upon it. At the same time the feeling of the City of London had risen to such a height that a scheme was on foot for raising a force for its defence—an ominous portent of a new and more bitter war! But the Commons did not lose their heads as yet. They dissented from the order given by the Lords, and left it to Fairfax to fix his head-quarters where he pleased, provided only that he did not approach within twenty-five miles of London.

On that day (March 11th) Cromwell wrote to Fairfax a short note tremulous with indignation and brimful of vague fears :*—

"There want not in all places men who have so much malice against the army as besots them. The late petition,† which suggested a dangerous design upon the Parliament in coming to those quarters doth sufficiently evidence the same . . . Never were the spirits of men more embittered than now. Surely the devil hath but a short time. Sir, its good the heart be fixed against all this. The naked simplicity of Christ, with that wisdom He is pleased to give, will overcome all this."

Then, in a hurried postscript, he adds :—

"Upon the Fast-day (10th) divers soldiers were raised, as I heard, both horse and foot, near 200 in Covent Garden, to prevent us soldiers from cutting the Presbyterians' throats! These are fine tricks to mock God with!"

What did Oliver mean by calling this City guard a "trick to mock God with?" To him the swift and marvellous triumph of the New Model Army was the result of manifest Divine intervention. And the will of God that the nation should be resettled on principles in fair accord with the religious inspirations of the army was as clear as though it had been proclaimed by an archangel from mid-heaven. Therefore to resist this destiny and threaten its appointed instrument was a mockery of omnipotence.

Meantime, the army began to think they had a right of petition as well as the Corporation of London. But for the present they confined themselves to addressing their own officers. Cromwell, writing again to Fairfax on the 19th, counselled prudence,

* Letter XLIII., in Carlyle.　　　　　† From the City, not the Essex one.

and especially a strict observance of the twenty-five-mile limit. But a natural blunder of the Commons widened the rift into an abyss. The army was not wanted in Essex, but it was wanted very much in Ireland. And if any considerable proportion of the men were drafted thither, the rest could easily be disposed of. But the members who met Sir Thomas Fairfax and his field-officers at Saffron Walden on this subject obtained little satisfaction. The officers would make no personal engagement until they knew who was to command, but they promised to further the drafting of their men for the service. To these officers a petition was presented from the soldiers to be submitted to the Lord-General, and by him, if he thought fit, to be sent up to Parliament. It contained nothing very formidable. It asked for payment of arrears, and for satisfactory indemnity against prosecution for acts done in war. It also requested immunity from pressing for foreign service,* and adequate provision for widows and maimed soldiers. But the Houses were now getting into a panic; and on hearing of this petition, both Lords and Commons passed a declaration severely condemning it, " as set on foot by some evil spirits purposely to raise a distemper and mutiny." Fairfax had sent up three officers, one of them being Colonel Pride, with an explanatory letter. But though this was received with some satisfaction, the censure was passed, and the officers were directed to return and suppress the petition. At the same time, in order to hasten the draft for Ireland, and also, perhaps, with the idea of severing the bond between the soldiers and their most popular commanders, Skippon was named General-in-Chief for Ireland, with the title of Field-Marshal, and Colonel Massey was appointed Lieutenant-General of Horse.

But the vote of censure roused uncontrollable irritation in the army. In the middle of April another and a more energetic effort was made to detach some of the troops for Ireland. A deputation from the Derby House Committee went down. Fairfax himself wrote a letter, to be read at the head of each regiment, reminding the men that they had free choice in the matter, but earnestly asking them to volunteer. The attempt, however, met with little success. The men were not satisfied with the commanders appointed. They shouted: " Fairfax ! Cromwell ! and we all go." Still less were they contented with

* This would include service in Ireland.

the proposal to give them eight weeks' pay when they were fifty-six weeks in arrear. A *ruse* to entrap part of a regiment into marching away only aggravated the prevalent ill-humour. Sixteen of these men, "though at first afraid," resolved to go back and acquaint their old general with the facts. Fairfax then remonstrated with the Commissioners, recommending open dealing as more effectual than "indirect ways." In a word, the army was immovable. The first result of this failure was a resolution, passed by the Commons on April 27th, at once to disband the army, both horse and foot, with six weeks' pay instead of the eight weeks' already offered. But such an order was easier to pass than to carry out.

During this time Cromwell was in attendance at the House of Commons. He had removed his family to London, and was residing with them in Drury Lane. Fairfax and Cromwell were manifestly of one mind. They sympathised with the army; they differed entirely from the majority in Parliament. But they were still hoping that a peaceful solution of the difficulty would be found. Their attitude is best expressed by Cromwell's own words : " He that ventures his life for the liberty of his country I wish he trust God for the liberty of his conscience, and you for the liberty he fights for." For the present they were endeavouring to keep the peace, and feeling their way from week to week.

At the end of April Skippon took his seat in the House as member for Barnstaple, and a substantial compliment was made to him by a vote of a thousand pounds. The vote probably expressed the high appreciation entertained by the House for generals who were not inconveniently brilliant or popular. On the next day after he had taken his seat, three troopers— Edward Sexby, William Allen, and Thomas Sheppard—requested an interview with him. These men—at any rate the two latter—were true types of the triumphant Ironsides, soldiers from conviction, bearing the sword of the Lord and of Gideon, but ready at any moment to throw over Gideon if he swerved by a hair's-breadth from the Divine Word. Allen especially had an intense belief in the power of prayer, and had no doubt whatever that it would bring clear revelations from heaven at every great crisis of duty. These men gave Skippon a letter from certain regiments of horse, explaining their reasons for declining to engage for Ireland.

This letter was communicated to the House. In fact, the men had adopted this method of presenting a petition without infringing the forms of military discipline. The Presbyterian leaders of the House, like all self-willed men when baffled, were greatly irritated. The men were summoned to the bar, and some members sneeringly asked these veterans of Marston Moor and Naseby whether they were not, in reality, Cavaliers. Imagine these grim men, in big boots and buff coats, standing, helmet in hand, at the bar of the House in whose cause they had fought for five years, only to be now asked whether they were not spies and traitors! Whatever were their feelings, they rightly judged that no retort could be so telling as a simple statement of fact. "They answered that they had been engaged in the Parliament's cause ever since Edgehill battle—some of their comrades wounded there. . . . And one of them particularly declared that when he was upon the ground with five dangerous wounds upon him, Major-General Skippon came by, and, pitying his sad condition, gave him five shillings to procure him some relief." * When questioned as to the precise meaning of terms used in the letter, they warily replied that, as the document was the expression of many minds, they could not answer till after consultation with their comrades.

Clearly, something must be done. In their extremity, the leaders turn to Cromwell. He is joined with Skippon, Ireton, and Fleetwood, in a commission to go down and assure the army that they shall have their money before disbanding; that legal indemnity shall be secured to them; and that all their other just demands shall be met. Ludlow says that on that very day there were not wanting suggestions that Cromwell himself should be arrested. It may have been so; † but, as it had happened before, and was to happen very often again, Oliver was felt to be most indispensable precisely at the times when faction was most eager to get rid of him.

Whatever confidence the officers might have in Cromwell and Ireton, they declined to enter upon any conference with the new Commissioners until they could consult the rank and

* Whitelocke.

† Ludlow betrays confusion; for he speaks as though Cromwell had gone away hastily on that afternoon to avoid detention, whereas he certainly went as Commissioner to the army.

P

file. Nothing is more noteworthy about this extraordinary
army than its union of democratic feeling and democratic
genius for organisation with perfect discipline in all military
duties. There is scarcely another case in history, unless it
be that of the Athenian citizen soldiers, in which officers and
men have met together familiarly for discussion and counsel
without slackening the cords of discipline. But these officers
and men had prayed together, had preached to each other,
and had stimulated one another's enthusiasm. They shared
in a common exaltation of spirit, which gave a sacred sanction
to command and obedience in their common work. And now,
when an unexpected peril required them to adapt their organisation to political ends, their enthusiasm supplied the place of
genius. Each troop or company elected two representatives,
called "adjutators;" or, by corruption, *agitators*. These together formed a representative assembly ; and the officers were
a sort of Upper House. But the adjutators and the officers
often met for counsel, and the result was a unanimity and
firmness of purpose which neither guile nor threats could ever
disturb.

When at length Cromwell and his colleagues met the officers,
the latter were informed that Parliament had ordered an inquiry
into "certain distempers and disorders" alleged to exist in the
army. The officers caught at those words. They knew nothing
of "distempers," they said; but if the subject were grievances,
then they could speak at large. They complained that the
petition of the army, addressed to General Fairfax, had been
taken as "putting conditions on Parliament." They insisted
that "instruments of difference" between the Parliament and the
army—that is Denzil Holles, Stapylton, Clotworthy, and other
Presbyterian leaders—should be put to the proof. They resented
the resolution to disband the army suddenly, without audit of
their arrears. They protested against being left at the mercy
of malignant accusers through want of an Act of Indemnity ;
and, capping several other grievances, they mentioned the
singular and significant slander " that a petition had been sent
from the army to the King, praying him to come to them, and
they would put the crown on his head." The origin of this
rumour was perhaps the certain fact that the King, on leaving
Oxford, had wished to surrender himself to Fairfax's army, and

had been referred to Parliament. But there is little doubt that the soldiers were now growing impatient of the ecclesiastical quibbles and wrangles which seemed mainly to delay a settlement with the King. They would have made no difficulty about letting Charles have as many parsons and bishops as he pleased, if only he would allow his subjects a similar liberty of worshipping God in their own fashion.

General Skippon was the spokesman of the Commissioners in making their report to the House ; and he acted the part of peacemaker, showing how far the army had reason on their side, and at the same time soothing the wounded dignity of Parliament. There were, however, some violent spirits, who broke out into denunciations and menace. Whereupon, Cromwell whispered to Ludlow, who was sitting by, " These men will never leave till the army pull them out by the ears."* The simple republican says that he was greatly shocked, and would have resented the speech if the state of affairs would have permitted him. But it would not; and Cromwell was beginning to think that the state of affairs would not permit a good deal besides which an effete and obstinate House was bent on doing. However, the House, unconscious of the treason he had whispered, voted thanks to the Member for Cambridge and his colleagues for their services, and resolved to improve upon the terms formerly offered to the army. It is noteworthy that the allegation of a design on the part of the soldiers to draw the King to themselves was left over for further consideration. It possibly occurred to the army, thereupon, that if they could not avoid the suspicion, they might as well have the advantage of such a course of action.

The crisis now ripened rapidly. On the last day in May, the army council resolved to contract their quarters, and insisted on a general rendezvous before they should be disbanded. Fairfax wrote apologetically to the Speaker, that he was forced to yield something to avoid worse inconveniences. The Commons, in distraction, now recalled the money sent for partial payment of the army. They passed vote after vote for expediting the audit and borrowing to pay off arrears. And, what was still

---

* Ludlow, fol. ed. of 1751, p. 73. One cannot help suspecting that what Oliver really said was, " These men will *never leave off* till," &c.—*i.e.*, " They will go on in their folly till forcibly stopped."

more ominous of their humiliation, they erased from the journals the censure they had passed on the army on March 30th. But all was of no use. The soldiers were convinced that the reins of power were in the hands of a few men who, after the army had been disbanded, would sacrifice almost everything for which Marston Moor and Naseby had been won. They dreaded resorting to violence. Indeed their bitterest accusation against Holles and his friends was, that they were preparing another civil war. But these troops had not been accustomed to surrender, and they were not going to learn it now. Still, they were at their wits' end what to do next, when, on June 5th, a startling rumour ran through their quarters that a troop from Oxford had gone to Holdenby House, and were now on their way to the army with the King at their head.

How Cornet Joyce came to conceive his happy idea will probably never be known. Fairfax, one of the last men we should suspect of lying, declared it had been done without his desire or knowledge, and he believed the same thing to be true of the body of the army. If it were proved that Cromwell had ever distinctly denied complicity in this stroke of policy, we should believe him too. But his alleged denials do not rest on very good evidence; and the transaction has an air of swift vigour well worthy of him. To take the King and carry him to the army was just one of those things at once obviously desirable and easily practicable, which are only detected by the eye of genius. The King himself, after the first uneasiness of the surprise was over, began to think he had made a change for the better; and he was especially gratified to find that these praying and preaching troopers had no objection to let him have his clergy about him, but were quite willing to extend to him the liberty of conscience which they asked for themselves.* It was on Friday evening, June 4th, that Cornet Joyce conducted the King to Huntingdon, where he rested for the night in the ancestral home of the Cromwells. The panic at Westminster was severe, and it was not much allayed by the General's letter explaining the action of the soldiers. All officers were ordered immediately to their posts. But Cromwell did not need to be ordered. He had already gone. For him the die was cast.

* The relations of Cromwell and Charles I. from this time to the tragedy at Whitehall will form the subject of a separate chapter (XVI.).

The army, and the army alone, had the power to re-settle the land, and therefore with the army he would be.

Those who can see in this resolve nothing but intriguing ambition, are for the most part misled by idolatry of constitutional forms. "Here is a man," they say, "who had fought for the supremacy of Parliament, and now, when that object is attained, he turns round and fights against it. There is no consistency in such a course. But when we look at what he gained by it, the motive of his inconsistency is clear." Yet we ought not to forget that precisely the same course was followed by Fairfax, Ireton, Fleetwood, Harrison, and twenty thousand of the purest-minded men who ever took up arms for any political aims. The mere fact that Cromwell's genius and inherent power carried him to the front cannot justify our applying one standard to them and another to him. The truth is—and it is peculiarly true of Cromwell—they fought for Parliament only because Parliament represented political and religious liberty. But when Parliament showed signs of treachery to this supreme object, they declined to lay down the spoils of victory at its feet. The obstinacy of the King had broken down the forms of the constitution. Revolution had supervened, in which the strongest elements of the chaos must prevail; and with an intensity of purpose burning within him like a consuming fire, Cromwell was resolved that political and religious liberty must, and should be, one of the survivals. To him, however, the issue did not present itself so. He believed God had manifested His will in signs and wonders. Parliament was rejecting that will, and he preferred to be on the side of divine destiny rather than on that of constitutional forms.

Thus it came to pass that he departed from Westminster to the army at the beginning of June, and was apparently present at Kenford, near Bury St. Edmund's, on the 4th, when Fairfax reviewed at that place seven regiments of foot and six of horse. The troops there presented a petition to their General, desiring that they might not be asked to acquiesce in any arrangement under which their enemies would be their judges. Fairfax was hailed with wild acclamations as he rode from regiment to regiment; and it was evident that amidst the breakdown of old institutions the army was the one remaining national organ of clear, definite, and practical purpose. It was national in this sense, that it represented better than the worn-out House of Commons whatever there was in the country of coherent, intelligent conviction, as distinguished from mere inertia or blind impulse. From Essex, Bucks, Norfolk, Suffolk, Hertford, and elsewhere, petitions were presented to the Commons, expressing sympathy with the army, opposing the attempt to disband it, and urging compliance with its just desires. These petitions were not the issue of dragooning. That from Hertfordshire was signed by twelve hundred residents, and was presented at Westminster by a deputation of two hundred knights and gentlemen.

Another general review took place on June 10th at Triploe Heath, where fresh Commissioners, headed by Skippon, tried to appease the men by reading new votes passed in their favour. But the troops declined to give any immediate answer; referred everything to their "adjutators;" and, in response to expostulation, filled the air with cries of "Justice! justice!" They had passed the stage when any vote would satisfy them, except one which should remove from power the Presbyterian *junto* whom they distrusted. The position was roughly analogous to that which arises in modern times when an unpopular ministry attempts to retain power in defiance of the constituencies.

From this army gathering, a letter was addressed to the Corporation of London, intended, if possible, to reassure the City and avert useless bloodshed. The Corporation, in a flutter of distracting alarms, was alternately petitioning Parliament for satisfaction to the army and offering to raise a force against it. The letter, signed by Fairfax, Cromwell, and all the chief officers, is regarded with probability by Carlyle as a hasty composition of Oliver's. It brought out clearly the truth that beyond "satisfaction to their undoubted claims as soldiers," the army were now determined to insist on the overthrow of the Presbyterian leaders, whose continuance in power threatened to make the past war fruitless and to kindle another. "We desire," they said, "a settlement of the peace of the kingdom and of the liberties of the subject according to the votes and declarations of Parliament, which before we took arms were by the Parliament used as arguments and inducements to invite us and divers of our dear friends out, some of whom have lost their lives in this war." This settlement, they said, ought to *precede* their disbanding.

They disclaimed any " desire for " an alteration of the civil government, or any factious hostility to the Presbyterian system. " Only we could wish that every good citizen, and every man who walks peaceably in a blameless conversation, and is beneficial to the Commonwealth, might have liberty and encouragement, this being according to the true policy of all States, and even to justice itself." They scouted the fear that the " poor hungry soldiers wanted to plunder the City." They valued their pay little " in comparison of higher concernments to a public good." " It's not your wealth they seek," said the letter, " but the things tending in common to your and their welfare." Yet there was not wanting a grim warning, that if after all this the citizens should be seduced to take up arms in opposition, the writers had at least " freed themselves from all that ruin which might befall that great and populous city." *

It was now clear that the army and not the House of Commons were masters of the position; and though the useless struggle, maintained for two months longer, has considerable dramatic interest, it has no such bearing on the development of Cromwell's career as to justify any attempt to describe it here. He began now to loom very large through the whirling mists of that stormy time. The resolute demand of the army for the suspension and trial of the eleven Presbyterian leaders of the Commons House was regarded as an impeachment of *his* enemies; and his growing influence was held to prove that he " carried his business with great subtlety." †

What, however, is most apparent in the records of the time is the marked change that came over the demands of the army after Cromwell had openly sided with it against the Parliament. Previously, the soldiers had put forward most prominently their long arrears of pay, and their requirement of security for the future. The request for a speedy settlement of the country had occupied only a secondary place. Now, on the contrary, their political requirements began to predominate over all considerations of their personal interests. After sending their manifesto to the City, they formulated in detail their accusation against the eleven members, which was entirely a political impeachment. It charged these leaders with a treacherous design to rob the nation of the fruits of victory won by the New Model,

* Rushworth, part iv., Vol. I., p. 554-5.   † Whitelocke.

and with a treasonable attempt to raise an armed force for that purpose. There is no doubt that these Presbyterians would have been very glad to checkmate the Independents by raising another army if they could; and in that case they would have retorted the charge of treason on Fairfax and Cromwell. The judgment of posterity is not decided by technicalities, but by a comparative estimate of the substantial ends sought by the contending parties.

The political aims of the army were defined afresh in a petition dated June 14th. The principal points insisted on were the purification of the existing House of Commons; the appointment of a time for its dissolution; triennial elections for the future; the right of petition; and an Act of oblivion after public justice had been satisfied " by some few examples." No Parliament was henceforward to be dissolved before its full period without its own consent; and it is noteworthy that this point being conceded, a desire was expressed to restore the King to his constitutional rights, and to confirm his family in the succession. In this petition the finger of Cromwell is evident, and especially, perhaps, in this reference to the King.*

The House, however, declined to entertain the question of its own dissolution, and refused also to discuss the article relating to the King. Neither would it suspend the eleven members, but rejected the request as an invasion of privilege. Thereupon the army drew nearer to London, lodging the King at Hatfield, and taking up their head-quarters at Uxbridge. On this the eleven members withdrew, some of them hurrying abroad, while others lingered in the City. The army could now afford to be gracious. The Council disclaimed any intention to invade privilege; commended the " modesty " of the accused members in wishing to retire; and expressed a hope that nothing would be done to hinder them.

Then followed a month of distracted disorder, in which the demoralised House was scolded and threatened by riotous citizens on the one hand, and overawed, on the other, by the thundercloud of the army, hovering now nearer, now further, according to the behaviour of members. It was the question of the City militia that drew down the lightning. At the request of the Corporation this force was placed under new

* See Chap. XVII.

management, in which the Presbyterian magnates had greater confidence. In obedience to the army, the House rescinded this order, and restored the City forces to the old management. This was indeed a vital question, admitting of no compromise. The only foe against whom the militia could be needed at present was the army ; and to the soldiers the new organisation was a revival of the stigma which branded them as public enemies. They had had quite enough of war, and they could not stand by while preparations for fresh hostilities were made before their eyes. They therefore insisted on keeping the militia weak, and at the same time demanded from Parliament an assurance that no foreign forces should be brought into the country. This was on July 20th. And as an illustration of the higher policy of the army leaders, it is interesting to note that, in addition to other demands, their Commissioners, among whom Cromwell was supreme, requested the discharge of all persons imprisoned for no other crime than maintaining " conventicles." The orthodox City bitterly resented these concessions. The apprentices took up the quarrel of their masters, and on the 26th the ill-feeling broke out in a riot which placed in a startling light the ignominious weakness of the once-omnipotent Parliament.

On that day a resistless rabble filled Palace Yard and Westminster Hall, blocked up the entrances of both Lords and Commons, invaded the lobbies, and insulted and hustled the members passing in. A number of sturdy lads climbed to the windows of the Upper House, and threw stones at the august legislators within. The proceedings of the Commons were disturbed by violent knocks at the door of their chamber. Some of the members indignantly drew their swords, and facing the mob in the lobby, drove them back. But the disorder and clamour making debate impossible, the House resolved to rise, affecting to disdain riotous threats. When, however, the Speaker essayed to pass through the lobby, he was violently driven back, and some forty or fifty of the mob rushed pell-mell with the retreating members into the House. The Speaker, forced into the chair, showed less firmness towards King Mob than he had exhibited on a former occasion towards more legitimate majesty. Gazing helplessly around him, he asked the rioters what vote they desired to have passed.

" That the King should be desired to come to London forth-with," was the answer. He then put the question in due form. " No ! " shouted Ludlow, but his voice was solitary, and the " Ayes" had it. " What more now ? " asked the Speaker. " That he should come with honour, freedom, and safety," bellowed the invaders of the House. This question also he put. " No ! " shouted Ludlow again. But the " Ayes " had it ; and then the House was permitted by its wild assessors to adjourn.

This, surely, was the bottom of the abyss. Lower than that an Imperial Parliament could hardly sink. The unnatural strain of war between organs of the same body corporate had exhausted the victors at the same time that it ruined the vanquished. Another month of this, and blank anarchy might efface all the results of a history rich in fruitful experience. In that time of despair even visionaries like Ludlow saw no hope except in the strong stern unity of purpose and disciplined vigour that knit the army into a type of orderly freedom. True, the army was subject to a man whose supremacy over elements of chaos threatened a new sovereignty of which they had not dreamed when they struck down the throne. But between the whirlwind and the waves welcome is any sturdy rock to which the ship-wrecked may cling with closed eyes till the hour of agony is past. No wonder therefore that Sir Arthur Haslerig persuaded the Speaker to go down to the army, or that he was joined in his flight by a hundred members, besides those of the Upper House.

The head-quarters of the army were now at High Wycombe. The anarchy of London left the officers' council obviously no choice but to advance at once ; and on July 31st the army reached Uxbridge. The City train-bands were called out, and for a day or two there was some risk that all previous miseries of war would be eclipsed by the horrors of a street fight in the crowded capital. On August 3rd the two Speakers, with fourteen Lords and a hundred Commons, met the generals and the whole army on Hounslow Heath, and were received with acclamation. " Lords and Commons ! " " A free Parliament ! " shouted the soldiers ; and honourable members took what comfort they could from this display of attachment to constitutional forms.

Meanwhile, the Commons who had remained in Westminster e ected another Speaker, and affected to proceed as though nothing had happened. The City made some show of resistance, but finally the Common Council despatched a submissive letter to Fairfax, beseeching peace. In response, the General demanded, and received, the surrender of all military posts on the west of London and in Southwark. Then, on the 6th, the New Model Army marched into Westminster, and brought its triumphs to a climax by submerging the Parliament it had been formed to defend. Every point of importance was occupied by soldiers, and at the entrances to the Houses a double line formed an avenue to the very doors of the chambers. By Hyde Park, St. James's, and Whitehall, the grim array of fighting saints moved on—first Colonel Hammond's foot, with steady tramp; then Cromwell and his renowned troopers, himself the centre of wonder and curiosity to both friends and foes; afterwards Sir Thomas Fairfax, amidst his life guards; and, finally, in a procession of coaches, the members of the two Houses.

On the following day the army marched through the City, preserving a gravity and order no less amazing than welcome to the alarmed citizens. In Parliament a month's pay was ordered as a gratuity to the men, an amount which there was much difficulty in borrowing; and then began a long wrangle, which does not concern us, about the validity of the proceedings since the riots of the previous month. The eleven members were judiciously permitted to escape; and towards the end of August the King was conducted to Hampton Court. The army had thus proved itself master of England's destinies. It remained now to be seen who was master of the army.

CHAPTER XV.

THE ARMY AND ITS MASTER.

FROM September 1647 to May 1648 Cromwell was continually occupied in futile negotiations with the King. A careful study of these negotiations is necessary to any right understanding of Oliver's character. In order, however, to exhibit at one view the causes of failure in those efforts, it will be best to give an entire chapter to the relations between Cromwell and the King, together with the dread issue at Whitehall. For the present, we may, as far as possible, confine our attention to parliamentary and military affairs, together with a glance at one or two incidents of more private interest. And the last may conveniently come first. It does not appear that the tithe-farmer of Ely had hitherto profited to any considerable extent pecuniarily by his services to the nation. At length, by the end of 1647, a grant out of the Marquis of Worcester's estates became substantially available. Cromwell estimated it at £1,600 per annum,* and the first use he made of it was to surrender a thousand pounds a year for five years, or until the end of the Irish war, towards the expenses of that service. At the time (March, 1648) there was an outstanding amount of £1,500 due to him as Lieutenant-General to the Earl of Manchester. Two years' salary was likewise owing to him as Governor of the Isle of Ely. These claims he also surrendered entirely.

Yet, when this sacrifice was made, the projected marriage of Richard suggested some considerable pecuniary demands on his father. Richard was not exactly a joy or a credit to his parents, nor was he, on the other hand, a disgrace. His was a negative character, without impulses, without susceptibilities, and well adapted to vegetate peacefully for eighty-six years. But he must have been a great disappointment to his father, and his insensibility to the questions of the age must have added

* Letter to the Derby House Committee, March 21, 1647–8; given by Carlyle.

untold bitterness to the loss of the two elder sons. However, he had to be married; and as the eldest son of a man now making a considerable figure in the State he must be enabled to keep up a fair appearance. According to the social notions of our own times he was still very young for marriage, being only twenty-one years of age. But in this matter alone he appeared disposed to follow his father's example. The young lady of his choice was Dorothy, the daughter of Mr. Richard Mayor, of Hursley Manor, near Winchester. Her father was a respectable, religious man, of orthodox Presbyterian associations. To this date he had not been prominent in the conflicts of the time; but in the process of the marriage negotiations, notwithstanding that many difficulties arose, Oliver seems to have taken a fancy to Mayor, and pushed him afterwards into the Little Parliament, and other positions of uncomfortable responsibility.

Richard had apparently made the acquaintance of Dorothy Mayor through Colonel Richard Norton, his father's fellow-soldier in the days of the Eastern Counties Association, but now residing in Hampshire, and, indeed, representing the county in Parliament.* To Colonel Norton Oliver wrote at the end of February, 1648, expressing his approval; and at the end of March the two fathers met at Farnham, in Kent. Cromwell was favourably impressed, but found that Mr. Mayor's opinion of him had been a little prejudiced. Writing to Norton the day after he says :—" Some things of common fame did a little stick : I gladly heard his doubts, and gave such answer as was next at hand—I believe to some satisfaction. Nevertheless, I exceedingly liked the gentleman's plainness and free dealing with me." The "things of common fame" were probably Oliver's dubious position between the Parliament and the army, and almost cer tainly his leaning to sectarian license.

A more real difficulty arose, however, when the marriage settlement came to be considered. In a letter to Norton on this subject Cromwell reckoned the value of his estate at little less than £3,000 per annum. This was to descend to Richard, an arrangement betraying the father's inherited sympathy with the ideas of the landed gentry. Meantime he was willing to set aside £400 or £500 a year for the maintenance of the young couple. But he insisted that Mr. Mayor, who had no son,

* He was one of the " recruiters " elected in 1645.

should settle the Manor of Hursley upon his eldest daughter. A more singular requirement was that Mr. Mayor should pay Oliver £2,000 in money. The explanation is that Mr. Mayor had already offered as much in a previously projected match for his daughter; and, besides, Oliver had other children to provide for. "The money," he says, "I shall need for my two little wenches,* and thereby I shall free my son from being charged with them."

Thereupon the treaty was broken off. But in the following year it was re-opened through the mediation of Mr. Robinson, a preacher of Southampton. The letters written by Oliver to Richard Mayor in the course of this revived negotiation are interesting from the light they shed on the character of the former, both as a father and as a man of business. He was eagerly desirous of effecting a union, the principal attraction of which lay in the moral influences likely to be exerted on his son. At the same time he stood firmly to the interest of the "two little wenches." "I may not be so much wanting," he says, "to myself nor family, as not to have some equality of consideration towards it. I have two young daughters to bestow, if God give them life and opportunity. According to your offer I have nothing for them—nothing at all in hand." Oliver was also of opinion that young people should not be too independent. He would leave a margin between legal obligation and paternal benevolence; or, as he put it, "he would have somewhat free to be thanked by them for." At the same time, he would have the engagement entirely dependent on the mutual liking of the young people. The marriage finally came off in the spring of 1649. When it is borne in mind that during the progress of this contract Oliver was already one of the foremost men in England, and likely, in the opinion of many, to become pre-eminent, it will be acknowledged that his conduct and correspondence on the subject are remarkable for the absence of pretence or assumption, and for the pure domesticity of feeling evinced.

Let us go back to the autumn of 1647. Notwithstanding army difficulties, a few troops had been got over to Ireland, mainly by the management of Colonel Michael Jones, late Governor of Chester, who was commissioned by the Parliament to accept from the Marquis of Ormond the surrender of Dublin.

* Mary, aged eleven; and Frances, aged nine.

For a long time the war in Ireland had smouldered uncertainly, fitfully blazing out and dying down under the vacillating policy of Charles, who would fain have pitted his rebels in Ireland against his rebels in England. But Colonel Jones showed the different temper of the Parliament by sallying from Dublin and gaining a considerable victory. The rebel army around London did not look very favourably on their comrades who had gone to Ireland without obtaining the conditions insisted on by the agitators. And Denzil Holles, in his vindictive "Memoirs," speaks of Colonel Jones as neglected by the army party. Whatever truth there may have been in this, it was not true of the man whom Holles himself regarded as the moving spirit of the army party. Cromwell felt impelled to write a note of warm congratulation to the new Governor of Dublin, and in doing so he naturally referred to the questionable conduct of himself and his colleagues at home :—

"Though, it may be, for the present a cloud may lie over our actions to those who are not acquainted with the grounds of them, yet we doubt not but God will clear our integrity and innocency from any other ends we aim at but His glory and the public good. And as you are an instrument herein, so we shall, as becometh us, upon all occasions give you your due honour." *

During the autumn and winter Oliver was constantly in his place in Parliament. Reform and pacification did not progress satisfactorily. One cause of failure was the decrepitude of the House of Commons, which, after sitting seven years, had "lost touch" with the country. Yet it may be questioned how far a general election could have helped matters in the desperate pass to which national affairs had come. Revolution had become essential to future political progress; and the proper instrument of revolution was not Parliament, but the army. Another reason for the helplessness of Parliament was the invincible ignorance of the King, whom no calamities and no terrors could divest of the delusion that he was as necessary to the British Commonwealth as the sun to the solar system. And a third reason was the deadlock in ecclesiastical affairs. If the country could have been polled on this question, there is little doubt that it would have supported a moderate episcopacy. The majority of those who had the art of making

* Letter XLVI., in Carlyle.

themselves heard in Parliament were in favour of rigid, uncompromising Presbyterianism.　But the army, now the arbiter
of the nation's fate, cared little what form of Church government were set up, provided freedom within tolerably wide
limits were given to separatists.

Cromwell, with his instinctive sense of practical possibilities,
knew that to oppose in Parliament the establishment of Presbyterianism was entirely hopeless.　All his efforts therefore were
directed towards a limitation of the time for which the Presbyterian experiment was to be tried.　On October 13th (1647)
he was teller in a division in favour of limiting it to three
years, but was beaten in a House of seventy-three by a majority
of three.　Again he was teller in favour of affirming the
principle of a limit, and carried this by fourteen.　On a third
division he supported a seven years' limit, but was defeated
by a majority of eight.　Such were the wrangles that occupied
the great council of a nation on the verge of disruption.　And
the moral cowardice characteristic of the worn-out House was
shown by the final adoption of unmeaning phraseology.　The
limit was to be " the end of the next session of Parliament after
the end of this present session."　Considering that the " present
session " had lasted seven years, and might last seventy, such a
term was doubtless accepted as equivalent to the Greek kalends.

But a question of a more vital character than any ecclesiastical controversies now demanded all the energies of Cromwell.
The army was quartered round London, mainly in the west,
having its head-quarters at Putney, within convenient distance
of Hampton Court, where the King was lodged.　In proportion
as the hopelessness of negotiation with Charles became more
and more apparent, the temper of the army grew more resolved.
Now that so many decent forms and amiable pretences had
been torn away from popular relations to the royal court, it
was inevitable that speculations should become rife, with which
the political capacities of that age were scarcely prepared to
deal.　In the army, a party of " Levellers " had arisen, whose
name is sufficiently indicative of their opinions.　And yet, at
this period of their history, perhaps the name does them injustice.　There was nothing very terrible or destructive in
their notions, for they only insisted, in effect, that rights and
responsibilities should be interpreted in the light of facts,

and not in that of fictions, legal or otherwise. Their chief fault was, that in their stage of the world's history their doctrines were impracticable, and in the eyes of Cromwell this was sufficient condemnation. The most obvious application of their main principle was to the case of the King himself, who was fictitiously irresponsible, but who as a matter of fact had obstinately refused the only system of government adapted to make royal irresponsibility endurable.

If we may judge by Cromwell's actions, there were in his view two limits to be observed in conceding to the army the freedom of discussion and political action justified by the extraordinary circumstances of the time and by the no less extraordinary character of the army itself. In the first place no factious section should be permitted to impose its will on the whole body, still less to sow dissension; and in the next place no disobedience to the commands of officers should be tolerated.

A perusal of the numerous documents put forth by the army about this time shows that these troopers, by virtue only of moral feeling and common sense, had ante-dated by two hundred years the slow conclusions of modern political experience. They would have abolished the privileges of rotten boroughs, and enfranchised more modern centres of population. They advocated something very like equal electoral districts. They were very careful of the power and dignity at least of any future Parliament, insisting emphatically that members should be free from the censure of any authority outside their own House. The making of war or peace was not to be without advice of Parliament. Bishops were to have no coercive power; but as to the abolition of their office, the army council was even yet comparatively indifferent.* Religious equality was laid down with a breadth marvellous for the time, but of course with the fatal exception of Roman Catholics. As Denzil Holles says in his criticism of these proposals—to him suggestive of epidemic lunacy—"there might be meetings to practise anything of superstition or folly!"

So far as such proposals went the army were practically unanimous, and Cromwell was heartily with them. But in regard to the fate of the King, and also as to the form of govern-

---

* This is certainly suggested by the "Army Declaration" of Aug. 1, 1647.

ment to be established for the future, there was not the same harmony. The Levellers, the extreme Radicals of the day, were already demanding vengeance on the " chief delinquent ; " while both in and out of the army Republican theorists were gaining strength and courage. Cromwell, not being a theorist, and finding, as yet, no sufficient indication as to the best practical issue, was anxious to prevent any premature declaration, much more any premature violence, on the part of the army. If he was rightly informed that there was a plot for the King's assassination, there must have been some worse elements in the army than its conduct otherwise would have led us to suppose. It is more than likely that his alarm on this subject hastened the King's departure from Hampton Court, as we shall see in the next chapter.

On November 15th, four days after that departure, there was a review of troops at Corkbush Field, near Ware. Sir Thomas Fairfax was in command, but his Lieutenant-General took the most active part in the unexpectedly precarious duties of the day. Two regiments came on the ground unbidden. Their defiant behaviour indicated mutiny, and their purpose was proclaimed by a document styled an "Agreement of the English People," copies of which were worn in their hats as cockades. The difference in force of character between Sir Thomas Fairfax and his second in command was very evident on this occasion. Fairfax had already apologised for disorders he could not repress, and had he been alone he must have done so in this difficulty as well. But Cromwell felt at once that the chaos in which the constitution had foundered was now threatening the army also. To maintain order here was an issue of life or death, to be decided on the instant. Therefore, taking with him a few resolute officers, he rode up to the mutinous regiments, and ordered them to take the papers out of their hats. There was a moment of hesitation, followed by sullen cries and general disobedience.

On board a war ship in action a man has been known to pick up from the deck a live shell, with the fuse rapidly burning, to carry it deliberately to the side, and drop it overboard. What his sensations may have been during the few seconds of suspense certainly no one could describe but himself, and probably he would afterwards be able to recall nothing but an intense conviction that he must and would succeed. It was not a bombshell

Cromwell had to quench at that moment, but a magazine of moral explosives, enough to rend into shreds whatever remnants of order and security existed in the land. If an order of arrest should spread the mutiny to the other regiments, from that hour the authority won on hard-fought fields would be of no more avail than the charred fragments of a man flung aside by an explosion. But the probability is Oliver had no misgiving.

He ordered the arrest of eleven ringleaders, who unresistingly surrendered. They were tried instantly by court-martial. Three were condemned to death. The sacrifice of one, however, was thought to be a sufficient lesson; and as no difference in degrees of guilt appeared, the three cast dice for their lives, and the one upon whom the lot fell was there and then shot to death by a file of his fellow soldiers. For this action Cromwell received the thanks of the House of Commons; but the republican Ludlow is careful to tell us that he disapproved, and vociferously voted " No." *

The departure of Charles from Hampton Court, his reception and virtual imprisonment at Carisbrooke, together with the vain attempts at a treaty with him, almost entirely occupied the attention of Parliament and army for several months. Meantime ominous tokens of inflamed feeling, boding a revival of civil war, appeared both north and west and south—nay, in the City of London itself. The most serious danger was threatened by a possible conjunction of 40,000 Scots, under the Duke of Hamilton, with English malcontents. In the spring of 1648, Sir Marmaduke Langdale, Cromwell's opponent at Naseby, joined Hamilton with 3,000 English horse. If they should effect a further junction with forces gathering in Wales they might become resistless.

It appears to have been this extreme danger that saved Cromwell from arrest and impeachment. There can be no wonder that the two-fold advantage he possessed from his power over the army and his influence in Parliament should excite jealousy. And Major Huntington, who had for some time been content with any menial employment from Cromwell, now

---

* In an interview with Ludlow, desired by Cromwell, in 1650, for the purpose of removing the dissatisfaction of the former with his conduct, the execution of this soldier was referred to. Cromwell defended it, " as absolutely necessary to keep things from falling into confusion, which must have ensued upon that division if it had not been timely prevented."—*Ludlow's Memoirs.*

thought to make some profit by furnishing the materials for an accusation. The charges against him were based on Oliver's difficult and ambiguous position between King, Parliament, and army. However, as usual, his services were indispensable even when most unwelcome, and his enemies came to the conclusion that "the preferring the accusation at this time was to weaken the army." The army was needed in Wales, and might soon be needed further north. And as Fairfax was engaged with disorders nearer home, in Kent and Essex, Cromwell was designated for the more distant service. The actual order was not given to him until the 1st of May. But he must have known very well that it was coming, and several days of the previous month were spent in a sort of preparation not very usual in the history of war.

In April 1648 a number of the officers and adjutators of the army, sick of fruitless treaties and party intrigues, agreed to meet together at Windsor Castle for prayer and self-examination. The human heart is proverbially deceitful, and we may well believe that with their pious aspirations not a little of self-will and party spirit was mingled. But they had at this time very serious cause to fear that all their hopes of a free, pure, and peaceable England would be blighted in the very moment of expected fruition. The terror-stricken advocates of a fatal compromise were nerved to desperate efforts by the returning clouds of war. If Royalists, Presbyterians, and Scots, should combine, it was little to say that home and peace and life had been sacrificed in vain. What was far worse in the eyes of these militant saints was that their country would be found fighting against God instead of fighting for Him, and that the succession of signs and wonders by which the Divine will had been declared in the past sanguinary years would be impiously rejected. How was it that they who knew God's will had become so powerless to do it? This was the question to which they determined to seek an answer in the very presence of the Eternal. One day spent in united prayer brought no light. "On the morrow," says Adjutant Allen,* whom we have seen before at the bar of the House of Commons, " we met again in the morning, where many spake from the word and prayed. And the then

---

* His account was written in 1659, when a more inevitable ruin threatened the life's work of himself and his comrades.

Lieutenant-General Cromwell did press very earnestly on all there present a thorough consideration of our actions as an army, and of our ways particularly* as private Christians, to see if any iniquity could be found in them, and what it was; that, if possible, we might find it out, and so remove the cause of such sad rebukes as were upon us by reason of our iniquities, as we judged, at that time." † What was done further, and what dread issues became clear, will be considered afterwards. Meanwhile, let us note that on the third day the light broke in, and they came with one heart and mind to the resolve that, instead of quitting the service and going back to their farms, as many had thought of doing, they would arise once more to the help of the Lord against the mighty. "It was the duty of their day," they saw, "with the forces they had, to go out and fight those potent enemies which that year in all places appeared against them; and this with a humble confidence in the name of the Lord only that they would destroy them." Does any one wonder that these men were invincible?

It was on Monday the 1st of May that Cromwell received the order to march, and on Wednesday the 3rd he started. His main object was to take Pembroke town and castle from Colonel Poyer, once an officer in the Parliamentary service, but now recalcitrant. The colonel had taken to drinking, and his conduct was eccentric and violent. But the advantages of the post he held induced the Royalists of South Wales to rally for his support. If he were suppressed, then Cromwell would be free to face the Scots. But his suppression proved to be so tedious a business, that if the northern invaders had been ably led they might have effected a junction with the Welsh insurgents before Cromwell could meet them except at the cost of surrendering South Wales. The detachment ordered on this service consisted of Cromwell's own regiment of horse, with another, and three regiments of foot. If we may believe a newspaper of the time,‡ the expedition was by no means popular in the army. Some men "were unwilling and refused, because they apprehended that all they had done had rather brought

---

* *I.e.*, individually.
† "Very unintelligible to posterity," says Carlyle. Why so? Have we ceased to believe in *any* power that justly exacts retribution? If not, differences of form, devotional or otherwise, are easily allowed for.
‡ *Moderate Intelligencer*, May 5, 1648, quoted in "Cromwelliana."

an increase of enemies than friends, of hatred rather than love; and therefore they could see no call to fight more, and adventure their lives to increase displeasures, and studies of revenge." We may presume these men had not been at the Windsor prayer-meeting, and did not belong to the Lieutenant-General's regiment. Nevertheless even these yielded to persuasion, "and gone they are, to the great grief of many, who were confident that the soldiers had been so tampered with since they left fighting, that they would be divided, and draw several ways."

As usual, Cromwell lost no time on the march, and reached Chepstow on May 11th. This town was in possession of the insurgents, and could not be gained by a sudden assault. It was, therefore, blocked by a force left under Colonel Ewer, and Cromwell pushed on by Swansea to Pembroke, where he arrived on the 21st. The needful artillery was sent by sea from Bristol, but the vessel struck on a bank, and the guns were not forthcoming. In this difficulty "honest Mr. Peters," who seemed always to have followed Cromwell with admiring zeal, went on board the *Lion* war-ship in Milford Haven, and borrowed six guns, for which batteries were erected. An attempted storm failed, and the siege was prolonged for six weeks. Both besiegers and besieged were hard pushed for supplies. Major-General Langhorne, a gentleman of the district, had shut himself up with Colonel Poyer, and was " very sick of body and mind."* The Parliamentary soldiers seized his cattle, whereupon his wife addressed herself to Cromwell, beseeching his consideration. In reply, he restored the cattle, on her promise that they should be forthcoming if required; and he also gave her leave to go to her husband in the castle, taking a doctor with her. A less amiable but more business-like aspect of his character is illustrated by a letter† written during this siege, giving minute directions to Major Saunders, an officer at Brecknock, how to proceed in the arrest of two suspected local magistrates. One was Sir Trevor Williams, of Llangibby, near Monmouth town; the other, Mr. Morgan, the High-Sheriff of Monmouth county. The thorough acquaintance shown with the disposition, temper, intentions, and habits of these men, and the curiously detailed directions as to Saunders's action in case of various possible contingencies, show the keen watchfulness of the writer's attitude,

* " Cromwelliana," p. 40. † Letter LX., in Carlyle.

and his extraordinary power of collecting and digesting in-formation.

As the siege lengthened out both assailants and defenders listened anxiously for news from the North. Poyer over and over again swore deep oaths that Langdale would send them relief in a few days, and at length confirmed his assurance by an offer that his men should hang him if it were not fulfilled. Cromwell, on the other hand, despatched six troops of horse and dragoons, by way of Chester, to render such service as might be feasible in preparing for the Scottish advance. At last, however, on July 11th 1648, both town and castle were surrendered on con-ditions stern towards Parliamentary deserters, who were required to surrender unconditionally, but moderate enough towards all others, who were guaranteed their life and liberty.

Cromwell now hurried away the whole detachment he had brought with him from Windsor, leaving local forces to finish the Welsh insurrection. His men at this time were in a very ragged condition, and a considerable number were absolutely without shoes or stockings. He marched through the Midlands by Leicester; and from Northampton—even then a metropolis of shoemakers—3,000 pairs of shoes were sent to the former town to be ready for him. Leicester was perhaps already strong enough in hosiery to provide him with stockings. What hap-pened when he reached Nottingham Mrs. Hutchinson tells us:—

"When he came to Nottingham, Colonel Hutchinson * went to see him, whom he embraced with all the expressions of kindness that one friend could make to another; and then, retiring with him, asked what thoughts his friends the Levellers had of him. The colonel, who was the freest man in the world from concealing truth from his friend, especially when it was required of him in love and plainness, not only told him what others thought of him, but what he himself conceived, and how much it would darken all his glories if he should become a slave to his own ambition, and be guilty of what he gave the world just cause to suspect; and therefore begged of him to wear his heart in his face, and to scorn to delude his enemies, but to make use of his noble courage to maintain what he believed just against all opposers. Cromwell made mighty professions of a sincere heart to him."

But from what happened afterwards Mrs. Hutchinson inferred

* Colonel Hutchinson had resigned his governorship of Nottingham. The post was now held by Colonel Poulton. Both Colonel and Mrs. Hutchinson held that the so-called "Levellers" had some very sensible notions

that her husband's frankness had determined Cromwell to beware of him as an obstacle in the path of his ambition.

Meantime the Duke of Hamilton, with an army of some 21,000 men, including 4,000 English under Sir Marmaduke Langdale, and some regiments of Irish horse under General Monro, had crossed the border, and was marching southward. It was uncertain whether he intended to advance through Yorkshire or Lancashire. Oliver, crediting his antagonist with the better strategy, joined his own little army at Wetherby on August 12th. Such reinforcements as he was able to sweep together raised his force to a little over 8,000, but the heart and soul of it was the detachment which since the beginning of May had marched from Windsor, fought its way through South Wales, and struggled, footsore and weary, into the North. Hearing now that the invaders had chosen the Lancashire route, he made a flank march, continued for four successive days, to Stonyhurst, near to which was a bridge over the Hodder, a tributary on the right bank of the Ribble. From that bridge to Preston the distance was nine miles, without any further impediment. Hamilton was marching in very loose order along and on either side of the great road stretching southwards through Lancaster, Preston, Wigan, and Warrington. His motive for preferring this road was the hope, cherished through defective information, that he would be joined in Cheshire by insurgents from Wales, and possibly reinforcements from Ireland. The three days' fight that began on August 17th was, in brief, as if a resolute man should find a long snake crawling stealthily by him, should cut it in two with a single blow of an axe, and then, seeing the fore-part still living and wriggling away, should follow it up until he had chopped it into bits.

On the evening of the 16th, before crossing the Hodder, it was ascertained that the Duke of Hamilton himself, with the main body, had reached Preston; that some of the hostile cavalry had gone on towards Wigan; that the rear was still straggling up from the north; and that Sir Marmaduke Langdale, with 7,000* men, lay between Stonyhurst and Preston. A council of war was then called, and Oliver laid before his comrades two alternatives—either to march southwards through Whalley and head the

* The force under Langdale here included some 3,000 additional to the numbers given by Whitelocke.

enemy off from London, or to break in upon his flank at once, and trust to the effect of a bold and sudden stroke. Such a council under a General who knows his own mind easily comes to a decision. It was resolved that "to engage the enemy to fight was their business," and few precious moments were lost from their brief night's rest before they crossed Hodder Bridge, and took up quarters in and around Stonyhurst Hall, "a Papist's house, one Sherburne's." During his march Cromwell had received various letters from discontented Republicans, who assured him that in this hour of extreme need they only desired to strengthen his hands.* But it is probable the object of their newly-awakened sympathy drew more inspiration from a remembrance of the Windsor prayer-meeting. Very early in the morning of August 17th all were on the alert, and an advanced guard of 200 foot and 400 horse was pushed on towards Preston to feel the way. Langdale believed that the unexpected enemy was Colonel Ashton, a local Presbyterian magnate, with a hastily-raised force of 3,000 men. Still, to make all sure, he ordered a concentration from his out-quarters, and drew up his force in a strong position amongst the enclosed fields, extending two miles from Preston. He had the river on his right, and a moor in front, on to which he sent a body of scouts and skirmishers. His communication with the advanced part of the main army towards Wigan lay across the Ribble Bridge. The position was approached by a lane from the moor, the ground on either side being soft and miry, besides being crossed by fences.

The "forlorns," as they were called, advanced cautiously, and it must have been nearly noon when the little band of 400 horse came upon Langdale's scouts and outposts. Neither side being disposed to retire, an obstinate skirmish ensued. The "forlorn of foot" hastened up, the main body being yet more than a mile behind. The order of battle was that Cromwell's own regiment

---

* "Some of us who had opposed the Lieutenant-General's arbitrary proceedings, when we were convinced he acted to promote a selfish and unwarrantable design, now, thinking ourselves obliged to strengthen his hands in that necessary work which he was appointed to undertake, writ a letter to him to encourage him, from a consideration of the justice of the cause wherein he was engaged, and the wickedness of those with whom he was to encounter, to proceed with all cheerfulness," &c. (Ludlow, p. 100, fol. ed.). "*That necessary work he was appointed to undertake.*" Were Ludlow and his friends always infallible judges of what was "necessary work?" Oliver thought not; and as to appointment, his notion was—"there be higher than they."

of horse, together with Colonel Harrison's, should charge up the lane. The foot soldiers were ranged on either side. Two regiments of horse were thrown out to the right—too far, as it turned out—and the remaining cavalry, with the exception of one regiment in reserve to ensure a passage through the lane, was placed on the left, down towards the river and the bridge. These dispositions being made, Cromwell himself rode forward to the front,* and found the advanced guards still skirmishing. The two poor companies of foot were drawn up waiting for supports, but Cromwell coming up wished them to march. The officers, not having half their men, " desired a little patience." But the only answer their general made was to give the order with his own lips—" March ! " Whereupon they did march, and so supported the skirmishing horse that opportunity was given to bring up the whole army.

Langdale's advanced guards being now driven in, an obstinate fight followed in the lane, in the fields at either side, and towards the river. The enemy had an eye to their communications by the bridge, and kept " shogging down " in that direction, so that Cromwell's right wing was left idle. Colonel Thornhaugh, in command there, fretted at this inaction. Alas, next day brought a glorious end to this and all other vexations for him ! At last, after four hours of hurly-burly, often at push of pike or clash of sword, with pistols fired close enough to singe each other's beards, the battle rolled down by the bridge and also back to Preston town, carrying disorder and dismay into the Duke of Hamilton's main body. They were not allowed any time for recovery. Four troops of Cromwell's own men, followed by Harrison's regiment, rode right into the town, sweeping their opponents along the streets. There was no hope of a rally on this side the Ribble. Some of Hamilton's horse, under Monro, galloped in headlong flight towards Lancaster, with Oliver's fierce saints following ten miles at their heels; nor did they escape without the loss of five hundred horses and many prisoners. But the main body of the invaders followed their distracted commander over Ribble Bridge, and streamed on mechanically towards Wigan.

* This appears from a comparison of Hodgson's account with Cromwell's letter about the battle. To learn anything of Cromwell's personal conduct in battle we always have to supplement his account by those of others.

There was little rest that night for either conquerors or conquered. When we remember that the victorious army, numbering scarcely more than 8,000 men in all, were on the march for seven days always on the alert, and for three of those days fighting at the same time, we may be sure that sleep was got somehow. But their General was ashamed of the necessity, and lamented that the enemy's rear should have marched three miles from Ribble Bridge before he was overtaken. That enemy was still 12,000 strong, and was chased by less than half that number all the way to Wigan. Here there was some skirmishing; but both pursuers and pursued were too weary for fighting, and lay in the town or in the field, exhausted, and bemired with "twelve miles of such ground as 'the General' never rode in all his life." On the way thither, Colonel Thornhaugh, "pressing too boldly," was pierced with three lance-wounds, and left dead on the field. When his men began to discuss his successor, their desires turned toward Colonel Hutchinson.

As soon as the summer morning broke the weary flight and chase began again, and flowed on, still along the great road towards Warrington. Within three miles of that town, at the village of Winwick, a resolute stand at length was made. Cromwell was with the advanced guard of his army, some distance before his main body, when he came upon the enemy in this position.* After losing a thousand killed and two thousand prisoners, the remnant retreated to Warrington, and barricaded the bridge over the Mersey. The Duke of Hamilton now went off with 3,000 cavalry, leaving General Baillie, with 4,000 horse and foot, to do the best he could for himself. But the only thing General Baillie could do was to surrender, on promise of life and " civil usage." The relentless persistency of Cromwell in pursuit was shown by the letters he at once sent off to ensure the capture of the Duke. The cavalry were too "miserably beaten out" to " trot after him." But he had no chance of escape, and was taken a few days afterwards in Staffordshire. Thus the whole of this invading army of 24,000† men was pulverised and scattered to the winds in a three days' fight by a force not more than one-third of its size.

By this extraordinary victory Cromwell was naturally much

---

* This is implied in the language of his despatch: " We held them in some dispute till our army came up."   † Including accessions in Lancashire.

elated, and his elation, as usual, has left its traces in the effusive religious phraseology of his letters. Writing to Lord Wharton, of the Derby House Committee, to congratulate him on the birth of a son and heir, he breaks out in ejaculation : " When we think of our God, what are we? Oh, His mercy to the whole society of saints—despised, jeered saints! Let them mock on!" It is impossible to repress the thought that such humility came very easy to the master of victorious legions, just as it does to the master of accumulated wealth in the Church of our own times. It is a cheap virtue to request the world to " mock on " when we have the world pretty well under our feet. But in Cromwell's case it is probable that this effusiveness was the forced outlet of an excitement that stirred the old morbid elements of hypochondria. In another letter of that time, addressed to Oliver St. John, there is surely a gleam of sheer fanaticism in the story of a dying man expiring in Preston the day before the battle. This man asked for a handful of grass, and when it was brought him, inquired "whether it would wither or not, now it was cut." Then, being answered " Yea," he prophesied that " so should this army of the Scots wither and come to nothing." Making all allowance for the puritanic habit of a too literal adherence to Old Testament precedents, we cannot help feeling that only morbid excitement would attach importance to an incident like this.

On the other hand, there is evident in all Cromwell's letters on such occasions a genuine desire to suppress any tendency to boastfulness. He had in him enough of the mystic to feel a keen joy in the idea of self-effacement before the Infinite Power. Compelled to the most vigorous self-assertion in the tumults of his time, he satisfied his own conscience, and found a real relief in passionate confessions of his nothingness before God. " I can say nothing, but surely the Lord our God is a great and glorious God! He only is worthy to be feared and trusted, and His appearances particularly to be waited for. He will not fail His people. ' Let every thing that hath breath praise the Lord!'" We cannot mistake the ring of genuine devotion in such words, but that is quite consistent with the existence in the same soul of a spiritual incontinence and lack of simplicity resulting sometimes in an unpleasant effusiveness.

Although there was now no enemy in the field—at least none

worth much attention—it was necessary, for the thorough completion of the work he had undertaken, that the commander of the North should go into Scotland. The Duke of Hamilton, though backed up by Presbyterians, had represented a Scottish party with whom Royalism stood before any ecclesiastical aims. It was not a large party, and the Preston rout had so paralysed it that Argyll and his friends, whose principle was the presbytery first and royalty afterwards, could now assume the government. To them, therefore, Cromwell addressed himself, explaining the benevolent intentions of their English brethren, and claiming the garrisons of Berwick and Carlisle. No resistance was offered him; but he thought it expedient, nevertheless, to advance into the Lothians, if only as a demonstration of the power of the English Parliament. Argyll and the new ruling committee were pleased rather than otherwise by his resolve, as it ensured the destruction of their political opponents.

Cromwell, on his part, maintained the strictest discipline among his troops, and declared his resolve to "be more tender towards the kingdom of Scotland, in the point of charge," than if he had been in England. Some local troops of the northern counties, disregarding the threat of death, ventured on plundering, no doubt in sore need, on which Cromwell wrote an anxious apology, and, as he could not fix the guilt on individuals, sent the whole of those troops back home. By such careful dealing with Scottish susceptibilities, and firm pressure where he knew the new men in power were ready to give way, he obtained the complete suppression of "incendiaries," and was himself welcomed to Edinburgh, and feasted there as a deliverer. Having seen a new Parliament summoned from which Hamiltonians were to be excluded, and leaving behind him, by desire of the new Government, a small detachment of horse and dragoons to see fair play, at length, towards the middle of October, he turned his face southward once more.

Marching by way of Yorkshire, he found Pontefract Castle held against the Parliament by Governor Morris, a former servant of Strafford's. The mischief of which such a desperate garrison was capable was shown by the murder of Colonel Rainsborough, who was stabbed at his lodging in Doncaster, not by a fighting party, but by disguised assassins from this Pontefract Castle. The place was so strong and so well-provisioned that its speedy capture was hopeless; and so, having written to the Derby House Committee to provide the requisite means, Oliver must needs leave the execution of the work to others. He was getting anxious to reach London once more, for reasons which will appear in the next chapter. Among these reasons, however, one may detain us for a moment here. Among the Welsh prisoners left in Nottingham Castle was a Colonel Owen, who had made interest with the Committee on Delinquents to be admitted to composition, and set free. Two members of the House of Commons signed an order to Colonel Poulton, Governor of Nottingham, to send up Owen, and this order the governor, somewhat informally, forwarded to Cromwell. The latter thereupon wrote to the members concerned, demurring to such ill-timed clemency. He reminded them that on the surrender of Oxford Fairfax and he had been blamed for moderation. Yet now, after a second war has been kindled by "a more prodigious treason than any that had been perfected before . . . for a little money all offences should be pardoned." But he declared it was not a love for severity that animated him, nor was it the notion that their blood was held so cheap which excited the officers " to amazement," but rather "to see such manifest witnessings of God, so terrible and so just, no more reverenced."

Here also we may note Mrs. Hutchinson's pique against Oliver for his vacillation about the appointment of her husband to Colonel Thornhaugh's regiment. When the men represented to the Lieutenant-General their preference for Colonel Hutchinson, he seemed pleased with their choice, and, according to Mrs. Hutchinson, promised to keep the post open till the colonel's answer could be received. Nevertheless, she says, Cromwell favoured the appointment of Major Saunders, and obtained his commission from Fairfax. This is perhaps one of the best authenticated stories we have of Oliver's proverbial "dissimulation." And it is very likely that in this as in other cases his lack of simplicity and his innate tendency to politic arrangements betrayed him into a demeanour that deceived the supporters of Colonel Hutchinson. But before convicting such a man of so paltry a lie, it is obvious to remark that Mrs. Hutchinson was not present when the soldiers had their interview with Cromwell, and had her impression only from men who interpreted his words by their own hopes. That Mrs. Hutchinson should think him afraid of her husband's uprightness we can well understand. It is just possible, however, that it was his unpracticality Cromwell really dreaded.

CHAPTER XVI.

CROMWELL AND CHARLES I.

AFTER the ill-judged invasion of the House of Commons by Charles I. in the beginning of 1642, it does not appear that Cromwell ever saw him again except on the battle-field, till after the exploit of Cornet Joyce at Holdenby House. There is no reason to suppose he had any personal hostility towards the King, or any feeling inconsistent with a desire to see him restored to his proper place in the constitution, provided sufficient guarantees could be afforded for his faithfulness to the constitution in the future. On the other hand, not sharing the republican theories of his friends Ludlow and Vane, he could not conceive of executive government except through "a single person" holding office for life. Whether that person should be called King, Stadtholder, or Protector, or whether the office should be hereditary or otherwise, did not seem to him a question of sufficient importance to fight about, because he thought a Parliament, secure of regular meetings, having the militia under its command, and able at any time to remove evil counsellors, would be strong enough to keep the chief magistrate tolerably straight in the discharge of his executive duties. There was no reason, therefore, why Cromwell should not be sincerely desirous of restoring Charles on fair terms. At the same time there were very strong reasons for his desire to have that restoration effected by the army rather than by the demoralised Parliament. For he knew that the influence of the eleven discarded members still survived, and that if Charles could only be got to abandon episcopacy, not only would religious freedom be excluded, but the political aims of the war would be so compromised as to be substantially lost.

There was one reason *against* negotiation with the King on the part of the army; and it proved in the end to be very formidable. This was the inconsistency of such a course with the new form now beginning to be assumed by the religious convictions of the soldiers. Charles was not exactly a godly man according to their ideas of piety. If they had been fighting justly, he must be guilty of innocent blood. And to bargain and chaffer with such a man savoured rather of carnal policy. Probably many in the army were of this opinion from the first ; and as soon as the insincerity of the King was perceived a strong revulsion of feeling seized the adjutators, and the catastrophe came.

While the King was still at Holdenby House, in the spring of 1647, one of the demands made by the army of the Parliament was, that their indemnity for acts of war should be guaranteed by the royal assent; for the men naturally argued that, after a dissolution, an order of Parliament would be disregarded by the judges. Oliver was at that time attending the House; and though there is no public utterance of his on this point recorded, the demand entirely coincided, as we shall see, with his opinions otherwise expressed. When Joyce and his men carried the King from Holdenby to Hinchinbrook, there was nothing in their demeanour inconsistent with the professed desire of the army to give the King his true constitutional position. His Majesty was, on the whole, rather gratified than otherwise with the change, and refused the offer of Fairfax to restore him to Holdenby. Persistently believing himself to be the indispensable centre on which all negotiations must turn, he was satisfied for the moment with the disadvantage inflicted on Parliament by the loss of his person. And he was no less pleased than surprised to find that his request for the attendance of clergymen, refused by the Parliamentary Commissioners, was at once conceded by the army.

Charles himself suggested Newmarket as his place of sojourn, and on the way thither, at Childerley House, between Huntingdon and Cambridge, Cromwell, in company with Fairfax, Ireton, and other chiefs of the army, was admitted to the royal presence. Fairfax testified his allegiance by kissing the hand of the King. Lord Clarendon, who in such a matter perhaps is credible, tells us that Cromwell and Ireton did not offer this sign of homage, but " otherwise behaved with good manners towards him." At the close of the interview Fairfax assured Charles of his desire to keep the army attached to the royal person. " Sir," replied Charles, " I have as good an interest in the army as you have."

R

How significant are these words of the unfortunate monarch's hopeless illusion as to his real position ! The difficulty in coming to any solid arrangement with him was illustrated already on Saturday, June 5th. On that day Lord Dunfermline communicated a royal message to a conference held by the Scotch Commissioners with a Commons' Committee. The King had commanded this nobleman to tell them "that His Majesty was unwillingly taken away by a party of the army ; that he desired both Houses to maintain the laws of the land ; and that, though His Majesty might sign many things in this condition, yet he would not have them believed till further notice from him." *   On that very day—it may have been at the same hour—Charles was resolutely refusing the offer of Colonel Whalley, on the part of Sir Thomas Fairfax, to conduct him back to Holdenby, and to reinstate the Parliamentary Commissioners who previously had charge of him.

Then followed the gathering of the army on Triploe Heath near Royston, and the vain attempts to effect an agreement with the Parliamentary Commissioners. In a paper dated June 14th, and containing the " further desires of the army " in addition to the impeachment of the eleven Presbyterian leaders, the restoration of the crown to its due place in the constitution was provided for.† During the marching and counter-marching consequent upon the negotiations that followed, the King was necessarily removed from place to place. But he was always treated with consideration ; and lodgings were found for him in suitable mansions or country houses at Hatfield, Caversham, Woburn, Stoke, and elsewhere. But the soldiers were determined not to lose him ; and an order of Parliament for his removal to Richmond was met by a petition that " the King might reside no nearer London than the quarters of the army would be borne."

Sir John Berkley, the former Royalist Governor of Exeter, had for some months been resident in France, and was mentioned to Queen Henrietta Maria as a person whose acquaintance with prominent officers of the New Model might make him a suitable emissary to assist the King in present straits. On the surrender of Exeter he had entered into friendly intercourse with his captors, and had ventured to prophesy that the Parliament, when they had done its work, would cast them aside as worn-

---

* Whitelock.   † Rushworth, part iv., Vol. I., p. 564.

out tools. Relying on the impression likely to be made by the
fulfilment of his prophecy, he volunteered to come over without
a safe conduct, and armed only with credentials to the King.
Cromwell had notice of his coming, and apparently at the
Lieutenant-General's instigation, Sir Allen Apsley,* Mrs.
Hutchinson's brother, went to meet Berkley. Sir Allen assured
him that the officers had not forgotten his former words to them,
and now began to think he had given them good advice. Berkley
was admitted to the King's presence by order of Cromwell, and
afterwards had an interview with the latter. In the conversation they had together, Cromwell confirmed Apsley's account of
the disposition of the officers, and volunteered the addition of
his own personal opinion, " that no man could enjoy his life
and estate quietly unless the King had his rights."

The flagrant contradiction between the King's language to
Colonel Whalley and his message to Parliament by Lord Dunfermline might well suggest doubt of any satisfactory issue.
But of course Cromwell and his colleagues had not now to
learn for the first time that Charles was often insincere; and
knowing his position to be so desperate, they might well hope
that the instinct of self-preservation, together with the common
sense of advisers like Berkley, might incline him to give reasonable guarantees of loyalty. Those guarantees were prescribed in
certain brief propositions drawn up by the army council—or
perhaps we may say, by Cromwell and Ireton. On the acceptance of these by the King, the army were to insist on the
opening of a " personal treaty " with Parliament for the arrangement of details.

The propositions varied in form from time to time in the
course of negotiation. But the "irreducible minimum" consisted of these heads : 1. The revocation of all proclamations
against Parliament. 2. The voidance of all titles of honour
granted by the King since he had left London. 3. The in-
capacitation of "malignants" for membership of Parliament or
any political office. 4. A general indemnity, with certain peremptory exceptions. 5. The absolute power of the two Houses
over the militia. It will be seen that, however insincere the

* Sir Allen Apsley was a Royalist, and had held Barnstaple for the King.
After the surrender of that place he compounded for his political opposition,
and was allowed to live in peace. It is strange that his sister does not mention
this mission of his. But Ludlow can hardly have been mistaken.

King might be, these propositions would go far to make him powerless for evil, while they would leave him ample influence for good. They were inevitable consequences of his appeal to arms. The proposed terms were shown to Berkley before they were submitted to the King; and Sir John thought it hard, as we should in these days, that the King's supporters in arms should be excluded from political life. But "Ireton told him there must be a distinction made between the conquerors and those that were beaten, and that he himself should be afraid of a Parliament where the King's party should have the major vote." * Cromwell, at the same time, urged a speedy arrangement; for he constantly declared that the present feeling of the army could not be of indefinite duration.† It was not however until two or three weeks after Berkley's arrival that the propositions were submitted directly to Charles.

Meantime, the army had advanced to St. Albans, lodging the King at Hatfield; and then, receiving temporary satisfaction from the city, had retired to Reading, while the King was removed to Caversham. However much we may condemn the overthrown monarch's judgment, his sorrows must move our sympathy. He longed to embrace his children who remained in England; but the timid Parliamentary leaders had been deaf to his desires. The future James II., then Duke of York, the Duke of Gloucester, and the Princess Elizabeth, all still of tender years, were at this time in the keeping of the Duke of Northumberland, and were well cared for. But the assurance of their welfare could not compensate their desolate father for the unsatisfied hunger of affection. In this matter Fairfax proved his friend. On July 8th from Reading he addressed to the Speaker a letter, hardly concealing under courteous phrases some honest indignation :—

"If it be in the prayers of every good man that the king's heart may be gained, the performance of such civilities to him is very suitable to those desires, and will hear ‡ well with all men, who, if they imagine

---

* "Huntington's Memoirs." Major Huntington seems to have been placed about the King by Cromwell, and to have got the impression that Royalism was likely to come uppermost after all. His narrative has a different colouring from Berkley's, but is in substantial agreement.

† *Ibid.* The words are: "always affirming that he doubted the army would not persist in their good intentions towards the King." This is *colouring.* What Cromwell meant was that the patience of the army was not exhaustless.

‡ Meaning, "sound well"—a common use of "hear" in that day.

it to be their own case, cannot but be sorry if his Majesty's natural affections to his children in so small a thing should not be complied with."*

The force of his appeal was probably not lessened by a spirited repudiation of the construction put by some upon the intercourse of his chief officers with the King, and his defence of their permission given to the Duke of Richmond and two prelatical chaplains to attend on his Majesty.   In the next words he certainly spoke the mind of his second in command, as indeed throughout the letter he professed to speak "not in his own name alone, but in the name—because he found this to be the clear sense — of the generality, or at least of the most considerable part, of the army."

"In general we humbly conceive that to avoid all harshness, and afford all kind usage to his Majesty's person in things consisting with the peace and safety of the kingdom, is the most Christian, honourable, and prudent way.   And in all things, as the representation and remonstrance of the army doth express, we think that tender, equitable, and moderate dealing, both toward his Majesty, his royal family, and his late party, so far as may stand with safety to the kingdom, and security to our common rights and liberties, is the most hopeful course to take away the seeds of war, or future feuds among us for posterity, and to procure a lasting peace and agreement in this distracted nation."

The truth is, that in the latter half of 1647 the army actually played the part of the Peace Society in our day.   They knew what war was, and they had had enough of it.   They wanted to get home to their farms, and wives, and children.   But go they would not until their country was settled.   The shortest way to that settlement appeared to be through an agreement between them and the King.   Whoever imperilled that settlement by stirring up the embers of war, such men they regarded as unpardonable traitors.   But they came afterwards to believe that the chief incendiary was Charles himself.   However, for the present, Cromwell and his friends were not without hopes that the policy described in the above-quoted letter of Fairfax would be successful.   The nominal law-givers at Westminster at once conceded to fear what they had refused to pity; and the royal children were sent to spend two days with their father.   Charles came to Maidenhead to meet them; and the occasion was seized by the country-side to make a great

* King's Pamphlets, No. 321, § 15.

display of devotion to the King. The roads by which parent
and children approached each other were lined with cheering
crowds, and strewn with greenery. All mothers and fathers in
villages for ten miles round were stirred by the " touch of
nature " revealing the loving heart beneath the crowned head;
and an impressive demonstration was made of the profound hold
retained by the instinct of royalism over the English populace.

The lesson was not lost on Cromwell, probably because he
little needed it, and because, despite his indifference to hand-
kissing, he shared that instinct himself. Besides, being a man
of strong family affections, with " two little wenches" still
brightening his home, and grandchildren beginning to expand
his range of love, he could not witness unmoved a sight like
that meeting; and indeed, in his emotional effusiveness he
appears to have been betrayed into exaggerated expressions of
feeling. For after having seen the King and his children
together in the pure delight of their reunited love, he met Sir
John Berkley, and told him it was the tenderest sight he had
ever beheld. In the reaction occasioned by strong sympathy
he went on, if we may believe Berkley,* to declare his admiration of the King and devotion to his interests. It seems probable that Oliver was on this occasion, as on many others, a trifle
too effusive. But what modern Radical who has been surprised
by the graciousness of royalty could fling reproach at him on
that account?

Soon afterwards the head-quarters of the army were removed
from Reading to Bedford, and the King went to Woburn.
There the proposals of the army were formally presented to him,
and it at once became apparent that any hope of an agreement
was futile. He assumed an air of offended majesty. He told
Sir John Berkley that the officers were merely trifling with
him, and that if they had been sincere in their desire to come to
an accommodation, they would never have imposed such conditions. Berkley showed himself a better adviser than courtier.
He bluntly said that, for his part, he should rather have suspected
they designed to abuse his Majesty if they had demanded less, and
that a crown so nearly lost had never been recovered on easier
terms. But Charles assured his faithful henchman that he

---

* We venture to doubt whether he went so far as to say that the King was
the best man in all his own dominions, as Berkley reports.

should see these men come down in their demands. The notion that he was indispensable to the victory of either Parliament or army was with him a fixed idea—the fruit of Stuart vanity grafted on Tudor arrogance. The same influences led him to merge all national questions in his official interests as king. It was not that he was selfish; but he, no less than Louis XIV., conceived of the State as summed up in himself. It was perfectly natural for him to say to Ireton, " I must play my game as well as I can." The obvious retort had never occurred to him as possible; and, probably, he thought it very impertinent in Ireton to say, " If your Majesty has *a game* to play, you must give us leave to play ours."

About this time John Ashburnham arrived. He was more of a courtier than a counsellor, and was proportionately valued above poor Berkley by all the King's connections and dependents, from Henrietta Maria to Edward Hyde. He corresponded with Cromwell and Ireton, but thought it clever to intrigue at the same time with the Scots through Lauderdale, and with Presbyterian London. He was credited, and probably enough, with sowing dissension in the city, and also with preparing the Scotch invasion. The effect he produced on the King was disastrous. Previously, Charles had been uneasy because Cromwell, Ireton, and other colleagues declined any honours or favours at his hands; and on this account he had been inclined to accept the invitation of the Parliament to go to Richmond. Whereupon Ireton said to him : " Sir, you intend to be arbitrator between the Parliament and us, and we mean to be so between you and the Parliament." But now, under evil advice, he boldly assumed the tone of a dictator. In an audience given to Cromwell, Ireton, and other chief officers, apparently at Woburn, in July, he commented haughtily on the proposal to inflict political disabilities on his adherents, and on the absence of any condition as to religion. He would have the Church restored according to his ideas. Without this concession he would not move a step. "Those of the army," says Berkley, " looked wishfully and surprised at me and Ashburnham." They had hoped to drop the religious difficulty till the secular government was settled, trusting that some practical compromise would emerge by leaving King, Presbytery, and sects for the present to do as they liked. They could only reply that the establishment of the Church was not their business; that they had thought it better to waive that question, and hoped the King would do so likewise. They reminded him also that he had consented to abrogate episcopacy in Scotland. To this he retorted it was a sin he had repented ever since. Thereupon, Berkley took an opportunity to whisper in his ear: "Sir, you speak as if you had some secret strength and power which I do not know of; and since you have concealed it from me, I wish you had kept it from these men also." Charles then felt he had gone too far, and resumed a more plausible tone. But the mischief was done. Colonel Rainsborough, whose sympathies were with the Levellers, hastened out and told the expectant soldiers that the case was hopeless.

But Cromwell pertinaciously hoped against hope. When the London riots at the end of July drew the army through Windsor to Uxbridge, Charles was lodged at Stoke. Sir John Berkley's account of what took place there is so curious and significant, that we cannot do better than extract it entire :—

"At this time those that were supposed best inclined to his Majesty in the army seemed much afflicted with his Majesty's backwardness to concur with the army in the proposals; and the rather, because they conceived great hopes that, within few days, they should be masters of London, which they doubted not might alter the temper of the army towards the King. Cromwell, Ireton, and the rest of the superior officers of the army knew that London would certainly be theirs, two days before they communicated it to the army; and therefore sent an express to Mr. Ashburnham and to me, to express to us that, since his Majesty would not yield to the proposals, yet he should at least send a kind letter to the army before it were commonly known that London would submit. We caused a meeting of the above named persons at Windsor, where the letter was immediately drawn. But his Majesty would not sign it till after three or four several debates, which lost one whole day's time, if not more. Mr. Ashburnham and I went with it at last, and upon the way met with messengers to hasten it. But before we came to Sion, the Commissioners from London were arrived, and our letter was out of season. For though his Majesty was ignorant of the success when he signed the letter, yet, coming after it was known, it lost both its grace and its efficacy. All that the officers could do they did, which was, whilst the army was in the act of thanksgiving to God for their success, to propose that they should not be elevated with it, but keep still to their former engagements to his Majesty, and once more solemnly vote the proposals; which was accordingly done.*

* "Memoirs of Sir John Berkley," in Maseres' Tracts, vol. i., p. 370. The reference of the phrase, "the above named persons," may be either to Crom-

This testimony strongly confirms the impression made by the general line of Cromwell's conduct at this time, that he was very loath to surrender the prospect of a settlement on the old lines of the constitution. But his persistency now began to expose him to suspicion and danger. When the King came to Hampton Court, and the head-quarters were fixed at Putney, Cromwell received almost daily messages from the King's attendants; and they were such frequent visitors at his lodging that he was generally believed to have made good terms for himself. John Lilburne, though a prisoner in the Tower, managed to spread this libel on his old defender. Lady Carlisle, a zealous Presbyterian, told Oliver she understood he was to be Earl of Essex and Captain of the King's Guard; she had it, she said, from Sir John Berkley. On the other hand, Berkley tells us he "would have lied if he had said anything to that purpose." The intrigues to make Cromwell odious to the army were so diligently pressed that he declared he was no longer safe in his quarters, and besought Berkley and Ashburnham to abstain from coming. "If I am honest," said he, "I have said enough; if I am not honest, nothing would be enough." The wrong-headed Ashburnham however would not listen. He told Berkley they must let these men see that their own disorders made their agreement with the King a necessity for them.

On September 7th, the King being now at Hampton Court, Parliament determined on a fresh attempt, in concurrence with the Scotch Commissioners, to get the King's assent to propositions substantially identical with those offered at Newcastle. These involved the adoption of the Covenant, with the iron yoke of the Presbytery, and would certainly not have been tolerated by the army. Cromwell and Ireton advised their rejection, and the proposal of a "personal treaty." This course the King took, suggesting also that the propositions of the army might be considered; and Cromwell supported that request in the House. But as Charles himself would not accept the army proposals, it was too obvious that he was satisfied with setting the two parties by the ears. This conduct of the King gave the Levellers fresh influence. The adjutators and the army generally began to declare that since their propositions were not accepted they would be

well and the officers, or to the King's advisers, mentioned by Berkley a few lines back. I think he meant Cromwell and the officers.

no longer bound by them, but do without the King, and set up a republic. This, says Ludlow, " struck terror " into Cromwell and Ireton. Perhaps that is too strong an expression; but there can be no doubt that even yet such a course was very repugnant to Cromwell's habits of thought. His trouble of mind was increased during the following month by rumours of plots to assassinate the King. Fanaticism is a disease that takes unexpected courses; and that, in some sections of both soldiers and people, zeal was now sinking into fanaticism is only too clear. Cromwell received such information on the 10th or 11th of November as made it in his view a plain duty to warn Colonel Whalley, who had charge of the King, to " have a care of his guards." " If any such thing should be done," he added, " it would be accounted a most horrid act." At nine o'clock on November the 11th, the King was missing; and the next tidings of him were received from the Isle of Wight.

The purpose of Charles in going away has never been made quite clear, and probably was not very clear to himself. There does not seem to have been any definite plan for his escape by sea; indeed he was quite unconvinced of the necessity for it, as he still considered himself secured by the very laws of nature against dethronement or death, except by assassination. It may be suspected that he had a forlorn hope of raising the country, and attracting a fresh army to his standard. Certainly there is good ground for thinking that he half-counted on seducing Robert Hammond,* the Governor of Carisbrooke, from his devotion to the Parliament. The paroxysm of anxiety and fear which seized this man when he heard of the King's approach betrayed a conflict of two loyalties, and showed that Charles's attendants had not been altogether without reason for their calculations. But the notion started by Restoration writers, that Oliver frightened his royal victim away, for the purpose of entrapping him in Carisbrooke, is now felt to be too absurd for discussion. It is clear from Oliver's letters that his knowledge of Hammond's nature gave him very serious anxiety as to what the result might be.

The sputter of mutiny at Corkbush Field, described in the last chapter, was one sign of the disgust now felt by the army

---

* Hammond's uncle, a clergyman and royal chaplain, had presented him to the King at Hampton Court.

at the wearisome and fruitless negotiations with the King. Cromwell himself was beginning to share that feeling, and Charles' flight of course absolved the officers from any obligation to carry the matter further. But they must needs be on their guard still against any arrangement, either with the Scots or the English Parliament, which would betray the cause they had at heart. Walking in the garden at Carisbrooke with his attendants, Charles amused himself with throwing a bone between his two spaniels ; and when the dogs began to snarl and fight over it, " Look you, gentlemen," said he, " that bone represents me between the Scots and the English." The bone was too hard for the little dogs to crack. Had a mastiff appeared upon the scene to arbitrate, the case would have been more typical.

For a while the Parliament meekly followed the counsels of the army, and the four bills submitted to the King to be passed as the preliminary conditions of a treaty were substantially identical with the proposals of the army, with one exception. One of the bills dealt with the Church Establishment, a question the army had " waived." But in the postponement of the Presbyterian Government for future consideration, the influence of the army was perceptible. However, it made little difference, as the King impartially rejected everything—no, not quite everything. At the very time when he was refusing the English proposals, he signed an engagement with the Scottish Commissioners,* by which he actually bound himself to confirm the Covenant, to settle Presbyterianism in England, and to humiliate his southern people by handing over Carlisle and Berwick to Scottish keeping. The reason for the difference of his conduct in the two cases is plain enough. The English Parliament offered a peaceful solution so guarded that he would not be able to extricate himself afterwards. The Scottish agreement promised him an army for the invasion of England ; and, should this prove successful, the northern lords broadly hinted to him that afterwards, so far as the southrons were concerned, he might explain the treaty in his own way.† This Scottish agreement was a secret one. But some suspicion of it probably hastened the Commons in their declaration of January 3rd, that they would

---

* Loudon, Lauderdale, and Lanrick.
† " Clarendon," vol. v., pp. 540, 541.

not, and no one else should, make any further addresses to the King for a treaty. On this occasion, Cromwell, rising just before the question was put, assured the House, " It was now expected the Parliament should govern and defend the kingdom by their own power and resolutions, and not teach the people any longer to expect safety and government from an obstinate man, whose heart God had hardened." And, in ominous tones, he emphatically warned the House against forcing the men who had won victory by their blood " to seek their safety by some other means than adhering to you, who will not stick to yourselves." *

There is surely no need to seek any recondite reason for Cromwell's change of attitude towards the King at this time. Those who assume that Oliver was consumed with ambition to be Earl of Essex and Captain of the King's Guard are naturally delighted with the ready explanation afforded by the romantic story of a letter from Charles to the Queen, concealed in a saddle, and cut out of it by Oliver disguised as a trooper, at the " Blue Boar Hostelry " in Holborn. In this letter it is said that Oliver found he was to have a hempen noose instead of the Order of the Garter. It is not at all unlikely that Charles wrote to that effect to the Queen, or that such a letter was intercepted, though the alleged mode of its interception is improbable, and not sufficiently supported by evidence. But those who believe that, whatever might be his faults, Oliver sincerely desired the security of civil and religious liberty, do not feel the need of any such melodramatic mysteries to account for his change of attitude. He changed because he found he might as well try to build a tower on a quicksand as to find any foundation for a lasting agreement in the weakness and faithlessness of the King. But he was yet far from seeing his way through the perplexities of the situation.

With an Englishman's confidence in the power of hospitality he gave a dinner, apparently at his own house in Drury Lane, to a number of leading Presbyterians and Independents, in the hope that he might effect a compromise ; but he did not make any progress. The parties differed fundamentally, the Presbyterians clinging to the divine right of institutions, and the Independents insisting on the divine rights of men. Where such a difference exists, compromise is hypocrisy.

* Walker's "Independency," Pt I., p. 71.

About the same period, the beginning of 1648, Cromwell also attended a conference in the city, where representatives of the Commons' House, the army-council, and the republicans debated theories of government. " But," says Ludlow, who was himself present, " the grandees of the army, of whom Cromwell was chief, kept themselves in the clouds, and would not declare their judgments, either for a monarchical, aristocratical, or democratical government, maintaining that any of them might be good in themselves, or for us, according as Providence should direct us." * On a more serious and practical point, the accountability of the King for the miseries of the country, and the duty urged by the republicans of bringing him to judgment, Oliver was now thinking there was very much to be said. If he did not commit himself, Ludlow believed it was not because he was unconvinced, but because he was hoping to make a better bargain with another party. But we are not told with what party, and we cannot conjecture which it could be. The Presbyterians hated and distrusted him ; with the Royalists he had broken. He could have no expectation from either of those parties now. If he hesitated, it was because of conservative instincts, which made him dread to enter on wholly new and untrodden ways. It is suggestive of a coarse vein in his nature that he escaped his perplexity for the moment by recourse to horseplay. Taking up a cushion, he flung it at Ludlow's head, and ran down stairs followed by Ludlow with another. He was noted for this kind of overgrown boyishness, and we may suspect it was occasioned by his morbid tendency to hysterical excesses of gloom or exuberance of spirits. The next day he told Ludlow at Westminster that he was convinced of the desirableness of what was proposed—that is, of the judgment and at least the deposition of the King ; but he doubted its feasibility. As to the republicans, however, he said " they were a proud sort of people, and only considerable in their own conceits." Yet he submitted with a good grace to be lectured by Ludlow on the sinfulness and danger of hankering after titles and gifts from royalty, and probably was more amused than edified. On the whole, we may venture to agree with Mrs. Hutchinson—no partial witness—that at this time Cromwell was " uncorruptibly faithful to his trust and the people's interest."

* " Ludlow's Memoirs," folio ed., p. 92.

At the end of March,* amidst rumours from all sides of fresh bloodshed through Royalist machinations, the army leaders and adjutators held that remarkable prayer-meeting mentioned in the previous chapter. In the depression and dismay then blighting patriotic hopes these men were determined to find out wherefore the Lord dealt so with them. And the course of self-examination they pursued is a remarkable illustration of the manner in which earnest Protestants will practise on themselves the arts left to trained spiritual directors in the Church of Rome. After prayers and exhortations, in which Cromwell took a prominent part, they resolved "to look back and consider what time it was when, with joint satisfaction, they could last say, to the best of their judgments, that the presence of the Lord was amongst them." Having fixed that date they were to feel their way forward again, down to the time of their meeting, and try all their actions as an army, till they could determine what it was that had made the difference in the Divine favour towards them. Following this method, they came to the conclusion that the point of departure from a right course lay in " those cursed carnal conferences which their own conceited wisdom, their fears, and want of faith had prompted them the year before to entertain with the King and his party." And in the end, after agreeing that their first business was on the battle-field, they resolved that if ever the Lord brought them back in peace, it would then be their duty "to call Charles Stuart, that man of blood, to an account for that blood he had shed, and mischief he had done to his utmost against the Lord's cause and people in these poor nations." †

For six months after this meeting Cromwell's energies were strained to the uttermost in Wales, Lancashire, and Scotland, and in the agony of a second civil war no progress could be made in the King's affairs. That the Lieutenant-General was kept informed of the feeling in Fairfax's army as well as in his own we may well suppose; but there is no evidence that he endeavoured in any way to inflame or aggravate it. The army-council

---

* " About the beginning of '48 "—that is O.S.—is the time fixed by Allen.

† It must have been immediately after this meeting, or even during its progress, that Cromwell's singular watchfulness enabled him to write to Hammond a detailed description of Charles's attempt to escape from Carisbrooke. For his part, he was determined that the King should neither be destroyed nor saved in an underhand manner. (Letter LVII. in Carlyle).

meetings were necessarily suspended during the war. But in the autumn, when Fairfax had finished his part of the work in Essex and elsewhere, and had fixed his head-quarters at St. Albans, the councils were held again, not without good reason.

When Fairfax had gone into Kent to suppress the insurrection there, the city council thought they had a good opportunity for petitioning Parliament to re-open a "personal treaty" with the King. The feeling in the Lower House was too obviously favourable to be resisted by Vane, Ludlow, and their party. All they could do was to delay the question. But in August (1648) the former vote against any address to Charles was revoked; and, finally, five Lords and ten of the Commons were appointed commissioners to hold a conference with his Majesty at Newport. Ludlow then applied to Fairfax, at that time before Colchester, urging him to interfere, on the ground that the whole scheme was only a stratagem to destroy the army. But Fairfax only gave a general answer, and Ireton thought the best plan was to await the conclusion of the treaty.* Perhaps the latter thought it would come to nothing. If so, he had not sufficiently estimated the effect likely to be produced on the Presbyterian party by the renewed successes of the army.

The Newport Treaty dragged on from September 25th, when the Commissioners arrived, till November 28th, when they departed. There is no reference to it in any of Cromwell's surviving letters until November 20th, when, addressing Fairfax, he signified his approval of a remonstrance from the army against it.† He did this at the request of the regiments stationed at St. Albans; and this fact does not look as if he had been forward to express his opinion in any lost documents. The adjutators had resumed their meetings, and needed no prompting. Indeed they presented their remonstrance to the House, without waiting for the Lieutenant-General's recommendation, on the same day when his letter was being written. The treaty was a mockery from beginning to end. Every one engaged in it knew that there was no prospect of a real agreement, and that they were only playing a match to see which side could out-manœuvre the other, so as to have the best vantage-ground for the real contest

* Cromwell also was of the same opinion. See his letter to Hammond of November 25th.

† Letter from Knottingley, in Yorkshire, No. LXXXIII. in Carlyle.

after the army had been disposed of. The King after wearisome haggling finally consented to recall his proclamations against the Parliament, to make a trial of Presbyterianism, to permit the imposition of the Covenant, himself being exempted, to concede the militia, and to disallow the peace made with Irish rebels. But he was moved to consent mainly by the argument secretly addressed to him * that all hope of preserving the crown lay in dividing the Parliament and army. And his intention to set the treaty aside as soon as he should obtain the power must have been transparent to every one. The genuine Presbyterians only quieted their consciences by their confidence that they could keep such power out of his hands.

In dividing the army and Parliament the treaty succeeded only too well. The House, after a debate, refused to take into consideration the remonstrance; and the inevitable consequences came quickly. On the 28th of November Colonel Ewer, with a detachment from St. Albans, removed the King to Hurst Castle; and on Saturday, December 2nd, Lord Fairfax † and his army marched into Westminster. The House of Commons was then debating the question whether the King's concessions afforded sufficient ground for a settlement. It was the conclusion of this debate that the army was so eager to hear. But it was not reached on that Saturday. On Monday the debate was resumed, and continued all night until five o'clock on Tuesday morning, when on a division 129 voted "Yea"—the King's concessions *were* a sufficient ground; and only 83 voted "No." The House then adjourned until Wednesday.

Cromwell was on his way from Yorkshire, but had not yet arrived. It is not likely that any arrangement had been made for military action in the event of such a vote; for, according to past experience, the presence of the army might be expected to prevent it. Lord Fairfax and his chief officers therefore had some anxious hours during that fateful Tuesday in their consultations with the Parliamentary minority. The decision to be taken, however, was obvious. The army—as Cromwell had distinctly and openly warned the House—had long been deter-

---

* "Clarendon," vol. vi., p. 169.

‡ Sir Thomas succeeded to the title on the death of his father in March, 1648.

mined that the victory purchased by their blood should not be squandered away by shifty compromises. Within the last day or two the men of Colonel Pride's regiment of foot had addressed an earnest petition to Fairfax, beseeching him that a way might be found for the co-operation of the army with the well-affected members of Parliament; and to these men the duties of the next day were entrusted. They were ranged in Westminster Hall and in the lobby of the House, while order was preserved outside by a regiment of horse. As the members approached the door of their chamber, they were met by Colonel Pride, to whom Lord Grey of Groby acted as "nomenclator." All members indicated to Colonel Pride as men on the proscribed list were conveyed to the Queen's Court, where they encouraged each other by denunciations of the violence done them. Over forty were thus secluded, and the majority was extinguished.

This, of course, was naked, undisguised revolution. No ingenuity could give such a proceeding any shadow of legality. But there was something very English in the fond notion that revolution wrought by something with the name of Parliament would feel more natural, even though that Parliament were hacked by the sword into a mere fag-end of one. Give a child a shapeless block of wood for a doll, and she will not thank you; but with the broken stump of what once *was* a doll, she will make believe as much as you like. Just so with good simple English souls and their rump of a parliament. It had once been one; and, however roughly it was used, somehow they found it easier to make believe about it than to regard the Commonwealth parliaments as legitimate.

Something of that kind was the feeling of Oliver himself as yet. He arrived in Westminster on the evening of that Wednesday. Finding what had been done, he said it was somewhat unexpected, but gave in his adhesion, and promised his support. That his colleagues might anticipate his support was sufficiently clear from a remarkable letter written ten days before to Robert Hammond. This letter was dated November 25th, and must have been written from Knottingley, near Pontefract. The fact that it was addressed to Hammond at Carisbrooke shows that Cromwell was not yet so entirely the director of the army's doings as is often assumed. For before the letter could be delivered Hammond was removed from his command and

S

recalled to head-quarters, nominally by Lord Fairfax, really by
the army-council. In this letter Cromwell met plainly the
question which has perplexed so many of his biographers—how
he, being the man he was, could consent to illegal violence.
Poor Hammond had been terribly troubled in mind by his office
as king's keeper, and by the steeper dip now taken by the stream
of events towards some unknown abyss. The defiant attitude
of the army seemed to him unconstitutional, and the designs of
the Levellers—the radicals of his day—appeared shocking.
Cromwell was evidently attached deeply to this man; and,
addressing him as "dear Robin," he reasons with him as an
elder with a younger brother. Oliver first speaks of his own
experiences, which are brighter in these busy times than when
he wrote to Mrs. St. John in stagnant days from the dreary
flats of Ouse River. With the reticence always characteristic of
him when his own exploits are concerned, he alludes to his
recent victories only as "some remarkable providences and
appearances of the Lord." Then he turns to the trouble of
Hammond's spirit, and his "dissatisfaction with friends' actings "
—that is, in preparing to force the Parliament and judge the
King. He urges that all human authority is limited, and
"that there are cases in which it is lawful to resist." "Whether
ours be such a case—this ingenuously is the true question."

To answer this question, he adduces the principle, "Salus
populi suprema lex"—the good of the people is the highest
law. Is that provided for, he asks, under this proposed settlement? Is not "the whole fruit of the war like to be frus-
trated?" Further, it was not the outward authority summoning
the army which made the quarrel lawful; but the quarrel
was lawful in itself. And the army has been so owned of
God that it was clearly called by Him; and as a divine
instrument, it may oppose one sort of legitimacy to another.
He insists on "providences; surely they mean somewhat.
They hang so together; have been so constant, clear, unclouded."

"I desire he that is for a principle of suffering * would not too
much slight this. I slight not him who is so minded; but let us beware
lest fleshly reasoning see more safety in making use of this principle than
in acting.† Who acts, if he resolve not through God to be willing to

* Unresisting submission to authority.
† *I.e.*, Lest, while we talk piously of obeying the powers that be, we are
really bent on "saving our bacon."

part with all? Our hearts are very deceitful, on the right and on the left."

*   *   *   *   *   *   *   *   *

"Thou mentionest somewhat as if by acting against such opposition as is like to be, there will be a tempting of God. Dear Robin, tempting of God ordinarily is either by acting presumptuously in carnal confidence, or in unbelief, through diffidence. . . . Not the encountering diffi-culties, therefore, makes us to tempt God; but the acting before and without faith."

*   *   *   *   *   *   *   *   *

"Dost thou not think this fear of the Levellers (of whom there is no fear), that they would destroy nobility, &c., has caused some to take up corruption, and find it lawful to make this ruining, hypocritical agree-ment? Hath not this biased even some good men? I will not say the thing they fear will come upon them; * but if it do, they will bring it upon themselves. Have not some of our friends, by their passive principle . . . been occasioned to overlook what is just and honest. and to think the people of God may have as much, or more good, the one way than the other? † Good by this man!—against whom the Lord hath witnessed, and whom thou knowest! Is this so in their hearts? Or is it reasoned, forced in?"‡

These words have the true ring of sincerity; but, as usual, they lack simplicity. What they amount to for us is this, that in a time of revolution we necessarily have recourse to first principles, and if we find a strong army on the side of justice, no considerations of ceremony or form shall prevent our using it.

Hammond was no longer at the post for which this letter was intended to strengthen him. But the writer was called sooner than he expected to act out on a conspicuous stage the advice he had given. No statute law could possibly be adduced to justify the proceedings against the King. They were revolutionary, undoubtedly. But to admit this is not to allow their injustice. When the proposal was brought forward in the mutilated House Cromwell rose, and said that "if any man had moved this from any private impulse,§ he should have thought him the greatest traitor in the world; but as Providence and necessity had cast them upon it, he should pray God to bless their counsels, though, for himself,

---

* Nor who will keep it off them.
† *I.e.*, The principles for which we fought are nothing if only we can be let alone now. Peace at any price!
‡ Letter LXXXV. in Carlyle.
§ "Upon design" is the phrase ascribed to him by Walker ("Indep.," Pt. II., p. 54).

he was not prepared on the instant to give them advice."
Then followed the declaration, that it is "treason in the King
of England to levy war against the Parliament and kingdom"
—a declaration which, for the first time in the history of
the world, illumined loyalty with its full meaning, and pronounced that faithlessness to the mutual bond is disloyalty,
treachery, treason, in the lord as well as in the vassal.

The part taken by Cromwell in the judgment on Charles I.
does not require any relation here of the unhappy monarch's
trial and execution. Oliver accepted full responsibility as a consenting member of Parliament, as a prominent commissioner in
the court, and as the third signatory to the fatal warrant.
Fairfax also had been appointed on the commission; but he
withdrew after the first day's sitting, apparently at the instigation of his wife. Cromwell, on the other hand, never to his
dying day repented the part he had taken in that dread deed,
but regarded it as a solemn, inevitable duty to his country and
his God. The stories of his levity in certain stages of the
proceedings are generally on a level with the ridiculous assertion
that he violently seized the hand of Colonel Ingoldsby, closed
the fingers over a pen, and by main force traced out the colonel's
signature to the warrant.* A man with Cromwell's undeniable
weakness for horse-play, especially considering its probable phy-
siological cause, would hardly pass through such a month as
January, 1649, without giving to the bitter passions of the time
some pretext for charges of the kind.

But when Cromwell looked, as it is said he did, upon the
royal face, now calm in death, his emotions, we fancy, were far
other than those of contempt or indecent joy. "The King was
a goodly man," he said, "and might have lived yet for many
years." But in his view those years were cut off by a union of
arrogant self-will with bottomless treachery. He held that a
breach of trust in a king ought to be punished more than any
other crime whatsoever.† However much Charles might protest
against the notion that the English throne was elective, the
assertion was true of the ancient constitution. And if, through
encroachments of the hereditary principle, the practice had

---

* A signature obtained in such a manner would surely bear obvious traces
of it.

† This, according to Burnet, was spoken to the Scotch commissioners, who
protested against the execution. Vol. i., p. 61.

changed, it was impossible in the very nature of things that his idea of a divine vice-regent ruling over awe-struck vassals could be tolerated by the English race. They had corrected similar errors in other kings by the vile means of assassination. It was high time that they asserted in a more formal manner their claim to loyalty from their sovereign. For that noble word, signifying devotion to the law of a social whole, came in feudal times to be applied specially to the relations of lord and vassal. But under the ancient gravitation of all advantage to the rich and strong it came to pass that only the faithlessness of the vassal was described as disloyalty, treachery, or treason. The insane pride of a wilful lord might be unwisdom or injustice, but the damning stigma of faithlessness to trust was never inflicted on him. Therefore the execution of Charles I. struck a deep note of the universal conscience in proclaiming that loyalty is required in a king as well as in subjects, and that his treason against them is at least as criminal as their treason against him. This may not be the letter of the law, but it belongs to that law which no letters can contain; it emerges from the very constitution of the universe as soon as rulers and ruled are born. The tragedy before Whitehall had its evil effects. It frightened a succeeding generation into a mere idiocy of royalist sentiment. It begot a spirit of abject flunkeyism, surviving even yet. But no monarch has ever since dared to face to the bitter end an issue between his desires and the national will.

CHAPTER XVII.

"THE LEVELLERS."

WITHIN a few days of the execution of King Charles, the House of Commons passed resolutions declaring the House of Peers to be "useless and dangerous," and the kingly office to be "unnecessary and burdensome." But with characteristic affectation of constitutional forms, even when all the pomp and circumstance of such forms were gone, they made the destruction of those old institutions the subject of Acts solemnly brought in and passed two months afterwards. During these months, with a vindictiveness against stone memorials more natural to Paris than to London, they ordered the late King's statues to be removed; and in a niche of the Royal Exchange, where the royal image had stood, they inscribed a record of "the tyrant's" departure, and of the beginning of "the first year of freedom." The same hopeful date was stamped on the Great Seal of the Commonwealth. They had yet to learn that, while anarchy and slavishness jostle each other in the passions and prejudices of a people, the violent removal of institutions is the beginning rather than the end of a problem.

The practical work of government required more immediate arrangements; and therefore a Council of State, consisting of forty members nominated by a Committee of the House, was at once appointed as an executive. Of this Council Cromwell was elected temporary president, and thus held already, in a manner, the first place in the Commonwealth. But it is noteworthy that the mutilated Parliament does not seem to have thought at this time that any permanent chief would be needed to take the place of the King. Were it not to be feared that their vote on this subject was owing to inevitable jealousies, we might credit them with more sense than modern republicans, who seem to think that a Commonwealth is impossible without a president. As long as that is the case, practical people may naturally prefer the harmless irrationality of hereditary succession to the most rational arrangement for a periodical fever of conflict for the supreme place. But, as we have seen, Oliver Cromwell was no republican. Both before the abolition of the throne and after the failure of the Council of State, his opinion as to the need for " a single person " was clear. And we have no reason to think that during this interregnum he held a different view. If then the gratification of his own ambition was his ruling motive, now was his chance; now was the time to remain watchfully at the centre of affairs on the look-out for any opportunity to turn his temporary presidency of the Council into a permanent headship of the State. No Napoleon would have allowed such an office to slip out of his fingers; and if Cromwell had cherished similar aims, he would never have gone to Ireland except as supreme magistrate and commander-in-chief of all the forces of the Commonwealth. Meantime he had a difficult task to set the new Council in operation. Many of the nominated members declined to subscribe a declaration, ordered by Parliament, that they approved of everything done in these months of revolution. As these scrupulous members included men like Vane and Fairfax, it was impossible to press the test; and it is natural to suppose that the substitution of a promise to be faithful to the new Commonwealth was the suggestion of the temporary president.

However untenable the position of the mutilated Parliament might be, their efforts were to a certain extent patriotic. They calmed popular fears by declaring their resolve to maintain the fundamental laws, and the security of life, liberty, and property. They sent the judges on circuit. They surrendered in certain cases their own immunity from arrest. But what chiefly concerns us is the burden they felt pressing upon them to avenge the massacre of Protestants in Ireland, and to restore order there. The submission of the rebel chief, Lord Inchiquin, to the Marquis of Ormond, and the union of Anglican Royalists with Papists, left the Parliament hardly a foot of ground outside Dublin. It seemed that the hopes from Ireland, vainly entertained by the late King, were likely to be realised by his son. Prince Rupert went to Kinsale with a fleet to prepare the way; and the council of young Charles advised the latter to land in Ireland himself. This plan was afterwards abandoned for a still more promising expedition to Scotland. But during the early part of 1649 Cromwell's unfailing apprehension of the main issue of the moment led him to urge the subjugation of Ireland. It may appear to us now a matter of course that the chief command of the expedition should be given to him. But it can scarcely have been so then. Remembering the difficulties of travel in those days, and the uncertainties of contrary winds, we may regard it as analogous to a proposal in our day to despatch the head of a great party, at a time of constitutional crisis, to settle affairs in Zululand. Fairfax could have been far better spared; but he had lost heart since the King's execution, and was apparently indisposed to any service. On the whole there is no reason to doubt that Cromwell's acceptance of a dangerous and distant task was prompted mainly by a conviction of manifest duty.

The abnormal political influence of the army had not been neutralised by the proclamation of a Commonwealth. There was much prayer and solemn inquiry among the troopers on this Irish business. And after the nomination of Oliver by the State Council, but before its confirmation by the House, the army representatives in conclave at Whitehall named delegates from every regiment, with instructions that they were " to seek God, to gather what advice should be offered to the General (Fairfax) concerning the expedition to Ireland."

In the week following this conclave the House confirmed the proceedings of the State Council, and agreed to a liberal provision of pay and supplies for the expedition. Magazines were to be collected at Bristol, Chester, Liverpool, Beaumaris, and Milford, while recruits were to be ready to supply the waste of war. On April 12th (1649) there was a gathering of citizens at the Guildhall, where Whitelocke, Vane, and Chief-Justice Wild, together with Cromwell and Fairfax, attended to explain the proposed expedition, and persuade the assembly to lend money. After the judges had spoken, Oliver addressed the meeting in a characteristic strain of mingled bluntness and plausibility. He apologised for asking their aid where his own interest might seem concerned, since he was himself designed for that service. But it was a public duty on which he was to be engaged, and he thought he could clear up some difficulties. " There was a fear abroad that after the money had been raised it would be diverted to some other object, and nothing would be done for Ireland; but he could assure the citizens that the Government were in earnest. Then it had been reported that there were divisions in the army. Certainly the attempt had been made to create division ; but it had failed. The officers were unanimous for this service ; and he doubted not the soldiers ; only it was necessary they should be encouraged." * The loan asked was £120,000, and that amount, or at any rate sufficient for a start, was obtained.

During these months it will be remembered that the marriage treaty for Richard, described in a previous chapter, was revived and carried on to its completion. The last letter on the subject was written three days after this Guildhall meeting. It was well Richard's father should have it off his mind, for the Parliament was threatened once more with the fate of Actæon ; and this time the danger was more formidable than even on Corkbush Field.

On Friday, April 20th, the Army Council met at Whitehall to select the regiments for service in Ireland. The mode of selection was not less extraordinary than the authority directing it. In the first place the officers and adjutators assembled gave themselves to " solemn seeking of God by prayer.". There were fourteen regiments of horse and an equal number of foot, out of which eight were to be chosen, four of either arm. Fourteen papers were cut to an equal size, and on four of them the word "Ireland" was written, the rest being left blank. The whole were then shuffled, and to prevent suspicion of collusion a child was brought in, who drew out the papers one at a time, and presented them in succession to the officers representing the horse. It was then found that the lot had fallen on Ireton's, Scroop's, Horton's, and Lambert's regiments ; and the same process having been repeated for the foot, Ewer's, Cook's, Hewson's, and Dean's were taken. The officers representing these regiments professed the readiness of their comrades ; and few if any sceptics were found to doubt that " the whole disposing thereof was of the Lord." All these troops were of the old army ; meantime three new regiments were being formed, including one of foot for Cromwell himself.

But the agreement in the army, to which Oliver had borne witness in the Guildhall, proved very superficial. The Levellers were disappointed to find that the " first year of freedom "

* Newspaper report in "Cromwelliana."

brought no sign of a new Parliament. During the previous year the notions of these men had spread beyond the army, taking exaggerated and fantastic forms. And the arrest in Surrey of some communists, who were proposing to throw down park palings and commence the Millennium by sharing the land together, suggested an anarchic spirit amongst the populace as well as the soldiers. Yet these "levellers" were no mere firebrands; nor is their mood to be confounded with the cantankerous temper of John Lilburn. That wrong-headed zealot was doing all he could to support them by books and pamphlets, and it had been found necessary to commit him to the Tower in consequence. But he would have done the same for any one who might afford a pretext for attacking the Government. Whenever the break-up of old institutions inspires half-educated men with the idea of judging everything by first principles, the best and bravest amongst them will often go farthest wrong. Knowing nothing of the conditions that make the process of evolution necessarily slow and apparently tortuous, they want to accomplish in a day, and at a stroke, what can only be achieved in a thousand years, by the slow co-operation of countless forces. They cannot understand that the fall of institutions leaves human nature still what those institutions have made it. Hence, the more earnest and daring and honest such men are, the more intolerant do they show themselves of accommodations, adaptations, and delays.

Such men were the Levellers, and most notably those of the army. They had a vision of a pure and patriotic Parliament, accurately representing the people, yet carrying out a political programme incomprehensible to nine-tenths of the nation. This Parliament was to represent all legitimate varieties of thought, and was yet to act together as one man. The necessity for a Council of State they therefore entirely denied; and they denounced it as a new tyranny. The excise they condemned as an obstruction to trade. They would have no man compelled to fight, unless he felt free in his own conscience to do so. They appealed to the law of nature, and found their interpretation of it carrying them further and further away from English traditions and habits, whether of Church or State. Into the church at Walton in Surrey, one Sunday afternoon at twilight, came six soldiers, whose leader carried a lighted lantern in one hand and four unlighted candles in the other. This leader would have gone up into the pulpit just vacated by the minister; but the parishioners would not let him. He declared he had a message to them from heaven, but they would not listen to it in the church; so he was fain to deliver it in the churchyard. There he announced that his message concerned "five lights," all to be symbolised by his candles. But the effect of the emblem was sadly marred, as in the wind that was blowing the candles would not burn. The first light was the Sabbath; it was his mission to declare this abolished "as unnecessary, Jewish, and merely ceremonial; and here, quoth he, I should put out my first light, but the wind is so high I cannot light it." * The next light was tithes; "abolished as Jewish and ceremonial, a great burden to the saints of God, and a discouragement of industry and tillage." The third and fourth lights were ministers and magistrates, both needless in the kingdom of the saints. And, finally, taking a Bible from his pocket, he declared it to consist of beggarly rudiments superseded by the fuller outpouring of Christ's Spirit. So, first setting fire to the book, he extinguished the lantern, and ended his message.

In some respects such men were precursors of the Quakers, with this formidable difference, that they had not yet reached the doctrine of non-resistance, and that most of them were armed veterans. Oliver Cromwell must surely have been haunted at times with the reflection that these men were his own disciples, improving on his own doctrines as to the freedom of the spirit, and as to the light of nature on the right of resistance to authority. But he never allowed such perplexities to hamper his action when the practical issue was clear. The moment the sect broke out in mutiny, he had it by the throat. Through the closed door of the council-chamber, the "sharp, untuneable voice" was heard proclaiming, with the added emphasis of a thump that shook the table, "I tell you, you must either break these people in pieces, or they will break *you!*"

On April 26th a part of Colonel Whalley's regiment, being under orders to leave London, though not for Ireland, broke out into open mutiny in Bishopsgate, and declared they would not go. Swiftly Fairfax and Cromwell were amongst them, and fifteen were arrested, whereupon the rest obeyed the order to

* Walker, "Hist. of Independency," Pt. II., p. 151.

march. Of those arrested six were condemned to death, and one was excepted from mercy. The case of this young man—Lockyer was his name—was pitiable indeed. He was only twenty-three years of age, but had served valiantly throughout the whole war, enlisting at sixteen. Apart from his present insubordination his fame was spotless. He was described in the papers of the day as "a pious man, of excellent parts, and much beloved." It seems to us now, and it seemed to thousands then, a cruel deed to take the life of this young hero for one act of sudden mutiny. But it was done. In the heart of London, beneath the shadow of St. Paul's, amidst horror-struck citizens and grimly-ranked comrades, he was shot dead, fronting his fate like a true man. We do not know all the circumstances that decided this stern judgment. Yet we can well understand that then, when all questions had been reduced to the issue of brute force, it was a matter of more than life or death to keep this weapon of force in the right hands. To hand it over to such guileless fanatics as those of the Walton incident would be to let loose, not exactly another war, but a sanguinary scramble, without definite issue, and with no conceivable end other than social disruption. But the execution of Lockyer proved a perilous deed, and the solemn procession of many hundreds at his funeral showed that popular sympathies had been touched. On May 6th, a delaration of the Levellers was scattered about the streets. On the 9th, a review was held in Hyde Park; and the Lieutenant-General, knowing well the limits of force in such a case, addressed himself to the reason of the men. He reminded them of what the Parliament had done, and assured them that a scheme was then in preparation for a "new representative." Great efforts had been made to raise money for the army. True, martial law was stern; but any who objected to that might have their discharge, and receive their arrears of pay in the same proportion as those who remained. A few troopers had green ribbon—the Levellers' colour—in their hats. They were ordered to remove it, and one, showing a disposition to be insolent, was arrested. But on the earnest solicitation of the men, Cromwell ordered him back to the ranks. All the obnoxious colours were removed, and discipline seemed to be restored.

But the mischief had spread far; and for some days in the

next week might have seemed beyond even Cromwell's control. Two of the regiments drawn for Ireland—Scroop's and Ireton's—were badly affected. Breaking from head-quarters at Salisbury, a great part of them endeavoured to join a Captain Thompson, who, with a number of Colonel Reynolds' men, broke out of Banbury. This captain, being attacked, dismounted three of his pursuers, and went off in search of the Salisbury men. But Fairfax and Cromwell were swooping down on them, unhesitating and relentless, as though the conscious ministers of a divine doom. The mutineers in anxious flight arrived tired and dispirited at Burford, in Oxfordshire, on Monday, May 14th, about 900 strong. Cromwell, tracking their uncertain march by reports, followed them pertinaciously like a sleuth-hound for nearly fifty miles that day. Resting his men for a brief hour or two before his final spring, he marched into Burford at midnight, when most of the weary mutineers were in deep sleep. Those who were awake or were roused by the clash of arms, sprang up and " bustled a little with the Lieutenant-General ; " but the whole 900, with the exception of one man killed, were made prisoners.

Then followed swift trial and condemnation—every tenth man doomed. On the 17th these condemned ones were stationed on the roof of the church, and one after another of the ringleaders was shot before their eyes in the grave-yard below. But when three corpses lay upon the sod, the fourth man coming forward to his death was reprieved. The condemned were brought down from the roof into the church, and to this gloomy congregation the Lieutenant-General, presumably from the pulpit, addressed a discourse such as could hardly fail to be impressive. Their lives were all justly forfeited, he told them, " the mutiny being of so high a nature, hazarding the ruin of both Parliament and kingdom, and delivering up all honest men to the cruelty of the common enemy, against whom they had fought so long." " Nevertheless, by the mercy of the General, they would be spared, and for the present would be quartered together until they were disbanded and sent home." The reprieved men however wept so plentifully under the sermon that hopes were entertained of their repentance, and they were finally allowed to serve in Ireland. It is scarcely just to speak of these men as the forerunners of " sans-culottism." According to the journals of the time, they were " great professors of the Gospel," but had " of late thrown off all ordinances, nay, some of them the Scripture itself, fancying to themselves that they lived above ordinances." When first overtaken they were "very high and peremptory in their language and carriage. But the sentence of death so struck them that when they had their moneys sent them to buy provisions, they all refused to accept of it, saying they must take care now to provide not for their bodies, but for their souls."*

It is difficult to conceive how after such a morning the great officers of the army could have been in a mood for festivity. But Oxford had been preparing to entertain them; and lodgings were provided for them in one of the colleges. How changed was the University now since the days when the Court resided there ! Victorious rebels now received honorary degrees, and learned dignitaries made fulsome speeches in their praise.

During these troubles it had been whispered about that Cromwell's own regiment of original Ironsides were infected by the Levellers, and were plotting to seize their illustrious colonel. The men were aggrieved at the story, and now drew up an address, which they presented to Fairfax, assuring him that the late mutiny met with their strongest reprobation, and that the story of their design against their colonel was a baseless slander.

It was surely the sense of a common danger that about this time prompted the most diverse sections of the Commonwealth to do honour to the one strong man in their midst. June 7th was kept as a thanksgiving-day for late deliverances ; and, after prayers and sermons occupying the whole morning, the city corporation entertained the Parliament, with the great officers of the army, at a dinner given in Grocers' Hall.† The Speaker, the Lord-General, and Bradshaw (now President of the Council) were there ; but the guest of the evening was certainly the commander for Ireland. The dinner was celebrated in the journals of the day as a type of what a godly festival ought to be.

" No drinking of healths or other uncivil concomitants formerly of such great meetings, nor any other music but of the drum and trumpet. A feast, indeed, of Christians and chieftains, whereas others were rather of Cretians and cormorants, and—which is to be remembered—the poor were

* " Cromwelliana."
† The halls of the City Companies seem to have been much more available for municipal purposes than they are now.

not forgotten at this feast. For, besides the overplus of victuals left at dinner, sent to several prisons in London, £400 was given and distributed among the poor of the several parishes in and about London."

What a triumph over the old. Adam! But surely the prevalence of " drums and trumpets " was ominous. Next day the wealthy corporation sent to the Lieutenant-General at his house a present of plate to the value of £300, and 200 pieces of gold. It would be equal to a present of something like £1,500 in our time, and would be a substantial help in providing for the " two little wenches," to whom the advent of the Lord Mayor's servants with their golden burden was no doubt an agreeable excitement.

Anxious to " provide things honest in the sight of all men," Oliver now requested of the House that before he went to Ireland he might render an account of the money entrusted to him in the previous year for Wales and Scotland. The regular auditing and printing of public accounts was one of the points insisted on by the Levellers, and the Lieutenant-General's care on this subject was perhaps among the points in his character that inclined them to trust him. Perhaps he was all the more anxious for an audit because a secretary of his, named Spavan, had been trafficking in his master's signature to passes. The man was condemned and imprisoned, but the scandal does not seem to have excited even vulgar suspicions of his employer.

On the recommendation of the Council of State, and after debate in the House, Oliver's Irish Commission was enlarged to include civil administration as well as military command ; and he was appointed Lord-Lieutenant, or Chief Governor of the island. His preparations were now complete. Men, arms, shipping, magazines, reserves of recruits—all had been provided according to his own plans. There had been more delay than was usual with him when a piece of work had been resolved on, and we cannot help suspecting that, in addition to the desire for a full equipment, he was actuated by a wish to watch personally over the first steps of the infant Republic.

At this time, there came secretly to London an Irish nobleman, Lord Broghill, of the Boyle family. He had fought against the Papists in Ireland ; but regarding all as lost after the execution of the King, he came secretly to London, intending to go thence to the continent, and offer his services to Prince Charles. Through the Earl of Warwick he sought a pass to go abroad, carefully concealing his intentions. One evening a messenger came to his lodgings to announce that Lieutenant-General Cromwell desired to wait upon him. Lord Broghill disclaimed the honour of such an acquaintance, and told the messenger there was some mistake. But presently Cromwell himself came, and assured the surprised nobleman he had no evil intention. Oliver then told him that the Council were fully aware of his design; produced copies of Broghill's correspondence; urged that he would do far better to help in restoring order in Ireland; and finally gave him the choice of instant arrest and imprisonment or acceptance of Parliamentary service against his old foes. Lord Broghill overcame his scruples, accepted a command, and became one of Cromwell's most faithful lieutenants.* The incident shows not only Cromwell's powers of persuasion, but his quick appreciation of available instruments.

At length, on July 10th (1649), in the early evening, the new Lord-Lieutenant took his departure in state. Oliver was but a bungler in pageantry. Nevertheless he always showed a clumsy sort of condescension to the weakness of humanity in such things. And so, on this occasion, as the vicegerent of English sovereignty over Ireland, he started on his mission in a grand coach, drawn by six light grey Flanders mares and surrounded by his life-guard of eighty gallant gentlemen, many of them colonels, and none lower than an esquire. With echoing hoofs, amidst the blare of trumpets and ringing cheers, he is gone : to such a height has the melancholy Ely grazier reached, since the days of his swollen throat and red flannel there. One cannot help hoping that his aged mother was present to see him.

His last days before embarking were occupied with family interests. On the day before his start he ventured to add to his public demands on the House a private request for consideration to his misguided cousin Henry, who had been blind to the justice of the Parliamentary cause. The request was granted; and Henry Cromwell's fine was remitted

---

* The story is given in Budgell's "Memoirs of the Boyles;" also in Morrice's "Life of Lord Orery."

—a subordination of public justice to private interest such as may be pardoned to human weakness.

Arrived at Bristol, he wrote to Richard's father-in-law at Hursley an affectionate letter. Mr. Mayor had been requesting some favour for a Major Long; and in response to this Oliver limits himself to a promise to do "according to his best understanding, with a due consideration to those gentlemen who have abid the brunt of the service." But the rest of the letter overflows with kindly feeling, with tenderness for the bride—a little sadly touched with anxiety for his spiritless son. While the father, at fifty years of age, is leading a noble life of toil and danger, the lazy Richard is gadding about on pleasure parties with his wife. "I am very glad to hear of your welfare, and that our children have so good leisure to make a journey to eat cherries; it's very excusable in my daughter! I hope she may have a good excuse for it."—Excusable in my daughter! Alas, not in my son.—"I wish he may be serious; the times require it." Nearly a month later, from Milford Haven, and already on board ship, he wrote again to Mayor, and at the same time to "his beloved daughter, Dorothy Cromwell." The young wife had been writing to her father-in-law a letter apparently carried by her husband. And the rough, strong man was evidently pleased. "Indeed I stick not to say I do entirely love you," he says, and then he goes on to distil for her in a few words the richest treasures of his experience. "Seek the Lord; . . . and be listening what returns He makes to you; for He will be speaking in your ear and in your heart, if you attend thereunto."

The letter to Dorothy's father is full of another victory won by the redoubtable Jones. Issuing from Dublin with some five thousand horse and foot, he had routed and scattered thrice that number under the Marquis of Ormond. "This is an astonishing mercy; so great and seasonable, that indeed we are like them that dreamed." Then, amid these ecstacies over the Lord's doings, comes the thought of lazy Richard. His father would have him comfortable, but not luxurious; nor wholly forgetful of what he owes his generation. "I envy him not his contents; but I fear he should be swallowed up in them. I would have him mind and understand business, read a little history, study the mathematics and cosmography:

T

these are good, with subordination to the things of God ; better
than idleness, or mere outward worldly contents. *These fit
for public services, for which a man is born."*

Very natural, very touching are these letters, bringing us
back to the heart that indited them. But they are not quite
what we should expect from a man whose prime motive was
ambition, or who was counting on making his lazy son hereditary ruler of England. Not long after these words were penned
the anchor was up, the sails were set, and Richard climbed down
the ship's side to row ashore, not, perhaps, without wonderment
at the strange passion of his father for wearing his life out in
arduous war and barren politics.

CHAPTER XVIII.

THE REMEDY OF FORCE.

CROMWELL's cruel violence in the conquest of Ireland is the darkest blot on his fame as a soldier. But it is unjust to exaggerate that stain by dwelling only on the frightful bloodshed of his victories, and forgetting the circumstances that occasioned it. Even in the nineteenth century, as the stories of the Indian mutiny and the negro riots in Jamaica prove, the English race, when wronged by those it esteems to be of a lower caste, is capable of reverting to the ferocity that made its primitive Saxon forefathers the terror of Northern Europe. But in the middle of the seventeenth century the vindictive passions of the nation were aggravated, not only by the inferior culture of the general population, but by the long prevalence of a bitter civil war; and, it must be added, by a misguided use of Old Testament precedents amongst the enthusiasts who determined national policy.

The rage and terror excited by the deeds of the Irish rebels in 1641 had never been appeased, nor even diminished, during the eight years that had now elapsed. The tales of massacre had been exaggerated, but they were still firmly believed. And the horror excited by vague stories of enormous slaughter was accentuated by accounts, unfortunately too true, of barbarities in detail. Crowds of miserable fugitives, women as well as men, had been stripped naked, and in the November nights hundreds of them perished of cold and hunger. The corpses lay about to be gnawed by dogs, till nothing was left but dry and scattered bones.[*] "Some women had their hands and arms cut off—yea, jointed alive—to make them confess where their money was."[†] The English passion had been sustained during all these years by a terror that Irish Papists were to be brought over to ravage England. Small detachments had indeed been brought, and

---

[*] Gardiner, "Fall of the Monarchy of Charles I.," vol. ii., p. 308, *seqq.* His authorities are unimpeachable.

[†] "Brief Declaration, &c., by G. E., minister of God's Word in Ireland," quoted by Gardiner, *l.c.*

T 2

were by order of Parliament adjudged to death without mercy, wherever captured. Their deeds in war, whether in England or Ireland, were perhaps the natural consequence of such a policy, but served to inflame the mutual detestation of the two races. Baillie, in 1644, says he had it from good hands that in Shropshire some Irish troops buried alive twenty-seven wounded men. And Whitelocke in April 1647 mentions letters from Ireland, describing how sixty Protestants in Kerry, women and children as well as men, were thrown into a deep, rocky cave, and lay there with broken arms and legs, till they died of their injuries, or were starved to death. The English and Scotch of that age were, with the exception of a few scholars, ignorant of the ancient culture of the Irish people, incredulous of their gifts and graces, and unable to conceive that the confusion and barbarism of the island were the result of English greed and misgovernment. The unity of the Aryan race and the place of the Irish in it were unknown. The native people were therefore regarded with the arrogant assumption, or contemptuous compassion, too often characteristic of British feeling towards alien populations of conquered lands.

We should think of Cromwell then at this time as impersonating the national judgment against the rebels, with its oblivion of history and its narrowness of sympathy. And we must remember that the English idolatry of force, conspicuous in his essential character, had been agravated in him by his fortunes. It was increased also by his plausible but superstitious doctrine of "providences" as revelations of God's will. How can we wonder at him when, in face of the Irish difficulties of the present day, the frank acknowledgment that "force is no remedy" has been greeted with a general cry of derision?

The expedition sailed from Milford Haven on the 13th of August 1649. It consisted in all of more than a hundred vessels, carrying a force of about 9,000 horse and foot. Ireton, who was Major-General of the army, was sent with Admiral Dean towards Kinsale, with a view of landing in Munster; but the prospects were not promising, and in a few days he followed his commander to Dublin without disembarking. On the 15th the new Lord-Lieutenant landed there. In his progress to the castle, crowds surrounded him with wild acclaim; and pausing by the way, he made them a speech declaring his confidence that by

Divine Providence he should "restore them all to their just liberties and properties." His first effort was to unite and inspirit the population forming the English garrison. He relieved of taxes the Protestants of Dublin and the neighbourhood, and, possibly in consequence, a number of gentlemen enrolled themselves in his life-guard at their own charges. With more doubtful wisdom he permitted, perhaps favoured, the invasion of the pulpits by his preaching troopers. "The buff coat appears instead of the black gown," said letters of the day; "not a word of St. Austin or Thomas Aquinas, nor any such hard words; only downright honesty is now given forth."

Inquiry showed that Jones's army, though it had fought well, had very different manners from the Ironsides, and especially much laxer notions on the subject of plunder. The Lord-Lieutenant therefore issued a declaration as to the principles on which he intended to conduct the war. He was resolved, "by the grace of God, diligently and strictly to restrain such wickedness for the future." He would have no wrong or violence of any kind toward people of the country, unless actually in arms, or employed with the enemy. He offered a free and secure market, and promised safety to all persons disposed to pursue their industry peaceably under protection of his army. Soldiers were warned that disobedience on these points would be visited severely.

Though Dublin had been freed from siege by the valiant Jones, Cromwell found that the city and its surrounding lands formed almost the only firm foothold of the Parliament. Only away in the north was another town, Derry, held for the Parliament, and that was closely besieged. Lord Ormond was now hand and glove with the Papists. But the misery of the unfortunate people, whether under patriots or invaders, was illustrated by his ravaging and burning the country in order that the people might be driven from their homes to fight. The marquis seems to have been uncertain and vacillating in his plans. He showed no disposition to risk a battle, but retired to a post between Trim and Drogheda (or Tredagh, as it was often called) to watch events.

Oliver's plan was soon formed. He would attack Drogheda. If Ormond threatened to interfere, he would fight him by the way, and take the town afterwards. Accordingly, on the 31st of

August he set out with eight regiments of foot, six of horse, and some troops of dragoons. Ormond made no attempt to stop him. His army was probably too badly organised and ill-fed. And on September 3rd, a singularly fateful day for Cromwell, the avenging army was before Tredagh. The town, standing on the Boyne, near the estuary, was divided into two parts by the river. It was strongly fortified, according to the notions of the age; and was commanded by Sir Arthur Ashton, with Sir Edmund Verney the standard-bearer at Edgehill, as his lieutenant. The garrison consisted of 3,000 regular troops, nearly all English Royalists, besides native auxiliaries. Cromwell invested the place on the south side of the river only, believing that the division of his army might expose either part to be crushed between Ormond and the garrison before the other part could cross the river to its assistance. At the south-east angle of the fortifications St. Mary's Church stood just within the walls, and two batteries were opened against either side of that angle. If a storming party could get in, they would lay hold of the church, and under its cover protect the entrance of their comrades.

Sir Arthur Ashton, being summoned, naturally gave no satisfactory answer. The summons offered mercy to the garrison on condition of instant surrender, with the usual alternative if refused. But this was the general formula in such cases, and cannot be pleaded as a justification for any exceptional course afterwards. On Tuesday, September 10th, two practicable breaches were effected on either side of the corner tower, the tower itself being also battered into ruins; and a storming party of a thousand men, headed by Colonel Castle, rushed into the gap. But the colonel received a fatal shot in the head, and so many of his followers were killed and wounded that the men gave back, and the assault failed. At the same time Captain Brandly of the navy got into an outwork on the south side; but the sally-port into that work through the town wall was blocked with a ghastly barrier of dead bodies, and proved impracticable. The day was already sinking; the inhabitants were hard at work on fresh fortifications within the breach. To let the night close on failure might be to bring Ormond down next day; and it was impossible to calculate the delays that might be caused. Nor was the Lord-Lieutenant thinking of Ireland only. Scotland was threatening; the Royalists were everywhere on the alert. The very life of the new Commonwealth depended on making short, sharp work here, by blows that should resound through the world. It was an occasion on which the Commander-in-Chief might well expose his own life to risks otherwise unjustifiable.

That this was Cromwell's view, we gather from his action, not from any words of his; for it is noteworthy and characteristic of him that in the despatch he wrote, otherwise copious in detail, there is not a syllable on the subject.* When the storming party recoiled, he himself took Colonel Castle's place, formed the men again, exhorted them to trust in God, and led them back to the breach. It was "a very hot dispute;" but, as their leader phrased it, "God was pleased so to animate them that they got ground of the enemy, and forced him to quit his entrenchments." They then seized the church, and the new barricades within the walls. Thus they protected the entrance of cavalry; and the neighbouring streets were speedily cleared. It was in this "heat of action," himself breathless with exertion, burning with excitement, his troopers madly charging past him into the doomed town, that he called out "No quarter!" and "forbade them to spare any that were in arms." On they went, cutting, slashing, and pistolling through the streets, the enemy flying across the bridge into the north town, or gathering into the "Mill-Mount, a place very strong and difficult of access." Alas! they might as well have taken refuge from a spring-tide on a sand-bank in the middle of their estuary. The Ironsides, following hard after them, surrounded them, burst in upon them, overpowered them, and "put all to the sword," not one escaping. At the same time, the chase went across the bridge, and was brought up round three towers, one St. Peter's Church steeple, the two others guarding gates of the town. The wretched fugitives in these towers were "summoned to yield to mercy." But the fate of their comrades gave them little hope, and perhaps they cast wild, forlorn glances toward the lurid west, where Ormond lay somewhere on the horizon in strange inaction while they were perishing. Cromwell thereupon ordered the church steeple to be set on fire, and night descending was made hideous by yells and curses from the flaming tower.

* Letter CV. His part in the storm is related in contemporary accounts.

So passed that night, the men in the remaining towers deaf to all demands for surrender, and their guards calming down through exhaustion, while the burning steeple, like a huge torch, shed a fitful light on the infernal work below. In the morning a peremptory summons was addressed to the refugees in the two towers; but they still refused, and the victors contented themselves with setting guards and awaiting the effects of hunger. But the desperate men in one of the towers fired on their besiegers still with fatal effect. When they at last came out, their officers were all killed, and every tenth man amongst the soldiers. Those in the other tower were all spared; but they and all who escaped with life were shipped off to the Barbadoes as slaves.

Thus did Cromwell begin to apply the remedy of force to the disorders of Ireland; and the warmest admirers of that method must acknowledge that it could scarcely have been applied by more vigorous hands. It would be doing him injustice to suppose that he had no misgivings. He explained that his stern orders were given in the heat of action, and he added arguments with which the press of our own day is familiar when the choice lies between the fallacious swiftness of brute violence and the more effective tediousness of moral remedies. "I am persuaded," he wrote, "that this is a righteous judgment of God upon these barbarous wretches, who have imbued their hands in so much innocent blood; and that it will tend to prevent the effusion of blood for the future; which are the satisfactory grounds for such actions, which otherwise cannot but work remorse and regret." Unfortunately it appears certain that the large majority of these "barbarous wretches" were English Royalists, who could not possibly have been concerned in the murder of Protestants.

This garrison was, as Cromwell said, "the flower" of Lord Ormond's army. The other forces of the enemy were comparatively undisciplined and wild. As the Irish had counted upon at least a prolonged resistance in Drogheda, the swift and terrible fate of the place struck terror far and wide. A detachment sent northwards under Colonel Venables found the garrisons generally deserted on their approach. Dundalk and Trim were given up without a blow, and before long the Lord-Lieutenant was able to turn southwards for the subjugation of

Munster. On the march, fortress after fortress was deserted at his approach, and on October 1st he reached Wexford. Ormond followed with a force of 3,000 or 4,000 men, and appeared on the north side of Wexford Harbour. But as the town declined to receive any more men, he marched away somewhat hastily, threatened and pursued by Lieutenant-General Jones. On the 3rd the town was summoned, and the governor, David Synnot, was not indisposed to yield, but asked terms too high for his circumstances. In reply to a long series of articles proposed by him, Cromwell wrote on the 11th a short note, offering life and liberty to the common men, life without liberty to the officers, and to the town protection from plunder. Meantime he had peremptorily refused any cessation of hostilities. While this note was being written, the end came unexpectedly.

Wexford Castle, standing at the south-east, was outside the walls. The commander there was one of the commissioners whom Governor Synnot had intended to send out for the arrangement of terms. This Captain James Stafford, seeing the hopelessness of his superior's proposals, appears to have unfaith-fully made terms for himself, and surrendered the castle. The appearance of Cromwell's men on its battlements caused a panic in the town garrison, who deserted the walls. Seeing this the assailants snatched up their scaling ladders, and in a few minutes were within the town. In the market-place the garrison foolishly attempted resistance. A fight ensued, and massacre followed. Some two thousand of the defenders were killed, and not twenty of the assailants. This slaughter was certainly not deliberately intended; but it followed inevitably from the sanguinary prece-dent of Drogheda. Cromwell however believed it to have been ordained of God, who would not permit His wrath to be turned aside by human counsels.

" And indeed it hath, not without cause, been deeply set upon our hearts, that we intending better to this place than so great a ruin, hoping the town might be of more use to you and your army; yet God would not have it so, but by an unexpected providence, in His righteous justice, brought a just judgment upon them, causing them to become a prey to the soldier, who in their piracies had made preys of so many families, and now with their bloods to answer the cruelties which they had exercised upon the lives of divers poor Protestants, two of which [cruelties] I have lately been acquainted with. About seven or eight score poor Protestants were by them put into an old vessel, which being, as some say, bulged by them, the vessel sank, and they were all presently drowned in the harbour. The other was this : they put divers poor Protestants into a chapel (which since they have used as a mass-house, and in which one or more of their priests were now killed), where they were famished to death."*

It is possible, indeed probable, that the garrison of Wexford contained a considerable proportion of Irish Papists, approvers, if not participants, of the crimes of 1641. To Cromwell's conscience this was a sufficient justification of the slaughter. In this age of the world, all except believers in the gospel of force can only wonder and regret that it should have been so.†

Still, in justice to Cromwell's stern calculations as to the effects of his severity at Drogheda, it must be conceded that after this affair at Wexford there was little more bloodshed, because in truth there was scarcely any more serious fighting, except at Clonmel next year; and, granting the necessity for the sub-jugation of Ireland, it is difficult to conceive how Cromwell, with the very limited force at his disposal, could otherwise have accomplished the work with an equal economy of time and suffering. The town of Ross, on the river Barrow, surrendered almost as soon as summoned, Ormond, as before, looking on sympathetically from the other side of the river. At this place Oliver himself remained for some weeks in poor health, and during part of the time quite helpless. Though muscularly a strong man, and presumably possessed of a vigorous vitality correspond-ing to his enormous energy, he had more fits of sickness than we should expect in a healthy man living so much in the open air. The attacks were probably traceable, like his hypochondria, to a morbid element in his nervous system. To Richard Mayor he writes, on November 13 :—

"I have been crazy in my health; but the Lord is pleased to sustain me. I beg your prayers. I desire you to call upon my son to mind the things of God more and more. Alas! what profit is there in the things of this world? Except they be enjoyed in Christ, they are snares."

In that time of sickness the disappointments of affection were more felt than the successes of war. A son with nothing else to do might have gratified a busy father with the home news for which he longed ; but "as for Dick," he writes, "I do not much expect it from him, knowing his idleness."

* Letter CVII. in Carlyle.
† The legend of the massacre of women at Wexford is absolutely without foundation. (See pp. 306-7.)

Meanwhile the formidable Irish conspiracy was melting away like accumulated snow under a sudden lava torrent. It would be fruitless to follow in detail events which have a certain monotony, as they consist of the successive surrender of garrisons, generally with Ormond looking on from the safe side of a river. Youghal and Cork thought well to "return to their obedience." During Cromwell's illness Ireton and Jones attempted to bring Ormond to an engagement; but he slipped away to Kilkenny, and they took Carrick instead without a blow. This gave an entrance into Munster, of which Oliver availed himself to besiege Waterford. That town however baffled him. He took the Passage fort, and obtained command of the harbour. But he was obliged to go into winter quarters without taking Waterford; and indeed the work was left for his successor. Kinsale surrendered on articles. By December he could report that the position of the English Government in Munster was "near as good as ever it was" since the civil war began. The greatest loss sustained was the death of Lieutenant-General Jones, who died of a fever resulting from exposure. Oliver, who had always generously estimated his worth, felt his loss deeply.

In his despatches the Lord-Lieutenant dwelt repeatedly on the need for reinforcements. The recruits, for whose training and transport he had made provision before he left England, do not seem to have been sent over as quickly as the drain upon his forces required. Yet he lost comparatively few men in battle. His difficulty was caused by the number of the captured places requiring garrisons. On November 14th he wrote, addressing the Speaker, "It is not fit to tell you * how your garrisons will be unsupplied, and no field-marching army considerable, if but three garrisons more were in your hands." And indeed when it is considered that the army he brought over could not have exceeded 10,000 men, while the only points in all Ireland then held for the Parliament were Dublin and Derry, it seems difficult to conceive by what economy and skill he could so direct and distribute his power as practically to secure the country within six months. Perhaps the most effective piece of artillery in the English army was the name of Oliver Cromwell. He made it a terror, and it has remained a curse.

* Letter CXV.

During the month of January 1650 the army took shelter in Youghal and Cork. The time of the Lord-Lieutenant was abundantly occupied with Irish business, reports from garrisons, orders to be given, government of the captured towns, decisions as to the fate of prisoners, besides much pondering on schemes for the re-settlement of this unhappy land. But in moments of rest—leisure it could not be called—his thoughts turned to the perils of the Commonwealth, and to the welfare of his own family. Lord Wharton, whom "if he knew his heart he loved in truth," was distressed that the revolution had not stopped short at what would have satisfied *him*. He was like a boy who looses his skiff from the river bank because to glide with the current is so exciting, but who is frightened by the inevitable rapids, and has not the courage to shoot them upright in his seat. He was right in a sense. The revolution *had* gone too far. But the only man who could have arrested it with safety to freedom was the late King; and as he stolidly refused, there was no help for it; the rapids had to be dared. To poor Lord Wharton wrote Oliver on January 1st, beseeching him to keep substantial issues in view, and not to be too readily scandalised by imperfections in the mode of working them out :—

"It is easy to object to the glorious actings of God, if we look too much upon instruments. I have heard computations made of members in Parliament—the good kept out, most bad remaining. It has been so these nine years. Yet what hath God wrought? The greatest works last. And he is still at work. Therefore take heed of this scandal. Be not offended at the manner; perhaps no other way was left. What if God accepted their zeal * as He did that of Phinehas, whom reason might have called before a jury . . . How hard a thing is it to reason ourselves up to the Lord's service, though it be so honourable; how easy to put ourselves out there, where the flesh has so many advantages."

What Oliver's homeward thoughts were we gather from letters written a little later. Always he was longing for some tokens of religious ardour or public spirit in his eldest son. Writing to Richard Mayor in April, he says, "Some letters I have had from him have a good savour. The Lord treasure up grace there, that out of that treasury he may bring forth good things." A letter of the same date to lazy Dick himself shows how the disappointed father tried to make the best of things as they were. It may be conjectured that Dick had

* *E.g.*, of Colonel Pride's regiment.

been writing plausible acknowledgments of spiritual prosperity, and insinuating that, for his soul's health as well as his body's comfort, he was better off in his peaceful quarters than anywhere else in the world. Whereupon, his father writes, half gratefully, half wistfully :—

" DICK CROMWELL,—I take your letters kindly. I like expressions when they come plainly from the heart, and are not strained, nor affected. I am persuaded it's the Lord's mercy to place you where you are. I wish you may own it, and be thankful, fulfilling all relations to the glory of God. . . . Take heed of an unactive, vain spirit. Recreate yourself with Sir Walter Raleigh's 'History.' It's a body of history; and will add much more to your understanding than fragments of story.* Intend to understand the estate I have settled. It's your concernment to know it all, and how it stands. I have heretofore suffered much, by too much trusting others. . . . I would not have (my brother Mayor) alter his affairs because of my debt.† My purse is as his. My present thoughts are but to lodge such a sum for my two little girls. It's in his hand as well as anywhere. I shall not be wanting‡ to accommodate him to his mind; I would not have him solicitous. Dick, the Lord bless you every way." §

One sentence in the above extract, referring to a habit of "too much trusting others," would seem to show but little self-knowledge. But then it is not political business, nor military duty, that is in question here. And in regard to money or estate Oliver certainly was never over-careful, as indeed is illustrated by his readiness to leave in the hands of Mayor the money for his two little girls. Again it occurs to us that this is scarcely the sort of letter a scheming usurper would write to the son he intended to make heir-apparent to a throne.

The Lord-Lieutenant did not linger in winter quarters. Rumours from England pointed to the proclamation of Charles II. in Scotland, and an endeavour on the part of his Scottish subjects to impose his royal yoke on England. This alarm indeed, together with the obvious indifference of Lord Fairfax to active service in their behalf, led the Parliament at the beginning of January to resolve on recalling Cromwell's victorious sword to their own side of the water. But, owing to contrary winds, their order did not reach him for more

* *Query* romances.
† Viz., Mayor's debt to Oliver : £2,000 as per marriage settlement.
‡ *I.e.*, I will not fail.   § Letter CXXXII., Carlyle.

than two months—a circumstance illustrative of what was said above as to the impolicy of so distant a service for any prominent man whose first consideration might have been his own interest. Still, rumour with its mysterious power of outstripping all known methods of communication brought hints of recall; and these added to the impatience of Oliver to get his Irish work out of hand.*

He therefore marched out in two divisions at the end of January. One division he committed to Colonel Reynolds, and sent him into Kilkenny County to keep the enemy in play, while he himself, with Ireton, now President of Munster, swept round by the borders of Limerick County into Tipperary, taking castles and towns, and thus enlarging the borders of the Parliamentary dominion. He met with little resistance; and within the first week of February was master "of all the land from Mallow to the Suir side." The discomfort occasioned to opponents by his incalculable swiftness and vigour was somewhat ludicrously illustrated at Fethard, in Tipperary, where he arrived in the night "very much distressed by sore and tempestuous wind and rain." He and his men found poor shelter in an old abbey, with the addition of some cabins and wretched houses; but he would not wait till morning without summoning the town. The garrison shot at his trumpeter; and then certain officers, knowing something of the defenders, were sent "to let them know the Lord-Lieutenant was there with a good part of the army." "We shot not a shot at them," says Oliver, as though astonished at their inhospitality to belated travellers, "but they were very angry, and fired very earnestly upon us; telling us 'it was not a time of night to send a summons.'" A very rude interruption to a night's rest! Nevertheless, on second thoughts, the governor decided that so importunate a guest was not to be refused; and the town was surrendered.

Pushing forward into Kilkenny County, he effected a junction with Reynolds, and then the whole army retraced its steps to take in Cahir and other strongholds, which fell like nine-pins before a well-aimed ball. Cahir had formerly occupied the Earl of Essex eight weeks, as Oliver mentions, for once a little boast-

---

* "A speedy period put to this work will break the expectation of all your enemies."—*Despatch of April 2nd*, 1650.

fully; or was it only to magnify "providences?" But the garrison had heard enough of the Ironsides, and there was no spirit left in them. Kilkenny, besieged toward the end of March, gave more trouble both in negotiation and fighting. Much ink was shed in correspondence with the governor, and after capturing one part of the town, forty or fifty men were lost in crossing the bridge to assault the other. After all, it was surrendered upon articles on March 28th 1650.

The storm of Clonmel on May 9th ended Cromwell's fighting in Ireland, and indeed also ended all real resistance to the Parliament. On this occasion the fighting was hardly less fierce than at Drogheda, but happily it was not followed by massacre or pillage. While the garrison drew out unobserved, the townsfolk succeeded in obtaining conditions, and these were faithfully observed, notwithstanding that the besiegers felt they had lost the garrison by a little sharp practice. The whole south of Ireland was now practically subject to the army. The power of the colonists in the north was restored; and the re-settlement could be conducted by men whom the Commonwealth might better spare than it could Oliver Cromwell.

In his despatch of April 2nd, recounting the capture of Kilkenny, Oliver complained, more in sorrow than in anger, of the Parliament's failure to supply him with money or men.* Out of 5,000 recruits raised in England, he declared he did not know of more than 2,000 that had come over.

After all, Cromwell did not rely only on force of arms. Hostile as he was to the leaders of the Irish race, he really intended well to the people themselves, desiring to make them share in the regeneration of England. The vehemence with which he dwelt on this purpose is conspicuous in the extraordinary "Declaration "† fulminated by him against the acts of "the Irish Popish prelates and clergy in a conventicle at Clonmacnoise." In its unconventional straightforwardness, and in the passion of moral conviction vibrating through its contorted language this declaration would be difficult to match among state-papers of the kind. In form, it was an answer to a sort

---

* "Sir, our horse have not had one month's pay of five. We strain what we can that the foot may be paid, or else they would starve."—*Despatch of April* 2, 1650. Why were the unpaid foot worse off than the unpaid horse? Was it that they were poorer men?

† Carlyle, vol. ii., p. 268.

of " pastoral " * put forth by the Romish clergy. But its real purpose was to explain to the people of Ireland the policy of Parliament. And those who had intelligence enough to understand it must have felt that this manifesto differed very much from the public utterances of any Ormonds, or Glamorgans, or O'Neiles. It differed in this respect, that both dynastic interests and class interests were conspicuously absent from it, that it was animated by devotion to principles rather than to men, while, at the same time, these principles were pushed even at the point of the pike, because they were expected ultimately to bless all men of every class throughout all great Britain and Ireland.

The pastoral appeal had expressed joy in the complete reunion between clergy and laity, and had expounded afresh how much the interest of the Church, of his Majesty, and of the nation depended on a persevering resistance to the Parliament. The clergy were much more prominent then as leaders of Irish disaffection than they are now. Yet the hold of Romanism upon the population was nothing like so strong as it is in our day. In his counterblast to the pastoral appeal Cromwell satirises the reconciliation of " clergy and laity "—terms " unknown to any save the Anti-Christian Church, and such as derive themselves from her. † Laity and clergy! It was your pride that begot this expression ; and it is for filthy lucre's sake you keep it up." But union or no union, it is for the people, not for himself, he fears.

"I say not this as being troubled at your union. By the grace of God we fear not and we care not for it. Your Covenant is with Death and Hell ! Your union is like that of Simeon and Levi. ' Associate yourselves and ye shall be broken in pieces ; take counsel together, and it shall come to nought.' For though it becomes us to be humble in respect of ourselves, yet we can say to you, God is not with you. You say your union is ' against a common enemy ; ' and to this, if you will be talking of union, I will give you some wormwood to bite on ; by which it will appear God is not with you."

By the " common enemy " he presumes they mean Englishmen, and he reminds them of the political union they have

---

* This consisted of the " Acts and Declarations " of Clonmacnoise. But it was in effect a pastoral appeal. The date of the meeting was December 4th, 1649. The reprint in London bears the " imprimatur " of Henry Scobel Cler. Parliamenti, which looks as if the Puritan " rebels " were not much afraid of prelatical rhetoric. But singularly enough the prelates were evidently afraid that Cromwell might gain the confidence of their flocks.

† One wonders what genealogy the " great Independent " would have assigned to modern nonconformist churches with their " clerical and lay brethren."

broken by their sectarian union. He is weak here; for he ignores the real facts of the past relations between the Celtic Irish and the stronger English race.

He then comes to the design of this sectarian union founded on political disunion. He quotes from the declaration of the Clonmacnoise meeting a long flourish about "the interests and immunities of the Church, and of every the Bishops and Prelates thereof," and "the honour, dignity, estate, right, and possessions of all and every of the said Archbishops, Bishops, and other Prelates." He insists that here is the secret of prelatic zeal, while the professed "advancement of his Majesty's rights and the good of this nation" are entirely secondary. He is very fierce against prelatic ambition and greed. As to "the interest of his Majesty," he asks "what Majesty they mean?" They would as readily support the King of Spain, or of France, to gain their ends. Then he comes to their plea concerning the welfare of the people:—

"In the last place, you are pleased,—having, after your usual manner, remembered yourselves first and 'his Majesty,' as you call him, next; like a man of your tribe with his *Ego et Rex meus*,—you are pleased to take the people into consideration, lest they should seem to be forgotten. Or rather you would make me believe they are much in your thoughts. Indeed I think they are,—alas, poor 'laity'!—that you and your king might ride them and jade them, as your Church hath done, and as your king * hath done by your means, almost in all ages. But it would not be hard to prophesy that, the beasts being strong and kicking, this will not last always. Arbitrary power men begin to be weary of † in kings and churchmen. Their juggle between them mutually to uphold civil and ecclesiastical tyranny begins to be transparent."

The prelates warn the people of their danger from England's threefold malignity in seeking the extirpation of the Catholic religion, the destruction of their lives, and the ruin of their fortunes. Oliver's dealing with the first point interests us from the light it sheds on his refusal to Romanists of the liberty he was eager to obtain for separatists. In the negotiations for the surrender of Ross the governor wished to make liberty of conscience one of the conditions. To this Oliver had replied— "I meddle not with any man's conscience; but if you mean a

---

* Is it the "*Prince of this world*" he means?

† Yet, two centuries later, what a picture does Europe present, from the Rhine to the Caucasus!

U

liberty to exercise the Mass, I judge it best to use plain dealing, and to let you know, where the Parliament of England have power, that will not be allowed of." This the prelates in their declaration called with much reason a "tyrannical resolution." The answer of the Lord-Lieutenant is not very clear on this point—that is, not verbally clear; but, after all, it glows luridly enough through the smoke of his wrath. He declines to regard priestcraft and the Mass as religious subjects. They are for him political engines, working the disintegration of the international union. And these engines he is determined to break up. But, on the other hand :—

"As for the people, what thoughts they have in matters of religion in their own breasts I cannot reach; but shall think it my duty, if they walk honestly and peaceably, not to cause them in the least to suffer for the same; and shall endeavour to walk patiently and in love toward them, to see if at any time it shall please God to give them another or a better mind."

Turning to the alleged intention of Parliament to exterminate the Irish race, he says this is only inferred from their resolution to put down Romanism. On this point he is needlessly subtle, as though his labyrinthine mind took a pleasure in beating the logic-chopping priests at their own weapons. But we are interested mainly in the method of conversion upheld by him, and described by him in a sentence that singularly illustrates his frequent habit of expressing downright honesty of intention in very tortuous language :—

"There may be found out another means than massacring, destruction, and banishment, to wit, the word of God, which is able to convert, a means which you know as little as practise; which indeed you deprive the people of, together with humanity, good life, equal and honest dealing with men of a different opinion, which we desire to exercise toward this poor people, if you by your wicked counsel make them not incapable to receive it by putting them into blood. And therefore by this also your false and twisted dealing may be a little discovered.

"Well; your words are ' massacre, destroy, and banish.' Good; *now give us an instance of one man since my coming into Ireland, not in arms, ' massacred, destroyed, or banished,' concerning the massacre or destruction of whom justice hath not to be done or endeavoured to be done.*" *

These last words are remarkable. It is obvious that the writer gave a tolerably wide interpretation to the phrase "in

* Italics, of course, the present writer's.

arms." He would include in that description all inhabitants who gave active aid in the defence of besieged towns, or who were so mixed up with the soldiery as not to be readily distinguishable. But the eagerness of the Lord-Lieutenant to add a controversial success to his martial victories would certainly prevent him from giving a challenge such as this, if he were not confident as to the result. At any rate the conspicuous absence of the beautiful women of Wexford both from the invective of the prelates and from all direct contemporary testimony quite justifies us in believing that when Oliver wrote these words that myth was quite unknown to him. As to banishment, he owns its severity, and denies that any had been or would be subjected to it whose lives were not justly forfeited. And, finally, as to confiscations, he contends that it was "a wise and just act in the State to raise money by escheating the lands of those who had a hand in the rebellion." *

"But what! Was the English army brought over for *this* purpose, as you allege? Do you think that the State of England will be at five or six millions charge, merely to procure purchasers to be invested in that for which they did disburse a little above a quarter of a million? †—although there be justice in that also, which ought, and I trust will be seasonably performed toward them. No! I can give you a better reason for the army coming over than this. England hath had experience of the blessing of prosecuting just and righteous causes, whatever the cost and hazard be. And if ever men were engaged in a righteous cause in the world, this will scarce be a second to it. We are come to ask an account of the innocent blood that hath been shed, and to endeavour to bring to an account—by the blessing and presence of the Almighty, in whom alone is our hope and strength —all who, by appearing in arms, seek to justify the same. We come to break the power of a company of lawless rebels, who, having cast off the authority of England, live as enemies to human society; whose principles, as the world hath experienced, are to destroy and subjugate all men not complying with them. We come, by the assistance of God, to hold forth and maintain the lustre and glory of English liberty in a nation where we have an undoubted right to do it; wherein the people of Ireland, if they listen not to such seducers as you are, may equally participate in all benefits, to use liberty and fortune equally with Englishmen, if they keep out of arms."

* In 1641 subscriptions were invited in England, and investors received a lien on forfeited Irish estates. The amount raised seems in all to have been about £250,000.

† An awkward sentence. "Would England spend five or six millions merely to protect a quarter of a million invested in Ireland?"—a question with bearings on modern policy in Egypt and elsewhere.

The last paragraphs of the manifesto assure all classes in Ireland that, while "leading persons and principal contrivers of the late rebellion" must be punished, all others may expect such a re-settlement of the island as will secure to them life, liberty, honour, and subsistence. How this promise was fulfilled is too long a story to tell here. But it *was* fulfilled. Ireland began to share with England the brief prosperity of the next few years. And the disturbance of Cromwell's settlement of that country was, like all effects of English revolutions on Ireland, a very questionable blessing.

Thus was the remedy of force tried in Ireland. Let those who advocate it now say whether they would carry it out with the same remorseless vigour. Even if they would, the only effect must be to add disappointment to horror. What is wanted is not Cromwell's violence, but his courageous recognition of facts, and his daring adaptation of remedies to the conditions of the times. The priests are invincible now, unless it should turn out that their influence is inconsistent with popular knowledge. The rights of cultivators are acknowledged, but they are minimised rather than generously conceded. Home Rule in some form is held to be inevitable; but it is withheld till evils are overcome, which it alone can cure. But we must be patient. Perhaps the time for heroes is gone by; and precarious majorities of mediocrities necessarily do their work piecemeal.

CHAPTER XIX.

DUNBAR.

THE recall of Cromwell from Ireland was suggested by the obvious probability of trouble with Scotland on account of the destruction of monarchy in England. The Scots, being an independent nation, had a clear right to choose their own form of government, and to crown the heir of the Stuarts if they pleased. But, practically, it would have been very difficult, if not impossible, to sever the fate of the southern country from that of the northern. The second Charles would have regarded Scotland only as a base for the conquest of his revolted kingdom of England. Besides, there was no genuine attempt at such a separation. The language of the Scots, and the bearing of the Royalists in England, showed that the design was to enthrone the Prince at Westminster by a combination of his adherents in both realms. Fairfax was not now to be counted on, and it was plain Cromwell must come back. But a summons delayed more than two months in transmission was regarded by the Lord-Lieutenant as allowing some discretion on his part. Therefore in the conclusion of his despatch from Kilkenny, he requested fresh instructions. At the same time he was most earnest in his profession of obedience to Parliament; so earnest, indeed, as to suggest the thought, he "doth protest too much." But he was really anxious to secure the subordination of the army to the civil government on one condition—that the civil government would complete the work it had employed the army to begin. In response the Parliament passed another order, that he should return if he saw it expedient to do so. In the end of April a frigate sailed from Milford Haven "to attend his pleasure ;" and at the end of May he went on board. He left Waterford still besieged. But the rebellion had been so broken that his deputy, Ireton, could easily finish the work. He left also his own son Henry, who had arrived in February and had now an opportunity of studying the country over which at a later time he presided as Governor.

Cromwell landed at Bristol, and was received there with loud acclaim. But this was only a faint prelude to what awaited him when on Friday, May 31st 1650, he drove into Westminster. London poured out its citizens and apprentices to line the roads as he approached. " What a vast multitude is come out to see your Lordship !" said an attendant. " Aye," replied Oliver, " but how many more would come to see me hanged ! " " There is many a true word spoken in jest," and Oliver's ideas of popular government were always strongly tinged with a distrust of unregenerate human nature. He did not return to his house in King Street. In consideration of his eminent services, and of his important official position, Parliament had assigned him a state residence in a building called the Cockpit, an appurtenance of Whitehall Palace, whither his wife had already removed—not very willingly, it is said. Her virtues were of a private character, and though her only surviving letter would indicate that, like all good wives, she tried to keep her husband up to the smaller duties of his position in letter-writing and social attentions, she herself seems to have shrunk from publicity, and bore as a martyrdom—

> " The burden of an honour
> Unto which she was not born."

On taking his seat once more in Parliament he received the formal thanks of the House from the lips of the Speaker. Nor was this gratitude an unsubstantial sentiment. The former vote of £2,500 a year for him still remained fruitless. And before his arrival the House had ordered immediate steps to be taken to realise it. Ludlow had interposed with an officious reminder of Skippon's claims. But to his astonishment and anger he was not heeded. Perhaps no previous achievement of Cromwell's, not even the suppression of mutiny in the army, had been so heartily appreciated as the stern vengeance he had exacted for the blood of Protestants in Ireland, and his reduction of the confusion there to the beginnings of order.

But the portentous cloud rising on the Scottish border threatened a speedy storm, and showed that Cromwell had very nicely calculated the time of his return. While the most formidable champion of the Commonwealth was still at death-grips with rebellion in Ireland, the Cavaliers and Royalist Presbyterians in the north had been wrangling, and fighting, and negotiating, as though to spin out the time for his convenience. The Marquis of Montrose, indignant at the conditions imposed on his master by the Covenanters, endeavoured to cut the tangle with his sword; but only with the effect of incurring death on a gibbet, under circumstances of intended humiliation converted by his heroic bearing into a halo of glory. After this sacrifice had proved the uselessness of force, Prince Charles lost no time in showing his unworthiness of such devotion by stooping to the hypocrisy of accepting the Covenant. When we remember how he afterwards publicly deplored his dead father's blood-guiltiness and his living mother's "idolatry," we are lost in amazement at the preposterous estimate men put on royal place, and also at the transparent pretences that are at a pinch satisfactory to holy sticklers for ecclesiastical forms. On the other hand we cannot wonder at the disgust which rent the feeble bond uniting his supporters, and still less at the new zeal inspired in the English army by moral indignation.

On June 12th the Parliament appointed Fairfax and Cromwell commanders of the inevitable expedition to the north. The Council of State then desired Lord Fairfax to say whether he would accept the command. He avowed that he had scruples on the subject, and resisted many importunities in which Cromwell joined. The latter then proposed to the Council that, notwithstanding the unwillingness of Fairfax to lead the army into Scotland, he should still retain the supreme command. For himself, Oliver declared that he would rather serve under Fairfax than command the greatest army in Europe.* But the Council were not satisfied to take this course; and Cromwell then suggested a committee to confer with Fairfax. Lambert, Harrison, St. John, and Whitelocke were named, and to these Cromwell was added. As they were leaving the chamber, Ludlow stepped up to Oliver and urged him "not to obstruct the public service out of mere compliment and humility."

When the committee met Fairfax, they first knelt down and prayed for Divine direction. Cromwell led, and was followed by Lambert and Harrison. That Fairfax was in perplexity there can be no doubt. He, at least, was not too splendidly successful

* Ludlow's "Memoirs." Ludlow himself was present at the Council. He says Cromwell "acted his part to the life, that I really thought him in earnest." When was he undeceived? Apparently when Cromwell consented to undertake an imperative duty absolutely refused by Fairfax.

to lose the credit of honesty; and if he had ever regarded this solemn opening of their conference as a mockery, we should have known it. But all of these men—unless Whitelocke was an exception—believed that they were instruments wielded by a divine power of regeneration. With pardonable inconsistency they thought also that the triumph of God's work depended on their discretion and faithfulness. In that hour they realised a crisis of their country's fate. Upon their decision might depend the continuance of the Commonwealth or the victory of allied bigotry and hypocrisy over its ruins. It is surely easier to believe that at such a moment they were over-mastered by sincere fanaticism than that they dared to look heaven in the face, and lie.

After prayers were over, Cromwell stated the purpose of their conference. Fairfax referred to the Covenant between the two nations, and denied that any just cause for invading Scotland was apparent. Cromwell agreed that an unjust invasion would be "abominable." But he argued that the Scots had first broken the Covenant by invading England under Hamilton; that there was reasonable ground for believing they were intending the same thing again, and that notoriously the only question to be decided was whether the scene of war should be in England or in Scotland. To these arguments Fairfax only replied that he could not overcome his scruples, and would resign his commission. If, as is sometimes held, he was tired of the form of chief command with the reality of a lieutenancy, the warm opposition of Oliver to his old leader's resignation might have prompted, if not concession, at least a generous response.

"I am very sorry," said Cromwell, "your lordship should have thoughts of laying down your commission, by which God hath blessed you in the performance of many eminent services to Parliament. I pray, my lord, consider all your faithful servants, us who are officers, who have served under you, and desire to serve under no other general. It would be a great discouragement to all of us, and a great discouragement to the affairs of the Parliament, for our noble general to entertain any thought of laying down his commission. I hope your lordship will never give so great an advantage to the public enemy, nor so much dishearten your friends as to think of laying down your commission." *

* Whitelocke's "Memorials," under June 25, 1650. Whitelocke was, of course, present; and though we cannot suppose he gives the precise words, he certainly gives them approximately, for he was a confirmed note-taker.

Notwithstanding this appeal, Fairfax resigned his commission as Lord-General on the 25th of June, and next day the appointment was conferred on Cromwell. Events had so clearly associated this name and victory that the suggestion of another candidate would have been in effect a proposal to deprive the Commonwealth of its trustiest weapon on the verge of a struggle for life. The promotion was a change of title rather than of of power. But it was a proud moment for the Huntingdon farmer; and, as is the case with all large natures, appreciation softened his heart toward detractors. He knew of course the part taken by Ludlow against the settlement of his income; and as they sat together in the House, Cromwell frankly referred to the change in Ludlow's bearing towards him, and said it seemed to insinuate some suspicion. But for his own part, he added, he was persuaded that both of them desired only the public good; and therefore he thought it would be well to talk over the matter. They had a private interview the same day in the " Queen's Guard Chamber." It was on this occasion that Ludlow, as previously mentioned, reproached Cromwell with his severity to the Levellers, and extorted an acknowledgment that necessity compelled his former friend to some actions contrary to the judgment of many about him. Beyond the severity to the Levellers, it does not appear what were Ludlow's complaints; but he was by no means satisfied with the Lord-General's soundness in the republican faith. Cromwell however assured him that he now felt a "free and equal commonwealth" to be inevitable.* It appeared to be the design of the Lord to free His people from every burden, and to accomplish what was prophesied in Psalm cx. Ludlow was impatient of Oliver's homily on this Psalm. But as we read it now, and remember Oliver's notion of the Bible, we can well conceive the fire that burned in his eyes as he spoke. There were two reforms, on the need of which he emphatically dwelt—those of the clergy and of the law. But he admitted " the sons of Zeruiah were too hard for him " at present. People said he and his friends wanted to destroy property; but he held that the law, as then constituted, served only to maintain lawyers, and encouraged the rich to oppress the poor. In Ireland, under the arrangements he had made, he declared that

---

* Like M. Thiers, in our own day, he thought that the republic divided them least.

more causes were decided in a week than in a year at Westminster; and he hoped to make Ireland in this respect a good
precedent for England.

Such ideas as these showed him to be what in modern times
would be called a decided Radical. The legal reforms he desired
have yet to be carried out; but in his recognition of the truth,
that Ireland's extremity might be the English reformer's opportunity, he showed a statesman's judgment, and a somewhat
striking anticipation of what is occurring in our own day.
His immediate purpose however was to interest Ludlow in
Ireland, and get him to go there as Lieutenant-General of
Horse. It has been suggested that it was very artful in Cromwell to send so impracticable a republican out of the way. The
simpler and more probable explanation is that he was not quite
satisfied about Lord Broghill, who held the post, and thought
Ludlow would do more service to the public there than by
theorising at Westminster. Ludlow gave in effect the Scriptural answer: "I have married a wife, and therefore I cannot
come." But he did go, after all.

On June 29th the new Lord-General left London. Already
troops had been collected from various garrisons and stations
on the northward route, and were streaming toward the border.
The Scotch were astonished that they were to have the conqueror
of Ireland amongst them so soon, and the terrors of his name
were increased by foolish exaggerations intended to animate
popular resistance, but more calculated to produce an opposite
effect. On the other hand the Parliament issued a declaration
of reasons for the invasion, and Cromwell, on the march, indited
an address "to the Saints in Scotland." The inscription indicated a possible source of perplexity that probably troubled many
in his army much more than himself. They were no longer
fighting against Papists and malignants. They were to contend
with brethren, who held them bound by a Solemn League and
Covenant. But the same circumstance might create doubt in
Scotland also. In fact, there were already three parties amongst
Charles's adherents. The main body, or centre, consisted of
rigid Presbyterians who insisted equally on Church and King;
the left was composed of zealots, caring more for Church than
King; while the right was formed by Royalists pure and simple,
who worshipped the King, and were hostile or indifferent to the

Kirk. The army's address to the Scottish "saints" was skilfully adapted to detach the zealots, and it was not without influence. It assured the northern brethren that "the inconsistency of English religion and liberties with the King's interest and the former constitution of Parliament did not arise from jealousies or pretences, but from the hardness of the King's heart and the backsliding of a greater part of those that were formerly trusted in Parliament." As to "presbyterial government," those who liked it should have all freedom to enjoy it, and if it were so much of God as some affirmed, it might be left to " God's own means, His word powerfully and effectually preached, without a too busy meddling or engaging with the authorities of the world."

Sir Arthur Haselrig was then Governor of Newcastle, and came to Durham to meet Cromwell. They had many religious exercises together, but there seems to have been feasting as well as fasting. From Alnwick a letter was despatched to Richard Mayor. The Lord-General is a grandfather now, and amongst all the cares of an opening campaign is anxious to "hear how the little brat doth ;" and then, after the usual indications of his perpetual disappointment in the "brat's" father, he adds : "I need pity. I know what I feel. Great place and business in the world is not worth the looking after. . . . I have not sought these things ; truly I have been called unto them by the Lord, and therefore am not without some assurance that He will enable His poor and weak servant to do His will." *

On the 22nd of July the army, passing through Berwick, crossed the border and encamped at Mordington. Here, says Captain John Hodgson,†

"The General made a large discourse to the officers on the bounds (boundary), showing he spoke as a Christian and a soldier ; and showed the inconveniency we should meet with in the nation as to the scarcity of provisions. As to the people, we should find them all soldiers, and they were very numerous, and at present, may be, unanimous : and much to that purpose. And he charged the officers to double, nay treble, their diligence in that place, for he was sure we had work before us."

That Oliver should speak in this style, not to a few select counsellors, but to the whole body of his officers, shows that he

* Letter CXXXIV.
† Who, by the way, scarcely deserves Carlyle's epithet, "pudding-headed," as this extract is enough to suggest.

counted confidently not merely on their pluck, but on their religious faith and devotion to the cause. To keep up mere physical courage, a general must often make light of difficulties even at the risk of begetting over-confidence. But when a leader can deliberately rehearse in the hearing of his supporters all their special disadvantages, with the certainty that his words will only inspire energy and watchfulness, it must be because a profound communion of spirit and purpose assures him of his ground. And indeed in this case the difficulties were formidenough. The Scottish army, under David Lesley, numbered about 20,000 men, and was increasing from day to day. The invading army was not more than 17,000 at its utmost strength, and would certainly decrease faster than recruits could be brought up. The country was so wasted and depopulated by order of the Scottish Government that nearly all Cromwell's supplies must be drawn from his ships. If a battle could soon be forced, the issue might indeed be expected confidently. But it was evidently Lesley's policy to avoid a battle, and to waste the English forces by delay.

On Thursday, July 25th, the invading army left Mordington, and marched to Cockburn's Path. This is a ravine, through which runs the main road from Berwick to Edinburgh. A small, resolute force might have inflicted great loss upon Cromwell at this pass; but no enemy appeared. In modern times a general engaged on such an expedition would keep up strong lines of communication with his base; and the fortification of Cockburn's Path would be essential. But Cromwell does not seem to have thought of it. If this was an error in generalship, it was unavoidable from the smallness of his army. But the seizure of this pass afterwards by Lesley constituted one of the most threatening features of his position in the retreat that followed. The only hope at that time was that Sir Arthur Haselrig might break through from Newcastle; but no arrangement of that kind appears to have been made beforehand.

On Friday Dunbar was reached; and supplies, very scanty says Cromwell, were obtained from the ships. Here the road turns sharply westward; and the next halt was at Haddington on Saturday. On Sunday came a rumour that the enemy would meet them at Gladsmuir, four miles nearer Edinburgh, where the road branches to either side of a long hill. But when Cromwell had pushed on his van in hot haste to seize the best ground, it turned out that the alarm was occasioned by mere scouting parties. Lambert and Whalley were immediately sent on to Musselburgh, with orders to attempt the enemy, if they could find him; and Cromwell himself brought up the main body in their rear. There was a little skirmishing of horse, but no serious resistance; and that Sunday night the English army lay at Musselburgh, a little port of much importance to them during the next week or two.

Here the mystery of Lesley's inaction was cleared up. The Scotch general had wedged his army in between the Calton Hill and Leith, and had strongly entrenched his front. He had outposts also on Salisbury Crags, to threaten and annoy the flank of the attacking army. No arrangement could have been more skilfully adapted to the strategy of delay. Before those bristling entrenchments and the craggy fortifications of Edinburgh Cromwell was as much baffled as a good hound might be that should come upon a hedgehog and a tortoise side by side. But in the case in hand the hedgehog was a formidable creature if unrolled; and any attempt, in its presence, to crack the shell of the tortoise was out of the question. On Monday, July 29th, an attempt was made to draw Lesley out. The outposts on Salisbury Crags were captured; and field-guns played on the Scottish lines. But Lesley's strength was to sit still; and he knew it. There was a soaking rain through the afternoon and night, while for many a dreary hour Cromwell's troops were kept in the field, watching for an opportunity; but in the early morning they were obliged, as Captain Hodgson phrases it, to go back to "their bread and cheese" at Musselburgh. Then Lesley launched his cavalry at their rear. But the English horse were ready for them; and as larger bodies were sent out by Lesley in support, there was a smart fight. Major-General Lambert was badly wounded and captured, but soon rescued again by Lieutenant Empson, of Cromwell's own regiment. The result was, that the Scots retreated, being followed by their foes up to the very trenches. But the Tuesday evening found both armies, except for the loss of killed and wounded, just where they had been on Monday morning.

The English forces—wet, muddy, wearied, and dazed with sleeplessness—crowded in and around Musselburgh, and tumbled down to rest as they could. They had not a long night's rest; for between three and four on Wednesday morning, there was an alarm of an attack in great force. The guards had been beaten in; a regiment of horse was retreating in disorder. But the sleepers were soon roused; the saddles were speedily filled; and the chase went back again to within a quarter of a mile of Edinburgh. In this rout Scottish officers of some consequence were captured or slain, and Lesley was confirmed in his policy of "masterly inaction."

That policy appeared likely to prove successful. No further attempt was made on either side for several days. But in the first week of August stormy weather prevented the approach of shipping to Musselburgh, and the army was threatened with starvation. It was necessary then to retreat to Dunbar, in order to obtain supplies. And the Edinburgh clergy gave public thanks that the Lord had put a hook in Oliver's nose, and led him back by the way that he came. At Dunbar he had to feed the Scotch inhabitants as well as his own army, for famine had reduced them to stealing horse-beans and picking up the leavings of the soldiers. On August 12th he was back in Musselburgh, but with no more prospect of a battle than before. Some new method must be tried, or his army would waste away.

Cromwell having the command of the sea, and being able to move around the south of Edinburgh at his pleasure, Lesley and the city drew their supplies down the Forth, or from its opposite shores. It occurred then to Cromwell that if he could threaten Lesley's communication with Linlithgow and Stirling, he might force him to fight. Accordingly, on August 13th, he marched round Edinburgh, by Colinton, so as to overlook the Stirling road. But this movement only made the advantages of Lesley's position still more apparent. Between Edinburgh and the Forth he could march parallel to Oliver's advance, but on a much shorter line; while the river Leith in this direction served much the same purpose of shelter in case of need as his entrenchments towards Musselburgh. Meantime, as supplies had to be drawn from Musselburgh, the English troops were a good deal harassed with marching backward and forward between the skirts of the Pentlands and that town. On the 27th of August Cromwell pushed on westward, towards Stirling. And when he saw Lesley's army emerging from between Edinburgh and the Forth, he rejoiced in the success of his manœuvre.

But he was deceived by his ignorance of the country. Lesley had drawn out his army where boggy ground prevented any general attack being made. There was an interchange of cannon-shot, and a little skirmishing, but nothing more. Half in impatience, half perhaps with the notion that the exposure of so valuable a prize might help to bring on a battle, Cromwell himself headed the charge of a forlorn hope. A Scottish carbineer took deliberate aim at him but missed; whereupon Oliver called out to the man that if a soldier of his had fired at such a distance from his mark, he would have dismissed him from the army.* All was of no use. Lesley, like a wise man, would not fight so famous an opponent, unless he could catch him at a great disadvantage. Provisions had fallen short, and on the Wednesday morning, August 28th, Oliver retreated once more towards Musselburgh. Lesley, seeing this, hurried to intercept him; but, as Cromwell puts it, "the Lord in mercy prevented" this, and the two armies resumed their former positions.

During these weeks a paper controversy had occupied the armies debarred from more carnal weapons. Both Scotch and English were most anxious to throw on each other the guilt of breaking the Covenant, and to maintain the consistency of their own godliness. That this should be so was a good sign, presaging the power of public opinion, which even in our own day has not attained maturity, but is destined yet to disarm the world. The General Assembly had issued a reply to the declaration of the army, and "some godly ministers" with the army drew up a rejoinder to that reply. In transmitting this rejoinder Cromwell assured the Assembly of his readiness ·to scatter broadcast amongst his men any papers they might send him. Accordingly, General Lesley sent him a Declaration of the Kirk as to the causes of the war, with a request to make it known to his officers. In reply Cromwell assured him that this had been done, as the trumpeter could testify. To this he added some strong reprobation of the purposes to which the Covenant was being wrested, and of the monstrous pretence that the godly interest could be served by forcing the young Charles Stuart on

* Mercurius Politicus, in King's Pamphlets, No. 478.

an unwilling people by means of his hypocrisies and Scottish arms.

Indeed the covenanting Charles was rather an incongruous monster to some amongst Lesley's own army. While Cromwell was hovering on the skirts of the Pentlands, Major-General Lambert had an interview with Colonel Strahan, and also with Colonel Gilbert Ker, both of whom were doubtful about the haste with which the Prince had been received before his godliness had been sufficiently tested. But poor Charles was just then being badgered to sign the unfilial declaration of his parent's sins, and both Strahan and Ker intimated that much depended on this. He did sign, however, and therefore these men continued to fight for him. The faith of a poor bewildered world in signatures of this kind is very strange. It arises presumably from association with the transfer of tangible possessions such as money or lands, or from the power of law to enforce a contract witnessed in this way. Such things are external to a man, independent of his character, and may therefore be secured through the outward hold on him given by his signature. But faith and faithfulness, belief and emotion, are so entirely matters of the inward man —of character, whether intellectual or moral—that the signature never can increase, though it may seriously diminish, a man's trustworthiness. In this case, Charles's signature could scarcely increase the moral enthusiasm of his army, and if self-respect had ever been a possibility with him, this must have robbed him of it.

When the army reached Musselburgh, on the evening of Wednesday, August 28th, it was already clear that a further retreat must be made. The men were sickening fast. About five hundred sick and wounded had to be shipped off at once from Musselburgh and Prestonpans to Berwick or Newcastle. The weather was extraordinarily wet and stormy for the season, and provisions had occasionally failed to get so far up the Firth. On the whole, it seemed best to retire to Dunbar, and make that the head-quarters. Thursday and Friday were occupied with preparations for removal, and particularly with embarking the sick. This work Cromwell superintended personally. It was barely completed when the van of the army reached Haddington on Saturday, August 31st; and in lingering behind to see the last of it, the Lord-General was nearly surprised at Prestonpans by the

advanced guard of the Scots, who hurried out of their entrenchments in pursuit.* There was some hard fighting between that
place and Haddington. But night came on, and as " the Lord
by His providence put a cloud over the moon," the rear brigade
of horse were enabled to rejoin their comrades. At midnight
the enemy, growing bold now, assaulted the western end of
Haddington, but were driven off more vigorously than they
expected. Indeed it was probably the ill-success of this assault
which disposed Lesley to resume his dilatory tactics next day.
For Cromwell would gladly have given battle ; only being now
much inferior in force, he was more anxious than hitherto to
have the fight on ground of his own choosing. On the Sunday
morning therefore he drew out his army in an open field on the
south side of Haddington, with a low, sloping hill in his rear,
and the little river Tyne in his front.† But Lesley would not
attack him there, and after waiting three or four hours, Cromwell continued his perilous retreat in the face of a much more
numerous and now confident enemy.

In following the record of these anxious days, it is difficult to
resist the impression that it was not so much generalship which
saved the English army, but rather its extraordinary moral tone.
To the ordinary bull-dog tenacity characteristic of the English
soldier, religious conviction in this case added the self-abandon-
ment of the martyr. Supplies were short ; comforts there were
none ; the weather was frightful ; exposure almost continuous.
At the same time discipline was rigorous. Soldiers of exceptional
moral weakness, who yielded to temptations of plunder, were
hanged without mercy. Yet the General, his officers, and his
men were united in an intensity of purpose and inspiring faith,
to which doubt of success was almost as impossible as fear of
death. This army was a portent, proclaiming to a frivolous
world the tremendous powers latent in the moral natures of
common men, and capable of being roused by a spark from

* See a letter in King's Pamphlets, No. 748, small 4to. The words are worth
quoting. " The Lord-General . . . . had still been there (out of that great
humanity and pious care of the soldiers, whereby, among other means, he hath
always been much in their hearts) to see the poor sick soldiers shipped away
and accommodated." That Cromwell should make no reference to this in his
description of the skirmish between Musselburgh and Haddington is only in
accordance with his uniform habit.

† The precise spot is not mentioned in Cromwell's despatch. But the " open
field " and the " south side " identify it.

v

heaven, which wraps them in a common flame. That the lesson should ever have to be applied in warfare again, may God forbid! But it is very applicable to contests of political principle; and wise are the leaders who heed it. Yet the wisdom of this world can never teach them to heed it—never! There were one or two keen strokes of something like military genius in this last campaign of Oliver's. But now, as he pensively rode his weary horse over wet moors, leading his draggled, sick, and half-fed soldiers to stand at bay in a nook of the sea-shore, it was as a preacher and a prophet, far more than as a general, that he kept his army unconquered.

Why did he not send a detachment to seize Cockburn's Path, and so re-open his land communication with Berwick? The only answer is, that he was not strong enough. To have divided his force while pursued by an enemy twice his strength would have been to insure the annihilation of one or both divisions. But Lesley, knowing the country well, sent a strong force across the hills to occupy that pass, while with his main body he encamped on Doon Hill to watch the refuge of his victim with very much the quiet confidence of a cat crouching above a mouse-hole. By the time Cromwell's baggage-train in the van had reached Dunbar, the Scots were streaming abroad to make sure of their vantage ground; and as night fell on that melancholy Sunday, he thought sadly of Essex, at Fowey, seven years before, and of the impatient judgments passed on the earl's generalship by himself and the promoters of the New Model. Here was Essex's chief critic in almost precisely a similar position now—only, if possible, more hopeless.

Heavily the train laboured up the slope on which Dunbar stands peering over the sea; and the carriages were ranged in the churchyard, then standing fifty or sixty yards outside the town. The troops, as they came up, were bivouacked across the base of the little peninsula. But the General, when he arrived —remembering perhaps the attack on the train at Marston Moor—ordered the carriages "to be brought down to a little poor Scotch farmhouse in the middle of the field where the army was quartered." * He apprehended apparently that the wave of attack might sweep round him where he lay—a sufficient indication of his sense of the danger.

* Letter in King's Pamphlets, No. 748.

And in truth the case was desperate. As his army faced southwards, with their backs to Dunbar, they had before them, within a little more than a mile, Doon Hill, a ridge running east and west, and rising to a height of nearly 600 feet. On its northern face it is somewhat steep towards the top, sloping out more gently below. Along these slopes Lesley's men were ranged, turning a little southward at his extreme right, so as to overlook and command the Berwick Road. That road was sealed up further on at Cockburn's Path ; and, therefore, should the English be foolhardy enough to attempt to pass the Scottish flank, they would be caught fast in a trap. Between the Scottish camp on its vantage ground and the forlorn English on the low fields was a water-worn ravine, so narrow and deep as to be called in the letters of the time " a ditch." Through this ravine runs the Brocksburn, flattening out its banks towards the sea. And here, towards the shore, the English left could look along the road crossing the burn towards Berwick, but, alas, first towards Cockburn's Path. Near this crossing, but still further towards the sea, stood Brocksmouth House, a seat of the Roxburgh family, and then occupied by the extreme left of Cromwell's army.

When Monday morning rose, the seriousness of the position must have been clear to every one. General David Lesley had not a doubt about the issue. Looking down from his height on the prospect below him, he declared that he would have the whole of that army down there, dead or alive, by seven o'clock next morning.* On the other side, Cromwell did not disguise from himself the fact that Providence had mysteriously brought him face to face with death and ruin. He wrote in the course of that day a short note to Haselrig ; and in one respect it is the most interesting of all his letters, because it shows how he bore himself in the darkest hour of all his active life. He knew Haselrig was in no position to send speedy help ; but there was a wider question than the fate of his army, and that was the fate of the Commonwealth :—

"Wherefore, whatever becomes of us, it will be well for you to get what forces you can together, and the south to help what they can. The business nearly concerneth all good people. If your forces had been in readiness to have fallen upon the back of Copperspath,† it might have

* Letter in King's Pamphlets, No. 478, small 4to.   † Cockburn's Path.

occasioned supplies to have come to us. But the only wise God knoweth what is best. All shall work for good. Our spirits are comfortable, praised be the Lord, though our present condition be as it is; and indeed we have much hope in the Lord, of whose mercy we have had large experience." *

During the greater part of the day there was little or no change in the position of affairs. Early in the morning a party of Lesley's cavalry had come down from Doon Hill towards Brocksmouth, and the horses were feeding in the corn-fields there; but the movement excited little attention. A little house on the margin of the "ditch" had been occupied by a party of Colonel Pride's men, because of a practicable passage across the burn there; and they were driven out of it, losing three killed besides several prisoners. But the stuff they were made of was shown by the answer of a one-armed man amongst them when carried before Lesley. "How will you fight," asked the Scottish general, "when you have shipped half your men and all your great guns?" "Sir," said the man, "if you will please to draw down your men, you shall find both men and great guns too."

At four o'clock an officers' dinner was provided in the town of Dunbar, at which, presumably, the Lord-General was present. Afterwards he went down with Major-General Lambert to Brocksmouth House, and, looking across from the grounds there, he noticed that the whole Scottish army was shifting its position. Rank after rank they were coming down the hill, and trending always towards the sea. So marked was this movement that some two-thirds of the left wing of horse were being drawn to strengthen the right on the lowlands about the Berwick road. The rest of the army—that is, mainly the foot—would evidently be ranged on the narrow strip of land between the "ditch" and Doon Hill. Lesley had apparently accepted the invitation of the one-armed man, and "was pleased to draw down his men."

Cromwell saw in an instant that his opportunity was come. Whether he exclaimed "the Lord hath delivered them into my hand" is not certain. At any rate he certainly thought it; and, turning to Lambert, he pointed out how a vigorous attack on the enemy's extreme right, before the new dispositions were fully

---

* Letter CXXXIX. This letter was delayed, and only reached its destination with another of very different tenor.

completed, might throw the whole Scottish army into confusion. Lesley had surrendered the advantage of the hill; and if his right on the comparatively open land could be broken, it would carry confusion into his main body jammed in between Doon Hill and the "ditch." With this view Lambert heartily agreed, and added that the scheme might be completed by the play of artillery against the enemy's left along the Brocksburn, while the right was assaulted as proposed.* The two then consulted Colonel Monk, who equally approved the scheme; and at nine o'clock a council was held, at which the various duties for the next morning were assigned. Six regiments of horse were to give the first shock, supported by three regiments and a half of foot. At the head of the horse were to be Lambert, Fleetwood, and Whalley, while Monk was to lead on the foot. Behind these, in rhythmical reiteration, two other brigades, under Colonel Pride and Colonel Overton, were to fall on; and two remaining regiments of horse were to come up with guns that might sweep the field. Their word was "The Lord of Hosts."

There was little time for sleep, and little opportunity amid driving showers of hail and rain.† What time there was seemed to these men better given to prayer. Hear what Carlyle's "pudding-headed friend," Captain Hodgson, has to say upon the matter. Rousing to his work at four o'clock—quite dark, on the third of September—he says:

"As our regiment was marching at the head of the horse, a cornet was at prayer in the night, and I appointed one of my officers to take my place. I rid to hear him, and he was exceedingly carried on in the duty. I met with so much of God in it as I was satisfied deliverance was at hand, and, coming to my command, did encourage my poor weak soldiers, which did much affect them."

Can we not imagine it? "Courage, men! *God is our refuge and strength, a very present help in trouble. Therefore, will not we fear though the earth be removed, and though the mountains be carried into the midst of the sea; though the waters thereof roar and be troubled, though the mountains shake with the swelling*

---

* I take this to have been Lambert's suggestion partly from Hodgson's report of the Major-General's observations at the council of officers, partly from the fact that he was so very anxious about the guns next morning as to keep Cromwell impatiently waiting while he directed them. Hodgson, indeed, attributes the whole plan of attack to Lambert.

† Merc. Pol. in King's Pamphlets, No. 479, small 4to, § 1.

thereof. . . . *The heathen raged, the kingdoms were moved: He uttered His voice; the earth melted. The Lord of Hosts is with us; the God of Jacob is our refuge.*" The scene about these men was very like what the Psalmist describes. They heard the roaring of the sea; the land was swept with the deluges of rain that now passed away, leaving a troubled sky. The tramp of war shook the sodden ground ; and, hidden in the dreary darkness before them, were the sharp issues of more than life or death—the Commonwealth or a covenanted Charles !

The day broke feebly as they moved on, and revealed much disorder and incompleteness. The Major-General was away ordering the artillery that was to play across the Brocksburn ravine, Cromwell waxing impatient and angry. The Scots were roused, and were preparing to dash across by the Berwick road. Then Lambert galloped up in hot haste, having settled his guns, and quickly ordered the assault. The horse and part of the foot spring straight at the foe. Cromwell's regiment, under Lieutenant-Colonel Goffe, and two other foot regiments are to go round by Brocksmouth House towards the sea. Cromwell himself rode in the rear of the regiment in which Hodgson was captain, and, as they crossed the stream, ordered them to incline still to the left, till they were clear of all bodies of men, and could wheel round full on the enemy's right flank. The shock of the first meeting—horse with horse—was tremendous. Cannon had damaged the Ironsides as they approached, but their swords now rang and clanged above the shouting and roar. The English foot that charged with the cavalry were at first repelled. But Goffe, coming round with his levelled pikes on the extreme flank, restored the balance of power. Horse and foot were now engaged all over the field; and then the sun burst forth in unveiled brightness above the sea. "Now let God arise," exclaimed Cromwell, "and let His enemies be scattered !" It was a moment of intensest passion, when faith, resolve, devotion, the fierce joy of battle, wrought up his energies to that white heat in which the mysteries of heaven as well as the counsels of earth seemed clear. And his voice, heard by all soldiers near him, was like that of God's messenger. The struggle was brief now. The English horse rode through and over the Scottish foot. The Scottish horse, recoiling, fell upon their own foot regiments coming to the rescue. "They run! I profess they run!" cried Oliver. But, poor wretches, thousands of them had no room to run. Those who advanced, being met and turned back by their own flying comrades as they hastened by the margin of the ravine, made faint attempts to rally, but were borne down by the rush of triumphant foes; and the whole of Lesley's army broke up into a rout of panic-stricken fugitives.

They fled this way and that, as they could — some to Cockburn's Path, some towards Edinburgh, some madly rushed into Dunbar itself. Three thousand lay dead. Ten thousand— about the number of the whole English army—were captured; fifteen thousand arms and two hundred colours were taken. Most marvellous of all, the victors did not lose thirty men. Cromwell's victories were usually of this kind—utter ruin and dissolution to his adversary. He knew how to follow up a success. And it is a curious illustration of the clear thought and perception he retained in his supreme moments of ecstasy, that, to make this pursuit more effectual, he called a halt, and gave out a Psalm to be sung while the horse were being collected and ordered for the chase. It had been impressed upon him that deliverance would come; and it did come. Imagine, then, that "sharp, untunable voice" ringing over the blood-stained field, and echoed by the hoarse music of inspired warriors triumphant in "the Lord of Hosts."

> "For great to us-ward ever are
> His loving-kindnesses;
> His truth endures for evermore:
> The Lord O do ye bless!"

CHAPTER XX.

AT A DEADLOCK.

THE annihilation of David Lesley's army left Edinburgh and Leith open to Cromwell; and on the day after the battle he sent Lambert with an adequate force to take possession. Edinburgh Castle however held out, and formed a temporary refuge for fugitive soldiers and ministers. The Lord-General remained still at Dunbar, having much to do. He was at his wits' end how to dispose of the ten thousand prisoners. He was obliged to dismiss between four and five thousand, who, being "almost starved, sick, and wounded," were little likely to fight against him soon. The remainder he sent by a convoy of four troops—so little was any rising of the border people feared—to Berwick; and thence to various English towns. The fate of these latter prisoners will not bear reflection. Sanitation and the machinery of supply were at best very imperfect in the seventeenth century; and the best was scarcely experienced by prisoners of war. They were nearly all swept off by pestilence.

On that 4th of September Cromwell had much writing to get through. In his despatch to the Parliament, after giving an account of the battle, he assumed a tone of exhortation. That a victorious general should do so might have been expected to excite uneasiness. But, so far as we know, it did not—at least among the friends of liberty. Ludlow, the zealous republican, tells us that he " rejoiced not more in the victory of Dunbar than in the excellent spirit of the Lord-General's words about the Commonwealth." The imputation of presumption was prevented not merely by the practical fact of Cromwell's great personal importance, but also by his position and privilege as a Parliamentary leader, and member of the Council of State. And indeed the public conscience allowed that there was some need for exhortation. Parliament was not making the progress it ought to have done in re-settling the country and preparing for a "new representa-tive." Meantime there was a growing discontent. In the week before Dunbar fight a petition had been drawn up—one' of many similar in tone—by "divers free-born Englishmen, in-habiting in the cities of London and Westminster, the borough of Southwark, hamlets, and places adjacent," calling to mind the professions of the Parliament and army, and praying that their promises might be fulfilled. In the existing state of things, " while the supreme trust * of Parliament is fixed in the persons of the same men during their own pleasures, . . . laws are made of so dangerous a nature, as men can scarce speak or do anything for fear of loss of life, or liberty, or estate." The upshot of the petition is to desire a new Parlia-ment and periodic elections, legal and regular gaol deliveries, and the universal restoration of trial by jury.† Some parts of this petition seem to show that the signatories had only a dubious attachment to the Commonwealth as then established. They may have been " Levellers; " and some who were Royalists at heart were perhaps glad to swell the voice of complaint. But, however that may have been, it is obvious they appealed to prevalent dissatisfaction with the prolonged continuance of revolutionary necessities. It was this state of feeling Cromwell had in his mind when he turned from the account of his victory to an exhortation of the Parliament :—

"Thus you have the prospect of one of the most signal mercies God hath done for England and His people this war. And now may it please you to give me the leave of a few words. It is easy to say, the Lord hath done this. It would do you good to see and hear our poor foot go up and down, making their boast of God. But, Sir, it's in your hands; and by these eminent mercies God puts it into your hands—to give glory to Him, to improve your power and His blessings to His praise. We that serve you, beg of you not to own us, but God alone. We pray you, own His people more and more; for they are the chariots and horsemen of Israel. Disown yourselves; but own your authority, and improve it to curb the proud and insolent, such as would disturb the tranquillity of England, though under what specious pretext soever. Relieve the oppressed; hear the groans of poor prisoners in England.‡ Be pleased to reform the abuses of all professions. And if there be any

* Responsibility—the trust reposed in Parliament by the nation.
† The Petition is in King's Pamphlets, small 4to, No. 478.
‡ It is to be feared he did not mean political prisoners. This and the next sentence point at debtors, and the oppressiveness of law courts and lawyers to the poor. (Compare the conversation with Ludlow.)

one that makes many poor to make a few rich, that suits not a Common-wealth. If He that strengthens your servants to fight, please to give you hearts to set upon these things, in order to His glory and the glory of your Commonwealth,—besides the benefit England shall feel thereby, you shall shine forth to other nations, who shall emulate the glory of such a pattern, and through the power of God turn into the like." *

If there were any who thought that at the head of an army Cromwell should have dropped the hortatory privileges of a Parliament man and member of the State Council, they were obliged to suppress their opinion in the outburst of jubilation called forth by his marvellous victory. Parliament ordered abundant supplies of all kinds—men, money, and provisions—to be sent to the conqueror, and accorded him a special letter of thanks "taking notice of his eminent services." The captured colours were ordered to be hung up in Westminster Hall. A medal also was struck, having on the obverse Cromwell's bust, with the Dunbar password, "The Lord of Hosts," and on the reverse the House of Commons. When the artist went to Edinburgh to prepare the design, Cromwell wrote to deprecate such an honour, and to suggest that a representation of the army should take his place. In addition to the duty of modesty, which most men who have achieved real honours recognise when formal honours are thrust upon them, it is quite possible he feared the misinterpretations not only of enemies but of friends. The time was indeed not far distant now when he would have to choose between seeing the ship of state founder and boldly seizing the helm himself. But that time was not yet.

On that same fourth of September, when he had so much on hand, his thoughts turned, as those of over-strained men will, to home and wife and children. Though the words he wrote were few, they are still touching :—

"*For my beloved wife, Elizabeth Cromwell, at the ' Cockpit.'* These :—

"*Dunbar, 4th September*, 1650.

"MY DEAREST,—I have not leisure to write much. But I could chide thee that in many of thy letters thou writest to me that I should not be unmindful of thee and thy little ones. Truly if I love you not too well, I think I err not on the other hand much. Thou art dearer to me than any creature. Let that suffice.

"The Lord hath showed us an exceeding mercy : who can tell how

* Letter CXL.

great it is ? My weak faith hath been upheld. I have been in my inward man marvellously supported, though I assure thee I grow an old man,* and feel infirmities of age marvellously stealing upon me. Would my corruptions did as fast decrease. Pray on my behalf in the latter respect. The particulars of our late success Harry Vane or Gilbert Pickering will impart to thee. My love to all dear friends. I rest thine,

"OLIVER CROMWELL."†

Poor wife ! Perhaps she felt it rather hard to gather particulars from Harry Vane, or Gilbert Pickering, or excited newsmongers dashing in and out. But a husband who has long state despatches to write, and 10,000 prisoners to dispose of promptly, cannot be as copious in his information as he would desire. A brief note also went to his " dear brother, Richard Mayor." "This is the Lord's doing, and it is marvellous in our eyes. Good sir, give God all the glory; stir up all yours and all about you to do so." Doll and her " little brat" were not forgotten by the grandfather. Not satisfied with public honours, he expressed a hope that she was about to make him still more a grandfather. But, alas, in other respects she had become like her husband, " both idle, and worthy of blame."

Before the end of the week he was in Edinburgh, and lodged in Murray House in the Canongate, a lodging already familiar to him in 1648. On the Sunday he noticed that the Presbyterian clergy were not at their work, and was told they had taken refuge in the castle. He therefore directed Whalley to write to Dundas, the governor, offering them free liberty of preaching and full security, if they would come down and attend to their duties. But they would not; whereupon the pulpits were occupied by Mr. Stapylton (of the marriage treaty) and other godly ministers from England. Nay, lest truth should fail in Edinburgh streets, troopers at a pinch could exhort with an unction peculiar to themselves. Hence arose much correspondence with the castle.

The ministers, through Dundas, reproached Oliver with the persecution of brethren in England and Ireland, and with his " unjust invasion." He replied that no man had been troubled for preaching the Gospel, but only for making this a pretext " to over-top the civil power." As to unjust invasions, time

---

* Fifty-one and a half. But what toil and strain during the last eleven years !

† Carlyle, Letter CXLIII.

was when a Scottish army came into England uninvited. "We have said in our papers," he continued, "with what hearts, and upon what account we came, and the Lord hath heard us, though you would not, upon as solemn an appeal as any experience can parallel." The ministers retorted with a cry of amazement that preachers should be prevented from bearing testimony "against the sins and enormities of civil powers." And having now heard how their deserted posts were being filled, they expressed solemn grief that "men of mere civil place and employment should usurp the calling and employment of the ministry." With more reason and dignity they protested that "they had not so learned Christ as to hang the equity of their cause on events"—namely, the providential judgments by ordeal of battle to which Oliver appealed—"but desired to have their hearts established in the love of truth in all the tribulations that befel them."

Against the scorn expressed for lay preachers Oliver's Independent soul flashed out in indignation. And finding himself at "reasonable good leisure" on September 12th, he expounded to them his view of this and other questions in a letter more remarkable for its burning intensity of conviction than for its literary style. As to the censure of ministers for testifying against the sins of the civil power, he asked, was it likely that when the authorities of a nation had turned out a tyrant "in a way which Christian times would mention with honour, and all tyrants in the world look at with fear," those authorities should submit "to be called murderers, and the like, for doing this thing?" In behalf of his preaching troopers, he asks :—

"Are you troubled that Christ is preached? Is preaching so inclusive in your function ? * Doth it scandalise the Reformed Kirks, and Scotland in particular ? Is it against the Covenant? Away with the Covenant, if this be so!† . . . Where do you find in the Scripture a ground to warrant such an assertion, that preaching is inclusive in your function ? Though an approbation ‡ hath order in it, and may do well, yet he that hath no better warrant than that hath none at all. I hope that He who ascended

* *I.e.*, included in *your* duties only. "So exclusively your function," as Carlyle puts it.
† This sentiment shows Oliver to be a "Leveller" at heart. " The thing may be right, but it is against this or that established institution," says the prudent Presbyterian. " Then down with the institution," says the Leveller.
‡ *I.e.*, the sanction of a presbytery, or of a congregation.

up on high may give His gifts to whom He pleases; and if these gifts be the seal of mission, be not envious though Eldad and Medad prophesy. . . . Take heed you envy not for your own sakes; lest you be guilty of a greater fault than Moses reproved in Joshua for envying for his sake."

In dealing with the objection that unlicensed preaching opened the door to error he laid down a noble doctrine of liberty, which the fatal incongruities of that chaotic time would not suffer him to carry out. In a singular anticipatory condemnation of the Maine Liquor Law, he says :—

" Your pretended fear lest error should step in is like the man who would keep all wine out of the country lest men should be drunk. It will be found an unjust and unwise jealousy to deprive a man of his natural liberty upon a supposition he may abuse it. When he doth abuse it, judge. If a man speak foolishly, ye suffer him gladly, because ye are wise; if erroneously, the truth more appears by your conviction (of him). Stop such a man's mouth by sound words, which cannot be gainsaid. If he speak blasphemously,* or to the disturbance of the public peace, let the civil magistrate punish him; if truly, rejoice in the truth."

In replying to the Scottish repudiation of the ordeal of battle as decisive of divine judgment he was of course on weaker ground. But there is this to be said for him, that the ministers would have made no difficulty about such an ordeal if the victory had been on their side. Besides, there was a certain element of truth underlying his argument—at least if the opinion be tenable that the Ironsides conquered quite as much by superior moral energy as by military genius. It would have been a fair enough argument, that the cause which inspired this elevation of character must have been of God. But that was not Cromwell's way of putting it :—

" But did not you solemnly appeal and pray? Did not we do so too? And ought not you and we to think with fear and trembling of the hand of the great God in this mighty and strange appearance of His? But [you]† can slightly call it an 'event'! Were not both your and our expectations renewed from time to time, whilst we waited upon God to see which way He would manifest Himself upon our appeals? And shall we, after all these our prayers, fastings, tears, expectations, and solemn appeals, call these bare 'events'? The Lord pity you!"

The invocation of the divine pity seems to have stirred afresh the sympathy of the indignant writer; for in a concluding para-

* An elastic term—best interpreted by the next words.
† The insertion of "you," easily omitted by a headlong writer like Oliver, makes it unnecessary to recast the sentence, as Carlyle does.

graph he expresses regret for occasional bitterness on his own part towards Presbyterian brethren :—

" We know there are stumbling-blocks which hinder you—the personal prejudices you have taken up against us and our ways, wherein we cannot but think some occasion has been given, and for which we mourn—the apprehension you have that we have hindered the glorious reformation you think you were upon. I am persuaded these and such like bind you up from an understanding and yielding to the mind of God in this great day of His power and visitation." *

With the letter were enclosed four queries for devout consideration—queries which other denominations besides Scottish Presbyterians would do well to ponder at the present day, especially when the writer asks whether their dissatisfaction with the course of events is not simply a sullenness assumed because " the great God did not come down to their minds and thoughts ? " The progress of an age is not necessarily towards the devil because it happens to move away from our ideas and creeds.

Oliver's epistle received no satisfactory reply ; nor did another, addressed by him from Linlithgow, on October 9th, " to the Right Hon. the Committee of Estates for Scotland." In this letter he besought the committee to consider whether " that Person in whom . . . malignancy and all malignants do centre " was worth the terrible cost they were paying for him— " the calamity of war lying upon the poor people of this nation, and the sad consequences of blood and famine likely to come upon them." There was no difficulty about peace between the two countries except this mad design to reinstate, through " hypocritical and formal shows of repentance," a family banned by heaven for accumulated blood-guiltiness. The appeal was unanswerable; and therefore it was not answered, except by a formal acknowledgment. Every one in Scotland, except the Royalist adventurers who coupled their fortunes with their king's, had an uneasy consciousness that a covenanted Charles bewailing the sins of his father and mother was a lie thrust into the very heart of the godly institutions which they supposed to constitute a revived theocracy. In fact the intrusion of this royal incongruity had split the nation into mutually mistrustful

* Carlyle, Letter CXLVIII.

factions; and after Dunbar resistance to Cromwell became more and more half-hearted.

In the western shires fresh troops were raised, who protested against the malignant influences around Charles, and declined the command of Lesley. Prominent in this movement were Ker and Strahan, who had no little sympathy for Cromwell. In the Glasgow presbytery they succeeded in getting a " re-monstrance" passed against the evil influences swaying the Committee of Estates; and another remonstrance, still stronger, was adopted by their army in the middle of October. The Kirk Commissioners, alarmed at this movement, and troubled in their own consciences, so worried Charles with their preachments and requirements that at last he fairly ran away from them, in-tending to remain with the Royalist Highlanders; but after a couple of days he was brought back again like a captured truant. On the other hand in their endeavours to transmute a lie into a fact the Kirk authorities and Committee of Estates, among whom Argyll was prominent, were hampered by Royalists pure and simple like the Marquis of Huntly, who were sick of covenanting quibbles, and wanted to postpone all controversies until, by a unanimous effort, the " King should enjoy his own again."

The head-quarters of Royalism were at Stirling. But Charles was for the most part at Perth; and to this town the Parliament was summoned to arrange for his coronation, which took place at Scone in the following January (1651). To accom-plish the purpose for which he came, Cromwell must either capture Stirling or draw the Royalists to a battle. With the aim of securing one of these alternatives, he marched towards Stirling on September 14th, and was within cannon-shot on the 17th. But the enemy would not be tempted out, and Cromwell, who rarely attempted what he was not sure he could perform, judged a successful assault on the town to be impracticable. He therefore returned to Edinburgh again on the 20th; and on his retreat heard of the work going on in the western shires.

He was not without hopes that the hostility of these western men might be averted; and partly with this view he still neglected Edinburgh Castle for the present, and marched across to Glasgow, where he stayed Saturday and Sunday, no resistance being made to his entry. On the way, he was careful to treat the country people in the most friendly manner; and a well-known Glasgow minister, Mr. Robert Baillie, the most profuse letter-writer of his age, testifies to the mild manners of the Ironsides in that town. He himself ran away. " I left," he says, " all my family and goods to Cromwell's courtesy, which indeed was great; for he took such a course with his soldiers that they did less displeasure at Glasgow nor if they had been at London, though Mr. Zachary Boyd railed on them all to their very face in the High Church." * But Ker and Strahan, with their western remonstrants—all honour to them!—were, after all, unwilling to concede to the English invader on their own soil all his demands. Instead of that, they started from Dumfries, apparently towards Edinburgh, and Cromwell hurried back to be beforehand with them; whereupon they desisted. During November the English army lay quietly in Edinburgh. Cromwell was awaiting the progress of faction in the Scottish ranks. He does not appear even to have taken any trouble about the castle, though he would of course prevent any supplies from being carried in. The season was not suitable for campaigning, and his army was in capital quarters.

Towards the end of the month the Committee of Estates sent Colonel Robert Montgomery into the west, to see if he could not bring the remonstrants to act with the army at Stirling. Cromwell thought it would be best to anticipate such a movement and to disarm the remonstrants by force, as he could not disarm them by argument. He was not, however, sure where he could find them. He therefore sent Lambert by Peebles to Hamilton, along the left bank of the Clyde, while he himself approached the same place from the north. Cromwell reached the rendezvous at the appointed time. But as Lambert did not arrive that evening, nor up to seven o'clock next morning, Cromwell concluded that he would not be able to reach the place at all because of floods on the line of march. He therefore retreated towards Edinburgh; and almost immediately afterwards Lambert marched into Hamilton. Meantime, Gilbert Ker was on the look-out for an opportunity of some stroke on his own account before Colonel Montgomery should arrive. He heard of Cromwell's departure and of

* Baillie's Letters, iii. 119, 120.

Lambert's position, and fell upon the latter in his quarters two hours before daylight on December 1st. He failed, however, and was not only beaten off but taken prisoner, while his whole force was ruined, and the army of remonstrants thus rendered useless to the royal cause. One result of this was that the kirk leaders through sheer necessity withdrew all opposition to the employment of any forces obtainable, however tinged with "malignancy." This concession rendered recruiting comparatively easy. But the zeal dependent on whole-hearted conviction was alienated from the Royalist camp.

All this time, as we have said, Cromwell had not troubled himself about Edinburgh Castle, except to try a little mining, which did not succeed. He had his reasons for thinking that the defence would not be obstinate. The garrison did not annoy the town, and he was therefore content to wait. The governor, William Dundas, was suspected by his spiritual pastors and masters of a leaning towards the opinions of the remonstrants. Being denied access to the estates at Perth, Dundas requested permission to confer with Alexander Jaffray of Dundee, and John Carstairs, a minister, both of whom had been prisoners since Dunbar, and were now left at liberty in Edinburgh on parole. This Cromwell conceded. But those gentlemen were much too "canny" to give advice under the circumstances. "Ye may do as you find yourselves clear, and in capacity," they wrote; "and the Lord be with you." On the 19th the castle was surrendered on terms very favourable to the garrison.

The English army now practically controlled the whole of Scotland south of the Forth and Clyde. Yet this army hardly exceeded twenty thousand men at its utmost strength, and was generally below that number. If the Scotch had been united, such a result would have been impossible. However, when Cromwell endeavoured to push his conquests north of the Forth, the smallness of the forces at his command proved to be an increasing difficulty. The position of Stirling, threatening the south, and supported by its communications with Perth made two armies necessary for the work to be accomplished : one to operate from the right bank of the Forth, and the other to be thrown between Stirling and Perth. But Cromwell's army was too small to be divided with advantage ; and he

w

therefore had to do the work of two armies with one. It was, naturally, not done so neatly as he would have desired; but it was done in a fashion that proved effective enough. But the difficulty had not to be faced just yet. Time was on the whole in his favour, because of the progress of faction among his opponents. He had no temptation therefore to risk a winter campaign. The Reverend Robert Baillie feared that this terrible Cromwell would disturb the sacred ceremony of his Majesty's coronation; but Oliver let them make their king in peace, being confident that, by God's help, he could unmake him in due time.

At the beginning of February he drew out the army and marched towards Stirling, though with what particular object is not quite apparent. He cannot have had any hope of capturing the Royalist head-quarters. Indeed from Falkirk he turned south-eastwards to Kilsyth. If the object was only to alarm and disturb the Royalist camp, it was attained at a very disproportionate cost. For the weather, both tempestuous and cold, drove him back to Edinburgh. Through exposure on this march the Lord-General took a chill, which settled into an ague, and laid him prostrate for a month. It was not until midsummer that his health was thoroughly restored. It may even be suspected that this sickness was the beginning of the end; for he never recovered his previous strength. During this illness he owed much to the affectionate devotion of his favourite servant, a Frenchman. The man's tender faithfulness was always gratefully remembered by his master; and in Oliver's will careful provision was made for him and his family. The illness was so serious that a rumour of Cromwell's death went forth, and was received by the Royalists with undisguised glee.* On the other hand, all, of every school, who cherished hopes of the Commonwealth, were struck with chill dismay. There were not a few who doubted now to what his overshadowing greatness might grow; and they could have wished him less important. But even these, when threatened with his loss, could not help fearing his knell might be that of the Commonwealth.

* "Shall no use be made of Cromwell's yet supposed death, against which we have yet nothing?"—Baillie, iii. 139.

And the outburst of joy on his recovery was correspondingly effusive.

In acknowledging, on March 24th, "with all humble thankfulness," "the high favour and tender respect" towards him expressed in a letter of President Bradshaw, "and the express sent therewith to enquire after one so unworthy," Cromwell shows the awe-struck feeling of one who has been consciously very near to death. He had often been so in battle; but that does not make the same impression. Yet in this solemnity of feeling he used strangely over-strained language. He spoke of himself as "a poor creature," "a dry bone," "an unprofitable servant to his Master and to the state." Was this merely hollow formality? Not quite; though there was certainly in it an element of conventionalism due to the religious fashion of the times. If the President had magnified the military services of any one, except his former leader Fairfax, beyond his own, Cromwell would have felt that injustice had been done. But in writing to Bradshaw he was not comparing himself with men. He was thinking of a divine call, and of his country's needs. In response to the former he would have sincerely considered self-contentment impious. And when he remembered the needs of his country, he might very well regard his service as utterly imperfect. For it was so. Vast as were his powers and enormous his energies, he could no more give to the England of his day the ordered liberty of which he dreamed, than he could give to her free trade or a penny post. Why he could not do it, he did not fully realise. But that his inevitable failure made him often unhappy, and gave him many an hour of sincere humiliation before God, is evident enough both from his letters and speeches.

One of the honours that may have helped to console him in his weakness and depression was his election, in the beginning of this year 1651, to the Chancellorship of Oxford University. His acknowledgment, dated February 4th, and addressed to the Vice-Chancellor Dr. Greenwood, shows that the distinction was very gratifying to him. The deprecatory language in which he speaks of his unworthiness and probable uselessness was fortunately contradicted by the practical reforms he was afterwards the means of introducing.

w 2

Amongst the documents remaining from this period of Cromwell's life is a letter to his wife, very suggestive of the freshness and tenderness of his domestic affections amidst the growth of his worldly fame and power. That she could fully enter into his plans, and thoroughly understand the scope of his patriotic ambition, is improbable. But that she unreservedly believed in him, there is no reason to doubt. And as opportunity leads us to dwell for a moment here upon Oliver's domestic relations, we may as well give in full the one letter of hers that has survived. It was written on the 27th December 1650, when the splendour of Dunbar victory had somewhat died away, and when the difficulty of further progress, together with the Lord-General's silence, was raising fresh anxieties amongst his friends, and apparently in his own home. Correspondence was never very certain of reaching its destination in such a time; and in his hunger for words from his own hearth Oliver had been, as the best husbands often are, a little impatient and unreasonable.

"My Dearest,—I wonder you should blame me for writing no oftener, when I have sent three for one; I cannot but think they are miscarried. Truly, if I know my own heart, I should as soon neglect myself as (omit*) the least thought towards you, who, in doing it, I must do it to myself (*sic*). But when I do write, my dear, I seldom have any satisfactory answer, which makes me think my writing is slighted, as well it may; but I cannot but think your love covers my weakness and infirmities.

"I should rejoice to hear your desire in seeing me; but I desire to submit to the Providence of God; hoping the Lord, who hath separated us, and hath often brought us together again, will, in His good time, bring us again to the praise of His name. Truly my life is but half a life in your absence, did not the Lord make it up in Himself, which I must acknowledge to the praise of His grace.

"I would you would think to write sometimes to your dear friend, my Lord Chief Justice, of whom I have often put you in mind. And truly, my dear, if you would think of what I put you in mind of some (*sic*), it might be to as much purpose as others; writing sometimes a letter to the President, and sometimes to the Speaker. Indeed, my dear, you cannot think the wrong you do yourself in the want of a letter, though it were but seldom. I pray think of; and so rest,—Yours in all faithfulness,†

"Elizabeth Cromwell."

* Word inserted by Carlyle to fill a lacuna in the original.
† There is no object in reproducing, as Mr. Forster has done, the spelling of the original. In those days spelling went very much by favour; and if Mrs.

The language of this letter is, in effect, "I cannot under-stand; I love." But the injunctions in the latter part show, besides a wife's faithfulness, also a wife's confidence in her superior judgment as to the smaller observances of life. What acknowledgment these anxious suggestions received we do not know; but when Oliver was convalescent in the following April, yet still liable to relapse, he had some practical hints to send to her in turn, besides expressions of gratitude for his recovery. Henry Somerset, Lord Herbert, the eldest son of the Marquis of Worcester, was inclined at the time to worship the rising sun for purposes of his own, and paid frequent calls to Mrs. Cromwell. But his family were not credited with faith-fulness to the Commonwealth, and the relations of the Lord-General to such people were scrutinised by unfriendly eyes. Mrs. Claypole's "necessity" was, no doubt, of an ordinary domestic kind, and it may easily be imagined how children who had been so rapidly elevated in the world with their father may have failed to take his view of life's responsibilities.

"*For my beloved wife, Elizabeth Cromwell, at the Cockpit. These* :—

"EDINBURGH, 12 *April*, 1651.

"MY DEAREST,—I praise the Lord I am increased in strength in my outward man. But that will not satisfy me except I get a heart to love and serve my Heavenly Father better, and get more of the light of His countenance, which is better than life, and more power over my corruptions. In these hopes I wait, and am not without expectation of a gracious return. Pray for me; truly I do daily for thee and the dear family; and God Almighty bless you all with His spiritual blessings.

"Mind poor Betty of the Lord's great mercy. Oh, I desire her not only to seek the Lord in her necessity, but in deed and in truth to turn to the Lord; and to keep close to Him; and to take heed of a departing heart, and of being cozened with worldly vanities and worldly company, which I doubt she is too subject to. I earnestly and frequently pray for her, and for him. Truly they are dear to me, very dear; and I am in fear lest Satan should deceive them,—knowing how weak our hearts are, and how subtile the Adversary is, and what way the deceitfulness of our hearts and the world make for his temptations. The Lord give them truth of heart to Him. Let them seek Him in truth, and they shall find Him.

"My love to the dear little ones; I pray for grace for them. I thank them for their letters; let me have them often.

"Beware of my Lord Herbert's resort to your house. If he do so, it

---

Cromwell's eccentricities in this respect were remarkable even for that day, the lack of culture shown is a confirmation of the view we have taken of her character.

may occasion scandal, as if I were bargaining with him. Indeed, be wise,—you know my meaning. Mind Sir Henry Vane of the business of my estate. Mr. Floyd knows my whole mind in that matter.

"If Dick Cromwell and his wife be with you, my dear love to them. I pray for them; they shall, God willing, hear from me. I love them very dearly.—Truly I am not able as yet to write much; I am weary, and rest thine,   "OLIVER CROMWELL."

The last words are pathetic in their indication of the languor that oppressed his over-wrought mind and body. It needs sympathetic imagination to read into the scanty records of the next few weeks, the struggle of strong will and faith against the paralysing spell of disease and against the persistence of baffling difficulties in his work. But surely the following letter, written just after a painful and fruitless march,* shows that so far from being embittered by pain and failure, his heart became more sensitive to the claims of love :—

"EDINBURGH, 3 *May*, 1651.

"MY DEAREST,—I could not satisfy myself to omit this post, although I have not much to write; yet indeed I love to write to my dear, who is very much in my heart. It joys me to hear thy soul prospereth : the Lord increase His favours to thee more and more. The great good thy soul can wish is that the Lord lift upon thee the light of His countenance, which is better than life. The Lord bless all thy good counsel and example to all those about thee, and hear all thy prayers, and accept thee always.

"I am glad to hear thy son and daughter are with thee. I hope thou wilt have some good opportunity of good advice to him. Present my duty to your mother, my love to all the family. Still pray for thine

"OLIVER CROMWELL."

In order to present at one view the illustrations furnished about this time by Oliver's letters of his domestic life, it will be better to introduce here one that was written at the end of July (1651) to Richard's father-in-law. The idle young man had been living beyond his income. It may be suspected that his father's rising fortunes appeared to him to make economy a matter of indifference. Such however was not his father's view. When speaking of the marriage treaty, we pointed out that the modest expectations implied therein were scarcely consistent with the arrogant schemes of ambition imputed to the master of a victorious army. And now, after the conquest of Ireland, and in the still higher position of supreme commander of the Commonwealth's forces,

* See next chapter.

the same simplicity marks these domestic letters. Those addressed "to his beloved wife, Elizabeth Cromwell," can hardly have issued from a mind in which thoughts of pomp and power were predominant. And in his mode of dealing with his son's extravagance we have only the feelings of a loving father, heartily disposed to be generous, yet firmly determined that his son shall not exceed the expenditure of a private gentleman in moderate circumstances; and above all, grieved to the heart that his son should find more attractions in luxury than in the service of his conntry. Dorothy is expecting another child, and therefore the grandfather is the more tender.

"I hear my son hath exceeded his allowance, and is in debt. Truly I cannot commend him therein, wisdom requiring his living within compass and calling for it at his hands. And in my judgment the reputation arising from thence would have been more real honour than what is attained the other way. I believe vain men will speak well of him that does ill.

"I desire to be understood that I grudge him not laudable recreations, nor an honourable carriage of himself in them; nor is any matter of charge likely to fall to my share and stick with me.* Truly I can find in my heart to allow him not only a sufficiency, but more—for his good. But if pleasure and self-satisfaction be made the business of a man's life—so much cost laid out upon it, so much time spent in it as rather answers appetite than the will of God, or is comely before His saints—I scruple to feed this humour. And God forbid that his being my son should be his allowance to live not pleasingly to our Heavenly Father, who hath raised me out of the dust to be what I am.

*　　*　　*　　*　　*

"Truly I love him. He is dear to me; so is his wife; and for their sakes do I thus write. They shall not want comfort nor encouragement from me, so far as I may afford it. But indeed I cannot think I do well to feed a voluptuous humour in my son, *if he should make pleasures the business of his life in a time when some precious saints are bleeding, and breathing out their last for the safety of the rest. Memorable is the speech of Uriah to David* (2 Sam. xi. 11)."

Do not the last words, given here in italics, open an inner sorrow deeper than any regrets about juvenile extravagance?" " And Uriah said unto David, The Ark and Israel and Judah abide in tents; and my lord Joab, and the servants of my lord are encamped in the open fields : shall I then go to mine house, to eat and to drink? As thou livest, and as thy soul liveth, I will not do this thing." These were the words that prompted in Oliver

---

* *I.e.*, it is not the money I hesitate about.

the vain wish, "O that there were such a spirit in my son!" There is no harshness in the regrets of this letter. There is only a painful wonder, pathetic in its wistfulness, that a son of his should have such ignoble ideas of happiness as to be content in sloth, when the cause of God and of humanity was calling to the keener joys of heroic strife.

CHAPTER XXI.

A "CROWNING MERCY."

THE army was not entirely idle during the Lord-General's illness. About the beginning of April they obtained possession of Blackness, a fortified village and castle on the right bank of the river Forth, near the mouth. Inchgarvie, an islet in the narrows opposite Queensferry, commanding the passage into the Firth, was also pressed by gun-boats, but could not be got till nearly four months afterwards. These movements were part of a plan, which Cromwell now had in view, for operating on both sides of the Forth at once. As we have already said, to do this effectively he ought to have had two complete armies strong enough to act independently, though in harmony. He could then have barred the road to England while striking at the Royalist camp from the north, where it was most vulnerable. Not having two armies, he tried to impose on the enemy by moving in both directions with detachments of one army. One of these movements would have to be sacrificed to the success of the other; but which it should be, must depend on circumstances.

By the middle of April, 1651, Cromwell thought himself sufficiently recovered to take the field in person. The relapse that followed showed he had been too sanguine; but he was becoming impatient of inaction, and anxious to get the business finished. On April 16th he reviewed at Musselburgh the greater portion of his force, about 17,000 men, equally divided between horse and foot. The shouts and acclamations that greeted him testified the joy and thankfulness of the men on seeing their invincible leader restored to life, and once more at their head. The army then marched off towards Linlithgow; but Cromwell himself remained behind. On the same day he sent Colonel Monk, now promoted to be Lieutenant-General of Ordnance, across the Forth with a number of gun-boats, to make an attack on Burnt-island. The idea seemed to have been that General Lesley, finding his northern communications threatened, would make some movement, of which Cromwell would know how to avail himself. At Linlithgow a detachment of the Royalist army attacked the English in their quarters; but they were beaten off, and no further result followed.* From this town the army marched to Hamilton on the Clyde, whither Cromwell came in person on the 18th. The garrisons at Edinburgh and Leith heard the big guns roaring far away at Burntisland; but no sufficient impression was made, and this part of Cromwell's scheme for the present failed.

On the next day, Saturday the 19th, he advanced to Glasgow, "with a body of his army," † apparently leaving the bulk of his forces at Hamilton. His arrival was unexpected; and to this he was indebted for the presence of many ministers, who would have fled if they could—amongst them, the Reverend Robert Baillie. On the Sunday the English General was a conspicuous attendant at two of the principal churches, where he heard two sermons and a lecture. In each of these, according to Baillie, the preacher "gave a fair enough testimony against the sectaries." A story told of one of these services is worth repeating, even though it may be considered doubtful. It was at the afternoon service, when Mr. James Durham preached "graciously and weel to the times as could have been desired." While the minister was making some obviously personal applications, a young man of the Lord-General's train was observed to leave his place and whisper in his master's ear, returning afterwards apparently disconcerted. It came out that the young man had sought permission to put a summary stop to the preacher's discourse. But the only answer he got was : " Begone, sir ; he is one fool, and you are another." ‡

The next day Cromwell sent an invitation to Mr. Durham and other ministers to a friendly conference; and, after a little hesitation, they came. The charges to be discussed were—(1) the alleged injustice of the English invasion; (2) the supposed contempt of Cromwell and his army for " ordinances ; " and (3) the reported persecution of ministers in Ireland.§ What Cromwell's arguments would be we know from his letters already quoted. As is usual in such cases, both parties were satisfied

* "Cromwelliana."   † Baillie, iii. 165.
‡ Pinkerton's Correspondence, I., 190. It is here said the young man wished to " *shoot* the parson."
§ Baillie, *l.c.*

with themselves—all the more so perhaps because "there was no bitterness nor passion vented on either side; all was with moderation and tenderness." *

Cromwell remained in Glasgow ten days, waiting apparently, to see if Lesley would make any movement. The reason for his choice of Glasgow is suggested by his conference with the ministers. He had still some hope that the "remonstrant" spirit of the western shires might be of use to him. He left in some haste, on account of a rumoured movement from Stirling. The rumour proved false, and he marched his army back to Edinburgh. On the way thither he passed, with a few of his officers, by the residence of Sir Walter Stewart, Laird of Allertoun; and a mistake of his guide necessitated his staying there some hours. Sir Walter, a staunch Royalist, was away from home, probably in Charles's service. His lady, left with a little delicate boy of ten, was naturally alarmed at such a visitor, but with a brave spirit did the honours of her house. She was soon put at her ease, for her guest claimed kinship with her husband, saying that by his mother's side he came of the Stewarts. The little boy, attracted by the kindly ways of the great soldier, began to scrutinise, as children will, the accoutrements of the party, and to handle one of the swords. Oliver stroked the child's head, called him "his little captain," and, remarking on his delicate appearance, suggested to his mother to try the south of France for him, specially recommending Montpelier. Lady Stewart was struck by the devoutness of the General's grace before meat and his thanksgiving after it. And when he was gone, as tradition will have it, she abated something of her zeal against the "rebels." She said she was sure Cromwell was one who feared God, and had the true interest of religion at heart.† This is only one illustration out of many of the favourable testimony borne to Oliver's natural kindliness, fairness, and rough courtesy by opponents whom chance brought face to face with him. The gossip of the Royalist camp, and the hearsay anecdotes of Restoration writers make him a miracle of hypocrisy. But whenever such men as Sir John Berkley, or the Rev. Robert Baillie, or Ludlow, or George Fox have actual personal

---

* " Cromwelliana."

† This story is from the " Coltness Collections," published by the Maitland Club, Glasgow, quoted by Carlyle.

experiences to relate, the impression made is a more or less favourable one, even against the will of the narrator.

The expedition to Glasgow brought on a serious relapse, causing grave anxiety to both Parliament and army during the month of May. And as Cromwell would not listen to a proposal that he should delegate some one to do his work for a time, Lord Fairfax despatched his own coach to Edinburgh with two doctors.* The doctors "were exceeding affectionately entertained by my Lord, as they deserved," says a letter of the time. "My Lord is not sensible that he has grown an old man," † says another writer from the army. "But if it please God to restore him now, I hope we shall prevail with him to favour himself.‡ The time for favouring himself, however, was not come yet, and in truth never did come. On June 5th he was able to drive out in his coach. It was indeed time for him to bestir himself, if at all possible. The Royalists everywhere were making such efforts as they could, though much more feeble than believers in the divine right of kings and the instinctive loyalty of subjects had expected. The Earl of Derby, titular King of Man, was laying his plans in his island fastness, and was relied upon to raise a large part of Lancashire to reinforce Charles, if only the Royalist army could break through to England. Presbyterian London was honeycombed with intrigue, and it was hoped that a road thither might be smoothed for a covenanted king. To Cromwell it was reported that Argyll and Huntly had gone north, expecting to raise additional levies of 15,000 men. He was now much perplexed, or, to use his own words, was "waiting upon the Lord, and not knowing what course to take." He would try again to tempt the enemy out of Stirling southward, or force him to do battle for his encampment at Torwood near Bannockburn.

Accordingly, at the end of June, the army took to the Pentland Hills again, and came down to Linlithgow. On July 2nd they left that town for Falkirk and Torwood. They could get plenty of skirmishing; but a stand-up fight they could not get. Bogs, and brooks, and finally entrenchments enabled the enemy

---

* One of these was George Bates, who afterwards reviled the memory of his patient.

† He is sensible enough of it, as we have seen. But he will not show it while "the Ark and Israel and Judah abide in tents."

‡ "Cromwelliana."

to strike what fugitive strokes they chose, and then secure themselves. Whether this failure betrayed the limits of Cromwell's military genius may be discussed by those better acquainted with the arts of mutual slaughter; but we may safely presume that the effective investment of Stirling and Torwood would have needed an army at least twice the strength of that under his command. On the 15th of July the seat of the Marquis of Calander was summoned in sight of the enemy. It was a sign of the growing heat of the conflict that the garrison were peremptorily and emphatically informed they should have no quarter unless they surrendered at once. Like brave men they refused; and in the assault sixty-two of the garrison were killed, only thirteen being made prisoners, besides some country people who were at once released. General Lesley must have received a very deep impression from "Dunbar drove," since he allowed this to be done in sight of his army, and would permit no movement to prevent it.

On Thursday, July 17th, Cromwell determined to strengthen his force on the other side of the Forth. He sent over Major-General Lambert with two and a half regiments of horse and three of foot. They crossed to the North Ferry at the mouth of the river, and the next morning had a smart action near Inverkeithing with a superior force of the enemy under Sir John Brown, formerly in the service of the English Parliament. The issue was as usual. Sir John Brown himself was captured along with five or six hundred of his men, and his troops were totally routed with a loss of some two thousand killed. In relating this success, Cromwell attributes the division of his army to divine direction. He had thought of "attempting the enemy within his fortifications, but the Lord was not pleased to give way to that counsel, proposing a better way." At the same time, as the human instrument is in this case his Major-General and not himself, he recommends Lambert for grateful notice. The victory was thought important enough to justify one of those hortatory discourses that now became familiar features of the Lord-General's despatches. Their frequency was ominous; but certainly not more so than the obvious paralysis now fallen on the remnant of the great Parliament.

"I hope that it becometh me to pray that we may walk humbly and self-denyingly before the Lord, and believingly also: that you, whom we serve as the authority over us,* may do the work committed to you with uprightness and faithfulness, and thoroughly, as to the Lord; that you may not suffer anything to remain that offends the eyes of His jealousy; that common weal may more and more be sought, and justice done impartially. For the eyes of the Lord run to and fro; and as He finds out His enemies here to be avenged on them, so will He not spare them for whom He doth good, if by His loving-kindness they become not good. I shall take the humble boldness to represent this engagement of David's in Psalm cxix. 134 :—'*Deliver me from the oppression of man, so will I keep thy precepts.*'"

Yes, without doubt, deliverance from a bad Government ought to lead to "sweeter manners, purer laws." But in the case of England such a deliverance did not seem to lead that way at all; and Oliver was sorely perplexed about this. It never occurred to him, apparently, that the violence and blood by which he triumphed had so disturbed the moral basis of constitutional equilibrium as to postpone to future ages the "peace and truth" he desired. But meantime he must go through with his hateful task. Hateful it was to himself, as is shown by his nervous dread, in his few following years, of any disturbance threatening civil bloodshed. Yet he was in a measure hardened to it now, and it could not appear so hateful to him as it does to a more peaceful generation. Almighty "loving-kindness" proved by the slaughter of 2,000 men! Would to God such horrible discords of phrase and fact might affect us as they ought whenever they occur, whether in the letters of the "great Independent" or in episcopal blessings on regimental flags!

But the enemy could not be drawn from his cover. Lesley did indeed threaten Lambert, and marched in great strength some four or five miles towards him. Cromwell thereupon pushed up to Bannockburn and Stirling, intending to cross the nearest ford, and so get the enemy between his Major-General and himself. But Lesley's information was as quick as Cromwell's, and on this movement. of the latter he drew back his army at once to its old positions. Again Cromwell looked anxiously and longingly at the Torwood defences. But they were "not advisable to attempt."

* Did this strike honourable members as a very odd sort of an acknowledgment? The constitution could hardly be regarded as settled while professions like this were necessary.

He was as much baffled as he had been before Leith. He might go on thus playing hide-and-seek with Lesley till the autumn was over, and sickness would again ingloriously waste the worn-out troops. At the same time the Royalists were being strengthened from the north, and might possibly at last overwhelm their opponents by sheer weight of numbers. It was time for some decisive stroke, even if considerable risk were involved; and probably it would not have been so long delayed but for the Lord-General's sickness and continued weakness. He now determined to throw the greater part of his army into Fife, so as to cut off Stirling from Perth and the north. His first intention was to leave on the right bank of the Forth a sufficient force to head off the enemy from any attempted invasion of England. But the work to be done in Fife required nearly the whole army, and therefore the plan was modified. Major-General Harrison was left with 3,000 horse. There were also some scattered regiments about the border. Otherwise England was left open to the Royalists, while Cromwell went round to their rear, and rather drove than tempted them in that direction.

This was a much bolder movement than the retreat in a somewhat similar difficulty from Musselburgh to Dunbar. It was indeed audacious from a political, as well as from a strategic point of view. It made enormous demands on the public confidence in the General, who thus sent the enemy into his own country; and it also showed a very daring trust, on the part of Cromwell, in the general attachment of the people to the Commonwealth. For if the people had felt any such devotion to the second Charles as they did afterwards to the Prince of Orange, the Royalist army, once in Lancashire or Yorkshire, would have become resistless.

One reason that induced Cromwell to concentrate nearly the whole of his army in Fife was the obstinate resistance offered by small fortresses such as Inchgarvie and Burntisland. But both of these fell when sufficient force was applied at the end of July, and Commissary-General Whalley marched along the Fife coast in co-operation with an attendant squadron of ships, thus securing command of both sides of the Firth. The capture of Perth (then generally called St. Johnston) was all that was now needed to make Stirling untenable; and this did not prove difficult. On

August 2nd Cromwell arrived before that town, and the next day it was surrendered without an assault. During the march, and before the town, reports came that Charles was breaking out southward. But the information being confused and contradictory, Cromwell determined to have Perth, if possible, while seeking better intelligence. When however the town had surrendered, he lost not a moment, but turned his army southward at once. Monk was left behind with a detachment strong enough to garrison Perth, and also, if the information turned out true, to besiege Stirling, and so secure to Parliament the control of Scotland. Having made these arrangements, Cromwell with the remainder of his army left Perth on August 3rd, and never made a halt for twenty-four hours, except once, until he reached Worcester on the 28th.*

On the way to Leith, the news of Charles's rush for England was confirmed; and in writing to the Parliament Cromwell shows far more anxiety about the temporary perturbation of spirit likely to be produced at Westminster by his strategy than about the substantial issue of the campaign. "This is our comfort," he says, "that in simplicity of heart as towards God, we have done to the best of our judgments, knowing that if some issue were not put to this business it would occasion another winter's war." He urges that all available forces should be gathered to hold the enemy in check, and he expresses his confidence that public feeling, being steadier now than it was at the time of Hamilton's invasion, is even less likely to give countenance to the invaders. In this opinion he was fully justified, and it illustrates his practical sagacity. The Royalists marched by way of Carlisle and Preston, fully expecting that the presence of King Charles's heir would reveal the re-action of feeling caused by that monarch's execution. In fact they were so weak, both in numbers and in munitions of war, that nothing but such an expectation could acquit them of insanity. But in this they were miserably disappointed. They found that, so far from joining them, the people rose against them, and cut off their stragglers.† Discipline was strictly enforced, as far as it could be, in such an army; and, in marked contrast with former

---

* The Parliamentary History.

† A Royalist officer, whose letter is given in the Parliamentary History, bitterly complains of this.

Royalist campaigns, plundering was prohibited. But the only effect of this care was, not to conciliate the people, but to disgust the soldiers.

Meantime danger gathered in their van and flank, while destruction chased them in the rear. Lambert was despatched from Leith with a large part of the cavalry to overtake Harrison, and with him to front the invaders. Until the Major-General reached him Harrison was to hinder and harass the enemy, as opportunity offered, on the left flank of the hostile advance. Lord Fairfax, true to his promise that he would defend England against invasion, gathered a force under his own command in Yorkshire. The Governor of Stafford contributed two thousand men to swell Lambert's force. Colonel Birch of Liverpool raised four thousand more. Colonel Lilburn with ten troops of horse fell upon the Earl of Derby at Wigan, and so mangled his promised reinforcements for Charles that the earl's appearance, wounded, and riding at the head of some forty or fifty demoralised horsemen, struck despair into the Royalist army. At Warrington Harrison skirmished with the enemy at the bridge; but was not strong enough effectively to bar it. " O you rogues!" cried the Royalist soldiers, "we will be with you before your Cromwell comes."

But their Cromwell was coming very fast. He chose the route through Yorkshire, partly perhaps because reinforcements would be more plentiful that way; partly also, it may be, to interpose more easily between London and the enemy. But all the information he received suggested that Charles would be more likely to turn aside into Wales, and content himself with kindling a guerilla warfare there in hopes of a better chance hereafter. The Scottish troops were wearied, half-fed, demoralised, and mutinous. Majesty was reported to have been seen, cap in hand, beseeching lame and fainting soldiers to march one stage further, on an assurance that all their wants should be soon supplied. The Lord-General of the Commonwealth's forces therefore had little anxiety during this march, except what was caused by a consuming impatience to get the business ended as soon as possible. The larger part of the troops retained by himself being foot soldiers, the pace was not that of the old times, when he rode thirty or forty miles in a day at the head of the Eastern Association

x

cavalry. But, as he never paused, he did not suffer the Royalists to gain on him. As he passed through Yorkshire by Doncaster and Rotherham, his old leader, Lord Fairfax, met him, and rode with him for some miles. At such a time there was no difference between them; and Oliver was cheered by the heartiness with which Fairfax assured him of his co-operation in saving the Commonwealth.* About the same time also he was overtaken by the news that Stirling had surrendered to Lieutenant-General Monk; so that Scotland would afford no refuge for the Royalist invaders, even if by a miracle they should escape from England. Continuing his march by Mansfield and Nottingham, he learned that the King of Scots had reached Worcester on August 22nd, and would probably get no further. At Coventry Cromwell met once more with his Major-Generals, Lambert and Harrison; thence, in company, they went by Evesham, and on the 28th appeared before Worcester from the south-east.

The Severn approaches Worcester from the north-west, then makes a bend to the south, and continues in this direction for several miles. The town, standing on the eastern bank, was connected with the opposite side by a bridge a little above the bend in the stream. Beyond this bridge was the suburb of St. John's, guarded on the west by a brook, running roughly parallel with the Severn. The brook flowed into the Teme, a tributary opening into the Severn about a mile from Worcester. Thus St. John's lay in an irregular parallelogram, surrounded on three sides by water. The road from the north passed straight through the town to near the southern end, where it diverged to the left, and made its exit by the Sidbury Gate at the south-eastern angle of the walls. Outside that gate, a few hundred yards along the road, was Fort Royal, a fortification crowning a steep knoll. The defences of Worcester had suffered during the wars; and of course could not be repaired in six days. On the western side there was no defence other than the river.

When the Royalists reached Worcester it was held by a small garrison for the Parliament. But the traditions of the place were Royalist. The Mayor, Edward Elvins, threw his

* "Cromwelliana." According to the newspapers, Fairfax undertook to raise additional forces if necessary.

influence on that side. It was the only town in which Charles was actively aided by the inhabitants. The garrison therefore after a few shots retired. But within a week the townsmen were cursing both their mayor and their own folly.

The position was nowhere very strong. But it was weakest on the river-side, where it lay open to attack by boats or across the bridge from St. John's. To break down that bridge would be to cut the line of retreat into Wales, the only refuge open. But to make the access to St. John's as difficult as possible for the enemy, another bridge at Upton, several miles below the city, had been destroyed as early as August 23rd. It was General Massey, formerly in the Parliamentary service, who undertook this piece of work. In his haste however he left certain skeleton beams hanging from pier to pier, such as could not conceivably to him be of any use to an army.

When Cromwell arrived at Evesham, within striking distance of Worcester, the first thing he did was to seek some means of getting at the suburb of St. John's. For almost the only time in his life, at any rate in any important battle, he commanded a force superior in numbers to the foe. His own troops, when re-united with Lambert's and Harrison's, numbered about 17,000 ; and the auxiliaries brought up, or so near at hand as to be easily available if wanted, were not less than 10,000 more. The Royalists on the other hand were not more than 16,000, if so many. There could be no possible doubt about his victory; but he desired to end the war here, and therefore he must cut off the access to Wales. Besides, weak as they were, the enemy were sure to fight desperately, because many of them were deserters from the Parliament, and had little mercy to expect if they were taken. It would make the victory easier to distract their energies by a twofold attack. Accordingly Fleetwood, with some of Lambert's men in addition to his own, marched direct from Evesham to the site of Upton Bridge on Thursday, August 28th. There a few troopers managed, by bestriding the hanging timbers, to get across to the further side in sufficient force to seize a church. Here they were attacked by General Massey, who had learned what was going on; but they beat off their assailants, and wounded Massey himself somewhat severely. Before any strong reinforcements arrived from Worcester they had made the bridge passable, and were established too securely to be meddled with. Between Upton and St. John's however there yet lay the river Teme. This was crossed by a bridge nearly two miles distant from the Severn, connecting the little town of Powick with St. John's; but that bridge was strongly held by the enemy. For greater facility of co-operation between the two attacks Cromwell designed to have a bridge of boats over the Severn just above the Teme. Another bridge of the same kind was to be laid over the tributary close to its mouth. For this purpose boats gathered from far and near were held in readiness about Upton.

The attack by way of St. John's was committed to the charge of Fleetwood; but the Lord-General himself visited Upton on the evening of Monday, September 1st, and when the day came, could not refrain from taking a prominent part in the work. By a welcome coincidence, promoted possibly by a little judicious delay, that day was the 3rd of September (1651), the anniversary of the battle of Dunbar. Although strongly opposed to the observation of times and seasons when celebrated on account of scriptural or historic associations, Cromwell's praying and preaching soldiers were just the sort of men to be impressed by omens, or, as they termed them, "providences." We may well believe therefore that the associations of this day intensified their confidence in battle. On the evening before, that is on Tuesday, September 2nd, Fleetwood crossed the Severn at Upton with a large part, perhaps fully half, of the army.

In the morning of the 3rd he led the main part of his division to Powick Bridge, to force that passage. He did not however reach the bridge till between three and four in the afternoon. During the morning the boats were brought up, and, in the face of the distracted enemy, laid across the Severn. Over this bridge the Lord-General in person led a column of horse and foot, and was the first man to step on to the contested ground.* At the same time boats were extended across the Teme, and a part of Fleetwood's division crossed thereby. The design against Powick Bridge diverted the enemy's forces, so that the passages both over the Severn and over the mouth of the Teme appear to have been easily effected.

The King of Scots with some of his lordly train was stationed on the roof of the Cathedral that rises from a lofty river terrace

* King's Pamphlets, small 4to, No 507.

overlooking the Severn.   Across the flat meadows and orchards
surrounding St. John's suburb, they could see the assailants
beyond the Teme converging in long lines like mere red and
brown ants towards two points—the one near Powick, the other
by the Severn.   From the south-east the guns of the Royal
Fort were thundering.   But what could it mean that troops
were emerging from that canopy of smoke beyond Sidbury Gate,
and massing themselves by Severn bank ?   The watchers could
see groups of boatmen and carpenters toiling and struggling up
stream with a little fleet of boats.   With anxiety the royal party
marked this clump of boats break up into two processions, and
range itself in lines that stretched from bank to bank, both on the
Severn and the Teme.   But surely some crushing ball will rend
those lines, or torches send them up in flame ?   Alas, no !   None
knew where these bridges were to be, and they are far away from
the most guarded points.   Flashes there are, and puffs of smoke
with the continuous crack, crack of musketry, as the armies front
each other more and more thickly at either side of the Teme.
But where those black bands lie across the water King Charles's
men are not in force enough to offer any effectual resistance.
Shrill trumpets shriek through the air, proclaiming the moment
of agony and fate.   The converging lines on the other side of
the Teme have joined in one.   It pushes toward the bridge of
boats.   And now from beyond Severn there is a rush across
the longer bridge.   The troops on this side yield, and run for
shelter to hedge-rows and orchards, where their fire is renewed
from cover.   A second living wave surges across the Teme.
Beneath rattling shot and blaring trumpets, a hoarse, continual
roar comes faintly up—" the thunder of the captains and the
shouting."

The moving lines break and spread out into serried ranks of
horse and foot.   Wherever a troop of Royalist foot appears in
the open it is ridden down.   The Scottish cavalry is too scanty
to avail much.   Where it shows itself, there is a rattle of pistols, a
clashing of swords, followed again by the onward movement of
the resistless wave that flows ever toward Worcester bridge.
But what is that smoke and rout farther away to the right ?
Surely, the rebels have carried Powick bridge, and from that
point too are driving their foes back toward the town.   And
worse still, over this line of boats across the Severn a column

of fresh troops—now horse, now foot—is ever moving from the left bank to the right. There must be three-fourths of Cromwell's army now on that side the river. What if the King himself were to head a vigorous sally from the Sidbury Gate? The garrison of the Fort Royal are diligently firing on the assailants. What if we burst forth there with all the strength we can gather, overwhelm the enemy with numbers, and raise a shout of victory? It might even yet be the saving of the day.

Such were the calculations of Charles's advisers, if calculation it can be called where there is but a forlorn hope. The beaten troops on the west were called in across Worcester bridge, and sent to swell the force of the sally through Sidbury Gate. Charles himself went out that way, and illustrated in his own person the frequent alliance of moral levity with physical courage. But Cromwell had interpreted the movement before its issue, and hastened over Severn again with ample force to redress the balance. Then followed a three hours' fight. For that doomed band of Royalists victory or death on the field was the only certain escape from a scaffold or slavery. Both leaders exposed themselves recklessly. Charles repeatedly charged. Cromwell was everywhere in the midst of the fight, and rode up to a still-firing body of foot to offer them quarter, an offer answered only by shot. It was " as stiff a contest as ever the Lord-General had seen." But it ended by the flight of some of the Royalists into the Fort Royal. That flight was followed by the capture of the fort. The guns were then turned upon the beaten army, who crowded in confusion toward Sidbury Gate. The confusion became panic, as they struggled through for shelter in the streets. A loaded hay-cart, hastily thrust into the open portal, gave a few minutes' delay, of which Charles availed himself to escape.* Seeing all was lost, he hastily changed his attire, and galloped off with one or two attendants by the north gate. Before ten o'clock at night the prospects of Stuart royalty were absolutely extinguished in the three kingdoms, for such time as it might please Heaven to keep Oliver Cromwell alive.

It is not quite clear why the north gate was not guarded. If that had been done, the Scottish King and all his army must have been captured at once. There was probably some reason

* Nash's "History of Worcestershire," vol. ii., Appendix, p. 106.

for what seems so obvious a defect in the strategy of the day. But after all, the loss by the omission was not great. It is by no means certain that Oliver was very anxious to capture Charles ; and leaving him out, the escapes of any importance were few indeed. Some six or seven thousand prisoners were taken, including the Duke of Hamilton, with the Earls of Rothes and Lauderdale. Hamilton was badly wounded, and Cromwell sent to him his own physician; but in vain, for the duke died in a few days. Earl Derby was sent to Chester, condemned there for treason, and executed at Bolton. A body of about 3,000 kept together and retreated towards the north, headed by David Lesley and Lieutenant-General Middleton. They were fiercely assaulted by the country people. Deprived both of sleep and food, they quickly wasted away. Their leaders deserted them, only to be themselves captured and sent to Chester. Few indeed succeeded in making their way back to Scotland.

The despatches of Cromwell describing this victory are brief. He expected soon to appear in Parliament again, and therefore spared himself in writing. He does not seem to have been quite certain that the war was at an end. For, on the day after the battle, he says—" It is, for aught I know, a crowning mercy. Surely, if it be not, such a one we shall have if this provoke those that are concerned in it to thankfulness." But when he realised its completeness, there was a radiancy about him which occasioned much discussion among his friends, and not a little foreboding among his enemies. The Reverend Hugh Peters must certainly be counted among the former, and the interpretation he put upon Oliver's jubilant gratitude and confidence was itself of doubtful significance. " This man," he said, " will be king of England yet." His only mistake was in using the future tense. The man was king of England already.

CHAPTER XXII.

WANTED, A SETTLEMENT.

THE almost unanimous hostility shown by the English people not only to the Scottish invaders but to their native allies had been a startling revelation to the Royalists; and it fully justified the confidence of Cromwell in his countrymen. Whatever might be in the future, the reaction had not come yet. The nation had paid a tremendous price for deliverance from Star Chambers, High Commissioners, and sacred prerogatives, whether royal or episcopal. For the present, it had shown no disposition whatever to surrender the prize. This state of feeling removed all taint of insincerity from the outburst of joy that greeted the " crowning mercy " of Worcester. It would be a mistake however to suppose that popular gladness took the form of grateful affection for the Parliament. Ever since " Pride's Purge " the ultimate authority had resided in the council of the army. The fact was decently veiled; and Parliament had hitherto prudently abstained from provoking its revelation. But amongst the people at large a dangerous habit had grown up, of regarding the army rather than the legislature as the instrument by which surviving abuses were to be swept away, and political perfection established.

The progress of opinion had concurred with the fortune of war to bring about this result. For the " New Model " army had consisted mainly of men in advance of their contemporaries. But by this time public opinion, so far as such a thing existed,* had moved sensibly nearer to the ideas of the army on such matters as toleration, equality, legal abuses, and, to a more limited extent, on government by representation. But the theorists then, as always, formed only a small minority amongst English people. What public opinion demanded was measures, not systems. The pressure of tithes, the cumbrousness and extrava-

* Public opinion is the resultant of many more or less divergent individual opinions. Amongst nations or classes where individual opinion does not exist, there may be panic or passion, but not public opinion.

gance of legal procedure, the appropriation of common lands by great owners, the misery of imprisoned debtors—such were a few of the evils denounced by reformers at that time. The continuance of war was supposed to have prevented their abolition hitherto. But now that " malignancy " was prostrate under the foot of the victorious Commonwealth, there could surely be no further delay. If the effete assembly at Westminster should hesitate, a patriotic army would now quicken their steps.

This state of feeling must be borne in mind if we would estimate rightly the popular enthusiasm that greeted the conqueror of Dunbar and Worcester on his triumphal entry into Westminster. Very soon after the battle it was clear that there would be no more fighting, and Cromwell set out for London. Four members of Parliament were sent down to Aylesbury as a deputation to meet him. Bulstrode Whitelocke, one of the deputation, evidently takes credit to himself, in his " Memorials," for a shrewd insight into the Lord-General's ambition; but on this occasion remembers only his affability, and says that, " now, and afterwards, in all his discourses about Worcester," Cromwell " would seldom mention anything of himself; mentioned others only, and gave, as was due, the glory of the action unto God." This is only what we should suppose from his letters. Whether pride had any great place in his character may be disputed. The flashes of scorn that look like this are better explained by another sort of fire. But of vanity there was not a puff in his whole nature.

The presents made by the Lord-General illustrate the distance between his times and ours. That he should give a horse to each member of the deputation was natural enough; but when we read that he gave each of them " two Scotchmen " as well, we can only lament that he was not raised above his generation in respect for human nature. Whitelocke, we are glad to learn, released his two prisoners freely, and sent them home. Others were held to ransom; but a great many such prisoners were sold as slaves to the infant colonies. It is satisfactory to know that—in the New England States at least—their masters demanded only a part of their labour, and suffered them to buy their emancipation if they could earn enough in their over-hours. Thousands of these miserable men were marched from Worcester to London, and led in shameful triumph through the streets. The fat citizens however were not without contemptuous pity for the gaunt, bony, ragged creatures, victims of an adventurer's ambition, and ostentatiously fed them with " good white bread," such as it was presumed they had never seen before.

On Friday, September 12th, the Speaker and many members, together with all the City magnates, drove out to Acton to meet the returning hero. The roads were lined with expectant crowds for four or five miles; and as the dust of the approaching cavalcade was seen all eyes eagerly watched for the one man who had tamed the Levellers, and quenched the rage of Papists, and mastered grim Scotland, in one unchecked series of victories. On came his life-guards—valiant gentlemen, with accoutrements, we may suppose, furbished up for the occasion, but stained and battered both by weather and battle. Then came a city troop of horse, afterwards many Parliament men and others on horseback. Next was the Speaker's coach, followed by some three hundred others. But where was the Lord-General? The sight-seers, who had counted on beholding him prancing on his charger, were doubtless disappointed to find he had taken refuge in the Speaker's carriage. But not the less they cheered, and shouted, and blessed the man who had saved the Commonwealth of England. Regiment after regiment, blue coats here and red coats there, fell in at the rear as the procession passed. Great guns were banging in St. James's Park; small arms were fired in the streets; the hoarse chorus grew louder, as the crowds thickened, down to Charing Cross; till at last, dazed and wearied, the hero of the day received the dearest welcome of all from the faithful wife and her " two little wenches."

On Tuesday, the 16th, he reappeared in his place in Parliament, and received the thanks of the House in an " eloquent oration " of the Speaker. A more substantial compliment was an additional grant of land to the value of £4,000 a year, together with the use of Hampton Court as a residence. It is certainly more than a mere coincidence that on this very day the House revived the subject of a " new representative." In the evening, he was entertained by the City, at a grand feast in Merchant Taylors' Hall; and afterwards the public business fell into its ordinary course—if, indeed, it had any ordinary course at that time. At least it became once more a drudgery of detail.

We must now consider how the public business stood. There was first the dreadful litter of war to clear away, prisoners to be disposed of, fortresses to be dismantled or repaired, temporary levies of troops to be disbanded, and stations appointed for the standing army. The future relations both of Scotland and Ireland to England, had to be determined. But before this could be done the constitution of England itself wanted re-settling. Meanwhile the people generally were more anxious for practical reforms such as have been mentioned. The Church also was in a confused condition, half reformed on no definite method, but vexed and perplexed with many anomalies. Foreign relations were unsatisfactory. The kings of Europe had not come to the help of the Stuarts, and had even shown a disposition to respect the stronger side. But the Dutch, as though jealous of a new republic, were not friendly; and a serious conflict for the command of the narrow seas was in prospect, indeed had already begun.

Considering the manners of the age, it cannot be said that the Commonwealth showed any cruel vindictiveness towards the defeated. Lord Derby had deliberately refused an offer of amnesty, had defied the Parliament from his little kingdom of Man, and had professed his intention, so long as he lived, to do all in his power against them. He had been as good as his word. His case was hopeless, and he met his doom bravely at Bolton. There were however other prisoners to be dealt with besides those captured in battle. So far back as the beginning of the previous year, when it had seemed possible, or probable, that the adventure of Prince Charles might succeed, a number of Royalist Presbyterians in London had met together at the house of the Rev. Christopher Love for the purpose of promoting that enterprise. This clergyman had a certain notoriety because of a sermon he had preached at Uxbridge before the Commissioners during the attempt at a treaty there. In that discourse he prophesied very evil things of the treaty; and in his zeal against episcopacy declared that an attempt at an agreement between heaven and hell would be as reasonable. In view of the treaty at Breda he now thought royalty might be preferable to a Parliament dominated by the army. The plot was discovered at the end

of April in this year, 1651, by the capture of a vessel on the coast
of Scotland with despatches for the Earl of Derby; and Love,
with one or two others, was condemned to die.   He wrote a full
confession, and great efforts were made to save his life.

It is said that Cromwell, on being appealed to, wrote in
favour of mercy, but that the letter was intercepted by the
Royalists, who kept it back, saying, " let the villain die."*   He
was executed on August 22nd, and several agents in the conspiracy
were yet in prison when the Lord-General returned to London.
John Maidston, writing to Governor Winthrop,† says that Cromwell procured the release of these men.   And this is confirmed to a
certain extent by what Ludlow says of a policy very surprising
to the inflexible republican.   Cromwell now, we are told, " endeavoured to oblige the royal party by procuring for them more
favourable conditions than consisted with the justice of Parliament to grant, under colour of quieting the spirits of many
people, and keeping them from engaging in new disturbances to
rescue themselves out of those fears which many who acted for the
King yet lay under."‡   Ludlow assures us that by this policy
" he designed nothing, as by the success was most manifest, but
to advance himself by all manner of means."   On this point
everyone must use his own judgment.   We are contented to
accept the fact that Cromwell was in favour of a merciful policy.
In pursuance of this he pressed an Act of amnesty and oblivion.
With all his efforts, however, he could not get it passed till
February 1652.

The progress of disarmament was not satisfactory.   It was
hindered by the necessity for keeping up a sufficient force
to meet promptly any new Royalist attempts on the Commonwealth.   New regiments, raised specially to meet the Scottish
invasion, were disbanded at once.   But the veterans of the
" New Model " were kept together, suitably recruited, and
maintained at a strength of about 20,000 men, distributed
through the three kingdoms.   On the other hand the fleet had
to be largely increased, owing to Dutch hostility.

The affairs of Scotland were entrusted for settlement to
eight Commissioners appointed in October.   The chief of

---

* Carlyle says of this story, " never repeat it more."   But it is worth
repeating if only to show the sort of influence believed by Royalists to be
exerted by Cromwell, actuated, of course, by " dissimulation."
† Thurloe, I. 765.   ‡ " Memoirs," p. 110, folio edition, 1751.

them were St. John, Sir H. Vane, Lambert, and Monk. We may safely assume that they carried out in general the ideas of Cromwell; and the upshot of their proceedings was a perhaps premature attempt to unite the two kingdoms in one Commonwealth under one Parliament.

In Ireland the war still lingered on. Rebellion had never raised its head with any vigour since Cromwell's tremendous blows. But his recall to meet the nearer danger of an invasion from Scotland had left the work in feebler hands. Ireton, his deputy, was a faithful and most pure-minded servant of the Commonwealth. His character was fairly illustrated by his refusal to accept a grant from Parliament additional to his pay. The Commonwealth had other debts, he said, which were more pressing. He was an honest man, but he was not a giant; and the struggle with the Irish chaos exhausted him. He caught a fever, which in ten days consumed his life, and laid him to his rest on the 26th of November, 1651. His body was brought over to England, and honoured with a stately funeral in Westminster Abbey. For the pomp of that ceremonial Cromwell was much blamed by severe republicans; but it was a tribute to patriotism rather acquiesced in than ordered by him. There was little need of envy. Ireton's corpse would have found a more sacred rest in any obscure " God's-acre" of his native county, hidden from the desecrating vengeance of the Restoration. Lambert's military genius and general capacity marked him out as Ireton's successor; but he was not satisfied with the terms of the proposed commission. He came from Scotland for the purpose of receiving it, but finally declined. Fleetwood then accepted the post, and being a widower soon married the relict of his predecessor. Bridget thus kept her honours. How far her affections were engaged we shall not presume to judge. Ireland, as well as Scotland, was made the subject of a Commission; and in the Irish Commission Cromwell himself took a prominent part. It did not come into operation till August 1652. But it is convenient to mention here the nature of the settlement proposed. In the preamble it was stated that it was "not the intention of Parliament to extirpate that whole nation; but that mercy and pardon, both as to life and estate, might be extended" to all labourers and others of the humbler sort.

There were a large number of exceptions amongst the higher classes. Some commanders were banished, and all of these lost two-thirds of their property. Others were allowed to remain at home under a similar confiscation. More lukewarm rebels lost one-third, or even only one-fifth, of their property. By an Act of the Little Parliament (1653), any surplus lands, after the satisfaction of adventurers, were to be devoted to the maintenance of free schools and manufactures. The same Act forbade any of the Irish race to live outside Connaught and Clare without a licence.

Foreign affairs now began to demand the serious attention of the Commonwealth; and unfortunately a foreign war prevented the economy imperiously demanded by the exhausted condition of the country. In the direction of the naval conflict with Holland, during the year following the battle of Worcester, Cromwell does not appear so conspicuously as to make the story of that war necessary to his biography. It is sufficient to bear in mind the outline of events which prepared the way for the supremacy at sea maintained by Great Britain under the Protectorate. Owing to the connection by marriage between the Stuart dynasty and the Orange family, and also by reason of commercial rivalries, the relations between the United Provinces and the new Commonwealth were not so cordial as might have been expected between peoples of such close religious and political sympathies. An agent of the English Commonwealth, Dr. Dorislaus, had been murdered at the Hague, and much diplomatic bickering had gone on for several years, when, in October 1651, the Parliament passed a Navigation Act, prohibiting the importation of goods into Great Britain or Ireland in foreign ships; the only exception being in favour of the native products of European countries, which were graciously allowed to send their own goods in their own vessels. The Dutch naturally resented such a blow at their carrying trade, and futile negotiations went on for six months; until, in May 1652, Admiral Blake fired upon Van Tromp's fleet near the English coast, and an engagement ensued. Blake was victorious, greatly to the joy of the republican party with Vane at their head. They had a notion that in the fleet they might find a make-weight against a dictatorial army. But the result was far from having a happy influence on the destinies of the Parliament. For war became inevitable; and the taxes, lowered in December 1651 by £30,000 a month, had to be raised again in the following December by a similar amount, not, however, until cruel pressure had been exerted to wring the uttermost farthing from political opponents admitted to compound for their delinquencies. The suffering and discontent thus occasioned had much to do with the public indifference to the fate of the Long Parliament.

Ecclesiastical affairs remained in an anomalous condition—episcopacy gone, presbyterianism not established, except to a very limited extent. Old-fashioned clergymen lingered on here and there in obscurity. In many parts the Independent system practically prevailed; while Parliament exerted an arbitrary authority whenever and wherever it pleased to do so at the instance of powerful members. The Church, pulsating everywhere with strong convictions and passionate impulses, was in fact a chaos, modified by occasional spasmodic radiations of centralised authority.

On all these matters of public business Cromwell had a potent, but by no means in all cases a decisive voice. It is too clear that he sympathised with the short-sighted policy of the Navigation Act and the Dutch war; and in May 1652 we find him down at Dover as a Commissioner, inquiring into the circumstances of the unexpected naval battle between Blake and Van Tromp.* On other points, as will soon be shown, he was sharply at issue with the Parliamentary policy; but for the present he threw himself eagerly into the multitudinous details of public work, hoping, with an ever-lessening hope, that by some new turn of events Sir Harry Vane and his friends would be induced to agree to a "settlement," and that the worn-out Parliament would make way for a "new representative."

Meanwhile he was very busy, as the Committees of Council on which he was engaged are enough to show. In September and October he was appointed on the committee for foreign and inland posts, and on the committee for trade; he was charged, along with others, to compose certain differences that had arisen between the Aldermen and the Common Council of London; he was called on to peruse and help in answering a

* Harris's Cromwell, p. 264.

letter of Manasseh Ben Israel, apparently seeking the removal of the ban that had rested on all Jews in England since the reign of Edward I. From Oliver's action afterwards it may be presumed that the arguments of Manasseh Ben Israel appeared to him convincing. With Whitelocke, Harrison, and others he was commissioned " to consider of some fit person to write the history of these times, and to take the oversight thereof." * He sat on the committee for carrying on the affairs of Ireland and Scotland ; and on another appointed to consider the reform of the law. He was a member of the Admiralty. In December, foreign affairs were referred to the committee on trade.† Altogether, we may conclude that peace brought him neither leisure nor rest.

Only one letter of any significance has been preserved from this period of Cromwell's career. It is addressed to his " esteemed friend, Mr. Cotton, pastor of the church at Boston, New England." This eminent Puritan divine had apparently written to him in terms of general approval and sympathy. In reply Oliver acknowledges the perplexity he had felt in the Scottish campaign, " by reason he had to do with some who were, he verily thinks, godly." But he protests that he had dealt with such in all possible tenderness and sincerity ; and he appeals as usual to the judgment of God, as manifested in the issue. " How shall we behave ourselves after such mercies ? " he exclaims. " What is the Lord a-doing ? " The conclusion suggests the " pride of humility." But one phrase in it is so true, that we cannot help regarding it as indicative of self-knowledge :—

" I am a poor weak creature, and not worthy the name of a worm, yet accepted to serve the Lord and His people. Indeed, my dear friend, between you and me, you know not me—my weakness, *my inordinate passions*, my unskilfulness, and every-way unfitness to my work. Yet, yet, the Lord, who will have mercy on whom He will, does as you see." ‡

Inordinate passions ! Yes, yet not in the vulgar meaning of the phrase could Oliver fairly be charged with these. But in the sense of a susceptibility to excitement, varying indefinitely

* It might be imagined that the " fit person " was not difficult to find. But the commission seems to have dropped through.

† His appointment to these committees, and several others on matters of detail, appears in the " Calendar of State Papers " (Domestic Series), 1651-2.

‡ Carlyle, Letter CLXXXIV.

amongst different people under the influence of the same cause, his passions were truly inordinate. His vehemence of feeling and determination about great purposes that he took to heart, and mainly about one—the formation of a theocracy in England—made him impatient of opposition, intolerant of delays incidental to the Divine laws of progress, reckless of method, so only that the end were gained. Hide-bound notions of church government, and wire-drawn theories of a republic, with all the wrangling and prattling they begot, stirred him more and more to wrath and indignation as he heard the people groaning under taxes, denouncing tithes, and cursing the delays and costs and oppressions of the law. Confiscations, he thought, were cruelly enforced by Parliamentary committees intent on raising money. Speaking afterwards of his experience at this time, Cromwell said :—

"Poor men under this arbitrary power were driven like flocks of sheep, by forty in a morning, to the confiscation of goods and estates, without any man being able to give a reason why two of them had deserved to forfeit a shilling. I tell you the truth. And my soul, and many persons' whom I see in this place, were exceedingly grieved at these things, and knew not which way to help them, except by our mournings and giving our negatives when occasion served." *

It did not seem to him to matter in the least how the thing were brought about, if only Divine righteousness could be made to rule in England as he believed it to have ruled in Israel of old. He did not and could not understand that method may sometimes be of even more importance than the definite result to be achieved.

There is proof enough that at this time the people generally looked to him rather than to the Parliament to secure to them the reward of all their sufferings. In the end of the same month of September that brought him back in triumph to Westminster one of the pamphleteers, who then played the part of our modern journalists, declared that all would be well now Cromwell was come back.

"His Excellency, the Lord-General, hath taken into consideration the grievous and heavy burdens of the people, and hath proposed a way for the speedy redress of all their calamities and troubles, by taking off taxes, excise, and other oppressures, which for so many years they have groaned

* Speech of September 12th, 1654   Carlyle, vol. iii., p. 377.

Y

under . . . Thus we may discern the great care and prudence of His Excellency towards this nation; who no sooner hath freed us from the tyranny of kings, but he immediately endeavours the restitution of a free state, and the freedom of the people; and in order thereunto the High Court of Parliament have made some progress therein for the choosing of a new representative, a work very acceptable and satisfactory, both to the people and the soldiery.*

The monthly assessment was, as we have seen, reduced considerably in the month of December; but the new representative, as ardently longed for then as a reformed Parliament in 1830, did not make much progress, notwithstanding the urgency of the Lord-General. He succeeded on September 19th 1651 in getting a vote that *some* definite time should be fixed for a dissolution, and the division—33 to 26†—showed to what a miserable remnant the great Parliament was now reduced. Not till November was the further effort made to say what the time should be; and then the House gave itself a respite of three years, till November 3rd 1654. When a new Council of State was to be appointed, the members mustered to the number of one hundred and twenty, though at other times they seldom exceeded fifty.

There was some reason in the arguments urged in favour of delaying the dissolution until the nation had recovered from the disturbance and disorders of war, if only the House had shown a practical desire to effect a settlement. But no such desire was apparent. The system of government had degenerated into an oligarchy, rich in patronage but poor in legislative power, and subject to the control of an army. It was, as we have said, to the Lord-General and his officers, rather than to the Parliament, that discontented classes addressed themselves. In October 1651 a petition from "divers persons"—presumably in London—was addressed to Cromwell, declaring that "the law was the badge of Norman bondage," that "prisons were sanctuaries to rich men prisoners and tortures to the poorer sort, who were not able to fee lawyers and gaolers." The petitioners prayed the Lord-General, "into whose hands the sword was put," to free them from oppression and slavery, to restore the nation's fundamental laws and liberties, and to gain a new representative, that the poor might have justice, and that arrests and imprisonments might be taken away.‡ In December petitions from several counties were sent up

* King's Pamphlets, small 4to, No. 507, § 24.
† The Parliamentary History.   ‡ Whitelocke.

to the army-council much to the same effect, with the ominous request " that, as God hath not put the sword into your hand in vain, you will mediate for us to the Parliament, that the oppressed people may be settled in freedom, which they cannot be while tithes continue, and covetousness excutes the law."

Amid such signs of general impatience the Lord-General had recourse to an old expedient of his—a conference of influential men. To prevent the appearance of faction, the meeting took place at the residence of the Speaker Lenthall. The attendance was numerous, including " divers members of Parliament, and some chief officers of the army."* Whitelocke, who reports the conference, does not mention many names, and amongst the few that are chronicled those of Bradshaw and Vane are conspicuously absent. We must conclude that they were not present, and we cannot wonder at it; for they were naturally suspicious of Cromwell's growing power, their notions of a settlement and his being very different. The attendants whose names are recorded were—Lenthall, Cromwell, Harrison, Whitelocke, Fleetwood, St. John, Whalley, Desborow, and Sir Thomas Widdrington.

The dialogue given by Whitelocke as the main portion of the conversation held was evidently elaborated from memory after the event, and most probably after the Restoration. But substantially it may be regarded as representing truly the positions held by the speakers. All thought it was high time " to come to a settlement." But whether that settlement should take the form of " an absolute republic, or should allow any mixture of monarchy," was an issue on which there was clearly no agreement. Cromwell was in favour of " monarchical power." The words attributed to him may not be literally accurate, but they certainly express his mind. " Really, I think, if it may be done with safety, and preservation of our rights, both as Englishmen and Christians, that a settlement with somewhat of monarchical power in it would be very effectual." Lenthall agreed with this view ; so did Whitelocke, St. John, and Widdrington. On the other hand it is noteworthy that Cromwell's connections and intimate associates—Fleetwood, Desborow, and Whalley— were either disinclined, or strongly opposed, to any " mixture of monarchy." Whitelocke thought it significant that Cromwell

* Whitelocke.

Y 2

would not entertain the suggestion of negotiation either with
Prince Charles or the Duke of York. To the chronicler the Lord-
General appeared to be "fishing for men's opinions," and it is
shrewdly insinuated that he objected to other nominations because he desired to be named himself. As to his desire to be
named himself, it is not improbable. According to Whitelocke's
recollection, the phrase used was "somewhat of monarchical
power." And it is very likely that he and Whitelocke were
thinking of different things.

That the state should have no personal head was, in Cromwell's opinion, a defect. The functions formerly discharged by
prerogative seemed to him indispensable to order. But whether
the personal head should be called Stadtholder, President, Protector, or King, was, in his way of thinking, a matter of quite
secondary importance. And if there was to be a personal head,
the man who held the balance of power as Captain-General
might well prefer to hold it in a civil capacity. His enormous
superiority as a candidate for such an office was too obvious to
be doubted by himself. He might be a "poor weak worm" in
his religious musings, but all the other worms around him were
indefinitely weaker and poorer. When the hostile fleet was to
be captured for Lilliput, Gulliver might well be acquitted of
presumption in feeling that the honour of the achievement should
be his.

The conference came to nothing, and the exhausted Parliament went stumbling on to its doom. The subject of law
reform had long been debated in vain; and at the end of
December 1651 the House agreed to refer the matter, for report,
to a committee selected from the outside world. Of this
committee Matthew Hale was chairman, and Hugh Peters,
Rushworth, and Ashley Cooper were members. Three months
afterwards they suggested, for one thing, a land register to
facilitate transfers, and to keep records of all "incumbrances."
A debate was then raised in the Parliamentary Committee as to
the meaning of "incumbrance," a question discussed by them,
off and on, until the end of the Parliament, without any result.
In April 1652 a bill for incorporating Scotland was read twice,
but it lacked vitality, and came to nothing, till Cromwell took
the matter in hand. In May the Parliament, supposed to be
busy preparing its own dissolution, took into consideration the

question how the House might be supplied with new members. The question was an ominous one. It suggested that after all the moribund House might seek to renew its youth and perpetuate itself. And this is what in the sequel the House did. For the notion prevailed more and more, and soon became a fixed idea, that the members of the expiring Parliament should not only have seats in the new one without election, but should sit in judgment on the claims of all who might be elected.

In August 1652 the patience of the army-council was already running out; and, after solemn prayer, as their fashion was, they adopted a petition demanding, with a kind of respectful peremptoriness, certain practical measures. First they placed a better provision for preaching the Gospel. Next they asked a reform of legal procedure, redress of abuses in excise, and—noteworthy in victorious soldiers—they insisted on a more faithful observance of articles of war granted to the enemy. They urged that the national revenues should all go into one treasury under officers appointed by Parliament, and that half-yearly accounts should be published. Finally they asked once more that the new representative should be hastened on, and the qualifications of future Parliaments should be stated. The House gravely thanked the petitioners, represented by General Whalley, but winced at the appearance of dictation, and some members appealed to the Lord-General whether this kind of thing should be permitted. He however did not take the same view—in fact, rather approved of it than otherwise. And so the months crept on in unsettlement, discontent, and heart-burning, the Parliament doing little or nothing, except provide for the expenses of the Dutch war, which went on victoriously for the English fleet, and perhaps lengthened out the patience of the country.

But in the autumn of this year, 1652, events began to gather to a crisis. On a fair evening in November Whitelocke, taking the air in St. James's Park, met the Lord-General, and the two had a long conversation. There is no reason to doubt that Whitelocke's notes of this conversation fairly represent the tendency of Cromwell's thoughts towards a system that should leave the chief executive power in the hands of a single person. After inveighing against the obstructiveness and love of patronage displayed by the Parliamentary remnant, he suddenly exclaimed, according to Whitelocke : " What if a man should take on him to be king ? " The wily serjeant endeavoured to soothe the excitement of his distinguished friend, assuring him that he in effect already possessed the necessary power to control the policy of the country. And then Whitelocke, if his memory is to be trusted, went on to suggest a negotiation with Prince Charles. Cromwell did not treat such an idea as impossible, but only pointed out that it would be a matter of great difficulty; and so the interview ended.

The impression we get from this reminiscence, taken together with hints from Oliver's own words and deeds, is that he did not think England could get on without a king, and that he conceived the want might be supplied altogether apart from the royal race of Stuart. Wielding the power he did, it was inevitable he should think of himself as possibly equal to the position ; but the notion that Oliver's soul was consumed by a slavish passion for the glitter and pomp of kingship is sufficiently rebutted by the fact, that the obstacles which finally deterred him from taking the crown were such as never in all history have prevented, or could prevent, a merely ambitious man from clutching so glorious a bauble. On this subject more must be said further on. But at that time, as Cromwell himself afterwards said, he found " the people dissatisfied in every corner of the nation, and laying " at the doors of the army " the non-performance of those things which had been promised." Under such circumstances, what was to be done ? The obvious answer is, that all parties sincerely anxious for a peaceful settlement of the country should have united to hasten the substitution of a vigorous and really representative assembly for an effete remnant of a Parliament. " The current of succeeding Parliaments is stopped," wrote a pamphleteer of the period, " and, if that continue stopped, we shall be more offended by an hereditary Parliament than we were by an hereditary king." *

But the problem did not admit of so obvious a solution ; and the pamphleteer just quoted himself suggested all unconsciously one insuperable difficulty. " I have asked divers soldiers," he says, " what they fought for. *They answered, they could not tell.*" If this was the case in the army, we may well conceive how profound was the political ignorance existing

* " The Law of Freedom in a Platform," &c.—King's Pamphlets.

amongst the thousands who had stolidly stuck to their farms, forges, and shops through all the excitements of civil war. Such a reflection however did not occur to the army leaders. They insisted persistently, and with increasing vehemence, on the election of a new Parliament; and if they were willing to wait till 1654, it was only to give time for the completion of a measure adapting the distribution of seats to the altered circumstances of the times, and arranging for the admission of Scotch and Irish members. But in the autumn of 1652 it had already become too clear that no such measure would ever pass the House, except in a form mutilated and marred by the resolve of the sitting members to retain their own supremacy. Meantime no practical measures were passed, and not the army only but the people generally were coming to the conclusion that they could not be worse off if they had no Parliament at all.

Cromwell then had recourse to his usual expedient of conferences. In October about half the ordinary attendants at the House were invited to meet the chief officers of the army. From time to time there were about a dozen of such meetings held, in which the officers besought the members " that they would be mindful of their duty to God and men in the discharge of the trust reposed in them." But the only result was that the Parliament, taking alarm, began to press on the " Act for a representative" in the form regarded by the army as simply an arrangement for enlarging and continuing the existing House. The last of these conferences was held on the 19th of April 1653. On that day, after the House rose, twenty-three members came to Cromwell's residence in Whitehall, where the officers were assembled; and the Lord-General was requested to express the views of the army. He then asked for a full explanation of the method to be followed in electing a new House, and of the qualifications to be required in voters. The only reply was that the continuance of the existing House was essential to the safety of the nation. Cromwell told them then that this was simply impracticable. Did they mean that the House was to be recruited by Presbyterians who had been faithless to the Commonwealth ? " It's one thing," he said afterwards, " to love a brother, to bear with and love a person of different judgment in matters of religion, and another thing to have

anybody so far set in the saddle on that account as to have all
the rest of his brethren at mercy."

Still the imperturbable refrain recurred—"that nothing
would save the nation but the continuance of this Parliament."
The officers then proposed that, as there was no prospect of
an agreement, the question should be left to "some well-affected
men," such as had an interest in the nation, and were known to
be of good affection to the Commonwealth. These men were to
constitute a commission, with temporary charge of the government, and to arrange the summoning of the new Parliament.
For this course it was alleged there were precedents in English
history. The members present did not absolutely reject the
expedient. They promised to consider it; and meantime, Sir
Harry Vane and one or two other leaders undertook that the
obnoxious measure before the House should be delayed until
another conference could be held. Thus they separated; and
every one thought the crisis to be adjourned.

Next morning, April 20th, the officers met again at Cromwell's
house, to discuss the details of the proposals to be made to the
members in the evening. While they were so engaged, word was
brought that the House was proceeding with the obnoxious bill.
The army-council was startled; but relying upon the word of Sir
Harry Vane that nothing irrevocable should be done, they still
continued their consultations. Presently however a second,
and soon a third messenger came, breathlessly now, to say that
the House was plainly bent on carrying the measure through all
its remaining stages at once, without even waiting to have it
engrossed, and dropping out of it even such political limitations
of the franchise as had been previously contained in it. Then
Cromwell rose in wrath. "It is contrary to common honesty!"
he exclaimed, and quitted the room.

He told no one what he was going to do. The real truth
probably is that he did not himself know. The bill had to be
stopped. This was no mere personal resolve of his; it was a
decree of Heaven. What more might follow, Providence must
determine. He summoned a company of soldiers—so slight was
the force he thought enough to overawe the Parliament of three
nations—and went down to the House. It would be curious to
speculate on his thoughts as he passed down Whitehall. But
such speculations would be vain; for his great straggling mind

was now wrought up to a white heat that fused all energies in
one consuming purpose, and concealed all processes of calculation
even from himself. That he had fought for Parliament only
to overthrow it,—that he had once protested against military
despotism and was now establishing the same thing,—that he
had struck down one system of arbitrary prerogative to set up
another—were thoughts that probably never occurred to perplex
him in that supreme hour. All he knew was that, if left alone,
the Parliament might in a few minutes more reduce the army
to the agonising alternative of a renewed civil war, or an abject
surrender of the noblest prize they had earned with their blood—
liberty of prophesying and worship.

Arrived at the House, he stationed his guards at the doors
and in the Lobby, and himself stepped quietly into his ordinary
seat. There were not many more than fifty members present.
He was in ordinary peaceful attire—black clothes and grey
stockings. Were not the members speedily aware of the extraordinary guard he had left outside? At any rate, the proceedings went on rapidly. A member was urging the necessity for
passing the bill at once. Cromwell listened for a while, and
then had a whispered conversation with Harrison—told him,
apparently, that this bill must be stopped at all hazards, even if
it involved the stoppage of the House itself. Cromwell had
been heard to say "that these men would never leave till they
were pulled out by the ears;" and Harrison understood him
well enough. "Think well, sir," said the faithful follower;
"the work is very great and dangerous." Yes; how great and
dangerous it was no one could judge after it had been done, and
least of all two hundred years after. If this thing should not
turn out to be the will of the Lord, it would recoil first upon the
man who did it, burying an illustrious life under shameful ruin,
and next it would drown in blood the human interests and divine
truths he sought to serve.

So he sat still for another quarter of an hour, with an
inward, ominous heaving of the coming storm. Then the debate
appeared exhausted, and the Speaker rose as though to put the
question. "This is the time," muttered Cromwell between his
teeth—"I *must* do it;" and so, putting off his hat, stood up to
claim a hearing. The Speaker sat down again; and amid deep
silence and eager attention on all sides, the member for Cam-

bridge began to speak quietly of the work of the Parliament now drawing to a close. Would that we had his speech! We only know that he said much in commendation of their public spirit and zealous labours; but afterwards, changing his tone, charged them with deterioration for some time past, accusing them of injustice, obstruction, and many other faults. His "sharp, untuneable voice" grew so incisive that, at length, Sir Peter Wentworth and others rose to order. "This was strange language," said Sir Peter, "unparliamentary, utterly unbecoming in a trusted servant, and one who had been so highly honoured." A trusted servant! Yes; one obedient to death in the work in which he had bound himself to help them. But for these men to think that they could use his victorious strength like the thews of a slave, to pull down and build up regardless of his own convictions and conscience, was a foolish assumption, and its announcement hastened the end.

Thrusting his hat on his head—an intimation that he regarded the authority there as defunct—he strode into the middle of the floor, and silenced Sir Peter Wentworth with peremptory contempt. "Come, come," he cried, "we have had enough of this. I will put an end to your prating! It is not fit you should sit here any longer. The Lord has done with you. You are no Parliament! I tell you, you are no Parliament!"—then, turning to Harrison: "Call them in, call them in." At that, some twenty or thirty musketeers tramped across the threshold hitherto impassable to arms, and stood silent, stiff, and attentive near the bar. Their General was now risen to a pitch of excitement which opponents affected to treat as madness. Consciousness of the supreme issues dependent on this stupendous stroke brought every faculty of his mind and every nerve of his body to its utmost tension. The accumulated indignation of months broke loose against men who had sacrificed the practical wants of a bleeding nation to metaphysics and eloquence, or love of place.

"Begone!" he shouted, all aflame with passion. "It is time you should give way to honester men. Some of you are drunkards! Some are adulterers—corrupt, unjust persons—scandalous to the profession of the Gospel!" Sir Harry Vane, chafing with natural wrath, insisted on making himself heard. "This is not honest," he exclaimed; "yea, it is contrary to morality and common honesty." But Cromwell, regarding him as the breaker of a compact, stopped him scornfully. " Sir Harry Vane! ah, Sir Harry Vane! The Lord deliver me from Sir Harry Vane!" Then, as the members, all with swords by their sides, meekly moved off, he protested that this odious work was not of his seeking. " It is you that have forced me to this," he cried; " I have sought the Lord night and day that He would rather slay me than put me upon the doing of this." " Sir," said Alderman Allen, " it is not too late. The members may yet be called back, and the sitting resumed." But Cromwell turned fiercely upon him with a charge of malversation in the handling of public funds, and ordered his arrest there and then. This quickened the retreat of the other members; but the Speaker still kept his place. " Fetch him down!" thundered Cromwell. General Harrison intimated respectfully to Lenthall that he had better descend. But the Speaker insisted on the show of violence. " Sir," said Harrison, " I will lend you a hand;" which he did, and the chair was vacated. The mace, now an inane formality, caught the destroyer's eye. " What shall we do with this bauble?" he asked. " Here, take it away;" and a musketeer took it up. The House was nearly empty now; but by the door Sir Harry Vane encountered, unmoved, the volcanic wrath once more. " *You* might have prevented this," said Cromwell; " but you are a juggler." The House was now cleared. Cromwell slammed the door, locked it fast, and walked off with the key in his pocket.

The Long Parliament had been dead some time. It was now buried—whether decently or not, opinions will differ. Its ghost arose some years after to " squeak and gibber " over the grave of the Commonwealth, and mournfully to dispute the patent fact of its own dissolution. But, in sober truth, it was now buried, having shared the fate of all institutions whose bodies make a hideous effort to survive their souls.

CHAPTER XXIII.

THE LITTLE PARLIAMENT.

In the afternoon of April 20th 1653 Cromwell visited the chamber in Whitehall where the Council of State was accustomed to meet. He found the members sitting, with their Lord-President Bradshaw in the chair. They probably felt an inward flutter when their disturber appeared; but outwardly they were calm, and apparently resolved to stick to their posts. The Lord-General himself was doubtless suffering some reaction from the volcanic explosion of the morning. He simply told them that if they were sitting there as a private company they were welcome to remain, but if as a council of state they could not but be aware of what had happened to the Parliament, and would feel that this was now no place for them in *that* capacity. " Sir," said Bradshaw, " we have heard what you did at the House in the morning, and before many hours all England will know it. But, sir, you are mistaken to think that the Parliament is dissolved; for no power under heaven can dissolve them but themselves. Therefore, take you notice of that." Nevertheless they yielded to the inevitable, and dispersed. As President Bradshaw prophesied, the report of the forcible suppression of Parliament spread very rapidly. But he was mistaken as to the effects he obviously expected to ensue. Within a very few days, addresses came in from all parts of the country, expressing hearty approval of what had been done, and—if we may use a modern phrase—confidence in the administration of the Lord-General. If these addresses had been the only evidence of national feeling, they might have been set aside as the result of Cromwell's management. But it is impossible to account in this way for the ready willinghood of almost all judges, sheriffs, justices of the peace, mayors, and other public officials, to co-operate with the new Government. The words of General Richard Deane, writing from the channel fleet to the

Admiralty Commissioners on April 22nd, may be taken as roughly expressing the general indifference to the fate of the Parliament if only the practical work of government could be got done. "My trust is in God," he says, "and I am not much solicitous though the world be turned upside down; only, you being the chief instruments in engaging me in this business, and promising me assistance, do not neglect me at such a time as this. I pray God to make us instruments to do His pleasure." This prevalent desire for measures rather than systems made Cromwell at that crisis a supremely representative man. This was the real reason why the change of government was effected so peacefully that at the end of May the council of officers could write to their brethren in Scotland: "There is not so much as a dog barking, or a serpent hissing, in the way of our great public affairs." To keep up this general confidence, it was necessary to convince the public that no military despotism was intended, and that the army had a more practicable settlement to propose than the late Parliament. It might also be needful, in some points, to anticipate reforms by at least temporary alleviations of abuses.

As an appeal to public opinion, the Lord-General and his chief officers issued on the second day after the dissolution an address to the people. After referring to the obstructiveness of the late Parliament, to the expostulations vainly addressed to them, as well as to the growing and dangerous discontent of the country, this document went on to describe the expedient rejected by the suppressed House, but now to be tried by the army. This was, to devolve the supreme authority "upon known persons, fearing God, and of approved integrity." To them the government of the Commonwealth was to be committed for a time "as the most hopeful way to encourage and countenance all God's people, reform the law, and administer justice impartially." With an honesty not often characteristic of such manifestoes the people were informed that this expedient was suggested with the view of giving time to wean them from their old constitutional habits. The army-council avowed that they had put it forward, "hoping thereby the people might forget monarchy, and, understanding their true interest in the election of successive Parliaments, might have the Government settled on a true basis, without hazard to this glorious cause, or

necessitating to keep up armies for the defence of the same."*
The document ended with a declaration that the authority of all
judges, magistrates, and other legal officials would meantime be
maintained intact.

To all impartial readers it must occur that this address
openly admitted the impossibility of entrusting the continuance
of the Commonwealth to the free suffrages of the nation. On
the other hand, it should be remembered that to issue writs for
the election of a Parliament would have appeared a much greater
stretch of authority than the summoning of a convention. Still,
the insistance of the army on the disfranchisement of all active
aiders and abettors of the Royalist cause, and indeed the plain
statements of the declaration, sufficiently prove that an unreserved
appeal to the hustings was distrusted. But it does not follow that
Cromwell and his colleagues were hypocrites playing fast and loose
with political principle. The doctrine of government by representation was not so matured nor so well understood then as it is
now. The ultimate appeal to physical force was always nearer
at hand than it is with us. And this fact had a twofold effect
on policy. The triumph of force was more readily accepted, not
only by the victors but by the indifferent majority as the true
test of opinion; and its sanguinary cost deterred men from
adventuring lightly any form of controversy that could excite
strong feeling. The risk of imbruing the country in blood was
a ready, often a real, justification for suppressing political opposition. In Cromwell's view, also, systems of franchise and
representation were entirely subsidiary to more immediately
practical issues. To the charge of inconsistency the theoretic
republicans, who persisted in treating the fag-end of a mutilated
Parliament as a representative assembly, were surely more obnoxious than the practical man who set it aside, and accomplished
by mere "rule of thumb" the most pressing desires of the nation.

On the 6th of June, accordingly, Oliver, as "Captain-General
of all the forces raised or to be raised within the Commonwealth," issued out a formal summons to about one hundred
and forty "persons fearing God, and of approved fidelity
and honesty," requiring them to come together on the 4th of
July to take up the "great charge and trust" of the nation's
affairs. The people thus selected by the General with the

* The Parliamentary History.

advice of his officers were not at all confined to any one party, ecclesiastical or political. The Presbyterians were well repre-sented. There were republicans, and there were those who would have been glad to have had a monarchy if they could have got it outside the Stuart family. They were alike in character rather than opinion. All had a high reputation in their own localities for uprightness and devotion. Otherwise, though there were few, if any, who could be called distinguished men, some of them afterwards became so. One of the most remarkable was Robert Blake, already famous on the sea.

It is a singular illustration of the perennial childishness of mankind that Mr. Praisegod Barbone, a leather dealer, of Fleet Street, who was summoned to this Convention, has not only been regarded as a ridiculous character himself, for no other reason in the world than the accident of his name, but has been supposed to stamp the whole assembly as a collection of laughable hypo-crites and oddities. Such however was not the opinion of their contemporaries. Whitelocke says : " It was much wondered by some that these gentlemen, many of them being persons of fortune and knowledge, would, at this summons, and from these hands, take upon them the supreme authority of this nation, considering how little authority Cromwell and his officers had to give it, or these gentlemen to take it. But it was accepted by them." The truth is, their notion of authority was different from that of Whitelocke. Like Cromwell, they believed that God had clearly declared His judgment. Like Cromwell, also, they believed in the authority of accomplished facts, at any rate when such facts were instinct with divine promise. Perhaps, on the whole, the most remarkable feature of the Convention was the summons of representative men from Ireland and Scotland. It was the first deliberative assembly that had ever been com-posed of men qualified to represent the interests of the whole British Isles.

Brief as was the interval between the suppression of the Par-liament and the meeting of the Convention, Cromwell was not willing it should pass without some foretaste of reform. Calling eight officers and four civilians to constitute, with himself, a new Council of State, he attempted at once to correct some of the most galling distresses of the time. One of these was the irrational system of imprisonment for debt. In the absence of any equitable bankruptcy law, there was no other resource for creditors than to test the resources of their debtors by the slow torture of imprisonment. Debtors, on the other hand, sometimes endeavoured to cheat their creditors by endurance rather than make a full discovery and surrender of their property. But it was a dangerous expedient ; for in the lapse of time it was quite possible they might be practically lost sight of, and spend their whole lives in gaol. The discontents and disorders of twenty-five years had of course increased the number of insolvent debtors, who were crowded into the prisons at the very time when more space than usual was needed both for criminals and political "malignants." The position of prisoners for debt also gave special facilities for corrupt gain to gaolers, who often enriched themselves at the expense of creditors. The sufferings directly and indirectly involved in such a system may be imagined ; but they were aggravated by rudeness of manners and defects of sanitation difficult to conceive in our times. So long ago as the morrow of Dunbar fight Cromwell had urged upon the Parliament to " hear the groanings of poor prisoners," but he had urged it in vain, and he now resolved to try what he could do himself.

Within ten days of the expulsion of the Parliament he appointed a committee of his temporary council to examine the grievances and oppressions believed to exist in the Upper Bench Prison, under the management of Sir John Lenthall. They were instructed to consider the wrongs suffered both by debtors and creditors, and to suggest remedies. On the fourth day after their appointment, they took the very obvious step of ordering the imprisoned debtors to " show cause why their estates should not be sequestered for payment of their just debts." Continuing their investigations, they found that there were in the Upper Bench Prison 399 debtors, with a total indebtedness of £900,000. The same committee was shortly afterwards directed to investigate the state of things in the Fleet Prison. One result of their inquiry was the publication of a complete list of all the debtors in the Fleet, with the dates of their first incarceration.* From this it appears that on the 25th of May 1653 there were in that prison thirty men who had been confined for debt more than five years. One had been there nearly thirty

* King's Pamphlets, No. 564, § 13.

years, having been arrested in 1624; and several had been detained since 1630. Evils of this sort affected Cromwell's mind far more than any theoretical defects of a constitution. But such a tangle was not to be cut by the sword; and it was left for his "Little Parliament," in the October following, to relieve imprisoned debtors by a system of county courts, in some respects anticipatory, as his legislation often was, of modern reforms. It is noteworthy that one of the county court judges appointed under this arrangement was his old enemy, Mr. Robert Barnard of Huntingdon.*

The miseries of impoverished Royalists were not excluded from the Lord General's sympathies. The Marquis of Worcester, out of whose sequestered family estates the Parliament had made a grant to Cromwell, was lying a prisoner in the Tower, and had repeatedly petitioned the House in vain for some relief of his necessities. An allowance of £3 a week had indeed been ordered, but it had never been paid; and, under a system making the comfort of prisoners wholly dependent on the means at their disposal, he was reduced to extremities. A fortnight after the expulsion of the Parliament he appealed to Cromwell; and in response obtained not only the payment of his allowance, but an order for the arrears as well. To the young Earl of Derby, whose father had been executed at Bolton, Cromwell awarded £500 a year, to be paid out of the sequestered estates. There was some difficulty in carrying out this arrangement; but the "Little Parliament" confirmed the allowance before they had sat a month. There is reason to believe that the tender side of Oliver's character, illustrated by such instances as these, was familiar enough to his contemporaries. A pamphleteer, discussing in June of this year "the Cause of the Poor," declares that—

"Worthy Oliver Cromwell deserves great honour and imitation. He gives more money to the poor than any I have heard of in our days— thousands a year. I would the rich would follow his steps. It is expected the Lord will use him, with some others who have the same spirit and merciful heart, to do great things for the good of this nation; especially to ease the oppressed, and to help them that cannot help themselves. . . . 'He hath put down the mighty from their seats, and hath exalted them of low degree.' 'Let every soul be subject to the higher

* Scobell.

Z

powers; there is no power but of God.' Those against whom none
are able to prevail are the greatest and highest power." *.

That Oliver was a power of this kind abundant proof was
afforded, if any had been needed, during the two months that
elapsed before his summons to "persons fearing God and of
approved fidelity and honesty" could be obeyed. Alderman
Allen, arrested in the Parliament House on April 20th, does
not seem to have been kept long in custody, and probably
inspired his city brethren with his own feelings. On May
30th several aldermen and others memorialised the Lord-
General to reinstate the late Parliament.† As soon as this
was known, a counter address was presented from other aldermen and citizens deprecating any such course. Thereupon
the first memorialists received "a notable tart answer," inti-
mating that if any blood were spilt on this occasion it would
be laid to their doors.‡

It is always a sign of health in a government to be able to
suppress incipient disorder with force sufficient to inspire respect
without striking terror. And this was characteristic of Oliver's
government from the very beginning. At the very crisis of his
fate complaints came from the Fen country that the company
for draining the Great Level were violently disturbed and hindered in their work by rioters. On the 23rd of April the "Lord
of the Fens," surely not unmindful of his old interest in popular
rights there, wrote to the company's agent :—

"I desire you to send one of my troops with a captain, who may by all
means persuade the people to quiet, by letting them know they must not
riotously do anything, for that must not be suffered. But if there be any
wrong done by the Adventurers, upon complaint such course shall be taken
as appertains to justice, and right will be done."§

This suppression of riot was followed up, in the month of
June, by the appointment of a commission of twenty-one
gentlemen acquainted with the Fens, to sit "at the 'Bell,' in
Ely," for the purpose of examining and reporting on claims
against the adventurers." ‖

* "The Cause of the Poor," by Samuel Richardson.—King's Pamphlets,
No. 569, § 9, p. 15.
† This was signed by a Thomas Allen; but the alderman arrested was
Francis Allen.—King's Pamphlets, 564, § 16.
‡ King's Pamphlets, No. 564, § 9.   § Carlyle. Letter CLXXXVIII.
‖ Calendar of State Papers (Domestic Series).

Alderman Allen and Sir John Lenthall were not the only men to experience Cromwell's intolerance of malversation in offices of trust. The Savoy Hospital and Ely House were important charities, which, as the tendency of such things is, had become the *peculium* of greedy managers and their needy dependents. At the end of May Colonel Pride, Colonel Packer, and others were commissioned to examine these charities with a view to providing " that the treasure be not wasted, and that only such men be admitted as are proved to be deserving of relief."

Meantime the fleet, once the hope of Royalists, had treated the expulsion of the Parliament with indifference, and was warmly loyal to the new Government. Van Tromp unexpectedly appearing off Dover on May 27th, when the English fleet was elsewhere, fired on the town, and did some damage to buildings. He was however speedily followed, and the insult was avenged by a victory thought to require a solemn and grateful national acknowledgment. But Oliver had not much faith in prayers or praises made to order. The " monthly fast " was dropped after the Presbyterian Parliament was no more, and the " great Independent " had a scruple about ordering a thanksgiving. He issued a " recommendation " that the 23rd of June should, as far as possible, be set apart for that purpose, while he expressly disavowed any intention of making it obligatory.

But naval victories were costly, and nothing shows the general favour of the public at that time to Cromwell's rule more conclusively than the ease with which he raised the monthly assessment once more from £90,000 to £120,000. Certainly the possibility of such a thing casts a strange light on the whole story of the civil war. It would not be true to say that Englishmen had surrendered their objection to being taxed without their consent. But events show that where that consent practically existed, they were not very particular as to the formal manner of its expression. If ship-money had been raised to meet a new Spanish Armada, Hampden would have met with no sympathy or support in resisting it.

It will thus be seen that, while no time was lost in summoning the Convention, Cromwell did not play the part of King Log even during the brief interval before its assembly. On July 4th, out of one hundred and forty members summoned, a

z 2

hundred and twenty appeared punctually to the day. Others came in afterwards; and in the end there were only two defaulters—a fair proof that, in the opinion of these "notables," Cromwell's assumption of power had been justified by the necessities of the nation.   Having given their names they were directed to enter the Council Chamber, where they "sat down, in chairs appointed for them, round about the table." One may imagine the subdued murmur of conversation of men at once eager and awed.   To many of them their surroundings were entirely strange; and to not a few even the person of the Lord General was unknown.   We can fancy the sudden hush as he at length entered, followed by a crowd of officers; and how all attention was fixed upon the burly form, the rugged features, and the commanding yet kindly eyes of the imperial man, who took his stand "by the window, opposite to the middle of the table." For some moments there was a bustle of officers thronging to fill up all available standing space.   Then a deep hush fell on the crowded chamber, and the Lord General spoke.

The speech he delivered may of course best be studied in Carlyle's skilfully edited version of it.*   For the purpose of this biography, a glance at its chief points must suffice.   If this historic utterance had been recovered for the first time now, the questions most eagerly asked about it would be—How did Cromwell defend his violent suppression of the Parliament? What new system of government did he suggest?   What principles did he recommend to the Convention?   What light, if any, did the speech cast on his own motives?   In the main we may here confine ourselves to answering such questions, for as they would naturally be first asked, so they are those of most permanent interest.   It is characteristic of the man that he never wrote his speeches.   To his practical temper the pen was the proper instrument for record, or communication at a distance. For direct utterance co-operation of tongue and brain was sufficient.   What might be lacking in form of expression was more than made up in power by tone, gesture, radiant looks, the vibration of his whole nature under the prophetic impulse.

In the opening of his speech Oliver dwelt upon the familiar theme, "that series of providences wherein the Lord hath appeared, dispensing wonderful things to these nations from the

* Vol. iii., p. 262.

beginning of our troubles to this very day." He referred specially to the formation of the "New Model" as a manifestation of God's purpose "to winnow the forces of the nation ; and to put them into the hands of other men, of other principles than those that did engage at the first." For mere " matters of fact " he contented himself with a vague reference to "stories that do recite those transactions "—surely a very modest way of saying that the chief hero of "those transactions" found a difficulty in dwelling on them. But there was another side to these events. They had a divine outlook ; and of that he will be bold to speak, though he does it in a lumbering sentence without beginning, middle, or end—a mere jumble of fuel for emotion, so to speak ; and some spark of the fire that burned in the speaker's soul is needed to make it shine.

"But those things wherein the life and power of them"—the events of the last few years—"lay; those strange windings and turnings of Providence; those very great appearances of God in crossing and thwarting the purposes of men, that he might raise up a poor and contemptible company of men, neither versed in military affairs, nor having much natural propensity to them—simply by their owning a principle of godliness and religion ; which, so soon as it came to be owned, and the state of affairs put upon the foot of that account, how God blessed them, furthering all undertakings, yet using the most improbable and the most contemptible and despicable means—for that we shall ever own—is very well known to you."

The Lord General, then, did not apparently regard himself as a man of military genius ? No ; his successes were in his view miraculous, bestowed upon him in spite of his incompetence, by the blessing of God on services offered in humble dependence on divine aid. Such a mode of thought is so utterly foreign to the present age that readers have some difficulty in realising it. But unless the effort be made, Oliver Cromwell cannot be understood. We might as well attempt to understand St. Paul on the hypothesis that he plumed himself on his gifts as an orator or a writer of letters, and traced his achievements to these.

What use, he went on to ask, did Parliament, after the crowning mercy of Worcester, make of these extraordinary blessings ? Their obvious duty was to realise that orderly, just, and pure polity, to make room for which God had overturned evil institutions. But the Parliament made no attempt of the kind. The army had been very loath even to petition, lest they should intrude beyond their province. But at last, "finding the people dissatisfied in every corner of the nation," and accusing the victors of the non-performance of those things which had been promised, "truly they did think themselves concerned, if they would, as becomes honest men, keep up the reputation of honest men in the world." Then came the conferences, and the revelation of a purpose to keep power in the hands of a party not at all representative of the nation. Was it to be expected that men who had fought through ten years of civil war for radical reforms—and above all for religious freedom—would now surrender them at the bidding of some fifty Presbyterian royalists and republican theorists?

It is curious to note that one of the chief offences of the Parliament in Cromwell's eyes was its neglect to seize the opportunity offered of reviving religion in Wales. It is not necessary to suppose that the Welsh blood in him gave him a special sympathy for the people. But it is clear he had perceived, what more recent experience has strikingly proved, their peculiar susceptibility to the sort of religion called "Evangelical." He assured his hearers that "God had kindled a seed* there, indeed hardly to be paralleled since the primitive time."

In a word, the army had been driven to the conclusion that from the late Parliament the "people of God," in "*the large comprehension of them, under the several forms of godliness in this nation*," had nothing more to expect. The words here italicised are worthy of note, for they imply much; and all the more because of their natural, unpremeditated utterance. The Parliamentary majority were zealous enough for *one* form of godliness. But they did not appreciate the power veiled under many forms. Now the power and life of religion, remaining the same through many changes of form, is moral rather than theological. It is not so much an opinion, as an affection of supreme loyalty. And it was this affection, with its fruits of "righteousness, peace, and joy in the Holy Ghost," on which the practical mind of Cromwell seized as the precious essence of religion. The sacrifice of this to a pragmatical uniformity in doctrine and discipline was, in his eyes, the unpardonable sin of the Parlia-

---

* Carlyle seems to regard this metaphor as incongruous. But surely "kindled" here means "quickened."

ment. Their utter incapacity for effective reforms—an incapacity shown by months of fruitless discussion on one word, " incumbrance "—was only an effect of unsusceptibility to divine judgments.

Having ended a somewhat rambling invective by an account of the treacherous attempt, contrary to agreement, to hurry through the obnoxious bill for a new Parliament, Cromwell proceeded to say that the object of calling the present assembly was to surrender to them the supreme authority, and " to divest the sword of all power in the civil administration." The future was to be wholly in their hands, within the limits of a certain " instrument of government " drawn up by the army-council, prescribing only that another Convention should be called by November, 1654, and that this second Convention should send out writs for a regular Parliament. No system of government was recommended to them. Leaving their commission perfectly blank in that respect, Cromwell went on to deliver an exhortation as to the spirit in which they should assume their responsibility. This exhortation was suggested by various passages of scripture.

He reminded his hearers of St. James's description of heavenly wisdom. He assured them that this would teach them the " judgment of truth," which would be as just towards an unbeliever as towards a believer; nay, would " rather miscarry toward a believer than an unbeliever." He longed that they might have such a spirit as Moses and Paul had, " which was not a spirit for believers only, but for the whole people." And then he launched out into a glowing exposition of some bright, prophetic symbols, in which his soul delighted. This rugged farmer captain, with so keen an eye for the chief practical issue of each day as it arose, had also, it would seem, his ideals, his imaginations, his passionate sentiments. But all these for him were clothed in the language of Zion. The visions of Isaiah, the ascent of Christ to heaven, the exultant songs of Hebrews who felt the very mountains reeling under the might of Jehovah, while " kings of armies did flee apace," and " the chariots of God, even thousands of angels," chased the foe,—such was the spiritual scenery amidst which his heart expanded with deep emotion, and triumphed in the strange fulfilment of divine promises to England.

Yet his practical sense was never far away; and noble utterances now and then assure us that all this supernatural glamour is only this eager soul's way of describing the splendour and the dread of the responsibilities, both individual and national, that confront him.

> "Truly seeing things are thus, that you are at the edge of the promises and prophecies—*at least, if there were neither promise nor prophecy, yet you are carrying on the best things—you are endeavouring after the best things.*"

Where a man's heart is in his words, the breaks and windings of his sentences, though they may obscure his grammar, reveal his soul. In that sudden turn of thought in the sentence just quoted, how clear it is made that the Hebrew imagery was but the accidental form, not the motive power, of Oliver's political emotion! To "carry on the best things," "to endeavour the best things," such was his simple rule; and it was not from the letter of the Bible, but in communion with the Eternal Spirit of all life and order, that he learned what those best things were.

So far, then, as we understand aright Oliver's speech to the Little Parliament, it answers clearly enough, though perhaps unexpectedly, the questions with which we supposed it to be approached. As to Oliver's defence, he did not seem to think that he much needed one. God had put on him the duty of saving the main ends for which, in Oliver's view, the war had been fought out. That was enough for him. As to a new form of government, he suggested none; nor did he, perhaps, sufficiently realise the fateful importance of the question. His notion of "healing and settlement" was the establishment of a Gospel ministry, protection for innocent differences of opinion, reform of legal abuses, promotion of trade, and the enforcement of foreign respect for England by an infusion of the spirit of his Ironsides into the fleet. He did not care much by what constitutional—or, for that matter, by what unconstitutional—methods these things were got done; but done they must be. The principles recommended to the Convention in their deliberations were simply those of sanctified common sense. And any one who reads this speech with open mind must surely be conscious that to retain suspicions of "dissimulation" and selfish ambition in the speaker requires some forced resistance of natural impressions.

In the deliberations of the assembly now dismissed to their work Cromwell himself did not take much part. One of the first things they did was to desire him to sit as a member; but he seems to have thought it was rather his business to carry on the executive government, leaving legislation to them. For a while it appeared likely that they would justify his expectations. They were men great in prayer, and commenced their labours by spending a whole morning in supplication, without any chaplain to assist their devotions. They elected as their chairman, with the title of Speaker, Francis Rous, Provost of Eton College, and more celebrated for psalmody than for statesmanship. They issued to the people a pious exhortation indicative of strong religious feeling in the authors. They revived at once the dropped bill of the Long Parliament for correcting the grievances and inconveniences of legal procedure. They appointed committees on trade and corporations, on the army, on the revenue and the treasuries, on public debts, on prisons and prisoners, on hospitals and their abuses. A more vague reference was made to a committee for the advancement of learning; and another sat " to receive proposals for the advantage of the Commonwealth." By their measure, already mentioned, for the relief of insolvent debtors, they set free several hundreds of hopeless prisoners in London gaols alone. They appointed commissioners to correct idle or immoral ministers; they even aspired to relieve agriculture of tithes, and to cleanse the Augean stables of Chancery by very simple processes of abolition.

Taking the Little Parliament as a whole, it seems to have been characterised by benevolence and by simplicity of purpose rather than by political knowledge or skill in statecraft. Men of liberal views and earnest devotion, but without experience of public life, sometimes imagine within themselves that, were they in office, they would find a short method of dealing with obvious abuses, apparently protected only by a network of red tape. They do not know how deeply the roots of abuses may be intertwined with the very vitals of a nation. If, by what they think a happy chance, such men should be suddenly placed in apparent power, they will probably find that their first vigorous grasp of the evils they would tear up excites a shudder and a convulsion, threatening a dissolution of the body corporate which they thought to save.

Such was the experience of the "persons fearing God and of approved fidelity and honesty" whom Cromwell had summoned to his aid. In disregard of political conventionalism there was much similarity between them and their convener. But he had an appreciation of opportunity and circumstance such as they evidently lacked; and in the sequel he came to look back upon his expectations from them as an instance of his own "simplicity." Chancery with its arrears of twenty-three thousand cases could not be got rid of by a stroke of the pen. Yet in their attempt to abolish it, these men perhaps intended only the reform recently accomplished, or said to be accomplished, in the incorporation of equity and law. Tithes were not, as they supposed, an unjust burden on the land. Perverted and squandered as tithes were and are, they remained, as they remain now, a precious reserve from an unwisely alienated public interest in the land. To have merely abolished tithes would have been then, as it would be now, to rob some men and to enrich others, in both cases alike unjustly, and without the slightest benefit to the nation. The reform needed was, and is now, to rescue for properly national purposes what is left of this revenue from land, at the same time so adjusting its pressure that the whole land charges on agriculture shall not amount to more than a fair rent with a reasonable proportion of rates. The time was not come, in the seventeenth century, for such proposals. The crude project of the Little Parliament only alarmed many interests, and strengthened the general desire that practical power might for the present remain with the Lord General's practical sense.

The public confidence in him was probably stimulated by the successes of the English fleet. Within little more than a month after the day of thanksgiving for one victory another followed, more sanguinary, but also more complete. Cromwell's extraordinary skill in collecting all the information he wanted now stood him in good stead. The Dutch envoys wrote home in July that "all secret actings" in the Netherlands, "and, were it possible, the very thoughts of those States, were most exactly, and weekly, presented in writing" to the English Council. On July 29th an engagement was begun between the two fleets, and lasted at intervals until August 1st. In this

battle, Van Tromp was killed, thirty-three Dutch ships were
sunk, and 1,200 prisoners were taken. Monk, at the beginning
of the battle, had declared that he would neither give nor take
quarter ; but the sight of the drowning wretches, struggling in
the whirl left by the sunken ships, seems to have made him
relent. The loss of the English was severe. But the remnants
of the Dutch fleet crept into Texel so utterly ruined that the
States now began to make earnest efforts for peace.

The negotiations were long, for Cromwell was imperious.
On one occasion, when the Dutch envoys said their countrymen
were of such generosity they would not listen to the terms proposed, his only answer was that *his* countrymen were English, and
had not lost their courage. Peace was not concluded indeed
until April, 1654. The terms were, briefly, a defensive alliance,
the perpetual acknowledgment of the superiority of England in
the narrow seas by the striking of Dutch colours on all occasions
to British men-of-war, compensation for English losses in Dutch
colonies, and in Copenhagen, under Dutch influence ; finally, all
commercial advantages possible under the then prevalent delu-
sions on the subject of trade. It is interesting to note that in
case of dispute as to the amount due for compensation, the
Swiss Cantons were to appoint arbitrators, whose decision should
be binding. In the course of these negotiations Oliver was
called upon for the first time to receive ambassadors, as the
sovereign ruler of his country. In a scene already described *
the former grazier of the fens bore himself in a manner which
showed at once grave consciousness of his surprising elevation,
and also a fear of unjustifiable assumption. This duty, like
all before, had come to him in the way of Providence, and
it was met in a mood too serious either for the anxieties of
vanity or the elation of pride.

While the members of the Little Parliament talked, Cromwell and his council worked. This council was supposed to be
the creation of the Parliament. And indeed on the 1st of
November, the existing council, including the Lord General
himself, went out of office, and the Parliament, 113 members
being present, proceeded to the election of a new one by a secret
ballot. When the scrutiny was taken, it was found that the
votes for Cromwell were exactly as many as the members pre-

* *Ante*, p. 2.

sent—113. That under the protection of secrecy this perfect unanimity should be shown, is proof enough that, in view of these notables at least, the choice lay between Cromwell and chaos. The only other man elected with anything approaching this unanimity was Sir Gilbert Pickering, uncle to the poet Dryden. Desborow had only 74 votes, and Harrison 58.

But when this new council was appointed the Little Parliament was already drawing near its end. Alarms of tithe-owners, uneasiness of clergymen, indignation of lawyers were sapping both its external authority and its internal harmony. Many of the members began to feel themselves in a false position. The real power was in the hands of Cromwell, not merely by the support of the army, but by a sort of inarticulate *plébiscite,* in which the members themselves concurred. Under such circumstances they began to think their discussions a waste of time ; and in the midst of a prolonged and often adjourned debate about tithes a resolution was hurriedly carried, early on Monday morning, December 12th, 1653, "That the sitting of this Parliament any longer, as now constituted, will not be for the good of the Commonwealth." The method of carrying out this resolution was as strange as everything else in the history of this singular body. The members hastened to Whitehall, and there drew up a resignation of their powers, the signatures being added on separate fragments of paper hastily fastened together. The Lord General received the document with expressions of surprise and deprecation ; and made as though he would refuse it altogether. The members present however respectfully insisted, and he had no choice but to yield. The conventionalities of life are often transparently insincere, and on this occasion perhaps Cromwell over-passed the absolute requirements of courtesy. But who is there that has not urged a troublesome guest to prolong his visit, when his absence was eagerly desired? There can be no doubt that the resignation relieved Cromwell of the growing anxiety he had felt about the impracticable temper of his unworldly legislators. The issue to which they were tending, he afterwards said, was "the confusion of all things." But on the other hand their failure was a great disappointment to him ; and this real disappointment underlay his polite regrets at their departure.

The Council of State disappeared with the assembly appointing it; and Cromwell once more held supreme power only as the Captain-General of the organised physical force of the nation. The army-council resumed its sittings; and the officers composing it betook themselves, as was their custom, to earnest prayer for divine direction. They held also several consultations apart from the Lord General; and, though people who lived in such intimate communion must have known each other's thoughts, there is no reason to doubt Cromwell's assertion that the issue of their deliberations was uninfluenced by any message or suggestion from him. They came to the conclusion that the Lord General should take it upon him to send out writs for a Parliament; and should also assume the power of adapting the representation to the existing distribution of population. To give some decent disguise of civil authority to his military office, they presumed to offer him a new title. They even suggested that he should assume the crown.* But on his rejection of this proposal, they insisted that at least he should style himself Lord Protector of the Commonwealth. Practical legislation being in their view what was wanted much more than an ideal constitution, they resolved to foreclose discussions on abstract principles by drawing up an "Instrument of Government."

This was a document of forty-two clauses, renewing in effect the ancient constitution of the country, with the substitution of a Protector elected for life instead of an hereditary monarch, and the omission of a House of Lords. These were of course great differences, the latter more important than the former. To make the sovereign ruler elective was to return to an original custom of the English race. To omit a House of Lords was to ignore an inveterate tradition and habit. But the rest of the "Instrument" contained nothing vitally inconsistent with the old constitution. The name "Protector" was adopted because recommended by precedent. All writs were to run in his name; all military and legal commissions to be issued by him; all national revenues and property to be vested nominally in him. There was no mention of "prerogative;" but almost everything that kings had claimed to do, the Protector could now do, with certain obviously necessary exceptions. During the sitting of Parliament he

* This rests on Cromwell's own statement as reported in "Burton's" Diary

could not dispose of the national forces, except by Parliamentary sanction. In decisions on war or peace he must have the sanction of his Council. He was compelled to summon Parliament at least once every three years; and until it had sat five months he was deprived of the power of dissolving it without its own consent. The Protector's power of absolute veto was confined to bills infringing the "Instrument." All other measures he could only suspend for twenty days, when, if he could not convince the Parliament, they would become law even against his will. But by a portentous stretch of the argument from necessity temporary power was conferred on the Protector, with the advice of his council, to issue Ordinances on any subject whatever, even the imposition of taxes, or the repeal of ancient laws; and these Ordinances were to have all the force of statutes of the realm until the new Parliament should otherwise resolve.

The clauses embodying the scheme for the new Parliament in some respects anticipated the reforms of two succeeding centuries. One Parliament of 460 members was to represent Scotland and Ireland, as well as England and Wales. But the assignment of 400 members to the two latter, while Scotland and Ireland had to be content with thirty each, was palpably unjust. The distribution of English seats was much more rational than in any previous or succeeding Parliament down to 1832. Manchester received a representative; and only twenty-one towns were allowed more than one member. In these it is noteworthy that Huntingdon and Cambridge were not included, while royalist Worcester was. The franchise, judged by modern ideas, was narrow and illiberal. It can cause little surprise that all who had fought for royalty should be disfranchised for twelve years. But the limitation of the power of voting to men who possessed property, real or personal, to the value of £200, must have excluded a large majority of the nation. Nor were the elected representatives to have unlimited power. The returns to the writs were to contain an express proviso, that the members should have no authority to alter the government as now settled in a single person and a Parliament. The meeting of the new House was fixed for September 3rd, 1654— a late date, but a glorious anniversary. Religious freedom, in the sense of liberty for all forms of belief and worship not

popularly identified with blasphemy or political reaction, was
made a fundamental article. Any proposal infringing this
might be absolutely vetoed by the Protector. "The Christian
religion, as contained in the Scriptures," was to be "held forth
and recommended as the public profession of these nations."
But another clause added that "to the public profession held
forth none shall be compelled by penalties or otherwise; but
that endeavours be made to win them by sound doctrine, and
the example of a good conversation."

A council was also nominated, consisting partly of military
officers and partly of civilians. Amongst the best known names
were those of Lambert, Desborow, Skippon, Fleetwood, Lord
Lisle, Sir Gilbert Pickering, and Sir Anthony Ashley Cooper.
Henry Lawrence became president. Francis Rous and Richard
Mayor were also named.

In urging their views upon Cromwell the council of officers
denied that he would be taking more power than he actually
possessed. On the contrary, they argued that the "Instrument
of Government" would limit his arbitrary authority, and in due
time transfer the supreme power to a Parliament. The new
constitution was instantly proclaimed with something of the
pomp usually observed on the accession of a king.

On December 16th, 1653, the Lord General went in state with
attendant grandees and lacqueys to the Court of Chancery, and
returned to Whitehall as Lord Protector of the Commonwealth.
The ceremony was not impressive, and the "gold band around
his hat" was surely a vulgar mockery of royal ornaments. It is
possible that Oliver's better judgment yielded to plausible platitudes about the effect of symbol and ceremony on the common
herd. But it would have been more becoming to the strenuous
reality of his life hitherto had he been content with the decent
garb of an ordinary English gentleman. No chair of state
could enhance the dignity, and no oath could heighten the
responsibility, of the office to which a divine destiny had now
raised him.

CHAPTER XXIV.

OLIVER, LORD PROTECTOR.

PERHAPS not half a dozen men in all human history have held so grand a position as that of Oliver, Lord Protector, at the beginning of 1654. Many an emperor and king has held sway over a wider territory, and has been obeyed with more slavish submission. But neither inheritance nor conquest, apart from nobler causes, could ever confer the extraordinary sovereignty wielded by this man. The peculiarity of his power was this, that it came naturally and inevitably to him as the impersonation of those qualities, convictions, and aspirations which for the time subordinated all other elements in the national character. "I was arbitrary in power," he said himself, speaking of this period, "having the armies in the three nations under my command; and truly not very ill-beloved by them, nor very ill-beloved by the people—by the good people." Of course there were also "good people" who did not love him at all, a circumstance he naturally overlooked. But the substance of his assertion is true, and might have been put much more strongly. The people who honoured human nature above political systems, the people who craved before all things civil and religious liberty, just laws, firm order, and national security, looked to him as the captain of their temporal salvation. They trusted everything to him; they hoped all things from him. They allowed him personally to wield the whole moral energy evoked in the nation by the strain and struggle of the past ten years. For nearly nine months, until the meeting of his first elected Parliament, he held this extraordinary dictatorship with full assurance that he was the very soul of the nation. And these nine months were probably the happiest time of his life.

He set himself at once to make full proof of his powers. But a prime condition of success was to nip in the bud all conspiracies against his government. The watchfulness and occasional severity required for this last purpose somewhat marred the peace of those otherwise prosperous months. Within four days of the inauguration of the Protectorate three colonels— Thomas Saunders, John Okey, and Matthew Alured—drew up a petition to " the Lord Protector and our General," denouncing the change of government as inconsistent with the aims they had fought for. But the petition was never presented, for Col. Alured was instantly arrested, his chamber searched, and the petition removed.* He was kept under arrest two days, and then released. The other subscribers of the petition appear to have passed without notice, though probably they were recommended not to meddle with such matters for the present. All three colonels were of the Anabaptist persuasion, and shared the reckless spiritual ardour characteristic of the sect in those days. Alured soon had an opportunity of redeeming himself. He was sent into Ireland in the spring to take charge of a military detachment from Ulster for the assistance of General Monk in his operations against royalism in the Scottish highlands. Now either the Anabaptist colonel should have refused this service, or he should have executed it faithfully. But he accepted it, and then, being at a distance, thought he might conspire with impunity. But Cromwell's eyes and ears being everywhere, the treacherous colonel was re-called, after which of course he had no further service under the Commonwealth.†

At the same time when the petition was impounded, the attention of the council was called to some fanatical utterances in an Anabaptist meeting-house at Blackfriars. On Monday evenings a sort of political club was held there for the discussion of prophecy and the signs of the times. The views of the " Fifth-Monarchy men," as they were called, found much favour at this meeting. Assyria, Persia, Greece, Rome—such were the four monarchies or dominions held to answer to the " four great beasts " in Daniel's vision. But the fifth monarchy was to be that of the Son of Man, the personal reign of Christ. And many Anabaptists believed that the time for this was at hand. Such a belief was harmless while it remained visionary. But fanatics sometimes do not scruple to lend a hand to the fulfilment of prophecy ; and there were those who thought they

---

* Cal. St. P. " Domestic Series," 1653-4.
† Letters XXXI. and XXXII. in Carlyle.

A A

could do this by taking Cromwell out of the way. It will be well to give here the Protector's own words about this Fifth-Monarchy superstition. They are very characteristic of the man, and though they were not uttered till September of this year in opening Parliament, they conveniently explain the action he took in regard to the Blackfriars meeting. After referring to some spiritual evils of the time, he proceeds :—

"But I say there is another error of a more refined sort (among) many honest people, whose hearts are sincere, many of them belonging to God ; and that is the mistaken notion of the Fifth Monarchy—a thing pretending more spirituality than anything else ; a notion I hope we all honour, and wait and hope for—that Jesus Christ will have a time to set up his reign in our hearts, by subduing those corruptions and lusts and evils that are there, which now reign more in the world than, I hope, in due time, they shall do. And when more fulness of the Spirit is poured forth to subdue iniquity, and bring in everlasting righteousness, then will the approach of that glory be. The carnal divisions and contentions among Christians, so common, are not the symptoms of that Kingdom ! But for men, on this principle, to betitle themselves that they are the only men to rule kingdoms, govern nations, and give laws to people, and determine of property, and liberty, and everything else, upon such a pretension as this is, —truly, they had need give clear manifestations of God's presence with them, before wise men will receive or submit to their conclusions ! Nevertheless, as many of these men have good meanings, which I hope in my soul they have, it will be the wisdom of all knowing and experienced Christians to do as Jude saith, when he reckoned up those horrible things, done upon pretences, and haply by some upon mistakes. ' Of some,' says he, ' have compassion, making a difference ; others save with fear, pulling them out of the fire.' I fear they will give too often opportunity for this exercise ! But I hope the same will be for their good. If men do but pretend for justice and righteousness, and be of peaceable spirits, and will manifest this, let them be the subjects of the magistrate's encouragement. And if the magistrate by punishing visible miscarriages save them by that discipline, God having ordained him for that end—I hope it will evidence *love* and not hatred to punish where there is a cause."

To the Protector it already appeared, in January of this year, 1654, that the Blackfriars fanatics were " giving opportunity for this exercise." Their preachers were warned by the council ; but two of them, named Feake and Simpson,* continued to indulge in fierce prophecies of speedy ruin to the head of the new government, prophecies too likely to excite murderous thoughts. These men therefore were committed to Windsor

* Cal. St. P. Domestic Series, 1653-4.

Castle, " in order," as the record states, " to the preservation of the peace of this nation."

But the most illustrious Anabaptist was Major-General Harrison, a man who in purity of purpose was worthy to rank with Eliot. No shadow of selfish ambition had ever perplexed the patriotic aims with which he had served throughout the war. The only doubts haunting his clear soul were occasioned by the heart-breaking contrast between his fervent hopes and the apparent issues of the war. Instead of the holy Commonwealth for which he had looked after that baptism of blood and fire, here was the old monarchy with a new name. The dearly-bought victory of prayers, and tears, and deadly strife was being turned to the glorification of one man. This man Harrison had loved and trusted with simple devotion, had stood by him in the strait between life and death when the Long Parliament was driven out, and had rejoiced in his appeal to the people of God. But the overshadowing personal predominance of Cromwell had given Harrison uneasy thoughts during the past year. Always living in a glow of devotion, he did not realise the prosaic problems of political detail on which national order and safety must depend. When therefore Cromwell calmly accepted the resignation of the assembly of saints, and set himself to bring up their arrears of work, Harrison was distressed. When the Protectorate was proclaimed he was dismayed, and determined to have no part in the shame of disloyalty to the Kingdom of God. In his unselfish anxiety he seems to have been attracted by the speculations of the Fifth-Monarchy men, and to have hoped that this dark cloud of personal ambition would soon be dispersed by some startling revelation of God's will. No offers, no friendship, no flatteries could bind such a man. " Those who had been to me as the apple of mine eye," he said on his trial as a regicide, " when they had turned aside, said to me, ' sit thou on my right hand; ' but I loathed it." And Cromwell saw that he loathed it; and then perhaps first realised the bitter cost of his lonely career, when he felt that Harrison distrusted him. But whatever dangers such a man's unworldly zeal might bring, no falsehood or treachery was to be feared from him. Cromwell therefore asked him whether he was prepared to own and obey the protectoral government. To this Harrison frankly answered " No ! " There was then no

A A 2

alternative but to deprive him of his commission, and soon afterwards he was requested to keep himself within his own county of Stafford.

The unopposed assumption of the Protectorate by Cromwell was a discouragement to the Royalists, who looked for their opportunity in the dissensions of the Commonwealth. In the month of February they made a feeble attempt to arrange a rising in several places at once. Part of the scheme was the assassination of the Protector as he went into the city to visit the Lord Mayor. But it came to nothing ; and though a few arrests were made, no one suffered any further penalty on account of it.

Prince Charles had been requested by the conspirators to be in readiness to come over, and it had even been proposed to bring him secretly into London. Charles, however, though never deficient in adventurous courage, found himself debarred from any bold stroke for what he considered his rights. Under evil advice he resorted to the pitiful expedient of offering bribes for his rival's assassination. " Whereas a certain mechanic fellow, by name Oliver Cromwell "—so the proclamation ran— " hath, by most wicked and accursed ways and means, against all laws both human and divine, most tyrannically and traitorously usurped the supreme power over our kingdoms . . . these are, in our name, to give freedom and liberty to any man whomsoever, within any of our three kingdoms, by pistol, sword, or poison, or by any other ways or means whatsoever, to destroy the life of the said Oliver Cromwell, wherein they will do an act acceptable to God and good men." Substantial motives were offered in the form of a pension, honours, and public employment—all secured on " the faith of a Christian king." This proclamation stimulated the ambition of Colonel John Gerard, a young man only twenty-two years of age, and belonging to a family with some pretensions. As his story was strangely linked with that of a foreigner condemned and executed for murder, and as both illustrate the imperturbable firmness of Oliver's administration, the two incidents naturally fell into one narrative.

Amongst the foreign powers at this time courting the English alliance not the least eager was Portugal, anxious for assistance against the decaying tyranny of Spain. The ambassador of that country was accompanied by his brother, Don Pantaleon Sa. On an evening in November 1653, Don Pantaleon was at Exeter Change, then a fashionable promenade frequented by lovers of elegant gossip. Colonel John Gerard was also present, and rudely jostled, or otherwise insulted the Portuguese nobleman. It is impossible to avoid a suspicion that the insult was suggested by the fervent young Royalist's contempt for a foreign embassy to rebels and traitors. The Portuguese, being worsted in the fight that followed, retreated for refuge to his brother's house. But the next evening he returned with a number of armed followers in the hope of finding Gerard. The intended victim however was not there ; but in the riot that ensued another man was killed by Don Pantaleon, either in mistake for him, or, as was alleged, in self-defence. The Portuguese rioters were then seized, and in the end, in spite of his brother's protests, Don Pantaleon was brought in guilty by a jury half composed of foreigners, and was sentenced to death.

But before that stern sentence could be carried out the intended victim had involved himself in a like condemnation. Early in the ensuing spring (1654), Gerard passed over into France, had an interview with Prince Rupert, was presented to Charles, and returned with a fully-prepared plan for an assassination and a rising, to be supported by the landing of foreign troops under Rupert. Gerard's most intimate associate in maturing the scheme was one Vowel, a schoolmaster in Islington ; but there were many others concerned in it. The conspirators arranged that a party of assassins should lie in wait for the Protector in a house on the road to Hampton Court, whither he was expected to go for his weekly rest on Saturday, May 20th. At the same time a party was to fall on the guard at Whitehall Mews, a number of troopers' horses in Islington fields were to be seized and mounted by Royalists, and the city was to be overawed pending the arrival of the invasion. On the fatal morning the conspirators were congratulating themselves on their successful secresy, and were counting confidently on the completion of their scheme. But the leaders, including Gerard and Vowel, were arrested within an hour or two of the appointed time. One of their accomplices, terrified by his position, confessed everything, and within a day or two the whole band were safe in gaol. Cromwell felt it was now time to prove that treason against his government was a dangerous adventure. In the end only two suffered death—Gerard and Vowel. Indeed only three, out of more than forty prisoners, were put on their trial. But to give that trial impressiveness, a special Ordinance was framed for constituting a high court of justice, consisting of four judges, the Recorder of London, seven aldermen, and twenty other members. Vowel was hanged, Gerard pleaded for death by the axe, and was beheaded on Tower Hill on the same day (July 10th) and on the same block as his intended murderer, Don Pantaleon Sa.

The execution of the latter was denounced by his brother, the ambassador, as a crime against the law of nations, an outrage on the sacred immunity of ambassadors. But in putting to death at once the contriver of his own death, and the intended murderer of the assassin, Cromwell gave not only to the nation, but to the whole world a conspicuous proof of the impartial and impregnable justice of his rule. At the same time the value set on his alliance was shown by the fact that the Portuguese ambassador, who left England on the day of his brother's death, signed before his departure a treaty conceding all the Protector's demands.

This complaisance of Portugal was in harmony with the extraordinary consideration shown by European powers at this time for the British Commonwealth. Civil dissension is generally followed by the indifference of foreign governments to a presumably weakened nation. But a single word of the Protector had more weight abroad than all the bluster and intrigues of Charles I. And this is the more remarkable, because the execution of that monarch sent a shudder through all the Courts of Europe. But with due subordination of sentiment to policy, all alike were now eager for Cromwell's favour. For this result the Protector was, of course, partly indebted to a fortunate balance of rivalries, that gave him a sort of casting vote in European councils. But it is also true that what made the casting vote obviously decisive was the vigour with which the resources of England were handled.

How the Dutch were humbled we have already seen. The attitude of Cromwell towards them was one of blundering patriotism, animated by a conviction that damage to the Netherlands was synonymous with benefit to England. There

was one condition alone which, in his view, would identify
their interests, and that was the incorporation of both in one
federal republic. That such a man should ever have entertained
so insane a project is a striking illustration of the backwardness
of political science in his day. No surer means could have been
invented for retarding political growth in England than a bond,
necessarily depriving the island of its happy immunity from
many conditions of continental national life. In this scheme,
at any rate, personal ambition can hardly have had place. For
the Protector could not have expected the same supremacy over
the united republics that he already possessed in the one. But
for many months, while the Dutch treaty was in progress,
Cromwell stuck to his purpose. He was attracted by the religious
sympathies of Holland, and by the additional guarantee to be
afforded by the union against a return of the Stuarts. But his
instinctive apprehension of the main immediate issue saved him
from fatal obstinacy. An honourable peace with the Dutch
would bring a great accession of strength both at home and
abroad; and he would not imperil this by his persistence. But
one of his aims, the ostracism of the Stuarts, he endeavoured
to obtain in another way. He insisted that King Charles's
grandson, the little William of Orange and all his descendants,
should be debarred not only from the office of Stadtholder,
which had been for a time abolished, but from any military
command in the republic. William was of course not a Stuart;
but Cromwell believed that the mother's influence would make
any real friendship between the two countries impossible unless
all her descendants were excluded from power. Little could he
have imagined that this child, after himself marrying a Stuart,
was to prove a more effectual destroyer of the dynasty than the
victor of Dunbar and Worcester. Under strong pressure the
States agreed to make this provision a secret article in the
treaty. But, needless to say, it was never carried out.

In April of this same year an advantageous treaty was also
concluded with Queen Christina of Sweden, the daughter of
Gustavus Adolphus. Bulstrode Whitelock had been persuaded,
or rather compelled to undertake the embassy to that princess
before the dissolution of the Little Parliament. Whitelock
himself generated the myth that his absence was necessary for
the accomplishment of Cromwell's ambition. But in truth the

man was too good a courtier ever to have given any trouble to a
rising power, and this easy complaisance was associated with
acquirements fitting him very well for the post. In the discharge
of his mission he won golden opinions from himself, as is amply
recorded in his memorials, and he also satisfied both the
Queen and the Protector.

Cromwell has been a good deal blamed, and with some
show of reason, for his policy toward France and Spain respectively. Looking upon the latter country as still the main
champion of the Papacy, he had a notion of reorganising a
Protestant League, in which England should take the place
that had belonged to Gustavus Adolphus. It is said that
he failed to appreciate the change caused in Europe by the
thirty years' war. The argument for this is that he acted
as though Spain were a formidable power, while he disregarded
the growing pretensions of France. But another view may be
taken of his policy. The very fact of Spanish decay suggested the possibility of securing the reversion of her American
trade and colonial dominion. And though France was
papistical, she was so in a worldly sort of way that has
not in the long run interfered with a ready welcome to the
progressive culture of each age. Not only neighbourhood
but a certain outlook towards the future makes the French,
notwithstanding differences of temperament, the natural allies
of the English race. The stupid and superficial prejudice
that plunged us into the anti-revolutionary war caused
probably the most ruinous blunder ever perpetrated in our
history. No Peninsula glories, no Waterloo laurels, no naval
traditions can compensate us for the waste of blood and treasure
that nearly bled the nation to death, and left behind the germs
of horrible social disease. The unnatural, fratricidal war of one
progressive race against another perverted the history of both,
and entailed at least a century of prolonged bondage on less
favoured nations. If we cannot credit the Protector with prophetic foresight enough to forecast the issues of modern European politics, at least we may allow that his instinctive preference
for the French alliance was true to the destinies of the two
countries.

But that preference was not shown by any subserviency,
nor even by solicitation. It was the inclination of a potentate

courted and feared by France and Spain alike. At the beginning of December 1653, Cardinal Mazarin, who administered the government of France, sent over the Duke of Bordeaux as an envoy to the Commonwealth. Causes of irritation then existed in the irregular hostilities of Blake, resulting in the capture of Dunkirk by the Spaniards. On the establishment of the Protectorate Bordeaux was made an ambassador; and an additional confidential agent, named De Baas, was sent over to take a part in intrigues unfitted for the dignity of an ambassador. When the Vowel conspiracy was concocted, Mazarin was persuaded to believe in its probable success. He knew Prince Charles and his courtiers well enough to be assured of the demoralisation and weakness in store for England if that prince should obtain the throne. With the usual morality of diplomacy he was of course anxious to secure that result; and he therefore ordered De Baas to favour and help the conspirators, if their schemes should appear feasible. But the treachery of this emissary did not escape the attention of Cromwell, who dealt with his conduct in a characteristic manner. He brought De Baas face to face with one of the conspirators, and having shamed him with the exposure of his intrigues, dismissed him. Mazarin became convinced that he must reckon on the permanence of the Protectorate, and henceforward treated the unfortunate Charles as little more than a distinguished nuisance. The farther development of Cromwell's relations to France and Spain belongs to a later period of his government.

While thus amply occupied in the suppression of conspiracy at home, and the maintenance of national influence abroad, the Protector made a daring attempt to bring up the arrears of legislation. By Section XXX. of the " Instrument of Government " he could, with the assent of his Council, issue Ordinances to have the force of law till Parliament should otherwise order. By virtue of this power he was able to keep up the revenue, and to make all needful arrangements for adapting the forms of administration to the change of government.

One of his first cares was to purify the fountains of justice. He filled up the roll of judges, and restored the regular assizes, which ever since the beginning of the war had been more or less intermittent. Amongst his legal appointments and promotions at this time some were remarkable; notably the elevation to the bench of Matthew Hale, a man whose character and legal knowledge were his sole recommendations, except perhaps this farther, that in the discharge of his duties he was capable of withstanding the Protector.

Before the new Parliament met on the 3rd of September, Cromwell promulgated nearly a hundred Ordinances, many of them of considerable importance, and of elaborate detail. Most of them were so obviously beneficial that they were readily confirmed by Parliament, notwithstanding the indisposition of that body to take anything on trust. As all these measures originated in Cromwell's determination to make up by the practical energy of the "single person" for the impracticability of Parliaments, and as they bear conspicuously the stamp of his individuality, it will be well to refer to the chief of them, and even to describe one or two.*

One of his earliest measures was the absolute repeal of an Act, passed by the Long Parliament in 1650, for subscribing the engagement to be true to the Commonwealth. The Ordinance added that if people had been prejudiced by not taking it, they were now to be admitted to full privileges. The purpose of this Ordinance has been disputed, and by some it has been supposed that it was intended to prepare for the restoration of the monarchy in the person of Oliver himself. Opinions on this point must be largely affected by the view we may take as to Cromwell's designs on the crown. It is not usually the fashion of eager, personal ambition of that kind to loosen the stringency of obligation to "the powers that be." It rather prefers to release men from one bond only when the other is ready. We know from other actions of the Protector that at this time he was indulging a vain hope of "healing and settling." And this desire, together with a repugnance to unnecessary oaths, is a sufficient explanation of his motives.

His Ordinance for the approval and correction of public preachers was specially characteristic. As we have already seen, he had no sympathy whatever with the objections made by any school of sectarians to the unsymmetrical and chaotic condition of the Church's outward organisation. But he strongly disapproved the laxity permitting men of loose manners, or destitute of pulpit gifts, to poison or cumber the

* They are given in Scobell's Volume, from which what follows is taken.

heritage of the Lord. His remedy therefore was aimed straight at this defect, while as to tithes, patronage, church government, or want of government, he left everything just as it was. A number of Commissioners, indiscriminately taken from Presbyterians, Independents, and Baptists, were appointed, whose duty it should be for the future to inquire into the fitness of all preachers nominated or presented to benefices. There was no direction to scrutinise the creed of any candidate before them; and all penalties for not reading the articles of belief were abolished. All that was to be decided was, whether the Commissioners considered the candidate " to be a person for the grace of God in him, his holy and unblameable conversation, as also for his knowledge and utterance, able and fit to preach the Gospel." Patrons were compelled to present within six months after a vacancy had arisen; and in the meantime the income was to go to the Commissioners, for the purpose of providing for the services. To meet the case of unfit preachers already in possession, other Commissioners were appointed in each county to hear and decide on complaints. Laymen were eligible both for the general and the county commissions. Indeed the latter consisted exclusively of laymen, except when questions of ignorance or inefficiency arose. Many eminent men undertook this service, as, for instance, Lords Fairfax, Say, and Wharton, Robert Blake, and Ashley Cooper. But, bearing in mind Oliver's letters to his eldest son, it must be owned that the appointment of Richard to such an office is surprising. To the satisfactory effects of this Ordinance Baxter has borne ample testimony.

Another important measure provided for the maintenance of roads. Two substantial householders were to be chosen yearly in each parish as waywardens. Within ten days after election, they were to inspect all roads, bridges, watercourses, and nuisances. Within six days after this inspection they were to levy, on personalty as well as on land and houses, whatever rate appeared to be needed, provided it did not exceed one shilling in the pound. All neglect of duty was guarded against by suitable penalties; and the whole scheme is remarkable for the practical insight shown, and the carefulness with which the details are worked out.

Perhaps the most extraordinary effort of Oliver and his

Council as legislators was the attempt made, notwithstanding the disastrous failure of the Little Parliament, to reform the Court of Chancery by an elaborate Ordinance of sixty-seven clauses. Proceedings, forms, clerkships, fees, all were regulated with punctilious nicety; but the details in this case are interesting only to the professional mind.

Scotland was the subject of several Ordinances. Pardon and grace were proclaimed, with some inevitable exceptions; and a reasonable provision was made for the wives and children of ruined delinquents. The northern kingdom was formally united with England in one Commonwealth; all customs or duties on commerce between the two were abolished, and the St. Andrew's Cross was incorporated in the national flag. Old feudal tenures of service and vassalage then surviving in Scotland were also done away with. An interesting effort to promote local self-government was made by the erection of Courts Baron in Scottish manors, with limited powers to make bye-laws and levy fines. Nor was Ireland forgotten. "Taking into consideration how much the honour and safety of this Commonwealth is concerned in the speedy settling of Ireland," the Protector ordered that all barriers against freedom of intercourse should be removed, and that, in form at least, complete political equality should be established between the two islands. As, however, the native race was in effect proscribed and outlawed, the equality hardly embraced more than the English settlers.

The drainage of the Fens once more demanded Cromwell's interference. The Adventurers had a difficulty in collecting rates, and in protecting their works against damage. But a stringent Ordinance, passed in May, put into their hands very drastic means for enforcing their claims. A curious clause tacked on to the end of this Ordinance gives a right to foreigners "in league and amity with the Commonwealth, being Protestants," to hold any land they might purchase out of the 95,000 acres allotted to the Adventurers. This looks as if it were intended for the benefit of the Dutch.

In social matters, cock-fighting, horse-racing, drunkenness, and profanity, of which the two latter were stated to be very prevalent in the east of London, all were rebuked and threatened by Ordinances. Duelling also was denounced. Both challenger and acceptor were to be punished with six months' imprisonment. The death of either party to a duel constituted the other a murderer; and persons challenged, if they did not within twenty-four hours discover the fact to the authorities, were liable to the penalty for acceptance. Soldiers who had fought for the Commonwealth were protected against the exclusiveness of trade-guilds, and authorised to set up business in any town where they might find an opening. Financial reforms of no small importance were inaugurated, by bringing all receipts into one Treasury at Westminster; by introducing English, instead of Latin, as the business language of the Exchequer; and by repression of the extortion exercised by clerks. The Act for the relief of creditors and debtors was found to need modification. Amongst other evils, property lawfully alienated by debtors had been wrongfully seized. A new Ordinance allowed debtors to go out of prison, on sufficient security, for the purpose of looking after their own affairs.

The last Ordinance passed at this time by the Protector and his Council was one for appointing visitors to the Universities. It was dated the day before the meeting of Parliament; but it was only the latest of many proofs given by Cromwell of his sincere anxiety for the promotion of learning. Since his appointment, in 1651, to the Chancellorship of Oxford University, he had lost no opportunity of directing towards salutary reforms the puritanic zeal which sometimes threatened destruction. He took an active interest in the selection of the best men to positions of influence; and his most remarkable appointment—that of John Owen to be Dean of Christchurch, and afterwards Vice-Chancellor—occasioned a signal revival of learning. Owen speaks emphatically of the wise and discriminative conservatism of the University's foremost defender, who "put to flight the lawless assailants of its honours and privileges."[*] Even Clarendon testifies that, when Charles the Second came to the throne, he found that University "abounding in excellent learning." And Wood, who was as little inclined to favour the Commonwealth, speaking of Greek discourses held at that time, adds: "Since the King's restoration we have had no such matters, which shows in some part that education and discipline

[*] " Oratio secunda," quoted by Godwin.

were more severe then than after, when scholars were given
more to liberty and frivolous studies."

Of one hundred and sixty-four sittings of the Council held
during 1654, the Protector was personally present at only
twenty-eight—a fact suggesting that he left a good deal to his
advisers. But his spirit animated them. He suggested their
efforts, and modified their conclusions. No Ordinance was passed
without his approval of every detail. And this amazing activity,
manifested in practical legislation suited to the felt needs of the
time, went far to override theoretic objections to the anomalous
authority by which the Ordinances were enacted.

CHAPTER XXV.

Of the Protector's private life—if indeed he had any—during these busy months, less record remains than of earlier periods, because his own letters almost fail us. In April 1654 he removed his residence from the Cockpit to Whitehall Palace. He also assumed more state and ceremony than he had been wont to do, or perhaps allowed it to be thrust upon him. Life-guards were unfortunately necessary for his safety, and indeed had attended upon him as Lord General. Ushers, flunkeys, and grand coaches were not so essential, but were supposed to impress the mob. Something in the nature of a Court naturally grew up around him; but, according to the testimony even of hostile critics, it was untainted by vice, or even looseness of manners.

Queen Christina of Sweden professed great admiration for his achievements, and the interchange of complimentary messages and presents between her and the Protector were marked by a certain affectation of gallantry. But when Whitelocke, on returning home, told Cromwell of the Queen's desire to visit him, he would not hear of it, declaring he could not tolerate the ill example she would set by her course of life. Count Hannibal Sesthed, connected by marriage with the King of Denmark, and previously Viceroy of Norway, came to England, and through Whitelocke was introduced to the Protector. Cromwell showed him much hospitality, and was pleased with the brilliancy of his conversation; but, on discovering that he was a man of vicious life, he refused peremptorily to receive him again.

Lieutenant-Colonel Joyce, more famous as a cornet, had in his latter days become a zealous Anabaptist, and like many others of his sect had grown disaffected to the Government. But surmise and rumour, never satisfied with obvious causes, had conceived far-fetched reasons for the Protector's disfavour. One insinuation, supported by Joyce himself, was that Richard Cromwell wanted a certain estate, called Fawley Park, in Hampshire, upon which Joyce also, having prospered in the world, had set his heart. The only private letter of Cromwell belonging to the first half of 1654 is addressed to Richard's father-in-law, Mayor, and refers to some projected purchase, apparently in Hampshire. Whatever it was, Cromwell backs out of the transaction. "Otherwise," he says, "the land in Essex, with some money in my hand, should have gone towards it." It is interesting to note the care needed to scheme private financial arrangements in the case of a man who publicly disposes, at his pleasure, of the revenues of three nations. "But," he adds, "I am so unwilling to be a seeker after the world—having had so much favour from the Lord in giving me so much without seeking—and so unwilling that men should think me so, which they will, though you only should appear in it (for they will, by one means or other, know it), that I dare not meddle nor proceed therein." How suggestive is that word "*I dare not*" from a man who had dared so much, and who, even now, depended for very life upon his power of daring justly! That this letter referred to the Fawley estate is only a probable conjecture.* But that, if Cromwell had dared to do such shabby deeds as Joyce insinuates, he could never have swayed Great Britain and Ireland by his moral vigour, is certain.

On June 1st, 1654, in accordance with the "Instrument of Government," writs were issued for the election of the new Parliament. The franchise was narrow, as we have seen, but otherwise the elections were free; and on this occasion no illegitimate influence was brought to bear on the constituencies. There was no reason to fear the return of a majority favourable to a restoration of the Stuarts. There was much more likelihood of a disposition to go behind the "Instrument of Government," and to insist on treating the existing administration as a temporary expedient. It naturally occurs to us to think that Cromwell ought to have been prepared for this, and to have submitted to it as an inevitable consequence of the revolution. But as he did not live in the nineteenth century, his notion of the functions of a Parliament was perhaps not so clear as ours. For him a Parliament was by no means the only way of ascertaining the national feeling, nor was the national feeling the only thing

* Made by Carlyle.

to be considered.   He believed God had declared His will, and the nation would be sinful to disregard it.   He regarded the army as the very soul of the nation, and the ready, indeed cordial, acquiescence of corporations and other representative bodies seemed to show that the better part of the people agreed with him.   On the other hand, the desire for measures rather than systems was little likely to be represented in proportion to its strength in the country.   It is not usually a very articulate feeling, and least of all likely to be found in candidates for a new Parliament at such a crisis.   Travelling up to London and residence there was a serious business for country gentlemen in those times.   Only men of social ambition, or of eager, enterprising natures were likely to make the sacrifice.   And in such a time these would be filled with ideals and theories.   Nevertheless the Protector and his Council trusted to the " Instrument," especially as the returns to the writs bore an express acknowledgment that the representatives sent were " not empowered to alter the government by a single person and a Parliament."

This acknowledgment did not deter the most distinguished men from seeking or accepting seats.   Bradshaw, who had so stoutly denied the dissolution of the Long Parliament, nevertheless came to this one.   Sir Arthur Haselrig was also returned, with a formidable knot of republicans, though Henry Marten and Algernon Sidney were wanting.   The younger Vane was not there, but his aged father was.   Fairfax and Blake were members, also Dr. John Owen, Vice-Chancellor of Oxford.   Matthew Hale by his membership proved that his alleged scruples against serving under a usurper did not interfere with his readiness to make new laws, as well as administer old ones, at the summons of the Protector.   Titled nobles were not wanting, as the Earls of Salisbury and Stamford.   All the Council, with the exception of Lord Lisle, had seats.   Fleetwood attended, leaving Ludlow behind him, a very half-hearted lieutenant.   Cromwell's two sons, Richard and Henry, were also members.

September 3rd this year fell on Sunday, and probably some difference of feeling between Oliver and the Presbyterians on the Sabbath question is indicated by his naming that day in the writ of summons. The proceedings commenced appropriately by the attendance of all members at St. Margaret's Church.

B B

After service they were received by the Protector in the Painted
Chamber, and he addressed them briefly in a speech, unreported
and unrecorded. The members then went into the House, and
immediately adjourned till the next morning. If we try to conceive what would at the present day be said of any Government
summoning Parliament on a Sunday only to seize on an
auspicious anniversary, the effort will suggest that there is an
unsuspected amount of difference between the tone of religious
feeling in those days and in our own. The same thing is suggested also by the fact that the Sunday's sermon was not
thought enough, but was supplemented on the following day by
another in Westminster Abbey, preached by Dr. Thomas Goodwin.
To the Abbey the Protector came in state, surrounded by Life-
Guards, gentlemen and officers before him bare-headed, pages
and lacqueys attendant. The son-in-law, Claypole, led a capa-
risoned horse after the carriage. Lambert and Henry Cromwell
sat in the coach uncovered. The Council followed at the heels
of the war-horse, and guards brought up the rear. The led horse
was a trifle in itself, but implied much. The people who demanded
ceremony of this kind would obviously not be long without a
monarchy. Sermon being ended, the great coach and paraphernalia
came into requisition again. The Protector was transported with
due dignity to the Painted Chamber, where he sat with his hat on
in a chair of state on a raised daïs. The members were accommodated with benches rising in steps round the room. All
uncovered in the presence of the Protector. There was the
usual bustle and shuffling, the usual breathless haste of late
comers outside the door, and subdued tiptoe steps as they passed
within. Then the silence of sudden attention fell on all. His
Highness had risen, and "putting off his hat" he made what
Whitelock calls "a large and subtle speech."

His address was somewhat subdued in tone as compared with
his opening speech to the Little Parliament. It was pervaded
by indications that the speaker was hoping against hope, yet
fixedly resolved to hold fast his faith to the end. He forbore to
reckon up the signs of Divine Providence, giving as his reason
the Psalmist's words, "They cannot be reckoned up in order unto
Thee. If I would declare and speak of them they are more than
can be numbered." He alluded also to Dr. Goodwin's sermon as
making such an effort needless. For the discourse had

treated of the delivery of the children of Israel—" the only parallel," said the Protector " of God's dealing with us that I know of in the world — Israel's bringing out of Egypt through a wilderness by many signs and wonders towards a place of rest—I say *towards* it." There is a mournful cadence in that reiteration, and yet a tone of courage too. It was not a time for speculations. Let the members mind practical business and hope for more leisure to theorise hereafter. " The remembering of transactions too particularly," he said, " perhaps, instead of healing—at least in the minds of many of you— might set the wound fresh a-bleeding. I must profess this unto you, whatever thoughts pass upon me : that if this day, if this meeting, prove *not* healing—what shall we do ! " The sentence seems to expire in a deep sigh. He knew very well the " thoughts" that would " pass upon him ; " the inevitable sneers at his prudent abstinence from " remembering of transactions too particularly." But let his critics stop the bleeding of a nation first ; and then they might sneer on.

Leaving that topic therefore he went on to speak of the condition in which the Convention had left national affairs, both civil and spiritual. A notable symptom of the instinctive conservatism of his temperament appears in his reference to the sentiment of equality.

" What was the face that was upon our affairs as to the interest of the nation ? —as to the authority in the nation ?—to the magistracy, to the ranks and orders of men, whereby England hath been known for hundreds of years ? A nobleman, a gentleman, a yeoman—that is a good interest of the nation, and a great one. The magistracy * of the nation, was it not almost trampled under foot, under despite and contempt, by men of levelling principles ? I beseech you—for the orders of men and ranks of men, did not that levelling principle tend to the reducing of all to an equality ? Did it think to do so ? † Or did it practise towards that for property and interest ? What was the purport of it but to make the tenant as liberal a fortune as the landlord ? "; Which, I think, if obtained, would not have lasted long ! The men of that principle, after they had served their own turns, would then have cried up property fast enough ! "

* Carlyle here interpolates "*natural*" magistracy. No doubt the epithet brings out the meaning of the speaker, who was too full of his practical aim to guard himself against the obvious retort that if the magistracy had been overthrown it was his own fault. But some magistracies are endurable and salutary, others not.

† *I.e.*, was this its animating principle ?

B B 2

Such words would appear at first sight to condemn some modern efforts at land-law reform. But there is an obvious distinction between such efforts and the designs of extreme Levellers. For the reforms now sought are intended for the protection of property, not for its destruction. They would merely secure to the farmer what surely ought to be treated as his own—the results of his own labour and expenditure in the improvement of his farm. On the other hand, a violent redistribution of property would only be a precedent for continually recurring catastrophes, in which the inevitable accumulations of the prudent and industrious would be divided again and again amongst the idle and useless. But the passage does indisputably suggest, nay prove, that the Protector had not a trace of genuine republicanism in his nature, and little anticipation of the modern sentiment of equality.

Proceeding next to speak of the religious condition of the nation, he condemned strongly the tendency to license, always treading on the heels of liberty. What he said about the Fifth-Monarchy men we have already quoted in illustration of his own action. But he was careful to add that if their doctrines " were but notions " they were best let alone. " Notions will hurt none but those that have them." On the other hand, " where every stone is turned to bring in confusion . . . this will be worthy of the magistrate's consideration." In addition to such causes of distraction, the revenue was insufficient, trade was depressed, and foreign affairs were threatening. The next words, homely and blunt as they are, give a singularly direct glimpse into the very heart of the man.

" Things being so—and I am persuaded it is not hard to convince every person here they *were* so—what a heap of confusions were upon these poor nations ! And either things must have been left to sink into the miseries these premises would suppose, or else a remedy must be applied.

" A remedy hath been applied. That hath been this government—a thing I shall say little unto. The thing is open and visible, to be seen and read by all men ; and, therefore, let it speak for itself. Only let me say this—because I can speak it with comfort and confidence before a Greater than you all—that in the intention of it, as to the approving of our hearts to God—let men judge as they please—it was calculated * for the interest of the people; for the interest of the people alone, and for their good, without respect to any other interest. And if that be not true—I shall be bold to say again let it speak for itself."

* *I.e.*, intended for.

This is scarcely the style in which flattering usurpers have usually gilded their acts of arrogant selfishness with ornaments of speech. Imperial Majesties use more polished periods, never roughened by the struggle of a soul with a great purpose. But in these rugged utterances of Oliver we see his spirit wrestling with a haunting dread, and pressing toward a blessed hope—the dread of worldly ambition, and the hope of a regenerated England.

As soon as the members had been dismissed to choose their Speaker, the Protector descended to his barge, and was quietly rowed back to Whitehall. He must have been anxious to hear how they were going on, and though there were none of the facilities of modern days, we may presume that he was kept constantly informed by his friends in the House. Their first proceeding could give him no uneasiness. They elected as their Speaker William Lenthall, who had for so many years held the same position in the Long Parliament. But he was not presented for approval to the Protector, as it had been customary to do to the monarch. On the next day Sir Arthur Haselrig, apparently on account of his strong republicanism, was appointed chairman of the Committee of Privileges. But a more ominous movement was the adoption of a resolution that the House should on the following morning take the matter of the government into consideration. It was not however until September 7th that the issue was raised, "whether the House did approve that the government should be in one single person and a Parliament." Haselrig and Bradshaw were strongly against the assumption that this should be taken as a matter of course; and after three days' debate they succeeded in carrying by a majority of five—141 to 136—a motion referring the question to a committee of the whole House.

Cromwell regarded this decision as inconsistent with the express provisions of the return to his writ, and as fatal to the practical legislation demanded by the needs of the time. No legal sanctions could very well be alleged, either for his view or for that of the majority of the House. The country was in process of revolution, and the real question was how the revolution might best be directed to issues satisfying the patriotic purposes of the war. On this point Cromwell had clear and definite convictions. Taking his soldiers as representative of the best elements in the population, he knew that they had been fighting for religious liberty, and for an infusion of natural justice into the operations of law. Such desires might speedily be satisfied if Parliament would accept the rough outlines of a constitution drawn out in the Instrument of Government. But theoretic discussions threatened to delay a settlement until conspiracy might make it impossible. On the other hand, the Republicans had no such definite plans. Their abstract ideas were noble enough, but for the practical embodiment of them they had no workable proposals.

They ought to have known their Protector well enough by this time to have anticipated some vigorous protest; but apparently they were scarcely prepared for its nature. On Tuesday morning, September 12th, the ninth day after their first meeting, they found the approaches of their House occupied by soldiers, the doors locked, and no admittance for them anywhere but to the Painted Chamber, whither they were directed. Such an act of violence might well astonish them. No king that ever reigned had dared thus to handle the representatives of the people. But in truth, the "single person" now in the place of kings was more representative than the representatives themselves. The difference of the position was seen in the fact that, whereas Charles I. had always to fear the interposition of London City for the Commons, Cromwell with confidence sent word to the Lord Mayor to be on his guard against any disturbance of the peace.

The members being assembled in the Painted Chamber, the Protector addressed them in, perhaps, the most vigorous speech he ever made. He did not so far transgress Parliamentary traditions as to take distinct notice of their proceedings, but the whole object of his expostulation was to expose the unreasonableness and danger of the debates on which they had entered. His argument was that his own assumption of authority had been no ambitious usurpation, but had been occasioned by a moral necessity, fairly interpretable as a divine call. Carrying this argument farther, he insisted that his government had been hailed with general signs of divine and human approval. "I do not know," he proudly said, "why I may not balance this Providence, in the sight of God, with any hereditary interest, as a thing less subject to those cracks and flaws, which that is commonly subject unto." His conclusion was that the House would be very ill-advised to bring into doubt the continuance of his government; that in fact they should not, and could not do it if they tried; and that, to save farther mischief, they would have to recognise afresh the conditions already imposed upon them by the returns to the writs for their election.

Still, he did not insist on all details of the Instrument. Some things were of secondary importance, others were fundamental. Amongst the latter were the conjunction of a single person with successive Parliaments, liberty of conscience, and the conjoint power of Protector and Parliament over the militia. Other things were circumstantial, and might be modified by agreement. But the fundamental points he would only surrender with his life.

"I would it had not been needful for me to call you hither to expostulate these things with you, and in such a manner as this. But necessity hath no law. Feigned necessities, imaginary necessities, are the greatest cozenage that men can put on the providence of God, and make pretences to break known rules by. But it is as legal,* as carnal, and as stupid to think that there are *no* necessities which are manifest, because necessities may be abused or feigned. And, truly, that were my case † if I should so think; and I hope none of you so think. I have to say, the wilful throwing away of this government, such as it is, so owned by God, so approved by men, so witnessed to (in the fundamentals of it), as was mentioned before, and in reference to the good of these nations and posterity, I can sooner be willing to be rolled into my grave and buried with infamy, than I can give my consent unto!"

The very chaos of this last sentence, like a great wave shattered in the act of sweeping down resistance, suggests the impassioned strength of purpose that must have been evident enough to hearers in the tone and bearing of the man. In conclusion, he cast scorn on the pretence that the members were quarrelling and wrangling for the liberty of England.

"Wherein, I pray you, for the liberty of England? I appeal to the Lord that the desires and endeavours we have had——nay, the things will speak for themselves. The liberty of England, the liberty of the people, the avoiding of tyrannous impositions either upon men as men, or Christians as Christians, is made so safe by this Act of settlement that it will speak for itself."

* *I.e.*, equally contrary to the freedom of the Spirit and the life of grace.
† Viz., stupidity, &c.

The conclusion of the whole matter was that every member of the House would be required, before taking his seat again, to sign an engagement promising faithfulness to the Lord Protector and the Commonwealth, and also recognising that the return to the writ bound him neither to propose nor to consent to any alteration of the Government, as it had been settled in a single person and a Parliament. It was a poor expedient at the best; and, like all such promises, a mere formality. But it had the advantage of proclaiming to the nation that its strongest man was not going to be displaced.

About a hundred and twenty signed in the course of the day, and, in a little time, three-fourths of the House had signed. But of course a Parliament that could be treated in this way had but little weight. If it had been fighting against preroga- tive, the case would have been different. But it was flouted by a man professing to be more representative than itself, and his profession had much reason in it. Such a Parliament was not likely to do much; and, as a matter of fact, it did nothing. Notwithstanding the engagement, almost the sole subject of debate was the Instrument of Government; and the debates had no issue. The power of the Protector and his Council to issue Ordinances ceased with the opening of Parliament; but his legislative activity had gone far towards meeting the prac- tical needs of the time; and the barrenness of the session was not felt as much as it otherwise would have been.

The Protector now gave his attention to the arrangement of two important naval expeditions. Tuscany, Algiers, Tunis, and Tripoli had all given offence to the British Commonwealth, either by favouring Royalist persons, as in the case of Tuscany; or by robbing and enslaving British mariners and merchants, as in the case of the Mahommedan States. To exact reparation for these injuries, Blake was despatched with thirty ships in October, 1654. The other expedition was one of more doubtful morality. A fleet was prepared under the command of Admiral Penn, the father of the great Quaker, and General Venables was associated with him to command the land forces embarked. The purpose of this armament was kept a profound secret, and the com- manders had sealed orders given them, which they were not to open until they reached a certain latitude. They then found that they had a commission to kill, burn, and destroy in the Spanish main; to plunder the treasure-ships, and conquer the island colonies of the hated nation. Proceedings like these have extorted the admiration of Cromwell's enemies. His most loyal admirers however find in them evidence that in regard to foreign affairs he was much less in advance of his times than in domestic policy.

In the end of September the Royalists had a tantalising disappointment, and the Ironside party an uncomfortable shock. On the 29th of that month, the Protector, accompanied by Secretary Thurloe and a few other gentlemen, held a picnic in Hyde Park. Six fine horses had been sent by Count Oldenburg as a present to his Highness; and after dinner his Highness took it into his head to drive these horses. Putting Thurloe inside the coach, he himself mounted the box. In his eagerness he excited the team so that they got beyond control. A postilion riding one of the foremost pair was thrown. The Protector himself was dragged off the box, and in his fall got his foot entangled, so that he was drawn along the ground for some yards. A pistol exploded in his pocket, adding to the alarm. Happily his foot was soon released; the coach passed on without hurting him; and he then rose from the ground only bruised and shaken. The unfailing panacea of these times, blood-letting, was prescribed; and after a week or two his Highness was himself again. The incident of the pistol was not needed to prove that Cromwell knew his life to be unsafe. But it was probably a warning to intending assassins that the mischief might not be all on one side.

The venerable mother of the Protector was still living, in her ninety-fifth year. The Huntingdon days, that seemed so far off to him, were doubtless very near and very precious to her old memory. Her declining days had but one object of thought, her son; and but one anxiety, his danger. She must needs see him at least once every day; and any chance gun-fire made her start and exclaim, " My son is shot ! " Poor mother ! she shared in a sacred experience : " *Yea, a sword shall pierce through thine own soul also.*" But her time of rest was now come. On Thursday, November 16th, the feeble current was ebbing out; and, as the pride of her eyes bent over her, she whispered her last blessing:—"The Lord cause

His face to shine upon you, and comfort you in all your adversities, and enable you to do great things for the glory of your Most High God, and to be a relief to His people. My dear son, I leave my heart with thee. Good-night!" When we bear in mind that she had buried a husband and a child years before Oliver was born, and that she must have remembered well the Spanish Armada, we may feel that few individual lives have ever embraced such a range of national events and individual experiences as hers.

The Parliamentary debates meantime often threatened fresh confusions. While no attempt was made to dispute the conjunction of the single person and a Parliament, other " fundamentals" were unmistakably threatened. Among the points on which the "Instrument" gave the Protector a final veto was religious liberty. But in December the House voted that this veto should not affect any bill passed to compel attendance on Divine worship, provided that no man was forced to attend any particular church. To this course the members were probably incited by the rapid growth of eccentric, and as the majority thought blasphemous, opinions. John Biddle, a schoolmaster, had published several works advocating heterodox, though certainly not rational, ideas. The Council ordered these books to be suppressed; and Dr. Owen was commissioned to answer them. But the Parliament was not satisfied, and committed Biddle to prison. A fanatic, styling himself Theror John, or Theauro John, burned the Bible in public, and laid about him with a sword at the door of Parliament; whereupon a committee received solemn instructions to inquire into his tenets, in order that they might be the better described in a Bill against all damnable heresies.

But the Bill was not destined to see the light. By January 17th 1655 the Act for declaring and settling the Government was ready to be engrossed; and it was resolved that unless the Protector and the Parliament agreed on every article, the measure should not pass at all. Here was fresh matter for discord and trouble. Meantime there were no money Bills passed, though the House had fixed the total cost of army, navy, and garrisons at the enormous sum of £1,100,000. The Protector had good reason to think that he had got on much better by himself, and had done more for the practical benefit of the people. The "Instrument" compelled him to allow them a session of at least five months; and he was anxiously waiting for the end of that time, which would expire on February 3rd, when it occurred to him, or some one suggested, that months as reckoned for soldiers' pay had only twenty-eight days. If Parliamentary months were reckoned in the same way, the time would be up on Monday, January 22nd 1655. It was an unworthy quibble; and Cromwell must have felt rather a contempt for the House than a fear of it before he could condescend to so undignified a trick.

Accordingly, on that morning the members were once more summoned to the Painted Chamber, where the Protector addressed them in a tone of grave disappointment, and even of indignant rebuke. The tenor of his argument—insistance on the need for practical legislation—was much the same as in his previous speeches, and need not here be detailed. But he added now, that while the House had been constitution-mongering the enemies of the Commonwealth, both Royalists and Levellers, had been endeavouring to unite their incongruous forces, and had seriously threatened a fresh outbreak of war. He was specially severe upon their pedantic meddlesomeness in regard to the rights of private conscience :—

"Is there not yet upon the spirits of men a strange itch? Nothing will satisfy them unless they can press their finger upon their brethren's consciences to prick them there! To do this was no part of the contest we had with the common adversary. . . . Those that were sound in the faith, how proper was it for them to labour for liberty, that men might not be trampled upon for their consciences! Had not they laboured but lately under the weight of persecution? And was it fit for them to sit heavy on others? Is it ingenuous to ask liberty and not to give it? What greater hypocrisy than for those who were oppressed by the bishops to become the greatest oppressors themselves, so soon as the yoke was removed?"

For this, and for other fundamental conditions of liberty and order the Instrument of Government had amply provided; nor was there anything in it to exclude amendments proved by experience to be necessary. The appointment of the chief magistrate by election was urged as a sufficient guarantee against tyranny; and the speaker took the opportunity of protesting emphatically against any proposal to make his office hereditary. "For as it is in the Ecclesiastes : 'who knoweth whether he may beget a fool or a wise man?' " In conclusion, he called heaven and earth to witness that he was now left under an imperative and inevitable necessity of doing the best he could for the country on his own responsibility ; and so he declared this Parliament dissolved.

CHAPTER XXVI.

BENEVOLENT DESPOTISM.

In his speech dissolving Parliament the Protector broadly hinted at the existence of a new danger in a secret alliance between Royalists and Republicans. The correctness of his information was very soon confirmed. Major Wildman, elected member for Scarborough in the late House, had persistently refused to follow the example of the majority in submitting to the test declaration imposed by the Protector. He retired indignantly to the west of England, where his conduct was diligently observed by the local authorities. On the 10th or 11th of February (1655) his arrest was deemed necessary, and was quietly accomplished. To do him justice, he appears not to have taken kindly to the underhand ways of a conspirator; for the officers and soldiers who siezed him found him seated in his apartment, with the door open, and lounging with his elbow on the table, while he composedly dictated to an assistant a revolutionary " Declaration of the People of England." With the motive principles of this declaration no fault can be found, except that they were applied in a manner unjust to the Protector, who held exactly the same principles, and only took a more effectual method of carrying them out. But the singular perversions to which an impracticable temper is liable are well illustrated by the odd turn given in the declaration to Oliver's depreciation of the arbitrary powers thrust upon him after the resignation of the Little Parliament :—

"He hath published to the world that he hath dissolved all civil government, and that he had in himself an absolute, unlimited, arbitrary power, without check or control, until he put some limits on himself, if he may be believed, in his paper of government."

The reference was to Cromwell's reiterated assertion that the " Instrument " had been his only available escape from government by martial law. It is, therefore, superficially justified by

the Protector's language. But, whereas Cromwell had urged
the fact as a reason for making the " Instrument " a transitional
step to more constitutional rule, Wildman seized upon his
acknowledgment as a sufficient reason for plunging the country
into civil war once more.

For some days previous to this arrest the Protector had himself been engaged in the examination of Royalist prisoners
charged with stirring up disorder in various parts of the country.*
On the 13th of February he sent for the Lord Mayor and a
number of city magnates, to secure their co-operation in guarding against any sudden surprise of the capital. To satisfy them
of the reality of the danger, he showed them an intercepted
letter, signed "Charles Rex," and inciting faithful subjects to
fresh bloodshed. He put before them the records of the exami-
nations made in his presence ; and he concluded by asking them
to raise additional forces, under the command of Major-General
Skippon. Six days afterwards, on the 19th, a number of city men
waited upon the Protector as a deputation from their municipal
brethren to assure him of support in preserving public order. About
the same time a proclamation was issued prohibiting all meetings
for horseracing, cock-fighting, or other popular amusements such
as might be made an excuse for political gatherings.† With the
sporting inclinations of the English character, Cromwell had,
unfortunately for his permanent success, a very imperfect sympathy. He entirely under-estimated the amount of discontent
and ill-feeling caused by prohibitions of this kind. True, the
godly did not care for such things ; and as to the ungodly, he
did not care to please them. But he did not reckon up fairly
the preponderant multitude, not belonging distinctively either to
the one class or the other ; and therefore he had no notion of the
enormous forces of reaction stored up by repression of this kind,
and ready to be liberated by any sudden disturbance. Up to this
time however the heroic impulse of the nation had not exhausted itself, and the strength of the old Adam was yet for a
while latent and passive. But if Cromwell had no misgivings
about putting down meetings for sport, he felt painfully the
necessity laid upon him to restrain Republican and Anabaptist

---

* " Cromwelliana."
† There had been a prohibition of the same kind for the last six months of
the preceding year. It was now renewed.

leaders. For Major-General Harrison he could feel nothing but respect and admiration—tempered, it may be, with regrets for his friend's unpractical turn of mind. Still, prudence required that such a man should be beyond the reach of conspirators, who knew his value for their purposes. He was therefore confined for a while, though not for long, in the Isle of Portland. Lord Grey of Groby was committed to Windsor, and other discontented Commonwealthsmen to various modes of mild imprisonment.

No wonder that Charles and his advisers thought the country already wearied of the Commonwealth, and believed the hour was come for a vigorous effort to be made simultaneously in several places, so as, if possible, to rouse the whole country at once. Major-General Sir Joseph Wagstaff, formerly of the Royalist army, was sent over to the western counties to prepare the way, if possible, for the Duke of York to command an army there. Lord Wilmot, now called Earl of Rochester, went into Yorkshire, and collected men on the ill-omened field of Marston, with the notion of surprising York. It was arranged that a force should be ready at the same time to capture Newcastle; and North Wales, with Shropshire, was to be the arena of a separate rising. The day fixed for firing the train was Monday, March 12th (1655). Charles came to Middelburg, in the Isle of Walcheren, to be ready for embarkation at any moment; and Cromwell's spy at Charles's court wrote that Hyde was "cocksure" of success.

It is more than doubtful whether this attempt ever had any chance of a triumphant issue. The popular yearning for "Charles Rex" was by no means so strong yet as it afterwards became, when the Protectorate fell into incompetent hands. But much disturbance and bloodshed would have been caused had not Cromwell combined in some sort the gifts of Argus and Briareus. His system of spies is repulsive to the more sensitive public honour born of the comparative security of later times. But in the absence of his faculty for multiplying and directing official eyes, modern governments are sometimes led to harass and worry a whole population by remedies of force which, after all, neither single out the guilty, nor prevent a repetition of their crimes. Before ever the fatal day arrived the most dangerous, because the most fanatical, conspirators had been secured.

Still the rising was attempted. Wagstaff slipped into the
country undiscovered, and on Sunday night, March 11th, came
into Salisbury, in company with Col. Penruddock, a country
gentleman, besides one or two other officers, and some two hundred rank and file. They had chosen wisely enough their place
of operations, for they were not expected in Salisbury; and for
some hours there was no force to resist them. The judges had
just come to the town on circuit. Wagstaff seized them and
the High Sheriff in their beds, and was bent on hanging them
all, as a terror to men taking office under a usurper. Penruddock however prevented this; and they contented themselves
with trying to get King Charles officially proclaimed at the
market-cross next morning. But the Sheriff and even the
town-crier proved refractory. Penruddock dragged the latter
to the steps of the cross, and by threats made him call out
"Oyez" four times. The colonel then proceeded to dictate to
the man the terms of a proclamation. But when it came to
"Charles II., King of England," the poor man stopped. "I
cannot say that word," he pleaded. Whereupon he was beaten.
But he said "they might kill him—yea, they might call for
faggots and burn him; but that word they should not get out of
him."* The obstinacy of the sturdy crier seems to have been
approved by his fellow townsmen, whom Wagstaff and Penruddock
found singularly insensible to the sacredness of royalty. In fact
they saw it desirable to move off, in the hope of gathering adherents as they went. But Captain Unton Crook, whose fidelity
Cromwell had already recognised,† was now in pursuit of them.
He came up with them at South Molton on Wednesday night,
and though a show of resistance was made, all the leaders except
Wagstaff were captured, and the insurrection was at an end.

In the trials that followed the Protector had some difficulties
with the judges. In their appointment he had certainly considered high character and learning more than a compliant
temper. Some of them, who were commissioned to the north
and west for the trial of captured conspirators, now scrupled
about condemning for treason men accused only under authority of an Ordinance passed by the Protector in council. On the
other hand, it was essential to the very existence of the Protectorate that the "Instrument of Government" and the Ordinances

* "Cromwelliana."   † Letter CXXXV. in Carlyle.

passed in accordance therewith should be treated as of equal validity with statutes of the realm. The difficulty was surmounted by a judicious balance of tact, persistency, and moderation. The scruples of judges were respected, and in some cases their resignations accepted. But the trials were insisted upon, and men of reputation and dignity were found to fill the vacancies. In the case of the rabble who had seized horses for the rising the charge was made horse-stealing instead of treason ; and the executions, considering the temper of the times, were very few. Wagstaff and Wilmot had escaped. Penruddock and a companion in misfortune, Major-General Grove, were beheaded at Exeter. Several of the followers were hanged, and a considerable number were transported to Barbadoes.

Even during these anxious months the legislative activity of the Protector and his Council was not wholly arrested. A proclamation was issued* enforcing a speedy and due execution of the laws for the suppression of drunkenness, profanity, and other offences against decency. The same proclamation regulated the assize of bread, ale, and fuel, and prescribed a careful inspection of weights and measures. Local authorities were incited to find work for the able-bodied poor, and also to make due provision for the helpless. Rogues, vagabonds, and sturdy beggars were not to be tolerated outside of a gaol. The accounts of churchwardens and other parish officials were to be properly rendered and audited. The Ordinance issued in the preceding year for the regulation of proceedings in Chancery had proved, or at least was alleged by the judges, to be in some points impracticable. Perhaps they expected it would be allowed to drop; but the only effect was that another Ordinance was issued to amend the former.

It may be convenient also here to mention by anticipation other Ordinances not passed until later in this year (1655). In November the Protector created a council of commerce, or board of trade, consisting mainly of mercantile men outside his own Council of State. Its duties were to watch the course of trade in the world, and to consider and recommend means for stimulating and extending the commerce of the country. A commission was also constituted to investigate charities, to report on abuses, and to suggest means by which the benefits conferred by

* "The Parliamentary History."

C C

such charities might be increased. Other Ordinances of more
doubtful justice and expediency will be better considered
together with the circumstances occasioning them. But by
such measures as are here mentioned Oliver sought to supply
the Parliament's lack of service, and to exemplify the sort of
legislation which, in his opinion, ought to have occupied the time
spent in constitution mongering.

But there was one Ordinance of the previous year (1654)
which almost brought the law-courts to a dead lock. Without
money the machinery of government must soon stop running.
By the " Instrument," the Protector in Council had the power of
levying necessary taxes until Parliament met. Availing himself
of this power, he had raised £60,000 a month by an Ordinance
expiring on the 24th of December. He had confidently expected
that before this date he would have obtained supplies from Parliament. But he had actually received nothing. It might be
held doubtful how far the financial article in the Instrument
was applicable to this unexpected state of things, and even that
article itself had been resisted as unconstitutional. In November, 1654, a London merchant, named Cony, declined to pay
customs which were levied, like the internal revenue, by an
Ordinance. The commissioners of customs fined him £500, and,
on his refusal to pay, sent him to prison for contempt. The
motion for a writ of *Habeas Corpus* was postponed for formal
reasons, and was not argued till May 17th, 1655.

The mention of *Habeas Corpus* suggests the awkward position in which the judges were placed. The only ground on
which the authority of the Ordinance could be maintained was
the success of a revolution. No precedent in the ancient course
of constitutional development could by any perversion be made
to justify the abrogation of statutes by a military council. The
view of Oliver was that the informal concurrence of the people
and the army had given him a moral right to wield the whole
forces of the nation for the good of all. That informal commission had been formulated in the " Instrument." But this, of
course, was revolution ; and who was to decide what part of the
ancient constitution the revolution had spared ? The obvious
answer would be that only those who held the commission to
carry out the revolution could decide that question. But from
such daring logic even Cromwell shrank. He knew very well

that an assumption of power to decide what was law and what was not would not be endured even from him. He therefore consulted law officers, and offered technical and legal pleas where the decrees of his government were concerned. But then these technical pleas had no force except what they could be shown to derive from the old constitution, which was thus acknowledged to survive where not abrogated by Parliament. And if the judges were to give validity to some parts of the ancient laws, how could they with any consistency be asked to ignore others, which, legally speaking, were of precisely the same validity? In other words, if the Protector allowed the continuance of *Habeas Corpus*, by the very fact of pleading against a writ, how could he possibly dispute *de tallagio non concedendo?* And if he did not dispute this, his case, legally, was at an end.

It was impossible that the judges, as faithful officers of the law, could give any other decision. On the other hand, it was equally impossible for Oliver to allow the efficiency of his revolutionary power to be doubted. Cony's advocates, Maynard, Twisden, and Windham, when the case came on again on May 17th, did not scruple to urge arguments which necessarily involved not only the immediate point at issue, but the whole foundation of the Protectoral Government. The result was that all three were committed to the Tower. On the next day Cony, in the absence of his counsel, pleaded his own cause with arguments open only to one answer—the accomplished fact of revolution; an answer not likely to be readily adopted by a judge. Chief-Justice Rolle, who presided, felt himself in a great difficulty, and eagerly seized on a trivial clerical error* in Cony's written response, as a reason for postponing judgment. An excuse was then found for throwing the case over into the next term. In the vacation Rolle resigned his commission, and Glyn was appointed to succeed him. But the case of Cony came no more into court. His advocates were very soon released from the Tower, and he himself was set at liberty. By some effective argument, the nature of which is unrecorded, he was persuaded to give no more trouble.

The irony of the situation was grim enough to satisfy the most bitter deriders of popular liberal movements. The

* The preposition " to " was omitted before the Protector's name.

c c 2

violence of the Protector in imprisoning Cony for resistance to
an unconstitutional demand of customs dues was precisely
parallel to the violence of the late King in imprisoning Chambers for the very same reason. The conqueror of despotism, the
man who in the hour of victory had tenderly besought Parliament to " hear the groanings of poor prisoners," was now seen
ruthlessly depriving of their liberty men whose only crime was
a bold insistance on the guarantees given by the ancient constitution against taxation without the consent of Parliament. To
such startling inconsistencies are even the best men condemned,
when events so hurry political progress as to involve them in
revolution. At the same time, it would be unfair to ignore the
substantial difference underlying the superficial resemblance
between the action of the Protector and that of the King.
Charles represented a reaction against the steady progress of
self-government. Cromwell on the contrary impersonated a
revolution in which the best energies of the nation were engaged
to secure at all costs, even at the cost of a temporary dictatorship, a victory over that reaction. Charles failed not merely
through incapacity, but also because he had the nation against
him. Cromwell succeeded not only because of his enormous
force of character, but because that force was exerted in accordance with what was, on the whole, the preponderant inclination
of the people.

In fact, Cony's opposition to the Protector's financial
demands was exceptional. In dismissing the Parliament,
Oliver " appealed to God, angels, and men," whether he was not
now justified in raising money by virtue of the article mentioned
above. Accordingly, on February 8th (1655), an Ordinance was
passed assessing at £60,000 the monthly revenue to be raised.
The amount was smaller than had been apprehended, and no
serious difficulty was encountered in its collection. He was
very watchful against waste or peculation. He had the art of
extracting its full value from money ; and, notwithstanding the
expense incurred in maintaining an imposing navy in addition
to a vigorous army, there was no great accumulation of debt
under his government.

At the same time when the relations between the Government and the exchequer bench were strained, as we have seen,
by the case of Cony, the Commissioners of the Great Seal also

resented Cromwell's unceremonious interference with the time-honoured practices of Chancery. On April 23rd there was an order in council that the Lords Commissioners* should act on the amended Ordinance for proceedings in Chancery. Commissioner Lisle was for complying; but his two colleagues, Whitelock and Widdrington, with Lenthall, Master of the Rolls, overruled him. After several colloquies, Whitelock drew up a portentous paper of reasons for refusal. Some of these are suggestive of red tape. But the fundamental difficulty was that the legality of the Ordinance was disputable. Into such a controversy Oliver would not enter. On May 1st an order in council was passed noting that the necessary attorneys had not been nominated according to the Ordinance, and directing this to be done at once. On the same day the commissioners returned answer that, " having sought to God " in their perplexity, they " were not free to proceed on that Ordinance." Some weeks now elapsed; but on June 6th the commissioners were directed to attend his Highness, bringing the seal with them. Whitelock's description of what followed is worth quoting :—

"The Protector gravely told us he was sorry some of us could not satisfy our own consciences to execute the Ordinance concerning the chancery, which they were informed had much good in it for the public. But he confessed that every one was to satisfy himself in the matters to be performed by him, and that he had not the worse opinion of any man for refusing to do that whereof he was doubtful. But in this particular the affairs of the Commonwealth did require a conformity of the officers thereof, and their obedience to authority. And, 'since' † some of us refused to execute this act as enjoined, they were compelled thereby to put this custody of the great seal into the hands of some others, who might be satisfied it was their duty to perform the command, and to put the Ordinance into execution."

On June 8th the seal was delivered to Fiennes and Lisle. The Master of the Rolls overcame his scruples and obeyed the Ordinance. But Whitelock did not lose much. As he himself tells us, " the Protector, being goodnatured," soon made him and Widdrington Commissioners of the Treasury by way of compensation.

But the chief fact of this year, and the most conspicuous illustration at once of Oliver's strength and weakness, was the

* Viz., Whitelock, Widdrington, and Lisle.
† In Whitelock, "being."

institution of Major-Generals—a sort of " home-rule " of the despotic sort, by which every district in England was endowed with a little Protector of its own. Cromwell called this a " little poor invention of his own," and was rather proud of it, as this deprecatory description shows. But so long ago as March 1654 the Grand Jury at York, when sending up a congratulatory address to the Protector, had suggested some such arrangement for their own county. After referring to various local needs, especially that of a godly ministry, they beg " for all these ends that some faithful and godly men may be empowered in this county, so as we may not be necessitated upon every occasion to repair to London, where many necessary things are not presented by reason of the tediousness and great expense of such journeys."* In many respects the Major-Generals who had been appointed during 1655 answered to this description, but they possessed more drastic powers than the Grand Jury presumably had desired.

The immediate occasion for the appointment of these officers was the abortive insurrection in the spring. At the end of May Desborow was commissioned in the West of England not only to command a new militia raised in addition to the regular army, but also to act as a supreme constable. The device appeared to work well; and other similar appointments were soon made. By the end of the year all England, with Wales, was divided into twelve districts, and in the March following London, under Skippon, was added. Over each of these a Major-General was appointed, and the instructions issued to them show that they were not merely to be military commandants, but deputies of the Protector in civil matters as well. They were not only to suppress disorders and to keep an eye on Papists and Royalists, but they were " to use their best endeavours to find out all thieves, robbers, highwaymen, and other dangerous persons, and the houses and places which they frequented and usually lodged in; and to take course for apprehending and prosecuting them and their receivers agreeably to law." They were to suffer no horse-races, bear-batings, cock-fights, or stage-plays. They were to " inform themselves of all idle and loose people who had no visible way of livelihood," and to consider how these might be made to work, or else sent out of the country. They were to

* " Parl. History," vol. xx., 278.

see that the Ordinance for ejecting inefficient ministers was carried out, and in every way they were " to promote godliness and virtue, and to discourage profaneness and ungodliness."

An institution like this, sustained by the most vigorous officers of the war—such as Lambert, Fleetwood, and Whalley, in addition to those already named—was a tremendous engine of despotism. That it was tolerable at all was owing partly to the exceptional character and aims both of the Protector and his subordinates, partly to the high strain of public feeling, which prompted the endurance of any sacrifice rather than a godless anarchy under either Levellers or Stuarts. But even thus it did not prove tolerable for long; and Oliver, responsive to the temper of the times as all born rulers are, had to withdraw it, even while protesting its excellence. Englishmen do not like to be too much governed, even for their own good, and by their best men.

But the heaviest burden lay on Royalists, Papists, zealous Anglicans, and other suspects. Not only was a registry of such persons kept, and a system of surveillance maintained, comparable to our ticket-of-leave system for criminals, but the expense of the system of repression was raised by a special tax of ten per cent. on their annual income. The proclamation put forth on October 31st, and signed by the clerk of the Council, betrays in many places the desire of Cromwell to justify himself to his own conscience for a policy evidently much against his desires. But he argued with some force that the new expenses were required solely because of Royalist machinations, and that it would be unfair to charge them upon the whole nation. The inveterate royalism of so many people surprised and disappointed him. Perhaps it set him thinking whether the prejudice could not be gratified in another way than by the restoration of the Stuarts. But for the present all he could do was to make the superstition expensive and inconvenient.

More odious than even such measures was an Ordinance issued in September for a more rigorous supervision of the press. Henceforth no newspaper was to be published without official permission. The rise of the Commonwealth had been signalised by a marked increase in the activity of the press; and its power had been recognised by an arrangement for publishing English news in the French and German languages. But now, under the blight of this decree, the number of newspapers fell from eight to two, and the public feeling of liberty and light was correspondingly diminished. Would it not have been better for Oliver's fame had he died in Worcester fight? No; for with certain exceptions due to theological bias his conception of the office of a ruler was noble, generous, and enlightened. Oliver Lord Protector, looms larger among the heroes of that strenuous time than Cromwell the Lord-General, and the lessons to be learned even from his failures are more impressive.

This year showed a rapid development of the Protector's foreign policy, and brought in its train the most decisive check ever experienced by his masterful spirit. The proceedings of his generals and admirals cannot be followed here in detail. But one instance of his interference in the domestic affairs of another nation must detain us a moment.

In pursuance of his inclination to a French alliance, Cromwell was about to conclude a treaty, when the news of a cruel persecution of the Vaudois peasantry determined him to make a noble use of Mazarin's anxiety for his friendship. In April 1655 a small army was quartered in the heretical valleys of Piedmont, and the inhabitants were violently evicted. Cruelty and brutality were inevitable in the execution of such a work; and when, at the beginning of June, the news arrived in England, natural compassion was heightened by religious sympathy. In this matter the nation was heartily at one with the Protector, who declared that "the calamities of these poor people lay as near, or rather nearer, to his heart than if it had concerned the dearest relations he had in the world." He was informed that a detachment of French soldiers marching into Italy had been lent to the Italian Duke for the enforcement of the cruel decree, and he at once determined there should be no treaty with France until the power of that kingdom had been used to redress the wrong it had abetted. He sent an envoy to Turin. He called to his aid the thunders of Milton's Latin eloquence, and proclaimed to the misguided Duke and to the world that "the rights of conscience are inviolable, and that God has reserved to himself all authority over it." In so doing he was not in the least troubled by the British prohibition of the mass in Ireland, nor by his own repression of the Anglican ritual in England. He satisfied himself with the idea that so long as he did not intrude on the silent thoughts or chamber religion of Romanists and Anglicans he kept his principle intact. He endeavoured to engage the Protestant powers of the Continent in a common remonstrance. And there can be little doubt that, if he had not succeeded otherwise, he would even have gone the length of landing his Ironsides in Italy. Happily this was not necessary. Cardinal Mazarin did not think the triumph of the mass in Piedmont worth the sacrifice of a powerful ally, and he put such pressure on the court of Turin that the Duke made a virtue of necessity, and asked the world to bear witness to the magnanimity of the pardon he extended to his rebels. But the incident delayed the treaty with France until the month of October (1655). Meantime Oliver did not confine his sympathy to political action. He recommended a day of national prayer to be observed on Thursday, June 14th, for the persecuted people. He ordered collections to be made in all the churches for their assistance, and he himself set an example of liberality by contributing from his own income £2,000.

During the spring, amid all his distractions, Oliver's thoughts were often with the fleets in Mediterranean and Atlantic waters, and he neglected no opportunity of keeping them reinforced and supplied. Blake, who had sailed in October 1654, was successful in all he undertook. The Grand Duke of Tuscany was made to pay £60,000 for favouring Prince Rupert and inhospitably expelling a Commonwealth squadron from Leghorn. Algiers, Tunis, and Tripoli were in succession compelled to give satisfaction for piracies. By the early summer, Blake was ready for other services, and the Protector directed him to sail westwards and prevent the Spaniards from sending any reinforcements to the West Indies.

The expedition of Penn and Venables turned out to be a humiliating failure. Oliver had intended it to seize Hispaniola ; and the force provided was quite sufficient for the work. But for once in his life he made an egregious blunder in the choice of men. Both the commanders were inefficient, and they made their misfortunes worse by quarelling with one another. However, being miserably beaten in Hispaniola, they made a more successful attempt on Jamaica, which was then added to the British Empire. But this success was not thought to compensate for the greater failure, and when at the beginning of June the two commanders returned to lay their excuses before the Protector, he committed them to the Tower. Within a month reinforcements were on their way to Jamaica. The conquest was completed, and Oliver made strenuous efforts, not at first very successful, to obtain colonists from Barbadoes, from New England, and from Ireland.

Cromwell had now reached the utmost height of power and contemporary fame. With rare exceptions men who raise themselves in the world by sheer force of practical worth have tact and temper to bear themselves in their higher place with a dignity surprising to the great ones amongst whom they intrude. Cromwell was not one of the exceptions. Even witnesses prejudiced against him allow that his earlier tendency to somewhat coarse, practical joking was not suffered to mar his grave and courteous manners in later life.* Sir Philip Warwick could never wonder enough at the fantastic fate that brought him, a born gentleman, to wait in custody on the leisure of a man formerly known only as an ill-dressed rustic. But he acknowledges that "a better tailor, and converse with good company" had given the rustic "a great and majestic deportment, and a comely presence." But, if we except occasions of mere pageantry incongruous with his homely nature, his dignity never betrayed the stiffness of assumption. It was the sincere attitude of a soul conscious that the right discharge of grave responsibilities required the sort of moral weight involved in due respect from others. This is well seen in his receptions of ambassadors, as in the case already mentioned, and another illustration occurred at the end of July in this year (1655). But space fails us to describe at length the reception of the extraordinary ambassador from Sweden. It is sufficient to note that both the envoy and the Protector used each his own mother tongue, and that an oral translation of the ambassador's speech into Latin by an interpreter was sufficient to make it intelligible to the Protector.

Oliver however often played the host in more homely fashion, and the grave entertainments, principally of sacred music, that followed his dinners or suppers at Whitehall, gave much satisfaction to godly preachers and to seriously-inclined officials. In such company might at times be heard the grave, sweet words of

* Yet in festivities of his own household his fun was still sometimes vulgar.

Milton, already passing from the light of earthly days to visions of a vanished Paradise. The less stately but more popular Waller was ever welcome to "the world's Protector," who prayed him to crown his kindness by saving his friend from self, as he had vindicated him against the world.* In strange contrast to his surroundings Hobbes of the Leviathan might sometimes be seen. Nor was any man of distinguished gifts unwelcome, whatever his opinions might be, if only he was of unsullied fame. Never, except in sheer superfluity of malice, was any insinuation ever made against the spotless purity of life preserved in the protectoral household. The man who could keep a camp sacred from vice even amid the fierce passions of war was not likely to permit the licentiousness of a court. One of the most singular guests he ever received was George Fox, who indeed came to him as a prisoner, but went away as a friend. The Quakers were causing a good deal of irritation by their indiscreet and, it must be added, their arrogant disregard of ordinary conventionalisms, and even of public order. But the interference of public authorities on such grounds too readily degenerated into persecution.

George Fox was brought up in custody from Leicester, and information was given to the Protector as to his peculiarities. A servant of Cromwell's, one Harvey, had been amongst the Quakers, though now a renegade; † and it was probably because of what he heard from this man that the Protector desired to see Fox for himself. George was brought into Oliver's bed-chamber, where Harvey was waiting upon his master. " Peace be in this house! " said George, solemnly; and then he exhorted the Protector to keep in the fear of God, that so " he might order all things under his hand to God's glory." George testifies that in their discourse about religion Cromwell " bore himself very moderately." We may suppose he was impressed with the rapt enthusiasm of his strange visitor. But he ventured to observe that the Quakers quarrelled needlessly with the preachers. Fox denied this, and said the quarrelling was all on the other side. He went on to illustrate his peaceable disposition towards them by denouncing all " who preached for hire, and were covetous and greedy, like the dumb dogs who could never have enough."

* Forster, "Statesmen of the Commonwealth," p. 50.
† "Fox's Journal," p. 127, 3rd ed., 1765.

He also discoursed on the uselessness of the Scriptures apart from the spirit and power that breathed them forth. We can well imagine that Cromwell's unconventional devoutness found something congenial in Fox's fervour. "Many more words I had with him," says Fox; "but people coming in, I drew a little back. As I was turning he catched me by the hand, and, with tears in his eyes, said, 'Come again to my house; for if thou and I were but an hour of a day together we should be nearer one to the other.'"

Another scene in Cromwell's household life is given by Whitelock, who describes a dinner, in the month of April, in honour of the board of "Triers," commissioned to secure a godly ministry. Their work was one that profoundly interested the Protector, and he was very cordial in his hospitality to them. Mrs. Cromwell, called "the Lady Protectress," was also gracious to them; and the evening passed with agreeable interludes of psalmody. "By such kinds of little caresses," says the narrator, "he gained much on many persons."

In his relations to his own family his affection did not diminish with advancing years—nor, indeed, did his authority. In a letter, dated June 22nd 1655, he pours out to Fleetwood his bitterness of soul at "the wretched jealousies" and "spirit of calumny" that are abroad :—

"It is reported that you are to be sent for, and Harry to be deputy, which truly never entered into my heart. The Lord knows my desire was for him and his brother to have lived private lives in the country. And Harry knows this very well, and how difficultly I was persuaded to give him his commission for his present place.* This I say as from a simple and sincere heart. The noise of my being crowned, &c., are like † malicious figments. . . . . Dear Charles, my dear love to thee, and to my dear Biddy, who is a joy to my heart for what I hear of the Lord in her. . . . . If you have a mind to come over with your dear wife, take the best opportunity for the good of the public and your own convenience. . . . . I bless the Lord I am not my own; but my condition to flesh and blood is very hard."

Fleetwood did take an opportunity to come over, and preferred to remain in England as one of the Major-Generals; and in the course of the following year Henry Cromwell succeeded to his Irish post. There is however no need to doubt Oliver's

---

* He was acting as sub-deputy, or lieutenant, to Fleetwood.

† *I.e.,* "similar."

sincerity in the above letter. The circumstances entirely changed after it was written; and it was only after long delay that he consented to Henry's appointment.

In the absence of Fleetwood Henry had to do the work of the deputy, and he found difficulties created for him by some persons—Ludlow had been amongst the number—who disapproved of his father's "usurpation," and were therefore not friendly towards himself. His father's advice, addressed to him in November, has under these circumstances a certain nobility of tone :—

"Son,— . . . . I do believe there may be some particular persons who are not very well pleased with the present condition of things, and may be apt to show their discontent as they have opportunity. But this should not make too great impressions in you. Time and patience may work them to a better frame of spirit, and bring them to see that which for the present seems to be hid from them—especially if they shall see your moderation and love towards them, if they are found in other ways towards you. Which I earnestly desire you to study, and endeavour all that lies in you. Whereof both you and I shall have the comfort, whatsoever the issue and event thereof be."

About this time Ludlow left Dublin, and after being, apparently by Cromwell's orders, delayed a while at Beaumaris, he came on to London. He had heard with anger and indignation of the system of personal rule established after the suppression of the Long Parliament; but being a man of theory rather than of action he submitted to the force of circumstances, and continued to discharge the duties of his subordinate position in Ireland. He did not however disguise the fact that he was one of those who, in the words of the above letter, "were not very well pleased with the present condition of things," and might be apt to show their discontent as they had opportunity. Still, he was not the man to conspire with Papists and Royalists; and the Protector thought he was conveniently situated in Ireland at a safe distance from men like Harrison. But after Fleetwood left the duties of his post to Henry Cromwell, Ludlow found his position insupportable, and insisted on coming over to England. To secure liberty to do so he gave Fleetwood (still nominally the Lord-Deputy of Ireland), a written engagement promising quietness, but in a conditional and unsatisfactory sense.

He had not seen his old comrade now for several years; and

since their parting Cromwell had risen to sovereign greatness.
It is never easy for once-familiar friends suddenly to accommodate their mutual bearing to such enormous alterations in relative
position; and the difficulty was heightened in this case by
Ludlow's anger, and by the necessity he felt for maintaining a
protest against what he considered a betrayal of trust. He has
described the interviews himself; * and it is creditable to his
candour that the impression conveyed is on the whole very
favourable to Cromwell. There appears to have been an entire
absence of assumption on the Protector's part—no trace of any
vanity of power. He was clearly anxious to establish any
tolerable understanding that should prevent the necessity of
restraining a man whom he respected; but at the same time
there was a sincere determination not to palter with any danger
to public security, and perhaps a tone of contempt for vapouring
sentiment.

Like George Fox, Ludlow was conducted to the Protector's
bed-chamber, which, in accordance with the manners of the time,
was often a consulting-room. Indeed, with a touch of coarse-
ness that belonged to the man rather than to the age, Oliver had
been in the habit of admitting familiar advisers not only to his
bedroom, but to his bed. That practice we may believe he had
abandoned since his rise to supreme dignity. But like kings the
Protector held his *levée*; and when Ludlow arrived he found
Lambert, Montague, and others present. Fleetwood came in soon
after. Cromwell without ceremony at once charged Ludlow with
unfair conduct in creating an impression of neutrality while
intending hostility. If he had continued to rely on Ludlow's
words, he said, he might have "been engaged in blood before he
was aware." And he asked earnestly "wherefore Ludlow would
not engage not to act against the present Government," adding
a maxim which the former member for Cambridge had certainly
not invariably observed, "that if Nero were in power it would be
a duty to submit." The republican then saw an opening for eloquent protest. He would suffer any extremities rather than acknowledge wrong to be right. "Yes, yes," Cromwell broke in; "we know
your resolution well enough, and we have cause to be as stout as
you. But I pray you, who spoke of your suffering?" "Sir," said
Ludlow, "if I am not undeceived, you mentioned the securing

* Ludlow's "Memoirs," p. 210, &c.

of my person." "Yea," rejoined Cromwell, waxing warm, "and great reason there is why we should do so; for I am ashamed to see the engagement you have given to the Lieutenant-General,* which would be more fit for a general who should be taken prisoner, and that hath yet an army of 30,000 men in the field, than for one in your condition." Then thoughts of old-comradeship probably intervened, and calming down he assured Ludlow he had always been ready to do him what good offices he could, and wished as well to him as to any of the Council.† But Ludlow must think of some pleasant place of residence, with good air and every other desirable qualification, for it was absolutely necessary he should live in retirement, and that the Protector should approve the place. In another interview Ludlow ventured to observe that he had been faithful to Cromwell in the difficulties of the latter. "I understand not what you mean by *my* difficulties," said the Protector, coldly. "I am sure they were not so properly mine as those of the public. For in respect to my outward condition I have not much improved it, as these gentlemen"—members of his Council—"well know." Finally the impracticable republican agreed to retire into Essex, where he lived in peace until he learned by sad experience that only Cromwell's strong hand had made it possible for him to continue in his native country at all.

When Ludlow visited Whitehall the bed-chamber Council were much occupied with overtures made on behalf of the Jews for re-admission to England after an exclusion lasting three hundred years. Manasseh Ben Israel, an influential Portuguese Jew, settled in Amsterdam, had been, as we saw, for some time past pressing the question. But neither the Long Parliament nor the convention of saints would listen to him. When Oliver became supreme, he commended the application to the consideration of his Council. He now summoned a conference of notables and clergy to debate the matter at Whitehall. He himself presided, and opened the discussion with an earnest speech from the chair in favour of the concession. The clergy however were averse to any hospitality to a race mani-

---

* Fleetwood.

† "His temper exceeding fiery, I have known," says John Maidstone, Oliver's steward, "but the flame of it kept down, for the most part, or soon allayed with those moral endowments he had."

festly under a divine curse, and the conclusion of the conference was unfavourable. Nevertheless the Protector so far stretched his power in favour of the Jews as to connive at their settlement. Little by little they began to come over, and happily for the commercial prosperity of the country have never been disturbed.

CHAPTER XXVII.

A QUIET YEAR.

THE year 1656 was perhaps the quietest Oliver had known since the first outbreak of the civil war. Faction and conspiracy, though not destroyed, at least became inactive. Trade and enterprise flourished under his strong government. Learning was pursued with grave earnestness. The majority of the nation were on the whole satisfied to leave their affairs in the hands of a ruler who clearly understood his business. At the same time, the renown of England and her authority in the world were greater than they had ever been except, perhaps, in in the days of Elizabeth. The exception is more than doubtful. For Cromwell commanded greater material resources than Elizabeth, and his tone, when speaking in the name of his country, was higher even than hers.

When Oliver told Ludlow that " in respect of his outward condition he had not much improved it " by his rise in the world, he referred, of course, to the expenses, responsibilities, and cares to be reckoned against his increased wealth. The allowance made for the Protector's family expenses was ample ; indeed, considering the greater value of money then, it was splendid. It ranged from £70,000 to £100,000 a year.* This was not generally thought extravagant, and it appears to have included the whole cost of his official residences, equipages, and attendants, besides the entertainments he gave to foreign ambassadors and domestic dignitaries. The national revenue was, in form, made payable to the Lord Protector. But great care was taken to distinguish between his private property and his official revenue. Neither he nor his family accumulated from public funds any secret hoard as a resource in a possible reverse of fortune.

His children, on the whole, did credit to their training.

* The former sum appears from a letter of John Maidstone to the Council, March 14, 1654–5. Cal. St. P. Dom. Ser. But the amount grew larger.

D D

Richard was weak and self-indulgent, but the influence of his father kept him at least as negative toward vice as he was toward virtue. Henry perhaps scarcely justified the confidence expressed by some, that he would have been equal to the burden of the Protectorate had it fallen upon him. He was sincerely devoted to the public good, but his character had nothing like the volume and power of his father's. The daughters, as might be expected, showed more pride in their elevation than ever their father did, and " the family," as appears from their extant letters, was a never-forgotten source of complacency. The title " her Highness " applied to a mother does not sound well from them. But they were good, faithful women, sincerely imbued with their parents' religion. The " two little wenches," Mary and Frances, were now grown-up girls with favoured admirers.

Mary was engaged to Lord Fauconberg, and " Frank," as she was familiarly called, was wooed by Mr. Rich, the grandson of Lord Warwick. But in the latter case the course of true love did not run smooth at first. Cromwell heard a bad report of the young man's morals, and this to his mind was fatal. Mary now behaved like her father's own daughter. She battled for her sister like an enraged hen defending a wounded chick. " Truly, I can say it," she wrote to her brother Henry in June this year, " for these three months I think our family and myself in particular have been in the greatest confusion and trouble as ever poor family can be in. The Lord tell us His mind in it, and settle us, and make us what He would have us to be ! " * The lovers had been allowed to pursue their courtship undisturbed for three months before the sentence of prohibition was uttered. It was generally believed that the Protector was not satisfied with the settlement proposed by Lord Warwick. But Frances was assured by her father that his real reason was the bad report he heard of her lover. The girl was incredulous of the report; maintained that such stories could not be true; they were the spiteful invention of interested people ; and her heart was too far gone to be changed without breaking. The two sisters had many an eager and tearful discussion of the difficulty. Frances " was resolved to know the truth," and believed she could prove the stories about her lover to be all lies. Mary bravely confronted her strong-willed father with

* Letter of Mary Cromwell, given in Carlyle, from Thurloe, v. 146.

rebutting evidence; but, alas, to little purpose. Only this was conceded, "that if he were satisfied as to the report, the estate should not break it off." And with that Frances, triumphant in her faith, was content.

It was said that Charles Stuart contemplated obtaining his father's crown by marrying one of Cromwell's daughters. But no thought of this kind prevented Oliver's approval of Mr. Rich. As to Charles, when Lord Broghill mentioned the report at Whitehall, Cromwell only remarked, "he is so damnably debauched, he would undo us all."* Poor Frances apparently convinced her father; for the marriage eventually came off, followed, alas, by widowhood within a few months. In fact Oliver, like many other strong-willed fathers, found that a daughter in love is more difficult to rule than an empire. Frances had inherited his firmness of resolve, and though she was only seventeen, her small persistency inspired by love was victorious. "Truly, I must tell you privately," wrote her sister, "they are so far engaged that the match cannot be broken off. She acquainted none of her friends with her resolution when she did it." †

While the "poor family" was thus distracted, the father was steadily bent on making his country supreme in trade, and the head of the Protestant interest of the world. A new treaty was in progress with Sweden, and Whitelock had much difficulty in escaping a second embassy. The propositions involved mutual concessions as to the enlistment of troops and hiring of ships by each Government in the dominions of the other.‡ The Protector desired so to limit this right that it might conduce to the establishment of a Protestant League; but Sweden was indisposed to commit herself to such a league, and the treaty hung fire, much to the indignation of the Swedish ambassador. Indeed Cromwell conducted himself throughout as one who had more to give than to ask. On one occasion the ambassador, after waiting more than an hour in an ante-chamber at Whitehall, was about to go away in high dudgeon. But Oliver made ample apology

---

* The story is told by Burnet, vol. i., p. 107. Like many other statements of the bishop, it is perhaps doubtful.

† The reference seems to be to a secret marriage. Any more ill-natured interpretation is excluded by the date of the nuptials, which were more than a year after.

‡ Whitelock: "Memorials," p. 633.

for the apparent discourtesy, declaring that the fault lay with his attendants, who had not informed him of the ambassador's presence.

At sea the newly-acquired naval supremacy of England was maintained; and Cromwell's letters bear interesting testimony to the care, diligence, and minute attention with which he watched over the fleet, and the new colony in Jamaica. Nothing decisive could be effected against the Spaniards for many months, because they shrank from conflict with Blake. But as though the number of enemies were a matter of indifference to him, the Protector in the month of May ordered Blake, with whom Montague of Hinchinbrook was now joined in command, to enforce on Portugal the instant ratification of the treaty concluded two years before, but still held in suspense. What specially offended Oliver was an attempt on the part of Portugal to alter one of the articles so as to make the religious privileges of English merchants in that country dependent on the consent of the Pope, " which, we hope, whatever befall us," says the Puritan ruler, " we shall not, by the grace of God, be brought unto." In the result, the King of Portugal not only at once ratified the treaty without waiting for the Pope, but also paid a round sum of money by way of compensation for delay.

In the comparative quietness of these months at home the Protector thought he had satisfactory evidence of the success of the Major-Generals. Before the end of the previous year the whole of England and Wales had been placed under their control, excepting only the City of London and its liberties. With this exception the Protector was not satisfied. He had no reason indeed to doubt that the security established by his government was very fairly appreciated by city men. But the confluence of strangers in the capital under various pretexts of trade and travel necessitated great watchfulness; and the density of the population in a thriving city, prohibited from extending its borders, gave facilities for concealment. But it was no easy matter to bring London under a Major-General without dangerously exciting ancient municipal sentiment; and, in the accomplishment of his project Oliver gave a singular illustration of the extent to which he combined firmness with tact and appreciative sympathy. On March 5th he invited the Lord Mayor, with the aldermen, and a deputation of common-

councillors, to attend him. He laid before them the evidences
he had of continued machinations for the disturbance of public
security. He explained the object he had in view in establishing his system of Major-Generals. He assured them that no
one could respect more than he did their corporate rights and
immunities; he had no idea whatever of interfering with these.
But he thought that their acceptance of a Major-General would
not in the least endanger their rights, while it would help him
very much in the maintenance of the peace of the Commonwealth. Of course his indisputable power added very much to
the persuasiveness of his argument, and consent was made all
the easier by the nomination of Major-General Skippon, who
was popular in the city. In fine, the Lord Mayor and his colleagues gave their consent with apparent heartiness, and the
scheme was thus complete. The Protector's engagements on
another day in this month illustrate the variety of his occupa-
tions. In the morning of March 25th, there was brought
before him a notable highwayman captured at an ale-house in
Old Street. This robber was alleged to have taken £10,000 in
twelve months—a sufficient hint of the insecurity of the roads
even under the strong government of the Protector. The man
was just mounting his horse to set out on a new expedition
when he was taken, and his fame amongst highwaymen secured
him the honour of special examination before the Protector.
After this the French ambassador was admitted to an interview,
and from stories of theft and murder on a small scale, the
supreme magistrate had to turn his mind to questions of international plunder and bloodshed.

The assizes in this spring were frequented by an unusual
concourse of the gentry in many parts of the country. On the
Grand Juries social dignity and wealth were more fully represented than they had been for years. From this it appeared
that the " usurpation " was beginning to be accepted, if not as a
gift of Providence, at all events as a decree of fate.

In the month of April, the Protector, always anxious to
encourage learning, endeavoured to bring to conclusion a scheme,
held in suspense during seven years, for the establishment of a
college at Durham. In 1650 the Long Parliament had ordered
that certain ecclesiastical endowments and buildings in the
cathedral city should be devoted to this purpose. Various

difficulties however had been interposed, and nothing had been accomplished yet. In his northern campaigns Cromwell had been impressed with the intellectual destitution of the people in these districts, and was resolved at length to bring the matter to an issue. The business was now actually achieved, and the college started. But it had not a long life, for it came to an end, with much else, at the Restoration.

In April Archbishop Usher, formerly of Dublin, died. For his learning and his character Cromwell entertained a very high respect; and though it is impossible to justify the excessive harshness with which he treated the Anglican clergy and their form of worship, it must not be forgotten on the other hand that, as though to prove how entirely he was governed in this matter by his notions of political necessity, he gladly took any opportunity afforded him of showing favour to distinguished episcopal clergymen, regarded only as scholars. As soon as he heard of Archbishop Usher's death he gave orders that he should be buried with public honours in Westminster Abbey, and provided £200 for the expenses.

To modern manners it seems strange to note how essentially religious was the view taken by the Protector and his colleagues of their duties and responsibilities. On May 2nd we find it announced in the journals of the time that "his Highness and the Council spent the day in private prayer and fasting, to seek a blessing from God upon our affairs and forces." To some it still appears paradoxical that rebels and regicides should have any pretence to religion. To us however the sanguinary employments to which the national forces were sent without any justification from imperious necessity appear more discordant with worship of the common Father. But to burn and drown Spaniards, to consume their ships, and to appropriate their treasures was then regarded as a mission incumbent upon Englishmen not merely on grounds of self-interest, but for the very highest reasons of devotion to God and His truth.

The implacable hostility of the Commonwealth to Spain had borne its natural fruit in negotiations between the domestic enemies of Cromwell and the foreign foe. The history of illegitimate alliances scarcely affords any more incongruous combinations than those that were formed about this time.

That Charles Stuart should seek the aid of Spain was natural enough; but that discontented Levellers, or Fifth-Monarchy men should go so near an alliance with the "Scarlet Woman" only shows how forgetful of principle even fanatics will become when actuated by disappointment and spite. Colonel Sexby, who once had confronted an effete Parliament with the imperious demands of his colleagues for a pure Gospel, impartial justice, and an equal Commonwealth, now so far forgot his zeal in passionate hate of his former General, that he was ready to combine with king, or Pope, or devil for the common purpose he shared with them of destroying the invincible Protector. When his new allies pointed out that beyond this aim his purposes were entirely different from theirs, he said he knew it, but at all costs he would get rid of Cromwell, and call a free Parliament. The free Parliament would doubtless recall Charles Stuart; but no matter; the accursed Cromwell would be gone. Amongst the designs formed under such incongruous auspices was one for an invasion of Ireland; and, in August of this year the Protector, who seems to have known as much of their designs as the conspirators themselves, wrote to his son Henry, directing him to contract the garrisons, to have a considerable marching-army in the field, and to pay very particular regard to the north, "where, without question, busy and discontented persons are working towards new disturbances."

According to the Instrument of Government the Protector was compelled to summon a Parliament at least once every three years. The summons might have been delayed till 1657. But Cromwell had no wish to govern without a representative assembly; and he hoped that the experience of two years would induce the constituencies to send up men prepared to abandon theoretic debate, and to give him practical aid in maintaining a government now proved to be advantageous to the nation. He therefore issued writs on July 10th, and the time of meeting was fixed for September 17th. All the influence of the Government was exerted to secure the return of suitable candidates. The system of Major-Generals gave great facilities for this purpose, and the Protector certainly made the most of it. At same time his opponents were not inactive. As soon as the approach of a general election was known a tract was widely distributed offering a "word in season" to all

Englishmen on their electoral duties. The writer altogether repudiated the notion that the choice should be limited to men who would be loyal to the Protectoral Government, and insisted on the exercise of the suffrage in accordance with abstract principles, regardless of all consequences.

Sir Henry Vane also issued a tract called a "Healing Question." It was not occasioned by the prospect of an election, but was suggested by Cromwell's recommendation of a fast for March 14th. In that proclamation the Protector exhorted the people to seek the Lord that they might discover "the Achan who had so long obstructed the settlement of these distracted kingdoms." Vane wrote his pamphlet as a contribution towards answering this question. He must have known that he would be regarded as identifying the Protector with the Achan sought. But his argument otherwise was neither disrespectful to Cromwell nor destructive to the existing government. Indeed he admitted that the concentration of executive powers in a "single person" might be convenient or even necessary. But the error of the last few years had been a departure from "the strait gate and narrow way of Parliamentary method." There was a sense in which Cromwell was quite ready to admit this; only he insisted that the error was unavoidable. He was earnestly preparing a return to the Parliamentary method when this pamphlet appeared. Nevertheless he considered Vane's argument dangerous, and summoned the writer to appear before the Council on August the 12th. His attendance at that time being inconvenient Vane excused himself, and was allowed to defer his appearance till the 21st. He was then ordered to give security in a bond of £5,000 against any attempt to disturb the existing government; and in default was committed to Carisbrooke Castle, where he remained till the end of December.

This arbitrary proceeding was wholly inexcusable. But the combination of calculation and impulse which betrayed Cromwell into so grave an error is not difficult to understand. That the coming Parliament should accept his government as an accomplished fact seemed a matter of life or death to the Commonwealth. He had information enough to make him certain that though the nation was settling down under him his removal might mean the return of the Stuarts. And history has justified him in believing the Stuarts to be impossible rulers of England. If he could only get one Parliament free from distracting theorisers he had plausible reasons for thinking that all would go well afterwards. And of all distracting theorisers alive it was most important to deliver Parliament from Sir Henry Vane. Ever since April 20th 1653 Cromwell had regarded Vane as slippery and treacherous. There were only two modes in which his influence might be neutralised; either to bind him over in a heavy penalty not to disturb the government, or to shut him up for a while. The former alternative was proudly declined by Vane, and Cromwell, not to be baulked, adopted the latter. Nor did he stop here. On the principle that what was worth doing at all must be done thoroughly, he arrested or re-arrested Harrison, Ashburnham, Lord Willoughby of Parham, and a number of others. But in these cases there was more justification than in that of Vane. The unprincipled alliance of republican and Anabaptist fanatics with Charles Stuart and Spanish Papists was creating a real danger, which it was surely better to prevent if possible by mild and brief imprisonments than to suppress by blood.

When to the exertion of official influence and the arrest of opponents we add the nomination by the Protector—for such it virtually was—of sixty members for Scotland and Ireland, we can easily believe that the representatives who came up to Westminster in September 1656 were as a whole much more likely to take the Protector's view of their duties than the previous Parliament had been. Still there were unconformable men returned, among whom Sir Arthur Haselrig, Ashley Cooper, and Thomas Scot, a strong republican, were prominent. As soon as the returns to the writs were made the Council were busy under the Protector's direction in considering the names of those elected, in order to determine whether their qualifications came within the conditions laid down in the Instrument of Government. For one of the worst features of that document was that it left the Protector and his Council to be judges on this question.

On September 17th the whole of the elected members met in Westminster Abbey to hear a sermon from Dr. John Owen; and then they adjourned to the Painted Chamber to hear a much more impressive sermon from the Protector. For Oliver's speech on this occasion was pre-eminently a religious discourse. It contained much unchristian sentiment; but it was unchristian only where it was intensely Jewish. It condescended with impatient disdain to some miserable details of assassination plots, but only to display in their failure the palpable reality of a divine providence. It reckoned up details of monthly assessments, of debts, and economies; but leaving them with a sigh of relief, the speaker broke into impassioned aspirations for an impulse from heaven to rouse his hearers to an earnest discharge of duty. The speech was very badly reported, and nowhere has the editorial skill and insight of Thomas Carlyle been more conspicuous than its rescue from obvious blunders, misprints, and confused punctuation. But it must have been very difficult to report, involved, often clumsy in expression, and rude even when grand—a long, rolling, thunderous cloud of speech, lit up here and there with sudden, blinding light. It begins heavily labouring; grows more electric as it proceeds; flames now and again with a truly sacred passion; and dies away in an infinite radiance of faith.

Professing to treat first of the "being and preservation" of the Commonwealth and its dependencies, the Protector hastened to vindicate his policy in making war on Spain. His reasons throughout were Jewish, and have no interest for us now, except as illustrations of the speaker's religion. "Why, truly, your great enemy is the Spaniard. . . . He is naturally throughout an enemy; an enmity is put into him by God. 'I will put an enmity between thy seed and her seed;' which goes but for little among statesmen, but is more considerable than all things." The Protector then showed how Royalists had not scrupled to avail themselves of Spanish help, and what intrigues had been the result. "We had that insurrection. It was intended first to the assassination of my person—which I would not remember as anything at all considerable to myself or to you, for they would have had to cut throats beyond all human calculation before they could have been able to effect their design." He expressed a hope, and indeed a belief, that discontented Republicans and Fifth-Monarchy men had not generally intrigued with Papists. But of Sexby he spoke with unrestrained anger, as "a wretched creature, an apostate from religion and all honesty."

"He went with letters to the Archduke Leopoldus and ⟶
. . . and hath been soliciting, and did obtain, monies, which ⟶
hither by bills of exchange. And God by His providence, we ⟶
exceeding poor, directed that we lighted on some of them, and some
the monies. Now, if they be payable let them be called for!"—"Her⟶
is your danger; that is it! Here is a poor nation that hath wallowed
in its blood—though, thanks be to God, we have had peace these four
or five years: yet here is the condition we stand in. And I think I
should be false to you if I did not give you this true representation
of it."

His Highness next proceeded to justify the institution of
Major-Generals. "When we knew all these designs before-
mentioned, . . . we did find out a little poor invention,
which I hear has been much regretted." He insisted that the
scheme had worked well, and gave no hint of surrendering it.
To this he returned in a later part of his speech. "It hath
been more effectual towards the discountenancing of vice and
settling religion than anything done these fifty years. I
will abide by it, notwithstanding the envy and slander of
foolish men."

Going on to the religious differences of the time, he declared
that "his practice since the last Parliament had been to let
all the nation see that whatever pretenders to religion would
continue quiet and peaceable, they should enjoy liberty." But
wherever there was reason to suspect factious designs, no pretence, however specious, should prevent his interference. So
also he endeavoured to maintain mutual tolerance amongst sects.
"If a man of one form will be trampling upon the heels of
another form; if an Independent, for example, will despise
him under baptism, and will revile him, and reproach, and
provoke him, I will not suffer it in him." Referring to the
reformation of manners he said:—

"Make it a shame to see men bold in sin and profaneness, and God
will bless you. You will be a blessing to the nation; and by this
will be more repairers of breaches than by anything in the world. Truly
these things do respect the souls of men, and the spirits, which *are*
the men. The mind *is* the man. If that be kept pure, a man signifies
somewhat; if not, I would fain see what difference there is betwixt
him and a beast. He hath only some activity to do some more mischief."

The inconsistencies and absurdities of existing law had long
pressed painfully on Oliver's sense of justice. He spoke now

with respect for the law in general, and with pardonable pride in his judges. But—

"the truth of it is, there are wicked and abominable laws, which will be in your power to alter. To hang a man for six-and-eightpence, and I know not what—to hang for a trifle, and acquit murder, is in the ministration of the law through the ill-framing of it. I have known in my experience abominable murders acquitted. And to see men lose their lives for petty matters—this is a thing God will reckon for. And I wish it may not lie upon this nation a day longer than you have opportunity to give a remedy."

Referring to finance he maintained that the Treasury had been managed "not unthriftily nor to private uses," and that the debt was considerably under the reported sum of £2,500,000. He had brought down the monthly assessment from £120,000 to £60,000. But the examination of these things was the Parliament's proper work, and therefore, leaving details, he uttered his whole soul in a concluding exhortation to practical earnestness in legislative work. It is impossible to mistake the true ring of genuine metal here.

"Now if I had the tongue of an angel,—if I was so certainly inspired as the holy men of God have been, I could rejoice for your sakes, and for these nations' sakes, and for the sake of God and of His cause which we have all been engaged in; I could move affections in you to that which, if you do it, will save this nation! If not,—you plunge it,—to all human appearance,—and all interests, yea, and all Protestants in the world, into irrecoverable ruin! . . . . . Therefore, I beseech you, do not dispute of unnecessary and unprofitable things which may divert you from carrying on so glorious a work as this is. I think every objection that ariseth is not to be answered; nor have I time for it. I say, look up to God; have peace among yourselves. Know assuredly that if I have interest, I am by the voice of the people the supreme magistrate; and, it may be, do know somewhat that might satisfy my conscience if I stood in doubt. But it is a union, really it is a union between you and me; and both of us united in faith and love to Jesus Christ, and to His peculiar interest in the world,— that must ground this work. And in that, if I have any peculiar interest which is personal to myself, which is not subservient to the public end, it were not an extravagant thing for me to curse myself; because I know God will curse me if I have! I have learned too much of God to dally with Him and to be bold with Him in these things. And I hope I never shall be bold with Him—though I can be bold with men, if Christ be pleased to assist.

"I say, if there be love between us, so that the nations may say, 'these are knit together in one bond to promote the glory of God against the common enemy; to suppress everything that is evil, and encourage what-soever is of godliness,'—yea, the nation will bless you! And really that and nothing else will work off these disaffections from the minds of men, which are great, and perhaps greater than all the opposition you can meet with. I do know what I say when I speak of these things. I speak my heart before God; and, as I said before, I dare not be bold with Him. I have a little faith. I have a little lived by faith, and therein I may be bold. If I spoke other than the affections and secrets of my heart I know He would not bear it at my hands! Therefore in the fear and name of God go on with love and integrity against whatever arises of contrary to those ends which you know and have been told of; and the blessing of God go with you—and the blessing of God *will* go with you!'"

Long before he came to these words the speaker had com-plained of weariness, and expressed sympathy with the cramped constraint of his crowded hearers. But his impassioned appeal to others brought fresh inspiration to himself. The visions he had seen in communion with Hebrew psalmists rose upon his soul again, fill-ing him with triumphant faith; and he could not cease. He went on speaking in the language of Sion—that tongue which has the strange gift of presenting the same eternal truths, the same immortal ideals in so many different forms to successive ages. He saw before him a holy land where strife was banished, where justice needed the sword no more. "'Surely His salvation is nigh them that fear Him'—ah!* 'that glory may dwell in our land! Mercy and Truth are met together: Righteousness and Peace have kissed each other. Truth shall spring out of the earth, and righteousness shall look down from Heaven.'" What hindered the entrance on that promised land? Fightings with-out and fears within. Hostile Papists, scheming priests, and murderous intrigues. But courage!

" If you set your hearts to it, then you will sing Luther's psalm. That is a rare psalm for a Christian; and if he set his heart open and can approve it to God, we shall hear him say 'God is our refuge and strength, a very present help in trouble.' If Pope, and Spaniard, and Devil, and all set themselves against us, though they should 'compass us like bees,' as it is in the hundred and eighteenth psalm,—yet 'in the name of the Lord we should destroy them.' And, as it is in this psalm of Luther's, 'we will not fear though the earth be removed, and though the mountains be carried into the midst of the sea; though the waters thereof roar and be troubled; though the mountains shake with the swelling thereof. There is a river, the

* The interjection in so exceptional a position is not likely to have been inter-polated by a reporter. It vividly suggests the intense feeling struggling in the heart of the speaker.

streams whereof shall make glad the city of God. God is in the midst of
her; she shall not be moved!' Then he repeats two or three times, 'the
Lord of Hosts is with us; the God of Jacob is our refuge!'

"I have done. All I have to say is, to pray God that he may bless
you with His presence; that He, who hath your hearts and mine, would
show His presence in the midst of us.

"I desire now that you will go together and choose your Speaker."

The moral effect of a speech like this in those times must
have been very great. And to succeeding ages it must appear
that it would have been well for Cromwell's reputation if he had
relied upon it. But in judging the necessities of his position
he took no counsel, and probably never allowed himself to be
influenced for a moment by any thought of his reputation.
When the members reached their lobby they found the doors
of the House guarded by soldiery. Every one who attempted to
enter was asked for a certificate under the hand of the chief
clerk in chancery. The certificate was to the effect that the
holder had been returned by such and such a constituency, and
had been approved by his Highness's Council. It appeared
that there were nearly one hundred members without any
such document in their possession; and these were inexorably
excluded.

The event, however, did not prevent the seated members from
proceeding to the election of a Speaker, and they chose Sir
Thomas Widdrington, who was entirely satisfactory to his
Highness. Grand Committees were appointed on privileges,
on elections, on religion, on courts of justice, and on trade. Sir
Charles Wolseley then obtained permission to introduce a Bill
renouncing and disannulling the pretended title of Charles Stuart
to the throne of Great Britain and Ireland.

Before the House adjourned a letter was brought to the
Speaker from the rejected members denouncing the outrage
inflicted in their persons on Parliamentary privilege. The
Clerk of the Commonwealth was thereupon ordered to appear
at the bar on the next day, and to bring with him all the
writs issued and the returns to them. In obedience to this order
he attended, only however to explain that he acted by direction
of the Council. On September 20th it was resolved that the
Council should be desired to give their reasons for this extraordinary procedure. On September 22nd Lord Commissioner

Fiennes brought a message to the effect that the Council had commanded him to give this humble reply—" That the twenty-first article of the Government of the Commonwealth imposed upon them the duty of examining the returns, to see whether the persons elected answered to the qualifications described. By the seventeenth article it was declared that the persons to be elected to serve in Parliament should be persons of known integrity, fearing God, and of good conversation. The Council had examined the returns accordingly, and had not refused to approve any elected members who came under that description. As to those who were not approved, his Highness the Lord Protector had given orders to some persons to take care that they should not come into the House." * When this message had been delivered, a resolution was moved to adjourn until the next morning; but it was lost by 115 to 80. Then by 125 to 29 it was resolved—" That the House do proceed with the great affairs of the nation, and that the excluded members be referred to the Council for redress."

These proceedings gave ample proof that the newly-elected Parliament was very much disposed to take Cromwell's view of its duties; and the Protector could therefore afford to treat with indifference the bold and vigorous protest which ninety-three of the rejected members proceeded to sign and publish. With great truth they said, " He hath now declared that the people's choice cannot give any man a right to sit in Parliament; but the right must be derived from his gracious will and pleasure with that of his councillors, and that his clerk's ticket only must be their evidence." With less truth, but with very natural feeling, they went on to say, " Thus hath he exalted himself to a throne like unto God's, as if he were of himself, and his power from himself, and we were all made for him, to be commanded and disposed of by him, to work for him, and only to serve his pleasure and ambition." That the Protector never at any time took any notice whatever of this protest is one amongst many illustrations of the entire absence of temper from his public policy; and this in one of his fiery disposition is not a little to his credit.

The House now gave itself to humble, practical work in a manner that must have rejoiced the Protector's heart. With due attention to form, they prescribed the simple ceremony to be

* " The Parliamentary History," xxi., p. 27.

adopted when the Protector should give his assent to Bills.
Parliamentary approval was asked by the Council for the appointment of Fiennes and Lisle to be Lord Keepers, and of John Glyn
as Chief Justice. They passed Bills against Charles Stuart;
also for the security of the Protector's person; for the abolition
of the Court of Wards; and for liberty of exporting certain
classes of goods at that time prohibited. They also passed a Bill
for uniting England and Scotland, a measure that had hitherto
depended on the Protector's edict. But when, in January 1657,
a Bill was introduced for continuing the extraordinary tax on
Royalists, it was rejected. This involved the abolition of the
system of Major-Generals, and what is very notable is that
Cromwell's family and connections especially used their influence to throw it out.

In February 1657 the budget of ways and means for carrying on the Spanish war was entered upon, and it was resolved that
£400,000 should be raised. The Spanish war continued to be
popular; and perhaps a great capture of treasure in September
1656 made the House more willing to part with the people's
money, under the idea that the war might after all prove a profitable speculation. After many disappointments a detachment of
Blake's squadron had fallen in with a Spanish West India fleet
of eight ships; two of these were captured, three (or four) were
sunk, and two (or three) escaped. It was a terrible affair, and
there were circumstances that made it peculiarly tragic. The
Governor of Peru, Don Francesco Lopez, was on board with his
wife, five children, and the treasure he had accumulated in his
office. The father, the mother, and the eldest daughter, who
was coming home to be married to the son of the Duke of
Medina Celi, were consumed with their ship. Two boys and
two girls were saved on board the English ships, and were
brought to London, where they were well cared for and afterwards sent home. For this atrocity a day of thanksgiving was
appointed on October 8th (1656).

The fierce temper of the times was shown not only in
public rejoicing over the robbing and burning of Papists, but
also in the cruel punishments of fanatics, whose worst crime
was disorderly conduct. The Protector was personally inclined
to regard Quakers as fit subjects for toleration ; but they
themselves made it very difficult for him to carry out his

views. In April 1656 the service at Whitehall Chapel was disturbed by a Quaker whom the Protector ordered to be taken before a justice of the peace. What became of him is not recorded, but the method of procedure is suggestive of the stocks, or a short imprisonment. The case of James Nayler, which occupied Parliament in the end of 1656, was more serious, and the admirers of Cromwell must wish that he could have seen fit to interpose between timid bigotry and its victim. Nayler had been a soldier of the Commonwealth, an Independent, and member of a church at Wakefield. Falling under the influence of George Fox he became a zealous Quaker, and then, as Fox himself laments, "ran out into imaginations."* His imaginations took the form of supposing himself to be a divine incarnation; and on entering into the town of Bristol he encouraged a display of wild excitement, such as looked painfully like a parody on Christ's entry into Jerusalem. He was naturally arrested, and nothing can more pointedly illustrate the difference between the 17th and the 19th century than what followed. In our time, if a noisy defender of the faith puts in motion some obsolete law against blasphemy, almost every one condemns his fussy zeal, and deplores the injury he does to religion. But James Nayler was solemnly examined by Parliament itself, as a portent of spiritual wickedness. The ordinary law was not thought adequate to his punishment. Contrary to Cromwell's view of the functions of Parliament, the House debated for many days what this poor fool's punishment should be; and, after many had clamoured for his death, at length passed a savage sentence, more worthy of Indians in their war-paint than of sober Puritans. He was to stand in the pillory at Westminster for two hours, to be then flogged at a cart's-tail from Palace Yard to the Old Exchange; his tongue was to be bored through with a hot iron; and the letter B was to be branded on his forehead. He was then to be conveyed to Bristol, carried into the town on horseback with his face to the tail, and there flogged again. Joshua Sprigge and a few others, true to the principles of Independency, petitioned against this barbarity. Desborow and Lawrence objected to boring the man's tongue; but the brutal sentence was carried out. In the interval between the punishments in London and at Bristol the Pro-

* "Fox's Journal," p. 205, 3rd ed., 1765.

E E

tector addressed a message to Parliament, asking in effect why they had thus taken upon themselves the execution of justice without consulting him. He doubted " how far such a proceeding might extend in the consequences of it." In conference with certain officers from the army on a different subject, about two months afterwards, he referred to this case of James Nayler as an illustration of the arbitrary tendencies of a single House unchecked by other constitutional powers. The sentence could not be in accordance with his feelings. We can only wish that he had seen his way to modify it. At the same time, it is difficult to say how he could have done so ; for the sentence was passed in virtue of the Parliament's supreme powers. It certainly deepened Oliver's objection to unlimited Parliaments.

In the same month when this barbarity was perpetrated the Protector gave proof of his sound common sense in regard to questions of religious difference in a letter he wrote to certain bickering Independents in the Newcastle corporation, who were offended at preferment being given in their neighbourhood to Presbyterians. He acknowledged the action, but denied that, where there was " an honest and Christian purpose," any question of Independency or Presbyterianism should weigh with him.

In a despatch to Cardinal Mazarin, dated December 26th 1656, and referring to some obscure dissensions in the Stuart family, by which both the writer and his correspondent hoped to profit, the Protector excused himself that he could not " at that juncture of time, and as the face of his affairs then stood," give open toleration to Catholics ; but he declared that he had been less rigorous than the Long Parliament, and hoped, as soon as he could remove some " impediments " and " weights," to make farther progress in the same direction. In truth, on such matters he was before his age; but he scarcely saw how far his principles would ultimately carry the world.

CHAPTER XXVIII.

THE REJECTED CROWN.

A WHOLE year had passed without any plot worth mentioning against the Protector's life, when on January 8th 1657 a man of weather-beaten form and furtive look was observed to be lingering about Whitehall Chapel after the usual Thursday evening service. His bearing betrayed the old soldier, and his interest in the place did not excite suspicion. Indeed he was known to trooper Henry Toope of the life-guard; but Toope was reticent about him for sufficient reasons; for this furtive loiterer was Miles Sindercombe, one of the mutineers captured and condemned at Burford in the days of the army revolt. He had made his escape then, and had seen service in Scotland since, but had been dismissed. Old comrades had noticed him about in town of late, but he had not encouraged advances, nor was his friendship inviting.

That night a sentry near the chapel sniffed the odour of a burning match; and, guided by his nose, groped his way into the chapel, where plainly there was something wrong. Quickly getting a light he found a slow match burning towards a packet of some inflammable composition, which, if it had caught fire, would soon have wrapped the whole building in flame. The alarm was given. The time was just upon midnight. The Protector was roused from his bed. Messages were sent to the Councillors. Some attendants wanted to ring an alarm bell and summon the train-bands, but such suggestions the Protector peremptorily silenced. Inquiries were made of the guards, and Henry Toope confessed a suspicion of Sindercombe, whose lodging he knew. To that lodging two guardsmen went, and soon returned with Sindercombe streaming with blood from a face-wound received in his desperate resistance.

He was removed to the Tower; and the inquiries that followed revealed a slowly-formed, often-defeated, and finally desperate scheme of assassination. Sexby had been the initiator

E E 2

of it—a fact not to be mentioned without sorrow. The grim trooper, who rebuked the effete Parliament eleven years before, seemed worthy of a better fate than to become a lurking murderer. But he had his money from a "Christian king," and he must give money's worth. It is incredible that he can have ridden in Cromwell's escort, as was said at the time; but at any rate he lurked about Westminster and Hampton Court, scheming with Sindercombe; always expecting an opportunity, but never finding one. At length he departed in disgust, and left the money with Sindercombe. The confederate did his best; hired a house at Hammersmith overlooking the road to Hampton Court; bought horses, secured riders, and planned a vigorous outburst of riot when the moment should come. At last, he thought if he could burn down Whitehall, the rioters might be turned to some use in the confusion. Hence the attempt. He was condemned to death; but by the help of his sister poisoned himself on the night before his execution. He did not fear death; for, said the newspapers, "he was infected with that unevangelical conceit of universal redemption." *
But he objected to being hanged, drawn, and quartered; and this he escaped. He was buried on Tower Hill with an iron bar thrust through his body and appearing above the ground to mark the infamous spot.

This discovery excited genuine emotion in Parliament. The sitting members almost unanimously agreed that security was beginning to be felt under Oliver, and that the continuance of his life and power was now the only safeguard against renewed civil war. The notion that Charles Stuart could secure a bloodless return would at this time have appeared ridiculous. The House had already passed a measure for the Protector's security. They now adjourned for a week; they appointed a day of national thanksgiving on February 20th, and on reassembling after their adjournment they resolved to wait on the Protector in a body to congratulate him on his escape.

This plot of Sindercombe's effected more than an interchange of sympathetic expressions between Protector and Parliament. Many began now to ask themselves whether the true mode of settling the nation would not be the coronation

* In "Cromwelliana"

of Oliver, and the restoration of the old order of things under a new dynasty. The changes of the last fifteen years had indeed been violent; but they had affected persons and parties more than institutions. The common law remained; and in its traditions it so enshrined old habits of public procedure that inconsistencies of language with fact were continually recurrent.* The repeals of statute law, though they had abolished abuses, left the great mass of legislation untouched. Bishops had been swept away; but the Established Church, with its territorial system, its tithes, and its patronage, remained so complete, that a nation accustomed now for a century to successive ecclesiastical changes noticed more the identity than the difference. The Crown and the House of Lords were wanting; but the result was that they were the more conspicuous by their absence. The majority of practical Englishmen under their Protector felt like a crew with a jury-mast. It does well enough to reach some harbour with; but they are always expecting to replace it. The Protectorate was at best a makeshift. How to reach a permanent settlement was a question asked by every one, and answered by none. Oliver, like a true Englishman, was for getting on as well as he could from one year to another, in the hope that prosperity and contentment would evolve a workable constitution. The Republicans on the other hand wanted a brand-new constitution, drawn up on abstract principles after exhaustive debates by delegates of the whole nation. But opinion amongst the trading classes was now favouring a reversion to the old system, with Oliver as king.

Among these trading classes, Alderman Sir Christopher Pack, formerly Lord Mayor of London, was a representative man. He had all the conservative instincts of prosperity, and while credited with considerable talent and power of speech he was not ashamed to devote his gifts to the support of monopolies. He was Master of the Merchant Adventurers, who had entirely engrossed the commerce in woollen goods; and on the occasion of a debate between them and free traders in the Committee of Trade, Pack is said to have "turned in the debate like a horse, and answered every man;" he spoke at least "thirty times," "did cleave like a clegg, and was

* *E.g.*, Oliver himself often speaks of the "three kingdoms."

very angry he could not be heard *ad infinitum.*" The same diarist,* from whom these expressions are quoted, also records that when the conference was held on the readmission of the Jews, " of all the head-pieces there, he was thought to give the best reasons against their coming."

On February 23rd 1657 this Sir Christopher Pack rose in his place in Parliament with a paper in his hand. It contained, he said, proposals tending to the settlement of the nation, and was in the form of a remonstrance to his Highness the Lord Protector. All he asked now was leave to read the paper. There was of course a good deal of difference of opinion on the point; but at last he obtained permission, and read his " remonstrance." In effect, it set forth the desirability of a more legal settlement of the nation than had yet been attained, and proposed a new " Instrument of Government," drawn generally on the lines of the former one, but in one or two points differing from it significantly.

The Protector was asked to undertake the government, with a title left suggestively blank; and he was also to name his own successor. There were to be two Houses of Parliament— the Commons, elected as under the former Instrument, and a second chamber, called vaguely " the other House," to be nominated by the chief magistrate, and approved by the Commons. The Protector's Council was to be relieved of the duty of scrutinising election returns. A tribunal of forty-one commissioners was to be appointed for the purpose, but was only to have a suspensory veto until the House was constituted and in a position to decide disputed returns for itself. Protestant evangelical Christianity was to be recognised and provided for as the religion of the State; but freedom of public worship was to be secured to all denominations not considered dangerous to political stability, or to decency and order.

The prime object of this proposal was to give the existing government a legal instead of a revolutionary sanction. The claim of Parliament to dispose of the crown was well established on old precedents; and although the new Instrument, in its first form as in its last, said nothing about the crown, it assumed that Parliament might mould the chief magistracy into accordance with the needs of the times. The anxious debates and

* " Burton's Diary," i., 308-9.

conferences occasioned by the blank at first left for Oliver's title distracted attention both then and ever afterwards from the real issue to fix it upon a subsidiary matter. The controlling motive of Pack and his supporters was not a wish to see Oliver made king, but a distrust of revolutionary government and a desire to build on ancient precedents. The question was felt to be of such solemn import that the whole of Friday, February 27th, was devoted by Parliament to prayers for divine guidance.

The republican officers of the army now took alarm. They foresaw that the blank in the remonstrance for the title of the chief magistrate would be filled in with the name of king. They therefore collected a strong deputation, consisting of a hundred officers, amongst them Lambert and Fleetwood; and while the Parliament was praying, they waited on the Protector to expostulate against his permission of such a scandal. Their master however soon made them understand that they were greatly mistaken if they supposed they could assume with him the dictatorial *rôle* of the Prætorian Guards. He had made them—not they him; and though he carried respect for their conscientious prejudices even to the extent of tenderness, he did not let it appear in this interview. He told them that the first intimation he had of the proposal was from the spokesman of the officers then present,* and that he had taken no part in any cabals about it. He said the time had been when they boggled not at the word [king]; for the Instrument, by which the existing government stood, was presented to him with the title in it, as some of the deputation could witness; and he had refused to accept it. For his part, he loved the title—a mere feather in a hat—as little as they did. Waxing warm, he taxed them with making him their drudge upon all occasions—as, for instance, to dissolve the Long Parliament—"though that was right enough, for the obstinate continuance of that Parliament had become unbearable." Then they had induced him to call a Parliament, or Convention, of their own naming. And what did that Convention do? "Why, fly at liberty and property. If one man had twelve cows, the Convention held that another who lacked cows ought to take shares with his neighbour. At the instigation of the officers he

* "Burton's Diary." It is not clear whether the intimation had been made previously or not.

had called the former and the present Parliament; and what settlement was there?" Finally he mentioned the case of James Nayler, as an illustration of the tendencies of unchecked Parliaments. "It might be your own case," he said; "by their judicial power they fall on life and limb; and doth the Instrument enable me to prevent it?"* In the issue, several of the highest officers surrendered their objections; and the opposition of others might evidently be overcome if it should appear worth while.

By the end of March, after many debates, Parliament matured Alderman Pack's remonstrance, and changed its name to that of "Petition and Advice." The last touch was the insertion of the title "King of England, Scotland, and Ireland." This was carried by 123 to 62; and it is very noteworthy that in the minority were eight members of the Protector's Council,† and some of his most intimate friends and supporters, such as his steward John Maidstone, Desborow, Whalley, and Pride. Richard Cromwell also voted against it, or at least abstained from voting. The last fact might be ascribed to a show of modesty; but it is impossible in view of the other names to endorse the statement, repeated even by enlightened historians, that "the proposal had been concerted between Cromwell and his most confidential advisers."‡ It is not thus that self-made kings and emperors usually manage their business. Had Cromwell been resolved upon the crown, or even had he been keenly desirous of it as a culminating honour, he would certainly have found means to prevent his own connections and personal dependents from risking the rejection of the vote. That he was not insensible to the attractions of a splendid and venerable title we may well believe. But the whole circumstances of the case go to confirm his own words, that he wished to be guided entirely by indications of the Divine will. Royalty has commonly been held to be so supreme a bliss, that historians have refused to credit the sincerity

* It may reasonably be held that the diarist, or his correspondent, being favourable to the kingship, was so pleased with a reported snub to the army that he rather exaggerated it. Still, he had good information, and was a dull man, not given to fancy. On the whole, the ideas and language are characteristic; and something may be allowed for Oliver's anger at the appearance of dictation.

† Viz., Henry Lawrence (President), Francis Rous, Sydenham, Fleetwood, Skippon, Pickering, Strickland, and Lambert.—"Parl. Hist." xxi.

‡ Godwin, iv., 348.

of men who, having that within their reach, have professed to be turned from it by considerations of duty or religion. But though Oliver had a great admiration for Queen Elizabeth, he appears to have thought the crown so tarnished and soiled by its late wearers that the honour of picking it up was not without some drawbacks.

On the 31st of March the whole House of Parliament went over to Whitehall, and by the hand of their Speaker delivered to the Protector their "Petition and Advice," which he was to accept or reject as a whole. The Speaker explained the purpose of the House to secure a permanent settlement, which, as experience showed, appeared most likely to be gained under some modified form of the old constitution. The document was then read by the clerk, and Oliver made a short reply, impressive not less by its reticence than by the emotion it betrayed. If he should hastily and unwisely accept such a proposal, he said "it had been better he should never have been born."

Three days afterwards he requested that a committee might be sent to receive his reply. His health was not good at this time. His enormous expenditure of energy during the past seventeen years was now telling upon him in feverish fits and exhaustion, foreshadowing the end. He received the committee with an apology—surely needless—for delay. It looks as though his mind, distraught with anxiety and bodily weakness, had magnified the lapse of time. His answer was brief and inconclusive. He appreciated the care shown by Parliament for securing liberty both religious and civil, but he did not see his way to accept the title.

"If the answer of the tongue as well as the preparation of the heart be from God, I must say my heart and thoughts, ever since I heard the Parliament were upon this business—though I could not take notice of your proceedings therein without breach of your privileges—yet as a common person I confess I heard of it in common with others,—I must say I have been able to attain no further than this: That seeing the way is hedged up so as it is to me, and I cannot accept the things offered unless I accept all, I have not been able to find it my duty to God and you to undertake this charge under that title."

But the question was not allowed to be closed thus. The practical arguments on the other side were very strong, and however the members of Parliament regarded Oliver's scruples—

whether as affected or real—they believed he only needed a little
pressure to give way. On April 8th therefore the House waited
upon him again, with their reasons for adhering to the Petition
and Advice. And a grand committee, numbering ninety-nine
members, was appointed to give him any farther satisfaction he
required as to the meaning of their "reasons."

On the 13th this committee had an interview with the Protector. After some preliminary and rather curious fencing as to
the method of procedure—whether the committee should state
their reasons and the Protector should retort his objections, or
whether the Protector should state his difficulties and the committee should solve them by elucidations of the proposed scheme
of government—Oliver prevailed, and the leading members of
the committee in turn, like a squadron of ships successively
delivering their fire on a battery, opened out their logical artillery.
Their arguments may, as Carlyle complains, be dull reading now;
but they showed a great deal of sound sense, and the chief points
are well worth repeating.

Whitelock* urged that, however carefully the powers of a
new office might be defined, unforeseen contingencies would arise,
and it would be impossible to resort in such a case to precedents.
But the advantage of the royal title was that, besides any limitations now to be imposed by statute, its prerogatives would in
omitted contingencies be limited by an exhaustless array of precedents. Glyn supported this by observing that " the prerogative
of the king is bounded as well as any acre of land." The Chief-
Justice also enlivened his argument by an illustration which
shows how free, and at the same time how real, the discussion
was. He supposed the case of a subject aggrieved by an act of
the Protector. Such a man says : " My Lord Protector, you are
sworn to govern according to the law, and yet you do thus and
thus." " Do I ? " says the Protector. " Why, what ought I to
do?" " Well, the king would not have done so," retorts the
aggrieved person. " But I am not the king," rejoins the Protector; " I am not bound to do as the king; I am Lord
Protector. If I have not acted as Protector, show me where the
law is." In a case like that, argued Glyn, the Protector might
" put any one to a stumble." Probably he had the case of

* As recorded in "The Case of Monarchy Stated."—"Somers Tracts," vi.,
352, &c.

Cony in his mind. Commissioner Fiennes endeavoured to clinch this argument by saying : "Either you must enumerate all the powers of the Protector, or what is left unenumerated must be the same thing as the law says is the duty of a king." But in this latter alternative, to which the judges inclined, Fiennes held that with the powers and authorities of a king the name also should go.

Glyn argued also that a *name* may be a substantial *thing*, and is so in the case of the royal title. "The whole body of the law is carried on this wheel." To this Lord Broghill added, that it was surely better to fit the supreme magistrate to the laws in being than to fit those laws to him. Fiennes strengthened the argument as to the significance of names by the fact that the associations of the title Protector implied a temporary arrangement, and led people to expect some change. Lisle added: "Though neither Parliament nor people have a jealousy of your person, yet of the title they have, for want of a right understanding." Glyn likewise urged that there were always incalculable hazards in the change of an ancient name, and reminded Cromwell that the Long Parliament, and notably Ireton, had on this ground resisted the change of the word Parliament to "Representative."

The Chief-Justice insisted farther on the binding force of the advice of Parliament, and the desire of a whole people. "This," he said, "is the first government tendered since these troubles by a general and universal consent of the people." Sir Charles Wolseley added that the people were much set on the title. "Your Highness," he said, "hath been pleased to call yourself— as when you speak to the Parliament—a servant. You are so indeed to the people ; and it is your greatest honour so to be. I hope then, sir, you will give the people leave to name their own servant. That is a due you cannot, you will not certainly, deny them." It seemed obvious to retort that the title had been formally abolished by an Act supposed to represent the national will. But Glyn, as though anticipating this, said "there never was any quarrel with the office ; only with maladministration."

Sir Charles Wolseley made a good point in showing that while as Protector Cromwell was "obliged to the law," yet he "had not the advantage of the law." He was bound to govern according to a system all the traditions of which were against him.

Lord Broghill raised a still more practical argument by referring to the statute of Henry VII., according to which obedience and service to a *de facto* king were made lawful, no matter how the crown had been obtained. Thus by his coronation Cromwell would relieve timid people of apprehensions about possible consequences of their obedience in any counter-revolution.

Such were the chief points raised by the committee* in favour of the royal title ; and it must be admitted that under the circumstances they had considerable force. Cromwell on the other hand said comparatively little, and it may be added, nothing very definitely to the purpose. He was not satisfied apparently with the form taken by the conference ; though what he would have preferred is not very clear. Carlyle says he wanted to be "drawn out." But this the committee, after some preliminary reticence, certainly tried to accomplish, and failed. Finally, acknowledging he had very little to say at that time, he adjourned the consultation over the Sunday to Monday, April 13th.

How the Sunday was spent by the Protector we can well imagine. He was in terrible perplexity ; not as some have supposed because he was " letting I dare not wait upon I would ;" but because his decision might confirm or ruin the whole public work of his life. There are strong reasons for thinking that as a matter of policy his decision was ultimately wrong, and that it did seriously affect for the worse the destinies of the nation he loved. But neither his decision, nor his character, nor his circumstances give any justification for the idea that in this interval of hesitation he was actuated mainly by personal hopes and fears. Surely he had given sufficient proof that there were hardly any limits to what he *dared* do, except the fear of mistaking Providence. As to his alleged fear of the army, his conduct at Ware and at Burford, when the army was far stronger and he far weaker than now, is a sufficient answer to that. Or, if more is needed, his proud rebuke of the recent military deputation, his possession of a new militia, and his proved mastery over his

* Not, of course, in the order given here. I have endeavoured to classify them.

greatest lieutenants, whom he cashiered or even imprisoned on the slightest sign of insubordination, are enough to show that with the Parliament and the majority of the nation at his back he could have held his crown even against his Ironsides.

On Monday, April 13th, he met the committee again, and made a long speech in reply to their arguments. He admitted the force of what they had urged in favour of the royal title, but still thought all practical advantages might be secured if a supreme executive officer were legally recognised under another name. The main object of their policy, he insisted, should for the present be to preserve peace. It was with that view he had assumed his place—" not so much out of hope of doing good, as out of a desire to prevent mischief and evil." He compared himself to " a good constable set to keep the peace of the parish." Then, with some frankness and some evident reticence, he spoke of the feeling entertained by many of his old soldiers. He was much more flattering to them behind their backs than to their faces. He told the story, as already quoted in an earlier chapter, of their enlistment; and with pride he added, " from that day forward they were never beaten." " I cannot think," he said, " that God would bless an undertaking of anything which would justly and with cause grieve them. True, they may be troubled without cause; *and I must be a slave if I should comply with any such humour as that.*" The national authority must be maintained; but perhaps factious division could best be opposed " by complying, indulging, and being patient to the weakness and infirmities of men who have been faithful, and have bled all along in this cause." Then, farther, it was a serious consideration with him that the providence of God seemed to " have blasted the very title." To assume it would seem to be like building Jericho again.

The speech did not announce any definite conclusion; but the Protector had by this time pretty well made up his own mind to refuse. If he did not say so yet, it was because he liked the Petition and Advice on the whole very well. If the royal title were dropped, and a few other amendments introduced, he thought the document well fitted to give a Parliamentary foundation to his government; and, alas, he did not count upon the nearness of his death. But the Parliament had insisted that he must accept the whole Petition or none; and this formal difficulty required some delay and management to overcome it. Meantime his health was bad; and another plot had exploded harmlessly, causing, however, considerable occupation to the wearied Protector.

On Thursday, April 16th, the committee returned to the charge, repeating for the most part the arguments they had already used. On Monday, the 20th, Oliver replied in a short speech, notable chiefly for his frank and emphatic acknowledgment that he had "no title to the government of these nations but what was taken up in a case of necessity, and as *a temporary means to meet the actual emergency.*" This is scarcely the language of a man bent on founding a new dynasty at all costs. But he now offered a paper of objections to various points of the Petition, and left the committee to consider them.

In a long and important speech to the committee next day (Tuesday, April 21st), he left the question of kingship on one side, and addressed himself to the other proposals in the document. To impress his hearers both with the importance of a settlement and with the difficulties that lay in the way, he returned to that narrative form of argument so dear to men who have reason to think they have accomplished somewhat in the world. Both the Long Parliament and the Little Parliament had failed to propound any plan for uniting religious liberty with secular order. Would the Petition and Advice succeed? He thought it would, with some amendments. But with those amendments we need not trouble ourselves, seeing how soon all came to nothing. Three points, however, illustrate the character and policy of the speaker. He desired and obtained a more strict exclusion from the franchise in Ireland and Scotland of disaffected persons; he required that the exclusion of "public preachers" from Parliament should not apply to any but acting pastors of congregations; and he added a hope that, though nothing to that effect occurred in the Petition, the Parliament intended a reform of the law, and also the reformation of public morals.

The Parliament readily amended their Petition as suggested; and, finally, on May 9th, the committee went to Whitehall, to receive, as they hoped, the Protector's assent. Just as they were going, a party of officers in the army requested permission to present a petition. They were called in, and offered their document at the bar. It was a petition against the restoration of the royal title. There was no time to consider it—scarcely even to hear it; perhaps indeed the committee did not hear it at all. But they went their way to the Banqueting House, and found that on the one point the Protector was immovable. He acknowledged that the document was "very honourable and honest, and the product worthy of a Parliament." But he added :—

> "I have only had the unhappiness, both in my conferences with your committees and in the best thoughts I could take to myself, not to be convinced of the necessity of that thing which hath been so often insisted on by you—to wit, the title of king—as in itself so necessary as it seems to be apprehended by you. . . . . At the best, if I should do anything on this account to answer your expectations, I should do it doubtingly. And certainly, whatsoever is so, is not of faith; and whatsoever is not of faith, is sin to him that doth it. . . . . I should not be an honest man if I did not tell you that I cannot accept of the government, nor undertake the charge of it—as to which, I have a little more experimented than everybody what troubles and difficulties do befall men under such trusts, and in such undertakings,—I say, I am persuaded to return this answer to you—that I cannot undertake this government with the title of king. And that is mine answer to this great and weighty business."

"I am persuaded," he says. What was it that persuaded him? Ludlow says it was the petition of military officers. But the answer was decided upon before that was drawn. Meantime several of the Major-Generals had begun to favour the title. But Oliver had a tenderness for the old soldiers who disliked it. He saw in their feelings a confirmation of his own fear, that the crown had become a cursed thing. There was some noble revulsion too from such a culmination to his career as the acquisition of "a feather in his hat." In a word, he was not inwardly free to accept without haunting doubts. And therefore he put aside what, to the vulgar—or, as he would have said, to the carnal—mind, was the most splendid prize the world had to give.

On the whole the policy of this decision was more than doubtful. A ruler, like every craftsman, must to some extent conform his work to his materials. Now at that time the little knot of Republicans had no appreciable weight with public opinion. That the English people generally craved a king is indisputable. Whether the precedents for Parliamentary interference with the succession would have reconciled public feeling to the establishment of an entirely new dynasty may be questioned; but certainly that was more probable than the continuance of a Protectorate.

The Parliament had now no alternative but to substitute the title of Lord Protector for that of King. With this alteration the Petition and Advice received Oliver's formal assent, and became an Act of Parliament. The most important purpose supposed to be gained by it was the conversion of a revolutionary government into a constitutional authority, ratified by the nation represented in Parliament. To point this significance of the new law, it was thought expedient to inaugurate afresh, by a solemn ceremonial, the Protector's acceptance of his office. This ceremony was held on June 26th 1657 in Westminster Hall. Great preparations were made for the event. The Parliament and all dignitaries, together with the foreign ambassadors, had places assigned them. As though to mark the Parliamentary basis of his authority, the Protector received from the hands of the Speaker the purple robe, the Bible, the sword, and the golden sceptre, the symbolism of each being duly explained by the mouthpiece of the national representatives. The Protector took an oath of fealty to the constitution. Mr. Manton, a favourite preacher of his, commended him to the Divine guidance and protection. Then trumpets blared, and heralds proclaimed, and the people shouted, and it was supposed a profound moral impression had been made. What was wanting however was just the mystic sacredness conferred by an appeal to dateless habits of reverence for traditional sanctions. In the ceremony there were all the elements of a coronation, except precisely what would have completed the spell,—the solemn Abbey and the ancient crown. To adopt all the childish paraphernalia of State, with the perverse exception of what gives to such things a consecrating charm, was entirely of a piece with the illogical and inconsistent methods of the English Commonwealth in all matters of external form.

After this ceremony, the Parliament rose until the following January (1658), when Alderman Pack and others hoped to occupy the Peers' Chamber; but by what title, except that of the "other House," was unfortunately not settled, and this merely nominal question eventually broke up the

Parliament. Nay, too probably it hastened the death of the Protector.

Meanwhile, whatever germs of disintegration within the Commonwealth were cherished by individual crochets and conceits, its external power and renown, being dependent on wisdom and vigour at the helm, were rising from year to year. Following the ideas of his age, Cromwell relied on French jealousy of Spain to gain for him that delusive object of traditional English ambition—a foothold on the northern shores of the continent. He negotiated a treaty, by which French and English troops supported by an English fleet were to take from Spain the towns of Ostend, Gravelines, Mardike, and Dunkirk. The last two were to be England's share of the spoil, Cromwell undertaking that the Roman Catholic religion should be freely tolerated.* Accordingly 6,000 Ironsides were landed at Boulogne in May; and such was the fame of these troops that Louis XIV. was highly gratified with the opportunity of seeing them. But the operations against the coast towns were delayed. The French found their advantage in the mere presence of the English armament, which, by keeping the Spaniards on the coast, facilitated more inland movements of French forces. They soon found however that Cromwell was not to be trifled with. He wrote to his ambassador, Lockhart, at the end of August, peremptorily requiring either that the operations agreed upon should be undertaken at once, or that his troops should return. Mazarin, who was said to be less afraid of the devil than of Oliver, at once took the hint. Before the end of September Mardike was captured, and delivered up to an English governor.

The chief reason for Mazarin's politeness to Cromwell was the now undisputed supremacy of the English Commonwealth at sea. A brilliant exploit of Blake in the spring had excited the admiration and terror of all foreign navies. In April he found the Spanish treasure-fleet from Mexico lying at Teneriffe, in the bay of Santa Cruz. The fleet, consisting of sixteen vessels, was itself strongly armed, and it lay under shelter of nine fortresses, disposed at intervals round the bay. Blake sailed into the bay early in the morning, and in a fight of nine hours battered all the fortresses into ruin, and sank, or drove

* Godwin, iv., 542.

F F

ashore, every Spanish ship. No plunder was obtained, but as affecting the national power the victory was worth more than any treasure. On the tidings of this achievement Cromwell wrote to Blake, sending a jewel voted by Parliament, and praising "the goodness and loving-kindness of the Lord, wherewith His people hath been followed in all these late revolutions." Blake did not long survive. He died within sight of home, and his body was laid in Westminster Abbey, till it was dragged thence in the drunken rage of the Restoration.

The slight sputter of conspiracy mentioned above as disturbing Parliamentary debates on the kingship did not cause much alarm. It was the work of Fifth-Monarchy fanatics without worldly alliances. Several people were imprisoned, but all were released without trial, and the leader of the movement, Venner, a wine-cooper, survived to try the same thing under Charles II.; after which, it need scarcely be said, he was not allowed to survive any longer.

An incident that quickly followed Oliver's rejection of the crown showed how little his decision had been influenced by fear of his leading officers. This was the dismissal of Major-General Lambert, and his relegation to private life. Lambert had been Cromwell's intimate associate from the days of the revolt of the army. He had supported his powerful colleague in most of the campaigns, and in all the revolutions that led to the Protectorate. But recently his conceit of his own capacity had tempted him to overlook the difference between mere subtlety of brain and mastery over men. His bearing led the Protector to ask him point-blank what his meaning was; and as the answer was unsatisfactory, he was called upon to resign his commissions. He was not illiberally treated, for he received a pension of £2,000 a year, and lived in rural retirement at Wimbledon.

The latter half of the year 1657 passed without any notable events, except the progress of the campaign in the Netherlands. The Protector was occupied with details of executive work, to which he always gave the most business-like attention. He had also, with the advice of his Council, to nominate the members of the "other House." In the month of November he enjoyed perhaps the last of his happy days, when his "two little wenches" were at length married to the husbands of their choice. Frances had succeeded in convincing her father that the stories about her Robert were a pack of lies. She was married at Whitehall on November 11th, all unconscious of the cloud of doom so near ; and her sister Mary became Lady Fauconberg, at Hampton Court, within a week after.

Parliament was duly summoned to meet again on the 20th of January 1658. The list of the " other House " included some able men, as Skippon, Desborow, Whalley, Maynard (Cony's counsel), and Lockhart, the ambassador to France. Whitelock of course had a seat there, and by a stroke of blundering policy Sir Arthur Haselrig was summoned. He however contemptuously rejected the doubtful honour, and insisted on admission to his seat in the Commons' House, from which he had been excluded. Six of the old peerage were nominated, but only one came. The new Instrument of Government gave the Commons entire control over the constitution of their own House, and Cromwell made no attempt to continue the exclusion of the members formerly rejected by his Council. All who took the oath according to the Instrument were admitted, and Sir Arthur Haselrig, making no scruple about that, came in with the rest.

The Protector, being weak in health, could not give a very long address at the opening of this session, and he followed the custom of previous monarchs in directing Nathaniel Fiennes, Commissioner of the Great Seal, to supplement his words. It is pathetic to find the weary Oliver still harping upon the eighty-fifth Psalm, and its aspiration " that glory may dwell in our land ! "

The " other House " proved to be not only a failure but a stumbling-block. On the very first day a difficulty arose. They sent a message to the Commons asking concurrence in a request to the Protector to name a day for public prayer. In the reply some name must be given to the senders of the message, and a squabble on this paltry issue was permitted to wreck the Parliament. Oliver, finding it difficult to believe that the majority of an elect assembly of Englishmen would imperil substantial interests for the sake of a word, appears to have thought they only needed a plain statement of what those interests were to awaken them to their responsibility. But he did not make sufficient allowance for the fact that during five years past the nation had been accustomed to leave its really pressing affairs in the hands of its strongest man, while Parliaments

F F 2

relieved of responsibility had debated and wrangled over theories without any immediate reference to facts.

However, he made a strenuous effort to convert the present Parliament to a more practical temper. He called the two Houses together within six days of their opening—so serious did the crisis appear to him; and he implored them by every consideration of patriotism and religion to prefer the interests of peace at home and persecuted Protestantism abroad to wretched crotchets about names and forms. He explained to them the situation abroad—how the resources of Spain and Austria and Hungary were likely to outweigh all the Protestant elements of Germany; how Pope Alexander VII. was making politic combinations, while Protestant Sweden and Denmark were flying at each other's throats, and the Dutch were valuing gain more than godliness. France, for the moment, was unconformable to papal designs. But there was no telling how long that would last, and if France and Spain should become friends, "then would England be the object of all the fury and wrath of all the enemies of God and our religion in the world!" Turning to domestic affairs, he insisted that the peace preserved amidst the persevering efforts of faction was a miracle of God's providence which ought to be gratefully guarded. "And whoever shall seek to break it, God Almighty root that man out of this nation! And He *will* do it, let the pretences be what they may." The horror with which Oliver contemplated the possibility of another civil war is evident in his unstudied language, coming straight from the heart.

"He that considereth not the 'woman with child'—the sucking children of this nation that know not the right hand from the left, of whom, for aught I know, it may be said this city is as full as Nineveh was said to be—he that considereth not these must have the heart of a Cain, who was marked, and made to be an enemy to all men, and all men enemies to him! For the wrath and justice of God will prosecute such a man to his grave, if not to hell!"

He declared that the Cavaliers were "inviting the Spaniard himself to carry on their cause, and he hinted at the possession of more knowledge on this subject than it would be prudent at that time to explain. In a word, he poured out his very soul in an entreaty to the Houses to provide for the maintenance of national security, and to leave subsidiary questions to a more convenient time.

But it was of no use. The Republicans had convinced themselves that the sort of acknowledgment to be extended to the other poor little House was a matter of more consequence than Protestantism abroad, or peace and progress at home. They succeeded in proving how accurate was the foresight which had excluded Haselrig and his friends at first; but more they were not permitted to do. On February 4th 1658 the Protector came unexpectedly to the House of Lords, and dissolved the Parliament. It is difficult to see what else he could have done at this time. Perhaps it might have been wiser to have dissolved immediately on his new inauguration. But his expectation seems to have been that the existing House of Commons would support a constitution of their own devising. And he underestimated the practical difficulties sure to arise on the inevitable return of the excluded members.

"That which brought me into the capacity I now stand in was the Petition and Advice given me by you; who, in reference to the ancient constitution, did draw me to accept the place of Protector. . . . Certainly I did look that the same men who made the frame should make it good unto me. I can say in the presence of God, in comparison with whom we are but like poor creeping ants upon the earth, I would have been glad to have lived under my wood-side, to have kept a flock of sheep, rather than undertaken such a government as this. But undertaking it by the Advice and Petition of you, I did look that you who had offered it unto me should make it good."

Instead of that, members of the House, notwithstanding their oath to the constitution, were known to be "enlisting persons by commission from Charles Stuart to join with any insurrection that might be made." The position had become intolerable. "I think it high time to put an end to your sitting," he exclaimed, "and I do dissolve this Parliament; and let God judge between you and me!"

CHAPTER XXIX.

THE WEARY TITAN.

THE dissolution of the Parliament left Oliver more than ever alone in his Titanic task. By his own unaided strength he had to hold up the firmament of authority and order. There were mutterings of earthquake within, and roarings of an outer deluge. But after six months of supreme and almost silent effort there was a portentous calm, in which he lay down to die, and left the world at gaze for more than a year longer before ruin came.

In addressing Parliament he had not exaggerated the dangers threatening the Commonwealth. With his curious faculty for obtaining always at the right moment the precise information most needful for his immediate duties, he could not fail to be aware that fresh schemes for combining invasion from abroad with conspiracy at home were now drawing to a head, and were very nearly ripe for prevention. One day about this time, when Lord Broghill was at Whitehall, the Protector suddenly told him, with a shrewd smile, that an old friend of his lordship had just come to town. "Why, whom can your Highness mean?" asked Broghill. "The Marquis of Ormond," answered Oliver, amused at the startled dismay evident on his faithful follower's face. Broghill, anxious to clear himself of any collusion with the organiser of papistic insurrection, protested that if it were so the visit was entirely without his privity. "I know that well enough," said Cromwell; "but if you wish to do your old friend a kindness, let him know that I am fully informed both as to his presence and his aims." Lord Broghill took the hint, and being directed by Cromwell to Ormond's lodging, told the Marquis what had passed, and had no difficulty in persuading him to go back hastily to his master.*

---

* This story is given in "Budgell's Memoirs of the Boyles." Thurloe, writing to Henry Cromwell on March 15, 1658, mentions Ormond's recent

At first sight such an action appears indicative of romantic generosity. But there was more in it than that. The Protector's best source of information at this time was open to him only on condition that it should be used so far as possible in such a manner as to prevent the Royalists from courting death. At the time of the Vowel plot in 1654 Sir Richard Willis, a devotee of royalty, had been amongst the arrested. With this man Cromwell had a personal interview, and suiting his arguments to the character he had to deal with, succeeded in convincing Willis that under the existing rule any farther attempts at insurrection would be a mere waste of loyal blood. Other inducements of the usual kind were added, and the result was that Willis undertook to keep the Protector informed of Royalist schemes on certain conditions. One of these was that conspirators betrayed by the spy should be spared, and another was that Willis himself should never appear openly as a witness. Such are the ignoble arts to which even a great soul can be constrained when once involved in the mining and counter-mining of political intrigue. Of course Cromwell knew better than to depend much upon testimony so tainted by falsehood at its source. But he had little difficulty in testing it for himself, or in following up the hints thus gained. The result was the discovery of the most formidable combination yet effected against him. Its danger consisted not in any engagement of popular sympathy, but in the preparations made by the Spaniards to send over from their Flemish ports a considerable and well-equipped force, which, if a landing were once effected, would be a strong nucleus attracting round it all discontented schemers, both among Republicans and Royalists. It was to promote this scheme that the Marquis of Ormond had come to London.

Secretary Thurloe, writing to Henry Cromwell on March 16th, said he believed that "Ormond's encouragements were not so great as he expected;" and on the previous day, in a letter to Lockhart, Thurloe said, "I must assure your lordship that there are no grounds at all for the falsehoods which are spread up and down of our disorders. I trust if they [the conspirators] ever go on with this attempt they will find it otherwise." The

presence in London. The essential feature of the story, the Protector's deliberate permission of Ormond's escape, is certainly historical.—Thurloe, "State Papers," vol. vii.

course of events proved that Thurloe was justified in this opinion. The virulence of the conspirators, as exemplified in the tract "Killing no Murder" issued in 1657, was caused not by hope, but by despair. The importance and the ability of that tract have been greatly over-rated. Its only merits, incisiveness of language and concentrated bitterness of satire, made it attractive, as it is even yet in parts, to lovers of vigorous invective. But a nation that enjoyed the order and prosperity resulting from the Protectoral Government was not greatly disturbed by it. And even its first avowed, and probably real author, the fanatic Sexby, is said to have acknowledged that the Parliamentary enactment of the Petition and Advice had now placed Cromwell's power on a legitimate foundation.* The Protector was fully aware of the constant risk of assassination, and took effective precautions. He made a practice of occasionally inspecting the guards himself, and when likely to be exposed to pistol bullets he wore a shirt of mail. But he had good reason for believing that his danger consisted in the vindictiveness of faction, and not in any widespread hostility to his rule.

Parliament having been dissolved on Thursday, February 4th, the Protector summoned the chief military officers to Whitehall on Saturday the 6th. In a long speech he explained to them the project of foreign invasion to support domestic conspiracy, and his vain attempts to awaken Parliament to a sense of the untimeliness of squabbles about form and ceremony. The officers in response declared their resolve to live or die with him in defence of the Commonwealth. But he felt neither desire nor necessity for an exclusive reliance on the army. On Friday March 12th he sent for the Lord Mayor, Aldermen, and Common Council, and addressed to them a similar speech. He specially "acquainted them with the reasons which moved him to dissolve the last Parliament," and they appeared to be "greatly satisfied" with his discourse.† Thus supported both by the army and by the city, he quietly laid hands on the chief agents of the conspiracy, and paralysed the whole scheme. Major-General

---

* Sexby was arrested in July, 1657, when already embarked for the continent. He was imprisoned in the Tower, and became distracted in mind. He died in January 1658. His avowal of "Killing no Murder," and his professed change of opinion are attested in "Thurloe" vi. 560. He said the book was printed before the adoption of the Petition and Advice: but he was incoherent.

† Thurloe to Lockhart, *l.c.*

Harrison had already been sent to the Tower—a measure of perhaps excessive caution. His imprisonment was brief. We may hope it was mild. But the necessity was a bitter one, and we believe Cromwell felt it so.

Prominent amongst the conspirators was Sir Henry Slingsby, who had taken part in the Penruddock affair, and had since been a prisoner in very lax confinement at Hull. It was proved that he was abusing the licence allowed him by giving commissions from Charles Stuart, and by endeavouring to seduce the garrison so that the castle and town might be made available for a landing of the invaders. Dr. Hewitt, an episcopal clergyman who had been allowed some measure of liberty to exercise his office, was proved to have likewise distributed commissions and to have been diligently engaged in preparing for a rising in London, when, as was hoped, the landing of Charles should draw the troops from the capital. With these were arrested three members of what was called the " sealed knot," a committee whose business it was to work separately without letting their followers know the members or even the existence of the other branches of the plot. Of this committee Sir Richard Willis was the apparent leader, and to keep up appearances he was arrested with the others.

That Cromwell was averse to political executions is sufficiently proved by their paucity during his precarious reign. But if an impression should be made that plots of this kind involved no risk of life to the plotters on discovery, Secretary Thurloe thought, and Cromwell now thought with him, that great encouragement would be given to conspiracy.* Stern measures therefore were determined on. A high court of justice was commissioned in accordance with the Act for the security of the Protector. It consisted of one hundred and thirty persons in addition to the judges and other great officials. By this court Sir Henry Slingsby and Dr. Hewitt were condemned ; and they were beheaded on Tower Hill on June 8th, 1658. It cannot be conceded that these men deserved more sympathy than we freely accord to all who stake their lives on their political opinions and prejudices. Dr. Hewitt indeed deserves rather less pity than his companion in misfortune, inasmuch as he misused the privileges of his sacred office to stir up a sanguinary strife, not for any

* Thurloe's " State Papers," vii., 84.

broad interests of mankind, but for the fiction of a divine right inherent in a God-forsaken family. Great efforts were made to save both of these men, and it is quite credible that Elizabeth Claypole interceded specially for Hewitt. But her own letter to her sister-in-law in Ireland proves that the story of her reproaching her father with cruelty in this case cannot be true.* Slingsby had married an aunt of Cromwell's son-in-law, Lord Fauconberg; and it is easy to conceive the pressure brought to bear in his case. But the exertion of private influence probably determined the Protector to be on his guard against his own natural feelings, and it is surely creditable to his impartiality that while a considerable number of arrested and condemned prisoners escaped for whom no such influence could be exerted, the only two brought to the block were men who had such powerful advocacy in their favour.

While these trials were in progress or preparation the Royalists of the city were irritated into recklessness by the proofs of their impotence, and on May 15th broke out into foolish and hopeless violence. A plan was concerted for capturing the Lord Mayor, and for simultaneously seizing various points in the city and Westminster. But as usual, Government had timely information, and an hour or so before the intended execution of the plot the train-bands fell in; the Lieutenant of the Tower marched through the streets with five small cannon; seventy prisoners were taken; and the plot was dissipated. Seven of the conspirators were brought to trial, and six condemned, of whom three were reprieved, and the rest executed.

The swiftness and punctuality with which every attempt at insurrection was suppressed at the very moment when performance fell due showed of course the watchfulness and vigour of Cromwell's Government; but on an impartial survey of the whole circumstances, something more than that is indicated. For in England no Government, however conspicuous its ability, has ever been able to maintain public order and security when the general feeling of the nation has been against it. Even in Russia

---

* The letter is dated four days after Hewitt's execution. "Truly the Lord has been very gracious to us in doing for us above what we could expect; and now He has showed himself more extraordinary in delivering my father out of the hands of his enemies, which we have all reason to be sensible of in a very particular manner. For certainly not only his family would have been ruined, but in all probability the whole nation would have been involved in blood."— Thurloe, vii.

that is [impossible; much more so is it in any nation with traditions of freedom. There is much reason for believing that while the bulk of the English people undoubtedly hankered after monarchy, as the Israelites after the flesh-pots of Egypt, still, to the end of Cromwell's life and even for a little while afterwards, they were averse to a return of the Stuarts. The Protectorate secured to them justice, order, and prosperity. It gave them a religious freedom, which, though very imperfect, generally satisfied the more earnest and opinionative amongst them. But perhaps what contributed more than anything else to the acquiescence of public feeling was the dignity and renown conferred upon the English name by Cromwell's now unrivalled empire of the sea, and the weight of his word with foreign potentates. It is impossible ever to justify the national vanity that prefers splendour abroad to prosperity and progress at home. But in Cromwell's case these latter had already been secured ; and his ambition, to make the name of an Englishman as awe-inspiring as that of a Roman in days of old, was at least more congruous with the condition of international relations in his day than any such preposterous conceit can be with times when we are almost within sight of a " federation of the world."

The fame and power of the Commonwealth were now at a culminating point. For more than two years France had refused an asylum to the claimant of the English throne, while at the same time receiving Cromwell's envoys with honours scarcely accorded to the ambassadors of the greatest monarchs. Spain, while anxious to avenge her lost fleets by raising a civil war in England, had shrunk from the enterprise as impracticable, and had implicitly confessed the inviolability of the British coast. But now Spain had to submit to military as well as naval humiliation, and surrendered to Ironsides garrisons that France had in vain sought to wrest from her. In May, under the command of Lockhart, Cromwell's ambassador, the English troops joined the French in the siege of Dunkirk. Louis XIV. and his cardinal minister were at Calais, and Lord Fauconberg was sent over as a special envoy on a complimentary mission. The magnificent king lavished upon his visitor all possible tokens of his sense of the honour thus done him, and Fauconberg felt highly flattered. But while the ceremonial minister of the Commonwealth was thus illustrating the vitality of the monarchical creed, the living pillars of the State were drawn up in grim rigidity on the sand-dunes of Dunkirk. The Spaniards, led by the Prince of Condé,* marched round to the north of the town, manœuvering to raise the siege, and on June 4th a decisive battle was fought. With Condé were the English princes, Charles's younger brothers. The six thousand Ironsides formed the left wing of Turenne's army, and extended across the sands to the margin of the sea. Their charge was resistless, carrying all before it, and as had been their custom on other fields, after securing their own side of the battle they went to the relief of the right wing, where Turenne was hard pressed. The engagement was hot, and the troops lost many killed and wounded. Their firmness, discipline, and resistless force extorted expressions of admiration from the future James II. It was the last conspicuous appearance of these fighting saints on any earthly field of battle ; and it is perhaps permissible to wish that their final effort had been made for a worthier cause than one of worldly policy and national aggression.

Dunkirk was surrendered a few days afterwards ; and in the middle of June a pompous embassy was sent over to deliver the keys to "the greatest captain on earth."† The Protector received the embassy in the Banqueting House at Whitehall. When the complimentary speech was concluded, the envoy handed to his Highness a letter from the French king. As the Protector took it, his eye seemed to be caught by something in the address. He looked at it for a moment doubtfully, and then put the letter in his pocket without opening it. The envoy asked Thurloe what was wrong with the letter. Thurloe replied that his Highness expected to receive from his Majesty the style of "brother." ‡

There is no doubt that Oliver was punctilious as to all observances supposed to involve the dignity of his government. But in his private life, so far as he could, he preserved the free habits of his earlier days. Thus on one occasion when he was driving in his coach near Hyde Park, George Fox, who was jogging along on horseback towards the modern

---

* Out of rivalry with Turenne he was serving against his own nation.

† An expression of the Duc de Crequi, on behalf of Cardinal Mazarin.

‡ Extracted by Godwin, iv., 548, from the diary of Dr. Henry Sampson, who gives it on the authority of Sir Thomas Rokeby, an eye-witness of the reception. The story goes on that Louis exclaimed in anger, "Am I to call such a fellow my brother?" "Aye," said Mazarin, "your father too, if you can gain anything by it."

Babylon, pushed his way to the side of the carriage. The life-guards would have driven him off, but Oliver bade them let the good man alone; and George came on at a foot-pace beside the window, solemnly discoursing till they reached St. James's Park. He "declared what the Lord gave him say of" Oliver's "condition, and of the sufferings of Friends in the nation; showing him how contrary this persecution was to Christ and His apostles, and to Christianity."* At parting Oliver desired his exhorter to "come to his house." The subject was one of much perplexity to Cromwell. For the Quakers themselves often made it easy for constables and magistrates to excuse as a necessary preservation of order what their prophet called persecution.

When Oliver reached Whitehall he sought his wife's apartments, and meeting a Quaker maid of hers, whose name was Mary Saunders, "Mary," said he, "I've some good news for you;" and when she asked, in some perturbation, what it could be, "Why," he replied, "George Fox is come to town." "That is indeed good news!" she exclaimed; for, as her prophet in his journal remarks, "she had received the truth." But her great master apparently was in the habit of joking with his servants, and on second thoughts she said she did not believe him; he was only fooling her. "Nay," he replied, "for truly I met him, and rode from Hyde Park to St. James's with him."† Then the Quaker maid was convinced; and, getting leave next day, sought out the lodging of her prophet to pay her devotion.

Shortly afterwards—whether in accordance with a message by Mary Saunders does not appear—Fox in company with Friend Edward Pyot went to Whitehall, and found Dr. Owen with the Protector. The discourse turned upon the "inward light," which Oliver would not allow to be supernatural. But George, standing by the table, continued discoursing in a very high tone of infallibility. Whereupon Oliver, exclaiming "Come, come! I will be as high as thou art!" sprang up from his chair, and seated himself on the table near George, as though to continue the conversation on easier and more familiar terms.

* "Fox's Journal," p. 208, 3rd edition, 1765.
† "Journal," *l.c.* The abbreviated conversation there is only expanded here by a probable word or two.

But Fox's prophetic solemnity was offended; and after Cromwell had provoked him still farther by his " light manner," they parted. Then when Oliver joined his wife and her friends, he seems to have thought with some compunction of his behaviour; for he was heard to say that he had " never parted so from the Quakers before." *

Nor was it only in such company that the natural man in Oliver broke out. Speaking of the perplexing negotiations about the kingship, Whitelock says :—

"The Protector often advised about this and other great businesses with the Lord Broghill, Pierrepoint, myself, Sir Charles Wolseley, and Thurloe; and would be shut up three or four hours together in private discourse, and none were admitted to come to him. He would be sometimes very cheerful with us, and, laying aside his greatness, he would be exceeding familiar with us, and everyone must try his fancy.† He commonly called for tobacco, pipes, and a candle, and would now and then take tobacco himself. Then he would fall again to his serious and great business, and advise with us in those affairs. And this he did often with us; and our counsel was accepted and followed by him in most of his greatest affairs."

The last words we may believe or not, as we like. The issue of the kingship business does not make them very probable. But the rest of the extract throws an interesting light on Oliver's bearing towards his intimates, and also suggests the permanence, though in a modified form, of that hysteric tendency which in earlier life made him liable to extremes of mirth and melancholy.

* "Journal," *l.c.* Mary Saunders, no doubt, was the informant.
† Perhaps in capping verses or other word plays.

CHAPTER XXX.

THE END.

BUT the end of all things earthly was for Oliver at hand. His stalwart frame showed outwardly few signs of decay; but he was inwardly consumed by care, and his attacks of sickness in Ireland, in Scotland, and occasionally within the last few years, had been of a nature to suggest a morbid element in his constitution, which under continued strain might bring about sudden collapse. He was not the man to carry lightly the vast burden of responsibility now incumbent upon him. It had come upon him late in life, when no genius can supply the facility of long practice. The statesmen of seventy or eighty years who to the wonder of the world have borne with apparent ease the enormous weight of State affairs, have usually been men to whom half a century's experience has made the use of office and responsibility a second nature. And besides they govern by help of an established order, providing for them a routine that saves half their seeming labour. But Cromwell had to sway the storm of revolution. He had to bring order out of disorder, stability out of earthquake. "Give me a fulcrum," said Archimedes, "and I will move the world." But Cromwell had no fulcrum, except his own tremendous will; and after the exhaustive struggles of the war, he had now borne alone for five years the strain of his unshaken resolve.

Perhaps even more wearing than public cares are the private griefs of susceptible affection. The tenderness that goes with giant strength has a far greater capacity for suffering than sentimental weakness can even conceive. There must be surely a vast disproportion between the reality of a great man's conscious being and the partial manifestation of it in his fame; as vast perhaps as the difference between the agitation of the sun's orb, shaken to its centre with molecular energies, and the calm radiance shed on the worlds around. In the inner being of the man domestic love and grief count for more than the outer world can ever know.

Hints given by his own words go far to prove that this must have been so with Oliver Cromwell; and now sharp sorrows were added to the trouble and vexation of which Mary's letter gave us a glimpse in the previous year. Not without tearful scenes and stormy protests on her part had Frances won her husband, nor without anxious consultations between father and mother. But in February 1658 young Rich had died, and left them the harder task of consoling a broken heart. A widow at nineteen years may be supposed to have other hopes in life, but if she has loved with all her heart and soul she cannot see them ; and such a dread eclipse of youthful joy paralyses all expressions of sympathy, except only the silent tears of those whom parental or fraternal love makes equal sufferers. Oliver might indite pious counsel to the bereaved grandfather, and the old man could respond with resignation of "hopes now withered and rebuked by a hasty and early death";* but with the passionate girl who had stormed even his firm will to gain the love now lost the father must have had a more pitiful and more hopeless task. Shortly afterwards the young man's grandfather, the Earl of Warwick, also died, and though this was a loss that did not come so nearly home, it deprived Oliver of a valued friend, whose absence deepened the gloom of gathering night.

In the beginning of July Elizabeth Claypole was taken ill at Hampton Court. Her seven years' reign at the beginning of her life as the youngest child had given her a special hold on her father's heart, and some congenial qualities of disposition enabled her to retain it afterwards. As soon as her danger became serious he waited at her bedside night and day. The terror of this new sorrow so broke his strength of will that he could not attend to public affairs ; and for the first time in his career his ministers had to lament that they could get nothing done. At the end of the month grief and watching prostrated him, so that anxiety began to be felt about himself. But on August 3rd Fleetwood wrote to Henry Cromwell that Lady Claypole was unexpectedly better, and her improvement had revived her father, who now had "a very good refreshment by sleep." But alas, the improvement was not for long. "Great

---

* The Earl of Warwick to Cromwell, in "Godwin," iv., p. 529.

extremity of bodily pain with frequent and violent convulsion fits "* carried her off on August 6th, and her father's anguish that he 'could not even relieve her suffering snapped his own hold on life.†

With the helpless craving that makes sorrow punctilious about funeral ceremonies, he laid her remains in sacred dust on Tuesday August 10th, and two days afterwards he was again seriously unwell.‡ Like David, he sought to "strengthen himself in the Lord his God," and often turned to the passages in the Bible from which he had drawn special inspiration in times past. At Hampton Court, sitting in his bed-chamber, he would have some Scripture read to him ; and thinking of the grave at Felsted, and of his triumph over bereavement there, he asked to hear once more St. Paul's words in his Epistle to the Philippians :—"*I have learned in whatsoever state I am, therewith to be content. I know both how to be abased and how to abound. . . . I can do all things through Christ, which strengtheneth me.*" Oliver was full of the past. As in the experience of the Psalmist, "while he was musing, the fire burned," and when silence followed the reading, he said, "This scripture did once save my life, when my eldest son died, which went as a dagger to my heart— indeed it did." § And then he repeated the words to himself, as though pondering and wondering ;—"how to be abased, and how to abound—both to be full, and to be hungry—both to abound and to suffer need. It's true, Paul, *you* learned this, and attained to this measure of grace ; but what shall *I* do ? Ah, poor creature ; it is a hard lesson for me to take out ! I find it so !—'*I can do all things through Christ which strengtheneth me.*' Surely He that was Paul's Christ is my Christ too !" With this reflection he seemed to gain the "faith that comes of self-control," and with it, peace.

During the week that followed Elizabeth Claypole's funeral,

---

* Thurloe, vii., p. 309.

† King's Pamphlets, small 4to, No. 792.

‡ The progress of his illness may be pretty closely followed by means of the letters in "Thurloe," vii., p. 294, &c.

§ In addition to what has already been said on the reference of these words to Robert, it may here be remarked that if Oliver had been meant, the words would have been "when my son was killed," for he was slain in battle. Besides, although a man may speak of his oldest surviving son as his "eldest," it is unnatural to give that title to the younger of two deceased sons.

G G

he was still able to mount his horse; and on one occasion,* as he rode into the park at Hampton Court, George Fox stood on the path near the gates. The expression of George was awe-struck; "for," says he, "I saw and felt a waft of death go forth against him; and when I came to him he looked like a dead man." It needed no supernatural sign to reveal the doom written on that weary and sorrow-laden face. The Protector stayed to listen to the catalogue of the woes of Friends, and parted as before with an invitation to George to "come to his house." But on the next day the doctors would not allow Fox to seek an audience; "so I passed away," he says, "and never saw him more."

On Thursday, August 19th, Cromwell's illness took the form of an ague—a form of disease to which he had been liable since his Irish and Scotch campaigns. On Saturday morning the fit returned, and the doctors pronounced the sickness to be a tertian; but they did not yet think his life to be in any danger. Still, his councillors and ministers could not but feel anxious about the question of his successor. By the new Instrument of Government he had the power of appointment; but he had not breathed a word on the subject to any one. Secretary Thurloe however understood that the Protector's nomination existed in the form of a sealed letter addressed to himself.† When Oliver felt his sickness increasing he despatched a gentleman, Mr. John Barrington, to Whitehall to fetch the document, telling him where to find it. It was not, however, in the place indicated, and in fact was never discovered at all.‡

Two days now passed without any recurrence of the fit; and on Tuesday, August 24th, the Protector removed from Hampton Court to Whitehall. It was his last journey. He was seized again in the evening after his arrival; but the fit was comparatively mild, and the doctors still encouraged hope. But on the following Friday the danger could no longer be disguised. "Truly the hot fit hath been very long and terrible," wrote

---

* Most probably Tuesday, August 17th. It was the last day that Cromwell could have mounted a horse; and certainly Fox's description of him as riding at the head of his life-guards could hardly be applicable to a carriage drive. On the Thursday (19th), the ague fits began.—Thurloe, vii., p. 354.

† Thurloe to H. Cromwell, vol. vii., p. 363. Thurloe does not say who told him, but it must surely have been the Protector.

‡ Thurloe, *l.c.*

Thurloe; " insomuch that the doctors fear he will scarce get through it." Anxiety now became consternation; and prayers inspired by alarm were offered in all churches. The preachers, relying on a literal interpretation of Christ's words concerning the prayer of faith, endeavoured to force a belief that their prayers *must* be answered, and then proclaimed that they would be. They could hardly conceive how Omnipotence itself could dispense with Oliver. But such was not his own thought. " I think I am the poorest wretch that lives," he murmured; " but I love God—or, rather, am beloved of God." * Yet, at first, he too thought that he *must* live. All witnesses testify that in these last hours his thoughts appeared to be occupied more with the prospects of the nation than even with his own family. His work was at best only half done. Healing and settlement still seemed far away; and if a new Parliament, with no strong hand over them, should fall to wrangling as the last had done, there was no possible issue but the return of the Stuarts, and the destruction of God's marvellous work in the land. " Lord," he sighed, " if I do desire to live, Thou knowest it is to show forth Thy praise, and declare Thy works."—" Is there none that says ' who will deliver me from this peril?' "—" Man can do nothing; God can do what He will."

But he soon felt that his confidence of life had some presumption in it. He had too often faced death to fear it now. But his was a faith that did not shrink from realising the dread solemnity of the coming change. He was heard saying, with deep emphasis, " It is a fearful thing to fall into the hands of the living God." A second and a third time he repeated the words. It was a habit he had. The repetition perhaps seemed to him to sink the truth more deeply into his soul. But it was not in terror that he spoke. " I am a conqueror," he said, " and more than a conqueror, through Christ that strengtheneth me." " The Lord hath filled me with as much assurance of His pardon and His love as my soul can hold."

On Saturday, August 28th, he had two fits in the twenty-four hours, and was much prostrated. The case was plainly hopeless; but even yet the men who could not conceive the future without him would not give him up. On Monday Thurloe

* King's Pamphlets, small 4to, No. 792.

G G 2

wrote to Henry Cromwell in terms that showed how gloomy he thought the outlook ; and he added :—

"Not that I think Charles Stuart's interest is so great, or his party so powerful in themselves ; but I fear our own divisions, which may be great enough if his Highness do not fix and settle his successor before he dies ; which, truly, I believe he hath not yet done."

Thurloe was afterwards told that on this very day Oliver, in the hearing of several witnesses, had named his son Richard as his successor. But the witnesses are not named, and the matter remains doubtful. On that Monday the wind began to rise, and in the night it swelled to a violent storm that swept over the land with destruction, snapping forest trees, unroofing houses, and keeping thousands awake with terror. Superstition or malignity whispered that this was the Prince of the power of the air come to claim Oliver's soul in fulfilment of the contract between them. And in that same storm young Isaac Newton was jumping backwards and forwards, now with the wind and now against it, in order to get data for a rough calculation of its force. But Oliver was occupied neither with dying superstitions nor dawning knowledge. He was thinking of " the Lord, whose way is in the whirlwind and the storm," and of England, yet in the midst of a moral revolution, so marvellously wrought, so fatally incomplete. Like the cornet overheard in the grim dawn at Dunbar, Oliver was impelled by fervour of desire to audible utterance in prayer ; and about this time he was heard to say :—

"Lord, though I am a miserable and wretched creature, I am in covenant with Thee through grace. And I may, I will, come to Thee for Thy people. Thou hast made me, though very unworthy, a mean instrument to do them some good, and Thee service. This people would fain have me live. They think it will be best for them, and that it will redound much to Thy glory. All the stir is about this. Lord, however Thou do dispose of me, continue to go on and do good for them. Give them consistency of judgment, one heart and mutual love ; and go on to deliver them, and with the work of reformation ; and make the name of Christ glorious in the world. Teach those who look too much on Thy instruments to depend more upon Thyself. Pardon such as desire to trample on the dust of a poor worm, for they are Thy people too. And pardon the folly of this short prayer, even for Jesus Christ's sake. And give us a good night, if it be Thy pleasure. Amen." *

* The pamphlet above referred to does not profess to be exact to a word. It

"His heart was so carried out for God and His people," says a recorder of these last moments, "yea, indeed, for some who had added no little sorrow to him, that at this time he seems to forget his own family and nearest relations." But no; he did not forget them. He had less fear for them than for the wider family of the nation. "Children," he said, "live like Christians. I leave you the covenant to feed upon. Love not this world. I say unto you, it is not good that you should love this world."

On Thursday another effort was made to have a valid appointment of a successor, which looks as though the nomination of Monday had been considered doubtful. But no satisfactory evidence is forthcoming as to what really took place, and it is impossible to repress a conjecture that while the circle at Whitehall thought the nomination of Richard on the whole likely to divide the nation least, and therefore endeavoured to engage his father's natural feeling in his favour, the father on the other hand knew his son too well to respond readily, and hardly realised what he did when at the last he was interpreted as assenting.

That night his speech began to fail. Again and again he reiterated, "Truly, God is good." "My work is done," he sighed; "but God will be with His people." He was restless, and his attendants offered him drink, wishing him to compose himself to sleep; but he said, "It is not my design to drink or to sleep, but my design is to make what haste I can to be gone." After that he did not linger long. In broken words, as the night passed by, "he used divers holy expressions, implying much inward consolation and peace; among the rest he spoke some exceeding self-debasing words, annihilating and judging himself. And truly it was observed that a public spirit of God's cause did breathe in him—as in his lifetime, so now to his very last." He seems never to have alluded to the nature of the anniversary dawning upon him. When the sun that had lighted Dunbar battle and Worcester fight shone through his chamber this 3rd of September, he was speechless. Between three and four o'clock in the afternoon the labouring breath ceased; and Oliver Cromwell was dead.

is here supplemented from Neale's version, in which are some characteristic expressions. As the writer of the pamphlet says, "So much is certain, that these were his requests."

To turn from such a death-bed scene to funeral ceremonies conceived in the worst taste of a tasteless time would be repulsive. Let it suffice that genuine feeling struggled through the grotesque forms imposed upon it. The stream of people who trod softly past the bed where a false effigy "lay in state," and the vaster throngs who lined the streets to watch the funeral procession, showed a very real sense of a loss too great and too vague in its consequences to be expressed by any words or signs. But after all the most noteworthy tribute to the power of the now silent form was the endurance of the Commonwealth for more than a year and a half under a feeble, helpless ruler, with distraction in the Parliament and faction in the army. As the gigantic Amazon river rolls such a torrent into the sea that it survives as a fresh-water stream for a hundred miles from the mouth, so the strong current of Oliver's purpose lived on, and the Commonwealth continued for a while with nothing to sustain it except his posthumous power. But it could not be for long. The Republicans soon learned their own helplessness; and the inevitable followed.

The preachers who had declared in effect that God could not do without this man did not understand the order of the world's progress. Certainly after his loss the Commonwealth soon became impossible, and the return of the Stuarts was a question of a few months, more or less. But that was the natural order of things; and in preventing it Cromwell would have been a hindrance rather than a promoter of real progress. For what was it that at the best could have been expected of him? Whether as Protector or as King, he would have continued to insist, as he had always done, on the adoption of practical measures favouring religion and morality, social peace and security, public justice, learning, and commerce. But he would have achieved all this, as he had done hitherto, by his immense personal superiority; and the education of the people in self-government must necessarily have been held in abeyance. He had already gone beyond public opinion; and though the substantial benefits of his government were acknowledged, yet as the volcanic eruption of abnormal reforming zeal cooled down, people fretted at the cold grey world that replaced the merry England of their youth. Cromwell and a strong successor might have maintained the new government through the time of reaction; but it would have been by holding the nation in leading-strings, and by sacrificing that which is better than all laws and all institutions—the political vitality of the English race.

The lesson of Cromwell's great career is really the very reverse of that which has with much applause been drawn from it. It is not enough that by force of circumstances a people lay hold on their ablest man and make him a beneficent despot. As soon as he ceases to be the executive of their will and imposes his will on them, their progress is arrested, and they become dependent for order and prosperity, not on their own wisdom and self-control, not on the abiding character of the nation, but on an accidental force of uncertain, but necessarily brief, duration. It was better then for the England of all time that the England of that day should lose a ruler too good for it, and should have free scope for an infatuated reaction. Only by experience of degradation and misery with every relapse into folly can a nation at last learn that there is no short cut to political beatitude. Neither the accidental genius of one man, nor the blind conservatism of the many can unite order and progress. That union is only to be achieved by general intelligence and moral effort, directing and enabling each unit in the multitude willingly to subordinate himself to the good of all.

But such considerations do not lessen—they rather enhance —the greatness of Cromwell. His worth to mankind lay in his power to meet a great emergency of revolutionary violence; in the frankness with which he accepted as the practical issue of the time a duel to the death between prerogative and self-government; in his capacity to inspire thousands with his own enthusiasm ; in his predominant energy, which forced distracted parties to unity of action; in the prophetic fire that kindled into one flame the religious zeal, the patriotic fervour, and the personal devotion of his followers. By such qualities alone, without aid of name or fame, he made of the Eastern Counties Association an impregnable stronghold for an otherwise desperate cause. By such qualities he made his armies of fighting saints a portent of sure destruction to opponents. And then, armed with these weapons of his own creation, he manifested in himself exhaustless reserves of force, that left him without a rival in the final achievement of victory.

When the victory was won, he alone saved the conquering

party from the shame of dissipation by shiftless and impracticable factions. The Republicans of the day counted some men of fine intellect and chivalrous ardour. But in numbers they were a small and feeble sect. Only the Protectorate or a new dynasty could have enabled England to prove to her ancient royal family her ability to do without them. If Oliver had not turned out the Long Parliament when he did, only a few months would have elapsed before it was done by Charles II. It is not just to say, as is often done, that he was without sympathy for the people whom he ruled. The only germ of truth giving plausibility to such a statement is, that his sympathies, being most attracted by the nobler elements in the English character—its rough practical justice, its religious faith, its enormous energy—he did not make sufficient allowance for the baser elements of sensuous indulgence, and superstitious conventionalism, and recurrent laziness. But he spoke the very heart of the commonplace Englishman when he bade republican theorists cease their prating and come to a practical settlement. He showed how deeply he was tinged with time-honoured traditions when he professed his inability to conceive how a Government could exist without " a single person " as a fixed head, or how society could get on without its three castes of nobleman, gentleman, and yeoman. And it was precisely this unreasoning sympathy with the social superstitions of the race which made the Protectorate possible.

In that supreme position to which Cromwell as truly as devoutly declared that he did not call himself, but had been called by duty and Providence, he made his brief rule on the whole the richest in suggestions and the most imposing in its combined strength and purity of all the Governments our land has yet known. In his insistance on an integral union of the three kingdoms he gave true interpretation, for the first time in our history, to the decree of nature stamped on the physical relations of the British Isles. In his re-constitution of Parliament and re-distribution of seats he anticipated, in some important points the Reform Bill of 1832. In his impatience of the bewildering coil of Chancery proceedings, and his bold efforts at simplification, he was two hundred years—alas, we may say three hundred years—before his time. In his pity for imprisoned debtors, and his practical measures for their relief, he made at least a substantial step towards the rational legislation of a still recent day. In his baffled efforts to give cheap justice, he left a hint to be yet taken up by some enlightened Government of the future. His ecclesiastical legislation was necessarily tinged by political necessities, and by the passions evoked in a civil war almost as much theological as secular. But this much at least may be maintained, that there was more religious liberty under his rule than had ever been known in England before, and that the national Establishment under his supremacy, in the greater prominence given to moral and practical requirements, in the diminished importance attached to all except central doctrines of Christianity, and in the freedom as to matters of form conceded to individual ministers, came nearer to the idea of a comprehensive Church than it has ever done before or since.

In finance Oliver was much hampered; but even in this his strong common sense introduced some excellent reforms by substituting English for Latin in account-keeping, by concentrating the treasuries in one, and by keeping a watchful eye on the effect of impost duties on trade.

If it be the glory of a ruler to make his country respected and feared throughout the world, not even Elizabeth can successfully rival Cromwell in this respect. Pitt, indeed, by exertions entailing on the nation exhaustion, debt, neglect of home interests, and popular misery, forced the nation into more dread prominence on the slaughter-fields of Europe. In making England a terror to others, he very nearly made her intolerable to herself. But the victor of Dunbar made her word potent from Stockholm to Tunis, while at the same time calling for no effort that was not well within the national capacity. When every fleet upon the seas deferentially saluted the British flag, and when the greatest monarch in Europe regarded 6,000 British soldiers as a sight worth travelling to see, the country was prospering in commerce, growing in resources, and advancing in all the arts of peace.

Indeed it was to the victories of peace, declared by his illustrious secretary to be no less renowned than those of war, that this true protector of British interests looked as his purest pride. War was to him a dread necessity, which none but a madman would lightly face, and none but prating fools would glorify as the chief end of man. But to be serviceable in any way in the promotion of learning, and in the accumulation of new mental treasures for mankind, was to him more than an honour— it was a joy that needed no praise or gratitude to recommend it. Oxford, Cambridge, Dublin, Durham, and Glasgow—all were indebted to him for wise arrangements, for precious manuscripts, for additional endowments, for enlarged libraries, or new buildings. He took a warm interest in the progress of Walton's Polyglot Bible, and ordered the paper for it to be imported free of duty. He was anxious for a new translation of the Scriptures, but opportunity did not serve. As in the case of Dr. Walton, so in that of Archbishop Usher and Dr. Seth Ward, a deserved reputation for learning was a sure passport to his respect and favour. And had he lived yet ten years more, the manifest tendencies of his mind and rule justify us in believing that he would have compelled the bigotry of the time to farther submission, and have made England as famous for catholic culture as for arms and commerce.

Such was the man whose body the creatures of the Restoration dragged from his grave that they might satisfy a vulgar and puny vengeance with outrages on a corpse. There are murders told of in English history which thrill us with horror; deeds of cruelty and injustice which are a lasting pain to the historic conscience. But the most of them had some poor excuse of brutal necessity or frantic passion. Perhaps if we could rightly estimate what goes to constitute baseness, not one of those sanguinary deeds would so sicken us with moral disgust and shame for our common nature as the impotent, cowardly, and needless deed wrought on Cromwell's dead body. In the Jews it was counted a crime that they built sepulchres for the prophets whom their fathers slew. So far as the Commonwealth is concerned, we are not open to that charge. Our fathers could not slay its great prophet and lawgiver. He was too strong and watchful for that. They rather satisfied themselves with rifling his tomb after he was dead, and mutilating his corpse. It is a shameful confession to have to make; but it is nevertheless true —that, so far as form and ceremony go, the national attitude towards this great memory is a tacit acceptance of that outrage. Our fathers emptied his sepulchre, and we make conspicuous by its absence from our historic monuments the figure of the most human-hearted sovereign and most imperial man in all our annals since King Alfred's days.

INDEX.

H H

SELECTIONS FROM VOLUMES

Published by Cassell, Petter, Galpin & Co.

NEW LIFE OF CROMWELL.
Oliver Cromwell : The Man and his Mission. By J.
ALLANSON PICTON. With Steel Portrait. Price 7s. 6d.

A Winter in India. By the Right Hon. W. E. BAXTER,
M.P. Illustrated. Crown 8vo, cloth, 5s.

Wealth Creation. By AUGUSTUS MONGREDIEN. Crown
8vo, cloth, price 5s.

Constitutional History and Political Development of
the United States. By SIMON STERNE, of the New York Bar. 5s.

The History of the Year. A Complete Narrative
of the Events of the Past Year. Crown 8vo, cloth, 6s.

England : its People, Polity, and Pursuits. By
T. H. S. ESCOTT. *Cheap Edition,* in One Vol., price 7s. 6d.

A History of Modern Europe. By C. A. FYFFE,
M.A., Fellow of University College, Oxford. Vols. I. and II. Demy 8vo,
12s. each.

Wood Magic : A Fable. By RICHARD JEFFERIES,
Author of "The Gamekeeper at Home," &c. *Cheap Edition,* cloth, 6s.

English and Irish Land Questions. Collected Essays
by the Rt. Hon. G. SHAW-LEFEVRE, M.P., First Commissioner of Works
and Public Buildings. Price 6s.

Local Government and Taxation in the United
Kingdom. Edited by J. W. PROBYN. Cloth, price 5s.

A Police Code, and Manual of the Criminal Law. By
C. E. HOWARD VINCENT, Director of Criminal Investigations. Cloth,
price 6s. *Pocket Edition,* for Policemen and Householders, with an Address
to Constables by Mr. Justice HAWKINS, 2s.

Land Tenure in Various Countries, Systems of. A
Series of Essays, published under the sanction of the Cobden Club. 3s. 6d.

The Landed Interest and the Supply of Food. By
Sir JAMES CAIRD, K.C.B., F.R.S. New and Enlarged Edition. Cloth, 5s.

English Land and English Landlords. By the Hon.
GEORGE C. BRODRICK. Price 12s. 6d. Published for the Cobden Club.

A Ride to Khiva. By Lieut.-Col. FRED. BURNABY.
Cheap Edition, 3s. 6d. ; *People's Edition,* 6d.

Cassell, Petter, Galpin & Co. : Ludgate Hill, London ; Paris ; and New York.

Selections from Cassell, Petter, Galpin & Co.'s Volumes (Continued).

The Life of the Rt. Hon. W. E. Gladstone. By
GEORGE BARNETT SMITH. With Two Steel Portraits. *Cheap Edition,* in One Vol., cloth, 5s. *Jubilee Edition,* 1s.

Russia. By D. MACKENZIE WALLACE, M.A. *Cheap*
Edition, in One Vol., with Two Maps, 10s. 6d.

The British Army. From the Restoration to the
Revolution. By Sir SIBBALD SCOTT, Bart. Demy 8vo, cloth, 21s.

Remedies for War, Political and Legal. By Prof.
SHELDON AMOS, M.A., Barrister-at-Law. Price 6s.

Universal History, Cassell's Illustrated. Vol. I. With
numerous High-class Engravings. 9s.

Gleanings from Popular Authors. Vol. I. With
Original Illustrations. Price 9s.

England, Cassell's History of. With about 2,000
Illustrations. Nine Vols., cloth, 9s. each. Or in library binding, £4 10s.

United States, Cassell's History of the. With 600
Illustrations and Maps. 1,950 pages, extra crown 4to. Complete in Three Vols., cloth, £1 7s.; or in library binding, £1 10s.

India, Cassell's History of. With about 400 Maps,
Plans, and Illustrations. Extra crown 4to, Two Vols., cloth, 18s.; or in library binding, £1.

The Russo-Turkish War, Cassell's History of.
Complete in Two Vols. With about 500 Illustrations. 9s. each.

✓British Battles on Land and Sea. By JAMES GRANT.
With about 600 Illustrations. Three Vols., cloth, £1 7s.; or in library binding, £1 10s.

Old and New London. A Narrative of its History,
its People, and its Places. With 1,200 Illustrations. Complete in Six Vols., 9s. each; or in library binding, £3.

Heroes of Britain in Peace and War. By E. HODDER.
With 300 Illustrations. Two Vols., 7s. 6d. each. Library binding, One Vol., 12s. 6d.

✓Decisive Events in History. *Fifth Edition.* With
full-page Original Illustrations. Cloth gilt, 5s.

Through the Light Continent; or, The United States
in 1877-8. By WILLIAM SAUNDERS. 10s. 6d.

Cassell, Petter, Galpin & Co.: Ludgate Hill, London ; Paris ; and New York.

2

NEW WORK BY CANON FARRAR.
The Early Days of Christianity. By the Rev. Canon
FARRAR, D.D., F.R.S. Two Vols., demy 8vo, cloth, 24s. *(Can also be had in morocco binding.)*

The Life of Christ. By the Rev. Canon FARRAR,
D.D., F.R.S.
Popular Edition, in One Vol., cloth, 6s. ; cloth gilt, gilt edges, 7s. 6d. ; Persian morocco, 10s. 6d. ; tree calf, 15s.
Library Edition. 29*th Edition.* Two Vols., cloth, 24s.; morocco, £2 2s.
Illustrated Edition. With about 300 Illustrations. Extra crown 4to, cloth, gilt edges, 21s.; calf or morocco, £2 2s.

The Life and Work of St. Paul. By the Rev.
Canon FARRAR, D.D., F.R.S. 19*th Thousand.* Two Vols., demy 8vo, cloth, 24s.; morocco, £2 2s.

THE NEW BIBLE COMMENTARY.
An Old Testament Commentary for English Readers.
By Various Writers. Edited by the Right Rev. C. J. ELLICOTT, D.D., Lord Bishop of Gloucester and Bristol. VOL. I., price 21s., contains the PENTATEUCH.

A New Testament Commentary for English Readers.
Edited by the Right Rev. C. J. ELLICOTT, D.D., Lord Bishop of Gloucester and Bristol. Three Vols., cloth, £3 3s.; or in half-morocco, £4 14s. 6d.
VOL. I. contains THE FOUR GOSPELS. £1 1s.
VOL. II. contains THE ACTS to GALATIANS. £1 1s.
VOL. III. contains the EPHESIANS to the REVELATION. £1 1s.

A Commentary on the Revised Version of the New
Testament for English Readers. By Prebendary HUMPHRY, B.D., Member of the Company of Revisers of the New Testament. 7s. 6d.

The Half-Guinea Illustrated Bible. Containing 900
Original Illustrations. Cloth, 10s. 6d. *Also in various Leather Bindings.*

The Bible Educator. Edited by the Very Rev. E. H.
PLUMPTRE, D.D. Illustrated. Four Vols., 6s. each; or Two Vols., 21s.

The Holy Land. From the Original Drawings by
DAVID ROBERTS, R.A. Divisions I. and II., with 42 Plates in each. Price 18s. each.

Sunday Musings. A Selection of Readings. Illus-
trated. 832 pp., demy 4to, cloth, 21s.

The Church at Home. Short Sermons, with Collect
and Scripture for Sundays, Saints' Days, and Special Occasions. By th Right Rev. ROWLEY HILL, D.D., Bishop of Sodor and Man. 5s.

The History of Protestantism. By the Rev. J. A
WYLIE, LL.D. With 600 Original Illustrations. Three Vols., 4to, cloth, £1 7s.; or in library binding, £1 10s.

Cassell, Petter, Galpin & Co.: Ludgate Hill, London ; Paris; and New York.

The Magazine of Art. Volume V. With about 400
Illustrations by the first Artists of the day, and beautifully-executed Etching, for Frontispiece. Cloth gilt, gilt edges, 16s. *The price of Vols. I., II., III., and IV. has been increased—Vols. I. and IV. to 21s. each, Vols. II. and III. to 15s. each.*

Evangeline. *Édition de Luxe.* With magnificent
Original Illustrations by FRANK DICKSEE, A.R.A., beautifully reproduced in Photogravure. *** Further particulars, with price, &c., may be obtained of any Bookseller.*

Longfellow's Poetical Works. With Original Engrav-
ings by the best English, American, and Continental Artists. Royal 4to, £3 3s.

Picturesque Europe. *Popular Edition.* Vol. I., with
13 Exquisite Steel Plates, and about 200 Original Engravings by the best Artists. Cloth gilt, 18s. N.B.—The *Original Edition*, in Five Magnificent Volumes, royal 4to size, can still be obtained, price £10 10s.

Egypt: Descriptive, Historical, and Picturesque.
By Prof. G. EBERS. Translated by CLARA BELL, with Notes by SAMUEL BIRCH, LL.D., D.C.L., F.S.A. With Original Magnificent Engravings. Cloth bevelled, gilt edges, Vol. I., £2 5s. ; Vol. II., £2 12s. 6d.

Picturesque America. Vol. I., with 12 Exquisite Steel
Plates and about 200 Original Wood Engravings. Royal 4to, £2 2s.

Landscape Painting in Oils, A Course of Lessons in.
By A. F. GRACE, Turner Medallist, Royal Academy. With Nine Reproductions in Colour. Extra demy folio, cloth, gilt edges, 42s.

Illustrated British Ballads. With Several Hundred
Original Illustrations by some of the first Artists of the day. Complete in Two Vols. Cloth, gilt edges, 21s.

Character Sketches from Dickens. Large Drawings
by FRED BARNARD of Sidney Carton, Mr. Pickwick, Alfred Jingle, Little Dorrit, Mrs. Gamp, and Bill Sikes. In Portfolio, imperial 4to, 5s. the set.

Pictures of Bird Life in Pen and Pencil. With Illus-
trations by GIACOMELLI. Imperial 4to, 21s.

The Changing Year. Being Poems and Pictures of
Life and Nature. With Illustrations. Cloth gilt, 7s. 6d.

The Doré Fine Art Volumes comprise—

	£ s. d.		£ s. d.
Milton's Paradise Lost	. 1 1 0	Purgatorio and Paradiso	. 2 10 0
The Doré Gallery	. 5 5 0	La Fontaine's Fables	. 1 10 0
The Doré Bible .	. 4 4 0	Don Quixote	. . 0 15 0
Dante's Inferno .	. 2 10 0	Munchausen	. . 0 5 0
	Fairy Tales Told Again . £0 5 0		

European Butterflies and Moths. By W. F. KIRBY.
With 61 Coloured Plates. Demy 4to, cloth gilt, 35s.

The Book of the Horse. By S. SIDNEY. With
Twenty-five Coloured Plates, and 100 Wood Engravings. *New and Revised Edition.* Demy 4to, cloth, 31s. 6d.; half-morocco, £2 2s.

The Illustrated Book of Poultry. By L. WRIGHT.
With 50 Coloured Plates, and numerous Wood Engravings. Demy 4to, cloth, 31s. 6d.; half-morocco, £2 2s.

The Illustrated Book of Pigeons. By R. FULTON.
Edited by L. WRIGHT. With Fifty Coloured Plates and numerous Engravings. Demy 4to, cloth, 31s. 6d.; half-morocco, £2 2s.

Canaries and Cage-Birds, The Illustrated Book of.
With Fifty-six Coloured Plates and numerous Illustrations. Demy 4to, cloth, 35s.; half-morocco, £2 5s.

Dairy Farming. By Professor SHELDON, assisted by
eminent Authorities. With Twenty-five Fac-simile Coloured Plates, and numerous Wood Engravings. Cloth, 31s. 6d.; half-morocco, £2 2s.

Illustrated Book of the Dog. By VERO SHAW, B.A.
Cantab. With Twenty-eight Fac-simile Coloured Plates, drawn from Life expressly for the Work, and numerous Wood Engravings. Demy 4to, cloth bevelled, 35s.; half-morocco, 45s.

European Ferns: their Form, Habit, and Culture.
By JAMES BRITTEN, F.L.S. With Thirty Fac-simile Coloured Plates, Painted from Nature by D. BLAIR, F.L.S. Demy 4to, cloth gilt, gilt edges, 21s.

Familiar Garden Flowers. FIRST and SECOND SERIES.
By SHIRLEY HIBBERD. With Forty Full-page Coloured Plates by F. E. HULME, F.L.S., in each. 12s. 6d. each.

Familiar Wild Flowers. FIRST, SECOND, and THIRD
SERIES. By F. E. HULME, F.L.S., F.S.A. With Forty Coloured Plates and Descriptive Text in each. 12s. 6d. each.

Cassell's New Natural History. Edited by Prof.
DUNCAN, M.B., F.R.S., assisted by Eminent Writers; with nearly 2,000 Illustrations. Complete in 6 Vols., 9s. each.

The World of the Sea. Translated by the Rev. H.
MARTYN-HART, M.A. *Cheap Edition,* Illustrated, 6s.

Transformations of Insects, The. By Prof. P. MARTIN
DUNCAN, M.B., F.R.S. With 240 Illustrations. *Cheap Edition,* cloth, 6s.

Cassell, Petter, Galpin & Co.: Ludgate Hill, London; Paris; and New York.

The Encyclopædic Dictionary. By ROBERT HUNTER,

M.A., F.G.S., Mem. Bibl. Archæol. Soc., &c. A New and Original Work of Reference to all the Words in the English Language, with a Full Account of their Origin, Meaning, Pronunciation, and Use. Three Divisional Volumes now ready, price 10s. 6d. each. Divisions I. and II. can also be had bound in One Volume in half-morocco, 21s.

Library of English Literature. Edited by Professor

HENRY MORLEY. With Illustrations taken from Original MSS., &c. Each Vol. complete in itself.

VOL. I. SHORTER ENGLISH POEMS. 12s. 6d.
VOL. II. ILLUSTRATIONS OF ENGLISH RELIGION. 11s. 6d.
VOL. III. ENGLISH PLAYS. 11s. 6d.
VOL. IV. SHORTER WORKS IN ENGLISH PROSE. 11s. 6d.
VOL. V. LONGER WORKS IN ENGLISH VERSE AND PROSE. 11s. 6d.

Dictionary of English Literature. Being a Comprehensive Guide to English Authors and their Works. By W. DAVENPORT ADAMS. 720 pages, extra fcap. 4to, cloth, 10s. 6d.

A First Sketch of English Literature. By Professor

HENRY MORLEY. Crown 8vo, 912 pages, cloth, 7s. 6d.

Dictionary of Phrase and Fable. Giving the Derivation, Source, or Origin of 20,000 Words that have a Tale to Tell. By Rev. Dr. BREWER. *Enlarged and Cheaper Edition*, cloth, 3s. 6d. ; superior binding, leather back, 4s. 6d.

Popular Educator, Cassell's. *New and thoroughly Revised Edition.* Vols. I., II., and III., price 5s. each. (To be completed in Six Vols.)

The Royal Shakspere. A Handsome Fine-Art Edition

of the Poet's Works. Vol. I. contains Exquisite Steel Plates and Wood Engravings. The Text is that of Prof. Delius, and the Work contains Mr. FURNIVALL's Life of Shakspere. Price 15s.

The Leopold Shakspere. The Poet's Works in Chronological Order, and an Introduction by F. J. FURNIVALL. With about 400 Illustrations. Small 4to, cloth, 6s. ; cloth gilt, 7s. 6d.

Cassell's Illustrated Shakespeare. Edited by CHARLES

and MARY COWDEN CLARKE. With 600 Illustrations by H. C. SELOUS. Three Vols., cloth gilt, £3 3s.

Figure Painting in Water Colours. With Sixteen

Coloured Plates from Original Designs by BLANCHE MACARTHUR and JENNIE MOORE. 7s. 6d.

Flower Painting in Water Colours. With Twenty

Fac-simile Coloured Plates by F. E. HULME. Crown 4to, 5s.

Sketching from Nature in Water Colours. By AARON

PENLEY. With Illustrations in Chromo-Lithography, after Original Water-Colour Drawings. Super-royal 4to, cloth, 15s.

Cassell, Petter, Galpin & Co. : Ludgate Hill, London ; Paris ; and New York.

Morocco : its People and Places. By EDMONDO DE
AMICIS. Translated by C. ROLLIN TILTON. With nearly 200 Original Illustrations. Extra crown 4to, *Cheap Edition*, cloth, 7s. 6d.

Our Own Country. An Illustrated Geographical and
Historical Description of the Chief Places of Interest in Great Britain. Vols. I., II., III., IV., & V., with upwards of 200 Illustrations in each, 7s. 6d. each.

Old and New Edinburgh, Cassell's. Vols. I. and II.
With nearly 200 Original Illustrations in each, specially executed for the Work. In crown 4to, cloth, 9s. each.

The International Portrait Gallery. In Two Vols.,
each containing 20 Portraits in Colours, executed in the best style of Chromo-Lithography, with Memoirs. Demy 4to, cloth gilt, 12s. 6d. each. ; or Two Vols. in One, 21s.

The National Portrait Gallery. Complete in Four
Volumes. Each containing 20 Portraits, printed in the best style of Chromo-Lithography, with Memoirs. Cloth gilt, 12s. 6d. each ; or Four Vols. in Two, 21s. each.

Science for All. Complete in Five Vols. Edited by
Dr. ROBERT BROWN, M.A., F.L.S., &c., assisted by Eminent Scientific Writers. Each containing about 350 Illustrations. Extra crown 4to, cloth, 9s. each.

Great Industries of Great Britain. With about 400
Illustrations. Extra crown 4to, 960 pages, complete in Three Vols., cloth, 7s. 6d. each. Library Binding, Three Vols. in One, 15s.

The Field Naturalist's Handbook. By the Rev. J. G.
WOOD and THEODORE WOOD. Cloth, 5s.

The Races of Mankind. By ROBERT BROWN, M.A.,
Ph.D., F.L.S., F.R.G.S. Complete in Four Vols., containing upwards of 500 Illustrations. Cloth gilt, 6s. per Vol.; or Two Double Vols., £1 1s.

The Sea : Its Stirring Story of Adventure, Peril, and
Heroism. By F. WHYMPER. Complete in Four Vols., each containing 100 Original Illustrations. 4to, 7s. 6d. each. Library Binding, Two Vols., 25s.

Illustrated Readings. Comprising a choice Selection
from the English Literature of all Ages. With about 400 Illustrations. Two Vols., cloth, gilt edges, 10s. 6d. each.

The Practical Dictionary of Mechanics. Containing
15,000 Drawings, with Comprehensive and TECHNICAL DESCRIPTION of each Subject. Three Volumes, cloth, £3 3s.; half-morocco, £3 15s.

Cassell, Petter, Galpin & Co.: Ludgate Hill, London ; Paris ; and New York.

The Countries of the World. By ROBERT BROWN,
M.A., Ph.D., F.L.S., F.R.G.S. Complete in Six Vols., with about 750 Illustrations. 4to, 7s. 6d. each. Library Binding, Three Vols., price 37s. 6d.

Peoples of the World. Vol. I. By Dr. ROBERT
BROWN. With numerous Illustrations. Price 7s. 6d.

Cities of the World. Vol. I. Illustrated throughout
with fine Illustrations and Portraits. Extra crown 4to, cloth gilt, 7s. 6d.

Sports and Pastimes, Cassell's Book of. With more
than 800 Illustrations, and Coloured Frontispiece. 768 pages, large crown 8vo, cloth, gilt edges, 7s. 6d.

In-door Amusements, Card Games, and Fireside Fun,
Cassell's Book of. With numerous Illustrations. 224 pp., large crown 8vo, cloth, gilt edges, 3s. 6d.

The Family Physician. A Modern Manual of
Domestic Medicine. By PHYSICIANS and SURGEONS of the Principal London Hospitals. Royal 8vo, cloth, 21s.

The Domestic Dictionary. An Encyclopædia for the
Household. Illustrated throughout. 1,280 pages, royal 8vo, *Cheap Edition*, price 7s. 6d.; half-roan, 9s.

Cassell's Dictionary of Cookery. The Largest,
Cheapest, and Best Book of Cookery. With 9,000 Recipes, and numerous Illustrations. *Cheap Edition*, price 7s. 6d.; half-roan, 9s.

Cassell's Household Guide. *New and Revised Edition.*
With Illustrations on nearly every page, and COLOURED PLATES. Complete in Four Vols., 6s. each.

Choice Dishes at Small Cost. Containing Practical
Directions to success in Cookery, and Original Recipes for Appetising and Economical Dishes. By A. G. PAYNE. 3s. 6d.

A Year's Cookery. Giving Dishes for Breakfast,
Luncheon, and Dinner for Every Day in the Year, with Practical Instructions for their Preparation. By PHILLIS BROWNE. *Cheap Edition*, cloth, 3s. 6d.

What Girls Can Do. A Book for Mothers and
Daughters. By PHILLIS BROWNE, Author of "A Year's Cookery," &c. Crown 8vo, cloth, *Cheap Edition*, 3s. 6d.

☞ Cassell, Petter, Galpin & Co.'s Complete Catalogue, *containing a List of Several Hundred Volumes, including Bibles and Religious Works, Fine-Art Volumes, Children's Books, Dictionaries, Educational Works, Handbooks and Guides, History, Natural History, Household and Domestic Treatises, Science, Serials, Travels, &c. &c., sent post free on application.*

Cassell, Petter, Galpin & Co.: Ludgate Hill, London ; Paris ; and New York.